WEAPONS & WARFARE

WEAPONS & WARFARE

Volume 1

ANCIENT AND MEDIEVAL WEAPONS AND WARFARE (TO 1500)

Editor
JOHN POWELL
Department of History and Political Science
Cumberland College

Managing Editor
CHRISTINA J. MOOSE

SALEM PRESS, INC.
Pasadena, California   Hackensack, New Jersey

Editor in Chief: Dawn P. Dawson
Managing Editor: Christina J. Moose
Project Editor: Heather Stratton
Production Editor: Joyce I. Buchea
Research Supervisor: Jeffry Jensen
Assistant Editor: Andrea E. Miller
Research Assistant: Jeff Stephens
Acquisitions Editor: Mark Rehn
Layout and Design: James Hutson
Illustrator: Kimberly L. Dawson Kurnizki
Photograph Editor: Philip Bader
Cover Design: Moritz Design

Copyright © 2002, by Salem Press, Inc.

Library of Congress Cataloging-in-Publication Data

Weapons and warfare / editor, John Powell.
   p. cm.
   Includes bibliographical references and index.
   Contents: v. 1. Ancient and medieval weapons and warfare (to 1500) — v. 2. Modern weapons and warfare (since 1500).
   ISBN 1-58765-000-2 (set : alk. paper)
   ISBN 1-58765-001-0 vol 1
   ISBN 1-58765-002-9 vol 2
   1. Military weapons—History. 2. Military art and science—History. I. Powell, John, 1954-
UF500.W48 2001
623.4′09—dc21

2001034150

Third Printing

PRINTED IN THE UNITED STATES OF AMERICA

CONTENTS

ANCIENT AND MEDIEVAL WEAPONS AND WARFARE TO 1500

PUBLISHER'S NOTE

Salem Press's two-volume set *Weapons and Warfare* is designed to meet the needs of college and high school students of history and sociology and others seeking information about weaponry, tactics, and modes of warfare from ancient times to the present, worldwide. Volume 1, *Ancient and Medieval Weapons and Warfare (to 1500)*, covers weapons and strategies from ancient through medieval times, and Volume 2, *Modern Weapons and Warfare (Since 1500)*, covers weapons and strategies from approximately 1500 to the present.

Users of this two-volume reference will find it a useful supplement to other publications: Salem Press's five-volume set *Magill's Guide to Military History*, which presents a survey of wars, battles, people, and groups and civilizations that played an important role in worldwide military history from ancient times to the twenty-first century, and Salem's four-volume *World Conflicts and Confrontations*, which examines current and historical world conflicts from a regional point of view. *Weapons and Warfare* complements both sets in its focus on the evolution of military theory and technology in the context of specific battles and conflicts.

More than 100 topics in *Weapons and Warfare* are organized thematically in articles ranging from 2,000 to 7,000 words (3 to 9 pages). Each volume opens with a series of overviews of major weapons groups, such as "Clubs, Maces, and Slings" in Volume 1 and "Rockets, Missiles, and Nuclear Weapons" in Volume 2, that discuss the development and the uses of each class of weapons. Volume 1 contains 14 weapons overview articles; Volume 2 contains 15. These weapons overviews are followed in both volumes by chronologically arranged sections covering major historical periods and regions of the world and their contributions to military weapons, technologies, and strategies. The geographical scope of the set is truly worldwide, including articles on Eastern and Southern Asia, the Middle East and Africa, and the Americas. The historical range of the set is equally broad,

covering the evolution of warfare from the time of the earliest Mesopotamian empires to the third millennium.

Weapons overview articles are consistently organized with sections on "Nature and Use" and "Development" of each weapons type. The geographically arranged warfare articles feature sections on "Political Considerations" where relevant, and on "Military Achievement," "Weapons, Uniforms, and Armor," "Military Organization," and "Doctrine, Strategy, and Tactics." Most warfare articles also feature a section on the primary sources from which historians base their observations that examines and evaluates the best sources for understanding the warfare of the period. Volume 1 ends with three transitional articles, "Handarms to Firearms," "Knights to Cavalry," and "Galleys to Galleons," which chart major innovations in gunpowder weapons, mounted warfare, and naval warfare from medieval to modern times. The organization of the articles and the twofold arrangement of the volumes allows readers to gain an integrated understanding of the subjects of weapons and warfare.

Weapons and Warfare contains a number of useful tools to help readers locate their areas of interest. Alphabetical and categorized lists of all entries, as well as a list of illustrations, appear at the beginning of both volumes. Volume 1 opens with a section on Research Tools that includes a Guide to Military Theorists, an essay on Geography and Military Development, a Time Line, and an Alphabetical Lexicon on Weapons of War. Volume 2 closes with a lengthy categorized Bibliography that lists recently published secondary print resources on weapons and warfare, a list of established Web Sites that provide reliable information on weapons throughout history, and a comprehensive Subject Index.

Written with the needs of students and general readers in mind, the articles contained in *Weapons and Warfare* present clear discussions of the topics, explaining any terms or references that may be unclear. Birth and death dates are given on first mention of all historical figures discussed in the text, as are the beginning and end dates of battles and wars. The focus, more on the technical and strategic development of weapons and tactics than on a narrative chronological history of events, allows students of history, political science, and science and technology alike to gain a broad understanding of the technological and strategic advances made over time and geography. Specific examples are discussed within the context of these developments.

The names of wars and battles and the names of military leaders and other personages vary from resource to resource and from country to country, depending on variables such as political perspective, the different methods of rendering foreign words (including anglicization), and customary usage over the years. In this encyclopedia, the names that are used in the essays, along with the date of the event or the life span of the person, are those that, over time, have proved to be the most common appellations and the spellings and renderings most familiar to the general audience. Chinese names have generally been given in their pinyin form, with Wade-Giles transliterations following in parentheses. For persons or places that are more commonly known by their Wade-Giles transliterations, such as Chinese Nationalist leader Sun Yat-sen, the pinyin (Sun Yixian) has been given in parentheses instead.

Distributed throughout *Weapons and Warfare* are more than 100 photographs, line drawings, and artists' renderings depicting the weapons discussed, as well as 35 maps that direct readers to the geographic areas inhabited or conquered by the empires, civilizations, and cultures discussed. More than 70 boxed "Turning Points" sidebars discuss, in time line format, the important concepts, key developments, and famous personages mentioned in the accompanying articles' text.

Reference works such as *Weapons and Warfare* would not be possible without the help of experts in the field. More than 78 contributors, including historians, political scientists, and other academicians, have lent their knowledge and insight to this project, and Salem's editors wish to extend their gratitude to them. We are particularly grateful to the project's editor, John Powell, Professor of History and Political Science at Cumberland College, whose guiding hand shaped this project and its contents at every step of the way.

CONTRIBUTORS

Stephen J. Andrews
*Morton-Seats Institute of
    Archaeology and Anthropology*

James A. Arieti
Hampden-Sydney College

Frederic J. Baumgartner
*Virginia Polytechnic Institute &
    State University*

Alvin K. Benson
Brigham Young University

Wayne H. Bowen
Ouachita Baptist University

Denvy A. Bowman
Coastal Carolina University

Joseph P. Byrne
Belmont University

Laura M. Calkins
Independent Scholar

Douglas Campbell
Independent Scholar

Frederick B. Chary
Indiana University Northwest

Douglas Clouatre
Kennesaw State University

Thomas I. Crimando
*State University of New York,
    College at Brockport*

Kenneth P. Czech
St. Cloud State University

John Daley
Pittsburg State University

John Coleman Darnell
Yale University

Touraj Daryaee
*California State University,
    Fullerton*

Jeffrey Dippmann
Central Washington University

Charles Mayer Dupier, Jr.
Cumberland College

Richard D. Fitzgerald
Onondaga Community College

K. Fred Gillum
Independent Scholar

Nancy M. Gordon
Independent Scholar

Robert F. Gorman
Southwest Texas State University

Oliver Griffin
Weber State University

Gavin R. G. Hambly
University of Texas at Dallas

Randall S. Howarth
Mercyhurst College

George Hoynacki
Merrimack College

Steven Isaac
Northwestern College

Robert Jacobs
Central Washington University

Lance Janda
Cameron University

J. E. Kaufmann
Palo Alto Junior College

Paul Bentley Kern
Indiana University, Northwest

Jacob P. Kovel
Kansas University

Mark S. Lacy
University of Wisconsin, Madison

John W. I. Lee
*University of California, Santa
    Barbara*

Keith A. Leitich
Seattle Central Community College

Van Michael Leslie
Union College

Eric v.d. Luft
*State University of New York,
    Upstate Medical University*

Joseph M. McCarthy
Suffolk University

Michael J. McGrath
Georgia Southern University

Carl Henry Marcoux
University of California, Riverside

Thomas C. Maroukis
Capital University

Jennifer P. Mathews
Trinity University

Timothy May
University of Wisconsin, Madison

Ruben G. Mendoza
Institute of Archaeology

Elizabeth L. Meyers
Independent Scholar

R. Scott Moore
University of Dayton

Walter Nelson
RAND Corporation

Oladele A. Ogunseitan
University of California, Irvine

R. K. L. Panjabi
*Memorial University of
Newfoundland*

Robert J. Paradowski
Rochester Institute of Technology

Brian A. Pavlac
King's College, Wilkes-Barre

Alan P. Peterson
Gordon College

Aaron Plamondon
Royal Military College of Canada

Mark Polelle
University of Findlay

John Powell
Cumberland College

Steven J. Ramold
Doane College

Eugene L. Rasor
Emory and Henry College

Kevin B. Reid
Henderson Community College

Burnam W. Reynolds
Asbury College

Edward J. Rielly
Saint Joseph's College of Maine

Charles W. Rogers
*Southwestern Oklahoma State
University*

Alison Rowley
Duke University

Joseph Rudolph
Towson University

Scott M. Rusch
University of Pennsylvania

James P. Sickinger
Florida State University

David Silbey
Bowdoin College

Michael J. Siler
*California State University, Los
Angeles*

Andrew C. Skinner
Brigham Young University

Roger Smith
Independent Scholar

Larry Smolucha
Benedictine University

Sonia Sorrell
Pepperdine University

James Stanlaw
Illinois State University

Cassandra Lee Tellier
Capital University

Jachin W. Thacker
Western Kentucky University

Louis P. Towles
Southern Wesleyan University

William T. Walker
Chestnut Hill College

John D. Windhausen
Saint Anselm College

Michael Witkoski
University of South Carolina

LIST OF ILLUSTRATIONS, MAPS, AND TIME LINES

VOLUME 1

ALPHABETIZED INDEX OF ESSAYS

CATEGORIZED INDEX OF ESSAYS

RESEARCH TOOLS

GUIDE TO MILITARY THEORISTS

Afonso de Albuquerque (Portuguese, 1453-1515): Albuquerque employed a system of strategically placed forts to expand Portuguese control of the trade route from the Red Sea along the coasts of India and Indonesia to Macao on the Chinese coast. Eventually Portuguese control was undermined by rival European powers and the Ottoman Empire.

Alexander the Great (Macedonian, 356-323 B.C.E.): Perhaps history's most famous conqueror, Alexander used a well-disciplined army inherited from his father, Philip II (382-336 B.C.E.), to dismantle the vast Persian Empire. Eventually his overreaching exhausted both his troops and himself; he died in Babylon returning from India. Alexander proved that smaller, better-trained armies with motivated troops could consistently defeat larger, more unwieldy forces.

Ardant du Picq, Charles Jean Jacques Joseph (French, 1821-1870): Killed during the Franco-Prussian War (1870-1871), Ardant du Picq is known for his posthumous work, *Études sur le combat: Combat antique et combat moderne* (1880; *Battle Studies: Ancient and Modern Battle*, 1914), which stressed the importance of morale in war. He believed that officers must instill confidence in their troops, especially given the impersonal nature of the modern battlefield.

Ashurnasirpal II (Assyrian, c. 915-859 B.C.E.): As creator of the Neo-Assyrian Empire, Ashurnasirpal established the traditions of military excellence and unrelenting cruelty that made Assyria a dominant and feared power from the Euphrates Valley to the Mediterranean.

Attila (Hun, 406?-453): By uniting all the Hunnic tribes from the northern Caucasus to the upper Danube, Attila led his armies on a swath of conquest that led to the gates of Rome itself. Attila's tactics relied on the speed, skill, and savagery of his troops, as well as the terror they inspired.

Augustus (Roman, 63 B.C.E.-14 C.E.): As first emperor of Rome, following the loss of three legions to German forces in the Teutoburg Forest in 9 C.E., Augustus fixed the boundaries of the Roman Empire along strong defensive lines.

Bayinnaung (Burmese, r. 1551-1581): As king of Burma (Myanmar), Bayinnaung unified the country and made it the most powerful in southeast Asia, dominating its neighbors and imposing Buddhism throughout the region.

Belisarius (Byzantine, c. 500-565): The greatest of Byzantine generals, Belisarius served on all imperial frontiers as well as crushing the Nika Uprising (532) that nearly toppled the emperor Justinian I (483-565). Belisarius wrested North Africa from the Vandals, conquered Sicily, and expelled the Ostrogoths from southern Italy—victories achieved with probably never more than about 18,000 troops at any one time.

Braun, Wernher von (German-American, 1912-1977): A pioneer in German rocketry and a visionary of space flight, von Braun helped develop the German rocket program during World War II, which included the V2, the first large military rocket. After the war he was a key member of the American space program.

Caesar, Julius (Roman, 100-44 B.C.E.): A nephew of the Roman general Marius, Julius Caesar rose rapidly in public life and in 60 B.C.E. was elected consul. The following year he was named governor of Cisalpine and Transalpine Gaul and seized the opportunity to conquer the whole of Gaul. Caesar next marched into Italy, precipitating a civil war with his rival, Pompey the Great (106-48 B.C.E.). In a whirlwind campaign, Caesar pushed Pompey out of Italy, captured Spain, and defeated Pompey at Pharsalus (48 B.C.E.). Master of the Roman world, Caesar was preparing for a campaign against the Parthian Empire when he was assassi-

3

nated. Caesar was bold to the point of rashness, but his brilliant mind and swift reactions made him master of any battlefield. He recorded his Gallic and civil war campaigns in his *Commentarii de Bello Gallico* (52-51 B.C.E.) and *Commentarii de Bello Civili* (45 B.C.E.), collectively translated as *Commentaries* (1609).

Charlemagne (Frankish, 742-814): King of the Franks and, after 800, Holy Roman Emperor, Charlemagne returned a strategic vision to European warfare. Thanks to an effective system of communications with his subordinate commanders, Charlemagne directed independent campaigns that established a large, relatively stable state in Western Europe.

Churchill, John, first duke of Marlborough (English, 1650-1722): During the War of the Spanish Succession (1701-1714) Marlboro made effective use of the allied forces through a blend of battlefield brilliance, logistical thoroughness, and diplomatic skills.

Clausewitz, Carl von (German, 1780-1831): Although he served as general in the Prussian army and fought against Napoleon in the Russian campaign of 1812, Clausewitz's major contribution was his posthumously published book *Vom Kriege* (1832-1834; *On War*, 1873). Clausewitz's representation of war as an instrument of the state to coerce an enemy into desired action is often paraphrased as "the continuation of politics by other means." Warfare, therefore, should be guided by political leaders who understand it. Political leaders and generals alike must also recognize what is known as the "Clausewitzian trinity" of violence, chance, and reason, represented in war respectively by the people, the military, and the government. Finally, war brings uncertainty—the "fog of war" and "friction"—in which military decisions must be made and executed.

Clausewitz thought commanders should reduce uncertainty, noting that courage and self-confidence are absolutely essential, especially for the general who seeks the most effective way to victory, that of destroying the enemy army in a single, decisive battle. Initially Clausewitz was regarded as a lesser military thinker, subordinate to

his near-contemporary Antoine-Henri Jomini, and some have faulted him for not presenting specific rules or principles for waging war. Although historical and technological changes have made parts of his work less relevant, Clausewitz remains one of the few essential military theorists in the history of warfare.

Colt, Samuel (American, 1814-1862): Colt invented the revolver that continues to bear his name, a pistol with a rotating cylinder holding six bullets that could be fired before reloading. It proved a success in the Mexican-American War (1846-1848), and by 1855 Colt had built the world's largest private gunmaking facility in Hartford, Connecticut, where he improved mass manufacturing through the use of assembly lines and interchangeable parts.

Crazy Horse (Native American, 1842?-1877): Chief of the Oglala Sioux, Crazy Horse joined with Sitting Bull (1831-1890) to use mobile warfare to destroy the forces under General George A. Custer (1839-1870) at the Battle of the Little Bighorn (1876).

Cyrus the Great (Persian, c. 601 to 590-530 B.C.E.): Founder of the Persian Empire, Cyrus was the world's first great cavalry commander and an expert at siege warfare. His conquests stretched from modern Turkey to the Persian Gulf.

Darius the Great (Persian, 550-486 B.C.E.): Darius established a strong central government in Persia with excellent roads and a powerful army. He extended the empire into northern India and conquered Thrace and Macedonia in Europe and Libya in Africa. Around 500 B.C.E. Ionian Greeks revolted, beginning the Persian Wars (499-448 B.C.E.). Darius died before he could mount his invasion of the Greek mainland.

Douhet, Giulio (Italian, 1869-1930): Originally an artillery officer, Douhet commanded Italy's Aeronautical Battalion from 1912 to 1915 and became convinced of the superiority of airpower. Like the American William "Billy" Mitchell, Douhet argued with such vehemence that he was court-martialed and forced into retirement. However, Italy's poor performance in World War I brought about his recall. Douhet's *Il Dominio dell'Aria*

(1921; *The Command of the Air*, 1921) argued for an independent air force capable of strategic bombing.

Drake, Francis (English, c. 1540-1596): Drake combined the roles of pirate, privateer, and admiral in England's struggle against Spain. He contributed to the tactics of fast, hard-hitting raids on Spanish ports and shipping. His concentration of the English fleet in the western entrance to the English Channel was a key factor in the defeat of the Armada in 1588.

Epaminondas (Greek, c. 410-362 B.C.E.): Commander of the Theban army at Leuctra (371 B.C.E.), Epaminondas defeated a much-larger Spartan force by concentrating his forces on his left wing and overwhelming the enemy's right. This use of the "oblique order" was an important development in phalanx warfare.

Eugène of Savoy (French, 1663-1736): Although French-born, Eugène was rejected by King Louis XIV (1638-1715) and became instead an Austrian general and statesman. He was a master of coalition warfare and cooperated successfully with the duke of Marlborough in victories over the French at Blenheim (1704), Oudenarde (1708), and Malplaquet (1709).

Fabius (Roman, c. 275-203 B.C.E.): Called to defend Rome during Hannibal's invasion of Italy, Fabius was nicknamed "the Delayer" for his refusal to meet his Carthaginian opponent in open battle. Instead, he wore down his foe by harassing his movements and denying him supplies, a logistical approach to warfare that had great implications for future commanders.

Fisher, John "Jackie" (English, 1841-1920): Fisher revolutionized naval warfare with the introduction of the HMS *Dreadnought* in 1906, the first all-big-gun battleship that began a new arms race. Fisher instituted other sweeping changes in British naval policy, including concentrating the Royal Navy in home waters for quicker mobilization against a European enemy.

Foch, Ferdinand (French, 1851-1929): A supporter of the offensive and the power of morale, Foch believed a defeat to be final only when an army lost the will to fight. In the last year of World War I the Allies named Foch as supreme commander, and his positive attitude, along with the arrival of American troops, brought an end to the war.

Frederick the Great (Prussian, 1712-1786): With the hope of promoting Prussia to great power status, Frederick relied upon both his superb army and his ability to draw the maximum from his troops. At battles such as Leuthen (1757) he used the famous "oblique order," massing troops on one flank to achieve a decisive local superiority. Even more important was his genius at combining his arms, as at Rossbach (1757). The result was to establish the Prussian army as the most powerful in Europe, a position that remained unchallenged for over a decade after Frederick's death.

Fuller, J. F. C. (British, 1878-1966): During World War I Fuller planned the Battle of Cambrai (1917), the first to employ tanks. As both an author and an instructor at the British Staff College, he strenuously advocated the extensive use of armor and airpower.

Genghis Khan, né Temüjin (Mongol, between 1155 and 1162-1227): Genghis Khan united the Mongol tribes and organized the Mongolian army into a powerful force. After his conquests of northern China and central Asia, he established a vast empire that was peaceful, well-administered, and strategically positioned. He encouraged trade and opening routes between Europe and China. Genghis Khan's military skill in battle was matched by his attention to organization and administration. His armies were highly disciplined and well supplied. Campaigns were carefully prepared using intelligence gathered by spies and scouts. His reputation and that of his army were his most powerful weapons.

Giap, Vo Nguyen (Vietnamese, born 1911): Viet Minh general Giap believed revolutionary warfare should follow a three-step progression: Guerrilla fighting; equality with the opponent; final victory. During the long struggle in Vietnam he employed this strategy against the French, South Vietnamese, and Americans, leading to military victories, such as that at Dien Bien Phu (1954), as well as politically beneficial military defeats such as the 1968 Tet Offensive.

Goddard, Robert H. (American, 1882-1945): The "father of modern rocketry," Goddard developed rockets using liquid hydrogen and liquid oxygen as fuels and invented steering systems, multi-staged rockets, and other elements of rockets used in modern warfare. From 1930 until the mid 1940's Goddard conducted much of his research in Roswell, New Mexico.

Gribeauval, Jean-Baptiste Vacquette de (French, 1715-1789): As inspector general of French artillery, Gribeauval significantly modernized that military arm. By making cannon bored instead of cast, he improved range, power, and accuracy. His cannon were smaller, lighter, and exceptionally mobile when harnessed to a new design of gun carriage.

Grotius, Hugo, also known as Huigh de Groot (Dutch, 1583-1645): The "father of international law," Grotius developed the first systematic set of laws to govern warfare. His masterpiece, *De Iure Belli ac Pacis Libre Tres* (1625; *On the Law of War and Peace*, 1654), was the foundation for international law regarding the conduct of warfare.

Guderian, Heinz (German, 1888-1954): A combat officer in World War I, Guderian recognized early the value of motorized armor. His book, *Achtung-Panzer! Die Entwicklung der Panzerwaffe, Ihre Kampfstatik, und Ihre Operative Möglickeiten* (1937; *Achtung-Panzer! The Development of Armoured Forces, Their Tactics, and Operational Potential*, 1937), outlined the tactics he and other German commanders would use in World War II.

Gustavus II Adolphus (Swedish, 1594-1632): Called the "father of modern warfare," Swedish king Gustavus II Adolphus improved infantry by mixing pikemen and musketeers in battalions. His lighter cannon introduced mobile field artillery that could support infantry on the battlefield. He also reintroduced cavalry, especially heavy cavalry, as a major element in warfare, giving it a critical role to play. Ironically, he was killed leading a cavalry charge in his victory at the Battle of Lützen (1632).

Hannibal (Carthaginian, 247-182 B.C.E.): Hannibal was a brilliant battlefield commander, and his victory at Cannae (216 B.C.E.) remains the standard by which all battles are judged. Hannibal's contribution to military theory comes mainly from his invasion of Italy during the Second Punic War. Hannibal cast himself as a "liberator" of the Italian cities and sought to detach them from Rome. When this proved unsuccessful, his unbroken string of tactical victories proved strategically useless.

Henry V (English, 1387-1422): In his victory at Agincourt in 1415, Henry skillfully employed the long-range firepower of English archers and mobile field fortifications consisting of sharpened stakes driven into the ground to defeat a larger army of mounted French knights, thus undermining the basis of traditional feudal military theory.

Heraclius (Byzantine, c. 575-probably 641): Threatened along his borders, Byzantine emperor Heraclius reformed the Byzantine military and administrative system by establishing the "theme system," in which military commanders were placed in complete control of provinces, or "themes."

Hideyoshi Toyotomi (Japanese, 1537-1598): A peasant who rose to command armies and ultimately Japan itself, Hideyoshi's combination of military ability, diplomacy, and political skills united the island. His career is an excellent example of the interrelated nature of warfare and politics.

Hitler, Adolf (German, 1889-1945): Influenced by his experience in World War I and his own racist views, Hitler believed that Germany must conquer both Western Europe, to gain security, and Eastern Europe, especially the Soviet Union, to secure *lebensraum*, or "living room," for its population. He was successful in wedding traditional military strategy to this malign political theory and in maintaining the support of the German people and military throughout most of World War II. Hitler was a supporter of new weaponry, such as the Luftwaffe's tactical bombers and fighters, the V-1 and V-2 rockets, and advanced submarines. He also encouraged innovative military techniques such as the Blitzkrieg.

Jomini, Antoine-Henri de (French, 1779-1869): A French general, Jomini entered Russian service after being denied a promotion. Jomini's *Précis de l'Art de la Guerre* (1838; *Summary of the Art of*

War, 1868) was a systematic distillation of his thoughts on military science. Jomini emphasized the immutable principles of war and the importance of maneuvering the mass, or main portion, of an army to make it most effective. He thought the mass should be concentrated at the decisive theater of war, threatening the enemy's communications if possible; that a commander should place the mass of his entire army against a part of his opponent's forces; that the mass of the army should concentrate on the decisive point on the battlefield; and that attacks should be coordinated for maximum impact. Jomini's ideas were highly influential, especially among commanders in the American Civil War (1861-1865).

Kangxi (K'ang-Hsi; Chinese, 1654-1722): The fourth emperor of the Ching Dynasty (1644-1912), who ruled China from 1669 to 1722, Kangxi consolidated Manchu power and legitimized Manchu rule in China. He defended his realm against incursions from the Russians to the north, seized the island of Taiwan, and overcame a serious internal revolt. In these efforts he made great use of Western technology, in particular cartography and cannons.

Khair ed-Dīn (Ottoman, 1483-1546): Creator of the Ottoman navy, Khair ed-Dīn was also known as Barbarossa because of his red beard. In 1533 Turkish sultan Süleyman I the Magnificent (1494 or 1495-1566) ordered him to reorganize the imperial navy, a task he accomplished with speed and ability. The new galleys were used in raids on Christendom and in the conquest of Tunis and Nice in France. Khair ed-Dīn used galleys to evacuate the Spanish Moors from Spain in 1533, a task of great logistic complexity.

Krupp family (German, 1587-1968): The Krupp family was for four centuries the premier military manufacturer in Germany and perhaps the world. Alfred Krupp (1812-1887) perfected techniques to manufacture modern weapons and was known as "the cannon king." Krupp guns contributed to Prussia's victory in the Franco-Prussian War (1870-1871) and were important to Germany's efforts in World War I. The Krupp family supported Adolf Hitler, and a second Alfred Krupp helped

devise the 88-millimeter gun, one of the most deadly artillery weapons of World War II. In 1968, following financial reverses, the Krupp family left the armaments business.

Lawrence, T. E. (British, 1888-1935): Part military advisor, part visionary, Lawrence directed operations of Arab irregular forces during World War I desert campaigns in 1917 and 1918 and helped the Arabs liberate themselves from the Ottoman Empire.

Lee, Robert E. (American, 1807-1870): Offered command of the Union armies at the start of the American Civil War, Lee sided with his native state of Virginia and rose to command the Army of Northern Virginia. He was noted for his aggressiveness, ever willing to defy military convention and divide his smaller forces in the face of the enemy to achieve a devastating flank attack.

Liddell Hart, Basil (British, 1895-1970): Liddell Hart's contributions to military theory include his concept of the "expanding torrent" of armed forces through the enemy's line, which was a precursor of the later German Blitzkrieg. He also advocated attacking key aspects of the enemy's civilian sector.

Louvois, marquis de (French, 1639-1691): As war minister under Louis XIV, Louvois strengthened the French army, making it possible for Louis to wage his numerous wars. Louvois also supported Sébastien Le Prestre de Vauban and others who helped modernize the French military.

Machiavelli, Niccolò (Italian, 1469-1527): Best known for *Il Principe* (1532; *The Prince*, 1521), Machiavelli also wrote *Dell' Arte della Guerra* (1521; *The Art of War*, 1560). Machiavelli looked to Republican Rome to argue that a truly stable and secure nation required a disciplined, well-trained citizen army instead of mercenaries. Machiavelli directly linked politics and war, anticipating the simplification of Clausewitz that "war is the continuation of politics by other means." *The Art of War* was held in high regard by readers such as Frederick the Great, Napoleon, and Clausewitz. Machiavelli wrote from experience: He drafted the Florentine *Ordinanza* of 1505, a military law to end use of mercenary troops.

Mahan, Alfred Thayer (American, 1840-1914): An American naval officer, Mahan published *The Influence of Sea Power upon History, 1660-1783* in 1890, arguing that sea power was the decisive factor in national strength. *The Influence of Sea Power upon the French Revolution and Empire, 1793-1812* (1892) extended and solidified his influence. Both books were widely read and studied in Great Britain and Germany prior to World War I and contributed to the naval arms race, which helped spark that conflict.

Mahan, Dennis Hart (American, 1802-1871): Instructor at West Point and writer, Mahan published editions of his *An Elementary Treatise on Advance-Guard, Out-Post, and Detachment Service of Troops and the Manner of Posting and Handling them in Presence of an Enemy* in 1847, 1853, and 1863. *Out-Posts*, as it was known, was a comprehensive review of strategy and tactics. Mahan helped teach Civil War generals to believe in an active offensive campaign of maneuver as a means of victory.

Mao Zedong (Mao Tse-tung; Chinese, 1893-1976): As a military and revolutionary theorist, Mao believed that the countryside, not the city, was the seedbed of a people's revolution and that "political power comes out of the barrel of a gun." He advocated a small but dedicated revolutionary force that would move among the general population until it could seize total control of the nation.

Marius, Gaius (Roman, 157-86 B.C.E.): Gaius Marius was the prime mover behind the second century B.C.E. evolution of Roman armies from groups of citizens serving for limited periods to standing armies raised and paid by their commander, to whom they were therefore loyal. He also instituted the cohort as a principal unit of the Roman army and improved training and discipline.

Maurice of Nassau (Dutch, 1567-1625): Commander of the Dutch forces in their revolt against Spain, Maurice introduced drill, discipline, organization, standardized equipment, and clear command structure. He drew upon classical examples to make his troops more flexible and responsive, and he effectively utilized artillery and engineers.

Maxim, Hiram Stevens (British, 1840-1916): Born in the United States, Maxim became a British subject in 1900. He invented the automatic machine gun, the basis for one of the most important of modern weapons.

Mehmed II (Ottoman, 1432-1481): The sultan Mehmed II completed the defeat of the Byzantine Empire with the Siege of Constantinople (1453), in which he used the largest cannons yet known, specifically cast for the purpose.

Minié, Claude-Étienne (French, 1804-1879): In 1849 Minié, a French officer, invented a bullet with a conical point and an iron cup at the bottom. When fired from a muzzle-loading rifle, the cup caused the bullet to expand and fit snugly against the rifling grooves of the barrel, increasing the accuracy. The Minié ball, as it was known, was quickly adopted by Western armies.

Mitchell, William "Billy" (American, 1879-1936): An advocate of airpower in armed forces and of the creation of a separate air force, Mitchell commanded the U.S. Army Air Service in Europe during World War I. He was a friend of British air corps commander Hugh Trenchard, an equally strong proponent of airpower. Mitchell's forceful arguments that airpower would be the decisive factor in warfare and his attacks on his superiors led to his court-martial and resignation.

Napoleon I, né Napoleon Bonaparte (French, 1769-1821): Napoleon's rise from a position of relative obscurity to that of emperor in 1804 and his final defeat at Waterloo (1815) and resulting exile to the barren island of St. Helena are romantic aspects of his life. His reputation rests on his reforms of the French legal and administrative system and, especially, his military genius. Napoleon inherited an army that had made major improvements in artillery, infantry tactics, and organization, and he incorporated these into a coherent system that improved the army's logistics, speed, and fighting power. He evolved a command system that allowed him to control operations in an extensive battlefield so he could menace one portion of an enemy's line and at the decisive moment strike at the most vulnerable point. With this flexibility he won complex battles at Castiglione

(1796) and Austerlitz (1805), both of which relied upon careful timing. Above all, Napoleon brought a vision to warfare that moved beyond the immediate battle to a strategic plan to win the war.

Nelson, Horatio (English, 1758-1805): During the Napoleonic Wars (1803-1815) Nelson's victories at the Battle of the Nile (1798), Copenhagen (1801), and Trafalgar (1805) ensured English naval domination. Nelson's innovative tactics, never formalized and always open to innovation, consisted of breaking the line of enemy ships and then concentrating upon the scattered elements.

Nimitz, Chester W. (American, 1885-1966): Commander in chief of the United States Pacific fleet during World War II, Nimitz used an "island hopping" strategy that seized key points and left Japanese forces isolated. Nimitz combined airpower and military intelligence to win the decisive battle of Midway in 1942.

Oppenheimer, J. Robert (American, 1904-1967): As director of the Los Alamos Laboratories during World War II, Oppenheimer was in charge of the team of scientists who developed the nation's first nuclear weapons. An excellent administrator as well as a scientist, he also was a member of the scientific panel that supported the use of the atomic bomb against Japan.

Philip II (Macedonian, 382-336, B.C.E.): As king of a marginal state on the edges of the Greek world, Philip transformed the Macedonian army into his era's most potent force, largely through effective use of the phalanx. He was preparing an invasion of the Persian Empire when he was assassinated by a Macedonian youth and succeeded in rule, ambition, and achievement by his son, Alexander the Great.

Qi Jiguang (Ch'i Chi-Kuang; Chinese, 1528-1587): Incorporated the precepts in Sunzi's (Sun Tzu's) *Bingfa* (c. 510 B.C.E.; *The Art of War*, 1910) in reforms that allowed larger Chinese armies to successfully cross the steppes against mounted, more mobile opponents and made China a more stable nation.

Schlieffen, Alfred von (German, 1833-1913): The German chief of staff from 1891 to 1905, Schlieffen devised an intricate plan for Germany to strike first against France and then move against the slower Russian armies. The plan was the supreme example of war by timetable and went through over fifty revisions. When war finally came, however, it failed.

Scott, Winfield (American, 1786-1866): A veteran of the War of 1812, a victor in the Mexican-American War, and a long-serving army commander, Scott instilled professionalism in the new American nation's army. His amphibious expedition against Mexico in 1847 used maneuvering more than frontal assault to achieve victory. In 1861 he proposed the "Anaconda Plan," which eventually defeated the Southern Confederacy by blockade, driving down the Mississippi River into the heart of the South.

Servius Tullius (Roman, 578-534 B.C.E.): A possibly fictitious Etruscan king credited with revising the Roman state, including its military. His army was organized around "centuries" of one hundred men capable of providing their own arms and armor. Servius is said to have built the first walls around Rome, the first bridge across the Tiber, and Rome's seaport at Ostia. During his reign (or during this time) Rome emerged as the leading power in central Italy.

Severus, Lucius Septimius (Roman, 146-211): Severus restored military strength to the Roman Empire after a period of civil war. He increased the number of Roman legions, created a mobile reserve, used more native troops, and tied the army to the throne by better pay. His dying words to his sons were, in effect, "Be generous to the soldiers and don't care about anyone else."

Shaka (Zulu, c. 1787-1828): Founder of the Zulu Empire in southern Africa, he introduced the *assagai*, or the short stabbing spear, and organized disciplined units that could be effectively commanded on the battlefield. The empire he founded resisted European control until 1897.

Sherman, William Tecumseh (American, 1820-1891): The commander of Union armies in the western theater during the American Civil War, Sherman declared that "war is hell and you cannot refine it," believing that the morale of an enemy civilian population was as much a target as its armies in the field. He employed this doctrine during his devastating March to the Sea (1864) and subsequent advance across the Carolinas.

Shi Huangdi (Shih Huang-ti; Chinese, 259-210 B.C.E.): The first emperor to rule a unified China, Shi Huangdi came to power in 246 B.C.E. as ruler of Qin (Ch'in), a feudal state that unified China in 221 B.C.E. He centralized government and military administration. He divided the country into 36 military districts and standardized weights, measurements, and even the axle lengths of carts to make roads more uniform. He built much of the Great Wall.

Shrapnel, Henry (English, 1761-1842): An English artillery officer, Shrapnel developed an artillery projectile with many small metal pieces which, when exploded, were effective against enemy troops. The name for his device, first used in 1804 and known as "shrapnel," has come to be used for similar fragments from artillery shells or bombs.

Sunzi (Sun Tzu; Chinese, fl. c. fifth century B.C.E.): Little is known about the author of *Bingfa* (c. 510 B.C.E.; *The Art of War*, 1910) except that he was active in military affairs during the Chou dynasty and had a profound influence on Asian military thought. He was largely unknown in the West until the eighteenth century and received widespread appreciation only in the twentieth. Sunzi stressed moral more than physical force, seeing defeat as a psychological condition that a successful commander imposes upon an opponent. A proponent of Taoist thought, Sunzi preached that a commander must use the natural flow of conditions—terrain, weather, enemy strength, or morale—to shape the battle plan. To dominate an enemy morally, one must understand the enemy completely, necessitating the use of intelligence-gathering, deception, and trickery. In Sunzi's concept of warfare, the ultimate goal is to make the enemy's plans fit one's own strategy so that his strengths become weaknesses and lead to his ultimate defeat.

Themistocles (Greek, c. 524-c. 460 B.C.E.): After the Greek victory over the Persians at Marathon (490 B.C.E.), Themistocles established a strong Athenian navy. In 480 B.C.E., the combined Greek fleet defeated the Persians at Salamis. Although Themistocles was exiled from Athens, he laid the foundation for the Athenian Empire.

Tiglath-pileser III (Assyrian, r. 745-727 B.C.E.): Assyrian ruler Tiglath-pileser III established a strong, centralized government and army that allowed the Assyrian Empire to conquer Syria, Phoenicia, Israel, and much of the Middle East.

Torstenson, Lennart (Swedish, 1603-1651): A Swedish general and artillery commander, Torstenson served under Gustavus II Adolphus and was expert in use of the new mobile field artillery. After rising to command of the Swedish army in 1641, he won a series of victories that relied much on his skillful use of field artillery.

Trenchard, Hugh (British, 1873-1956): After serving in the British Army, Trenchard became the Royal Flying Corps' field commander in 1913. In 1918 he established the Independent Air Force as a separate branch. He supported strategic bombing and instituted its first use against Germany in the closing days of the war.

Trotsky, Leon (Russian, 1879-1940): Known as a political leader of the Bolshevik Revolution (1917-1921), Trotsky was the creator of the Red Army during the Russian Civil War (1918-1921). As the first modern military force motivated and guided by ideology, the Red Army preserved the Soviet revolutionary government against its internal and external enemies.

Vauban, Sébastien Le Prestre de (French, 1633-1707): Vauban is chiefly remembered as Europe's best and most prolific military engineer at a time when siegeworks and fortifications were crucial to the art of military affairs. He developed a system of geometric, angular, defensive works that were mutually reinforced by firepower and difficult to attack. Vauban was equally adept using counterwalls or circumvallations; indirect approaches, such as zigzagging trenches; and explosives, such as mines, in capturing enemy fortresses.

Vegetius Renatus, Flavius (Roman, fifth century C.E.): Vegetius's *De Re Militari* (between 383 and 450 C.E.; *The Fovre Bookes of Flauius Vegetius Renatus: Briefelye Contayninge a Plaine Forme and Perfect Knowledge of Martiall Policye, Feates of Chiualrie, and Vvhatsoeuuer Pertayneth* *to Warre*, 1572; also translated as *Military Institutions of Vegetius*, 1767) remained a highly influential work well into the nineteenth century, providing an excellent description of Roman infantry doctrine, especially its emphasis on drill and maneuver. This work was consulted as a practical manual on military matters for centuries.

Wallenstein, Albrecht Wenzel von (Bohemian, 1583-1634): As a general in the forces of the Holy Roman Empire during the Thirty Years' War (1618-1648), Wallenstein raised his own armies and provided for them from the lands of his opponents. His maxim was that "war must feed war."

Whitney, Eli (American, 1765-1825): American inventor Whitney perfected the manufacture of interchangeable parts in 1798, standardizing the machine-made parts of a musket to predetermined specifics and bringing mass production to warfare.

Yamamoto, Isoroku (Japanese, 1884-1943): Japan's most successful admiral during World War II, Yamamoto devised the surprise attack on Pearl Harbor. He forced the "decisive battle" with the American fleet at Midway; the American victory there was the turning point in the Pacific war.

Yi Sun-Sin (Korean, 1545-1598): Yi developed probably the first ironclad battleship, the *kobukson* or "turtle ship," whose upper deck was covered with iron plates with cannon mounted along the sides and stern. When the Japanese invaded Korea in 1592, Yi's fleet cut them off from supplies and reinforcements. His naval victories are ranked with those of Lepanto (1571) and the Spanish Armada (1588).

Žižka, Jan (Bohemian, c. 1360-1424): Military leader of the Hussites, Žižka used linked, stoutly built wagons filled with troops and small cannon as mobile field fortifications. Žižka was never defeated in battle despite the fact that he was, for much of his life, blind.

Michael Witkoski

GEOGRAPHY AND MILITARY DEVELOPMENT

DATES: TO C. 1500 C.E.

SOME GEOGRAPHIC CONSIDERATIONS

Warfare takes place within natural contexts that humans can do little to affect. Whether in military action, gathering to fight, campaigning, or fighting in pitched battle, geographical factors such as terrain, food resources, water, weather, and climate have played major roles in shaping the nature and conduct of organized human conflict. Natural features such as ore fields, natural harbors, and mountain passes, or human-made features such as roadways, cultivated fields, and cities have provided both the means for waging war and the targets of territorial aggressors.

Natural resources dictate the availability of military matériel: wood for ships; plentiful grass for herds of horses; and iron, copper, or tin for weapons. Geographic access is necessary for trade that can enhance natural resource deficiencies, and natural trade routes themselves can become military targets, for either control or plunder. In the premodern world, climate tended to dictate where people congregated, and weather tended to restrict military campaigning to the summer months between spring planting and fall harvest.

Human interaction with the landscape shaped the course of warfare in China, the West, and other rather limited regions in the premodern world. Organized cultivation of the land provided rich stocks of food that attracted hungry nomadic peoples who took what they wanted and were able to take. Walled cities, in which people, wealth, and industry concentrated, developed both defensive and offensive capacities that revolutionized military thinking and action. Developed ports became wealthy points of trade and colonial expansion, as well as cradles of naval development and warfare, especially around the Mediterranean basin. Chinese, Persian, Roman, and Incan roads channeled armies quickly within their empires, enabled rapid communication, and consolidated expansion into neighboring areas. Bridges afforded the easy crossing of natural obstacles such as rivers and gorges. Fortification of natural strongpoints along frontiers, coastlines, and travel routes defended political boundaries and economic interests. Finally, great walls such as those of China and Rome's frontier in Britain clearly marked territory and limited depredation by invaders.

Military technology and the changes in thinking and fighting that both drive its development and are in turn affected by it seem to have evolved most rapidly and thoroughly in regions of the world where geographical access encourages contact among varied human groups. Natural obstacles such as heavy forests, jungles, deserts, and mountains tend to insulate peoples from one another and place limitations on effective interactions among even neighboring groups. Where mobility is limited, advances in military technology (and, arguably, in all phases of technology) are likewise limited. Even far-ranging contact by sea, such as that of the Athenians, Vikings, or Polynesians, revolutionized neither the native peoples nor the colonizers. Across the face of the great Eurasian landmass, however, the use of metallurgy, wheeled vehicles, cavalry, and gunpowder technology spread and found ready acceptance along the way. Perhaps because the Western peoples—from Persia to Britain and from Scandinavia to the Sahel—remained in some form of sustained contact from the mid-first millennium B.C.E. through the Persian, Hellenistic, Roman, Celtic, and Islamic empires, major technological innovations developed, took hold, and spread rapidly. Aside from the lack of major geographic obstacles to invasion—the Alps are passable in summer and the Mediterranean is as much a highway as a barrier—early urbanization and intense rivalries both within and among regions account for much of this dynamism.

A range of shifting political and even religious foundations for warring societies may also have played a part in military development. In Mesopotamia, Akkadian king Sargon the Great (c. 2334-2279 B.C.E.) melded the independent, feuding city-states into an empire and created the core of a limited imperial army drawn from throughout the region. In their movement from kingship to functional democracies to imperial subjection, the ancient Greeks shifted from an organization of heroic warriors to a phalanx of citizen shock troops, a force of multiethnic mixed arms with a heavy reliance on cavalry. The Greeks' proximity to and contact with their many neighbors, such as the Persians, Egyptians, Romans, Etruscans, and Carthaginians, resulted in trade, competition, and conflict that necessitated unprecedented innovations. Not least among these areas of development were naval technology and strategy. Rarely outside the West was sustained land and naval competition so fierce and so regular.

Religious considerations drove the Hebrew people to conquer and dominate much of the Levant, and the terrific successes of Islam stemmed far more from aggressive religious fervor than from military innovation or organization. The conflicting desires to create a territorial Hebrew Promised Land, to spread the *Dar al-Islam*, and to reconquer the same Promised Land for Christian purposes from the *Dar al-Islam* all speak to the geographic expressions and impulses upon which Western religions as well as political entities have relied.

GEOGRAPHIC RESOURCES AND WARFARE

Humans have certain needs for food and shelter that nature must supply. Historically humans largely have occupied a zone of the globe in which climate is conducive to food crops and extremes in temperature and weather are minimal. Some communities shifted from hunting and gathering to herding or domesticating animals and cultivating the soil. After settling in one place, people began to create and store food surpluses and to build permanent shelters. People who remained wanderers (nomadic peoples) or who were perhaps displaced from their own settlements preyed upon these centers of primitive wealth, necessitating the construction of defensive walls and the earliest cities.

Although cattle raids among the Irish, described in the Irish epic *Táin bó Cúailnge*, exemplify the precivilized expression of tribal rivalry, struggles over cultivated lands and the cities they sustained typified warfare in the ancient world. Surplus in food led to the creation of other forms of valuables through specialization of labor. In some of these settings, warriors stood apart from cultivators, protecting them and living off their labor. In others, the cultivators themselves served as soldiers, denying a basic class distinction. In either case, the initial impulse was defensive, although in the former, the urge to display one's virtues as a warrior or leader may have fueled rivalries or conquests of neighboring lands. In many cultures that practiced primitive warfare, conflicts were strictly limited, highly ritualized, and rather bloodless. Resources might have been exchanged but not destroyed or plundered outright. Because of the traditional nature and functions of these battles, little change took place over time. The likeliest events to upset rituals and shape new forms and meanings for organized conflict were major environmental changes (such as disease or sustained weather problems), inmigration, or conquest.

Warrior societies were generally poor materially and relied upon predation for their own wealth. They evolved among cultivators of poor soil, as in the case of the Vikings, or from herdsmen, as did the Central Asian peoples of the steppe. In both of these cases the warriors gained tremendous mobility from clinker-built longships and mounted horses, respectively. In both Viking and steppe nomad societies, trade was as important as plunder, but their native territories provided little of value to others. These warrior groups ranged widely and sought to despoil where defenses were weak; they shared no ritual niceties with their enemies and terrified the people who did. With limited resource bases of their own and without any clear sense of territoriality, these groups could not take and hold power for any sustained period without adapting to the material and social cultures of the conquered, as did the Mongols in China and the Vikings in Normandy.

GEOGRAPHY AND EMPIRE BUILDING

Long-term military success lay, in ancient times, with those who controlled resources and the means of transforming some of them into weapons. Those societies with this power were able to consolidate and control territory that contained raw materials and to defend it from invaders. Indeed, territorial lordship seems to have evolved out of these needs in the Nile Valley, Mesopotamia, China, and parts of the Indus Valley. Land-based empires tended to expand into contiguous areas until forced by geography to halt or to vault barriers. The deliberate expansion of Rome in Italy, of Alexander in the Persian territories, of the Franks in Western Europe, and of Islamic warriors along the Mediterranean littoral and into Persia all followed this pattern. Lands with valuable resources or connections to other such territories were brought under political and military control. However, with trade and ultimately colonization, a society could transcend both its own home territory and its direct neighbors to draw upon far-flung resource centers. Early examples of such societies are the Polynesians, Greeks, Phoenicians, and later the Carthaginians. Seaborne Arabs sailed the Indian Ocean. In more modern times, the Spanish, Dutch, and English all expanded their territory to acquire resources. In each of these cases, expansion into immediately neighboring territories was unfeasible, undesirable, or thwarted, and maritime and naval technology opened distant doors.

The expansion of land-based empires relied upon superior technologies and skillful uses of them, and military organization that could allow operation at a distance from home bases. It also could require adaptation of tactical and sometimes strategic assumptions and factors. Assyrian and Hyksos warriors created and ruled their empires from horse-drawn chariots. Alexander the Great's (356-323 B.C.E.) combination of sarissa-wielding phalanxes and su-

perb cavalry spelled the end for the Persian charioteers and lightly armored infantry. Frankish heavy cavalry bested the lighter Arab horsemen on open fields in central Gaul, and the articulated Roman maniples maneuvered skillfully through rough Italian mountain terrain in ways no massed phalanxes could have. Roman soldiers were also road-builders and connected their conquests directly with urban supply bases and ultimately with Rome itself.

The Assyrians were apparently the first people systematically to utilize protected lines of communication, supply depots, and baggage trains. Alexander's widely ranging army often relied upon supply from both coastal ships and stocked depots, and they suffered tremendously when these failed them. Persian king Xerxes (c. 519-465 B.C.E.) lost his bid for control of southern Greece when his supply ships and their escorts were destroyed at Salamis in 480 B.C.E. In his fourth-century B.C.E. *Bingfa* (c. 510 B.C.E.; *The Art of War*, 1910) the Chinese military theorist Sunzi (Sun Tzu) recommended that the armies of invading commanders carry their own equipment from the homeland but rely on enemy lands for provisions.

Seaborne empires require unobstructed sailing channels that connect the home ports to those of the colonies. Ships had to be adaptable for either trade or battle and ideally could carry on both simultaneously. Ships sought either friendly or directly controlled ports as safe havens along the routes, and those that harbored hostile ships were given a wide berth. Open sea could not be controlled effectively, and individual ships were very vulnerable to predators either alone or in groups. Control of surrounding land could be a factor protecting shipping, but, as Venice discovered in its own Adriatic Sea, it was no guarantee of insulation from bold, swiftly moving enemy fleets.

Ports, as interfaces between land and sea, enjoyed the strengths and weaknesses of both elements. A stout wall, such as that of Constantinople, could hold enemy armies at bay indefinitely, while supplies could flow in from the sea. A blockading fleet could bottle up the harbor, but unless an army controlled the land approaches to the city, its hinterland could provide for its needs. By its very nature a port city was likely to be well stocked in needed provisions and thus likely to withstand any but the most determined siege. Constantinople fell only when the Turks brought to bear cannon that were capable of breaching its land-side wall in 1453. Ports were, however, vulnerable to raids by fleets that were naturally invisible in the vastness of the open sea or that lay in wait in nearby friendly waters. Before telescopes and artillery, there was little time between spotting raiders and setting out a naval defense, and no way of striking back beyond a bow shot.

Throughout history, invading groups have been drawn to the rich ports of Mediterranean mercantile nations: Iberian pirates in the first century B.C.E., Vandals in the sixth century C.E., Arabs in the ninth, Vikings in the tenth, and feuding Genoese and Venetians in the fourteenth. As trade and conquest extended out of the Mediterranean, ship technology evolved to accommodate oceanic conditions and eventually transoceanic voyages, by which time shipboard cannon and small arms had begun to replace crossbows and javelins. There is an interesting parallel between the development of weapons for use on land and those for sea warfare: Most weapons used at sea were first developed for land fighting. Even the ramming prow began as the battering ram; the Roman *corvus* as a siege tower bridge; Greek fire as a weapon against wooden gates. These modifications make sense if one views a ship as a small, mobile castle at sea.

Although the creation and maintenance of seaborne empires required resources and techniques of attack and defense rather different from those of land-based ones, the fundamental human needs for movement, provisions, and effective weapons remained the same. When peoples such as the Persians, Romans, Arabs, or Byzantines could manage the resources to afford both formidable armies and fleets over the long run, the power of their empires was awesome. For some, such as the fifteenth century Chinese, the matériel was there, but the will to project power and awe was not. For others, such as the Phoenicians and later Carthaginians, vulnerability of the home base spelled doom, while Athens and its empire suffered defeat in the Peloponnesian War (431-404 B.C.E.) when the superb Spartan army allied itself with the Persian fleet.

GEOGRAPHY AND MOBILITY

The ability to build and manage ships enormously enhanced people's ability to treat water as a pathway rather than an obstacle. Wide rivers provided easy downstream movement and ready, if difficult, upstream travel and shipping. When an army in motion needed to cross a river, its width and depth determined the means. When fording proved impossible, bridging on pontoons, usually small boats lashed together, did the trick. The Assyrians were apparently the first to use regular bridge engineers, but the Romans developed efficient bridging on the march to an art form. Permanent bridges, however, provided ready access for enemy armies coming from the opposite direction and had to be fortified or guarded with care. Armies could also be ferried across broad expanses of river, but boats brought to or created on the scene were necessarily quite small and light.

Armies that could not use ships to attain their goals were forced to use land routes to maneuver, within both their own and enemy territory. When in motion, the premodern army relied predominantly on human feet and legs, which could traverse a wide variety of terrain and cover great distances when provisions were at hand. Pack animals that could cover the same ground carried supplies but required fodder, which was either carried or found along the way. The Macedonian armies used servants as carriers, but the Roman legions employed about eight hundred pack animals for each legion. Part of the reason for these differing choices may stem from the Macedonians' heavy reliance on cavalry: limited fodder went to Alexander's war horses instead of pack animals. Sledges provided platforms on which provisions and supplies could be carried, dragged by either human or limited animal power.

After armies began using wheeled conveyances, the need arose for fairly smooth and consistent pathways unrestricted by obstacles such as strewn rocks, swamps, or overly steep or narrow passages. Unpaved roads, as found in the Persian Empire, proved perfectly passable in good weather but turned into muddy morasses when heavy rains came. Romans and Chinese created artificial surfaces that retained the road's integrity in all but the worst weather. Carts might be drawn by people or draft animals, such as oxen. The use of horses did not become widespread until after breeders had developed animals of suitable size and strength, and carters had created appropriate harnesses. Progress at human and draft animal speed was steady but slow on easily traversed terrain without steep grades and somewhat faster on paved roadways.

Before horses were ridden, they were harnessed to light chariots. Developed earliest on the Iranian Plateau, horses provided warriors and soldiers much greater speed and range, both prior to and during battle. Organized aggression on a large and mobile scale began with the charioteers. Flat, hard terrain was a necessity, however, and chariots triumphed only where this was in abundance: in Mesopotamia, China, Egypt, and parts of Celtic Western Europe. Before battle, Persian soldiers swept and leveled the field to aid the maneuver of their wheeled warriors. Aryans initially invaded the Indus Valley in chariots, and Mycenean Greeks and Etruscans also used war chariots, but the rocky geography of Italy and Greece limited their usefulness in large formations. Chariots provided platforms from which to shoot arrows or hurl missiles and could easily run down broken formations of lightly armed infantry. Although the fielding and maintenance of a corps of chariots was an expensive proposition, chariot warfare became a standard part of empire building in both China and western Asia. Horses needed large amounts of grass or grain, however, and when dessication set in, as in Mesopotamia, their days were numbered.

Where the availability of grasses allowed, horses were eventually bred, raised, and used for cavalry, first perhaps on the Iranian Plateau around 1400 B.C.E. By around the eighth century B.C.E. horses with backs strong enough to be ridden forward, rather than on the haunches, provided people of the Eurasian steppe between the subarctic northern forest and the great Asian deserts with devastating power and mobility. These horse people had the run of their own vast seas of grass, but were drawn to the civilization and wealth of India, China, and the West. Scythians, Cimmerians, Huns, Mongols, and Turks each in turn terrorized civilized peoples and forced them to adapt to the horseman's threat. However, these were cultur-

ally nomadic peoples, and only those Mongols settling in China and those Turks remaining in Asia Minor were transformed into a stable populace. The mobility of the steppe nomads provided their freedom and defined their military tactics: bow-, sword-, and spear-wielding hordes aligned in a great crescent that thundered across the open plain. They were quick to fire their missiles and disperse, reforming and charging again as needed. They could bleed or milk their mounts for food, and as long as the grass was plentiful, they could maintain their control. Beyond the steppe, however, they could not long survive without adapting or retreating.

Arabs and Europeans adopted cavalry as an arm of mixed-force armies, and Western armies gained clear, if limited mobility, from the use of cavalry. Islam was spread as quickly as it was by fervent horsemen who established both the religion and its rulers from southern Gaul to India. These Islamic warriors arrived in desert areas by camel and fought on horseback. Their goal was not territorial conquest per se, but the diffusion of the truth of Islam and worship of Allah. Yet their tremendous mobility spurred the post-Roman West to create its own cavalry, with enormous repercussions for medieval European society and politics. Western cavalry units were quite small relative both to those of the steppe hordes and to the size of their own societies because local Western economies were settled and agricultural rather than nomadic. The warrior class was supported by the agricultural and trading classes, and the European idea of the chivalry of the mounted knight dominated in Europe as part of a larger social, political, and economic reality.

When horsemen introduced themselves into areas previously lacking in horses, such as South Africa, the Americas, and Australia, the enormous advantage in range and speed, as well as accompanying firepower, gave these intruders a huge advantage over local warriors. Nonetheless, areas of extreme heat or cold and mountainous, heavily forested, jungle, and swampy regions have all proven inhospitable as theaters of operation to bodies of cavalry.

In general, the same routes that provided the most direct pathways for merchants, pilgrims, diplomats, and migrating peoples also served the needs of campaigning armies. The paths of least geographical resistance have been trod for centuries, if not millennia. Just as cities are rebuilt time and again upon the ruins of their predecessors for reasons of geography, so battles will repeatedly occur on the same spots as armies vie to enter or defend territory that retains its importance. If the province of Edirne, formerly Adrianople, is the most contested spot on the globe, however, it is not because of its natural resources, but rather because of its position along the southern bridge between Europe and Asia. Nature has provided the obstacles to human movement as well as the highways along which the armies of the world have campaigned.

TERRAIN AND WARFARE

Sunzi, in his *The Art of War*, stated that "Those who do not know the conditions of mountains and forests, hazardous defiles, marshes and swamps, cannot conduct the march of an army." Of Sunzi's five fundamental factors of war, two are geographical: climate and terrain. The fifth century Roman military historian Vegetius posited that each of Rome's major military arms had its own terrain-specific role: the cavalry had the plains; the navy had seas and rivers; and the infantry had hills, cities, and flat country. The peoples of the great riverine civilizations of China, India, and the West created the great armies of conquest and consolidation. The peoples of the littoral regions of the Aegean, the northern fjords, Oceania, and the Indian coast sent out their seaborne forces of trade, plunder, and colonization. The steppes bred and unleashed on the world the nomadic hordes of charioteers and horsemen. The open terrains of plain, sea, and steppe fostered types of warfare that pitted relatively mobile forces against fixed targets, such as towns, ports, castles, and walls; highly mobile forces, such as fleets and cavalries, against one another; or relatively static armies against each other on the battlefield. Less open terrains, such as mountains, swamps, heavy forests, or jungles, called for conflicts in which neither the massing of troops nor the nimble maneuvering typical of other settings was desired, or even at times possible. Poorer terrain tended

to be economically poorer as well, and war tended to flow out of these areas into the wealthier and literally more attractive regions. Territorial defense by the world's early civilizations often meant pacifying surrounding hills and forests occupied by these outsiders.

Warriors who developed their skills in these less accessible areas had often acquired tactics and weapons that complemented those of the larger armies they joined, as either allies or willing captives. In general, fighting men from these marginal regions were considered "irregular," whether fighting or joining highly organized armies. Mountain and forest terrain lent itself to relatively small, highly mobile, independent parties who would strike and retreat quickly. Such fighters often proved resistant to both authority structures and the discipline necessary to phalanx warfare. Their fluidity and their tendency to raid and ambush, major parts of their strength, have frustrated regular troops from ancient Persia to twentieth century Vietnam. Tu Mu, a ninth century commentator on Sunzi, suggested avoiding or at least scouting areas of danger to chariots and armies: mountain passes, river crossings, and the places where vegetation is luxuriant.

The use of javelins, bows, and slings enabled irregular fighters to engage at a distance, ensuring a buffer that allowed for escape when necessary. The Chinese, Persians, Macedonians, and Romans all incorporated irregulars into their service, adding a needed dimension to their infantry and cavalry arms. The wilderness areas from which irregulars came also provided places of resistance and refuge in times of upheaval or invasion. The difficulty of operating either deterred incursion by regular armies, hampered it effectively, or led to disaster, as in the Teutoburg Forest in 9 C.E., when Germanic warriors annihilated a Roman army that had pursued it too far.

By the time of the first Sack of Rome (410 C.E.), the Roman soldier had become increasingly barbarized and was expected to wield the sling, bow, and even darts. Vegetius Renatus recognized the barbarian origins of the sling in the Balearics and suggested its use derived from the waging of war in stony places. He cited the need for mounted archers to count the same among their enemies and mentioned the origin of the "lead-weighted darts" among the Illyrians. Vegetius also recognized the untrained and undisciplined nature of the *auxilia* soldiers drawn from diverse barbarian peoples. Roman adaptation to the strengths and weaknesses of their enemies had evolved by Vegetius's time, so that the use of concealment and ambush played major roles in his thinking. He believed that a good generals would not attack in open battle where the danger is mutual, but rather from a hidden position. The nature of the battlefield is also of major consideration to the commander and should be studied as to its appropriateness to either the cavalry or infantry.

The difficulties of forcing large groups of foot soldiers to cross desert environments meant that battles in truly desert terrain generally occurred between bodies of men on camel- or horseback. The heat and lack of water allowed for armies of only limited size, and generally lightly armed and armored characters took part in desert warfare. On the fringes of these areas fought the Byzantine *cataphracts* and crusading knights, relatively heavy shock troops whose enemies generally wielded the bow and maneuvered agilely into the desert wasteland itself when retreat was warranted. Fluidity and expectations of minimal gains influenced their tactics and strategies, as they did peoples of the mountains and forests. From horseback slings, bolos, and even lassoes could be used by light cavalry to hamper heavy formations in open field.

CLIMATE, WEATHER, AND WARFARE

In temperate zones early military campaigning was generally a summertime activity, conducted by civilized peoples between the spring planting and the fall harvest. For professional armies, the winter season presented conditions of cold, wind, and precipitation that were best avoided. In spring, flooding rivers often proved impassable, and spring and fall rains turned marching routes into morasses. Chinese, Incan, and Roman roads alleviated some of the last inconvenience, but seasonal campaigning remained the norm. Vegetius recommended conducting naval maneuvers only between late May and mid-September. Foul-weather attacks presented both risks and the opportunity for surprise. Long-term sieges of cities or fortresses had necessarily to last beyond the campaigning season, and while the inhabitants often suffered from lack of food and other supplies, those blockading, relegated to second-class field quarters, often endured worse. Sunzi, who always argued against protracted warfare, advised against sieges of cities under even the best of conditions.

In hotter zones periodic monsoons made military maneuvers all but impossible, and desert conditions affected the size, movement, and armament of military bodies. The Crusaders quickly found that their heavy armor was a deadly encumbrance rather than an aid in the Levant. Lighter clothing and lighter armor characterize warm-climate warriors and soldiers. As such, lighter weapons could kill them. Native allies often became very important when an empire struck too far north or south from its homeland, and adaptations to local conditions became mandatory. Deaths from dehydration, heat stroke, and unfamiliar diseases had to have been plentiful when men from the temperate zones marched south. One explanation for Attila's (c. 406-453) refusal to march south into Italy is his fear of the area's summertime heat and disease.

Ships at sea are far more vulnerable than land armies to occasional storms, and occurrences of storms breaking up large fleets are not rare in ancient chronicles. Perhaps the most famous is the *kamikaze*, or "divine wind," that destroyed the Mongol invasion fleets that threatened Japan in 1274 and 1281.

THE HUMAN LANDSCAPE

The development of cities, more than any other human activity, focused military aggression and provided the means for increasing the scope and deadliness of warfare. Cities became targets of predatory nomadic peoples and of each other. Banded together under a single leader, the combined surpluses of a city provided the wherewithal to carry on protracted campaigns of conquest. Between cities stretched roads along which merchants and armies traveled, and urban wealth grew with the trade that followed.

The oldest known urban place, Jericho, sported walls in its earliest form: walls clearly meant to keep out challengers. The desire to defend and defeat these human landmarks led to an entire branch of military science. Like cities, fortified outposts within which soldiers huddled to defend frontiers and approaches developed defenses appropriate to current siege technologies. At the extreme, these developed into curtain walls.

For Sunzi and his commentators cities were, like other geographic obstacles, to be avoided by the campaigning army. When cities or large fortifications were not the objective, careful consideration had to be made in deciding whether to attack. Unlike mountains, forests, or marshes, cities and fortifications certainly held people, and probably armed men who could cut supply and retreat lines. The Chinese seem to have assumed rather quick and shallow offensive sallies, on which their supply lines and escape routes would be minimally vulnerable. Alexander was willing to bypass strongholds, the major exception being Tyre, which he besieged at a great cost in time and energy from January to July 332 B.C.E. Empires and kingdoms tended to fortify along their frontiers, leaving the interior relatively unprotected. The decision of the Roman emperor Aurelian (c. 215-275 B.C.E.) around 270 C.E. to build up the city of Rome's walls speaks to the Romans' very real fear of the Germanic tribesmen, as distant as they were. After all, fortified cities were needed along the imperial boundaries, not deep within. Where and when the political geography was fragmented—as in classical Greece, China during the Warring States period, feudal Europe, and Renaissance Italian city-states—every center was vulnerable and had to be defended.

Few premodern city walls were spared the experience of siege, and great innovations accompanied the evolving practice of siegecraft. It has been suggested that the first true professional soldiers evolved from the need for protracted and well organized sieges. Professional soldiers were neither elite warriors nor citizen soldiers. They brought the patience and skill necessary to invest a fortified area successfully. Weapons and techniques for gaining forced entry developed as simple blockades of city gates proved of little practical use. Egyptians may have used batter-

ing rams as early as 1900 B.C.E.; siege towers were depicted from the eighth century B.C.E.; and catapult-like machines for hurling projectiles against the walls or into the protected areas emerged in the fourth century B.C.E. The use of scaling ropes and ladders and the practice of undermining walls are probably of even greater antiquity: The earliest levels of Jericho show signs of a dry moat. Other methods of defense included bastions that jutted out from the walls to provide flanking fire by archers and others; towers that protected vulnerable corners and gates; crenellations; machiocolations; battering (sloping out) of wall bases; and, at least during the high Middle Ages, increasingly ingenious ways of defending gateways. Like other types of military technology, siege engines and defensive forms migrated: The round towers and curtain walls of Edward I's (1239-1307) Welsh castles have their origins in the Islamic Near East.

Geography above all other considerations determined the locations of cities and fortifications. When defense was a major factor, location on hills or along ridges provided the best position from which to resist and repel attackers. After laying siege to Celtic and Etruscan strongpoints, the Romans either destroyed them or forced the inhabitants to move to the valley below, as, for example, at Gubbio in Umbria. Here the medieval citizens relocated to the side of the hill, where the main civic structures remain. Human needs also dictated sufficient living and storage space, a source of fresh water, and easy access in time of peace. When garrisons were consistently small, as in the Roman forts along the Saxon shore or along the frontier of the Sienese Chianti, the needs were small and there was little need for growth. As fortified cities expanded, however, the urban geography changed as the location of the site became less important than the human alterations to it.

Strings of forts marked the Incan and Roman frontiers, but the greatest expressions of the siege mentality were the great walls of the Roman emperors Hadrian (76-138) and Antoninus (188-217) in Britain, and the crowning achievement of Chinese engineering, the Great Wall. The Great Wall stretches for some 4,000 miles and initially linked a series of hilltop fortifications along a border of steppe and mountain, wilderness, and civilized terrain during the Qin (Ch'in) Dynasty (221-206 B.C.E.). Climatic shifts in the region to and from desertification made its rein- forcement of a natural physiological boundary irrele- vant, and the Great Wall's failure to hold back the Mongol advance is legendary.

BOOKS AND ARTICLES

Contamine, Philippe. *War in the Middle Ages*. New York: Blackwell, 1986.

Engels, Donald W. *Alexander the Great and the Logistics of the Macedonian Army*. Berkeley: University of California Press, 1980.

Keegan, John. *A History of Warfare*. New York: Vintage, 1994.

McNeill, William H. *The Pursuit of Power: Technology, Armed Force, and Society Since* A.D. *1000*. Chicago: University of Chicago Press, 1984.

Preston, Richard A., Sydney F. Wise, and Alex Roland. *Men in Arms: A History of Warfare and Its Interrelationships with Western Society*. 5th ed. New York: Holt, Rinehart and Winston, 1991.

Joseph P. Byrne

Time Line

Date	Event
c. 13,000 B.C.E.	Spears and spear-throwers appear as weapons.
c. 10,000 B.C.E.	Bows and arrows appear as weapons in Neolithic cave paintings.
c. 9th millen. B.C.E.	The sling makes its first known appearance.
c. 7000 B.C.E.	The inhabitants of Jericho construct massive fortifications around their city.
c. 7th millen. B.C.E.	The stone-headed mace makes its first known appearance.
c. 5000 B.C.E.	The city of Jericho becomes arguably the first town to be fortified with a stone wall.
c. 5000 B.C.E.	Sailing ships make their first appearance in Mesopotamia.
c. 4000 B.C.E.	Horses are first domesticated and ridden by people of the Sredni Stog culture.
c. 4000 B.C.E.	Copper is used to make the first metal knives, in Middle East and Asia.
c. 3500 B.C.E.	The Sumerians employ wheeled vehicles.
c. 3200 B.C.E.	The Bronze Age is inaugurated in Mesopotamia as new metal technology allows more lethal weapons and more effective armor.
c. 2500 B.C.E.	The Sumerian phalanx is first employed.
c. 2500 B.C.E.	Metal armor is developed in Mesopotamia, making the stone-headed mace obsolete.
c. 2300 B.C.E.	After the composite bow is introduced by Sargon the Great, the use of the Sumerian phalanx declines.
c. 2250 B.C.E.	Composite bow is depicted in Akkadian Stele of Naram-Sin.
c. 2100 B.C.E.	The Sumerians reassert their supremacy over southern Mesopotamia, precipitating a renaissance of Sumerian culture and control that lasts for approximately 200 years.
c. 2000 B.C.E.	The first metal swords, made from bronze, appear.
c. 1950-1500 B.C.E.	Assyrians first rise to power during the Old Empire period.
c. 1900 B.C.E.	Primitive battering rams are depicted in Egyptian wall paintings.
c. 1810 B.C.E.	Neo-Babylonian leader Hammurabi unifies Mesopotamian region under his rule and establishes capital at the city-state of Babylon.
c. 1800-1000 B.C.E.	Aryan invaders conquer India, mixing with earlier cultures to produce a new Hindu civilization in the area of the Ganges River Valley.
c. 1700 B.C.E.	Assyrians employ integrated siege tactics with rams, towers, ramps, and sapping.
c. 1674 B.C.E.	The Hyksos people introduce the horse-drawn chariot during invasions of Egypt.
c. 1600 B.C.E.	Chariot archers are increasingly used in warfare.
1600-1066 B.C.E.	Shang (Shang) Dynasty rules in China.
c. 1500-900 B.C.E.	During their Middle Empire period, the Assyrians drive the Mitanni from Assyria, laying foundations for further expansion.

DATE	EVENT
1400-1200 B.C.E.	Mycenaean civilization flourishes, with a wealth of political, economic, and religious centers.
c. 1384-1122 B.C.E.	The crossbow is originated during China's Shang Dynasty.
c. 1300 B.C.E.	Chariot design undergoes major innovations, with an increase in the number of spokes and the relocation of axles.
c. 1300-700 B.C.E.	Semitic desert dwellers infiltrate southern Mesopotamia to establish Chaldean culture during period of Assyrian domination in Near East.
c. 13th cent. B.C.E.	The Hebrews conquer Transjordan and Canaan under the leadership of Joshua.
1204-1194 B.C.E.	The fortified city of Troy is besieged by the Greeks for ten years and falls only after succumbing to the Greek deception tactic of the Trojan Horse placed outside the city's gates.
c. 1200 B.C.E.	The use of the chariot in warfare declines and foot soldiers increasingly come into use, as "barbarian" tribes, fighting on foot and armed with javelins and long swords, overrun many ancient Middle Eastern kingdoms.
c. 1200 B.C.E.	The chariot is introduced to China from the northwest and is later adapted for use in siege warfare.
1200-1100 B.C.E.	Mycenaean order collapses during a period of upheaval.
c. 1122 B.C.E.	Shang Dynasty armies introduce the chariot to northern China in warfare against the Zhou (Chou) Dynasty.
1100-750 B.C.E.	In the period known as the Greek Dark Age, petty chieftains replace the Mycenaean kings.
1066-256 B.C.E.	Zhou Dynasty rules in China.
c. 1000 B.C.E.	Metal-headed maces become common in Europe.
c. 1000 B.C.E.	Cimmerians first produce bronze battle-axes.
c. 1000 B.C.E.	Iron begins to replace bronze in the making of weapons in Assyria.
1000-990 B.C.E.	David consolidates the reign of Judah and Israel and defeats neighboring kingdoms of Moab, Edom, Ammon, and Aramaea, among others.
c. 1000-600 B.C.E.	Aryan Hindu civilization comes to dominate most of northern and central India while smaller states wage war for control in the South.
c. 900 B.C.E.	Cavalry begins to compete with chariotry as a method of warfare in the Neo-Assyrian Empire.
c. 900 B.C.E.	Scyths and succeeding steppe warriors master the use of bows while on horseback.
c. 900 B.C.E.	Iron weapons become increasingly popular.
c. 900 B.C.E.	Smiths master the use of iron to make stronger, more lethal swords.
900-600 B.C.E.	Assyria undergoes Late Empire period, its greatest era of military expansion.
850 B.C.E.	The principles of fortress-building are evidenced in an Assyrian relief sculpture.
753 B.C.E.	The city of Rome is said to be founded on the banks of the Tiber River by Romulus, one of the twin sons of Mars, the Roman god of war.

Date	Event
c. 750-650 B.C.E.	Hoplite armor and tactics are developed.
745-727 B.C.E.	After years of domestic turmoil, Tiglath-Pileser III reestablishes control over Assyrian homeland and institutes military reforms.
721 B.C.E.	Sargon II conquers Israel.
705-701 B.C.E.	Judean king Hezekiah leads rebellion against Assyrian domination.
c. late 7th cent. B.C.E.	The Greeks develop the trireme, a large ship powered by three rows of oarsmen.
c. 700 B.C.E.	Tight-formation hoplite tactics, well-suited to the small plains of the ancient Greek city-states, are first introduced in Greece.
626 B.C.E.	Nabopolassar Nebuchadnezzar leads revolt against Assyrian rule and establishes Chaldean, or Neo-Babylonian, kingdom.
612 B.C.E.	Assyrian city of Nineveh is conquered by Medes and Babylonians, marking the final destruction of the Assyrian Empire.
c. 6th cent. B.C.E.	The lance is first used by the Alans and Sarmatians, and the chariot is first used by various tribes in battle.
587 B.C.E.	Jerusalem falls to the Neo-Babylonians.
587-586 B.C.E.	Nebuchadnezzar II uses siege warfare to conquer Jerusalem.
c. 546 B.C.E.	Persian king Cyrus the Great uses chariots to great advantage at the Battle of Thymbra.
539 B.C.E.	Chaldean Empire is conquered by Persian king Cyrus the Great.
c. 5th cent. B.C.E.	The crossbow is developed in China, providing more power, speed, and accuracy than the composite bow.
c. mid-5th cent. B.C.E.	Athens establishes itself as a major naval power in the Mediterranean.
499-448 B.C.E.	The Persian Wars are fought between Persia and the Greek city-states.
431-404 B.C.E.	The Peloponnesian Wars are fought between Athens and Sparta.
c. 429-427 B.C.E.	A wall of circumvallation is used in the Siege of Plataea by Sparta and Thebes at the beginning of the Peloponnesian War.
c. 401 B.C.E.	Slings are used to great effect against the Persians at the Battle of Cunaxa, outranging Persian bows and arrows, and charioteers are overwhelmed by more flexible cavalry, ending the dominance of chariots in warfare.
c. 400 B.C.E.	The development of the *gastraphetes*, or belly bow, allows the shooting of more powerful arrows.
c. 4th cent. B.C.E.	Earliest known stirrups, made from leather or wood, are used by the Scyths.
c. 4th cent. B.C.E.	Onboard catapults are added to ships, effectively rendering them as floating siege engines.
c. 4th cent. B.C.E.	The *Arthasastra*, an influential treatise on Indian politics, administration, and military science, is reputedly written by the prime minister Kautilya.
c. 4th-3d cent. B.C.E.	Mediterranean city-states undertake massive building of walls during a period of warfare.

DATE	EVENT
c. 4th-3d cent. B.C.E.	The use of protective bone breastplates is regularly adopted.
c. 399 B.C.E.	The catapult is invented at Syracuse under Dionysius I, significantly advancing the art of siege warfare.
c. 390 B.C.E.	Gallic warriors overwhelm the Republic's forces, capturing and plundering the city of Rome.
371 B.C.E.	Thebes defeats Sparta at Leuctra, ending Spartan supremacy in hoplite warfare.
c. 350 B.C.E.	Philip II of Macedon develops the Macedonian phalanx and adopts the use of the sarissa, a pike of nearly 15 feet in length wielded with two hands.
338 B.C.E.	Philip II of Macedon defeats united Greek army at Chaeronea.
334 B.C.E.	Alexander the Great uses stone-throwing torsion catapults at the Siege of Halicarnassus.
333 B.C.E.	Alexander uses combined infantry and cavalry forces to route the Persian cavalry under Darius III at the Battle of Issus.
332 B.C.E.	Alexander begins the Siege of Tyre.
331 B.C.E.	Alexander defeats main army of Darius III at Gaugamela.
326 B.C.E.	The Indian king Porus employs war elephants against Alexander's forces at the Battle of the Hydaspes, seriously disrupting the Macedonian phalanx.
c. 321 B.C.E.	Chandragupta Maurya expels Alexander's forces from India and establishes the Mauryan Dynasty.
307 B.C.E.	King Wu Ling of Zhao (Chao), inspired by steppe nomad tribes to the north, introduces the use of cavalry in China.
305-304 B.C.E.	Macedonians employ a huge siege tower known as a *helepolis* during the Siege of Rhodes.
c. 3d cent. B.C.E.	The Parthians, a steppe nomad people, perfect the Parthian shot, fired backward from the saddle while in retreat.
c. 3d cent. B.C.E.	Romans utilize the corvus, a nautical grappling hook that allows sailors to board and capture opposing vessels.
c. 274 B.C.E.	Aśoka the Great, grandson of Chandragupta Maurya and a military genius in his own right, solidifies the strength of the Mauryan Empire.
247 B.C.E.	Hamilcar Barca is appointed Carthaginian military commander, marking the emergence of Carthage as a major military threat.
241 B.C.E.	In the final naval victory of the First Punic War, Rome expels the Carthaginians from Sicily.
237 B.C.E.	Hamilcar begins Spanish military campaign, in preparation for ultimate war with Rome.
221 B.C.E.	Hamilcar's son Hannibal takes command of Carthaginian military.
221-206 B.C.E.	Qin (Ch'in) Dynasty rules in China.
218 B.C.E.	Hannibal leads a force of war elephants, cavalry, and foot soldiers across the Alps to trap and defeat the Romans at Trebia.

DATE	EVENT
216 B.C.E.	Hannibal issues Rome its greatest defeat in battle at Cannae.
214 B.C.E.	Chinese emperor Qin Shi Huangdi (Ch'in Shih Huang-ti) orders that the many portions of the Great Wall be joined to form a unified boundary.
c. 206 B.C.E.-220 C.E.	Crossbows come into regular usage in China.
206 B.C.E.-220 C.E.	Han (Han) Dynasty rules in China.
197 B.C.E.	The Romans defeat main army of Macedonian king Philip V at Cynoscephalae.
168 B.C.E.	The Romans defeat Philip V's son, Perseus, at Pydna, eventually organizing Macedonia as a Roman province.
167-161 B.C.E.	Judas Maccabeus leads campaigns against Greek rule.
146 B.C.E.	Rome defeats Carthage in the Third Punic War, destroying its greatest enemy and assuring its long-term dominion.
58-45 B.C.E.	Julius Caesar employs independently operating cohorts in the Gallic Wars and the Roman Civil Wars against Pompey.
53 B.C.E.	Parthian mounted archers defeat heavily armed Roman infantry at the Battle of Carrhae.
c. 50 B.C.E.-50 C.E.	The earliest horseshoes are made in Gaul.
39-37 B.C.E.	Herod is named king of Judea by the Roman Senate and leads campaigns to establish his kingdom.
c. 31 B.C.E.	Specialist corps of slingers largely disappear from ancient armies.
c. 1st cent. C.E.	Aksumite Ethiopians emerge as dominant players in the control of Red Sea trade.
66-70	The Jews wage war against the Romans.
70	The Romans besiege Jerusalem, taking the city's population captive and leveling its buildings to the ground.
73	The Romans employ ramps and siege towers in their successful three-year Siege of Masada.
c. 2d cent.	The use of armor spreads from the Ukraine to Manchuria.
c. 100	With the increasing use of cavalry in Roman warfare, the *spatha*, a longer, slashing sword, becomes popular.
c. 122-136	Hadrian's Wall is constructed in northern England, marking northernmost border of Roman Empire.
c. 3d-4th cent.	Despite the increasing role of cavalry due to barbarian influence, infantry remains the dominant component of the Roman legions.
220-280	Wei (Wei), Shu (Shu), and Wu (Wu) Dynasties rule in China during Three Kingdoms period.
265-316	Western Jin (Chin) Dynasty rules in China.
c. 4th cent.	The use of stirrups is introduced in China, allowing cavalry armor to become heavier and more formidable.

DATE	EVENT
300-1763	During the miasma-contagion phase of biological warfare, environments are deliberately polluted with diseased carcasses and corpses.
317-420	Eastern Jin Dynasty rules in China.
320	Chandragupta II establishes the Gupta Dynasty, recalling the glory days of the Mauryan Empire and employing a feudal system of decentralized authority.
324	Roman emperor Constantine builds a new eastern capital at Constantinople.
370	Rome rebuilds its walls as protection against barbarian invasions.
386-588	Southern and Northern Dynasties rule concurrently in China.
c. 400	The bow and arrow is introduced in eastern North America.
c. 400	Cavalry replaces infantry as the most important element in Roman armies.
c. 400	Horseshoes come into general use throughout Europe.
c. 400	The Chinese first make steel by forging cast and wrought iron together.
451	Attila the Hun invades Roman Gaul.
476	The Sack of Rome by barbarians brings about an "age of cavalry," during which foot soldiers play a diminished role in warfare.
500	Central Asian invaders appear in India, bringing superior fighting techniques and concentrated use of cavalry.
507	Clovis defeats the Visigoths at Vouillé and unifies Gaul.
527-565	Roman emperor Justinian reigns, definitively codifying Roman law, waging war against the Germans and Persians, and changing the nature of the empire from that of a constitutional to that of an absolute monarchy.
553	Eastern T'u-chüeh Empire founded in Mongolia
c. 7th cent.	Aksumite kingdom is weakened by the spread of Islam throughout Arabia and North Africa.
610-641	Heraclius reigns over the Byzantine Empire, Hellenizing the culture and introducing the theme system of Byzantine provinces ruled by military governors.
622	In a journey known as the Hegira, the Islamic prophet Muḥammad (c. 570-632) flees from Mecca to Medina to avoid persecution.
632-661	Muḥammad is succeeded after his death in 632 by the four legitimate successors of the Rāshidūn caliphate.
674-678	Greek fire, a flammable liquid, is used by the Byzantines against Arab ships during the Siege of Constantinople.
680	The forces of Muḥammad's grandson Ḥusayn are ambushed and massacred at the Battle of Karbalā, marking the beginning of Shia as a branch of Islam.
687	Pépin of Herstal wins the Battle of Tertry, solidifying rule over all Franks, and unifies the office of Mayor of the Palace.
c. mid-8th cent.	Islam becomes the dominant religio-political power structure of the Middle East, from the Atlantic to the Indian frontier, including the Mediterranean coast and Spain.

DATE	EVENT
c. 700-1000	Ghana emerges as the dominant kingdom and military power of the Western Sudan.
714	Pépin's illegitimate son, Charles Martel, seizes control over Frankish kingdom in a palace coup.
740-840	Uighurs destroy T'u-chüeh Empire and dominate Mongolia.
c. 750	Carbon-steel swords first appear in Japan.
c. 757-796	Offa's Dyke is built in the kingdom of Mercia to protect the kingdom's Welsh border.
793	Vikings sack Lindisfarne Abbey in northern England.
800	Charlemagne is crowned Holy Roman Emperor by Pope Leo III.
840-920	Kirghiz invade Mongolia and drive out Uighurs, continuing to dominate the region.
843	Vikings sack Dorestadt and Utrecht.
845	Charles the Bald, king of the Franks, pays Vikings money to retreat.
880's	King Alfred the Great begins constructing a series of *burhs*, or garrisons, to defend Wessex from Vikings.
886	Last Viking siege of Paris.
891	The Vikings suffer a rare defeat at Louvain.
c. 10th cent.	Ghaznavid Turks invade India from Afghanistan, introducing an Islamic influence that will continue almost uninterrupted until the early sixteenth century.
911	Rollo receives county of Normandy from the French king.
920	Khitans drive out Kirghiz and establish empire in Mongolia and China.
c. 930	Vikings settle Iceland.
954	English expel the last Viking king from York.
990's	The first stone keeps appear in northwestern Europe.
c. 10th-11th cent.	The crossbow makes its first European appearance, in Italy.
1013	Danish king Sveyn I Forkbeard defeats English king Ethelred I and forces him into exile.
1017-1035	Sveyn's son Canute rules both England and Denmark.
1044	The first precise recipe for gunpowder is given, in a Chinese work.
1066	William of Normandy defeats English at the Battle of Hastings, and a rapid proliferation of motte-and-bailey castles follows.
1095-1099	During the First Crusade, initiated by Pope Urban II, European crusaders, fighting to protect the Holy Land for Christianity, capture Jerusalem.
1100	European knights adopt the use of the couched lance, which provides more force than previous hand-thrust weapons.
1125	Jürcheds conquer northern China and drive out Khitans, and Mongolia descends into tribal warfare.
1139	The use of the crossbow in Christian Europe is prohibited by Pope Innocent II at the Lateran Council.

DATE	EVENT
1145-1149	The Second Crusade, unsuccessfully led by the kings of France and Germany, is prompted by Muslim conquest of the principality of Edessa in 1144.
1187-1192	The Third Crusade succeeds, especially through the efforts of English king Richard I, in restoring some Christian possessions.
1192	The samurai Minamoto Yoritomo establishes the first shogunate at Kamakura, bringing order to Japan after four centuries of feudal chaos and political vacuum.
1196-1198	King Richard I of England builds Château Gaillard with three baileys, which had to be captured before the castle could be taken, serving as multiple lines of defense.
1198-1204	The Fourth Crusade, initiated by Pope Innocent III, captures Constantinople and damages the Byzantine Empire.
c. 1200	In North America, the southwestern Anasazi culture is destroyed, possibly by raiding Ute, Apache, Navajo, and Comanche tribes.
c. 1200	As forged steel processes are refined, several European cities, including Sheffield, Brussels, and Toledo, emerge as swordmaking centers.
1206	Genghis Khan is named ruler of the Mongols.
1213	The Mongols invade China.
1217-1221	The Fifth Crusade, organized to attack the Islamic power base in Egypt, succeeds in capturing the Egyptian port city of Damietta but ends in defeat when the crusading army attempts to capture Cairo.
1228-1229	In what is sometimes referred to as the Sixth Crusade, the excommunicated Holy Roman Emperor Frederick II sails to the Holy Land and negotiates a reoccupation of Jerusalem.
c. mid-13th cent.	The cog, with high sides that offer protection against other vessels, is developed in Northern Europe.
1230	The kingdom of Mali is founded by a Mandinka prince after the defeat of the Susu kingdom.
1236-1242	The Mongols make conquests in Russia, Eastern Europe, Iran, and Transcaucasia.
1248-1254	The Seventh (or Sixth) Crusade is led by Louis IX of France and follows a course similar to that of the Fifth Crusade.
1258	Mongols capture Baghdad and end the ʿAbbāsid Caliphate.
1260	Mongols invade Syria and capture Damascus but are defeated at the Battle of Ain Jalut by Mamlūk slave cavalry, trained by the Egyptians to steppe nomad levels.
1261	Civil war between Il-Khanate of Persia and the Golden Horde of Russia begins.
1269-1270	Eighth (or Seventh) Crusade is organized by a now-elderly Louis IX, who dies upon landing in Tunisia, leading to the breakup of his army.
1270-1272	Edward I, the son of Henry III of England, decides to press on alone to Palestine after the French abandon the Eighth Crusade and achieves some modest success with a truce before the ultimate fall of Acre, the last bastion of the crusader states, in 1291.

DATE	EVENT
1272	Kublai Khan establishes the Yuan Dynasty.
1277-1297	King Edward I of England builds a series of ten Welsh castles, with an implicitly offensive function as continuances of the king's campaigns.
1298	The English army uses the longbow to great effect against the Scots at Falkirk.
c. 14th cent.	An "infantry revolution" spurred by the greater use of the pike and bow takes place in Europe.
c. 1300	An increase in separate tribal identities among North American indigenous peoples develops in response to increasing importance of agriculture and clearer definition of gender roles.
c. 1300	The Chinese first use black powder to propel projectiles through bamboo tubes, revolutionizing warfare.
1300	Japanese craftsmen perfect the art of swordmaking, creating the *katana*, a curved sword used by samurai warriors.
1302	Flemish pikemen defeat French knights with advantageous choice of terrain at Courtrai.
1314	Emperor Amda Tseyon comes to power in Ethiopia, expanding and solidifying the Solomonid Dynasty.
1315	Swiss pikemen begin string of victories against mounted knights by defeating the Austrians at Morgarten, leading to their fourteenth and fifteenth century dominance of infantry warfare.
1331	First known use of gunpowder weaponry occurs at the Siege of Friuli in Italy.
1335	Il-Khanate of Persia ends.
1340	The first definitive use of gunpowder weapons is made at the Siege of Tournai.
1346	English longbowmen defeat French knights at the Battle of Crécy, which also marks the first definitive use of gunpowder artillery on a battlefield.
1346-1347	Cannons are deployed by the English at the Siege of Calais.
c. mid-14th cent.	The carrack, an efficient sailing ship with multiple masts, becomes popular in Atlantic and Mediterranean waters.
1368	The Chinese Yuan Dynasty ends, and the Mongols are driven back to Mongolia, where a period of civil war ensues.
1369	Tamerlane becomes ruler of Central Asia.
1377	Cannon are first used successfully to breach a wall at the Siege of Odruik, the Netherlands.
1398	Mongol invasions by Tamerlane devastate North India.
c. 14th-15th cent.	The increasing predominance of firearms in Europe results in the diminishing use of archers in warfare.
1415	English archers and infantry inflict a major defeat upon mounted French knights at the Battle of Agincourt, initiating the decline of the heavily armored cavalry knight.

DATE	EVENT
c. 1420	Corned powder and matches are developed.
1420	Hussite leader Jan Žižka stymies German knights during the Hussite Wars with his *Wagenburg*, a defensive line of wagons and cannons.
c. 1425	The corning, or granulating, process is developed to grind gunpowder into smaller grains.
1450	Songhai incorporates the former kingdom of Mali and comes to control one of the largest empires of that time.
1450-1700	Sword blades become lighter, narrower, and longer, gradually evolving into the familiar rapier design.
1453	With use of large cannons, the Muslim Turks besiege and capture Constantinople from the Byzantines and establish the Ottoman Empire.
1468	Songhai armies invade Timbuktu, execute Arab merchants and traitors, and sack and burn the city, thereby heralding a period of anti-Islamic sentiment in West Africa.
1477-1601	Perpetual civil war is waged throughout the Sengoku, or "Warring States," period.
c. 1480	Fortifications begin to undergo design changes, such as lower, wider walls, to accommodate the use of cannons.
1494	Charles VIII introduces the modern siege train in his invasion of Italy, confirming the obsolescence of high medieval defenses.
c. 1500	The Iroquois Confederacy, an alliance of separate tribes formed to fight hostile western and southern neighbors, is established in the American Northeast.
c. 1500	The development of gunpowder muskets, pistols, and cannons forces tactical and strategic changes in the use of spears, bows and arrows, swords, cavalry, and armor.
c. 1500	As European plate armor becomes more prevalent, the sharper, more narrow rapier is developed to combat it.
c. 1500	Leonardo da Vinci draws a design for what could arguably have been the first helicopter.
c. 1500	A Chinese scientist is killed by the explosion of gunpowder rockets he had tied to a chair in an effort to develop a flying machine.
1501	The development of gunports allows a ship's heaviest guns to be mounted on its lowest decks, stabilizing its center of gravity.
1503	The first effective use of the combination of firearms and pikes, a formation called the "Spanish Square," is made at the Battle of Cerignola.
1522	Spanish harquebusiers slaughter Swiss pikemen in the service of the French at the Battle of Bicocca.
1525	The Spanish Square formation of pikemen and harquebusiers is used to slaughter French cavalry at the Battle of Pavia.
1526	Bābur makes effective use of artillery to defeat Sultan Ibrāhīm Lodī at the famous Battle of Pānīpat on April 20, 1526, and establish the Mughal Empire.

Date	Event
1527	The Mughals defeat the Rajputs at the Battle of Kanwa.
1529	The Mughals defeat the Afghans at the Battle of Ghāghara.
c. 1530	King Henry VIII of England builds series of forts on southern coastline to guard against European invasion.
c. mid-1500's	European cavalries begin to appear armed with short muskets that can be fired from both mounted and dismounted positions.
1541	Portuguese musketeers arrive to help defend Ethiopia, ending the Islamic threat two years later, under the emperor Galawdewos.
1543	Firearms are first used in Japan.
1544	At Cerisolles, French knights fighting in the traditional style play a major role in gaining victory over the Swiss, the last battle in which they are to do so.
1556	Bābur's grandson Akbar is victorious at the second Battle of Pānīpat, against the Sur descendants of Shēr Shāh, and eventually conquers most of northern and eastern India, Afghanistan, and Baluchistan.
1562	The *caracole* maneuver is first executed by Huguenot pistolers against Catholic forces at the Battle of Dreux.
1565	The Siege of Malta ends the Turkish advance across the Mediterranean.
1571	The Battle of Lepanto II, fought between the Ottoman Turks and the Christian forces of Don Juan de Austria, is the last major naval battle to be waged with galleys.
1575	Three thousand musketeers help General Oda Nobunaga win control of central Japan.
1588	The English employ galleons to individually attack the larger ships of the formidable Spanish Armada, defeating the Spanish and revolutionizing naval tactics.
1591	Songhai is conquered by a Moroccan army consisting primarily of European mercenaries armed with muskets, the first to be used in West African warfare.
1592	Muslim leader Aḥmad Grāñ defeats forces of Lebna Dengel at the Battle of Shimbra-Kure, opening southern Ethiopia to Islamic rule.
c. late 16th cent.	Japanese swordmaking techniques reach a peak of sophistication, with a variation of the hammer-welding process.
c. 17th cent.	The howitzer is developed by the English and Dutch for use against distant targets.
c. 1600	The military reforms of Maurice of Nassau reduce the size and depth of pike formations to facilitate maneuverability and increase the number of muskets in units.
1600	The Battle of Nieuwpoort in the Netherlands is the first battlefield test of Maurice of Nassau's linear infantry tactics.
1603	Tokugawa Ieyasu establishes the Tokugawa shogunate, with its capital at Edo, marking the beginning of early modern Japanese history.

DATE	EVENT
1609	The Netherlands forces Spain to grant a truce tacitly recognizing Dutch independence after over thirty years of revolution of Dutch Protestant provinces against Spanish occupation.
1631	Gustavus II Adolphus's military reforms prove their value at the Battle of Breitenfeld, as Gustavus's disciplined cavalrymen combine firepower and shock tactics.
1632-1653	The fifth Mughal emperor, Shah Jahan, builds the Taj Mahal as a monument to his love for his wife Mumtaz Mahal.
1642-1649	During the English Civil War, the Royalist Army is the first to use horse artillery in the form of a small brass cannon mounted onto a horse-drawn cart.
1653	The line of battle is developed as a naval tactic, allowing for more effective use of broadside firepower.
1657	ʿĀlamgīr becomes the sixth Mughal emperor and ultimately expands the Mughal Empire to its greatest extent.
c. 1660	Sébastien Le Prestre de Vauban emerges as a genius of military engineering, designing bastioned fortifications.
1673	The use of saps and parallels is introduced by Sebastién Le Prestre de Vauban at the Siege of Maastricht.
1673	Dutch scientist Christiaan Huygens develops a motor driven by the explosion of gunpowder.
1688	Sebastién Le Prestre de Vauban introduces the socket bayonet, which fits over a musket's muzzle and allows the musket to be loaded and fired with the bayonet attached. As the socket bayonet replaces the pike, specialized pike troops disappear from use.
1690	The Brown Bess flintlock musket is developed, and its variations remain in use by all European nations until the mid-nineteenth century.
1696	Ricochet fire is introduced by Vauban at the Siege of Philippsburg.
c. 1700	The introduction of rifling and patched-ball loading increases the accuracy of firearms.
c. mid-1700's	Advances in cannon technology allow smaller guns to shoot farther with less powder.
1712-1786	King Frederick the Great of Prussia is the first to use Jägers, or "huntsmen," expert mounted marksmen.
1754-1763	Large muskets are first used successfully by Americans in the French and Indian War.
1757	Frederick the Great wins renown and respect with his masterful use of the oblique attack at Leuthen.
1759	Frederick the Great introduces the first true horse artillery units, which, because of their unprecedented mobility and firepower, are quickly adopted by other European nations to become a staple of most eighteenth and nineteenth century armies.

DATE	EVENT
1763-1925	During the fomites phase of biological warfare, specific disease agents and contaminated utensils are introduced as weapons, with smallpox, cholera, and the Bubonic Plague as popular agents.
1769	French military engineer Joseph Cugnot develops a steam-driven carriage, arguably the first true automobile.
1775	David Bushnell invents a one-man submarine, the *Turtle*, which is used in the American Revolutionary War.
1778-1779	Frederick the Great begins deploying semi-independent detachments during the War of Bavarian Succession, foreshadowing use of independent army divisions.
1781	The Siege of Yorktown effectively ends the American War of Independence.
1790's	British artillerist Henry Shrapnel invents the "shrapnel shell," packed with gunpowder and several musket balls and designed to explode in flight.
1792	Modern French military techniques and arms are introduced into Turkey.
1792	War rockets are used by the sultan of Mysore to terrorize British soldiers.
1798	British admiral Horatio Nelson abandons traditional line tactics in victory over French as Abū Qīr Bay.
1804-1815	French emperor Napoleon Bonaparte develops his cavalry to the height of its quantity and quality, making it as significant as infantry in the outcomes of battles and campaigns.
1805	British artillerist William Congreve develops first warfare rockets and launching tubes.
1807	American inventor Robert Fulton invents the first steamship, which by the time of the Crimean War, has largely replaced the sail-powered ships in British, French, and American navies.
1826	The janissary corps are destroyed and the Turkish army is modernized.
1832	The last of the classical sieges occurs at Antwerp.
1834	Turkey creates its first military academy.
1835	The Colt revolver is patented by its inventor, Samuel Colt.
1840's	The telegraph becomes widely used and links governments with field commanders.
1845-1920	Asphyxiating gas weapons developed for chemical warfare include chlorine and phosgene.
1846-1848	Although military swords have entered a period of decline, cavalry sabers prove decisive during the Mexican-American War.
1847	Anesthesia is first used during a battlefield operation.
1848	The Sharps carbine, a single-shot, dropping-block breechloader firing paper and metallic cartridges, is developed.
1856	The Bessemer process of economical steel production is invented.
1860	England launches HMS *Warrior*, its first ironclad warship.
Apr. 12, 1861	Confederate forces attack Fort Sumter, South Carolina, initiating the Civil War.

DATE	EVENT
Mar. 9, 1862	The Battle of Hampton Roads between the ironclads USS *Monitor* and CSS *Virginia* revolutionizes naval warfare.
May 5, 1862	Confederate General Gabriel J. Rains uses the first land mines to cover his retreat from Williamsburg, Virginia.
May 31-June 1, 1862	At the Battle of Seven Pines (Fair Oaks), Virginia, a machine gun is used for the first time in war.
Feb. 17, 1864	The Confederate submarine CSS *H. L. Hunley* becomes the first underwater vessel to sink an enemy ship, the USS *Housatonic*, near Charleston, South Carolina.
1866	British engineer Robert Whitehead develops the first practical torpedo.
1867	The last Tokugawa shogun surrenders power to imperial forces, paving the way for the Meiji Restoration and Japan's reentry into world politics and culture.
1873	German arms manufacturer Alfred Krupp invents one of the first practical recoil systems for field artillery pieces.
1880's	The French develop high-explosive artillery, rendering all existing forts obsolete.
1884	Hiram Maxim invents the first practical machine gun.
1898	Mauser Model 1898 produced; culmination of military bolt action design.
1900	The zeppelin, also known as a rigid airship or dirigible, a steerable lighter-than-air aircraft, is invented in 1900 by German Count Ferdinand Graf von Zeppelin.
1903	The Wright brothers, William and Orville, launch the first successful airplane at Kitty Hawk, N.C.
1904	Japan attacks the Russian-controlled port of Lüshun, traditionally known as Port Arthur, beginning the Russo-Japanese War, fought between Russia and Japan for control over Korea and Manchuria.
1904-1905	Trinitrotoluene (TNT) is first used as a military explosive during the Russo-Japanese War.
1904-1905	The effective use of indirect fire during the Russo-Japanese War spurs American and European leaders to adopt it for their own armies in order to defend their guns against counterbattery and infantry weapon fire.
1905	The Japanese navy wins a stunning victory at Battle of Tsushima, devastating the Russian fleets and forcing Russia to surrender Korea and other territory to Japan.
1905	The French build the first airplane factory, near Paris.
1906	HMS *Dreadnought*, the first all-big-gun battleship, is launched at Portsmouth, England.
1908	The Luger P.08 is adopted as the official German service pistol.
1910	A plane takes off for the first time from the deck of a ship, presaging the modern aircraft carrier.
Oct. 11, 1911	After an Italian pilot flies the first combat mission, using his plane for reconnaissance, during the Italo-Turkish War, Italy begins using airplanes and dirigibles for bombing attacks.

DATE	EVENT
1914-1918	World War I armies form large cavalry components, which are converted into infantry as the war evolves into stagnant trench warfare, and high casualty rates occur.
Aug. 1914	German planes bomb Paris.
Sept. 1914	German U-9 submarines torpedo Allied ships.
Apr. 1915	First aerial "dogfight" takes place, after German aircraft are fitted with machine guns that are coordinated to fire between the blades of a moving propeller.
May 1915	German zeppelins bomb London.
May 1917	Allies establish Atlantic convoy system.
Nov. 20, 1917	British make successful tank attack at Cambrai.
1919	The restrictions imposed on the German military by the Treaty of Versailles at the end of World War I meet almost universal disapproval across the political spectrum in Germany.
1920	American John Taliaferro Thompson invents the most famous submachine gun, known as the "tommy gun," fully automatic and small and light enough to be fired by a single individual without support.
1920-1960	Nerve gases, such as tabun and sarin, are developed for chemical warfare to inhibit nerve function, leading to respiratory paralysis or asphyxia.
1923	The Treaty of Lausanne creates the Republic of Turkey, bringing the Ottoman Empire to its official end.
1923	HMS *Hermes*, the first purpose-built aircraft carrier, is commissioned.
1925-1940	During the cell culture phase of biological warfare, biological weapons are mass-produced and stockpiled; Japan's research program includes direct experimentation on humans.
1926	Robert Goddard achieves the first free flight of a liquid-fueled rocket.
1928	Chiang Kai-Shek captures Beijing and, as leader of Nationalist Party, heads China's first modern government.
1930's	As the building of extensive fortified lines begins, the French complete the Maginot Line along eastern border of France.
1930's	German scientist Wernher von Braun develops the first liquid-fueled rockets
1933	Adolf Hitler, leader of the National Socialist German Workers' (Nazi) Party, is appointed chancellor of Germany and calls for the abolition of the Treaty of Versailles and the rearmament of Germany.
1934-1935	Mao Zedong leads his Chinese Communist forces on 6,000-mile strategic retreat known as the Long March.
1935	British scientists develop the first radar.
Oct. 1936	The First tank-versus-cavalry and tank-versus-tank engagements of the Spanish Civil War take place near Esquivias, south of Madrid.
1936	The M1 Garand rifle is the first standard-issue semiautomatic military rifle.

DATE	EVENT
1936	The first practical helicopter is developed by German engineer Heinrich Focke.
Apr. 1937	German air forces supporting the Nationalist cause in the Spanish Civil War bomb the Spanish town of Guernica, killing approximately 2,100 of the town's 8,000 inhabitants in arguably the first premeditated use of terror bombing.
July 1937	Japan invades China, initiating Second Sino-Japanese War (1937-1945).
1939	German chancellor Adolf Hitler uses combined arms forces to invade Poland, which is then partitioned between Germany and the Soviet Union.
May 10, 1940	The German Luftwaffe conducts the first combat parachute and glider troop landings to open Germany's western front attack.
Aug. 1940	Germans begin the Battle of Britain, a series of air raids over Britain, aimed at destroying British infrastructure and morale.
Nov. 10, 1940	The British Royal Navy produces a decisive aerial victory at Taranto Harbor, Italy, crippling the anchored Italian fleet with nighttime bomb and torpedo attacks.
1940-1969	During the vaccine development and stockpiling phase of biological warfare, there are open-air tests of biological dispersal in urban environments in the United States.
June 1941	The Germans begin Operation Barbarossa, their invasion of Russia, advancing as far as Moscow and Leningrad.
Dec. 7, 1941	The Japanese navy launches a morning surprise air raid against the U.S. fleet at Pearl Harbor, Hawaii, sinking or damaging several U.S. battleships and bringing the United States into World War II.
May 1942	The Battle of the Coral Sea is the first naval battle fought entirely by carrier-based aircraft.
Aug. 1942-Jan. 1943	With the use of aerial resupply, the Russians withstand the German Siege of Stalingrad, marking the ultimate German failure on the Russian front.
July 1943	The Russians defeat the Germans at the Battle of Kursk, one of the largest tank battles in history.
1944	Germany launches the first long-range ballistic missiles, the V-1 and V-2, against England during World War II.
June 6, 1944	On what is known as D day, Allies begin invasion of Normandy, France, the largest amphibious operation in history and the beginning of Allied victory in Europe.
1944	The Japanese begin kamikaze attacks on Allied ships in the Pacific.
Apr. 1945	In the last major amphibious offensive of World War II, U.S. forces invade Okinawa and, after meeting fierce resistance, seize the island from Japan.
Apr.-May 1945	The Russians wage air, artillery, and tank attacks in the Battle for Berlin that ultimately bring about German surrender.
July 16, 1945	First successful test of the atomic bomb is made at Alamogordo, New Mexico.
Aug. 6, 1945	The first atomic bomb to be used against a civilian population is dropped by the United States on the Japanese city of Hiroshima, killing more than 70,000 people and hastening the end of the war.

DATE	EVENT
Aug. 15, 1945	Emperor Hirohito announces Japan's surrender.
1945	As World War II concludes, Indochinese Communist Party leader Ho Chi Minh proclaims a Democratic Republic of Vietnam, and France begins reasserting its colonial rule in Indochina.
Feb. 22, 1946	George F. Kennan's "Long Telegram" articulates the rationale behind Soviet aggression and advocates a firm U.S. response, with force if necessary, beginning the Cold War era.
1946-1949	Civil war rages in China between Nationalist and Communist Party forces, resulting in the triumph of Communism and in Chiang Kai-shek's flight to Taiwan.
1947	The Kalashnikov AK-47 becomes the first widely deployed modern assault rifle.
Mar. 12, 1947	U.S. president Harry S. Truman introduces the "Truman Doctrine," committing the United States to responsibility for defending global democracy, a clear signal of U.S. intention to check Soviet expansion and influence.
1949	The Soviet Union tests its first atomic bomb.
1952	The world's first hydrogen bomb is exploded at Enewetak Atoll in the Pacific Ocean.
1953	The Soviet Union tests a hydrogen bomb.
1954	The Geneva Conference calls for a partition of Indochina into four countries—North Vietnam, South Vietnam, Laos, and Cambodia—and for an election within two years to unify the two Vietnams.
1954	The USS *Nautilus*, first nuclear-powered submarine, is commissioned.
1955	The United States assumes political control of South Vietnam from the French.
1955	The first practical hovercraft is developed by Christopher Cockerell.
1956	The United States and the U.S.-backed South Vietnamese president, Ngo Dinh Diem, reject the Geneva-mandated reunification elections, knowing that the popular Ho Chi Minh would win.
1957	The Soviet Union successfully tests an intercontinental ballistic missile.
Oct. 4, 1957	The Soviet Union launches the world's first artificial earth satellite, inaugurating the space race, sparking a reassessment of U.S. military and technologic capabilities, and providing impetus for the development of both a space program and more sophisticated weapons-delivery systems.
1959	North Vietnam begins armed struggle against U.S. soldiers and South Vietnamese loyal to the Diem government.
1959-1970	Psychoactive chemical weapons are developed to produce hallucinations in exposed individuals.
Oct. 14, 1962	A U.S. pilot takes pictures indicating that Soviets are placing missiles on Cuba, and the ensuing crisis takes the world to the nuclear brink before ending on October 26.
1964	The People's Republic of China conducts its first successful nuclear weapons test.
1965	The United States pursues a policy of escalated military involvement in Vietnam.

DATE	EVENT
1966	Mao Zedong initiates a decade-long Chinese Cultural Revolution to purge his opponents from the Communist Party and renew the people's revolutionary spirit.
June 5, 1967	The Israeli Air Force (IAF) launches devastating surprise counter-air raids against threatening Arab nations, beginning the Six-Day War.
Oct. 21, 1967	Egypt sinks the Israeli destroyer *Eilat* with a Soviet Styx cruise missile.
1968	The Soviet Union invades Czechoslovakia, establishing the Brezhnev Doctrine of Soviet military domination over Warsaw Pact states.
1968	North Vietnamese and Viet Cong launch the Tet Offensive, which, although unsuccessful, contradicted U.S. reports that a decisive end to the war was near at hand.
1969-present	During the genetic engineering phase of biological warfare, recombinant DNA biotechnology opens new frontiers in the design and production of biological weapons.
1970-1979	During an era of détente, more stable relations prevail between the Soviet Union and the United States and their respective allies.
1970-present	Binary chemical weapons, stored and shipped in their component parts, are developed to increase quantities that can be safely transported to deployment sites.
Oct. 6, 1973	Egypt launches air strike against Israel, beginning Arab-Israeli October War.
1973	The final American fighting forces withdraw from Vietnam in late March, following a January 27 peace agreement.
1975	Saigon finally falls to the North Vietnamese forces, and Vietnam is united under Communist rule.
1978	The United States begins production of the first precision-guided artillery munitions.
1979	Soviet forces enter Afghanistan ostensibly to overthrow the government of Prime Minister Hafizullah Amin and install a puppet government loyal to Moscow.
1979	The Iranian Revolution ends Iran's close military ties with the United States.
Jan. 23, 1980	After an Iranian mob takes over the U.S. embassy, and the Soviet Union invades Afghanistan, U.S. president Jimmy Carter declares that the United States will consider any threat against the Persian Gulf a threat against its vital interests and will react, if necessary, with military force.
Mar. 1981	Soviets launch their first well-planned offensive in Afghanistan.
Mar. 11, 1985	Mikhail Gorbachev is chosen as the new General Secretary of the Soviet Union, and his reforms initiate a thaw in relations between the United States and the Soviet Union.
1985	Mikhail Gorbachev is chosen as the new general secretary of the Soviet Communist Party, and his reforms initiate a thaw in relations between the Soviet Union and the United States.
July 28, 1986	Soviet leader Mikhail Gorbachev announces a limited withdrawal of Soviet troops from Afghanistan.

DATE	EVENT
Dec. 8, 1987	U.S. president Ronald Reagan and Soviet general secretary Gorbachev sign the INF Treaty governing intermediate nuclear forces (INF) and calling for the destruction of U.S. and Soviet missiles and nuclear weapons.
1988	After Pan American Flight 103 explodes over Lockerbie, Scotland, killing hundreds, state terrorism mounted by Libya is suspected as cause.
1989	Gorbachev is elected state president in the first pluralist elections since 1917, and by the end of the year all Warsaw Pact nations had overthrown their communist leadership.
1989	The Afghan Interim Government (AIG) is established, and the Soviet Union completes its withdrawal from Afghanistan.
1989	The dismantling of Germany's Berlin Wall signifies the end of the Cold War, as U.S president George Bush promises economic aid to the Soviet Union.
Jan. 17, 1991	A U.S.-led U.N. coalition leads a well-orchestrated air attack against Iraqi dictator Saddam Hussein in an effort to oust his forces from Kuwait.
Feb. 1991	U.N. forces undertake a decisive ground assault on Iraqi positions in Kuwait.
Apr. 1991	No-fly zones are established and enforced in Iraq to prevent repression of Kurds in northern Iraq.
1991	After the Baltic States of Estonia, Latvia, and Lithuania are granted independence and other former soviets join the Commonwealth of Independent States, Gorbachev resigns as president and the Soviet Union is officially dissolved.
1993	A bomb attack on New York's World Trade Center kills 6 people and injures more than 1,000.
1995	The April bombing of a federal office building in Oklahoma City, Oklahoma, by one or more individuals allegedly affiliated with militia groups kills 168. Within the same week, a Japanese religious cult mounts gas attack in a Tokyo subway, hospitalizing 400.
Jan. 1996	An international force composed largely of NATO troops is deployed in Bosnia to ensure the implementation of the Dayton Accords.
1996	Millionaire Islamic extremist Osama bin Ladin issues a declaration of war against United States.
1998	The simultaneous bombings of U.S. embassies in Kenya and Tanzania in August kill 224, and bin Laden group supporters are suspected. United States conducts counterattack shortly thereafter against bin Laden training base in Afghanistan.
2000	The October 12 suicide bombing of USS *Cole* in the Persian Gulf kills 17 sailors.

WEAPONS OF WAR
ALPHABETICAL LEXICON

Aircraft carrier. Large motorized warship with a flat topdeck to serve as a runway for fixed-wing aircraft. Invented by the British in 1918, developed by most major navies in the 1920's and 1930's, and first used in World War II, its effectiveness was dramatically proved at the Battle of Midway, in June of 1942, when planes from three American carriers, *Enterprise*, *Hornet*, and *Yorktown*, commanded by Admiral Raymond A. Spruance, destroyed four Japanese carriers, *Akagi*, *Hiryu*, *Kaga*, and *Soryu*, commanded by Admiral Isoruku Yamamoto. The carrier immediately superseded the battleship as the primary instrument of naval firepower.

Antiaircraft gun. Machine gun, often with two or more barrels for wide-pattern fire; pedestal-mounted with rapid 360-degree traverse in fixed batteries, land vehicles, or ships; designed for accurate, long-range, high-angle fire to shoot down enemy aircraft. Developed late in World War I and known as ack-ack, both from its sound and from British signalmen's variant pronunciation of its acronym, AA, it was a standard weapon in World War II, but was superseded by guided antiaircraft missiles in the late twentieth century.

Antiballistic missile (ABM). Developed by the United States in the late 1950's and widely deployed by both the United States and the Soviet Union by the 1970's, any guided missile, either ground-launched, sea-launched, or air launched, with a nuclear warhead designed to explode in the vicinity of incoming enemy missiles, rendering them harmless. ABM systems were supposed to be severely limited as a provision of the 1972 Strategic Arms Limitation Talks (SALT 1), but verification proved difficult.

Antimissile missile. Any missile intended to destroy an incoming enemy missile before it can do any damage. Satellite-guided antimissile missile systems were a fundamental component of President Ronald Reagan's Strategic Defense Initiative (SDI), known as "Star Wars," in 1983, but their technology was still not practical as of 2001. Antiballistic missiles are a special type of antimissile missile.

Antitank gun. Rifled firearm specifically designed to destroy tanks. The earliest was in 1918, the German 13.3-millimeter Mauser Tankgewehr bolt-action rifle, firing armor-piercing bullets. By World War II, antitank weaponry was recognized as very important. Most were field pieces, such as the German 37-millimeter Panzerabwehrkanone (PAK36) and the Soviet 100-millimeter M-1944, all firing armor-piercing shells. After World War II, recoilless guns, mortars, and rocket launchers firing guided armor-piercing missiles replaced antitank guns.

Arbalest. Originally, after about the eleventh century, the French word for crossbow, derived from two Latin words, *arcus*, or bow, and *ballista*, or big, rock-shooting crossbow. Around 1400, the term also began to mean a particular type of large, very powerful, heavy-draw Northern European crossbow, whose bow was shorter than average and either reinforced with steel or made entirely of steel.

Armor-piercing shell. Special antitank or antiship artillery ammunition, in two varieties: kinetic and chemical. The former is a hard, high-velocity, usually pointed shell that punctures the armor then explodes inside the target; the latter is designed to explode either near or on the armor, shattering it from the outside. Development of armor-piercing ammunition was necessitated by the introduction of ironclad warships in the American Civil War and tanks in World War I.

Artillery. Sometimes called ordnance, the term comprises all firearms, or weapons powered by explosions, that must be operated by more than one soldier for maximum effectiveness, such as cannons, most rockets, and most missiles, as well as some pre-gunpowder heavy siege weapons such as catapults, onagers, trebuchets, and large varieties of crossbow. Artillery is traditionally classified as either heavy or light.

Assagai. Short-handled, long-bladed, double-edged traditional spear of the Zulu nation of South Africa. Used mainly as a multiple thrusting weapon, it could also be hurled as a javelin or wielded for slashing. It fit well into the standard "chest-and-horns" assault and surround tactics of the Zulu, in which a large body of troops in close ranks would run suddenly at the enemy to gain advantage in hand-to-hand combat, as they did when they destroyed the British at Isandhlwana in 1879.

Assault helicopter. Versatile fighting aircraft developed by the United States in the 1950's, first used extensively in the Vietnam War (1961-1975) and refined by the Soviet Union in the 1970's. The mainstay of modern air cavalry, its tactical equipment includes computerized search-and-destroy weapons, antitank guns, machine guns, rockets, air-launched minelaying systems, and sophisticated navigation devices for rapid, ground-hugging flight. Among the most prominent types are the Soviet Mi-24 and Mi-28 and the American Apache and Black Hawk.

Assault rifle. Fully automatic rifle that can fire either single-shot or rapid fire, developed by many nations during World War II, but primarily by Mikhail Timofeyevitch Kalashnikov (b. 1919) for the Soviet Union between 1941 and 1944. His AK-47, named for the year of its invention, is the most famous weapon of this type. Others include the Israeli Uzi and the American M-16. Most models have a straight stock to prevent the recoil from pushing successive shots gradually too high during rapid fire.

Atomic bomb (A-bomb). Extremely powerful explosive device involving the fission of radioactive elements, invented during World War II by an American team of scientists in fulfillment of the secret, federally funded Manhattan Project. It was first tested on July 16, 1945, at Alamogordo, New Mexico; first used on August 6, 1945, when the United States dropped Little Boy, a uranium bomb, on Hiroshima, Japan; and used for the second and last time in the twentieth century on August 9, 1945, when the United States dropped Fat Man, a plutonium bomb, on Nagasaki, Japan.

Automatic firearm. Any firearm that loads automatically, usually from either a bandolier belt or a magazine, and fires more than one shot for each squeeze of the trigger. The reloading process is typically powered by the energy from each previous shot, as hot gas, recoil, or blowback. The first sustained use of automatics in warfare was as the various Browning, Maxim, Spandau, and Vickers heavy machine guns that caused millions of casualties in World War I.

Ballista. Gigantic crossbow used in both ancient and medieval warfare, developed by the Romans but patterned after the mounted crossbows invented by Archimedes. Tactically employed as a catapult, it was cocked with a winch and ratchet, usually wheeled, and capable of hurling bolts or stones of up to about 10 pounds (4.5 kilograms) accurately for relatively long distances (about 400 yards or meters) at tolerably low trajectory.

Ballistic missile. Large, long-range guided missile, usually with a nuclear warhead, developed by the United States in the late 1950's, self-propelled by a rocket engine on a high-trajectory, often stratospheric, course, guided in its upward arc but usually free-falling in its descent. Its earliest prototype was the Nazi V-2 (Vergeltungswaffe Zwei) rocket, used with a high explosive warhead against London from September, 1944, to March, 1945.

Ballistite. Smokeless powder introduced in 1887 by Alfred B. Nobel (1833-1896) and consisting of 40 percent low-nitrogen nitrocellulose and 60 percent nitroglycerin. The product could be manufactured as small flakes and was a common propellant for firearms until after World War II. In the English-speaking world, cordite, a similar mixture invented shortly after ballistite, was more common.

Bangalore torpedo. Indefinitely long metal tube, consisting of a series of short lengths screwed together, with an explosive charge at one end and a fuse inside the tube. By pushing it slowly toward or under its target, demolition teams could remain in positions of cover and cut paths through barbed wire, neutralize mine fields, or blast fortifications. The Allies, notably the amphibious forces on D-Day, used it extensively during World War II.

Barbed wire. Thick wire with sharp metal points built in at regular intervals, first patented in the United States in 1867, first used for civilian purposes to mark boundaries, and extensively deployed as a defensive obstacle in both world wars. Since the late twentieth century, varieties have been manufactured with imbedded fiber optic cable so that computerized sentry systems can determine precisely where the enemy breaches it and immediately direct defensive fire to that spot.

Barrage balloons. Defensive antiaircraft apparatus used in both World Wars, especially by the British. Small balloons trailing long cables or nets were tethered at high altitude in the hope that enemy aircraft attacking below the balloons would catch their wings on the dangling obstacles.

Baselard (or *basilard*). Double-edged European dagger common from the fourteenth to the sixteenth centuries, typified by two prominent cross pieces, one at the pommel, or the end of the hilt, the other at the guard, or the joint between the hilt and the blade.

Battering ram. Ancient and medieval siege engine for breaching enemy walls, consisting of a large pole, usually a tree trunk, with a metal head, sometimes pointed, slung horizontally from ropes under a sturdy frame so that it could be swung back and forth with great force. The frame, covered with water-soaked hides to prevent defenders from burning it, could be wheeled up to the target wall by soldiers underneath it, chocked, and put to work.

Battle-ax. Slicing and chopping weapon invented in the Stone Age when someone lashed a sharp stone to the end of a stick, developed throughout the Bronze Age, and nearly perfected during the Iron Age, when more sophisticated versions evolved from both the mace and the hand ax. Although warriors needed great strength to wield it well, it proved popular in all pre-firearm cultures, especially in the eighth to eleventh centuries among the Vikings, who revered their axes and often gave them proper names, such as Skarphedin's gigantic Rímmugýgr, or "Ogress of War," in *Njal's Saga.*

Battleship. Gigantic, armored, motorized ship bristling with long-range, large-caliber, breech-loading cannon, mounted mostly in turrets, intended primarily for ship-to-ship combat. It dominated naval warfare from the late nineteenth century until the aircraft carrier was proved superior at Midway in 1942. Before 1906 it was relatively slow, with the intermediate battery larger than the main battery, but thereafter the standard was the dreadnought, faster, larger, more heavily armed and armored, and with its strength disproportionately concentrated in the main battery.

Bayonet. Edged weapon attached to the muzzle of a firearm, usually a musket or rifle, first used in Europe in the seventeenth century to substitute for a pike. The earliest, the plug bayonet, was inserted into the muzzle itself. The socket bayonet includes a sleeve to fit over the muzzle; the sword bayonet has a regular sword hilt with an adapter slot that slides under the barrel; and the integral bayonet is permanently affixed to the firearm. Bayonet tactics evolved into complex and deadly offensive maneuvers in the eighteenth and nineteenth centuries. Since the twentieth century, bayonets have mostly been multipurpose survival knives conveniently detachable from a soldier's personal weapon.

Bazooka. American recoilless antitank weapon, the M9A1, common in World War II. A short-range, hand-held, direct-fire, line-of-sight weapon firing unguided projectiles, it was superseded after the war by more sophisticated recoilless guns and especially by mortars firing guided antitank missiles.

Big Bertha. Any of several large German howitzers mounted on railway cars and used extensively in World War I on the western front until 1916, when the newer Allied heavy artillery outranged them. The designation especially refers to the Krupp 42-centimeter L-14, because Gustav Krupp's wife's name was Bertha.

Bilbo. High-quality, wide-bladed, double-edged, fancy Spanish rapier of the Renaissance, so called from the place of its manufacture, Bilbao, Spain.

Bill. Type of pole-arm whose head includes a regular spear point, a hook for unhorsing mounted knights or cavalrymen, and numerous perpendicular spikes. One of the first pole-arms, it evolved from the pruning hook, or billhook, and was in use from the early Middle Ages until the end of the eighteenth century. Many variants exist, some resembling the *voulge*, with a small ax-blade instead of the spikes, but the required feature is the hook.

Biological weapons. Organic substances introduced into enemy areas by bombing, artillery, or infiltration, designed to cause debilitating disease outbreaks. Sometimes, but not quite accurately, known as germ warfare, the employment of such weapons includes loading medieval trebuchets with dead horses, tampering with water supplies, and releasing noxious aerosol particles in enemy airspace. Among the diseases that could be caused by these tactics are cholera, influenza, anthrax, typhoid, dysentery, encephalitis, malaria, typhus, yellow fever, bubonic plague, and smallpox.

Bireme. Galley with two banks of oars. Shortly after the naval ram was invented around 800 B.C.E., the Greeks and Phoenicians developed fast galleys to exploit this weapon. More oarsmen meant more speed and power, but, since single-banked ships long enough to hold crews of more than 50 were impractical, the bireme was developed around 700 B.C.E., with an upper bank of oars on outrigger fulcrums so as not to interfere with the lower bank. It was between 25 and 35 meters long, carried a crew of about 100, and reached top oared speed between seven and nine knots.

Blockbuster. Popular name for the high-capacity bomb, the giant aerial bomb dropped by both the Allies and the Germans in World War II, so called because each one was capable of demolishing an entire city block. Developed first and best by the British, the largest could hold 22,000 pounds (10,000 kilograms) of TNT, RDX, PETN, or some combination of these explosives.

Blowgun. Long, straight, thin, smallbore, hollow tube through which light projectiles, usually darts, are driven with amazing accuracy to surprising distances, solely by the force of rapidly but smoothly exhaled breath. Independently developed by many preliterate tropical cultures, such as those of Malaysia, Indonesia, and Brazil, its darts are sometimes poisoned and a flared mouthpiece is often added to concentrate the breath for more power.

Blunderbuss. Short-range, short-barrelled, muzzle-loading, smoothbore, personal firearm developed in either Holland or England early in the seventeenth century and common through the eighteenth, characterized by a flaring muzzle to facilitate loading and to scatter the shot, which could be either a single bullet or a pellet load. Extremely inaccurate, with the effect of a sawed-off shotgun or scattergun, it was typically used as a defensive or deterrent weapon for property owners, ships' officers, and stagecoach drivers.

Bofors gun. Type of light, mobile, antiaircraft gun, usually 40 millimeters, intended especially against low-flying planes, named after the Swedish company that introduced it in the 1930's. Naval varieties are typically mounted with double, quadruple, sextuple, or octuple barrels.

Bolt-action rifle. Any breech-loading rifle that uses the manual action of a sliding bolt to open the breech block and eject the spent cartridge. The bolt handle is pushed up out of a slot to unlock the breech and down into the slot to lock it. The weapon can be either repeating, if it can take a magazine, or single-shot, if it cannot. Typically, the repeaters have military application, while single-shot bolt-actions are for sport. Developed in the 1860's and 1870's, bolt-action weapons were the norm in the Boer War and World War I.

Bomb. Any offensive explosive device designed to detonate only under certain conditions, but especially, since World War I, one dropped from an airplane, thrown, or otherwise delivered aerially, but not by artillery.

Bombard. Primitive smoothbore mortar, probably dating from the early fifteenth century, characterized by a narrow powder chamber; an extremely short, sometimes flaring, barrel; and a huge-caliber bore, sometimes as wide or wider than its length.

Bomber. Aircraft designed to drop explosive devices accurately on target. The first bombers were observation planes dropping hand-held bombs early in World War I. By the end of that war, both sides had planes specialized for bombing missions, particularly the British DeHavilland and the German Gotha. The Spanish Civil War and World War II were the first wars in which airpower played a dominant role, and during their course, aerial bombing became a carefully studied science.

Booby trap. Offensive obstacle designed to kill, maim, or terrorize unsuspecting soldiers or passersby. Extensively used by the Viet Cong against the Americans in Vietnam, by native populations against invading forces, by fortress defenders, and by terrorists, the wide variety of booby traps includes car bombs, mines, mail bombs, pitfalls, nets, tripwires, spikes, spring traps, snares, positioned firearms, and time bombs.

Boomerang. Aboriginal Australian aerodynamically enhanced throwing stick, designed in two basic forms: the one flying a curved path and returning to the thrower, the other flying straight, far, end-over-end, but not returning. The former is used mainly for hunting and exhibitions, the latter for war. War boomerangs exist in many styles, but are generally heavier and may have cutting edges or protuberances.

Bow. Invented in the Stone Age, a simple combination of string and spring to hurl projectiles, usually arrows, much farther, more powerfully, and more accurately than they could be thrown by hand. The shape, tension, material, length, weight, and curve of a bow all affect its spring energy. Bows are of four basic kinds: simple, made of a single piece; backed, two pieces of different materials glued together; laminated, three or more pieces of the same material glued together; and composite, three or more pieces of different materials glued together.

Bowie knife. American single-edged fighting knife about 20 inches long overall, named for American frontiersman James Bowie (1796-1836), but actually designed by his brother, Rezin. Evolved from the frontiersman's hunting knife and the straight-bladed "Arkansas toothpick," it featured a simple hilt; a flat, wide crossguard with a prong at each end angled about 45 degrees toward the point; a tempered steel blade, mostly straight, but, from the point toward the hilt about 3 inches, convex in front and concave in back; and a strip of soft metal, such as brass, inlayed along the back of the blade to catch enemy blades. It was edged blade-length in front and along the concave portion in back.

Breechloader. Any firearm that loads its ammunition through the rear of the barrel. Attempted for centuries, but barely practical in time for the Crimean War and the American Civil War, it soon thereafter superseded muzzle-loaders and made repeating arms and automatic weapons possible.

Bren gun. British light machine gun, the Bren Mk1, first produced in 1937 and used extensively in World War II. Because the British based its design on the Czech ZB/vz26, invented eleven years earlier, they coined its name from the "Br" in Brno, where the Czech gun was made, and the "En" in Enfield, where the British gun was manufactured. The Royal Small Arms Factory, Enfield, North London, was founded in 1804 and has been responsible for a great number of historically important weapons.

Brig. Sailing, two-masted, square-rigged, wooden warship, related to the nonnaval brigantine, smaller than a frigate but bigger than a sloop of war or corvette, carrying between 12 and 32 guns on one or one-and-a-half decks. Brigs were common from the eighteenth century until the end of the age of sail.

Broadsword. Large straight European sword dating from the early Middle Ages, usually double-edged, often two-handed, intended for slashing, chopping, and cutting, rather than thrusting.

Browning automatic rifle (BAR). American light machine gun, the .30-06-caliber M-1918A2, invented by John M. Browning (1855-1926). Weighing only 20 pounds, air-cooled, with gas-powered reload and a bipod at the muzzle, it was well known as the squad automatic of World War II.

Caltrop. Small, throwable, defensive obstacle consisting of four metal spikes protruding from a central vertex, each at an angle of 120 degrees to the other three, so that whichever three form a tripod on the defended ground, the fourth will be sticking straight up. At Bannockburn in 1314, Robert the Bruce devastated the English cavalry with caltrops.

Canister shot. Type of case shot, preloaded into a brittle tin shell designed to disintegrate immediately upon firing and thus add its own fragments to the antipersonnel pattern of projectiles. It differs from grapeshot by being sealed in a container and from case shot by specifically incorporating a tin shell. Its advantage over both was ease of loading.

Cannon. Firearm too big to be carried by an individual soldier, an artillery piece, invented early in the fourteenth century, that exists in three basic forms: gun, howitzer, and mortar, which are distinguished by caliber, trajectory, projectile velocity, range, and barrel length.

Carbine. Rifle with a short barrel designed to be convenient for cavalrymen. Developed by the French during the wheel-lock era, it achieved its greatest renown in the nineteenth century, when early breech-loading carbines such as the Sharps, Enfield, Springfield, and Winchester became standard British and American cavalry issue.

Carronade. Short-barrelled, large-caliber, relatively lightweight, smoothbore naval cannon, inaccurate but highly effective at short range, introduced by the Carron Company of Scotland in 1779 and common until the mid-nineteenth century.

Case shot. Short-range, wide-dispersion, antipersonnel muzzle-loading artillery ammunition. Consisting of small metal balls or shards and common during the last hundred years of the muzzle-loading era, it differs from grapeshot by being sealed in a container, which would either break, burn, or disintegrate as soon as the charge was fired, thus allowing the load to spread. A variety of case shot sealed specifically in a tin shell is canister shot.

Catapult. Ancient and medieval artillery engine using a lever to hurl large projectiles. Its power came from either a leaf spring; the torsion of a twisted skein, as in the onager; or a huge counterweight, as in the trebuchet. Made obsolete by the development of the cannon, catapults nevertheless re-

mained fairly common in warfare until the sixteenth century and were used as recently as World War I to hurl grenades into enemy trenches. The term also refers to devices used to launch planes from aircraft carriers.

Chain shot. Type of ammunition for smoothbore, muzzle-loading cannon. Compact when loaded, but expanding when fired, it was designed for naval use in the sixteenth century to cut the rigging of enemy ships. Later it was also used by ground troops as an antipersonnel charge.

Chariot. Ancient attack vehicle, a two-wheeled backless cart with high front and sides, pulled by usually one or two but sometimes as many as four horses. It could contain either a single occupant, who both drove and fought, or two, one to drive and the other to shoot arrows, thrust spears, or slash with his sword. At Gaugamela in 331 B.C.E., the Persians used chariots with protruding scythes affixed to rotate with the axles, but the maneuvers of Alexander's phalanxes snagged the scythes with one another and rendered the chariots ineffective.

Chassepot. Bolt-action 11-millimeter rifle invented in 1866 by Antoine Alphonse Chassepot (1833-1905) and carried by French soldiers in the Franco-Prussian War. Based on the Dreyse needle gun that was standard in the Prussian Army after 1848, it used a combustible paper cartridge. When the trigger was pulled, a needle pierced the cartridge from behind before hitting the primer and firing the charge.

Chemical weapons. Organic or inorganic agents, usually delivered by shell, intended to poison the enemy. Safety for the attacker is often achieved through the binary system, whereby two ingredients are kept isolated from each other within the shell until impact, when they combine to create the poison. Since World War I, various provisions of the Geneva Conventions and other international treaties have limited chemical warfare, especially the use of poison gas.

Cheval de frise (pl. *chevaux de frise*). Literally, Frisian horse, a late medieval and early modern defensive obstacle consisting of many long spikes protruding radially from a central log, barrel, or other convenient cylindrical object serving as an axis. A good anticavalry defense for musketeers, it could safely be moved into position by four soldiers, two at each end. Not much used after the eighteenth century, it was finally superseded by barbed wire in the late nineteenth century.

Claymore. Gigantic two-handed Scottish broadsword with a blade up to 6 feet long. The traditional blade of Scotland, known in Gaelic as claidheamh mòr, it was developed in the late Middle Ages and used extensively throughout the Renaissance and Early Modern Era.

Club. Short, stout, heavy, sticklike object, usually wooden, with a large knob on one end to crush skulls or break bones. Of prehistoric origins, it could have either a plain, blunt warhead or a spike driven through the warhead for added deadliness. Almost exclusively a weapon of traditional, preliterate, or aboriginal cultures, it nevertheless appeared also in more advanced cultures as armor-breaking weapons: the mace and the war-hammer. Perhaps the most famous club is the Irish shillelagh, cut from the blackthorn tree.

Cluster bomb. Developed by the Soviet Union in the 1930's and common since the 1960's, an aerial bomb that jettisons its casing at a predetermined altitude to release dozens or even hundreds of small bombs, or bomblets, typically used as an antitank, antivehicle, or antipersonnel weapon.

Composition B. Also called cyclotol, a castable mixture of 60 percent RDX and 40 percent TNT, insensitive to temperature and shock, commonly used as a military explosive because of its tremendous power to crush and shatter. It was the usual load of Allied bangalore torpedoes in World War II.

Composition C. Plastic explosive consisting of 80 percent RDX and 20 percent plasticizing agent, designated C-1 through C-4 according to which plasticizer is used. Like all practical military explosives, it is insensitive to environmental conditions, safe to handle, and long-lived. It is frequently used in land mines.

Cordite. Efficient form of smokeless powder invented in Britain in 1889 by Sir Frederick Augustus Abel (1827-1902) and Sir James Dewar (1842-

1923), consisting of nitroglycerin, guncotton, petroleum jelly, and acetone pressed into thin brown cords. Similar to ballistite, it was used extensively in small arms ammunition throughout the twentieth century.

Crossbow. Shooting weapon invented in China about 500 B.C.E. and known in Europe by the end of the first millenium, consisting of a short, thick bow transversely attached to a wooden stock that featured a trigger, a groove to guide the projectile, and usually a detachable cranking mechanism to draw the string. Its ammunition was either stones, pellets, or short arrows called bolts, or quarrels. With a range of about 400 yards (370 meters), it was so accurate and powerful that in 1139 the Lateran Council banned its use against Christians. After Crécy in 1346, the British preferred the longbow, which could shoot six times as fast, but the crossbow, with its longer range, remained dominant on the continent through the fifteenth century. By the mid-sixteenth century, it was obsolete in warfare, superseded by firearms.

Cruise missile. Tactical, self-propelled, ground-hugging, guided missile developed by the United States and the Soviet Union in the 1960's and 1970's. A "smart bomb," capable of pinpoint accuracy, it can carry either nuclear or nonnuclear warheads and can be launched from land, sea, or air. The American sea-launched Tomahawk and the air-launched ALCM turbofan-powered cruise missiles proved devastating against Iraq in the 1991 Persian Gulf War.

Culverin. Long, smoothbore, muzzle-loading, medium- to large-caliber European field cannon of the fifteenth to seventeenth centuries. Since cast iron technology was not yet dependable for large objects, its barrel was not cast, but constructed of overlapping and superimposed hoops of wrought iron. A typical culverin had a 6-inch bore and fired an 18-pound ball.

Cutlass. Short, curved, wide-bladed saber with a thrusting point and a stout handgaurd, developed in Europe in the seventeenth century, remotely related to the English falchion of the thirteenth century, and used mostly in naval warfare and by pirates.

Dagger. Next to stones, probably the most ancient of all weapons, originally made of chipped flint. A sharp-pointed, straight-bladed knife intended primarily for stabbing, it can be held with the little finger toward the blade for powerful downward stabbing or with the thumb toward the blade for more versatile thrusting and slashing.

Defoliant. Chemical weapon intended to destroy plant life and thus prevent the enemy from taking cover in the forest or living off the land. The most notorious was Agent Orange, used extensively by the United States in Vietnam and subsequently discovered to have debilitating long-term side effects on exposed personnel.

Depth charge. Antisubmarine high explosive device, first used in 1916 by the British against the German U-boats in World War I. Since World War II, depth charges have been standard armaments on destroyers, destroyer escorts, and PT boats. Typically, several are catapulted overboard simultaneously in different directions, set to explode at different depths to maximize the chance of hitting the target either directly or with shock waves.

Derringer. Small, easily concealable, short-barrelled, medium- to large-caliber, usually single-shot, rifled pistol, first manufactured about 1850 by Henry Deringer (1786-1868) of Philadelphia. With the "D" in lower case and another "r" added, the name became generic. John Wilkes Booth (1838-1865) used a derringer to assassinate Abraham Lincoln (1809-1865).

Destroyer. Fast, relatively small, motorized warship of the twentieth century, intended to defend fleets and convoys from all sorts of attack: surface, undersea, and air. It is armed with a great variety of weapons, including torpedoes, depth charges, antiaircraft guns, medium-caliber cannon, and sometimes missiles.

Destroyer escort. Motorized warship, smaller and usually slower than a destroyer, developed by the United States early in World War II to support destroyers in their mission to defend fleets and convoys. Since 1975, it has been also known in the U.S. Navy as a frigate.

Dirk. Dagger used by the British navy in the eighteenth and nineteenth centuries and by Scots generally since the Middle Ages. This traditional Scottish weapon, regularly issued to regimental pipers, is characterized by a wide, straight, symmetrical, double-edged, tapering blade about one foot long. The genuine Scottish dirk has no guard, but the naval dirk does.

Dive-bomber. Small, maneuverable, propeller-driven airplane capable of steep, steady dives and abrupt, rapid climbs, intended to drops bombs accurately at low altitude and escape before antiaircraft fire or enemy fighter aircraft could bring it down. Armed with either bombs or torpedoes, it is especially effective for attacking ships broadside. Dive-bombing originated as a tactic in World War I, but achieved prominence in World War II through such planes as the German Junkers Ju-87 Stuka, the Japanese Aichi D3A and Yokosuka D4Y, and the American Douglas SBD Dauntless and Curtiss SB2C Helldiver.

Dumdum bullet. Hollow-point or soft-nosed bullet designed to expand quickly upon impact, causing tremendous internal damage and leaving a horrible exit wound. Developed around 1891 by the British at their colonial arsenal in Dum Dum, India, near Calcutta, they used it in India and the Sudan in the 1890's until it was banned by the Hague Convention of 1899.

Dynamite. Powerful high explosive invented in 1867 by Alfred B. Nobel, consisting of an inert, porous substance saturated with nitroglycerin. Its greatest advantage is rendering nitroglycerin safe to handle, but because it cannot be stored for long periods without becoming unstable, it has limited military application.

Elephants. Not only transportation for soldiers and equipment, but also the first tanks. Used in warfare in India from prehistoric times, and by the Persians against the Greeks in the fourth century B.C.E., the military importance of elephants was made most famous by Hannibal's crossing the Alps to attack Italy in 218 B.C.E. Elephants, aside from being monstrously strong, are fearless, difficult to kill, and a terror to enemy horses.

Explosive projectile. Any hurled device designed to explode either on impact or at a predetermined point in its flight, not limited to artillery shells, but also including hand grenades, long-range guided missiles, and even medieval fire pots.

Falchion. European short, single-edged sword popular from the thirteenth to the sixteenth centuries, featuring a wide, heavy, straight-backed blade, a convex cutting edge near the point, and usually an S-shaped crossguard. It evolved into the cutlass.

Falconet. Very light, smoothbore, muzzle-loading, small-caliber European field piece of the sixteenth and seventeenth centuries, characterized by a long, narrow, cast metal barrel, usually bronze. The largest known was a 3-pounder, that is, it fired a 3-pound ball. The name means "little falcon."

Farm tools. Throughout history, when large numbers of peasants either revolted or were impressed into service, their weaponry included their familiar tools from home. Scythes, sickles, threshing flails, pitchforks, and pruning hooks were extensively used in such conflicts as the Crusades (1095-1270), the Thirty Years' War (1618-1648), and the French Revolution (1789-1799). Minor modifications turn a sickle into a curved dagger or a pruning hook into a pole-arm.

Felucca. Slender, swift, lateen-rigged, wooden sailing ship of the Mediterranean, developed in the sixteenth or early seventeenth century. Favored by the Barbary corsairs until their demise at the beginning of the nineteenth century, it typically carried ten to fourteen guns and seldom as many as twenty.

Field piece. Any light or medium-weight cannon designed to be highly mobile and versatile in the thick of battle. The term especially refers to the horse-drawn cannon of the muzzle-loading era. Most of Napoleon's victories involved his expert use of such artillery.

Fighter aircraft. Early in World War I, personnel in observation planes would fire pistols at enemy observation planes. Soon two-seater planes were equipped with a swivel machine gun for the copilot. In 1915 Anthony Fokker (1890-1939) invented for the Germans a gear system to allow mounted machine guns to fire forward without hitting the propeller, thus creating the first practical fighter planes. Ideal fighters are small, fast, and maneuverable. Propeller fighters such as the Japanese Mitsubishi Zero, the German Messerschmitt, the British Spitfire, and the American Flying Tiger reached their zenith in World War II and were superseded by jets in the late 1940's.

Fighter jet. Although developed first by the Germans and later by the Allies during World War II, jet fighter aircraft did not see much action until the Korean War. Outstanding jet fighters include the Russian MiG (Mikoyan-Gurevich) series and the American F-11 Tiger, F-86 Sabre, and F-104 Starfighter.

Fire pot. Ancient and medieval incendiary weapon, consisting of a ceramic container filled with an inflammable substance. Flung from a catapult, onager, or trebuchet, it was designed to ignite easily upon impact.

Fire ship. Derelict wooden sailing ship or barge, set afire and sent among the enemy's wooden ships. It represented an effective and common naval tactic from ancient to early modern times.

Flail. Type of mace with one, two, or three warheads, usually solid iron spheres studded with spikes, attached to the thick reinforced wooden handle by short lengths of chain. It was used for the same purpose as the mace, to crush armor, but the chains provided a whiplike effect that added velocity and force to the warhead.

Flak. Invented by the Germans in 1936, the 88-millimeter Flugabwehrkanone (FLAK36) automatic cannon, with an effective range of about 26,000 feet (8,000 meters), was the standard Nazi antiaircraft gun of World War II and the basis of several further antiaircraft and antitank weapons. Allied airmen soon applied the term to antiaircraft fire in general, especially the hazardous flying debris from exploding antiaircraft shells.

Flamethrower. Offensive incendiary device whereby a single infantryman can safely and effectively shoot a stream of burning liquid from a high-pressure nozzle to distances of about 200 feet (60 meters). Developed during World War I and used extensively in World War II and Vietnam, it was a significant advance in military technology because fire is often as dangerous for the attacking and attacked armies alike. Soldiers using flamethrowers typically wear flameproof armor, head to toe.

Flintlock. Dominant muzzle-loading firearm ignition mechanism, invented around 1610 and common from 1650 until the end of the muzzle-loading era in the mid-nineteenth century, a simple improvement of the snaphance, from which it differs by being single-action rather than double. When its trigger is pulled, the hammer pushes the pan cover away from the pan, thus creating sparks, igniting the primer, and firing the weapon.

Fragmentation bomb. Invented during World War I, an artillery shell or aerial bomb whose thick but brittle metal casing is scientifically designed to shatter upon impact, sending jagged debris in all directions as antipersonnel projectiles.

Frigate. Sailing, square-rigged, three-masted wooden warship larger than a brig but smaller than a ship of the line. It usually carried between 20 and 48 guns on two decks. The USS *Constitution*, "Old Ironsides," launched in Boston in 1797, was a 44-gun frigate. From 1950 to 1975 the U.S. Navy designated some large destroyers as frigates, and after 1975 used the term to refer to destroyer escorts.

Fusil. Light, small-caliber, French flintlock musket of the seventeenth century. British soldiers armed with these weapons were called fusiliers. Subsequently, *fusil* became the ordinary French word for rifle.

Galleon. Warship developed in Spain and England in the fifteenth century, trimmer and more streamlined than the floating fortresses of the fourteenth century. Without their high, overhanging forecastles and poops, but with three or four full-rigged masts, it was the first ship able to hold position against the wind while delivering broadsides to the enemy. The British victory over the galleons of the Spanish Armada in 1588 was not only because of the weather, but also because Sir Francis Drake's galleons were smaller, shallower, faster, and more maneuverable. The galleon was superseded in the seventeenth century by the British man of war.

Galley. Long, low, slender, shallow-draft warship of the Eastern Mediterranean, usually rowed, but equipped with a single square sail. Developed in either Greece, Crete, or Phoenicia around the ninth century B.C.E. and later adopted by the Romans, it was the primary warship until the fall of the Roman Empire. With the foremost part of the prow at or just below the waterline reinforced and sharpened, its basic tactics involved ramming the enemy ship broadside, then either boarding it, sinking it, or setting it afire. Galleys were used in war as recently as Lepanto (1571).

Garand rifle. Semiautomatic .30-'06 caliber rifle invented in the 1930's by John C. Garand (1888-1974), engineer at the U.S. Armory, Springfield, Massachusetts. Also called the M-1, it had an eight-round magazine. When the U.S. Army made it the standard infantry weapon in 1936, it was the world's first semiautomatic rifle to be so honored. American ground troops carried it in World War II and the Korean War.

Gas shell. Basic element of chemical and biological warfare, an artillery projectile filled with poison gas that is released at or just before impact. Used extensively in World War I, armed chiefly with mustard gas, phosgene, or lewisite, it differs from a gas grenade by being fired rather than thrown. Even though military poison gas was outlawed by the 1925 Geneva Protocol, most countries have continued to develop such weapons.

Gatling gun. Primitive machine gun invented in 1862 for the Union army in the American Civil War by Richard Jordan Gatling (1818-1903), characterized by several, usually six to ten, revolving barrels that were cranked around to produce rapid fire. The Gatling gun was superseded by Maxim's machine guns in the 1890's, but the Gatling principle was employed for airborne and antiaircraft weapons in the late twentieth century when very high rates of fire, in excess of 6000 rounds per minute, were desired.

Gladius. Short, straight thrusting sword carried by the Roman infantry legions. From its name derives the word "gladiator." It was superseded in battle by the *spatha* in the Christian Roman Empire.

Glaive. Type of pole-arm whose head consists of a single blade resembling that of a sword. Common variants include a curved, single-edged, saberlike blade and a broadsword blade. It was developed by the French during the High Middle Ages and used primarily for slashing.

Grapeshot. Type of spreading antipersonnel and anticavalry muzzle-loading artillery ammunition, consisting of 10 or 20 loose, grape-sized, solid metal balls packed as a group into a cannon. Very common in warfare from the eighteenth century until the end of the muzzle-loading era, it differs from case shot and canister shot by not being sealed in a container. The effect was like that of a giant shotgun. The Russians fired grapeshot into the Light Brigade at Balaklava in 1854.

Greek fire. Early medieval, and perhaps ancient, incendiary mixture of unknown ingredients, usually delivered by catapult in breakable containers and extensively used in naval warfare because it was unaffected by water. Some say it ignited on contact with salt water and was first used in 673 by the Byzantines defending Constantinople against the Arabs. Others, who discount the story that Archimedes set Roman ships afire with mirrors during the Second Punic War, suggest that he may have been the inventor and first user of Greek fire.

Grenade. Small bomb, either thrown by hand or launched from a hand-carried device. Developed in Europe in the sixteenth century, it originally contained either gunpowder or an incendiary mixture, but later versions contain smoke screen, poison gas, or other chemical agents. Grenades are detonated by percussion, impact, or a short time fuse activated just before throwing or launching.

Grenade launcher. Dating from the fifteenth century and in constant military use ever since, any short-barreled, wide-bore, muzzle-loading, personal firearm designed to throw grenades farther and more accurately than they can be thrown by hand. Some muskets and rifles can be temporarily converted into grenade launchers with specialized muzzle attachments. The 40-millimeter American M203 grenade launcher, standard infantry equipment in the 1990's, is easily combined with the M-16 rifle to create a double-barreled weapon.

Guided missile. Developed by the United States, the Soviet Union, and many other industrialized nations after World War II, a self-propelled, usually rocket-propelled, air- or space-traversing missile, distinguished from an ordinary missile by its being capable of having its course corrected during its flight. It can be ground-launched, air-launched, surface-ship-launched, or submarine-launched. Among water-traversing missiles containing guidance systems, guided torpedoes are generally not called guided missiles, but sea-launched tactical antiship missiles, such as the French Exocet and the American Harpoon, are. Inventing missile guidance systems required the prior development of radar, radio, and computers.

Guisarme. Type of pole-arm whose head includes two blades curving away from each other, sharpened on the outer, or concave, edges. Invented in Europe in the eleventh century, it was used until the fifteenth for slashing, unhorsing, tripping, and thrusting.

Gun. In military parlance, always a cannon, never a personal firearm. As a piece of ordnance, it is usually a big, powerful, long-range cannon firing with a flat trajectory and is thus distinguished from howitzers and mortars.

Guncotton. Explosive compound, also called nitrocotton, a variety of nitrocellulose invented by German chemist Christian Friedrich Schönbein (1799-1868) in 1845 and produced by soaking plain cotton in nitric acid and sulfuric acid. Guncotton burns too fast to be a safe and efficient smokeless propellant for firearms, but it was later used in the invention and manufacture of practical smokeless powders.

Gunpowder. Although Roger Bacon (1220-1292) was the first Westerner to give exact directions for making gunpowder in 1242, it had been developed by the Chinese many centuries earlier. A simple mixture of potassium nitrate, sulfur, and charcoal, gunpowder revolutionized warfare by enabling projectiles to be fired long distances from hollow tubes closed or partially closed at one end. Later improvements, such as powder B, ballistite, and cordite, include less volatile and less smoky varieties.

Halberd. Versatile type of pole-arm whose head includes an ax on one side, a spike, pick, or hook on the other side, and a spear point at the tip. Developed in Switzerland in the thirteenth century, gradually improved through the sixteenth, and still carried by the Swiss Guards of the Vatican, it was an important multipurpose weapon of European foot soldiers during the Renaissance, employed to unhorse, thrust, parry, or slash. Horsemen would frequently become intimidated by companies of well-seasoned infantry armed with halberds.

Hand-cannon. Primitive European muzzle-loading personal firearm, developed about 1400, featuring a long stock, short barrel, smooth bore, and large caliber. Intended to be fired from a benchrest position, it featured, under the stock near the muzzle, a protruding spike to hook over the rest to prevent recoil. It was superseded by the harquebus about 1450.

Hand grenade. Invented in the sixteenth century and in constant military use ever since, small explosive device designed to be thrown by hand and detonated by either impact or a time fuse. Among its most prominent users were the British Grenadiers of the eighteenth century. Twentieth century examples include the German *Steilhandgranate* "potato masher," the Japanese 97, and the American Mk2 "pineapple."

Harquebus. European muzzle-loading firearm developed about 1450. Fired by either a matchlock or a wheel-lock mechanism, it was in general use until about 1550, when the snaphance was invented and the flintlock musket became possible. Also called arquebus, hackbut, or hagbut, it evolved from the hand-cannon, was heavy, bulky, short-ranged, and inaccurate, and was typically fired from a monopod or tripod.

Heavy artillery. Large cannon that differs from light artillery not only by weight, but also by caliber, mobility, and purpose. Such guns are suitable for fortress defense, shore batteries, and siege work, but not for battlefield situations where quick adaptability could be the key to victory. The peak use of heavy artillery was in World War I, when guns of 40 centimeters and larger were moved by railroad or mounted on battleships.

Horse artillery. Type of field artillery in which the gunners ride horses. Until the end of the eigh-

teenth century, guns, carriages, and caissons were pulled by horses while the gun crews and drivers walked. One of Napoleon's most important tactical innovations was to develop the horse artillery, dramatically increasing the versatility, mobility, and effectiveness of his cannon. In the American Civil War, the term referred to the Confederate practice of disassembling small howitzers, loading the components on pack horses, running them with the cavalry through terrain where normal gun carriages could not pass, then quickly assembling them at the next battle.

Howitzer. Type of cannon, originating in the seventeenth century, with a barrel longer than that of a mortar but shorter than that of a gun, designed to fire medium-velocity projectiles at medium to high trajectories.

Hydrogen bomb (H-bomb). Thermonuclear device that uses the power of an atomic fission reaction to fuse heavy hydrogen atoms, deuterium and tritium, into helium. Fused in this way, hydrogen releases about four times as much destructive energy as the same mass of uranium or plutonium in an atomic bomb. The United States tested its first hydrogen bomb in 1952; the Soviet Union in 1953.

Incendiary bomb. Any chemical device intended to cause outbreak of flames among the enemy, including fire bombs, napalm bombs, Molotov cocktails, and fire pots. Some commonly used inflammatory agents are white phosphorus, gasoline, thermite, and magnesium.

Intercontinental ballistic missile (ICBM). Strategic weapon of mass destruction, focus of the Cold War arms race between the Soviet Union and the United States, a very long-ranged, nuclear-armed guided missile, such as the Soviet SS-9, SS-16, SS-17, SS-18, and SS-19, and the American Minuteman III and Titan II, land-launched from underground silos. Similar, but shorter-ranged, missiles, such as the American Polaris and Trident, can be launched from submarines.

Ironclad. Motorized or, less commonly, sailing wooden warship armored with metal plates on its hull and topsides, developed early in the American Civil War. As demonstrated in the classic draw between the USS *Monitor* and the CSS *Virginia* (formerly the USS *Merrimack*) at Hampton Roads, Virginia, on March 9, 1862, it revolutionized naval warfare.

Jacketed bullet. Small arms projectile consisting of a soft metal core, usually lead, coated with a harder metal, often copper, which is still soft enough to grip the rifling inside the barrel. Standard military issue throughout the world since the late nineteenth century, the main advantage of such ammunition is that it can be fired at higher velocity, thereby gaining a flatter trajectory and a longer range.

Javelin. Generic term for any light, usually short, spear whose sole purpose is to be thrown, sometimes with a throwing device to extend the arm and increase its range. Invented during the Stone Age, it was common among most ancient troops, especially the Greek hoplite infantry. One famous type of javelin is the Roman light *pilum*.

Jeddart ax. Type of pole-arm whose head consists of a grappling hook on one side and, on the other side, a long ax-blade with an undulating edge and a spear point. Developed from the halberd and *voulge*, contemporaneous with the Lochaber ax in the sixteenth century, it could be used for scaling walls and unhorsing riders, as well as for thrusting, chopping, and slashing.

Jeep. Named by altering the acronym "GP" for "general purpose," a small, light, fast, tough, dependable, all-terrain motor vehicle with four-wheel drive, an 80-inch wheelbase, and often a machine gun mounted in the back, developed by the Americans in the late 1930's and used extensively in World War II, Korea, and Vietnam. (Jeep is now a trademark for a civilian vehicle based on the military original.)

Jujitsu. Unarmed Japanese martial art whose origins are lost in antiquity, but whose basic principles were codified by samurai in the seventeenth century. Named from two Japanese words meaning "gentle skill," it is not the same as judo, "gentle art," a more recent derivative that emphasizes leverage and throwing. True jujitsu also involves complex maneuvers of kicking, punching, and holding.

Karate. Based on ancient Chinese boxing techniques, this hard-hitting, unarmed Japanese martial art that features extraordinary leaps, chops, and kicks became systematized during the seventeenth century on the island of Okinawa and was named from two Japanese words meaning "empty hand." Tae kwon do, or "Korean karate," evolved from it in the 1950's.

Kidney dagger. Sometimes called ballock dagger, a symmetrical, double-edged, usually ornate European dagger of the thirteenth to seventeenth centuries, so called from the shape of its guard.

Knife. Hand weapon with a multipurpose short cutting blade, dating from prehistoric times and differing from a dagger by its versatility, from a sword by its length, and from a bayonet by its independence.

Knobkerrie. Zulu striking or throwing club, carved from a single piece of hardwood, with a long, thin, straight handle and a smooth, small to medium-sized, spherical or ovoid knob for the warhead.

Kris. Traditional Malay dagger, common throughout Southeast Asia, characterized by a long, asymmetric, double-edged, distinctively wavy or serpentine blade. A spur on one side of the base of the blade typically blends into a sort of hand guard. The handle is often ornate and the blade is sometimes ridged, laminated, and inlayed with elaborate designs or battle scenes.

Kukri. Traditional, single-edged, guardless, long knife or short sword of the Gurkhas of Nepal, characterized by the distinctive shape of its blade: straight out from the hilt to about a third of its length, then bent abruptly downward toward the edge at an angle of about 35 degrees. The back of the blade thus resembles a hockey stick, but the edge is sinuous and, from the vertex of the angle to the point, usually convex.

Lance. Light, long, narrow spear, often with a handguard, carried by horsemen. An ancient weapon, it was used for tournament jousting in the Middle Ages, fell out of military favor in the Renaissance, but was revived by Napoleon. Throughout the nineteenth century until World War I, the lance was common among European and Asian cavalry regiments and Native American horsemen.

Land mine. Explosive obstacle or booby trap, typically buried just under the surface of the ground and easily detonated by pressure or tripwire. A mainstay of twentieth century warfare, most are antipersonnel devices, but some, set to detonate only from heavy pressures, are used as antitank or antivehicle weapons.

Langue-de-bœuf. Type of pole-arm whose head consists mainly of a long, double-bladed spear point named for its shape, like that of the tongue of an ox, or *langue de bœuf* in French. Developed by the Swiss and French in the fifteenth century, it was an early form of the partisan.

Laser. Originally LASER, acronym for light amplification by stimulated emission of radiation. Developed in the late 1950's, it emitted light in a continuous narrow beam of all the same wavelength, either visible, ultraviolet, or infrared. Its most successful military use is in rangefinding and guidance systems for precision-guided munitions (PGM). The United States used laser-guided bombs with great effectiveness in the 1991 Persian Gulf War.

Lewisite. Poison blister gas, $C_2H_2AsCl_2$, a colorless or brown fast-acting blistering agent and eye irritant, smelling of ammonia and geraniums, synthesized in 1918 by Winford Lee Lewis (1878-1943), then a captain in the U.S. Army Chemical Warfare Service; used briefly by the Americans toward the end of World War I.

Light artillery. Cannon with a small to medium caliber and a light barrel, distinguished from heavy artillery mainly by its superior versatility. Usually wheeled, and sometimes portable by as few as two or three soldiers, it can be quickly redeployed, realigned, and redirected amid volatile battlefield predicaments. The category includes field artillery, tank guns, automatic cannon, antiaircraft guns, antitank mortars, and most howitzers.

Limpet mine. Named after the marine gastropod mollusk that clings to undersea surfaces, a twentieth century naval explosive device containing magnets for divers or amphibious saboteurs to attach it to an enemy ship's hull below the water line. American versions from World War II weighed about 10 pounds and used a time-delay fuse to detonate a high explosive charge, usually torpex.

Lochaber ax. Type of pole-arm whose head includes, on one side, a hook for scaling walls or unhorsing riders, and on the other side, a long, wide, convex blade. About half the length of the blade extends beyond the end of the staff. Developed in Scotland late in the sixteenth century, it was popular with clansmen in their struggles against the English until Culloden in 1746.

Longbow. The mainstay of English military success from the thirteenth to the sixteenth centuries, it made archery more accurate and deadly, as well as inexpensive and uncomplicated. It was a simple bow about 6 feet long, drew about 80 or 90 pounds, and shot a 3-foot arrow about 270 yards (250 meters). In its time, the only personal weapon that could outrange it was the crossbow, but the crossbow was slow, and a practiced archer could shoot ten or twelve arrows per minute. The longbow proved devastating against the French at Crécy in 1346.

Long-range bomber. During World War II the Americans developed aircraft that improved offensive punch by flying faster and farther for bombing runs. Early in the war, they replaced their B-17 Flying Fortress with the B-29 Superfortress, which flew at 350 miles per hour and could bomb a target 2,000 miles from base and return safely. The *Enola Gay*, which dropped the atomic bomb on Hiroshima, was a B-29. From the 1950's until the 1990's, the B-52 Stratofortress was the world standard for long-range jet bombers.

Longship. Long, low, slender, shallow-draft vessel of the eighth to eleventh centuries, usually propelled by a single square sail amidships, but also equipped with oars. Developed in Scandinavia by expert seafarers, it was the swiftest ship of its time and struck terror throughout coastal Europe as the preferred raiding ship of the Vikings. From the name of its flat rudder, "steer-board," always lashed to the right side of the ship, derives the word "starboard."

Lucerne hammer. Type of pole-arm that evolved from the *voulge* in the fifteenth century and whose head consists of a heavy, four-pronged warhead: a stout, thick spear point for thrusting; a pick perpendicular to the staff; and two claws opposite the pick and also perpendicular to the staff. Its sole purpose was to smash or penetrate armor.

Mace. Type of club, developed early in the Bronze Age and refined during the Middle Ages, consisting of a short, thick staff and a massive metal warhead with between four and six blunt blades or flanges parallel to the shaft and equally spaced around the head. Alternately, a mace warhead could be a solid metal sphere studded with spikes. It was used extensively by mounted knights to smash or dent armor. After knights in armor disappeared from warfare, the mace continued to be used as a ceremonial symbol of authority.

Machete. Long knife or short sword that originated in the tropical Spanish colonies in the sixteenth century, with a short, thick, single-edged, heavy blade for cutting sugarcane, hacking through jungle, or slashing enemies.

Machine gun. Developed in the second half of the nineteenth century, a complex automatic rifle capable of rapid fire with ordinary small arms ammunition. Prototypes were developed by James Puckle (1667-1724), Richard Jordan Gatling, and Thorsten Nordenfelt (1842-1920), but the first successful true machine gun was invented around 1884 by Hiram Stevens Maxim (1840-1916) and adopted by Britain, Germany, and the United States in the 1890's. Loosely, the term can refer to any automatic weapon.

Man of war. Developed in Britain early in the seventeenth century, any large sailing warship, especially either a frigate or a ship of the line, square-rigged and with at least two gun decks. Bigger, faster, more fully rigged, and more heavily armed than the ship it replaced, the galleon, it survived until the end of the age of sail and made the British navy supreme.

Mangonel. Medieval torsion-powered catapult closely related to the onager, but smaller and, because its throwing arm travelled through an arc of only 90 degrees, less efficient. When cocked, the arm was horizontal; when released, it hit the padded leather buffer at the vertical, thus dissipating all its follow-through energy. Like all torsion en-gines, it was adversely susceptible to changes in humidity affecting the twisted skein.

Matchlock. Introduced in Europe in the early fifteenth century and used until the early eighteenth century in the West and until the mid-nineteenth century in Asia, muzzle-loading firearm ignition mechanism consisting of a lighted wick or match that the trigger action brought into contact with the pan of powder after the pan cover was lifted by hand.

Metal case cartridge. The earliest cartridge cases were either paper or cloth. They were satisfactory for muzzle-loaders, but impractical for breech-loaders, especially when the shooter wanted to reload quickly and cleanly. The metal case that replaced the paper case in the 1870's had several important advantages, chief among which was that it expanded to seal the breech as soon as the weapon was fired. It not only made breech-loading efficient, but also made automatic weapons possible.

Mine. Naval or land booby trap, an explosive weapon usually set to detonate by pressure. Floating mines, moored just below the surface, were typically equipped in both World Wars with Herz horns, a German invention that, when hit, triggers an electrochemical reaction that detonates the high explosive charge. Land mines can be laid by sappers or sown by mortars or from cluster bombs. Anti-mine apparatus includes probes, metal detectors, bangalore torpedoes, tanks equipped with flails, ploughs, or rollers, and minesweeping ships.

Minenwerfer. Literally, mine-thrower, a rifled, muzzle-loading, short-barrelled, 25-centimeter German mortar of World War I, often loaded with gas shells.

Minié ball. Not really a ball, but a conical lead bullet with a hollow, expanding base, invented in 1849 by French army officer Claude-Étienne Minié (1804-1879). Firing the weapon pushed the bullet tightly into the rifling of the barrel, thus dramatically increasing its range and accuracy. The Crimean War and the American Civil War proved the superiority of the Minié rifle over both the smoothbore musket and the rifled musket that used spherical ammunition.

Missile. Any self-propelled ammunition or projectile. Its three main types of self-propulsion are jet engine, propeller, and rocket. Because rocket propulsion is by far the most common, some missiles, especially small ones, are loosely called rockets. In the late twentieth century, the term became mostly synonymous with "guided missile." Loosely, the term can mean any hurled object.

Mitrailleuse. Hand-cranked machine gun developed in 1869 for France and characterized by 37 barrels in a hexagonal pattern inside a single air-cooled barrel. A metal ammunition block inserted vertically into the breech, transverse to the barrels, held all 37 rounds. The French used the *mitrailleuse* too far back from the front lines for it to be effective in the Franco-Prussian War (1870-1871). The term later became the ordinary French word for machine gun.

Molotov cocktail. Terrorist and insurrectionist incendiary weapon developed in Europe in the early twentieth century and named after Soviet statesman Vyacheslav Mikhailovich Molotov (1890-1986). Consisting of a glass bottle filled with gasoline and plugged with an oil-soaked rag, it is thrown like a hand grenade as soon as the rag is ignited.

Mortar. Short-barrelled, large-caliber, usually muzzle-loading cannon designed to lob shells at low velocity and high trajectory with moderate accuracy for short distances, such as over the walls of a besieged fortress. It has been in constant military use since the fifteenth century, but in the late twentieth it became mostly an antiarmor, guided missile launching weapon.

Multiple independently targetable reentry vehicle (MIRV). Type of nuclear warhead on either an intercontinental ballistic missile (ICBM) or a sea-launched ballistic missile (SLBM), developed in the 1970's, consisting of a cluster of guided missiles to saturate the general area of the target and make antimissile defense more difficult for the enemy.

Musket. Any muzzle-loading, long-barrelled, personal firearm, originally smoothbore, but could be either smoothbore or rifled. Invented in the fifteenth century, it was a standard infantry weapon for four hundred years until superseded by the breech-loading rifle in the 1860's.

Mustard gas. A poison gas, $C_4H_8Cl_2S$, an acrid, noxious substance that penetrates and irritates skin, causes severe blisters, and can cause blindness; used extensively by both sides in World War I.

Muzzle-loader. Any firearm, either personal weapon or artillery piece, that loads its charge and projectile through the front end of the bore. Muzzle-loaders dominated for almost 600 years, but, with the exception of mortars, most military firearms since the late nineteenth century have been breechloaders. The greatest drawback to muzzle-loaders is that they cannot repeat.

Naginata. Traditional Japanese pole-arm whose head consists of a long, high-quality, curved, saberlike sword blade rigidly attached to the staff with an overly long shank or tang. An expert in *naginatajutsu*, the martial art of wielding this weapon, was a very deadly warrior.

Nao. Sailing, deep-draft, broad-beam Portuguese merchantman and warship, called *nau* in Spain and carrack in England, developed in the late thirteenth or early fourteenth century, probably by Basque shipbuilders. Usually with three or four masts, armed with one or two decks of bronze cannon, and full-rigged, it was sturdy but slow. Famous *naos* include the *Santa Maria*, Christopher Columbus's flagship; most of Ferdinand Magellan's fleet that circumnavigated the world from 1519 to 1522; and the *Henry Grâce à Dieu*, Henry VIII's naval flagship.

Napalm. Incendiary substance, ammunition for flamethrowers and firebombs, developed by the United States in 1942 and used extensively in the Pacific theater of World War II and in Vietnam. Also called jellied gasoline, especially in its early years, it exists in several formulas, the most successful of which is napalm-B: 50 percent polystyrene, 25 percent benzene, 25 percent gasoline. The name derives from two of its original ingredients, naphthenic acid, or aluminum naphthene, and palmitic acid, or aluminum palmate. Napalm adheres to its target, making it difficult to extinguish.

Neutron bomb. The so-called dirty bomb, developed in the 1970's, an enhanced radiation bomb intended as an antipersonnel tactical nuclear weapon, designed to do minimal damage to non-living structures, but to kill or incapacitate all animal life within a certain radius.

Nuclear-powered warship. The technology of substituting nuclear fuel for diesel is especially effective for submarines, enabling them to stay submerged much longer and refuel less frequently, thus increasing the threat of the sea-launched ballistic missile (SLBM). The first nuclear-powered submarine, the USS *Nautilus*, was launched in 1954.

Oil pot. Defensive weapon for besieged medieval garrisons, a large metal cauldron containing hot oil to be poured on attackers trying to scale the walls.

Onager. Light, versatile, mobile catapult developed by the Romans in probably the third century, so called because, after launching its load, when the throwing arm landed on the padded leather buffer at the front of the stout wooden frame, it kicked like its namesake, the Asian wild ass. Its power came from a skein twisted around one end of its arm, which travelled through an arc of about 135 degrees.

Ordnance. A term which has two distinct meanings in military parlance, depending on context. On the one hand, it means military equipment and hardware in general, not only weapons and ammunition, but also vehicles, tools, and durable supplies. On the other hand, and more properly, it means artillery, cannons, and their ammunition. Ordnance officers are responsible for procuring and maintaining this materiel, and ensuring that the artillery is in good working order.

Parang. Malay name for the jagged-edged, oddly-angled sword traditionally used by the Dyak headhunters and pirates of Borneo. The tip is sometimes squared off, with three or more separate points in line. The hilt is usually guardless and often elaborately decorated with horn, hair, or feathers.

Partisan. Type of pole-arm whose head consists mainly of a long, broad, double-bladed spearhead, characterized by two small winglike extensions or flanges at the base of the spearhead curving up toward the point. It evolved from the langdebeve in the sixteenth century and was common throughout the seventeenth. In William Shakespeare's *Hamlet*, I.i.144, Marcellus asks whether he should strike the ghost with his partisan.

Patrol-torpedo (PT) boat. Very small, very fast, shallow-draft, motorized vessel, typically armed with torpedoes, machine guns, and depth charges, used extensively by the Americans in the Pacific Theater of World War II. John F. Kennedy became a war hero while commanding PT-109.

Percussion cap. Small container of priming substance which is detonated when struck in a specific way, thus setting off the main charge and propelling the projectile down the barrel of the firearm. Alexander John Forsyth (1769-1843), a Scottish minister, patented the first practical percussion firing mechanism in 1807. His invention proved to be among the most important in the history of firearms, because it eventually made possible metal-case cartridges, breech-loading, rapid fire, and quick reloading. Cartridges are designated according the placement of their internal percussion caps: rimfire, centerfire, and the obsolete pinfire.

Petard. Explosive demolition device of the sixteenth century, consisting of a container of gunpowder which could be placed against a wall, gate, portcullis, or drawbridge, then detonated in an attempt to open a breach. Because of its extraordinarily loud report, it was named after the French word for "to break wind." Because so many of its users were killed by the explosion before they could get away, the phrase, "hoist with his own petard" arose, meaning "defeated by his own designs."

Petronel. Large-caliber matchlock carbine developed in France in the late sixteenth century, featuring a banana-shaped butt, curved sharply downward for bracing the weapon against the chest.

Phosgene. Poison gas, $COCl_2$, colorless lung irritant, smells like freshly cut grass, causes choking death by pulmonary edema, that is, by drowning in one's own mucus; used extensively by both sides in World War I.

Pike. Very long type of pole-arm whose head consists mainly of a heavy but narrow spear point rigidly attached to the staff with a long metal shank. The pike dates from ancient times, but its most celebrated tactics involved infantrymen creating defensive formations such as the mobile *cheval de frise* against enemy cavalry in the sixteenth to eighteenth centuries to allow musketeers safety while reloading. Such pikes could be 16 feet (5 meters) long.

Pilum. Roman spear, standard equipment for foot soldiers in the legions. It existed in two forms: one long, heavy, often with a handguard midway down the shaft, and used mainly for thrusting; the other short, light, without a handguard, basically a javelin with a small head designed to break off upon impact.

Pistol. Short-barrelled handgun, invented in the late fifteenth or early sixteenth century, frequently in military use as an officer's sidearm. Its one-handed operation made it suitable for cavalrymen. In automatic or semi-automatic pistols, the magazine can be conveniently contained in the handle.

Plastic explosive. Stable, moldable, high explosive mixture created by combining a plasticizing agent such as oil or wax with a high explosive compound such as RDX or TNT. First developed in the 1890's, plastic explosive research expanded dramatically during and after World War II, resulting in such products as composition C.

Pole-arm. Long, multipurpose spear developed at every time and in every culture, but especially in Europe throughout the Middle Ages. Used extensively by foot soldiers and palace guards until the nineteenth century, it consists of a large, finely crafted metal head rigidly affixed to a wooden staff. Varieties include the bill, *guisarme*, glaive, halberd, jeddart ax, *lang-de-bœuf*, Lochaber ax, Lucerne hammer, partisan, pike, poleax, *spetum*, and *voulge*.

Poleax. Type of pole-arm whose head includes a broad-bladed ax on one side. There may be a spear point at the tip of the head and either a spike, pick, or hook on the other side, so that the weapon would resemble a halberd. It was developed in Europe in the late Middle Ages and used throughout the Renaissance and early modern era.

Pom-pom. So named from the sound of its report, small-caliber automatic cannon whose reloading mechanism is powered by the firing of each previ-

ous round. Developed in the 1880's and 1890's by Hiram Stevens Maxim and originally intended as a mounted naval gun, its first use was as a field piece by both the British and the Boers in the Boer War. In subsequent naval and antiaircraft use, it was typically mounted in pairs. The British used a 37-millimeter version as a field piece in World War I.

Poniard. Renaissance French dagger with a long, slender, triangular or square blade, somewhat resembling a stiletto. In combat it was often wielded in conjunction with the rapier as a parrying weapon. The name derives from *poing*, the French word for fist.

Powder B. The first successful smokeless powder, invented in 1885 by Paul Vieille (1854-1934) and soon adopted by the French army. It consists of nitrocelluose gelatinized with ether and alcohol, evaporated, rolled, and flaked.

Pursuit plane. From 1920 to 1948 American fighter aircraft were officially designated "pursuit" and were numbered with the prefix "P." Among the outstanding planes in this series were the Curtiss P-1 Hawk, the Boeing P-26 Peashooter, the Lockheed P-38 Lightning or Fork-Tailed Devil, and the Curtiss P-40 Flying Tiger.

Quarterstaff. Particularly stout medieval English stave of oak or ash, about 8 feet long and 1.5 inches thick, occasionally banded with iron at both ends, usually wielded with one hand in the middle and the other near one end. A surprisingly versatile weapon in the quick hands of an expert, it can stun, stab, crush, unhorse, fracture, or even kill. The legendary meeting of Robin Hood and Little John involved their famous quarterstaff duel on a narrow bridge.

Rapier. Long thrusting sword developed in Europe in the sixteenth century and popular until the eighteenth. With a rigid, slender, straight blade of fine steel and usually an elaborate hilt and handguard, it served the privileged classes, both civilian and military, as a dueling weapon, an instrument of stealth and assassination, and a symbol of rank and authority.

RDX (cyclo-1,3,5-trimethylene-2,4,6-trinitramine). Also called cyclonite or hexogen, one of the most common military explosives of the twentieth century, especially in World War II. Invented in 1899 by the Germans and named by the British, its name is an acronym for "Research Department Explosive." More powerful than TNT and comparatively stable, RDX is often mixed with TNT, as in torpex, the standard torpedo load, or in aerial bombs and artillery shell fillings.

Recoilless rifle. Invented by the Americans during World War II, a hollow tube, open at both ends, allowing a single soldier to fire an artillery shell from the shoulder. The American M20 superseded the M9A1 after World War II. The Swedish Miniman and the German Armbrust are late twentieth century disposable recoilless antitank guns firing just one load of shaped charge, that is, a shell that explodes on the outer surface of the armor and bores a hole through it.

Repeating rifle. Breech-loading personal firearm, using manual action to feed the next round from a magazine into the firing chamber. Developed independently and gradually by many inventors in the mid-nineteenth century, its eventual perfection early in the twentieth century was made possible by two innovations: the metal-case cartridge and smokeless powder. The repeating action can be lever, as in the Winchester 1873; slide, as in the Colt Lightning; or bolt, as in most World War I repeaters.

Revolver. Type of breech-loading pistol, invented in the mid-nineteenth century, classified in four basic kinds according to how the multichambered cylinder is exposed for reloading: side-gate, where a flap opens on one side of the weapon; break-open, where the barrel swings down on a hinge; swing-out, where the cylinder swings to one side on its hinge; and removable cylinder. A revolver is either single-action, if it needs to be cocked manually, or double-action, if the trigger cocks the hammer. Famous manufacturers include Tranter, Webley, Colt, and Smith and Wesson.

Rifle. Any long-barrelled personal firearm, either muzzle-loading or breech-loading, that has spiral grooves machined inside the barrel to spin the bullet, thus increasing its accuracy, range, and power. Invented in the fifteenth century and first popularized by the American colonists in the mid-eighteenth century, it superseded smoothbore weapons in the 1860's. Outstanding examples are the Winchester, M-1, Springfield, and Enfield.

Robot bomb. Early type of guided missile developed by both sides in the European Theater late in World War II, a small drone, or pilotless airplane, loaded with high explosives and sent on a descending course toward its target. The best known is the jet-powered Nazi V-1 (Vergeltungswaffe Eins), used against England in 1944.

Rocket. Self-propelled airborne missile, powered by the rearward thrust of gases from burning either solid or liquid fuel, invented by the Chinese about 1000, developed in Europe in the sixteenth century, made practical for warfare by Sir William Congreve (1772-1828), and evolved into a major element of modern warfare by Konstantin Eduardovich Tsiolkovsky (1857-1935), Robert Hutchings Goddard (1882-1945), and Wernher von Braun (1912-1977). The first important military rocket was the German V-2 of World War II.

Rocket launcher. Developed by all sides during World War I, any device designed to make small rockets more portable, versatile, and mobile as artillery ammunition. In the form of a mortar or recoilless rifle, a rocket launcher and its ammunition can be mounted on a tank, jeep, or gun carriage, or carried by one or two infantryman, who fire it either hand-held or from a bipod or tripod mount.

Rubber bullet. Also called baton round, large-caliber antimob projectile, typically 37-millimeter, developed by the British in the 1960's and designed to stun and intimidate rather than kill, although it can kill if fired at close range. The same specialized weapons that fire it can also fire canisters of tear gas, smoke screen, and other antiriot ammunition.

Saber. Long slashing sword invented in Europe in the eighth century. Used in most wars since then, it achieved its greatest prominence as a cavalry weapon in the nineteenth century. Usually curved with a blade-length single edge on the convex side, it could also be edged a few inches down from the point on the concave side for back-slashing.

Samurai sword. Traditional weapon of the feudal Japanese warrior class who followed the military religion of bushido. This high-quality, gently curved, single-edged, two-handed, long sword features a small guard, long handle, and elaborate workmanship. Known in Japan as daisho, nodachi, tachi, or katana, depending on length and style, its standard design was established in the early ninth century by the great swordsmith Yasutsuna.

Sax. Also called *scramasax*, long dagger or short, straight, iron sword of the Northern European tribes in the Dark Ages.

Scimitar. Traditional saber of Islamic nations, developed prior to the Crusades, characterized by a long, thin, single-edged, crescent-shaped blade. Varieties include the Persian *shamshir*, the Turkish *kilij*, and the Arab *saif.*

Scud missile. Soviet tactical nuclear or high explosive missile, liquid-fueled, relatively short-ranged, equipped with an inertial guidance system. Scuds with nonnuclear warheads were used ineffectively against Israel by Iraq in the 1991 Persian Gulf War.

Semiautomatic firearm. Any firearm that loads automatically but fires only one shot for each squeeze of the trigger. Mechanically, it is midway between a repeating rifle and a fully automatic weapon. The earliest was the 1893 Borchardt pistol.

Shell. Any cannon-fired projectile filled with explosive, typically designed to explode at a given point in its flight or upon impact. The earliest artillery shells, in the fifteenth century, were hollow iron spheres filled with gunpowder and fitted with fuses. Besides varieties of gunpowder or black powder, common explosive shell fillings include picric acid, ammonium picrate, TNT, amatol, RDX, and pentaerythitol tetranitrate (PETN).

Ship of the line. Large three-masted, square-rigged, sailing warship with at least two and usually three fully armed gun decks, carrying between 64 and 140 guns, so called either because it was powerful enough to hold the line of battle or because, with sister ships fore and aft, they formed an impregnable line. Developed by the British in the seventeenth century, it was the mainstay of naval power in general and the British navy in particular for the next 200 years, superseded only by ironclad and motorized vessels.

Shrapnel. Antipersonnel explosive shell invented in the 1790's by British artillery officer Henry Shrapnel (1761-1842), consisting of a case of small shot with a fuse designed to detonate over the heads of enemy soldiers. The term also loosely refers to any small airborne metal fragments or debris from an explosion.

Siege artillery. Class of large weapons, originally only mechanical instruments such as catapults and trebuchets, but later also explosion-powered weapons such as mortars and other large firearms, employed during sieges to breach walls, destroy defensive works, and keep besieged garrisons confined.

Siege tower. Tall, shielded platform that could be wheeled up to a besieged wall for archers inside the platform to shoot down on defenders. Because they were so vulnerable to fire, siege towers were covered with water-soaked hides or metal plates. In a famous incident during the Siege of Acre (1191) by King Richard I of England (1157-1199) in the Third Crusade, the Muslim defenders first saturated a huge copper-plated Christian siege tower with a flammable liquid, then set it afire with a burning log hurled from within the fortress by a trebuchet.

Sling. Invented in the Stone Age and existing in myriad forms ever since, a simple flexible or elastic device for extending the range and velocity of hurled objects. The basic weapon is just a small pouch in the middle of a thong. The warrior places a stone in the pouch, grabs both ends of the thong, whirls the sling, and releases one end at the optimal moment, as David did in his famous encounter with Goliath in 1 Samuel 17. Slings are sometimes attached to certain kinds of catapults, such as the trebuchet.

Sloop of war. Single-masted, sailing, wooden warship, rigged fore and aft with a lone jib, carrying between 10 and 28 guns on a single deck. Sometimes called a corvette, a ship of this class could also have a small foremast, and if so, it could be square-rigged. Developed by the British in the late seventeenth and early eighteenth centuries, it was a staple of naval warfare until the middle of the nineteenth century.

Smokeless powder. Several attempts were made in the mid-nineteenth century to find an explosive that would burn more completely, produce less smoke, and thus be a more effective propellant for firearms than gunpowder. Prussian Major Johann Schultze offered a prototype in 1864, but it burned too quickly, violently, and uncontrollably. The first successful smokeless powder was powder B, developed in France in 1884. The French produced the first smokeless powder cartridge in 1886. Other successful smokeless powders include ballistite and cordite. Such powders are either single-base, consisting of mostly nitrocellulose or guncotton, or double-base, consisting of nitrocellulose or guncotton and nitroglycerin. Conventional munitions typically use double-base powder.

Snaphance. Invented in Europe, perhaps by the Dutch, some time from 1550 to 1570, a major technological advance in muzzle-loading firearm ignition mechanisms. When the trigger is pulled, the powder-pan cover swings up and the hammer swings down so that, when the two collide, sparks are produced which, as the hammer continues down into the pan, ignite the priming powder and fire the weapon. The snaphance achieved great popularity in the seventeenth century and made the flintlock possible.

Snickersnee. From two Dutch words meaning "thrust" and "cut," a large knife or short saberlike sword used in Europe in the eighteenth century for both thrusting and cutting. The term has also become generic for any swordplay.

Spatha. Ancient Roman sword with a broad blade for slashing. Longer than the gladius, it was used by both infantry and cavalry in the last centuries of the Roman Empire.

Spear. Long pointed shaft for either thrusting or throwing. In prehistoric times it was first just a sharp stick, but later in the Stone Age hunters and warriors added sharp heads of stone, bone, teeth, or ivory. As knowledge of metallurgy grew, so did the sophistication and keenness of spearheads. By the Renaissance, European spears were highly specialized, some involving the functions of the ax or sword as well as the spear. By the twentieth century, most spears were only ceremonial.

Spetum. Type of pole-arm evolved from the trident. In the middle of the warhead was a langdebeve spear point and at the sides were a symmetrical pair of shorter pointed blades, each with one or more bill hooks on the outer edge. A very versatile weapon for both thrusting and slashing, it combined the best features of the partisan, the *guisarme*, and the bill.

Star shell. Nineteenth century artillery projectile that explodes in mid-air, optimally at the high point of its arc, releasing a bright display of sparks, either to illuminate a target or to signal friendly forces. Used during the British night attack on Fort McHenry on September 13, 1814, these shells were immortalized by Francis Scott Key (1779-1843) in "The Star-Spangled Banner" as "the bombs bursting in air."

Stave. Peasant weapon of the Middle Ages, especially in England, where it evolved from the walking stick into a long club and became the standard defense for pedestrian travelers as well as a popular infantry weapon. The toughest kind of stave is the quarterstaff.

Stealth bomber. The American B-2 Spirit bomber, developed in the 1980's as part of President Ronald Reagan's Strategic Defense Initiative (SDI), characterized by its unique bat-wing appearance and its ability to avoid detection by enemy radar. Even though it first flew in 1988, it was not flown in the 1991 Persian Gulf War because it was not capable until 1996 of delivering nonnuclear bombs. It flew against Serbia during the Kosovo crisis of 1999.

Sten gun. British 9-millimeter light, simple, inexpensive submachine gun invented in 1940 by Major Reginald Vernon Sheppard and Harold John Turpin. The name comes from the "S" in Sheppard, the "T" in Turpin, and the "En" in either Enfield Small Arms Company or England. Versatile, effective, and often having a collapsible stock, nearly four million Sten guns were manufactured during World War II. American soldiers in the European Theater, equipped with more sophisticated weapons, called it the Stench gun.

Stiletto. Thin, symmetrical, Renaissance Italian dagger with a round, square, or triangular blade and no edge, used only for stabbing. Also called stylet, some round-hilted varieties were used by infantrymen as plug bayonets. A highly specialized stiletto, the fusetto, had a slender, graduated, cone-shaped or isosceles-shaped blade for early artillerymen to gauge the bore, clean the vent, and puncture the powder bag of muzzle-loading cannon.

Stones. Always available, and with deadly power obvious to even the most prehistoric of our hominid ancestors, small jagged rocks picked off the ground and hurled are the most ancient of all weapons. Still in prehistoric times, early humans learned to chip stones into sharper hand weapons, rudimentary knives, and later into arrowheads, spearheads, and ax-heads. Naturally smooth or artificially smoothed stones became ammunition for slings.

Submachine gun. Fully automatic personal firearm, small and light enough to be fired by a single individual without support, developed between the World Wars, in particular by John Taliaferro Thompson (1860-1940), inventor of the most famous submachine gun, the "tommy gun." The "sub-" prefix refers only to size and weight, not to either the mechanism or the degree of automatic operation.

Submarine. Undersea naval craft. David Bushnell (1742-1824) used a one-man submarine, the *Turtle*, in the American Revolution (1775-1783). A Confederate nine-man, hand-cranked submarine, the CSS *Hunley*, sank the USS *Housatonic*, and itself, in 1864. The first practical motorized submarines were developed in the United States by John Philip Holland (1840-1914). The deadliness of the German U-Boat wolf packs proved submarines an indispensable aspect of effective naval warfare since World War I. The first nuclear submarine, the USS *Nautilus*, was launched in 1954. Torpedoes are the standard armament of submarines, but since the Cold War many have also carried missiles.

Surface-to-air missile (SAM). Small, defensive, guided missile launched from a usually mobile ground station toward an airborne target. As either an antimissile missile or an antiaircraft weapon, it can be equipped with a small nuclear warhead. The smallest have a range of about 6 miles (10 kilometers) and can be fired by one soldier from a shoulder-held recoilless launcher. The largest have a range of about 40 miles (65 kilometers) and are launched from a semi-permanent launch vehicle.

Sword. Edged weapon with a long blade and usually a sharp point. Invented in the Near East about 6000 B.C.E., it may have been one of the earliest things that humans learned to make out of metal, though its technology did not become practical until the Iron Age, about 1000 B.C.E. Some varieties of sword, such as the rapier, are mainly for thrusting; others, such as the saber, mainly for slashing; and a few, such as the cutlass, are dual purpose. A basic weapon in nearly every war until the end of the nineteenth century, the sword's use since then has been mostly ceremonial.

Tank. Motorized, fully armored, attack vehicle running on self-contained tracks, usually with guns mounted in a revolving turret, invented by the British in 1915 and first used in battle at Flers-Courcelette on September 15, 1916. The Allies used nearly 500 tanks at Cambrai in November, 1916. The Germans were slower to recognize the value of this new technology, and the first tank-versus-tank battle occurred at Villers-Bretonneux on April 24, 1918. Early in World War II, German Panzers dominated and it was the Allies' turn to play catch-up, which the Americans did very well with the Sherman tank. Tanks were a mainstay of ground warfare throughout the twentieth century.

Thermonuclear device. Any bomb that relies upon the principle of the fusion of atoms of low atomic weight. At the dawn of the twenty-first century, they are the most powerful bombs yet produced. To fuse the nucleus of one atom with another requires tremendous heat as a trigger and produces tremendous heat when accomplished. Since the early 1950's, these bombs have been extensively tested, manufactured, deployed, and stockpiled, but, as of 2001, never used in warfare.

Time bomb. Any explosive device with a time delay fuse set to detonate at an exact, predetermined time and usually hidden in or near its target. Invented in the nineteenth century, there are three types, classified according to their means of detonation: burning fuse, the most primitive, first made practical in 1831 by the British; clockwork fuse, developed in the twentieth century and used extensively in World War II; and chemical reaction fuse, the most sophisticated, invented by an Anglo-American team in World War II and common among demolition engineers, terrorists, and saboteurs ever since.

TNT (trinitrotoluene). High explosive first synthesized in the 1860's, but not used as a military explosive until the German armed forces adopted it in 1902, and not extensively in warfare until World War I. Ideal military explosives are powerful, nonreactive, safe to handle, have a long storage life in any climate, and can detonate only under specific conditions. TNT meets all these criteria. The power of nuclear bombs is measured by kiloton, a unit equal to one thousand tons of TNT, or by megaton, equal to one million tons of TNT.

Toledo. Finely tempered, very sharp, elegant steel sword produced in Toledo, Spain. Swords manufactured in this Spanish city have had the reputation for high quality since perhaps as early as the first century B.C.E. They have been commonly called Toledos since the sixteenth century.

Tomahawk. Small, light ax or hatchet invented in pre-Columbian times, probably by the Algonquins, but carried by most Eastern North American native tribes. Its head was originally stone, but metal after the seventeenth century. It could be either wielded as a hand weapon or thrown. Also, the name of the best-known cruise missile.

Torpedo. Naval waterborne antiship missile, either guided or not, launched from a ship, submarine, patrol-torpedo boat, or aircraft, and driven by a propeller. The first practical torpedo, developed by British engineer Robert Whitehead (1823-1905), was invented in Britain in 1866. Earlier, for example in the American Civil War, the word referred to antiship mines. The first extensive use of true torpedoes in war was by the German submarines (U-boats) in World War I. Among the explosives commonly used in torpedo warheads is torpex, a mixture of 42 percent RDX, 40 percent TNT, 18 percent aluminum powder, and a tiny bit of wax, developed by the British during World War II.

Tracer bullet. Used in the nineteenth century, but developed comprehensively in the twentieth, any projectile, usually from a machine gun and often for antiaircraft fire, either containing or coated with chemicals to produce a visible trail of luminous smoke, especially useful at night to verify the gunner's aim. A variant is the spotter bullet, which contains chemicals to provide a visible flash upon impact. Tracers or spotters can also be armor-piercing or incendiary.

Trebuchet. The largest, most efficient, and most effective of medieval catapults, developed in the thirteenth century and used exclusively as a siege engine. Essentially a first-class lever whose effort was about 20,000 pounds (9,000 kilograms) of rocks in a bucket on the short arm, whose load was a boulder of about 300 pounds (140 kilograms) at the end of the long arm, and whose fulcrum was a massive wooden frame, it had a range of about 300 yards or meters at medium to high trajectory. Often the throwing arm incorporated a sling to increase the range and velocity of the projectile. As the short arm was very short and the long arm could be up to 50 feet (15 meters), the machine had to be cocked with a complex system of pulleys.

Trident. Ancestor of most pole-arms except the pike, it evolved from the agricultural pitchfork and at first was indistinguishable from it. Intended only for thrusting, its three points created a broad warhead that increased the likelihood of wounding the enemy. It was used in most ancient and medieval wars, but is best known as a weapon of Roman gladiators. A later, more sophisticated version is the spetum.

Trireme. Galley with three banks of oars. Developed from the bireme for speed and power around 650 B.C.E. and reaching its height of development during the fifth century B.C.E., it had an overall length between 35 and 40 meters, a crew of about 170, a draft of only one meter, and a top oared speed between nine and eleven knots. Each higher bank of oars was mounted on outrigger fulcrums farther abeam than the next lower bank. Because rowing required precise timing by all crew members, only carefully trained freemen, not slaves, were used, to ensure high morale. By 500 B.C.E., the trireme dominated the Mediterranean.

Tulwar. Traditional saber of India, characterized by a large, disk-shaped pommel, a knobbed cross piece at the guard, and a broad, deeply curved blade sharpened along the length of the convex edge. Some varieties had knuckle guards, and many had elaborately engraved or inlaid blades.

Voulge. Type of pole-arm whose head consists of a very large, broad single-edged ax-blade with small, sharp spikes or hooks at the top and back. One of the earliest pole-arms, it evolved from the ancient pruning hook, a farm tool. The Lochaber ax, the jeddart ax, and the Lucerne hammer all evolved from it.

War-hammer. Medieval, especially late medieval, sophisticated, metal-headed, European club, sometimes called battle-hammer, either a short-handled hand weapon or a pole-arm, designed with both a pick head to break armor and a blunt head to cause concussions, trauma, or fractures inside the armor without breaking it.

Wheel lock. Complex muzzle-loading firearm ignition mechanism, invented around 1500. When the trigger was pressed, a wheel turned, opening the pan, creating sparks from friction with iron pyrites, and igniting the powder. It was superseded by the snaphance in the mid-sixteenth century.

Whizbang. British trench soldiers' onomatopoeic name for a German high-velocity, low-trajectory artillery shell in World War I, usually 88-millimeter. The soldiers believed that if they could hear the "whiz," then the "bang" would not get them.

Yataghan. Turkish short saber without a crosspiece or handguard. The blade is nearly straight, but in the shape of an S-curve with the edge concave near the hilt and convex near the point.

Zeppelin. Rigid airship or dirigible, a steerable lighter-than-air aircraft, as opposed to the blimp, which is nonrigid, and the balloon, which is rudderless. Invented in 1900 by German Count Ferdinand Graf von Zeppelin (1838-1917), it was originally intended for civilian passenger service and performed that function until the *Hindenburg* disaster in Lakehurst, New Jersey, on May 6, 1937. The Germans bombed England by zeppelin during World War I, but abandoned that practice because airships are difficult to defend.

Eric v.d. Luft

WEAPONS AND FORCES

CLUBS, MACES, AND SLINGS

DATES: TO C. 1500 C.E.

NATURE AND USE

Clubs, maces, and slings, originally appearing in primitive times, are alike in their antiquity and concussive effect. Clubs are stout sticks, weighted at the striking end and usually made of hardwood, although bone, horn, and stone were also used. Clubs, the oldest weapons, have taken many forms throughout history. As small personal weapons, less than 2 feet in length, they could be thrust into belts and carried anywhere. Larger war clubs—from 2 to 3 feet in length—were wielded with one hand, and very large clubs, from 3 to 6 feet in length, were used with both hands. Shafts could be straight or curved, with cylindrical, ball-shaped, or broad, flat heads. Shaft edges could be sharpened, knobbed, spiked, or fitted with naturally sharp items, such as shark's teeth, rays' tails, or obsidian blades.

Although hand weapons could be used with more accuracy and force than thrown ones, clubs meant for throwing were also used. These "throwing sticks" were usually 2 to 3 feet long and could be curved, such as the Australian boomerang, or could have a ball and handle, such as the African knobkerrie. Users of these weapons hoped either to kill an enemy outright by crushing its skull or to incapacitate it by breaking its bones or stunning it. The club has seen worldwide use among primitive tribal peoples and early civilizations, and simple forms were wielded by early hominids.

Developed from the club, the mace is a heavy weight attached to the end of a handle. Stone maces appeared during the seventh millennium B.C.E. in the Neolithic Near East, and their use spread into Europe, Egypt, and India, where they were employed into the early Bronze Age. A mace was made by inserting 2- to 3-foot-long handles into holes bored through stones that had been worked into spherical, or at least symmetrical, shapes. Maces with bronze or iron heads became popular during the medieval era

Greek slingers, circa 400 B.C.E.

(approximately 500-1500 C.E.), and their use spread from Central Asia and the Near East into Europe, the Far East, and North Africa. Although intended to injure people, maces were also designed to damage armor: smashing it with blunt heads, penetrating it with spiked or knobbed heads, or cutting it with flanged or winged heads. Maces could also be thrown, although this was an unusual usage. The military flail, which had mace heads or clubs attached by chains to the handle, also appeared during the medieval period but may have been more of a demolition device for siege warfare than a combat weapon, at least in Western Europe.

The sling was most likely a product of the Neolithic Near East (ninth millennium B.C.E.) but may have had earlier origins. It was probably derived from throwing stones whirled about by attached lashes; the South American *bolas* is an example. The most common sling, the hand sling, consisted of a 3-foot-long strap with a pouch in the center in which a missile, usually a stone, was placed. The user would take both ends of the sling in one hand, whirl the stone around quickly, and then let go of one end of the sling. The released stone would then fly toward its target. Hand slings—made of leather, wool, woven grasses, sinew, or human hair—have been used by many primitive peoples worldwide for hunting, warfare, and protection from predators. They were popular among civilized peoples in the Indus Valley, the Near East, Greece, Sicily, Spain and the Baleares, Celtic Europe, Mesoamerica, and the Andes.

TURNING POINTS

9th millen. B.C.E.	The sling makes its first known appearance.
7th millen. B.C.E.	The stone-head mace makes its first known appearance.
c. 2500 B.C.E.	Metal armor is developed in Mesopotamia, making the stone-headed mace obsolete.
c. 1000 B.C.E.	Metal-headed maces become common in Europe.
401 B.C.E.	Slings are used to great effect against the Persians at the Battle of Cunaxa, outranging Persian bows and arrows.
c. 31 B.C.E.	Specialist corps of slingers largely disappear from ancient armies.

Skilled slingers could hurl heavy stones to damage armor out to 15 yards, strike small targets with stones out to 30 yards, shatter skulls out to 50 yards, hit man-sized targets out to 180 yards, and throw light lead shot over 360 yards. In battle, slingers were employed to harass enemy formations before hand-to-hand combat began, to pursue routed foes, to ward off enemy cavalry and elephants, and to protect one's own troops from missile attacks. During sieges slingers provided covering fire, harassed working parties, and hurled incendiaries into buildings or siegeworks.

Another type of sling was the staff sling, apparently invented in the Roman Empire and used at sieges in medieval Europe. It was essentially a hand sling attached to a 4-foot staff. The user held the staff horizontally in both hands, then swung it upright, flinging the missile from the sling attached to the end of the staff.

DEVELOPMENT

The club's developmental history is largely lost, because of the perishability of wood. By approximately 50,000 B.C.E., humans had developed the creativity and skill to produce any of the many club designs found among modern tribal peoples. In combat, prehistoric hunter-gatherers and small groups of farmers and herders probably preferred, whenever possible, to ambush or raid their enemies, thereby avoiding the hazards of close combat made more dangerous by their lack of armor, numbers, and strong leadership. Clubs would have been used mainly to finish off wounded or trapped foes. In direct confrontations hunter-gatherers would have hurled missiles, including throwing sticks or slingstones, at one another from a safe distance, contenting themselves with low casualties.

As populations expanded in Neolithic Europe and in the Near East, more complex societies arose in which powerful chiefs led their warriors into close combat. This ex-

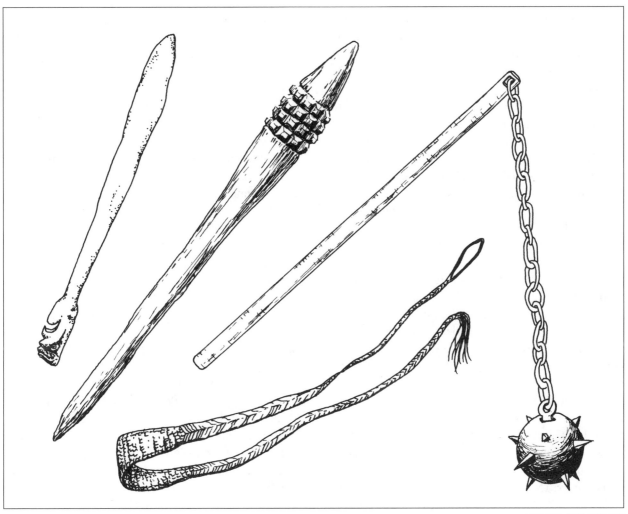

Kimberly L. Dawson Kurnizki

From left to right, an Iroquois club from eastern North America; an Aboriginal throwing stick from northwestern Australia; a spiked Swiss "morning star" mace; and a braided sling from the Pacific Islands.

plains the appearance of the stone-headed mace and of new sling projectiles that were added to the usual water-worn stone. Worked spherical stone projectiles appeared by about 6000 B.C.E., kiln- or sun-hardened clay balls by about 5000 B.C.E., and biconical-shaped missiles by about 4000 B.C.E. Such aerodynamic shapes and regularized sizes allowed slingers to shoot farther and with more accuracy.

In open combat, warriors probably exchanged fire with slings and bows for some time before advancing to fight with spears, maces, and clubs, hurling throwing sticks as they neared their opponents. Piles of

slingstones found in the destruction horizons of Neolithic and Chalcolithic settlements also indicate sling use in early siege warfare. Incendiary projectiles, in the form of heated clay shot or grasses plaited around stones, probably also made their initial appearances during Neolithic sieges.

As early civilizations developed in both hemispheres, so did armies. Units of like-armed men organized either as light infantry outfitted with missile weapons or as heavy infantry equipped with close combat weapons. Light infantry began battles by showering enemy formations with missiles, hoping to disrupt them. The heavy infantry then charged, fought the enemy infantrymen, and put them to flight, whereupon the light troops pursued. Slingers served as light troops in Bronze Age Mesopotamia, the Indus Valley, and Greece.

Throwing sticks were used in Mesopotamia until about 2000 B.C.E. and for another millennium in Egypt. Stone-headed maces played an important role in infantry combat in Old and Middle Kingdom Egypt (c. 3100 to 1674 B.C.E.), in Canaan during the same era, and in the Indus Valley's Harappan civilization (c. 2500 to 1750 B.C.E.). In the Americas, the Incas (c. 1200 to 1572 C.E.) used a combination of slingers, spearmen, and macemen, the maces having circular bronze heads with six points. The Aztecs of that era employed slingers and club bearers, some of whom utilized the *maquahuitl*, a powerful two-handed, obsidian-edged sword-club.

The stone-headed mace had virtually disappeared in Mesopotamia by approximately 2500 B.C.E., probably because the area's fierce military competition spurred the development of metal arms and armor. Bronze could be turned into sickle swords, socket axes, and other new weapons, while copper helmets backed with leather spread the impact of a club or stone macehead blow enough to prevent their wearers from being stunned or killed. By time of the New Kingdom (c. 1570 to 1085 B.C.E.), Egypt had adopted armor as well. As armor and metal weapons became common, clubs and stone-headed maces disappeared. Maces with metal heads were used in the Incan Empire, and mace-like bronze weapons continued in use in Egypt. Bronze maceheads similar to medieval weapons have been discovered in Armenian tombs of the second half of the second millennium B.C.E. Maces had long been associated with authority: Narmer, one of the first Egyptian pharaohs (c. 3100 B.C.E.), is depicted wielding a mace. Other evidence suggests that mace use was restricted to officers, such as those of the Neo-Assyrian Empire (911 to 612 B.C.E.), and kings, such as the Scythian monarchs (seventh to fourth centuries B.C.E.) for some two millennia.

It was not until the early Middle Ages that metal-headed maces became popular. Steppe nomads and Muslim warriors—Arabs, Iranians, Turks, Mongols—

employed them as an important secondary weapon for their lance- or bow-armed cavalry, an alternative to the sword and ax. The Chinese, Indians, Byzantines, Russians, Eastern Europeans, and, after about 1000 C.E., Western Europeans then followed suit. Infantry only occasionally used maces, because foot soldiers could accomplish more with staff weapons. The mace was more useful to cavalry in easy reach of foot soldiers' heads. As long as mail or lamellar armor remained the norm, maces could be rather light, with rounded heads, either symmetrical or nonsymmetrical in form, or equipped with knobs or spikes. Flange-headed maces also appeared early and became common in Europe once plate armor came into use. However, lighter maces survived as emblems of authority. The club also survived as an ersatz weapon or police arm: William the Conqueror is depicted bearing one at Hastings, where he defeated the English in 1066 C.E. The club probably denoted William's rank, distinguishing him from lesser men carrying maces.

The sling enjoyed more common usage than the mace. David's slaying of Goliath is only the most famous use of the sling by the ancient Jews. The Neo-Assyrian Empire considered its slingers so valuable it armored them. Certain peoples were noted as skilled slingers. The Baleares, inhabiting the Balearic Islands off the coast of Spain in the western Mediterranean, used slings from childhood. They carried three slings of different sizes—short, medium, long—for various ranges. They could allegedly hurl stones weighing up to 14 ounces, smashing armor at close range. Assyrian slingstones, by contrast, averaged only 7 to 9.5 ounces in weight. Balearic slingers served with Hannibal (247-182 B.C.E.) and Julius Caesar (100-44 B.C.E.) and remained known into the Middle Ages for their skill with slings. Another noted group of slingers were the Greeks of Rhodes. During the Battle of Cunaxa (401 B.C.E.), slingers from Rhodes used lead shot to outrange Persian bows and slings—the latter with heavy stones—to help the Greek army make its escape.

Lead shot first appears in the late second millennium B.C.E. on Crete and Cyprus. Cast in molds and weighing 0.7 to 4.5 ounces, lead shot was often marked with insults, invocations, or identifications. It outranged clay or stone shot and was more difficult to see, and thus harder to dodge. It could bury itself in the target's flesh, requiring careful surgery to extract. In the second century B.C.E. the Greeks invented a sling that fired a *kestros*: a bolt with a pointed iron head 6 inches long, set in a winged wooden shaft 9 inches long. However, the use of the *kestros* never spread beyond Greece.

After the Pax Romana, a period of peace within the Roman Empire that began in approximately 31 B.C.E., specialist corps of slingers largely disappeared. The Imperial Roman army tried to compensate by training all recruits in use of the sling. It is unlikely, however, that men introduced to the weapon late and on a part-time basis became strong, accurate slingers. The staff sling, easier to use than a hand sling, is a likely response to this situation. Although the sling never attained the popularity in medieval times that it enjoyed in antiquity, it remained in use in militias and peasant revolts. Monarchs such as King Frederick I Barbarossa of Germany (r. 1152-1190), King Edward I of England (r. 1272-1307), and Ottoman Sultan Mehmed II (r. 1451-1481) also recruited slingers to engage in siege warfare. In Spain the sling remained especially important: At the Battle of Nájera in 1367 C.E., for instance, English longbowmen suffered heavily from Spanish slingers before finally defeating them. Spaniards in turn suffered at the hands of Mesoamerican and Andean slingers. In various regions the weapon is still used by shepherds, sportsmen, hunters, and rioters.

BOOKS AND ARTICLES

DeVries, Kelly. *Medieval Military Technology*. Lewiston, N.Y.: Broadview Press, 1992.

Gabriel, Richard, and Karen Metz. *From Sumer to Rome: The Military Capabilities of Ancient Armies*. New York: Greenwood Press, 1991.

Keeley, Lawrence H. *War Before Civilization: The Myth of the Peaceful Savage*. Oxford, England: Oxford University Press, 1996.

FILMS AND OTHER MEDIA

Arms in Action: Slings and Spears. Documentary. History Channel, 1999.

Scott M. Rusch

PICKS, AXES, AND WAR-HAMMERS
DATES: TO C. 1500 C.E.

NATURE AND USE

Picks, axes, and war-hammers are shock weapons. Like all members of this weaponry class, they are designed to be held rather than thrown and to multiply the amount of force that can be brought to bear upon an opponent, while also extending the warrior's deadly range beyond the length of the arm.

Prehistoric picks, axes, and war-hammers were variations on a single basic design. A wooden or bone haft, or handle, served as an extension of the user's arm, so that the bone, horn, wood, stone, or metal head could be swung through a larger arc, thus acquiring more speed than could be achieved with the arm alone. When the head struck an enemy, its speed and mass transferred sudden, intense pressure to a small area and thereby delivered a wound that could be either disabling or fatal, depending upon the part of the body struck. The three weapons differed only in the impacting surface delivering the force and the type of damage that ensued.

The pick had a pointed head and was meant to puncture. The natural and most force-efficient method for wielding the pick was a overhead stroke, which meant that the head, shoulders, and frontal chest cavity of the opponent were the primary targets. Slanting and even horizontal strokes to the body trunk, although more awkward to perform, could also cause deadly injuries. Furthermore, should the pick point pierce the chest cavity, even if the blow was not swiftly mortal, the small, deep wound that the pick head made was likely to become infected.

The ax-head was a wedge with a sharpened edge that ran parallel to the haft. The battle-ax almost invariably had a single leading edge rather than double blades. It was for cleaving, slicing, and cutting. Like the pick, the ax was most easily swung vertically, but it was a more versatile weapon because of its broad edge. Although the head and shoulders were the pri-

mary points of attack, the entire body, in fact, was at risk. If the ax-head had a sharpened rather than a blunt edge, slanting or horizontal strokes could do severe damage to the arms and legs, breaking bones or severing limbs entirely. Even a glancing blow or partial contact could open a long gash or slice and cause massive bleeding. Because of this utility, axes were nearly universally employed prehistoric weapons, from the first flint heads lashed onto sticks to such specimens as finely crafted North American tomahawks and ornately inlaid Scandinavian two-handed battle-axes.

The head of the war-hammer, or war-club, was blunt, often only a sturdy wooden knob or lump of stone, and its purpose was to shatter and crush. Although the war-hammer could break leg, arm, and rib bones, the primary target areas were, again, the head and shoulders. A direct blow to the head killed by causing massive hemorrhaging even if the skull was not caved in, but even a light or partial impact was likely to stun, at the very least. Likewise, a blow to the shoulders, with their relatively delicate clavicles, could disable enemies and leave them unprotected against further attack. A variation on the war-hammer, the mace, had short flanges or spikes protruding from its head. Thus, it pierced and tore the flesh as well as shattered bones.

The great advantages of shock weapons were their accuracy, power, and economy. Even an unskilled warrior was capable of swinging and striking home with a pick, ax, or club, whereas it took considerable training and skill to use successfully such stand-off weapons as javelins or bows. Moreover, unlike javelins and arrows, which once sent in flight were difficult to retrieve for reuse, shock weapons posed a threat as long as warriors had the strength to wield them. On the other hand, picks, axes, and war-hammers were very short-ranged, seldom extending the warriors' effective battle reach more than twice that of the arm alone. The warrior, in close proximity to his enemy, was in imminent danger.

Combatants using shock weapons had to exploit these advantages while mitigating the disadvantages. Archaeological evidence, anthropological studies of nineteenth and twentieth century primitive societies, and surviving weapons reveal three often-employed tactical uses. Most often, battles opened with an exchange of fire from standoff weapons by the front ranks of opposing groups separated by an empty zone. If one group stopped fighting and fled, the second might pursue to kill or capture the enemy. The pursuers then used shock weapons after closing with the foe. Picks, axes, and war-hammers also proved effective for fighting in confined spaces where standoff weapons were impractical: for example, a forest ambush or an assault on a fortified area. The weapons could be used to break apart defensive works and to destroy property as well as to harm people.

Last, shock weapons were occasionally used for close combat. A high degree of discipline is required for troops to meet face-to-face in a battle line, but by the Bronze Age, societies were sophisticated enough to support the requisite level of training, and this basic battle doctrine lasted into the Middle Ages. Engagements almost certainly began with exchanges of arrow or javelin fire, but then the front ranks of warriors advanced on each other until the lines collided, and warriors fought directly with shock weapons. In this hand-to-hand combat, comrades-in-arms had to be close to one another in the line, practically shoulder-to-shoul-

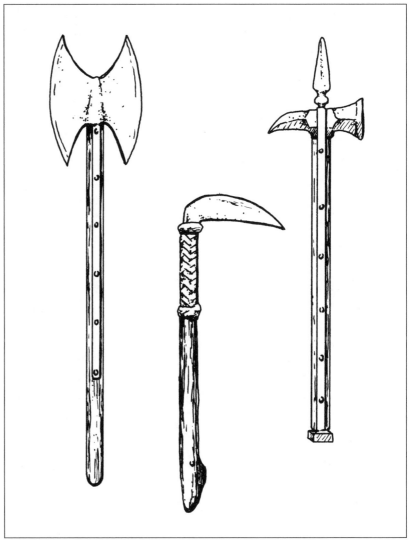

Kimberly L. Dawson Kurnizki

From left to right, an early sixteenth century European battle-ax with a double-headed blade; an early Japanese pick with a stone blade bound to a wooden haft; and a late fifteenth century Italian war-hammer with langets securing the head to the haft.

der, so that their sides were protected while they concentrated their attack on the enemy warriors directly in front of them. Wood shields were developed to protect their fronts, and the initial clash involved each opponent striving to shatter the opponent's protection in order to force an opening for a killing blow. The side that succeeded in penetrating the line and dividing its enemy usually won the battle.

During the Iron Age, however, swords and lances increasingly became the main battle weapons. Axes, picks, and war-hammers were used more and more as auxiliary weapons.

DEVELOPMENT

By about 1.5 million years before the present, the first small hand axes were being produced as part of the Acheulean tool tradition of the Lower Paleolithic era, the earliest part of the Old Stone Age. Probably first used as tools, these axes, or bifaces, were about 4 to 6 inches in length and were made by flaking both sides of a stone to form an edge. The affixation of this biface to a handle was an innovation of the Upper Paleolithic era (35,000 to 10,000 years ago), as was the development of hammers, an evolution of the simple club. The use of obsidian or flint, which could be chipped into a much sharper edge than could other types of rock, began during the Mesolithic, or Middle Stone Age, period in Europe (10,000 to 8,000 years ago). Likewise, picks probably began as simple sticks with pointed ends more or less perpendicular to the handle and evolved in tandem with the ax, as pointed rocks or horns were attached to handles. Picks, axes, and battle-hammers appear to have been employed as weapons generally throughout the prehistoric world during the Mesolithic period, depending only on the availability of suitable materials to make them. Isolated, preliterate cultures continued to use such weapons, in some cases, well into the twentieth century. Indeed, highly developed non-Western armies used such weapons—for example the Zulu knobkerrie, a short, heavy, wooden club that could be swung or thrown—to telling effect against Western forces with firearms through the nineteenth century.

The addition of the haft, or handle, to a shaped head was the key technological step in producing shock weapons. Three common methods of attachment developed: lashing the head into a wooden sleeve, as in the vee formed by two branches of a limb; binding the head into split wood; and inserting the head into a bone socket. Rawhide or animal tendons served as lashings. During the Neolithic period (8,000 to about 4,000 years ago), stoneworkers learned to drill holes into flint by applying alternately heat and water. This process allowed them to insert a haft through the head and wedge it in firmly with shims, improving the strength of the ax.

With one face left blunt and the other shaped to either a point or a blade, the Neolithic weapons could function as combination hammer-axes or pick-axes. When artisans learned to grind the edge, rather than to form it by flaking off chips of flint, they were able to produce slimmer ax-heads with sharper edges, which enhanced the power of the weapons to pierce and slice. These finely wrought axes were valuable commodities. In some areas, notably prehistoric England, axes were highly prized for barter. In fact, archaeologists debate whether the axes were intended to be wielded or to serve strictly as a kind of currency, although they might well have served both functions.

Another innovation occurred when humans began to use copper to make ax-, pick-, hammer-, and mace-heads. The molten metal could be poured into a mold and, after cooling, cold-hammered and whetted to a fine edge. However, copper is soft and the edges quickly dulled. Bronze, an alloy of copper and tin, is much harder, and became the standard material for tools and weapons beginning about 3000 B.C.E. in the Near East. This technical advancement launched the Bronze Age. About 1600 B.C.E. Roman artisans began making tools and weapons from brass, a zinc-copper alloy harder and more durable than bronze. About 2500 B.C.E. in Sumer, craftspeople moved the socket holding the handle to the back of the ax-head, reducing its weight and giving the weapon better balance.

In Europe during the Neolithic period, maces were more common than axes, and at Çatalhüyük in modern Turkey, the site of a large Neolithic settlement, archaeologists uncovered copper maces dating from as early as 7000 B.C.E. Because they were difficult to make, these early copper maces may have been the weapons of leaders. An indication of their status appears in a small relief sculpture dating from around 3100 B.C.E., showing Menes (c. 3100-3000 B.C.E.), the first pharaoh to rule all of Egypt, striking an enemy's head with a mace.

The advent of iron and steel made it possible to shape more elegantly flared, sharper ax-heads with thinner heads, as was true, for instance, with the two-handed Viking battle-ax. Maces became common weapons during the Middle Ages, whereas picks were relegated to use in warfare primarily for digging and breaking down defensive structures. These weapons became obsolete after the introduction of firearms, and by the beginning of the sixteenth century, European armies were unlikely to carry them into battle.

BOOKS AND ARTICLES

Ferrill, Arther. *Origins of War: From the Stone Age to Alexander the Great*. Boulder, Colo.: Westview Press, 1997.

Hogg, O. F. G. *Clubs to Cannon: Warfare and Weapons Before the Introduction of Gunpowder*. New York: Barnes & Noble Books, 1993.

Keely, Lawrence H. *War Before Civilization*. New York: Oxford University Press, 1996.

Roger Smith

BOWS AND ARROWS

DATES: TO C. 1500 C.E.

NATURE AND USE

Bows and arrows are among the oldest and most popular weapons of all time. Although simple in design, their invention represented one of the most important technological innovations of primitive humans, one that allowed individuals to attack both animal and human targets with greater force, from longer range, and with a more rapid rate of fire than had been possible with the spear or other handheld projectiles. Bows and arrows were presumably first used for hunting, perhaps as early as 30,000 B.C.E., but Neolithic cave paintings show them deployed as weapons against other humans by about 10,000 B.C.E.

In its most basic form the bow consists of a shaft of wood with a string attached to both its ends. When this bowstring is drawn back, the energy of the archer's pull is transferred to the bending bow, and after the bowstring is released, this energy is channeled through the bowstring to project the arrow forward. The arrow's speed and distance depend on the flexibility of the bow; a stiffer bow requires more strength to string and shoot, but this added resistance translates into greater velocity and distance for the arrow itself.

The varieties of ancient bows were as numerous as the peoples who made them, but they generally fall into two categories. A self bow—also called a simple bow, stave bow, or longbow—was constructed from a single piece of wood, although bows of reed and other materials are known. They measured from 1.5 to more than 6 feet in length, and their effective range could extend to more than 200 yards. Self bows were extremely simple to make, but a suitable type of wood was required: Too pliant a wood packed little power, whereas one that was too stiff might break or prove difficult to use efficiently.

The second basic type of bow was the composite bow. It consisted of either a single piece or several pieces of wood glued together. This wooden core was reinforced by bone on the interior, or belly, and by sinew on the outside, or front, lending the bow

A fourteenth century English longbowman with a quiver of arrows poised to fire his weapon.

76

greater elasticity. Composite bows were extremely strong and difficult to string, but they had an effective range of up to 300 yards, far greater than that of the self bow. They were also smaller and easier to carry, making them more versatile, especially for firing from horseback.

Arrows also came in different types, but their basic design was simpler and changed little over time. Ancient arrows typically consisted of two parts: a light, slender shaft of wood or reed and an arrowhead of stone, bone, or metal. Arrowheads could be flat, leaf-shaped, or triangular and were sometimes barbed. They were attached to their shafts either by a hollow socket, into which the shaft was inserted, or by means of a tang, a flat projection that fit into a notch in the shaft itself. Feathers were frequently affixed to the opposite end of the shaft to maintain an arrow's speed and accuracy in flight.

Virtually all ancient civilizations, from China and the Near East to Greece and Rome, employed bows and arrows in some capacity. Archers were common in siege warfare, in which both attackers and defenders routinely harassed their opponents with volleys of arrows. Their use in battle, however, varied, seemingly along geographical lines. In Europe archers tended to be stationed on the wings, in front of, or behind a battle line of infantry or cavalry, and they tended to provide cover as these other forces prepared to engage the enemy at closer range. In the ancient Near East and Central Asia, however, bowmen on foot or horseback played a more decisive role in warfare; they made up the bulk of many armies and often determined the outcome of battle itself.

DEVELOPMENT

As noted above, bows and arrows appear as weapons in cave paintings of the late Neolithic period (8,000 to 4,000 years ago), although their use in combat may be much older. Surprisingly, however, evidence for

TURNING POINTS

c. 10,000 B.C.E.	Bows and arrows appear as weapons in Neolithic cave paintings.
c. 2250 B.C.E.	Composite bow is depicted in Akkadian Stele of Naram-Sin.
c. 1600 B.C.E.	Chariot archers are increasingly used in warfare.
c. 400 B.C.E.	The development of the *gastraphetes*, or belly bow, allows the shooting of more powerful arrows.
53 B.C.E.	Parthian mounted archers defeat heavily armed Roman infantry at the Battle of Carrhae.
1346 C.E.	English longbowmen defeat French knights at Crécy, demonstrating the importance of archers to English warfare.
c. 14th-15th cent.	The increasing predominance of firearms in Europe results in the diminishing use of archers in warfare.

archers in the warfare of early civilizations is sparse. The Sumerian hero Gilgamesh carried, along with several other weapons, a bow in the Gilgamesh epic (c. 2000 B.C.E.; English translation, 1917), and the so-called Stele of Naram-Sin (c. 2250 B.C.E.) shows the Akkadian king Naram-Sin (c. 2254-c. 2218) carrying what appears to be a composite bow. The Egyptians may have been the first to employ archers on a large scale. By 2000 B.C.E. their armies included a corps of Nubian archers, who presumably supported native Egyptian infantry armed with spears and daggers.

The bow and arrow acquired more importance when they were combined with the war chariot. Chariots had been used as transport vehicles in Mesopotamia in the third millennium B.C.E., but by the sixteenth century B.C.E. they had become the preeminent weapon of war throughout the Near East and Egypt. The chariot functioned as a mobile firing platform, carrying a driver and archer armed with a composite bow. As the driver brought the chariot within range of opposing forces, the archer released his arrows, seeking to create confusion and disorder in the enemy line. In some armies archer-bearing chariots numbered in the thousands, and the union of bow, arrow, and chariot figured prominently at the Battles of Megiddo (1469 B.C.E.), between the Egyptians and a coalition of forces from the Levant, and Kadesh (1274 B.C.E.), between the Egyptians and the Hittites.

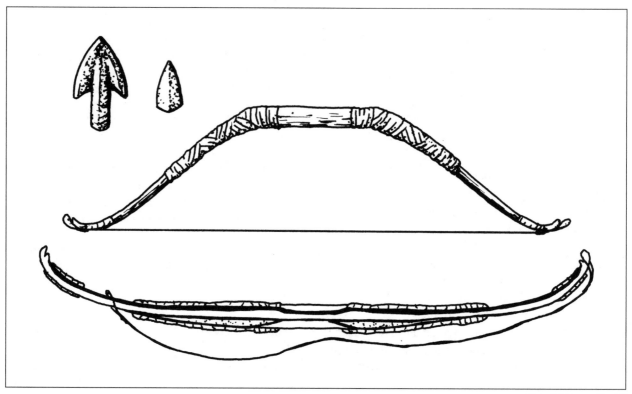

A simple bow, the joints bound with animal sinew, shown in both strung and unstrung positions. Also shown are barbed and leaf-shaped arrowheads.

The significance of the bow in the latter battle is reinforced by wall carvings; an Egyptian relief commemorating the battle shows the pharaoh Ramses II (c. 1300-1213 B.C.E.) standing on his chariot and shooting his bow, seemingly mowing down the opposing Hittites single-handedly.

Chariot archers survived into the first millennium B.C.E. under the Assyrians, who dominated the Near East from the ninth through the seventh centuries B.C.E., but bows and arrows also found greater use in other units. Assyrian infantry consisted primarily of archers wearing heavy armor, who released their arrows under the protection of body-sized shields held by attendants. More significant, the Assyrians were instrumental in developing cavalry, including mounted archers. Like their counterparts on foot, Assyrian horse archers worked in pairs, as one rider shot his arrows while a second held the archer's reins and a shield. The combination of foot and horse archers

was also adopted by the Persians, who became the preeminent power in the Near East in the sixth century B.C.E. Their tactics are well illustrated at the Battle of Plataea (479 B.C.E.) during the Greco-Persian Wars (499-448 B.C.E.). At the start of the battle, Persian cavalry harassed the Greek infantry with a constant onslaught of missiles, while refusing to engage the Greeks at close range. The Persian infantry soon followed with its own barrage of arrows, which were unleashed from behind a shield wall. The intention, it seems, was to weaken the Greeks with missile weapons, so that the infantry could emerge from behind its shield wall and overcome the remnants of the Greek infantry with the spears and daggers they also carried.

The heavily armed Greek spearmen, however, proved superior to the lightly armed Persian archers at Plataea, and the Greek victory in the Greco-Persian Wars signaled the end of the archer's prominence in

Near Eastern and Western warfare for several centuries. The Greeks were familiar with the bow and arrow; the Athenians had a contingent of archers at Plataea, and bowmen from the island of Crete were popular as mercenaries throughout the Mediterranean from the fifth century B.C.E. onward. Indeed, Alexander the Great (356-323 B.C.E.) utilized Cretan and Macedonian archers effectively throughout his conquest of the Persian Empire. The Greeks, however, despised the bow and arrow as cowardly and effeminate weapons, and archers generally played only a supporting role in combat.

The Romans, too, originally had little use for bows and arrows. They possessed no native archers of their own, and they relied on mercenaries or allies to supply archers when needed. Only as the nature of Rome's enemies changed in the first, second, and third centuries C.E. did archers take on an increasingly significant role in Rome's armies. Among these enemies were the Parthians, who in the second century B.C.E. had established an empire where the Persian Empire had once stood. The Parthians fought with composite bows on horseback and were best known for the so-called Parthian shot, in which Parthian horse archers would charge an enemy and, as soon as they released their arrows, would immediately reverse direction and ride quickly out of range of enemy missile fire. Such tactics proved highly successful at Carrhae (53 B.C.E.), where Parthian mounted archers annihilated seven Roman legions, approximately 40,000 men.

Developments in China mirrored those of the Near East and Europe. Archers on chariots were known as early as 1200 B.C.E., and they remained the elite weapon of war throughout most of the Zhou (Chou) Dynasty (1066-256 B.C.E.). Archers also served in Chinese infantry, but not until the fourth century B.C.E. did the Chinese begin to develop an effective cavalry. The incursions of nomadic horse archers from the steppes of Central Asia forced the Chinese to adopt their own mounted cavalry, which they did in the third, second, and first centuries B.C.E.

It was in the hands of nomadic peoples skilled in horsemanship that the bow and arrow achieved their greatest successes in warfare. Beginning in the seventh century B.C.E. the Iranian Plateau and Eurasian steppes produced several cultures whose movements threatened and sometimes overthrew the more sedentary civilizations of Europe, the Near East, and China. These peoples included the Scythians, Huns, Avars, and Turks, who shared with one another a life seemingly lived on horseback and a reliance on the composite bow. They wore little armor and were extremely mobile, and with their large numbers they could inflict heavy damage on an opposing force while avoiding direct contact against a more heavily armed foe. The most formidable of these horse archers were probably the Mongols, who emerged from Mongolia in the twelfth century C.E. Fighting on horseback and carrying one or more composite bows and sixty arrows, Mongol warriors were highly disciplined, and they used both mobility and deception to overwhelm their opponents. Under Mongol leader Genghis Khan (between 1155 and 1162-1227), Mongol armies swept across Asia and the Near East and into Europe. They established their own dynasty in China early in the thirteenth century, and by 1250 their empire stretched from Asia to Eastern Europe.

While Mongol horse archers were terrorizing Asia and Eastern Europe, the English were experimenting with the longbow, a development that changed the nature of Western warfare. Longbows had been known in Europe for centuries and had played no small role in the victory of William the Conqueror (c. 1028-1087) over the English at Hastings in 1066, but their role in battle was marginal until the English adopted the Welsh longbow in the twelfth century. Made from the wood of the yew tree, the Welsh longbow reached almost 6 feet in length and required considerable strength and skill to wield. It was also inexpensive, and, with training, common soldiers could learn to shoot with enough distance, speed, and power to penetrate even the thickest suits of knightly armor. Edward I (1239-1307) was the first English king to enlist large numbers of longbowmen (mostly Welshmen) in his armies, with whom he defeated the Scottish pikemen at Falkirk in 1298. During the fourteenth century, however, native English archers took up the longbow in greater numbers and proved their worth against heavily armored knights, especially during the Hundred Years' War against France (1337-

1453). At Crécy (1346) the English longbowmen first routed the mercenary Genoese crossbowmen before wreaking havoc on successive charges of French cavalry, killing more than one thousand knights by the end of the battle. Similar charges by armored knights on horseback at Poitiers (1356) and on foot at Agincourt (1415) brought similar results, and helped hasten the end of the dominance of mounted cavalry in European warfare.

The rise of gunpowder ultimately brought about the demise of the bow and arrow in battle. That demise, however, did not occur overnight, and for centuries after the introduction of gunpowder (c. 1300), archers remained an important component of most armies. Only with the development of effective and reliable handheld firearms in the sixteenth century did bows and arrows become obsolete.

BOOKS AND ARTICLES

Bradbury, Jim. *The Medieval Archer.* Rochester, N.Y.: Boydell & Brewer, 1999.

Drews, Robert. *The End of the Bronze Age: Changes in Warfare and the Catastrophe Circa 1200* B.C. Princeton, N.J.: Princeton University Press, 1993.

Ferrill, Arther. *The Origins of War.* Boulder, Colo.: Westview Press, 1997.

Hardy, Robert. *The Longbow: A Social and Military History.* London: Bois d'Arc Press, 1998.

FILMS AND OTHER MEDIA

Arms in Action: Bows. Documentary. History Channel, 1999.

James P. Sickinger

CROSSBOWS

DATES: TO C. 1500 C.E.

NATURE AND USE

The crossbow was a handheld weapon consisting of a short bow made of either composite materials such as wood and horn, or iron, mounted on a stock, generally of wood. The bowstring was usually drawn by a type of mechanical device and fired by a trigger mechanism. The crossbow's missile, called a quarrel, or bolt, was short and heavy, designed to penetrate armor at close range. Various devices were employed to cock the bow, with its short limbs and heavy draw weight. The crossbow's power and short-range accuracy were counterbalanced by the length of time required to arm the weapon and its lack of range. Sometimes called arbalests, crossbows have been used as infantry weapons, and in heavier, more complicated versions as siege weapons.

Evidence points to the Chinese of the Shang Dynasty (1600-1066 B.C.E.) as the originators of the crossbow. Early missiles included stones and fire arrows. By the time of the Han Dynasty (206 B.C.E.-220 C.E.), crossbows had come into regular use among Chinese troops, particularly along the northwestern frontier. Soldiers stationed on the Great Wall could use the protection of the wall as they loaded and fired their bolts at invaders. Chinese crossbows featured bows of laminated bamboo, specially glued and covered with lacquered silk, which were fitted onto lacquered, wooden stocks. Chinese bolts were usually about 12 inches long with bronze heads capable of puncturing the quilted silk, padded leather, and metal armor of the era.

Another refinement was the repeating crossbow, fitted with a wooden, boxlike magazine holding from ten to twelve bolts and appearing in China in the first century C.E. The hinged magazine could be moved forward and back, thus serving as both a loading mechanism and a cocking device. Although the magazine increased the output of the archer, the magazine system was awkward and time consuming to reload. There is evidence, however, that types of magazine-fed crossbows were still in use during the First Sino-Japanese War (1894-1895).

Crossbows spread from Asia to Europe at some unspecified date. The Romans used large, complex versions of the crossbow as siege engines capable of firing heavy missiles against walled cities. In terms of infantry use, however, fragments of tombstone carvings from Le Puy and Polignac-sur-Loire in France dating roughly from the fourth century C.E. indicate that Roman legions may also have had crossbowmen using a basic model of laminated wood with a manual cocking arrangement. There is no evidence to show that the Romans employed the weapon on a broad scale.

DEVELOPMENT

Although there have been allusions to the crossbow's use in fifth and sixth century England, the first Western written record of its use appears in a manuscript from 985 C.E. Derived from the Latin *arc*, or bow, and *ballista*, or missile thrower, the weapon became known as an *arcuballista*, or arbalest. Several eleventh century references note that William the Conqueror (c. 1028-1087) included crossbowmen in his Norman army, which invaded England in 1066. By the time of the Crusades of the eleventh through thirteenth centuries, crossbows had become a standard and valued part of European armies. Anna Comnena of Byzantium (1083-c. 1148) provided one of the most complete descriptions of Crusader crossbows, noting that soldiers had to strain with both arms to cock, or span, the bow.

Among the most proficient soldiers using crossbows were the Italians, particularly the Genoese. Hired as mercenaries by a variety of European

TURNING POINTS

c. 1384-1122 B.C.E.	Crossbow is originated during China's Shang Dynasty.
c. 206 B.C.E.-220 C.E.	Crossbows come into regular usage during China's Han Dynasty.
10th-11th cent.	The crossbow makes its first European appearance, in Italy.
1139	The use of the crossbow in Christian Europe is prohibited by Pope Innocent II at the Lateran Council.
1191	Christian crossbowmen are instrumental in defeating Muslim warriors at the Battle of Arsuf during the Third Crusade.
1415	English longbowmen prove more effective than Genoese mercenary crossbowmen hired by the French at the Battle of Agincourt during the Hundred Years' War.

crowned heads, Italian crossbowmen were noted for their accuracy in battle. Simple soldiers could be trained in the use of the crossbow in a matter of weeks, whereas longbow archers required years of strengthening and practice to become expert. The use of the crossbow allowed a common soldier with minimal training to dispatch a well-armored, professional knight. So devastating had the crossbow become in conflicts raging across Europe that Pope Innocent II (d. 1143), at the Lateran Council (1139), prohibited their use. The prohibition did not extend, however, to use against infidels, and even in Europe the ban was generally ignored.

Although the crossbow had been used in the First (1095-1099) and Second Crusades (1145-1149), it had its greatest impact during the Third Crusade (1187-1192). King Richard I of England (1157-1199), a proponent of crossbow use and an accomplished marksman, was reported to have used the weapon to slay a Muslim archer high atop a wall during the Siege of Acre (1189-1191). In various skirmishes throughout the campaign, crossbowmen successfully defended supply routes and garrison posts. At the Battle of Arsuf (1191), Christian crossbowmen wreaked havoc against the lightly armored Muslim bowmen of the sultan Saladin (1138-1193). Muslim arrows did not easily penetrate the thick felt overcoats and mail shirts of the Europeans, whereas the short, heavy quarrels pierced the light armor of Muslim soldiers and horses. At Jaffa (1192) crossbowmen played a key part in Richard s victory over a numerically superior force. Later, after returning to

England, Richard was mortally wounded by a crossbow quarrel while laying siege to the castle of Chalus, in the Limousin, France (1199).

The cocking mechanisms of crossbows went through a variety of developments during the Middle Ages. Although dates of innovations are unknown, evidence shows the weapon's evolution. As armor increased in strength, crossbows increased in power. The simple method of cocking, or spanning, by hand was replaced with both a stirruplike device at the head of the stock and a pair of belt hooks known as the "belt and claw." By placing the bowstring in the hooks, and the foot in the stirrup, sufficient leverage and power could be exerted to cock the weapon.

With the desire to increase range, even more radical spanning devices were needed. The *arbalest à tour* utilized a pulley system hooked to the string rather than the belt claws. By drawing on the pulleys, the string could be more easily cocked. In the fifteenth century, a "screw and handle" device consisting of a threaded rod hooked to the string and cranked at the rear of the stock by a handle, created a powerful weapon. The "goat's foot lever" employed hinged double levers, which bent the bow and cocked the string. This system was particularly efficient in the lighter-weight crossbows favored by European cavalry. A French innovation called the *cranequin*, or ratchet-winder, utilized a handle connected to a pair of cogs enclosed in a drumlike attachment hooked to the string by a rail. By cranking the handle in a circular motion, the rail drew the string to the cocked position. Each time a *cranequin* was used, however, it had to be removed in order to fire the crossbow and then reattached for reloading. Such a device was especially necessary as laminated bows were replaced with stiffer, more powerful metal limbs.

Perhaps the most complicated version of crossbow mechanisms was the windlass, or *moulinet*, system. A combination of fixed and free pulleys was attached to the stock of the bow, and the free-running pulleys hooked to the string. By inserting a foot into the stirrup to stabilize the weapon, crossbowmen would then crank a pair of handles engaging a windlass to wind the fixed pulleys. This marriage of pulleys and handles could span even the heaviest of crossbows used in besieging castles and other fortifications. As with the *cranequin*, however, the *moulinet* system had to be removed to shoot, thus creating a slow rate of fire.

As crossbows evolved, so too did quarrels. Wooden shafts fitted with iron heads remained the standard missile for centuries. Quarrels were usually

from 9 to 12 inches long. To stabilize the quarrel in flight, fletchings of wood, leather, or feathers were used, although these were much shorter and shallower vanes than those of longbow arrows. With the development of mechanical spanning devices, all-metal bolts became the most lethal of projectiles, particularly when used on heavier crossbows.

In English and continental European armies, crossbowmen were generally placed in the front line of battle to pepper foes with their bolts. At the Battle of Taillebourg (1242), England's King Henry III (1207-1272) was defeated by French king Louis IX (1214-1270) even though the English counted some 700 crossbowmen in the infantry. During the Hundred Years' War (1337-1453), Genoese crossbowmen in the employ of the French dueled English longbow archers at Crécy (1346) and Agincourt (1415). In both engagements, the longbowmen prevailed with their greater range and accuracy.

Corps of crossbowmen were included in most Eu-

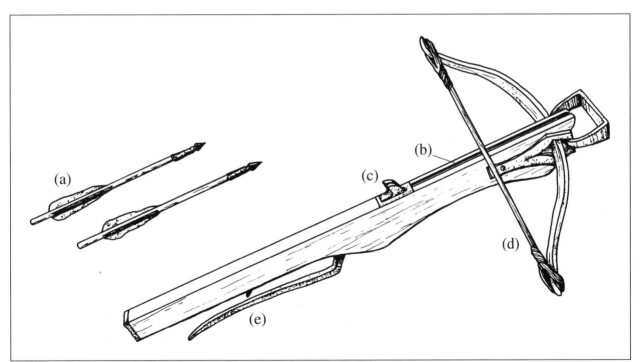

Kimberly L. Dawson Kurnizki

A crossbow shown with two quarrels, or bolts (a), which are fitted into the groove (b), with their butt ends against the nut (c) after the bowstring (d) has been drawn back and held by the nut. When ready to fire, the operator aims from the shoulder and presses the trigger (e) to release the bolt.

ropean armies into the sixteenth century. At the Battle of Marignano (1515), a bodyguard of two hundred mounted crossbowmen helped Francis I (1494-1547) of France defeat the duke of Milan. When Spanish adventurer Hernán Cortés (1485-1547) trekked into Mexico (1521), he brought with him a company of arbalesters, as did Francisco Pizarro (c. 1478-1541) in his invasion of Peru (1524). As late as 1570, Spanish marines stationed aboard galleons were still armed with crossbows.

With the advent of gunpowder and handguns, the military use of the crossbow dwindled. By the seventeenth century, it had primarily become a tool for hunting and target practice. During World War I (1914-1918), medieval crossbows were stripped from armories and converted into grenade launchers for use in the trenches. More recently, some modern military special forces have adopted crossbow use for clandestine operations.

BOOKS AND ARTICLES

Gardner, Charles W. "Weapon of Power: Slower than the Longbow, the Crossbow Offered Deadly, Accurate Simplicity." *Military History* 6, no. 3 (1989): 18, 70-74.

Heath, E. G. *The Grey Goose Wing*. Greenwich, Conn.: New York Graphic Society, 1971.

Hurley, Vic. *Arrows Against Steel: The History of the Bow*. New York: Mason Charter, 1975.

Payne-Gallwey, Sir Ralph. *The Crossbow*. 1903. Reprint. New York: Barnes & Noble Books, 1995.

Kenneth P. Czech

KNIVES, SWORDS, AND DAGGERS

DATES: TO C. 1500 C.E.

NATURE AND USE

Almost every human culture and civilization in the world has used knives and daggers. A knife is one of the most basic tools, used for cutting any number of materials, from food to fibers. Knives were also used as weapons to kill humans. A dagger could be considered a long, double-edged knife, ranging from 15 to 50 centimeters and meant specifically as a weapon. Knives and daggers have two basic parts: first, the blade, a flat surface with one sharp edge or two, usually narrowing to a point; second, the hilt, covering the tang, which extends back from the blade, and providing a handhold. The hilt itself has two parts: the grip, perhaps with some sort of guard to protect the hand, and a pommel, which is a piece at the end of the grip to back up the hand and provide balance. For protection from the sharp blade, knives were carried in sheaths or scabbards while not in use.

Some knives were meant to be thrown. Otherwise knives and daggers were usually wielded either overhanded, with the blade extending down from the fist, or underhanded, with the blade sticking up from the fist. These weapons also had the advantage of concealment when worn underneath clothing. In the warfare of all but the most primitive societies, the knife or dagger was usually the weapon of last resort, after other weapons had been lost.

Most cultures have also developed swords, which could be considered extended daggers, with blades longer than 40 centimeters. Swords could, given their weight and length, more effectively hack, slash, puncture, or cut an enemy. Grooves in blades, or fullers, are often believed to have been channels to drain away blood but were usually built into the blade to add flexibility, lightness, and strength. The limited reach of the sword, compared to that of the spear or bow, often meant that it was a secondary weapon. Although rarely decisive in itself during battle, the sword was one of the most widely used weapons for close combat before 1500 C.E.

The history of knives, daggers, and swords has perhaps been more influenced by fashion than by application in warfare. These weapons and their sheaths have often been made with great care and decoration, conveying the status of their owners. The sword, especially, became a work of art, status symbol, magisterial emblem, and cult object. The right of knights or samurai to wear swords indicated their social positions, and men defended that rank in sword duels. In medieval Europe a squire was dubbed to knighthood with a sword blow, known as an accolade. Large ceremonial swords of state were carried in processions or displayed in court to illustrate a ruler's power over life and death. Swords or daggers also embodied religious significance, such as sacrificial daggers made of chalcedony used by the Aztecs for human sacrifice. The similarity of a sword's shape to that of a cross also lent it a Christian symbolism. Legends concerning Arthur's Excalibur and Roland's Durandal celebrated the sword in Europe, and many Japanese believed that certain old swords embody the spirits of Shinto deities.

DEVELOPMENT

The earliest humans made the first knives and daggers from stone, such as flint or obsidian. They shaped blades through "pressure flaking," banging pieces of stone against one another so that chips of stone broken off would leave a blade form behind. By the time of the agricultural cultures of the New Stone Age (Neolithic times), a grip made of wood or bone was then formed and attached with lime or binding to the tang. The peoples of the Americas and the Pacific rarely progressed beyond stone technology, and so did not develop significant swords. The Aztecs, how-

TURNING POINTS

4000 B.C.E.	Copper is used to make the first metal knives, in Middle East and Asia.
2000 B.C.E.	First metal swords, made from bronze, appear.
900 B.C.E.	Smiths master the use of iron to make stronger, more lethal, swords.
100 C.E.	With the increasing use of cavalry in Roman warfare, the *spatha*, a longer, slashing sword becomes popular.
1300	Japanese craftsmen perfect the art of swordmaking, creating the *katana*, a curved sword used by samurai warriors.
1500	As European plate armor becomes more prevalent, the sharp, narrow rapier is developed to combat it.

ever, may have been able to dominate their neighbors in the thirteenth century C.E. with the interesting sword-club, the *maquahuitl*, which set obsidian blades on either side of a wooden shaft. They also used special stone knives to cut out the hearts of human sacrificial victims.

The essential change came with the beginnings of metallurgy. Copper was the first metal to be used for knives, probably beginning around 4000 B.C.E. in the Middle East and East Asia. The invention of bronze, usually copper alloyed with tin, led to a great improvement in the strength and durability of weapons. In "grip-tongue" blades, whether cast in one piece or two, hilts were attached to the blade or reinforced with rivets. By the second millennium B.C.E. hilt and blade were forged from one piece of metal, with flanges between hilt and blade to protect the user's hand.

As blades began to get longer, the resulting weapons became known as swords. Some were curved, based on the sickle, an agricultural implement used for harvesting. Curved blades were better suited to cutting, whereas straight blades were better at hacking and thrusting. The Minoans and Mycenaeans of the Eastern Mediterranean from about 1400 to 1200 B.C.E. began to develop not only decorative long swords but also highly useful short swords. The curious "halberd" of the Early Bronze Age looked like a dagger set at right angles to a shaft, creating a kind of dagger-ax.

Swords became more lethal after smiths had mastered the use of iron, beginning around 900 B.C.E. In-

stead of being cast from liquid metal, iron weapons were beaten out of ingots heated in forges. Because the hardness of ancient iron varied considerably, a key development toward improving the swords was pattern welding, which was the combining or plaiting together of different strips of iron into formations or patterns. This technique blended the weaker and stronger parts of the iron into a more uniformly strong and flexible blade. Although ancient smiths might not have understood the scientific basis of making steel, iron hardened with carbon, many swordmakers developed techniques that guaranteed its use in the sword.

With the Iron Age, the sword became a standard, if not always decisive, weapon. In the Greeks' phalanx method of combat, the opposing formations of spear and shield were most important, but swords were used in close combat, often as a desperate measure. The hoplite sword, intended mainly for slashing, had a wide bulge about one-third of the way down from the point, narrowing to a waist until widening at the hilt again. Some Greeks also used a *kopis*, a heavy, single-edged, downward-curved sword.

The Roman legions made their short "Spanish" sword, the *gladius hispaniensis*, a more essential part of their fighting system. After weakening the enemy with thrown spears, they closed and smashed their large shields against their opponents. Then, while the enemy usually used an overhand sword blow, caught by the Roman shield, the Roman legionary would thrust his short, stabbing sword underneath into the stomach, where its long point could penetrate most linked armor. The Romans also carried fine daggers, but they seem not to have been used in battle. By the time of the early empire, the infantry preferred the short, hacking, "Pompeian" sword. Beginning in the second century C.E., with the rise of cavalry, a more suitable, longer (80 centimeters), slashing sword, the *spatha*, began to dominate in the Roman armies. This sword was the ancestor of medieval European swords.

The Roman Empire was brought down by Germanic peoples using long swords. Through the early Middle Ages, the sword became the basic weapon of a warrior. Battle would often begin with a charge, on foot or on horseback, using spears or lances. Once those weapons were spent, however, the warriors would hack at their armored foes with swords. Axes and maces were also popular, as well as the *seax*, a heavy, single-edged, broad-bladed chopping sword which had evolved by 900 into the *scramasax*, a short chopping blade. With the rise of knighthood by the eleventh century, warfare with lances and swords allowed Europeans to push back their opponents in the Crusades. After armorers developed better armor to help knights survive in battle, swordsmiths devised blades that would break through metal. The falchion, a broad-bladed, cleaverlike sword addressed that need. Thirteenth century knights also began to use heavier and longer one-and-one-half-handed ("bastard") or two-handed swords. By 1500 infantry, especially the Swiss and German *Landsknechte*, had developed huge swords, up to 175 centimeters long.

Another solution to European plate armor was to emphasize the swords' thrusting ability. The blade became thicker and more rigid, so the user could pierce weaker joints in the armor. In order to improve grips on such swords, protective rings began to be added to the cross-guard. Guards became more elaborate, including a curved bar stretching from cross-guard back to pommel, while the blade became narrower and sharper at the point. Thus the modern rapier appeared, which began to dominate after 1500.

Daggers were worn by European warriors throughout the Middle Ages. Daggers played only a minor role in combat, with one exception: Should a knight through exhaustion or wound be found on the ground, his enemy might dispatch him with a "misericord" dagger thrust through a chink in the armor. The popular late-medieval *baselard* and rondel daggers with their long, narrow blades were used for this purpose. The former had a curved cross-guard and pommel, whereas the latter had a disk-shaped guard and pommel. The rondel dagger also evolved into the Scottish dirk.

Sub-Saharan Africa was not using bronze weapons by the Bronze Age and began to use iron by the third century B.C.E. By the fourth century C.E., the use of iron tools and weapons had spread throughout the continent. A shortage of iron, however, meant that sub-Saharan peoples had to import many weapons from European and Islamic civilizations. In some cultures, the Kuba kingdom of the Congo, for instance, daggers and swords with unusual blade shapes acquired great cultural importance. Africans also developed a unique throwing knife, the *hungamunga*, with several blades branching out at angles from a main shaft.

Islamic swords, whether Arab, Turk, Persian, or Indian, were often typified by the scimitar, a curved, single-edged blade meant for slashing, which developed in the eighth or ninth century C.E. Scimitars predominated by 1400 C.E. but never entirely replaced straight blades. Until the fifteenth century the city of Damascus not only made famous swords but also

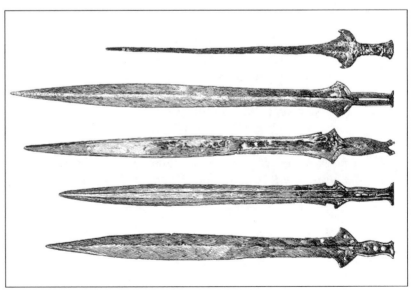

North Wind Picture Archives

A collection of Bronze Age Celtic swords.

served as a trading center for weapons made elsewhere. Persian weapons were famous for "watered" steel, in which the combination of higher and lower carbon content created a wavy pattern in the blade visible after an acid wash. Islamic dagger shapes varied widely according to region, although the *jambiya*, or curved ceremonial dagger, is most famous. Persian and Indian versions have a double curve. Interesting daggers from India included the Gurkha's *kukri*, with a downward-curved, single-edged, leaf-shaped blade, and the *katar*, or punch dagger. The unusual Malayan kris had a blade that could be wavy and widened from the point to a thick wedge at the hilt, which itself was set at an angle down from the blade. Throughout Southeast Asia, machetes, or parangs, were used as jungle knives for both clearing vegetation and fighting.

In China, straight bronze swords of various lengths dominated until the establishment of the Chinese Empire in the third century B.C.E. Iron weapons were then introduced, which led to long (90-centimeter) straight swords. Cavalry, charioteers, and infantry all used swords, although an important side weapon was also the dagger-ax. The scimitar-like cavalry sword, probably introduced by Turkish peoples of Central Asia, became more popular after the eighth century C.E.

The high point of swordmaking skill lay in Japan. Japanese swords were made with a highly sophisticated folding of metals: millions of times for the cutting edge, mere thousands for the spine. With polished blades and decorative hilt fittings, Japanese blades were unsurpassed in both beauty and lethality. The earliest swords in Japan, around 700 C.E., were based on straight Chinese blades. During the Heian period (794-1185 C.E.) the blades of the long *tachi* used by samurai horse warriors began to be curved. These types of swords were perfected in Japan during the late eighth and early ninth centuries. Although the primary weapon of the samurai was originally the bow, failed attempts by the Mongols to invade Japan in 1274 and 1283 C.E. led to a new emphasis on the sword in combat. In the fourteenth century the Soshu tradition of swordmaking was founded, creating the curved sword that became the *katana*. By the fifteenth century, the samurai warrior class had the sole right to carry swords, normally both the long sword, the *katana*, and the short sword, the *wakizashi*. The Japanese also had equally fine knives, ranging from the dagger, or *tanto*, carried with the swords, to smaller blades that fit into the scabbards of other weapons. Knives had various uses: as a replacement for chopsticks, for throwing at an enemy, for committing ritual suicide, or for giving the *coup de grâce* to an opponent.

BOOKS AND ARTICLES

Coe, Michael D., et al. *Swords and Hilt Weapons*. New York: Barnes & Noble Books, 1993.

Oakeshott, R. Ewart. *The Archaeology of Weapons: Arms and Armor from Prehistory to the Age of Chivalry*. Reprint. Mineola, N.Y.: Dover, 1996.

Warner, Gordon, and Donn F. Draeger. *Japanese Swordsmanship: Technique and Practice*. 2d ed. New York: Weatherhill, 1993.

FILMS AND OTHER MEDIA

Arms in Action: Swords. Documentary. History Channel, 1999.

Samurai Sword. Documentary. Panther Productions, 1995.

Brian A. Pavlac

SPEARS AND POLE-ARMS

DATES: TO C. 1500 C.E.

NATURE AND USE

The spear is among the simplest and most universal of early weapons: a simple penetrating point secured to a shaft that adds either aerodynamic qualities or leverage and distance from the target. Evidence for the manufacture and use of such weapons exists among every major population group in the world and stretches back to Paleolithic times. A basic spear consists of a long shaft of wood, bamboo, or iron with a sharpened head or point attached to one end. If the head is long and provided with a sharpened edge, the spear may be used as a slashing weapon. However, most spears were designed either to be hurled, as were javelins, or to be used as thrusting weapons held in one or both hands.

Used by infantry against other infantry or cavalry, pole-arms encompass a range of weapons consisting of a long, sturdy pole, or haft, with a pointed, hooked, or edged blade attached to one end. The heads of these weapons—consisting of the blades plus the sockets and side braces used for attachment—varied in length and complexity. Hellenistic sarissas (*sarissophoroi*) and late medieval pikes were fairly simple iron spear points at the ends of 16- to 18-foot poles. Medieval and early modern halberds were complex combinations of thrusting points, blades, and hooks used to unseat horsemen. Some scholars categorize any thrusting spear as a pole-arm, while others define pole-arms as having specifically evolved during the Middle Ages from agricultural implements such as pruning hooks, axes, forks, and hammers. The widest variety of these latter weapons is to be found in the European and Mediterranean regions and in Japan.

DEVELOPMENT

Early humans created the first spears by sharpening and later hardening in fire the ends of long, straight, wooden shafts. At some time people began to attach pointed heads of sharpened bone or flaked flint by notching the shaft end, inserting the flange, or tang, on the head behind the point, and lashing the two together. Javelins had light shafts and triangular or even barbed heads that helped the weapon remain in its victim. Prehistoric Europeans as well as peoples of the Americas, Oceania, and Asia also developed spear-throwers, which were short handles of carved horn, wood, or ivory cupped at one end. The cup held the butt of the shaft, and the handle acted as a lever or rigid sling that hurled the spear with greater accuracy and force than could an unaided human arm. Thrusting spears developed longer, leaf-shaped heads that could be more easily withdrawn after penetration.

Copper, and later bronze, spearheads first appeared in Mesopotamia and were used along with stone spearheads. Beaten or cast metal allowed for the creation of sockets behind the heads. These sockets could be as long as 2 feet, making for a more secure attachment than lashed tangs and reducing the likelihood of the shaft breaking. The heroes of Homer's epics the *Iliad* and the *Odyssey* (both c. 800 B.C.E.) fought their individual combats with two javelins with 6-inch heads, as well as stout 10-foot olive-wood spears with sharpened butts and 2-foot bronze heads with straight, rather than leaf-shaped, edges and a prominent median ridge running back from the tip.

Iron heads emerged in tenth century B.C.E. Greece and among the Celts of the Hallstatt culture (c. 700 B.C.E.). The latter created leaf-shaped heads with short wings, or lugs, at the base of the point to prevent overly deep penetration—perhaps a development from hunting practice. Later La Tène-era (c. 500-50 B.C.E.) graves contained heads that display a wide variety of shapes and sizes, including triangular, wavy-edged, and leaf-shaped. Celtic charioteers hurled

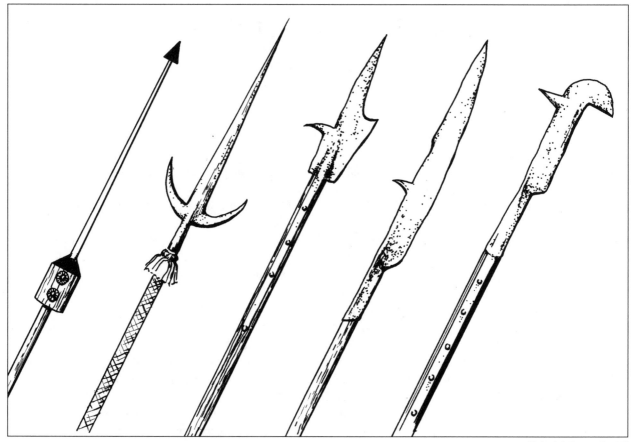

From left to right, a pilum, *with a leaf-shaped tip and an iron neck weakened to break on impact; a* corseque, *with a triangular blade and wings; a halberd, displaying a characteristically complex combination of thrusting points, blades, and hooks for unseating horsemen; a glaive, with a spike and a long, gently curving blade, like that of a knife or single-edged sword; and a bill, with a broad outward-curving blade for cutting or grabbing horsemen.*

iron-tipped javelins, as did eastern Mediterranean light infantry, or *akonistai,* at the beginning of Greece's classical period. Fifth century B.C.E. Greek hoplites, or infantry soldiers, fought with stout 9-foot spears in phalanxes several men deep. Vulnerable Persian infantry armed with shorter spears had to rely on archers. The armies of Alexander the Great, king of Macedonia from 336 to 323 B.C.E., and his successors also relied on phalanxes of spear-throwers in ranks of up to five men deep with ash-shafted sarissas of up to 21 feet in length. Some Hellenistic cavalry also used sarissas, while others wielded shorter spears for under- or overhand thrusting. The Roman

victory at Pydna (168 B.C.E.) ended the dominance of the sarissa.

The standard Roman javelin was the *pilum.* One third of its 5.5-foot length was a long iron neck with a leaf-shaped tip. To prevent the *pilum* from being hurled back, its wooden socket was weakened to break upon impact. Later, under Julius Caesar (100-44 B.C.E.), the iron neck was weakened so that it would bend after penetration and render the enemy's shield useless. From either the Sabines or the Celt-Iberians, the Romans borrowed the *verutum,* a curved-bladed javelin thrown with a leather sling, or *amentum,* that wrapped around the shaft. The *verutum* largely replaced the *pilum* in the second century C.E. The *falarica*, or Saguntine spear, was a javelin with a foot-long head of triangular section; balls of fiber soaked in pitch could be attached and ignited to make an incendiary missile.

In Asia, Tibetans wielded the *dung*, a spear 7 to 10 feet in length with a long, narrow, two-edged head on a socket. The shaft was often wrapped with iron bands, tipped at the butt end with an iron cap, and was used by cavalrymen for vaulting into the saddle. Japanese armies carried several types of pole weapons, beginning with the *take-yari* or *take-hoko*, a 6.5- to 8-foot bamboo pole tipped with a simple jagged edge. The traditional *yari* usually had long tangs that attached either triangular or diamond-sectioned tips with pegs and metal collars, called *habaki*. Some heads were as long as short swords, and spear-fencing emerged as a respected martial art. Wings, hooks, and curved blades eventually were added, as in the forked or crescent-headed *sasumata* or the cross-shaped *maga-yari*. Other Japanese pole-arms included the *ono*, a poleax with a hammer or peen opposite the blade, and the *kama-yari*, with a picklike head. Hafts were usually of wood, lacquered or plain, and sometimes wrapped in silk thread.

In Africa, native and Arab warriors hurled the 4-foot-long *assagai* or *zaghaya*, with a long, barbed lancet head whose tang was lashed to a wood or bamboo shaft. At lengths of up to 36 inches, the shorter javelin known as the *jarid*, or *djerid*, with its square-sectioned steel head was used in most Islamic-dominated areas.

In medieval Europe the use of the spear continued while other pole-arms were developed. Frankish warriors borrowed the Roman *pilum* (*angon*), barbing the tip and sheathing nearly the entire shaft in iron. Frankish thrusting spears had leaf-shaped tips with short lugs or wings at the base. Scandinavians used a variety of spears, including those designed for slashing (*hoggspjot*), hurling (*gaflak*), and flinging with an *amentum* (*snoeris-spjot*). They also employed thrusting weapons with long spikes. Hundreds of iron heads with bronze or gold inlay and ashwood shafts of 6.5 to 11 feet have been found in Danish graves. Norse warriors often named their weapons, usually incorporating serpent imagery. Eu-

ropean infantry continued to use thick-shafted spears tipped with lugged, leaf-shaped, or triangular heads until well after 1500 C.E.

Stirrups and deep-welled saddles allowed cavalry to wield spears more effectively in both over- and underhand motions, as shown in images such as the Bayeux tapestry (c. 1080 C.E.), which depicts the Norman Conquest. The lance developed as a shock weapon couched close to the body for charging other cavalry. Roman and early Byzantine *cataphracts* lashed their long spears against their horses' necks, supporting the butt by a rope sling at the croup. In the high Middle Ages, the 9- to 11-foot-long shaft had uniform thickness and a small, leaf-shaped tip. Tournament jousters used a three-pronged tip, or *cronel*, designed to grab, rather than to penetrate, the opponent's shield or armor. Hilts were added in the fourteenth century to absorb recoil upon impact, and conical vamplates that also served to deflect the enemy's lance tip appeared in the fifteenth century. Jousting shafts composed of bundles of thin staves (*bourdonass*) designed to shatter upon impact replaced those of solid wood, and plate breast armor sported small brackets, called arrests, that cradled the butt of the knight's lance.

Infantry spears evolved in two directions after about 1200 C.E. On one hand, the sarissa emerged again as the pike, with its small diamond-sectioned head at the end of a 12- to 18-foot-long ash shaft. Phalanxes or squares of up to four effective men deep could withstand the most determined cavalry charge with their leveled weapons, as at Courtrai (1302 C.E.) and Bannockburn (1314 C.E.), but archers easily decimated the unprotected ranks at Falkirk (1298 C.E.). Nonetheless, armies of pikemen proved successful until effective firepower broke their ranks, as at Bicocca in 1522 C.E.

On the other hand, spears with short wings or lugs evolved into more complex thrusting weapons as the tips lengthened and the wings arced out from the base. The *langue-de-bœuf* (ox tongue) began as a long, two-edged blade with a short socket and no wings; in the fifteenth century wings were added, and the resulting weapon became known as the partisan. The Italian *corseque*, with a broad, triangular blade and generally longer wings evolved similarly. The wide, flat surfaces of the *corseque* served Renaissance decorators well, and the weapon ended up as the ceremonial weapon of bodyguards.

Although ancient Egyptians had fought with an axlike blade attached to a long pole, most slashing pole-arms evolved from the agricultural implements that European peasants used to defend themselves against mounted warriors. The English bill, designed for pruning, consisted of a long and broad cleaverlike blade that curved outward at the top. It could strike downward or horizontally, and the hooked top could cut or grab mounted men. Iron sleeves that protected the shaft from blows gradually evolved, as did the blade's design. The fully developed bill of the fourteenth century sported a long, curved fluke on the backside, a pointed thrusting blade on the top, hooked and sharpened lugs at the base, and a peen or spike that projected perpendicularly from the haft, or pole. The top blade or spike could penetrate breastplates and the peen could penetrate helmets, while the fluke could hook and pull knights from horses or trip foot soldiers. The French *guisarme* retained more of the early bill's cutting edge, while the symmetrical Italian double-bill resembled a fleur-de-lis mounted on a long, broad leaf-shaped cutting blade.

Axes came with short or long hafts, and long hafts were favorites with the Norse, Russians, and Anglo-Saxons. Poleaxes developed in the later Middle Ages and were surmounted by long, straight, or curved Danish ax-heads, perhaps with rear-projecting flukes. When a thrusting point was added, in approximately 1300, a proper halberd was born. Swiss halberdiers slaughtered Austrian troops at Hildisrieden and at Sempach in 1386 and at Näfels in 1388, and later became the Pope's bodyguards. Various combinations of flukes, points, and blades often make differentiating between bills and halberds difficult, but the halberd is generally distinguishable by its salient convex ax-blade. The glaive, or broadsword, evolved during the fifteenth century from the long-hafted scythe, with its long, gently curving blade. The concave edge was inverted to convex, like that of a knife or single-edged sword, and spikes or flukes were added to the back of the blade. The *fauchard*, with its distinctive crescent fluke, derives from the glaive. The practical value of these weapons declined after the late fifteenth century, and bills, halberds, and glaives became highly decorated ceremonial weapons.

Other farm implements, including hammers, flails, and forks, were also mounted on poles for military use. Pole hammers might also sport hooked flukes or long spikes, whereas military forks with two tines were sometimes supplied with blades or hooks. Spiked maces with long hafts and even spiked balls with one long spike extending as a thrusting point also appeared on high and late medieval battlefields.

BOOKS AND ARTICLES

Nicolle, David C. *Arms and Armour of the Crusading Era.* 2 vols. White Plains, N.Y.: Kraus International, 1988.

Puricelli-Guerra, A. "The Glaive and the Bill." In *Art, Arms, and Armour,* edited by Robert Held. Chiasso, Switzerland: Acquafresca Editrice, 1979.

Snook, George A. *The Halberd and Other European Pole Arms.* Bloomfield, Ontario: Museum Restoration Service, 1998.

Spring, Christopher. *African Arms and Armour.* London: British Museum, 1993.

Swanton, M. J. *The Spearheads of the Anglo-Saxon Settlements.* London: Royal Archaeological Institute, 1973.

FILMS AND OTHER MEDIA

Arms in Action: Slings and Spears. Documentary. History Channel, 1999.

Joseph P. Byrne

CHARIOTS

DATES: TO C. 401 B.C.E.

NATURE AND USE

The chariot derived from the four-wheeled wagon, and was replaced by a two-wheeled vehicle after the original wagon was found to be too cumbersome for combat. While the precise origin of the chariot remains unknown, it is known that the Hyksos, of Semitic origin (c. 1700 B.C.E.), introduced the horse-drawn chariot during invasions of Egypt (c. 1674 B.C.E.). Hammurabi, ruler of the Amorite Dynasty (c. 1750 B.C.E.) in Mesopotamia, was driven from the Near Eastern sphere of power when conquered by the Hittites, a people from the northern mountain regions of modern Iran and Iraq whose spearmen fought from chariots. In Asia Shang (Shang) Dynasty (1384-1122 B.C.E.) armies introduced the chariot to northern China in order to overrun the earlier Chou (Zhou) Dynasty (1122-221 B.C.E.).

The rapid development of the chariot, the breeding of horses, and the ability to control them with a bridle and bit allowed for efficient use of the chariot in battle. Chariots drawn by horses were yoked horizontally in pairs. Two wooden, Y-shaped forms attached to the yoke were fitted to the horses but limited the terrain over which they could be used effectively for battle. As chariot use increased, so did the need for professional charioteers and chariot-warrior teams, each consisting of a driver and an archer. The Hittites were credited with the expansion of the chariot crew to include a third man, the guard or shield bearer. The Hittites also used the chariot defensively against enemies. Reconstructions of early chariots found primarily in Egyptian tombs of New Kingdom (c. 1550 B.C.E.) kings reveal a hard, dense wood used to prevent cracking of the hub, an inflexible wood for the spokes, and a flexible wood for the wheel rim, or segments of the wheel rim, called fellies.

Initially, the chariot provided armies with speed and thus the potential for surprise attacks. This new form of attack forced military leaders to adopt new battle tactics. When integrated into the battle-field, the maneuverability of the chariot allowed the chariot-warrior to perform an outflanking maneuver. In early use, archers were able to use the chariot as a mobile platform from which to shoot. The mobility increased the damage inflicted on enemy troops and enabled chariot soldiers to chase down fleeing enemy soldiers.

In the Near East, the chariot became an effective offensive weapon. Often more disruptive than destructive, aggressively mobile chariot forces could gain control over the east-west and north-south trade routes to the sea, as well as inland access to natural resources, eliminating the need to mount an expensive army campaign.

Treaties formed with opposing enemies combining a large kingdom and vassal-states within one area of influence illustrate the important role chariots played in the history of the Near East. Even the show of force by aggressive chariot tactics helped to dissuade confederations of opposition.

Egyptian tomb paintings (c. 1700 B.C.E.) depicting the design and manufacture of early chariots show a vehicle with four-spoked wheels and a single axle centered under a single platform, on which the chariot driver stood directly over the axle. The light weight of wooden chariots provided Egyptians with needed mobility in battle. At approximately 1300 B.C.E., two changes in chariot design were made. The first innovation was an increase in the number of spokes, from four to six, in order to sustain a heavier weight on the wheels. The second was the relocation of the axle from the center of the chassis to the edge of the platform, which was open at the end of the chassis.

Early chariot tactics were immediate and intrusive; the charioteers would rapidly advance and encircle the enemy at a distance of approximately 100

TURNING POINTS

c. 1674 B.C.E.	The Hyksos people introduce the horse-drawn chariot during invasions of Egypt.
c. 1300 B.C.E.	Chariot design undergoes major innovations, with an increase in the number of spokes and the relocation of axles.
c. 1122 B.C.E.	Shang Dynasty armies introduce the chariot to northern China in warfare against the Chou Dynasty.
546 B.C.E.	Persian king Cyrus the Great uses chariots to great advantage at the Battle of Thymbra.
401 B.C.E.	Charioteers are overwhelmed by more flexible cavalry in the Battle of Cunaxa, ending the dominance of chariots in warfare.

yards and then use the chariot as a mobile platform from which the archer would shoot. This method permitted both speed and a greater ability to maneuver on the battlefield than had war wagons or troops on foot. The result left an enemy defenseless to form a counterattack.

In a two-wheeled, four-spoked Greek chariot, there was a chariot-warrior group of two: the driver and the archer. The two-wheeled Greek chariot did not provide an archer with protective cover, and no spear-throwing could be accommodated in the two-wheeled chassis, or in the battle strategy, without bringing the chariot to a stop. The open-framed chassis had bentwood rods with leather sheets stretched between them. These light chariots allowed for side screens but required the attachment of metal plates for protective purposes. The characteristically curved draught-pole, connecting the yoke to the chassis, was supported at the yoke end by a leather swathe and then continued back to the protective chassis screen.

DEVELOPMENT

The component parts of the chariot—wheels, draught-pole and yoke, chassis, and fittings for harnessing—developed independently in different regions. Wheels were made either as a single unit or as segments of smaller pieces of wood, often fastened together with leather. The spoke wheel derived from the earlier three-part wheel. Implementation of the hub permitted a lighter-weight chariot with the spoke used to disperse the weight density. Spoke wheels were more expensive to produce than were the earlier three-part wheels, and their production demanded a higher level of technology, as well as a skilled work force. The finished wheel consisted of a hub to hold the axle, as well as sockets for each spoke end.

To lessen the stress of the chariot's dispersed weight, spokes were of precisely equal lengths. The spoke was trimmed to fit, like a dowel, into the hub holes and wheel rims. Egyptian spokes were carved separately to fit the hub hold and were connected by mortise-and-tenon joints borrowed from Old Kingdom furniture-making techniques. Bent wood, in either single pieces or segments, heated to form the circular shape, was used for the wheels. In Bohemia, the Rhineland, and possibly India, the spoke was held together with overlapping metal strips wrapped to envelop the join. In Shang Dynasty China (1384-1122 B.C.E.), chariots utilized a spoke wheel. Both six- and eight-spoked wheels were used in the Near East (c. 1900 B.C.E.), and the six-spoked wheel was standard for Hittite- and Syrian-designed chariots (c. 1400 B.C.E.).

Unlike Egyptian chariots, the Greek light chariot rotated on a fixed axle held by a metal linchpin. Iron linchpins coated with bronze were used in the Celtic chariot. The Greeks used a four-horse chariot team, which continued to be employed by the Etruscans (c. 900 B.C.E.) and the Northern Europeans. After the fall of the Roman Empire, little is known about medieval chariots until the twelfth century. Apart from new technology evidenced by a lathe-turned and mortised hub, chariots of this period do not show much technical innovation. Instead, a series of wheeled vehicles served mainly as carting or farm vehicles and, in battle, moved men and weapons.

Iron Age wheelmakers often lined wheel hubs with bronze and then fitted them with an iron collar.

Roman designs introduced a gear-like set of rods made of wood to form channels inside the hub or to turn between the hub and axles.

The harness remained unimproved beyond the yoke until the twelfth century introduction of the traction harness. In Han Dynasty China (207 B.C.E.-222 C.E.) and in third century C.E. Persia, girth bands were developed to harness horses without choking them. The leather breast band fell horizontally to respond to the horizontal pull of the horse.

During the second millennium B.C.E., the horse-drawn light chariot provided armies with new mobility and speed. In early battles, chariots were used to create confusion in enemy ranks in preparation for coordinated chariot and cavalry charges. In China (c. 1400 B.C.E.) the chariot was a mobile command post. Chariots and cavalry were used on flanks or sometimes in front with the objective of outflanking the enemy and gaining rear access to the enemy's

vulnerable infantry. At the Battle of Thymbra (546 B.C.E.), Persian king Cyrus the Great used the chariot to take advantage of gaps in the Lydian chariot wings.

Once coordinated teams of chariots and cavalry organized, the role of the chariot diminished, especially in difficult terrain. Charioteers formed elite corps in Near Eastern and Egyptian armies for nearly a thousand years. In Greece, however, where the terrain varied, cavalry replaced the chariot. The Hellenic army consisted of a line of infantry, known as hoplites, in a formation of eight-deep units. The hoplites advanced with the object of smashing through the enemy's front line. Flanking the hoplites were armed spearmen with javelins and shields. The success of the Greek system depended on the hoplites' ability to penetrate the enemy's front line so that in retreat the enemy would be vulnerable to Greek missile weapons. Apart from the two classes of Greek infantrymen, hoplites and spearmen, there was no

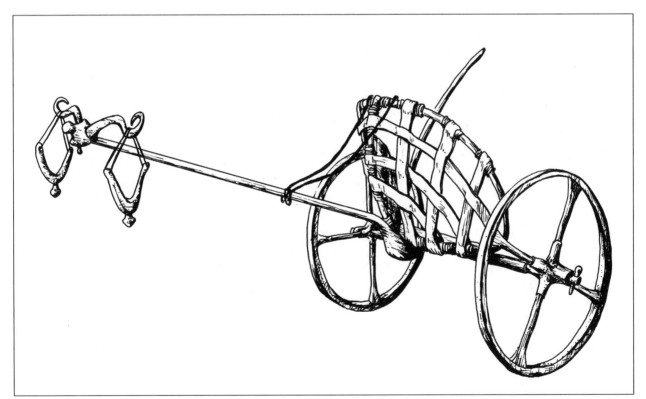

Kimberly L. Dawson Kurnizki

A two-wheeled, four-spoked Bronze Age chariot constructed with bent wood, showing the Y-shaped forms that fitted the pair of horses to the yoke.

cavalry force, nor was the composite bow used extensively in conjunction with chariot attacks. With these battle tactics, the need for chariots disappeared.

The characteristics of the Greek fighting style were established in the decisive Battle of Cunaxa (401 B.C.E.), in which Persian prince Cyrus the Younger attempted to seize the throne from his brother Artaxerxes II (r. 404-359/358 B.C.E.). The hoplites easily dispersed the Persian infantry and drove Cyrus's forces off the battlefield, killed him, and isolated the Greek infantry in Cyrus's employ. Here the cavalry replaced the chariot because the cavalry could exploit tactical maneuvers on the battlefield and added a flexibility not possible with the chariot. The lesson was not lost on the Macedonian army led by Philip II (382-336 B.C.E.).

Philip's Macedonian army formed a core around the "Companion cavalry." This group numbered about two thousand, and Philip added about six thousand other armed cavalry from previously conquered Near Eastern groups. This calvary was joined by an infantry of about twenty-five thousand men divided into three main groups: the phalanx, a highly trained group twice as deep as the earlier hoplite formation that provided freedom of movement on the battlefield; the *hypaspists*, a secondary shield-bearing corps of soldiers similar to those of the phalanx; and a group of lightly armed soldiers equipped with javelins and bows. Because these forces were effective against chariots and horses, the art of chariots soon disappeared from battle formations and became limited to observation posts or command posts.

BOOKS AND ARTICLES

Littauer, M. A., and J. H. Crouwel. *Chariots and Related Equipment from the Tomb of Tut'ankhamen*. Oxford, England: Griffith Institute, 1985.

Shaw, Ian. *Egyptian Warfare and Weapons*. Risborough, Buckinghamshire, England: Shire, 1991.

Yadin, Yigeah. *The Art of Warfare in Biblical Lands*. 2 vols. New York: McGraw-Hill, 1963.

Elizabeth L. Meyers

FIREARMS AND CANNON
DATES: TO C. 1500 C.E.

NATURE AND USE

The first precise recipe for gunpowder, a Chinese invention dating to before 1000 C.E., is found in a work from 1044. Long before it gained any military significance, gunpowder was used for holiday displays of colored smoke and fireworks. The earliest evidence of gunpowder weapons is a set of figurines dating from 1128 found in a cave. One figure holds a device that appears to be a potbellied vase with a blast of fire coming out, within which is a disk that probably was intended to portray a ball. Further evidence from Chinese records and art indicates that gunpowder weapons were in widespread use by 1280. These weapons seem to have included the three essential elements of true gunpowder weapons: a metal barrel, an explosive powder similar in chemical makeup to that of black powder, and a projectile that filled the barrel in order to take full advantage of the propellant blast.

The consensus among historians is that the Mongols carried gunpowder westward from China in the thirteenth century, but there is no agreement on whether gunpowder weapons were brought to Europe with the powder. The first European mention of gunpowder was by thirteenth century scientist and educator Roger Bacon (1220-1292), who recorded a recipe in 1267. His term, "fire for burning up the enemy," suggests that Bacon regarded gunpowder as an incendiary, not a propellant. Late thirteenth century gunpowder recipes called for saltpeter, sulfur, and charcoal in the proportion of six parts saltpeter for every one part each of sulfur and charcoal—a more explosive combination than that used by the Chinese and therefore better for projectile weapons. There is no convincing evidence for the existence of such weapons before 1326, although several earlier sources have been interpreted as referring to them.

Although a reference to the making of gunpowder artillery found in a 1326 document from Florence is widely accepted as the first reliable mention, it is less informative than an illustrated English manuscript from the following year. This illustration shows a large pot-bellied vessel lying on its side on a table with a large bolt projecting from its mouth, which is aimed at the gate of a walled place. Behind the device stands an armored man with a heated poker, which he is about to put to its touch hole. Such a device became known as *pot de fer* (iron pot). As that illustration reveals, these early gunpowder weapons were largely associated with sieges. The first definitive mention of them in action came from a siege of Tournai (1340). Whether the English deployed cannon in the Battle of Crécy (1346), the first decisive battle in the Hundred Years' War, is disputed, but they did use them at the Siege of Calais (1346-1347).

In field warfare, early gunpowder weapons—both firearms and artillery—lacked the technical quality to compete effectively with longbows and crossbows. Their weight, unreliability, inaccuracy, and slow rate of fire made them inferior in most respects to traditional combat weapons for more than a century after 1327. In sieges, however, these defects were less problematic. The cannonball's flat trajectory assured that the ball would strike low against the high walls of medieval fortifications and be more likely to open a breach than would mechanical artillery, which had a high trajectory. The first known instance of gunpowder artillery bringing a siege to a successful end occurred in 1377 at Odruik, the Netherlands.

By the late fourteenth century, the size of gunpowder artillery had increased greatly. Huge bombards—so called because their hewn stone cannonballs buzzed like bumblebees when fired—reached twenty tons in weight. Balls weighed as much as one thousand pounds, a weight attributed to the balls fired by the largest bombard used by the Turks against Constantinople in 1453. Although a direct hit from a ball

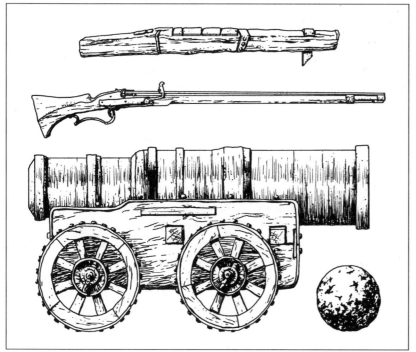

From top to bottom, a harquebus, the first effective matchlock firearm, dating from around 1470; a more evolved matchlock musket, dating from around 1600; a muzzle-loading bombard, known as "Mons Meg," dating from around 1440.

suggested that the term "harquebus," the common word for the first effective firearms, came from the German for such hook guns.

DEVELOPMENT

It is difficult to date the development of effective firearms because most of the people who created and used the new weapons were illiterate and did not leave written records. A chronology of firearm technology depends on a few surviving examples, as well as drawings and sketches that are not detailed enough to show the changes involved. Corned powder, which provided greater explosive power than did earlier serpentine powder, appeared around 1420. Corned powder produced higher muzzle velocities and could fire balls capable of penetrating the plate armor worn by the knights who were the mainstay of most fifteenth century armies. Higher muzzle velocity, however, could be achieved only with a barrel longer than that of the hand-cannon. Because of such defects, hand-cannons were not competitive with bows until 1450. By then gunsmiths had found the right compromise between ballistic performance and weight by fitting hand-cannons with barrels of about 40 inches in length. The first known illustration of a long-barreled firearm shows it being used for duck hunting. Hunting requirements often produced technological changes that later appeared in weapons.

Another innovation toward more effective firearms was the match-string; soaked in saltpeter, it burned slowly but with enough heat to touch off gunpowder. The match also was developed sometime around 1420, replacing the clumsy and unreliable burning stick. The match, however, created the same problem for its users as had the burning stick: It had

of that weight had a good chance of collapsing a wall, bombards were extremely difficult to move, and the amount of gunpowder they required was expensive and difficult to procure. Smaller pieces of artillery went by names such as *ribauld* and *serpentine*.

In Bohemia military leader Jan Žižka (c. 1360-1424) used small cannon in the Hussite Wars (1419-1434) against the forces of the Bohemian king Sigismund (1368-1437). Forced to fight German knights with poorly trained foot soldiers, Žižka developed the *Wagenburg*, a defensive line of wagons. On some were placed small cannon, and on others, men with firearms. The Germans on horseback presented large targets for the inaccurate gunpowder weapons in use, and the smoke and noise of the weapons frightened their horses. Some of the Hussites' primitive firearms had hooks attached that fit over the upper edge of the wagons' sideboards to absorb the recoil and provide a steady base for firing. It has been to be held in one hand and touched down into the chamber to fire the powder. That meant that only one hand could be used to hold the piece, butted up against the chest, not the shoulder. Too large a charge of powder could result in a broken breastbone. The solution was the matchlock. The matchlock evolved in Germany to include springs, a trigger, and a clamp for holding a smoldering match so that when the trigger was pulled, the match's burning tip was thrust into the powder and touched it off. After the shoulder stock, borrowed from the crossbow, was added to reduce the impact of the recoil from the greater muzzle velocity, the firearm was made up of the proverbial lock, stock, and barrel.

The users of the matchlock device found that coarse powder often failed to ignite and fine powder often created too forceful a recoil. The innovative solution to this problem was to place a small pan filled with fine powder behind the chamber of the barrel and to put coarse powder in the chamber. The match touched off the fine powder in the pan, blowing flame through a small hole into the chamber, igniting the coarser powder there, and firing off the ball. Often, however, the powder in the pan ignited with fire and sparks without touching off the powder in the chamber.

The harquebus, as the first matchlock firearm became known, was developed by 1460, but its impact on the battlefield was slow to appear. As a smoothbore weapon, it was inherently inaccurate: The spin of a ball tumbling down a smoothbore barrel is determined by the last point on the barrel the ball touches as it leaves the muzzle. The user has no idea what direction the spin will cause the ball to take; balls fired from smoothbore weapons never have the same trajectories. Consequently, the harquebus was reasonably accurate for only a short distance, before the uncontrolled spin took over. The impact of the ball on its target, even an armored cavalryman, was great at close range, but that advantage was largely negated by the long time it took to reload a harquebus. If the harquebusier missed the charging knights with his first shot or if he had a misfire—a common occurrence with the harquebus—they would be on top of him before he could reload. Before the seventeenth century invention of the paper cartridge that combined a ball and a measured amount of powder, reloading a harquebus, even under the best conditions, took well over a minute. In the confusion and disorder of a battlefield, especially with lance-wielding knights bearing down, many harquebusiers took several minutes to reload or were never able to reload and fire a second time. Compared to longbows, the early harquebus performed poorly in reliability, rate of fire, and accuracy.

The harquebus found its first niche as a siege weapon, where it replaced the crossbow. Firearms were good weapons for urban militias guarding city walls across Europe. A minimal amount of training was required to use the harquebus effectively on walls, and, although the weapon was more expensive than the crossbow, it was still affordable to the artisans and merchants who belonged to the urban militias. The harquebus was probably introduced to the field armies, which doubled as siege forces, in the context of sieges.

The harquebus served for a time as a useful weapon for defending a fortification, but improvements in gunpowder artillery quickly negated the defensive advantage. Because late medieval iron casting produced a poor product, barrels made of cast iron frequently burst, killing gunners and bystanders.

TURNING POINTS

1044 B.C.E.	The first precise recipe for gunpowder is given, in a Chinese work.
1340 C.E.	The first definitive use of gunpowder weapons is made at the Siege of Tournai.
1346-1347	Cannons are deployed by the English at the Siege of Calais.
1377	The first siege won by cannon is ended at Odruik, the Netherlands.
c. 1420	Corned powder and matches are developed.
1503	The first effective use of the combination of firearms and pikes, a formation called the "Spanish Square," is made at the Battle of Cerignola.

Pieces of better quality were made by forging iron bars arranged in a circle and banded by hot metal hoops that tightened down as they cooled. These hooped bombards were the weapons first associated with the name "cannon," which came from a Latin word for "tube." Early cannons, with short barrels and large muzzles, used stone balls. Smaller pieces often were equipped with breech pans, which were loaded in advance and were set in the piece in rapid succession for firing. Another solution to the poor quality of pieces made with cast iron was to use bronze instead. Europeans were familiar with the casting of bronze bells, and that technology was easily transferred to the making of weapons. The use of bronze allowed gunmakers to manufacture long-barreled pieces with smaller muzzles—called culverins, from a French word for serpent—that were capable of using iron or lead balls. The French led in the development of high-quality culverins and of the gun carriage, with high wheels and long tail, that defined gun carriages until the nineteenth century. With an artillery train of some eighty bronze culverins on mobile carriages, French king Charles VIII (r. 1483-1498) had great success in reducing Italian fortifications during the initial phase of the Italian Wars of 1494-1559. In the Battle of Fornovo (1495) the French artillery also played a significant role as an effective field weapon.

During the wars in Italy after 1494, field armies began to include harquebusiers. At the Battle of Cerignola (1503) in the French-Spanish war over Naples, the Spanish commander Gonzalo Fernández de Córdoba (1453-1515) devised a way to make effective use of harquebusiers by digging trenches in front of their lines. This action transformed the battlefield into a fort and imitated a siege, a situation in which the harquebus had long proven itself. Harquebus fire raked the French forces as they approached the Spanish trenches. Over the next twenty years, the Spanish rapidly increased the number of handgunners in their forces and developed the infantry formation called the "Spanish Square," in which pikemen and harquebusiers provided mutual support for each other. It remained the dominant infantry system until the beginning of the Thirty Years' War in 1618.

BOOKS AND ARTICLES

Buchanan, Brenda, ed. *Gunpowder: The History of an International Technology.* Bath, England: Bath University Press, 1996.

Hall, Bert. *Weapons and Warfare in Renaissance Europe.* Baltimore: Johns Hopkins University Press, 1997.

Lu, Gwei-Djen, et al. "The Oldest Representation of a Bombard." *Technology and Culture* 29 (1988): 594-605.

Lugs, Jaroslav. *Firearms Past and Present: A Complete Review of Firearms Systems and Their Histories.* 2 vols. London: Grenville, 1973.

Frederic J. Baumgartner

ANCIENT FORTIFICATIONS

DATES: TO C. 370 C.E.

NATURE AND USE

Fortifications are structures built by human beings for the purpose of warding off attacks by hostile animals or humans. In the broadest sense, fortifications can be forms of protection, such as armor, inoculation, or even insect repellent, worn by an individual to protect against harm. Fortifications can also be communal defenses, such as forts, moats, walls, or the "strategic missile defense," a proposed network of satellites positioned in outer space to protect against attacking ballistic missiles. In the study of warfare, "fortifications" generally refers to temporary or permanent communal defenses against attacks by human enemies. Temporary fortifications for immediate use in battles or other engagements are called "field fortifications" to distinguish them from permanent structures such as castles, stone walls, and forts.

DEVELOPMENT

In Neolithic times, small villages were located either on high ground or in barely accessible areas reached only with considerable difficulty. Where nature did not provide a barrier to intruders, human ingenuity placed trenches, palisades, or moats over which bridges could be placed or removed. These three types of defenses, when intended to protect against other humans, were the first military fortifications.

It seems likely that permanent fortifications evolved in response to the settling of agricultural communities. Early fortifications did not require much sophistication, because threats came mainly from weak and desperate nomadic individuals or from small raiding parties. Jericho—an agricultural community in the Jordan Valley north of the Dead Sea, settled in part because of its celebrated spring, which provides a thousand gallons of water every minute—is believed to have been the first town to build an encircling fortification, around the fifth millennium B.C.E. The town was surrounded by a stone circle and a massive tower, also of stone, that enabled lookouts to spot potential enemies long before they arrived. It is not currently known whether there were such fortifications in the Old Kingdom of Egypt, though fortifications on a large scale would certainly have required an advanced degree of political organization.

In an era when the principal weapons were spears, swords, and arrows, permanent fortifications were an effective defense against swift and vigorous frontal attack. The safest and most effective means of conquest was by siege: an attack on or blockade of a city or castle, in which the inhabitants would be starved, frightened, or bored into submission. The Trojan War (1204-1194 B.C.E.) was basically a ten-year siege of Troy by the Greeks. Legend indicates that even after such a long period of time, Troy would not have fallen but for the Greek stratagem of the Trojan horse. The Trojan horse was a large, hollow, wooden horse placed outside the Trojan gates. The Trojans were deceived into tearing down their own gates so that the horse, and the Greeks hidden within it, could enter.

The difficulty of a successful siege lay in maintaining an army in the field for a sustained length of time. Without regular supplies, the army laying siege would be compelled to withdraw, especially if the besieged party had, as in the case of Jericho, access to water and food. Even if the fortification could hold out, a siege might end if there were a betrayal, stirred by civil strife or bribery.

Assyrian reliefs show that by 850 B.C.E., the principles of fortress building were already in place. Portrayals of military camps of the period show them as round and reveal curtain walls, or protective walls between gates or bastions; loopholes, small holes for shooting arrows; parapets, guarding walls at the edge

The remains of a Roman fort along Hadrian's Wall, one of the most famous ancient fortifications (c. 122-136 C.E., in Northumbria, England.

or terraces of a building; crenelation, or repeated depressed openings; strong, fortified gates; and towers or bastions, projections from the curtain walls. With all these defenses, no part of the wall went unobserved or undefended. As more and more of the world became civilized, city walls became regular parts of landscapes. Rare was the city, such as Sparta or Rome for a good part of its history, that could boast of its security with an absence of walls. It was a glaring indication of Rome's decline when, in the third century C.E., Aurelian built new walls for the imperial capital. When siege equipment, such as battering rams and catapults, came into use in the West, walls were thickened and made higher, and moats were dug more deeply to provide further protection. Eventually, as better organization and more money became available, empires were able to construct mon-

umental fortifications such as the Great Wall of China, built in the third century B.C.E. during the Qin (Ch'in) Dynasty (221-206 B.C.E.) and Hadrian's Wall in northern England, built on the orders of the Roman emperor Hadrian around 122-136 C.E. These fortifications were the greatest military structures of the ancient world.

AFRICA

Egypt is a land blessed with natural defenses. To the west of the Nile Valley lies the immense Libyan Desert, to the east, the Arabian Desert. To the south are the high rocky ledges of the Nile River cataracts and, to the north, the Mediterranean Sea. Beyond the cataracts to the south was Nubia, a land inhospitable to agriculture but valuable for its copper, gold, semi-precious stones, and exotic animals. Here, during the

Middle Kingdom (c. 2000 B.C.E.), Egypt set up a system of forts to protect its conquests of Nubia. These fortifications stretched for 250 miles between the first and fourth cataracts and gave protection to the settled areas of both river and desert. They were constructed close enough to one another that communication by fire or smoke signals was possible. The first forts, in Lower Nubia, close to the first cataract, seem to have been planned to support the agricultural communities living along the banks of the Nile; the later forts, in less civilized areas to the south, probably were established to serve as a military line marking the southern frontier of Egypt. Garrisons were maintained to administer, rule, and protect the populations, and perhaps also to intimidate them into continued submission to the central authority.

ASIA

Sumeria, the world's oldest known civilization, was located in southern Mesopotamia, the fertile land between the Tigris and Euphrates Rivers. The Sumerians created walled communities at the foothills of the Mesopotamian alluvial plain. By about 3000 B.C.E., the Sumerians were building independent cities, among which Ur, Uruk, and Kish were the most prominent. These cities did not at first have walls, perhaps suggesting an absence of warfare. However, peace did not last, and between 3100 and 2300 B.C.E., war seems to have been a regular part of life and death. By 2700 B.C.E., the city of Uruk had erected walls of about 5 miles in length. The Akkadian king Sargon (c. 2334-2279), one of the first great Mesopotamian conquerors, conquered Sumeria and upper Mesopotamia and may have organized the various fortified communities he encountered into an interconnected whole. Rock sculptures depicting Sargon's grandson Naram-Sin (c. 2261-2224 B.C.E.) seem to show well-defined fortifications, as well as some of the methods of siegecraft, particularly the breaching and scaling of city walls.

The ancient Mesopotamian city of Babylon, capital of the Babylonian Empire first established in the early eighteenth century B.C.E., serves as an excellent example of a city well fortified for defense. The ancient account by historian Herodotus (c. 484-424 B.C.E.) tells of a wall 15 miles long, 85 feet thick, and 335 feet high, surrounded by a broad, deep moat. Queen Nitocris, he adds, altered the straight-flowing Euphrates so that boats sailing to Babylon would pass the city three times before flowing through a tunnel under the wall and into the city itself. The same queen diverted the river and excavated a huge lake in order to slow the river's course, again giving Babylonians time to prepare a defense. Persian king Cyrus the Great (c. 601-590 to c. 530 B.C.E.) conquered the city by diverting the river from its course and then marching his soldiers over the drained riverbed and through the wall. A generation later, around 520 B.C.E., when Babylon rebelled against the Persian king Darius I the Great (550-486 B.C.E.) and appeared likely to withstand a protracted siege, the city was taken by trickery, when one of Darius's men, pretending to be a defector to Babylon, opened the gates to the Persians.

The walls of Babylon required immense size to resist siege engines, battering rams, scaling ladders, siege towers, and catapults. Powerful battering rams are depicted in a Mesopotamian palace relief sculpture dated to 883-859 B.C.E. A mobile siege tower has been dated to 745-727. The biblical book of Chronicles speaks of King Uziah's stone-throwing machines, which protected Jerusalem, although most historians believe this reference to be an anachronism inserted by a later writer. These sorts of weapons did not come into widespread use in Europe until the fourth century B.C.E.

Fortified cities appeared later in China than in Egypt, sometime during the Shang Dynasty (c. 1523-1027 B.C.E.). Because the land did not provide trees, earthen walls were used there instead. The Great Wall, perhaps the world's most famous fortification, was made by connecting many small, local walls that had been constructed previously by regional rulers. The line of the wall kept changing until, by the third century B.C.E., it lay on the border between the agricultural areas, where irrigation was possible, and the unsettled pastoral lands, where nomadic life predominated. The line of the wall varied as it moved north to enclose the Ordos plateau or extended toward the west to the Tibetan plateau. The wall was relocated as changes in climate, landscape, and population caused shifts in the frontier between civilized and uncivilized regions. In the end, the length of the wall, with all its extensions and branches, was nearly 4,000 miles.

The wall's purpose is ambiguous: It may have been principally to keep the population in or to keep marauders out. Only a wealthy and powerful bureaucracy could have afforded to build and maintain such a structure. Only a well-organized army would have dared to oppose it. That China did not rely on the wall for its sole defense is clear from the fact that the Chinese never tore down the walls around the cities where irrigated farming communities had developed. Yet the wall must have intimidated any nomads contemplating attacks upon the awesome might of the wall's builder.

EUROPE

The earliest defensive structures in Europe seem to have been built in about 2200 B.C.E. in Britain, perhaps as early agricultural communities began to wage war with one another for resources or political power. In Dorset, a gate with massive timber posts 5 feet across has been dated from this time.

The Greek city-states that developed during the barbarous period known as the Greek Dark Age (about 1100-900 B.C.E.) at first fortified only an acropolis, a citadel located on a hill used as a refuge in times of war. Poverty was surely the reason for the limited defense; walls were expensive, and a sparsely populated agricultural society would not have been able to afford them. In the flush of success after the Greco-Persian Wars, however, the Athenian general and statesman Themistocles (c. 524-c. 460 B.C.E.) persuaded his fellow Athenians to rebuild the city's walls and its harbor, known as the Piraeus. About three decades later, his successor, Pericles (c. 495-429 B.C.E.), persuaded them to build the Long Walls between Athens and the harbor, so that even during a long siege the city would have access to supplies from the sea. Battles in Greece traditionally had been fought outside the cities. However, during the Peloponnesian Wars (431-404 B.C.E.) and increasingly throughout the fourth century B.C.E., cities themselves were targeted directly. Throughout the Hellenic world, cities used their wealth to expand their fortifications, so that by the third century B.C.E., places such as Rhodes and Pergamum had fortresses as strong as any found in later times. These fortresses possessed multiple walls that provided mutual cover, so that if the exterior walls were scaled by invading enemies, the enemies would find themselves trapped between the scaled exterior wall and additional interior walls.

The account by ancient Greek historian Thucydides (c. 459-402 B.C.E.) of the Spartan siege of Plataea (429-427 B.C.E.) is perhaps the most revealing ancient account of siege warfare before the adoption in Greece of sophisticated siege engines. It also illustrates the use of field fortifications. While the Plataeans themselves were enclosed behind their walls, the Spartans worked continuously for seventy days to put up a palisade, or fence of stakes, made from fruit trees. They added timber and laid it in a lattice to support a mound of wood, earth, and stones.

TURNING POINTS

c. 5000 B.C.E.	The city of Jericho becomes arguably the first town to be fortified with a stone wall.
1204-1194 B.C.E.	The fortified city of Troy is besieged by the Greeks for ten years and falls only after succumbing to the Greek deception tactic of the Trojan Horse placed outside the city's gates.
850 B.C.E.	The principles of fortress-building are evidenced in an Assyrian relief sculpture.
214 B.C.E.	Chinese emperor Qin Shuangdi orders that the many portions of the Great Wall be joined to form a unified boundary.
4th-3d cent. B.C.E.	Mediterranean city-states undertake massive building of walls during a period of warfare.
c. 122-136 C.E.	Hadrian's Wall is constructed in northern England, marking northernmost border of Roman Empire.
370	Rome rebuilds its walls as protection against barbarian invasions.

For their part, the Plataeans built up their wall opposite the mound to a great height, protecting it with hides against hostile burning arrows. In addition, they pulled down part of the wall where the Spartan mound abutted so that they could carry its dirt into their city, thus forestalling the mound's growth. The Spartans took the countermeasure of twisting clay in wattles of reeds to prevent the soil from being carried away, and the Plataeans responded by digging a tunnel under their wall to the mound and using it to carry away more mound material. The Plataeans also built a crescent wall inside their outer wall, so that if the first wall were taken, the enemy would have to begin anew with a fresh mound. When some simple siege engines and an attempt to burn the city also failed, the Spartans built a wall, or circumvallation, around Plataea and left a small force to continue the siege. After two years, the Plataeans ran out of provisions and surrendered to the Spartans, who killed them all.

Macedonian conqueror Alexander the Great (356-323 B.C.E.) conducted at least twenty sieges during his conquests, succeeding under the most difficult of circumstances. His 332 B.C.E. victory at Tyre, an island fortress that he attacked by means of a mole constructed from the shore to the island, and that against Prince Ariamazes of Sogdiana, whose mountain fortress Alexander captured in 328 B.C.E. by means of mountaineers from above, are perhaps his most splendid triumphs over seemingly insurmountable fortifications.

In Roman mythology, Romulus and Remus, the twin sons of Mars, the Roman god of war, founded the city of Rome. After a quarrel, Romulus supposedly killed Remus and built walls around the city. However, whatever walls Rome may have had in its early period were insufficient to keep out the Celts, who sacked the city in 390 B.C.E. Although this attack may have had a psychological impact on the city of Rome, it seems to have had no major political results. A few years later, the Romans built a massive wall, parts of which still stand. As Rome grew, however, it gave up its walls, so proud of its might and its policy of offensive preemptive strikes against enemies that it felt no need to fortify the city. During the Empire, Rome rarely faced enemies capable of organizing the siegecraft and supplies that would allow them to undertake long sieges against the well-stocked Roman garrisons. The would-be challengers functioned at little more than a tribal level and could not afford fortifications that would have been able to withstand the imperial army.

Toward the end of the third century C.E., Emperor Aurelian (c. 215-275) fortified Rome with a wall 12 miles around and 40 feet high, a structure that no doubt protected the citizens against the increasingly frequent barbarian forays into Roman territory, but the perceived need of which foreshadowed the precarious state of the Roman Empire. Cities in Gaul and Spain were also fortified with walls from this time, though at a fairly slow pace. Rome accelerated its building of chains of forts along the North Sea and Atlantic coasts, but when these frontier defenses were overcome by the Huns, the empire lay vulnerable.

To maintain their empire, the Romans built a system of forts, first in open territory, for the purpose of controlling the surrounding countryside, and later on hilltops where there were extensive views for keeping watch. It is likely that a coherent imperial policy dictated a standard form of forts and their distances from one another. In general, Rome used a cordon system of forts and watchtowers without running barriers.

It is believed that a Roman army on the march erected a temporary camp every night. As part of their individual equipment, soldiers carried stakes with which to construct a palisade on top of a bank of earth, which was made by digging a ditch around the camp and piling the earth on the inside perimeter. Although Flavius Vegetius Renatus, a late fourth century C.E. Roman military theorist, lamented in his time the fact that soldiers no longer carried the tools or were trained to construct such camps, by Vegetius's time, Rome's military was used primarily for defense and its system of permanent forts was already in place.

THE AMERICAS

The principal weapons used in the Mayan lowlands, which were populated as early as 1000 B.C.E., seem to have been spears, though clubs and knives were also used. Because these weapons did not pose the same dangers as did arrows or other projectiles, Mesoamerican fortifications did not need overlapping fields of vision. Thus, walls projecting outward from the main fortress—an identifying characteristic of forts in Europe and Asia—were unnecessary. As a result, it is at times difficult to identify certain archaeological sites as fortifications. What appear from the bottom of a mountain looking upward to be walled fortifications may appear from above to be terraced retaining walls. One might wonder whether the appearance as a fortification was designed to discourage would-be attackers or merely was a result of construction methods and topology. Although these questions cannot be answered, freestanding walls with moats in front of them do suggest strongly that these structures were fortifications. The fighting among early American peoples was intense and continuous, and its aim seems to have been, not the death, but the capture of the enemy for sacrificial purposes.

Before 600 B.C.E., there do not seem to have been major permanent fortifications, but, from 600 to 300 B.C.E., as dispersed settlements were replaced by larger societies, more hilltop sites were constructed. Lowland fortifications, generally embankments surrounded by ditches, seem not to have been very intimidating structures, but perhaps were adequate to the military requirements of those early periods. Inhabitants of Mexico's Valley of Oaxaca developed probably the most complex Mesoamerican culture in the centuries before the Christian era. Its religious center, Monte Albán, rose on a series of hills. Monte Albán was fortified around 200 B.C.E. with an earthen wall of 1.8 miles, a height of between 10 and 13 feet, and a width at its greatest of 60 feet. A large reservoir was also built that could hold enough water to sustain a siege of several years. In short, it was a structure that was as well suited for its purposes as some of the contemporaneous fortresses elsewhere in the world.

BOOKS AND ARTICLES

Armillas, P. "Mesoamerican Fortification." *Antiquity* 25 (1951): 77-86.

Ferrill, Arther. *The Origins of War from the Stone Age to Alexander the Great*. New York: Thames and Hudson, 1985.

Johnson, A. *Roman Forts of the First and Second Centuries* A.D. *in Britain and the German Provinces*. New York: St. Martin's Press, 1983.

Johnson, Stephen. *The Roman Forts of the Saxon Shore*. New York: St. Martin's Press, 1976.

McNicoll, A. *Hellenistic Fortifications from the Aegean to the Euphrates*. Oxford, England: Clarendon Press, 1997.

Southern, P., and K. R. Dixon. *The Late Roman Army*. New Haven, Conn.: Yale University Press, 1996.

Toy, Sidney. *A History of Fortification from 3000* B.C. *to* A.D. *1700*. London: Heinemann, 1955.

Waldron, Arthur. *The Great Wall of China: From History to Myth*. New York: Cambridge University Press, 1989.

Winter, F. E. *Greek Fortifications*. Toronto: University of Toronto Press, 1971.

Yadin, Yigael. *The Art of Warfare in Biblical Lands in the Light of Archaeological Discovery*. Translated by M. Pearlman. New York: McGraw-Hill, 1963.

James A. Arieti

MEDIEVAL FORTIFICATIONS

DATES: C. 500-1500 C.E.

NATURE AND USE

In even the earliest and most primitive societies, the need to stave off attackers led to the construction of defensive physical structures. The variety of such responses naturally became ever more diverse as groups worldwide had to meet the intersecting challenges of the foe, their own resources, climatic and geographical constraints, and anticipated forms of organized violence. Fortification is thus any construction, permanent or transitory, earthen, organic, or stone, designed to shield defenders from an attacker while those defenders either await help or resist assaults themselves. Even with the rather limitless bounds of human ingenuity, fortifications nonetheless tend to fall within four somewhat interrelated categories: refuges, strongholds, fortified lines or zones, and urban walls.

DEVELOPMENT

By 500 C.E., each type of fortification had appeared numerous times in human conflicts. A stronghold differs from a refuge in that it is a place that hosts an active defense; from its walls, defenders may launch offensive sallies. The refuge, by contrast, is primarily defensive, a place to wait out the enemy in such a position of strength that the enemy will forgo the costs of attack. The final types of military architecture are even less distinct; city walls are in one sense fortified lines. Here, though, the concern is with those fortified zones meant to secure the peace of whole regions.

All types appeared concurrently and in overlapping cycles of need and development worldwide before Europe's medieval period. The Roman Empire had its own strategic mix of city walls, fortified frontiers, and the near-instant fortress otherwise known as an encamped army. After the Empire's fall in Western Europe, its legacy continued in the walls that surrounded many cities, the fortified zones of northern England and the Rhine and Danube Rivers, and the defenses of Constantinople, which stymied and stupefied many an invader. In Asia the tradition of long walls was already centuries old, having been initiated by the first Qin emperor in 221 B.C.E. In the Americas, the lack of metallic technology severely constrained the forms warfare might take; moreover, the earliest Mayan societies may well have not had, in the traditional Western sense, cities to defend. In sub-Saharan Africa and Australasia, the archaeological record has been less forthcoming. Doubtless, the inhabitants shaped earth as needed into ditches and ramparts, the latter surmounted even today by thorny hedges, known as *bomas* or *zarebas*, to keep out predators.

FORTIFIED LINES

Despite the remaining fortifications that surrounded them, the Europeans of the Germanic West had difficulty reaching the level of defensive sophistication of the Roman Empire. Even with the extant physical reminders of the Roman fortified lines, especially Hadrian's Wall in Britain, they declined to maintain such lines and delayed a long time building their own. Perhaps they saw little point to such defenses, which had failed to keep them out of the Roman heartlands. The permeability of such zones has raised a number of debates as to their real purpose, and whether they were meant to prevent invasion, to slow invaders, or to keep internal populations within limits. The Saxons, who invaded Britain after the 450's, found the defenses of the Saxon Shore did little to slow their conquest. To the north Hadrian's Wall likewise hindered the Picts little in their raids.

TURNING POINTS

c. 757-796	Offa's Dyke is built in the kingdom of Mercia to protect the kingdom's Welsh border.
880's	King Alfred the Great begins constructing a series of *burhs*, or garrisons, to defend Wessex from Vikings.
990's	The first stone keeps appear in northwestern Europe.
1066	Rapid proliferation of motte-and-bailey castles follows the Norman Conquest of England.
1196-1198	King Richard I of England builds Château Gaillard with three baileys, which had to be captured before the castle could be taken, serving as multiple lines of defense.
1277-1297	King Edward I of England builds a series of ten Welsh castles, with an implicitly offensive function as continuances of the king's campaigns.
1494	Charles VIII's invasion of Italy confirms the obsolescence of high medieval defenses.

Hadrian's Wall stretched for 117 kilometers across northern England, ranging in thickness from 2.3 to 3 meters and averaging a height of from 5 to 6 meters. The wall was part of the Roman strategy of defense in depth. In the absence of manned watchtowers and fortified camps to the rear, the Saxons were hardly set to use the wall to its best advantage. Even so, the wall did form, in its less than pristine state, something of a hindrance to the return of raiders northward. Northumbrian pursuers could count on it slowing marauders if those raiders tried to get their spoils through or over the fortifications.

It would appear that Offa's Dyke, built during the reign (757-796) of that Mercian king, was meant to achieve an effect along the Welsh border similar to that of Hadrian's Wall. An earthen rampart 18 meters wide formed in part by the ditches that bracket it, Offa's Dyke meandered for 192 kilometers through regions that had little in the way of leftover Roman defenses or roads. There was little hope of keeping out Welsh raiders, especially since the dyke was virtually unmanned. Again, though, its physical bulk would slow the exodus of such raiders, especially if they were driving stolen livestock, permitting Mercian forces to catch up with the marauders. In addition, the dyke provided a roadway that cut across the ranges and rivers of the Welsh marches, thus eas-

ing both the report of such raids and the speed of reaction.

The impassability of terrain might make fortified lines not only a cost-prohibitive measure but also a rather unnecessary one. In Mesoamerica contending empires could keep invaders at bay simply by blocking well-established paths. In the absence of siege equipment and draft animals, such structures would not have needed much complexity to be effective. In Europe fortified bridges developed not only to secure lines of communication and transport but also to block the progress of Viking raiders up the river systems. Thus a number of such bridges controlled the rivers below Paris after the 880's to prevent direct access or indirect efforts by portage. When Vikings actually did besiege Paris in 885, it took them over four months just to reach the city.

The most famous and latest of all fortified lines are of course those of China. The Great Wall is not actually a single wall curling along China's northern borders, nor does its current condition date back to 221 B.C.E. The earliest (Qin) walls were earthen, tamped down by forced labor between retaining wooden walls that connected watchtowers. The actual remains of this wall are now in the realm of conjecture. The current masonry walls—which are actually many sets of walls, not always connected, and not one continuous line—date from the Ming Dynasty (1368-1644) emperors, who reigned after the expulsion of the Mongol Dynasty. The facts of these fortifications are impressive: 2,400 kilometers in length, 7.6 meters high at a minimum, often 9 meters wide, and sometimes scaling 70-degree slopes. Like their European counterparts, however, they proved less than impermeable, again raising the question of whether the walls were more clearly intended to keep the native population contained within and untainted by exterior contact.

As the Germanic groups, especially the Franks, entered the deteriorating Roman Empire, they brought a new structure to the landscape: the private fortress. Although these small refuges, which utilized so little stone, have left few archaeological remains, contemporaries noted their appearance in rural and isolated areas. Most important, commentators of the day stressed the remoteness or inaccessibility of such sites. Because of the new inhabitants' rudimentary technology, these protocastles relied on their physical surroundings to deter would-be invaders. On isolated summits, crowning precipitous sites, these forts gave some protection to the rural regions of Gaul and Visigothic Spain; their small size and private ownership, however, limited their value as refuges for a harried populace. Instead, the later Frankish kings found them to be troublesome centers of resistance, because it was so difficult to bring an army to bear on such places.

The situation differed in eighth and ninth century Anglo-Saxon England, especially Wessex. By the 870's, after Viking invaders had occupied much of England and pushed into Wessex, King Alfred the Great (r. 871-899) secured a truce after his victory at Edington (878). During the cessation of active campaigning, Alfred devised a sophisticated defensive strategy centered upon thirty-three refuges. These *burhs*, as they were called, were scattered over the kingdom, seldom more than a day's ride apart, and usually near major transportation routes. Often quite sizable and well provisioned, the *burhs* were meant both to house a large garrison and to provide ample room into which a refugee population might flee. Alfred's strategy, which would prove successful in 896, was to have the population and movable wealth protected in the *burhs* while he shadowed the invading Vikings with the Wessex army. By hampering the Vikings' ability to forage or pillage, Alfred simply made his kingdom an uninviting prospect to Viking plunderers.

These fortifications did not have to be terribly complex, because the Vikings had little in the way of siege weaponry. Nonetheless, Alfred's administration prepared the *burhs* well, as is known from a document called the *Burghal Hidage* (c. 920), which lists them. By dividing the resources of the kingdom into units called hides, each of which was sufficient to provide one man for *burh* garrisons, the Anglo-

Saxons assigned enough hides to each *burh* to assure that its walls were defended by one man for every 4.25 feet. Because some *burhs* had circumferences of over one mile, this meant that Viking invaders had to sense the sizable numbers of uncowed foes they left in their wake as they bypassed the *burhs*. The *burhs* themselves were formidable: The first barrier was an exterior ditch perhaps more than 30 meters wide and sometimes as deep as 8 meters; an earthen bank came next, reaching up to 3 meters in height; timber defenses surmounted this ringwork in most cases, but stone walls were put in place at major sites, especially those that housed the royal mints. Many *burhs* took advantage of natural defenses, such as swamps and rivers, whereas others were built upon the remains of previous Roman fortifications.

The advantages offered by *burhs* or even the most simple defenses naturally drew people to those fortified locales. This rationale appears to explain the growth of the stone enclosures at Great Zimbabwe centuries later. The original impetus for the southern African plateau's settlement remains debated, but the availability of iron doubtless held part of the appeal. At all three parts of the site, the most restricted sites are those where archaeology has found iron stores or iron-working tools. Between 1100 and 1500, the Great Enclosure was built, with walls of quarried granite 32 and 37 feet in height and without any mortar, encompassing first a hilltop and later a site across a small valley. Early in the twentieth century, the archaeological record at Great Zimbabwe was greatly altered or nearly destroyed, and the reason for the site's abandonment by 1700 is unknown. However, no one has supposed a victory by besiegers.

STRONGHOLDS

The transition in Europe from simple refuges to castles came with the motte-and-bailey structure, whose origins lie in the tenth and eleventh centuries. The heart of this fortification was the motte, a steeply conical mound surrounded by a ditch and crowned by a timber palisade. Within this enclosure, a wooden tower originally rose, most often on stilts. The bailey was a secondary enclosure at the base of the motte, somewhat kidney-shaped as it fit alongside the motte. Separated from the motte by ditches and protected by its own palisade and ditches, the bailey formed a living area and an extra line of defense. From the bailey, a bridge either spanned the ditch on a more convenient gradient to the motte's gate or reached only to steps cut into the motte's steep slope. If the bailey became lost to attackers, the bridge was easily disposable. The quick proliferation of the motte-and-bailey lay in its most basic advantage: It provided a maximum amount of defense at the lowest cost of construction. Moreover, it was possible to build one within days.

In addition to its defensive capabilities, the motte-and-bailey had an offensive potential. As an easily built, forward base for troops, mottes were useful in subduing hostile regions. One of the earliest builders of mottes, Fulk III (c. 970-1040), the count of Anjou, used castles to push his borders farther toward Normandy. In turn, the Normans learned from this tactic and applied it most dramatically in the conquest of England. William the Conqueror (c. 1027-1087) built motte-style fortifications immediately upon his arrival in England, a fact graphically illustrated in the Bayeux tapestry. After his victory at the Battle of Hastings (1066), William and his chief followers brought the whole of England under control by establishing motte castles at crucial points throughout the kingdom. After the transition to stone castles became widespread in the twelfth century, many mottes did not have the stability to support massive keeps as replacements for the wooden towers. Instead, the palisade was rebuilt as a "shell keep," so that the weight of the new masonry was dispersed over the mound.

Although the use of timber castles continued into the thirteenth century, the transition to stone appears to have begun in the late tenth or early eleventh century, owing in part to the innovations of Fulk III.

Library of Congress

The twelfth century attack and defense of a city wall, with numerous types of siege engines in use.

Some scholars have convincingly argued that the bulky, rectangular towers at Langeais and Montbazon, reaching to 16 and 30 meters high respectively, were Fulk's constructions and that Fulk may well have been responsible for a number of other stone castles in the region. Not surprisingly, many of the stone castles surrounding Anjou date from soon after this period, as Fulk's rivals and successors imitated his new building program. These new keeps, or donjons, were massive, multistoried edifices that could house many troops. Fulk's two towers had walls between 1.5 and 3 meters thick and up to 30 meters high. The White Tower in London, begun by William the Conqueror, had walls as thick as 4.5 meters and as tall as 27 meters, with the corner turrets reaching above that height. It comprised 30 square meters, and the keep at Colchester was even larger.

The new preference for such expensive and mammoth constructions physically reflected the increasing wealth of the feudal nobility as principalities such as Anjou, Normandy, and of course, England, stabilized. The ability of these lords to command greater resources also meant they could put better-equipped armies into the field. Thus the siege weapons of antiquity, which had never completely been forgotten, began reappearing: battering rams, ballistae, onagers, and later, the trebuchet, as well as the old standby, fire. Successful defense against these weapons required the use of stone. The spread of castles was dramatic: The French province of Poitou had only three castles before the Viking incursions, but at least thirty-nine castles dotted the province by 1100. No archaeological evidence has been found of castles in the northwestern region of Maine before 900; two centuries later there were sixty-two. Other regions saw similar levels of castle-building. Such numbers do not take into account fortified residences, which lacked the defensive power of castles.

The intensified wealth and warfare of Europe did not account alone for the spread of more sophisticated defenses; inspiration came also from Constantinople and the Muslim fortresses taken only with the greatest effort during the First Crusade (1095-1099). The earliest castles that the Crusaders built were the rectangular keeps to which they had been accustomed in Europe, but the needs of these exposed states and sites soon mandated a change. Larger complexes became the rule in order to house both greater garrisons and the supplies necessary so that such a force could hold out, possibly for years, until relief could arrive from other allies or from Europe. Saphet had a garrison of between 1,650 and 2,000 men, while Margat's 1,000 defenders were supposed to be able to hold out for five years; the cisterns at Sahyun held ten million liters of water. These fortresses reflected Byzantine reliance on high, massive walls studded with towers to provide enfilading fire. These walls could actually be built more quickly than one of the rectangular keeps; moreover, they provided space for vitally necessary cisterns and reservoirs. Some castles still had keeps, but these were a final defensive point rather than the primary one.

The most famous of the Crusader castles is Krak des Chevaliers, which remains impressive even in its ruined state. Occupying a hilltop in Syria that had formerly been a Muslim stronghold, it began with the advantage of difficult access. Its outer wall was added in the 1200's even as the inner defenses were strengthened. This wall encompassed an area of 210 by 140 meters and had both semicircular towers and machicolations, or openings in the overhanging battlements that protected defenders who fired missiles, rolled stones, or dropped combustibles upon attackers at the wall's base. In forested Europe machicolations were only slowly adopted, because wooden overhangs, or hoardings, were so easily built for the same purpose. The higher inner circuit of walls could complement the outer defense with missile fire. Two towers flanked the small gate, which gave access either to the forecourt or to a series of gateways that protected the entrance into the fortress proper. The inner wall, or *enceinte*, was anchored by five large towers. In addition to these defenses, a massive talus, or sloped base, made the walls on the southern and eastern sides virtually impervious to mining and scaling ladders. Apart from its defensive function, the castle's increased lower bulk also protected Krak des Chevalier from the earthquakes that had damaged it in the mid-twelfth century. In later centuries, Japanese castles would also contend with natural catastrophe. Below the talus was an artificial reservoir, and granaries and armories lined the walls. Little

Krak des Chevaliers, in modern Syria, the most famous of the Crusader castles.

wonder, then, that the Mamlūk armies that took Krak in 1271 opted to trick the defenders into surrendering rather than risk an unsuccessful siege.

The lessons learned in the Middle East soon wrought changes in the structure of castles in Europe. Circular towers came to predominate, as castle builders realized that square angles gave attackers extra blind spots to exploit; more important, curved surfaces resisted the projectiles of pregunpowder artillery better than flat ones. King Richard I (1157-1199) of England, also known as Richard the Lion-Heart, would apply this principle liberally at his "saucy castle," the Château Gaillard, where the exterior wall of the inner bailey had a rippled surface. Although keeps continued to be built, including the huge circu-

lar donjon at Coucy, which was 31 meters in diameter, the emphasis moved to multiple lines of defense. Gaillard had three baileys to be captured before attackers faced the keep. Barbicans appeared as new fortifications in front of gateways that provided further fire support for this weakest point in a wall. Concentric walls, with the second overtopping the first considerably, became the new fashion in fortification; towers often broke the continuity of such wallwalks so that one portion of the walls could be lost without losing the entire circuit.

The most distinctive examples of concentric castles were Edward I's (1239-1307) Welsh castles, ten fortresses built between 1277 and 1297. Like their motte-and-bailey predecessors and the Crusader outposts, they had an implicitly offensive function, as their dominating presence and garrisons were meant as continuances of the English king's campaigns. Edward turned primarily to Master James of St. George, a Savoyard architect, to oversee the project. The show of strength may have been as much in the swift construction of the expensive castles as in the high curtain walls pierced with arrow slits, protective drum towers at each angle, and heavily defended gateways. Only one of these castles had a keep, so the emphasis was on the concentric walls. The inner walls loomed high over the outer walls, so that defenders could fire missiles from both. At Harlech and Beaumaris, the successive gates were sandwiched between flanking towers, whereas the entry itself went through a passage. Attackers within the passage would find themselves at the mercy of archers firing through *meurtrières*, or murder-holes.

Although castles would appear during Japan's Sengoku, or Warring States, period (1477-1601), they differed markedly from European models in both geographical and cultural considerations. A typical *hirojiro*, or lowland fortress, had a broad stone base with a curving face which, it was hoped, would offset the threats of earthquake or rain-sodden soil giving way. The towering superstructures above this foundation were actually lightweight wood and plaster, again so built as to survive repeated tremors. Despite the immensity and complexity of Japanese castles, they were rarely the focus of battle, because samurai preferred to display their prowess in the field against individual foes. Such battles also had the advantage of leaving intact buildings to the victor. The Japanese reluctance to adopt Western styles of warfare also meant that artillery had a minimal impact on Japanese castles until the 1800's.

In very different circumstances, the Maoris of New Zealand likewise showed a predilection for ritual combat and the preservation of defenses. The Maori *pa*, the first evidences of which date to 900, seem similar to the motte-and-bailey. At their height, such strongholds often occupied hilltops with difficult access; a wooden palisade surrounded the summit, with ditches in front and embankments within that allowed defenders to hurl weapons upon attackers. The wall was regularly pierced with openings, so

defenders could jab spears at those trying to scale the palisade. Close by was a less fortified village whose residents would retreat into the *pa* when warned by alarms. Long sieges, however, were rare. Attackers would challenge defenders to come out before the *pa* and engage in single or group combat. If the defenders declined, then a frontal assault might ensue, with the intent of capturing without destroying the fortification and its supplies.

WALLED CITIES

The defensive importance of cities marked both the beginning and the end of the medieval period. The Romans left a legacy of urban fortification: In Gaul alone, nearly 90 of the 115 cities received new walls, smaller in circumference but imposing still with their 10-meter height, 4-meter width, and foundations reaching from 4 to 5 meters underground. These defenses usually withstood Germanic assaults with ease but were rendered irrelevant if the walls were breached by trickery or treachery. Although rare, a long siege likewise could succeed by starving towns into submission. These conditions held true throughout the Merovingian period also, and one is reminded that the Crusaders only gained Antioch through bribery. During the Carolingian period, defenses were often neglected or even quarried for other projects, but repairs began anew with the Viking invasions. As towns grew in wealth and population from the 1100's onward, they had to erect new defenses to safeguard both. This would occur all over Europe, but the most striking example may well be the double curtain at Carcassonne, in southern France, which incorporated lessons learned from the cities of the eastern Mediterranean.

The techniques adopted by European cities may be highlighted by comparison with contemporary settlements in Mesoamerica. Maya centers show remarkable stonework, but it appears that these sites functioned more as royal residences and religious sites than as economic centers. Thus, the majority remained unfortified. Other sites, such as Becan or Mayapán, did have enclosing ditches, large embankments, and wooden palisades, and a few had stone walls topped again by palisades. Sometimes these defensive lines surrounded only core areas of the city. In all cases, however, this military architecture remained rather simple, because besiegers could bring so little weaponry to bear against it.

In Europe, though, the pendulum of innovation was already swinging away from the high walls of concentric castles and cities. Gunpowder artillery may have been present by 1340, and it made itself felt at the Siege of Calais from 1346 to 1347. Gunpowder weapons became increasingly refined, until they became the primary means of siege warfare. In the early 1400's the English used them successfully against both Scottish and French cities. More dramatically, in 1453 the land walls of Constantinople were breached by Turkish bombards after a millennium of successful defense. The high walls of medieval fortification were now considered a liability, but they could not easily be abandoned. At first, many curtain walls were pierced to admit cannons to be fired outward, but this had limited success. Outworks began to appear so that defenders could keep besiegers distant with their own cannons. These low-profile embankments foreshadowed the future of fortification. Military architects began to propose a new style of defense: low-profile, wide walls that could hold artillery, even wider ditches to distance besieging artillery, and still more outworks, or bastions, to provide flanking fire. Italian cities were the first to adopt this new form of siege warfare. When French king Charles VIII (1470-1498) invaded Italy in 1494, his artillery made a shambles of the medieval defenses in his way, and the Italians adopted the new techniques.

BOOKS AND ARTICLES
DeVries, Kelly. *Medieval Military Technology.* Lewiston, N.Y.: Broadview Press, 1992.
Higham, Robert, and Philip Barker. *Timber Castles.* London: Batsford, 1992.
Kenyon, John. *Medieval Fortifications.* New York: St. Martin's Press, 1990.
Rogers, Randall. *Latin Siege Warfare in the Twelfth Century.* Oxford, England: Clarendon Press, 1992.

Steven Isaac

SIEGES AND SIEGECRAFT
DATES: C. 7000 B.C.E.-1500 C.E.

NATURE AND USE

Siege warfare is the art of taking a fort or fortified city. In a passive siege, the besiegers attempted to starve the defenders by sealing off the city or fort from the outside world by circumvallation, which means encircling with a wall or rampart. Active siege tactics assaulted the fortifications by attempting to go over, through, or under the wall. The main weapons and tools for an active siege were ladders for climbing walls, drills and battering rams for punching through walls, and spades for undermining walls. Catapults and siege towers provided support.

Fortifications go back at least to Neolithic times. Seven thousand years B.C.E., the inhabitants of Jericho constructed massive fortifications that included a stone wall 10 feet thick and 13 feet high, a moat 10 feet deep and 30 feet wide, and a stone tower 28 feet high and 33 feet in diameter. By the time of the early civilizations in Mesopotamia and Egypt, the art of fortification had already been well developed. Walls featured balconies that allowed defenders to shoot straight down at the enemy, as well as towers and bastions from which defenders could rake besiegers with flanking fire. Gates were the most vulnerable points in a wall, and ancient architects spared no effort to secure them. Pilasters, bastions, towers, and balconies protected them. Metal plating covered the gates to prevent fire. Narrow, winding entryways made it more difficult for attackers to enter the city if they succeeded in breaking through the gate.

Although besiegers undoubtedly circumvallated cities almost from the beginning of siege warfare, the ancient Greek historian Thucydides (c. 459-402 B.C.E.) provides the first detailed account of the construction of a wall of circumvallation in the Siege of Plataea by Sparta and Thebes (429-427 B.C.E.) at the beginning of the Peloponnesian War (431-404 B.C.E.). A mile in circumference, it was a double wall with

space between in which to quarter troops. It took two and a half months to build. Battlements and towers strengthened the wall, and the digging of clay for the bricks left a moat on both sides. Plataea was thoroughly isolated but it held out for two and one-half years, revealing the weakness of passive sieges.

To shorten sieges, more aggressive methods were necessary. Escalade, or scaling, was perhaps the earliest means of overcoming fortified walls. A twenty-seventh century B.C.E. Egyptian wall painting at Dehashe shows soldiers trying to pry the gate open with poles while assault teams attack the wall with scaling ladders and archers attempt to drive the defenders from the wall. Escalade was not effective, however, against walls higher than 10 meters. The long ladders needed to scale greater heights were unwieldy and collapsed under the weight of too many soldiers climbing them.

Because walls in ancient Egypt and Mesopotamia rose as high as 20 meters, means other than escalade were necessary to assault them, and battering rams soon came into use. An Egyptian palette dating from around 3000 B.C.E. shows creatures that may be symbolic of battering rams attacking a wall. More clearly, a twentieth century B.C.E. Egyptian wall painting depicting a siege shows three men protected by a mobile hut using a long beam to pry stones from the wall. By the eighteenth century B.C.E. the Assyrians were deploying battering rams in integrated assault tactics that included the use of not only rams but also siege towers, siege ramps, and the method of sapping, or undermining walls. Lack of remaining evidence precludes a clear picture of the earliest Assyrian rams, which were probably prying devices used to dislodge bricks from walls. It is not until the Neo-Assyrian Empire in the ninth century B.C.E. that Assyrian rams are seen in palace wall paintings. Assyrian emperor Ashurnasirpal II (r. 883-859 B.C.E.) deployed huge rams that required six wheels for support. A domed

TURNING POINTS

c. 7000 B.C.E.	The inhabitants of Jericho construct massive fortifications around their city.
c. 1700 B.C.E.	Assyrians employ integrated siege tactics with rams, towers, ramps, and sapping.
c. 429-427 B.C.E.	A wall of circumvallation is used in the Siege of Plataea by Sparta and Thebes at the beginning of the Peloponnesian War.
c. 399 B.C.E.	The catapult is invented at Syracuse under Dionysius I, significantly advancing the art of siege warfare.
334 B.C.E.	Alexander the Great uses stone-throwing torsion catapults at the Siege of Halicarnassus.
305-304 B.C.E.	Macedonians employ a huge siege tower known as a *helepolis* during the Siege of Rhodes.
70 C.E.	Romans employ catapults during their Siege of Jerusalem.
1304	English king Edward I employs thirteen trebuchets at the Siege of Stirling.

turret from which archers could fire protected the front of the ram, and wicker shields also covered the sides and front. The machine was about 5 meters long and from 2 to 3 meters high. The battering pole hung like a pendulum from a rope attached to the roof. It had a metal blade at the end, which the crew could jam between bricks to pry them loose from the wall. The wheels provided mobility, but the ram was so heavy it was difficult to maneuver. Future Assyrian emperors sacrificed weight for mobility, but Tiglathpileser III (r. 745-727 B.C.E.) used lighter four-wheeled rams that were more maneuverable.

Siege towers were in use in both Egypt and Mesopotamia at least by the early second millennium B.C.E. They rested on wheels or rollers and could be pushed forward into position, providing a means of crossing the wall by dropping a boarding bridge from the tower to the wall. They also gave archers and slingers a better angle of fire to drive the defenders off the wall.

The construction of siege ramps goes back to the third millennium B.C.E. Siege ramps helped attackers cross walls and provided a means of bringing battering rams across moats, outer walls, or slopes at the base of the wall known as glacis. They allowed attackers to attack the wall toward the top, where it was thinner than at the base. Ancient Babylonian mathematics problems show that engineers could calculate how long it would take them to construct a ramp. If these problems reflect reality, the Babylonians could build a ramp to the top of a 22-meter wall in five days with 9,500 men working at the task.

By at least the early second millennium B.C.E. Mesopotamian engineers had developed the art of collapsing walls by sapping. Sapping involved either boring through a wall or undermining it. To undermine a wall, sappers dug a tunnel and then set the support beams on fire to collapse both the tunnel and the wall above. The depth of the tunnel had to be exactly right; if it was too shallow, the weight of the wall might collapse the tunnel on top of the sappers, if it was too deep, it would not collapse when the support beams were burned.

The Assyrians were the first to develop tactically integrated siege armies. Siege warfare was like a giant construction project. The construction of siege towers and siege ramps and the undermining of walls required large amounts of manpower and the ability to organize labor. Assyrian siege armies deployed a variety of skilled troops—sappers, archers, slingers, assault troops, and battering ram crews—and Assyrian commanders knew how to coordinate them toward a common tactical purpose.

DEVELOPMENT

The most important development in siege warfare was the invention of the catapult. The first catapult was probably invented by an unknown craftsman under the employ of the Greek tyrant Dionysius I of Syracuse (r. 405-367 B.C.E.). Dionysius had brought a large number of craftsmen from Sicily, Italy, and Greece to Syracuse to manufacture arms for his war against the Carthaginians in Sicily. One of them devised the *gastraphetes*, or belly bow, which is considered the first catapult. The archer could, by bracing the bow against his stomach, use both hands to pull back a slider with more strength than he could muster with one arm. A trigger, when pulled, then released the arrow. These catapults helped Dionysius take the city of Motya, a formidable Carthaginian stronghold on the west coast of Sicily, in 397 B.C.E. It is probable that winches were added to the *gastraphetes* early on to pull back the slider with mechanical power.

The next step in the development of catapults was the application of torsion power in which ropes were wound tightly with a windlass. The sudden release of the tension released a powerful burst of energy. Little is known about the origins of the torsion catapult. The Macedonian king Philip II (382-336 B.C.E.) used arrow-shooting torsion catapults that may have been invented by his engineers. Philip's son Alexander the Great (356-323 B.C.E.) deployed stone-throwing torsion catapults in the Siege of Halicarnassus in 334 B.C.E. Catapults more often strengthened the defense than the offense. For example, in the Roman Siege of Syracuse in 213 B.C.E. the Syracusans used catapults of various sizes to keep Roman ships away from their walls.

In Hellenistic times, siege warfare became more technical and the equipment more complicated. The Macedonian commander Demetrius Poliorcetes (336-283 B.C.E.) employed a huge siege tower called a *helepolis*, literally translated as "taker of cities," at the Siege of Rhodes in 305 B.C.E. Protected by iron plates, the tower rose nine stories and was large enough to carry catapults. Twelve hundred men pushed it forward on its eight iron-rimmed wheels. The *helepolis* provided cover for two gigantic rams. When the *helepolis* advanced, the Rhodians were able to knock loose some of its iron plating with stone-throwing catapults and set it on fire with flaming arrows shot from catapults. After repairs, Demetrius attacked again. The huge rams did batter down a part of the Rhodian wall, but Demetrius failed to take the city and, in the end, his acceptance of a negotiated end to the siege was a testimony to the difficulty of capturing a well-defended city.

Although the siege equipment of republican Rome was somewhat haphazard, siege machinery was a regular part of the Roman imperial army's equipment. Each legion was equipped with ten catapults as well as engineers and sappers. A Roman battering ram was a heavy beam with an iron head in the shape of a ram's head. The Romans used all sizes of catapults. In general Romans seemed to have called their smaller catapults *scorpions* and the larger ones *ballistae*, but there was no real consistency in the terminology. Later the word "onager" came into use to describe large catapults. "Onager" means "ass," and the catapults were so-called because of the way the

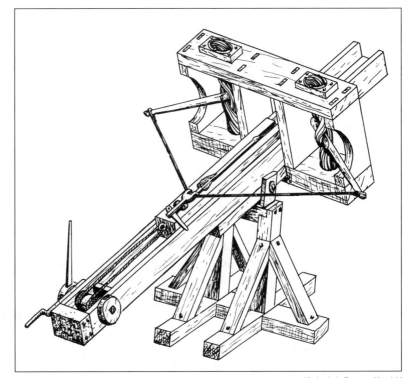

Kimberly L. Dawson Kurnizki

The Roman ballista, circa 50 B.C.E., a two-armed torsion weapon used to hurl large arrows or stones.

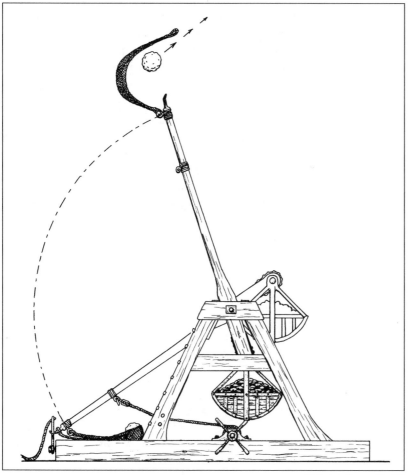

Kimberly L. Dawson Kurnizki

A drawing of a trebuchet, after Sir Ralph Payne-Gallwey (1842-1916),
A Summary of the History, Construction, and Effects in Warfare of
the Projectile-Throwing Engines of the Ancients *(1907). Such siege
weapons reappeared throughout the medieval period, as the building of
castles proliferated.*

shorter than the end throwing the missile. When released, the counterweight forced the short end down, lifting the long end with enough force to hurl a stone a considerable distance. The earliest trebuchets used men for counterweights. Several men would simultaneously pull on ropes with all their weight to force down the short end and propel the stone. By the early thirteenth century trebuchets with much heavier dead weights required fifty men to operate them and were capable of throwing a 250-pound stone about 150 meters. The biggest Roman catapults could throw a 70-pound stone about 225 meters.

Large trebuchets were expensive and relatively rare. In the Siege of Holyrood (1296) the English king Edward I (1239-1307) deployed three trebuchets, which threw 158 large stones in three days. In 1304 he used thirteen trebuchets to throw 600 stones during the Siege of Stirling.

Despite the impressive array of siege machinery, the reduction of powerfully fortified cities remained difficult throughout ancient and medieval times. Sieges were often time-consuming and expensive. Well-defended, well-provisioned cities could hold out for months or even years. Ancient armies fed themselves by foraging, and when they stopped moving, they soon exhausted food supplies in their immediate area, presenting siege commanders with difficult logistical problems. Siege armies labored in unhealthy circumstances. The disposal of human and animal waste was difficult. Disease was a major killer.

Against this background, psychological warfare was of great importance. Siege commanders tried to

rear kicked up, like that of a donkey, when they were fired. Ancient historian Flavius Josephus (c. 37-c. 100 C.E.) claimed that Roman catapults were capable of throwing 55-pound stones to a distance of 400 yards at the Siege of Jerusalem in 70 C.E., although he probably exaggerated their range.

Medieval siege warfare evolved little from that of ancient times. The outstanding medieval innovation was the trebuchet, a stone-throwing catapult powered by a counterweight. The throwing arm rested on a pivot so that the end with the counterweight was intimidate cities into surrendering by offering relatively lenient terms but threatening dire consequences if resisted. The common practices of sacking, rape, transportation, enslavement, and massacre added credibility to the threats.

Ruse and treachery were the preferred means of taking a city. The legend of the Trojan horse reflected the reality that often the only way to gain entry to a city was by trickery. The ancient historian Herodotus (c. 484-424 B.C.E.) tells the story of Zopyrus, a fanatically loyal Persian soldier who mutilated himself so that he could pose as an aggrieved deserter in order to gain entry to Babylon, which was under siege by the Persian emperor Darius (550-486 B.C.E.). Once in the city, Zopyrus opened the gate to the Persians.

Sieges placed cities under great stress, and siege commanders attempted to exploit any social or political fault lines in the hope that traitors would betray the city. This ploy was especially useful in Greek siege warfare. During the Peloponnesian War (431-404 B.C.E.), more cities fell by betrayal than by any other means.

The introduction of gunpowder in the fourteenth century brought an end to a long epoch in siege warfare, which had changed little since ancient times. By the fifteenth century cannon were a regular part of siege warfare for which stone walls were no match. Thus the ancient art of fortification was revolutionized and, with it, the art of siegecraft.

BOOKS AND ARTICLES

Bradbury, Jim. *The Medieval Siege*. Woodbridge, England: Boydell Press, 1992.

Kern, Paul Bentley. *Ancient Siege Warfare*. Bloomington: Indiana University Press, 1999.

Marsden, E. W. *Greek and Roman Artillery*. Oxford, England: Clarendon Press, 1969.

Yadin, Yigael. *The Art of Warfare in Biblical Lands in the Light of Archeological Discovery*. London: McGraw-Hill, 1963.

Paul Bentley Kern

ARMIES AND INFANTRY
DATES: C. 2500 B.C.E.-1400 C.E.

NATURE AND USE

Infantry is that part or those parts of an army trained and organized to fight on foot with handheld weapons. Foot soldiers have formed the largest component of most armies throughout history. Infantry forces are attested in ancient Mesopotamia, Egypt, Assyria, Greece, Rome, and China, where they were used both in battle and in assaulting and defending fortified positions.

Infantry forces were termed either "light" or "heavy," according to the weapons carried and armor worn by individual foot soldiers. Light infantrymen were equipped with little if any armor, and they used missile weapons such as javelins, bows, and slings to engage the enemy from a distance. Because of their greater mobility, light infantry units were effective in rugged terrain and using guerrilla tactics, but lightly armed soldiers could also be deployed as skirmishers fighting in front of or along the flanks of heavy infantry. Heavy infantrymen usually wore heavy defensive armor, carried weapons suited for close combat, such as swords and spears, and fought in dense, compact units. They were most effective in pitched battles fought on open plains.

In loosely organized armies foot soldiers often relied more on numerical superiority than on tactical maneuvering, achieving victory by simply overwhelming enemy forces. Infantrymen were most effective, however, when deployed in organized formations. The phalanx and the legion are the best known formations from ancient and medieval times. The phalanx was a square or rectangular formation in which foot soldiers stood shoulder to shoulder in files several ranks deep. When the soldiers of the front line locked their shields together, they presented an impenetrable wall capable of withstanding charges by chariots, cavalry, and even other infantry. On the attack members of a phalanx wielded either thrusting spears or pikes, and a well-disciplined phalanx could overrun many types of opposition. The phalanx was utilized with great success in antiquity by the ancient Greek city-states and the Macedonian Empire. In the fourteenth and fifteenth centuries Swiss pikemen readopted the phalanx to defeat mounted knights.

The legion was the basic infantry formation of the Roman army. Its size varied over time, but during the third and second centuries B.C.E. it consisted of 4,000 to 5,000 men, mostly heavy infantry. Legionaries wore a helmet and carried a tall body shield called the *scutum*. They carried a javelin (*pilum*) and sword (*gladius*) as close-combat weapons. Unlike the phalanx, the legion did not fight in a single massed formation. Each legion was subdivided into several smaller tactical units usually deployed in three lines that attacked in successive waves. Mobile and flexible, the Roman legion proved to be the preeminent infantry force of the ancient world.

DEVELOPMENT

Written records of battles from ancient Egypt and the kingdoms of the Middle East frequently mention infantry, but it is difficult to determine what role foot soldiers played and how important they were in combat. The Sumerian Stele of the Vultures, dating from about 2500 B.C.E., depicts spearmen in a phalanx-like formation, but during the second millennium B.C.E. infantry may have fought primarily as skirmishers in support of chariots. One theory holds that the foot soldiers rose in prominence only around 1200 B.C.E., when "barbarian" tribes, fighting on foot and armed with javelins and long swords, overran many of the kingdoms of the ancient Middle East. A similar transition away from chariot warfare to infantry began to occur in China in the fifth century B.C.E.

The Assyrians organized their infantry into specialized units in the early first millennium B.C.E., but the armies of the ancient Greek city-states were the first to rely almost exclusively on soldiers fighting on foot. Around 700 B.C.E. they began to deploy infantrymen called hoplites in densely packed phalanxes. Each hoplite wore a bronze helmet, corselet, and greaves, or shin guards. He carried a circular shield for protection and used a thrusting spear as his primary weapon. The phalanx was suited to the small plains of Greece, and in battle it attacked in tight formation. As they neared the enemy, hoplites in the front ranks of the phalanx raised their shields and spears and jabbed at their opponents, while those in the rear pushed on the backs of those ahead of them. Hoplite battles resembled shoving matches, as a phalanx sought to overwhelm its opponent by its momentum. The success of the phalanx ultimately depended on the cohesion of its members.

The superiority of the Greek hoplite army was demonstrated first at the Battle of Marathon (490 B.C.E.), where the Athenian hoplite phalanx charged and defeated a numerically superior but more lightly armed Persian force. A second Persian campaign against Greece met a similar fate during the Greco-Persian Wars (499-448 B.C.E.). Spartan hoplites held the narrow pass of Thermopylae (480 B.C.E.) for several days against vastly superior Persian numbers, and at Plataea (479 B.C.E.) a hoplite army drawn from Sparta, Athens, and other Greek city-states defeated the Persians decisively. Greek hoplites remained the elite warriors of the Mediterranean world for nearly a century and a half.

The prominence of infantry battle in Greek warfare declined somewhat during the Peloponnesian Wars (431-404 B.C.E.), which pitted the naval strength of Athens against the land-based power of Sparta. Few infantry battles were fought, and the war was ultimately decided at sea. Decisive hoplite battles did take place during the fourth century B.C.E., but new developments changed the face of Greek warfare. At Lechaeum (390 B.C.E.), on the Gulf of Corinth, a force of peltasts, light infantry armed with javelins, decimated a Spartan regiment and illustrated the vulnerability of heavy infantry to light-armed troops. At

Kimberly L. Dawson Kurnizki

Greek hoplite, circa 700 B.C.E., wearing a bronze helmet, corselet, and shin guards, and carrying a circular shield and a thrusting spear.

Leuctra (371 B.C.E.) the Theban commander Epaminondas (c. 410-362 B.C.E.) employed novel tactics to defeat the Spartan phalanx. Epaminondas strengthened the left wing of the Theban phalanx to a depth of fifty men and charged the Spartans at an oblique angle. The weight of the Theban left flank ripped through the Spartan line, and the supremacy of the Spartan hoplite was ended forever.

More significant were the innovations of Philip II of Macedon (382-336 B.C.E.), who reformed the Macedonian army, including its infantry. Philip increased the depth of the Macedonian phalanx and reduced the size of the shield carried by its members. He also armed his infantry with sarissas, pikes nearly 15 feet in length and, unlike the spears of the Greek hoplites, wielded with two hands. At Chaeronea (338 B.C.E.) Philip combined the new Macedonian phalanx with his cavalry to rout a hoplite army of Thebans and Athenians. Philip's son, Alexander the Great (356-323 B.C.E.), employed similar combinations of infantry and cavalry charges at Granicus (334 B.C.E.), Issus (333 B.C.E.), and Gaugamela (331 B.C.E.) to break the Persian army and conquer the Persian Empire. The size of the Macedonian phalanx grew in the armies of the Hellenistic kingdoms

founded after Alexander's death, but infantry was increasingly used in conjunction with other forces, including chariots and elephants.

As the Greeks and Macedonians employed phalanx tactics, the Romans developed a style of infantry warfare based on the legion. The legion evolved over the course of the Roman conquest of Italy in the fifth and fourth centuries B.C.E. Its heavy infantrymen were deployed in three lines, each made up of ten units called maniples. In battle the first line of maniples, the *hastati*, advanced first. When they neared the enemy they released their javelins and then drew their swords and charged, seeking to take advantage of the confusion caused by their missiles. If the *hastati* failed to defeat the enemy, they were joined by the second line of maniples, the *principes*, who used similar tactics. The third line of maniples, the *triarii*, were armed as spearmen, and they engaged only when the situation became critical.

With their legionary tactics, the Romans overcame the peoples of Italy and the western Mediterranean. Roman legions, however, were not invincible, and the Roman infantry met defeat in battles against Pyrrhus and in the Second Punic War (219-202 B.C.E.) against the Carthaginian general Hannibal

TURNING POINTS

c. 1200 B.C.E.	The use of the chariot in warfare declines and foot soldiers increasingly come into use, as "barbarian" tribes, fighting on foot and armed with javelins and long swords, overrun many ancient Middle Eastern kingdoms.
c. 700 B.C.E.	Tight-formation hoplite tactics, well-suited to the small plains of the ancient Greek city-states, are first introduced in Greece.
c. 350 B.C.E.	Philip II of Macedon develops the Macedonian phalanx and adopts the use of the sarissa, a pike of nearly 15 feet in length wielded with two hands.
58-45 B.C.E.	Julius Caesar employs independently operating cohorts in the Gallic Wars and the Roman Civil Wars against Pompey.
3d-4th cent. C.E.	Despite the increasing role of cavalry due to barbarian influence, infantry remains the dominant component of the Roman legions.
476	The Sack of Rome by barbarians brings about an "age of cavalry," during which foot soldiers play a diminished role in warfare.
1298	The English army uses the longbow to great effect against the Scots at Falkirk.
14th cent.	An "infantry revolution" spurred by the greater use of the pike and bow, takes place in Europe.
1315	Swiss pikemen begin a string of victories against mounted knights by defeating the Austrians at Morgarten.

(247-182 B.C.E.). The Romans were able to draw on enormous reserves of manpower to replenish their losses, and they learned from their defeats. They lost battles but won wars. In the second century B.C.E. the experience gained by decades of fighting in Italy helped Roman infantrymen defeat the Macedonian phalanx in the Second and Third Macedonian-Roman Wars (200-196 B.C.E., 172-167 B.C.E.). Thus, although the Macedonian phalanx initially carried all before it at the Battle of Pydna (168 B.C.E.), it lost cohesion as it advanced, allowing Roman legionaries to pour into gaps in its line and cut down the Macedonians at close range with their swords.

The Roman legion underwent further reforms during the second century B.C.E., and by the time of the general Gaius Marius (157-86 B.C.E.) ten cohorts had replaced the thirty maniples as the legion's tactical units. With the change to cohorts the distinctions between *hastati*, *principes*, and *triarii* disappeared, so that all legionaries were armed and fought in the same fashion. The legion continued to deploy for battle in three lines, with four cohorts in the first line and three cohorts in the second and third, but this arrangement could be varied, and unlike maniples, individual cohorts could operate independently. Julius Caesar (100-44 B.C.E.) employed cohorts very effectively in the Gallic Wars (58-52 B.C.E.) and in the Roman Civil Wars against Pompey (49-45 B.C.E.).

Under the Roman Republic, the infantry of Rome's legions was an offensive force. With the establishment of the Empire, Roman infantry forces acquired a defensive role. Rome's legions manned the frontiers of the Roman Empire and engaged in few pitched battles in the first few centuries C.E. The size of the legion decreased, and legionaries discarded their heavy armor and adopted missile weapons. Cavalry acquired a more important role in Rome's armies as a result of barbarian incursions across the Empire's borders during the third and fourth centuries C.E. Infantry remained the dominant component of the legion into the fourth and fifth centuries C.E., and in pitched battle Roman foot soldiers were vastly superior to their barbarian counterparts, as demonstrated in 357 C.E., for example, at Strasbourg, then called Argentoratum. Even the defeat of the Roman army at Adrianople (378 C.E.) was due largely to the

flight of the Roman cavalry, not to the weakness of its infantry. After that point, however, foot soldiers became increasingly dependent on mounted soldiers, and cavalry gradually assumed a more decisive role.

The millennium following the fall of the Roman Empire is sometimes labeled an age of cavalry. Although cavalry charges often determined the outcome of battle, it would be a mistake to discount altogether the importance of foot soldiers in this period. Frankish armies fought on foot well into the time of Charlemagne (742-814 C.E.), and Anglo-Saxon armies in England relied on foot soldiers up until the Battle of Hastings (1066 C.E.). Well-disciplined infantry could also withstand a charge of mounted knights, as did the Milanese at Legnano (1176 C.E.). Something of an infantry revolution, however, took place in the fourteenth century, spurred in part by the greater use of the pike and bow. At Courtrai (1302 C.E.) Flemish infantry, armed with pikes, withstood a charge of French cavalry and then slaughtered the knights who had fallen from their mounts. In 1314 English cavalry suffered a similar fate against the Scottish pikemen at Bannockburn. Use of the crossbow, capable of piercing the armor of a mounted knight, had also begun to challenge the supremacy of cavalry during the twelfth century, but the longbow proved more effective in terms of cost, rate of fire, range, and accuracy. By the late thirteenth century a majority of English foot soldiers carried the longbow, and their large numbers proved decisive against the Scots at Falkirk (1298), and later in the Hundred Years' War (1337-1453) against the French at Crécy (1346), Poitiers (1356), and Agincourt (1415).

The most significant infantry innovation was the development of the Swiss phalanx. Swiss infantrymen wore little armor and carried no shields, but they carried either a pike 18 feet in length or a halberd, both of which were wielded with deadly effect. After infantrymen in the outer ranks of the phalanx delivered the initial blows with their pikes, soldiers armed with halberds emerged from the phalanx and engaged enemy cavalry and foot soldiers at close quarters. When harassed on all sides by cavalry, the Swiss phalanx could also adopt a "hedgehog" formation, with pikes turned outward in all directions. A string of Swiss victories over mounted knights began early in the fourteenth century at Morgarten (1315) and by the end of the fifteenth century, European monarchs were either recruiting Swiss infantrymen into their armies or modeling their own infantry units after the Swiss. Infantry had again come to dominate Western warfare.

BOOKS AND ARTICLES

DeVries, Kelly. *Infantry Warfare in the Early Fourteenth Century: Discipline, Tactics, and Technology.* Woodbridge, England: Boydell Press, 1996.

Drews, Robert. *The End of the Bronze Age: Changes in Warfare and the Catastrophe Circa 1200 B.C.* Princeton, N.J.: Princeton University Press, 1993.

Hanson, Victor. *The Western Way of War: Infantry Battle in Classical Greece.* 2d ed. Berkeley: University of California Press, 2000.

FILMS AND OTHER MEDIA

Weapons at War: Infantry. Documentary. History Channel, 1992.

James P. Sickinger

CAVALRY

DATES: TO C. 1500 C.E.

NATURE AND USE

Historically, cavalries were military forces that traveled and fought on horseback, unlike mounted infantrymen, who traveled on horseback but fought on foot, and charioteers, who fought from carts pulled by horses. Cavalry was less expensive and more mobile than was chariotry and could move two to three times faster than could infantry, covering at least 30 to 40 miles a day for an indefinite period. The physically and psychologically imposing combination of man and horse made resistance difficult for foot soldiers.

Cavalry in antiquity fell into two basic categories: light cavalry, unarmored or lightly armored men on small, swift ponies or horses, and heavy cavalry, moderately or heavily armored men on large, sometimes armored, horses. The principal cavalry weapons were the composite bow, javelin, and lance. Almost every cavalryman used at least one of these weapons; light cavalrymen emphasized the bow or javelin and heavy cavalry the lance. However, many other combinations of weapons were used. On the march, light cavalry would scout ahead, protect the flanks and rear of their army, and raid enemy forces. In camp, at sieges, or on garrison duty, cavalry would patrol and undertake escort duties. In battle, light cavalry would ride at the enemy, fire missiles, and then gallop out of the range of return fire. Skilled horse archers could turn in their saddles and fire while withdrawing, a maneuver known as the Parthian shot, for the Parthians (third century B.C.E.), a nomad steppe people who perfected the technique. Heavy cavalry would mass and charge enemy forces, hoping to rout them. If this happened, the light cavalry would pursue. If things went badly, the light cavalry would instead try to cover the retreat of friendly forces. Finally, cavalry and mounted infantry used the horse's high march rate to perform raids. After short-range raids, the raiders quickly returned to the safety of their border forts. In long-distance raids, traversing hundreds of miles of enemy territory, the raiders used speed and unexpected movements to avoid interception.

The first known cavalry appeared in the Near East, around 1200 B.C.E., after the collapse of the Bronze Age civilizations there. Armies dominated by cavalry were fielded by Eurasian steppe nomad groups, such as the Cimmerians, Scythians, Sarmatians, Huns, Avars, Turks, and Mongols. Combined forces of cavalry and infantry were fielded by the agricultural peoples of Europe, Asia, and North Africa, notably the Assyrians, Achaemenid Persians, Greeks, Macedonians, Celts, Spaniards, Numidians, Carthaginians, Romans, Chinese, and Indians. Cavalry enjoyed a dominant position in the armies of many peoples, beginning with the Parthians and Sassanian Persians and continuing with the Byzantines, Arabs, Russians, and medieval Europeans.

DEVELOPMENT

The horse was first domesticated and ridden six thousand years ago by the Sredni Stog culture of the North Pontic region in the modern Ukraine. The development of horseback riding and, several centuries later, the wheeled cart allowed nomads to exploit the resources of the prairie steppe that runs from Hungary past the Ural and Altai Shan Mountains of Central Asia to Mongolia and Manchuria in the east. Because chariotry preceded cavalry everywhere in the Bronze Age, the first mounted warriors probably fought dismounted, adopting the chariot because it allowed them to fight on foot, as they were accustomed, and leaving control of the horses to the charioteers. Armed riders are depicted in late Bronze Age (c. 1550-1200 B.C.E.) Greek, Egyptian, and Near

Eastern art, but they appear sitting "donkey seat," on the animal's rump, not up on its shoulders: an inefficient position that is also harmful to the horse. It is likely such riders were only scouts or messengers, armed for self-defense.

After the collapse of the Greek and Near Eastern Bronze Age civilizations (around 1200 B.C.E.), cavalry gradually began to replace chariotry. The process is clearly depicted in reliefs of the Neo-Assyrian Empire (911-612 B.C.E.). The earliest cavalrymen, of the ninth century B.C.E., unarmored and still sitting donkey seat, were chariot riders on horseback. The "chariot warrior" wielded a bow, and the accompanying "charioteer" managed the reins of both his own and the bowman's horses and carried a shield and spear for self-defense. By the mid-eighth century B.C.E., each horseman controlled his own mount, sat on the horse's withers, used lances as well as bows, and, in some cases, wore lamellar corselets as body armor. By the end of the eighth century B.C.E.,

corseleted cavalrymen equipped with both bows and lances appeared, supported by horse archers. Half a century later, horses were outfitted with cloth armor similar to that of chariot horses.

CAVALRY ACCOUTREMENTS

Like most cultures in and after the ninth century B.C.E., the Sredni Stog culture managed its horses by directly controlling their heads, using reins connected to bits held in place in the horses' mouths by antler cheekpieces attached to bridles. Even this was not always necessary; the Numidians, raised on horseback, controlled their small, swift, and obedient Libyan steeds with only a stick or cord around the neck. Throughout the first millennium B.C.E., most horsemen rode either bareback or seated upon a saddle cloth. The first saddles, consisting of a pad with two cushions resting on either side of the horse's spine and held on by a girth, appeared around 400 B.C.E., used by nomads in the Altai Shan Mountains

Kimberly L. Dawson Kurnizki

A Parthian horse archer of the third century B.C.E. practicing the Parthian shot, a maneuver in which the rider turns in his saddle and fires while withdrawing.

of central Asia. It took five centuries for saddles to become commonplace. Whips or goads were favored by Asian horsemen, but spurs were used in Greece during the fifth century B.C.E. and in Celtic lands soon afterward.

To protect horses' hooves from the wet conditions of the northwestern European climate, the Celts began making horseshoes. The earliest horseshoes were made in Gaul between 50 B.C.E. and 50 C.E., and horseshoes also enjoyed some popularity in Roman Britain. Elsewhere in the Roman Empire, temporary "hipposandals" of woven grass or leather and metal predominated. Horseshoes did not come into general use until after 400 C.E.

The earliest known stirrups, made of leather straps or wood, or featuring metal hooks, appear in Scythian contexts in the fourth century B.C.E. and in India around the end of the first millennium B.C.E. Although stirrups may have been a necessity for the heaviest cavalry forces, they were rarely depicted in art of the period, perhaps because men reared in the saddle found the use of stirrups embarrassing. Only in fourth century C.E. China was the full metal stirrup adopted; by the seventh century C.E. it had made its way west with the Avars. Although none of the aforementioned inventions can be demonstrated clearly to have had a decisive impact upon cavalry operations during the first millennium C.E., they must have made the creation of mounted forces easier for peoples unaccustomed to riding, such as the Chinese and the Franks.

By around 1100 C.E., Western European knights had discovered the use of the couched lance. Held onto the horse by a high saddle and stirrups, the knight could hold the lance firmly under his arm, adding far more force to the blow than any thrust by hand could do. However, because the massed charge of Western European knights had long been considered irresistible by their Byzantine and Arab foes, the couched lance would seem to be only a tactical refinement, not a decisive advance.

TURNING POINTS

c. 4000 B.C.E.	Horses are first domesticated and ridden by people of the Sredni Stog culture.
c. 900 B.C.E.	Cavalry begins to compete with chariotry as a method of warfare in the Neo-Assyrian Empire.
c. 4th cent. B.C.E.	Earliest known stirrups, made from leather or wood, are used by the Scyths.
c. 3d cent. B.C.E.	The Parthians, a steppe nomad people, perfect the Parthian shot, fired backward from the saddle while in retreat.
333 B.C.E.	Alexander the Great uses combined infantry and cavalry forces to route the Persian cavalry at the Battle of Issus.
53 B.C.E.	Parthian horsemen devastate the Roman legions at the Battle of Carrhae.
50 B.C.E.-50 C.E.	The earliest horseshoes are made in Gaul.
400	Horseshoes come into general use throughout Europe.
1100	European knights adopt the use of the couched lance, which provides more force than previous hand-thrust weapons.
1260	Mongol warriors are defeated at the Battle of Ain Jalut by Mamlūk slave cavalry, trained by the Egyptians to steppe nomad levels.

CAVALRY DEVELOPMENT IN CIVILIZED NATIONS

There were two general lines of development in cavalry: that of the civilized nations of the Mediterranean and that of the steppe nomads and those who imitated them. For the first group, the problem was in integrating cavalry into armies that were composed predominantly of infantry. The Achaemenid Persians, who reigned from 560 to 330 B.C.E., followed the Assyrians' example and used light foot archers and spearmen with missile-armed cavalry that did not try to charge massed infantry forces. This combination worked well in the Near East but failed in offensives against the Greeks and the steppe nomads.

The Greeks themselves came to realize by the fourth century B.C.E. the value in the coordinated use of heavy and light infantry and cavalry together.

Macedonian conqueror Alexander the Great (356-323 B.C.E.) used this strategy in the eventual defeat of the Achaemenid Persians. Alexander's heavy, pike-armed infantry provided a solid base, and the light infantry provided missile fire wherever needed. Thessalian light cavalry, armed with javelins, guarded his left flank, and other light cavalry were positioned on the far right flank. The elite Companion heavy lancers and supporting *hypaspist* infantry massed farther in on the right. At both Issus (333 B.C.E.) and Gaugamela (331 B.C.E.), after the other units had drawn out the enemy, the Companions charged into the Persian left flank cavalry, ruptured the enemy line, and then rallied and charged into the enemy flanks and rear, achieving the victory in both battles.

Alexander's "combined arms" approach was adopted by the Carthaginians and, eventually, by the Romans as well, after the Carthaginian general Hannibal (247-182 B.C.E.) had demonstrated its effectiveness. Although the Romans experimented with heavy cavalry, they generally preferred light cavalry, relying upon their superb legion infantry for shock action.

CAVALRY DEVELOPMENT AMONG STEPPE NOMADS

The second main line of cavalry development occurred among the steppe nomad peoples, who enjoyed far more pasturage than did the peoples of Western Europe, the Mediterranean region, and China. Because the steppe nomads spent so much time on horseback, their armies were dominated by cavalry, a tactical development imitated by Iranian monarchies and Chinese dynasties. The Cimmerians, a people who inhabited southern Russia and were driven to Turkey by the Scythians in the eighth century B.C.E., were the earliest known steppe nomad horse archers. As evidenced by later steppe nomad tactics, these people probably stressed hit-and-run attacks from front, flanks, and rear by small, scattered bodies of horse, using feigned retreats and ambushes to draw out and destroy enemy forces. As the Cimmerians passed over the Caucasus in the eighth century B.C.E., they wrecked kingdoms throughout Anatolia before finally being destroyed. Their Scythian and Sarmatian successors fielded both light-armed horse archers and heavy cavalry, equipped with lances and armor covering man and, often, horse as well. Such heavy cavalrymen, called *cataphracts* by the Greeks, would charge and rout enemy forces already weakened by the horse archers' attacks. The Parthians, a steppe people who seized Persia from the Macedonians, exploited the matchless advantages of Iran's wide pasturelands and unique Nisaean breed of horse—larger and better bred to carry weight than most steppe or western animals—to field numerous *cataphract* and horse archer units. The effectiveness of the Parthian force was displayed in 53 B.C.E., when a Roman army under Marcus Licinius Crassus (115-53 B.C.E.) invaded Parthian territory at Carrhae. Commanded by a noble known as Surenas, the Parthians lured Crassus into open desert terrain, where Parthian horse archers shot his infantry to pieces. When Crassus's Gallic horses charged to drive them off, the *cataphracts* countercharged and crushed them. The Roman army was destroyed, and Crassus killed.

THE RISE AND FALL OF CAVALRY

Parthia, not Rome, influenced the development of cavalry over the next millennium. In the late Roman Empire and its Byzantine successor in the East, the balance tilted in favor of the horse, with infantry forming a defensive body in battle and serving chiefly as a refuge for the cavalry. Others who adopted this pattern were the Indians; the Chinese; the Arabs, who quickly moved from camels to horses; and, more gradually, the European peoples as well. Whether the adoption of saddle and stirrup drove this development, or was driven by it, is unclear. Heavy cavalry service eventually became a justification for aristocratic political power and encouraged cavalry's growing predominance. However, large infantry forces were still needed, if only for siege warfare. Thus, aside from cavalry raids such as the long-distance *chevauchées* of the Hundred Years' War (1337-1453 C.E.), offensive operations necessarily tied cavalry to an infantry pace. The Mongols under Genghis Khan (died 1227 C.E.) solved this problem: Their armies of highly trained, fast-moving horse archers and *cataphract* lancers simply rounded up local peasants by the thousands and forced them to perform siege warfare duties. The epitome of steppe nomad armies, the Mongols were hindered only by environmental factors and internal political problems until they suffered their first defeat in 1260 C.E. at Ain Jalut, Israel, at the hands of the Mamlūks, Egyptian slave cavalry, trained to steppe nomad levels. Toward 1500 C.E., infantrymen began to return to prominence in Europe; notable examples are the English long-bowmen, Swiss pikemen, and Hussite *Wagenburg* soldiers. The development of gunpowder artillery and firearms ultimately spelled the end of cavalry dominance in Europe and, eventually, everywhere that European armies marched.

BOOKS AND ARTICLES

DeVries, Kelly. *Medieval Military Technology.* Lewiston, N.Y.: Broadview Press, 1992.

Ellis, John. *Cavalry: The History of Mounted Warfare.* New York: G. P. Putnam's Sons, 1978.

Hyland, Ann. *Equus: The Horse in the Roman World.* New Haven, Conn.: Yale University Press, 1990.

_____. *The Warhorse, 1250-1600.* Stroud, Gloucestershire, England: Sutton, 1998.

O'Connell, R. L. *Ride of the Second Horseman: The Birth and Death of War.* Oxford, England: Oxford University Press, 1995.

Scott M. Rusch

Warships and Naval Warfare

Dates: To c. 1200 c.e.

Nature and Use

From ancient times, the principal warship of the Mediterranean Sea was the oared galley, which was used to ram and sink opposing ships. The galley typically had fore and aft decked platforms with a lower, usually open, area for the rowers. The galley was built using a "shell-first" construction, in which the planks of the galley's hull were edge joined with mortise-and-tenon joints, to which a system of frames was later inserted. Joints typically were made out of oak for strength, and the other sections were constructed from lighter woods, such as pine or fir, for speed. From the bow of the vessel at its waterline projected a sharp beak, or ram, usually made of bronze, which was used to puncture the sides of opposing ships and cause them to sink.

Control of the sea and protection of merchant shipping were important for many Mediterranean civilizations. Although the Phoenicians and Etruscans previously had developed navies to defend their trading interests, the Greek city-state of Athens was the first to actively use its navy in efforts toward imperial expansion. Even a largely land-based power such as Rome was eventually forced to develop a navy to deal with naval threats such as the Carthaginians and the Vandals.

The oared galley also predominated in the Atlantic Ocean for many centuries. Raiders such as the Vikings used their oared galleys, known as longships, to make raids along the coast of Europe. In response to the more strenuous maritime conditions along the

A Greek trireme, which employed three banks of rowers to achieve the superior speed, handling, and power that enabled Athens's growth as an imperial power in the mid-fifth century B.C.E.

coast of northern Europe, these vessels did not use mortise-and-tenon joints, but instead were clinker-built. Clinker-built construction, sometimes called clench-built construction, is a method of shipbuilding in which overlapping planks are fastened to one another using wooden pins, called treenails, or iron clench nails. Next, a form of caulking, consisting of animal hair dipped in pitch to prevent leaking, is placed in the seams between the planks.

The oared galley remained the dominant warship until the development of the cog in the thirteenth century C.E. The cog was a large merchant vessel associated with the development of the Hanseatic League, a commercial union of German, Dutch, and Flemish towns. It had very high sides and a flat bottom and was propelled by a single square sail. Although the cog was a poor sailer, its high sides offered protection against smaller oared vessels, such as the Viking longships. The addition of fighting castles at the bow and stern allowed the vessel to be used to fight wars and blockade towns. The cog was soon replaced, however, by the carrack, a sailing ship with multiple masts and a combination of square and lateen, or tri-angular, sails. The carrack was a very efficient sailing vessel that became popular in both the Atlantic and the Mediterranean. After cannons were added to the carrack, many Western European countries utilized the vessel to become worldwide naval powers.

DEVELOPMENT

The Greek civilization was one of the first to develop naval power. The first Greek warships, consisting of a single level of oarsmen with one rower per oar, were called *triacontors* and *pentecontors* (thirty- and fifty-oared ships). By the end of the eighth century B.C.E., a second level of rowers was added, in an effort to improve the vessel's speed and to increase the force of the collision between the vessel's ram and the opposing ship. After the addition of a third row of oarsmen in the late seventh century B.C.E., the resulting vessel was known as a trireme. According to the Greek historian Thucydides (c. 459-c. 402 B.C.E.), the trireme was invented by a Corinthian named Ameinocles. However, other ancient sources credit the Sidonians

Kimberly L. Dawson Kurnizki

with the innovation. Because only the wealthiest cities could afford to build and maintain a trireme, these vessels were not used extensively for several centuries, after which the Phoenicians and Egyptians began to incorporate triremes into their fleets. It was during Athens's growth as an imperial power in the mid-fifth century B.C.E. that the superior speed, handling, and power of the trireme firmly established its position as the premier warship.

The design of the trireme slowly evolved during the Hellenistic Age into that of a much larger and bulkier vessel. To increase the ship's speed and power, extra men were added to each bank of oars, leading to quadriremes and quinqueremes. A quadrireme was not a vessel with four banks of oars, as the prefix "quad-" suggests, but rather it was a trireme with a top row of oars with two oarsmen to each oar and two lower rows of oars, each manipulated by one man. A quinquereme, also known as a *pentereis*, or a "five," had two rows of oars manned by two men and one row manned by one. The new configuration of oars and oarsmen brought about several changes in the design of the vessel's hull, among which was its increased breadth. The longer oar length changed the stroke of the oarsmen. Because a seated stroke did not allow the full power of the oar to be utilized, a full stroke had to be performed from a standing position by the man on the inside end, as the oar rose and fell during the course of one revolution. More room between decks was also needed, as the men were standing instead of sitting. These adjustments led to larger and larger ships.

CONSTRUCTION OF LARGE SHIPS

Among the most important reasons for the construction of larger ships were technological advances in weaponry. The torsion catapult had been invented around 400 B.C.E. but did not play an important role until the campaigns of Alexander the Great (356-323 B.C.E.). A logical next step was the mounting of catapults on board galleys to use against other ships, as seen in the famous battle for Cyprus between Demetrius Poliorcetes (336-283 B.C.E.) and Ptolemy in 306 B.C.E. To mount the catapult, a larger ship and a sturdier deck, to absorb the weapon's recoil, were needed. Because smaller ramming ships were easy prey for long-range weapons, warships were built larger to offer protection from aerial bombardment. As the ships became larger, however, their mobility was retarded. This gigantism saw the construction of "sixteens," "twenties," "thirties," and culminated in the huge ship constructed by Ptolemy IV around 200 B.C.E., which was referred to in the ancient literature as a "forty."

When Demetrius Poliorcetes attacked Rhodes in 305 B.C.E., he was forced to experiment with new naval tactics, in response to the strength of the city's defenses. To attack the harbor, he built a floating siege machine that was mounted on the hulls of two cargo ships. He constructed four towers, or "penthouses," for use against the harbor's fortifications. These penthouses were taller than the city's harbor towers and permitted arrows and javelins to be directed at the defenders manning the harbor towers. Demetrius Poliorcetes also planked over several of his

TURNING POINTS

c. late 7th cent. B.C.E.	The Greeks develop the trireme, a large ship powered by three rows of oarsmen.
c. mid-5th cent. B.C.E.	Athens establishes itself as a major naval power in the Mediterranean.
c. 4th cent. B.C.E.	Onboard catapults are added to ships, effectively rendering them as floating siege engines.
c. 3d cent. B.C.E.	Romans utilize the *corvus*, a nautical grappling hook, allowing sailors to board and capture opposing vessels.
674-678 C.E.	Greek fire, a flammable liquid, is used by the Byzantines against Arab ships during the Siege of Constantinople.
mid-13th cent.	The cog, with high sides that offer protection against other vessels, is developed in Northern Europe.
mid-14th cent.	The carrack, an efficient sailing ship with multiple masts, becomes popular in Atlantic and Mediterranean waters.

lighter boats, into which he placed archers and catapults, who fired through ports that could be opened and closed.

During the First Punic War (264-241 B.C.E.) Rome found that, despite the strength of its army, its Carthaginian opponent was a superior naval power. In response, the Romans utilized the *corvus*, or raven, a nautical grappling hook. This device was simply a long, spiked gangplank mounted on the bow of a Roman warship and dropped onto the deck of a Carthaginian ship, securing the two ships together and allowing a Roman contingent to board and capture the opposing vessel.

After its final defeat of Carthage in the second century B.C.E, the Roman navy began a slow decline in strength. The only real need for a continued naval presence was the protection of merchant ships, especially the annual grain ships coming from Egypt, from piracy. The large quadremes and quinqueremes of the Hellenistic Age were phased out, and smaller, faster ships better able to combat the pirates were increasingly produced. New vessels, such as the *liburnian* and the *dromon*, were introduced into the Imperial fleet and soon replaced the trireme as the main warship of the Roman navy.

THE *DROMON*

The *dromon* was built for a specific purpose: to combat a different type of enemy than had the trireme, which was typically used against other triremes in pitched naval contests. During the years of the Roman Empire, vessels became smaller and faster. A military vessel was needed that could catch these smaller vessels and still be powerful enough to fight in large-scale naval battles against organized opponents. The *dromon*, with its various capabilities, was the solution. It was fast—in fact, its name means "runner" in Greek—yet it was still large enough to carry the weapons required during large naval conflicts.

North Wind Picture Archives

An engine for launching Greek fire, a flammable liquid that would burn even in water and was used to great effect by the Byzantines during the first Arab siege of Constantinople (674-678 C.E.).

Perhaps the best-known offensive weapon of the Byzantine fleet was "Greek fire," invented by a Syrian, Callinicus, in Constantinople and used in 674-678 C.E. during the first Arab siege of Constantinople. Greek fire was a flammable liquid that would supposedly burn even in water. It was shot through a metal tube, or siphon, onto enemy ships, causing them to catch fire. Most Byzantine ships had a siphon, protected by the forecastle, mounted at the bow. Larger vessels sometimes had siphons mounted on each side of the ship, as well as small siphons that could be used for boarding actions or for repelling boarders. Although the Byzantines zealously guarded the secret makeup of Greek fire, the Arabs eventually produced a similar flammable liquid in the ninth century C.E.

Dromons also carried other offensive weapons, for both long-distance attacks and close ship-to-ship action. They had large crossbows, known as *toxoballistrai*, mounted on deck. Small catapults capable of launching stones or pots containing vipers, scorpions, quicklime, or Greek fire were also used. Deck crews were armed with bows and crossbows. For close work, cranes were used to drop heavy stones onto and hopefully through the decks of opposing ships.

Byzantine naval supremacy remained unchallenged until the seventh century reign of the Byzantine emperor Heraclius (c. 575-641). In 626 C.E., a Persian army and an Avar fleet threatened Constantinople, but the Byzantines destroyed the Avar ships, forcing the besiegers to withdraw. Soon afterward, the Arabs, realizing the importance of naval power, developed a fleet based upon the Byzantine model and began to challenge the Byzantines for control of the Mediterranean. This fleet proved to be quite successful, defeating the Byzantines in 655 C.E. at Lycia (Dhat al-Sawari), off the Syrian coast. In 717 C.E.

Constantinople was attacked by a large Arab flotilla, but the Byzantines were able to destroy the attacking fleet with Greek fire, lifting the siege and allowing Emperor Leo III (c. 680-741) to drive off the Arabs.

Although the Byzantines were successful in fending off Arab attacks on Constantinople, they were less successful in 1204 C.E. during the Fourth Crusade. In a carefully planned amphibious assault using both soldiers and warships, the crusaders were able to capture the city that had withstood capture for nearly nine hundred years.

BOOKS AND ARTICLES

Casson, Lionel. *Ships and Seamanship in the Ancient World*. Baltimore: Johns Hopkins University Press, 1971.

Gardiner, Robert, ed. *The Age of the Galley: Mediterranean Oared Vessels Since Pre-Classical Times*. London: Conway Maritime Press, 1995.

Lewis, Archibald, and Timothy J. Runyan. *European Naval and Maritime History, 300-1500*. Bloomington: Indiana University Press, 1985.

McGrail, Sean. *Ancient Boats in North-West Europe: The Archaeology of Water Transport to A.D. 1500*. New York: Longman, 1987.

Morrison, J. S., J. F. Coates, and N. B. Rankov. *The Athenian Trireme*. 2d ed. Cambridge, England: Cambridge University Press, 2000.

Throckmorton, Peter. *The Sea Remembers*. New York: Weidenfeld & Nicolson, 1987.

R. Scott Moore

THE ANCIENT WORLD

EGYPT AND THE MIDDLE EAST

CITY-STATES AND EMPIRES THROUGH OLD BABYLON

DATES: C. 3500-1595 B.C.E.

MILITARY ACHIEVEMENT

The evolution of warfare in ancient Mesopotamia led to the creation of large, powerful empires in the Near East, the weapons and formations of which influenced classical civilization. Historians believe that the beginnings of organized warfare coincided with the dawn of written history in both Mesopotamia and Egypt, probably independently of one another. Around 4000 B.C.E. the Sumerians, a people of unknown ethnic origin, settled in southern Mesopotamia, building their cities and fortifications out of mud bricks. They failed to create a stable, unified kingdom, however, living instead in a cluster of independent city-states, such as Ur, Kish, Lagash, Erech, Suruppack, Larsa, and Umma, and constantly warred with each other for supremacy over the region.

The first steps toward unity were taken in southern Mesopotamia when King Lugalzaggesi (r. c. 2375-2350 B.C.E.) of Uruk created a temporary Sumerian Empire by subduing his rivals and ultimately establishing nominal control over all of Mesopotamia as well as parts of Syria and Asia Minor. He was defeated by the Akkadian king Sargon the Great (c. 2334-2279 B.C.E.), who led a Semitic band of warriors in conquest of Sumer, unifying upper and lower Mesopotamia and creating the first real empire in history, which lasted nearly three hundred years. In thirty-four major battles Sargon used new technology to establish a domain that stretched eventually from the Mediterranean Sea to the Persian Gulf. Akkadian civilization eventually succumbed to an invasion of barbarous mountain dwellers from the east called the Gutians, who were victorious not because of their superior technology but because of their intensity in combat. Some time after 2100 B.C.E. the Sumerians reasserted their supremacy over southern Mesopotamia, which precipitated a renaissance of Sumerian culture and control in the area that lasted for approximately two hundred years.

After the beginning of the second millennium B.C.E. a new Semitic race of people, the Babylonians, perhaps from the area of modern Syria, rose to prominence in Mesopotamia. With its capital established at the city-state of Babylon, the whole region once again became unified under the rule of the powerful Babylonian leader Hammurabi (c. 1810-1750 B.C.E.), the famous lawgiver, warrior, and strategist.

Hammurabi's death was followed by an outburst of revolts that led to the rapid disintegration of his

TURNING POINTS

c. 3200 B.C.E.	The inauguration of the Bronze Age in Mesopotamia enables more effective weapons and armor.
c. 2500 B.C.E.	The Sumerian phalanx is first employed.
c. 2300 B.C.E.	After the composite bow is introduced by Sargon the Great, the use of the Sumerian phalanx declines.
c. 2100 B.C.E.	The Sumerians reassert their supremacy over southern Mesopotamia, precipitating a renaissance of Sumerian culture and control that lasts for approximately 200 years.
c. 1810 B.C.E.	Neo-Babylonian leader Hammurabi unifies Mesopotamian region under his rule and establishes capital at the city-state of Babylon.
1595 B.C.E.	Mesopotamian Empire falls to the Kassites.

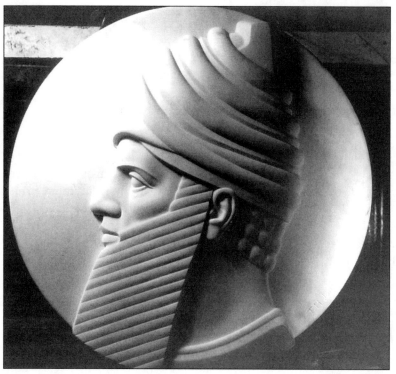

A relief of Hammurabi, the powerful Babylonian leader who united the Babylonian kingdom and codified its laws.

kingdom. In the late seventeenth century B.C.E. the Hittite Empire, centered in Asia Minor, began expanding with the aid of early iron technology. In 1595 B.C.E. Mesopotamia fell to the Kassites and entered into a long period of lethargy.

WEAPONS, UNIFORMS, AND ARMOR

Ancient weapons in Mesopotamia can be divided into two categories: shock weapons, for striking the enemy in hand-to-hand combat, and missile weapons, for shooting or throwing at the enemy. The earliest weapons were crafted from stone and included the mace and stone-ax. The inauguration in Mesopotamia of the Bronze Age (c. 3200 B.C.E.), so called for the introduction of new metal technology, was roughly contemporaneous with the beginnings of city-state civilization and ushered in the use of metal weapons, making warfare much more lethal than it

had been previously. The use of metal transformed shock weapons. Brittle stones were unsuited to producing lasting sharp edges used for striking opposing combatants. The introduction of metal helmets, shields, and body armor with bronze scales eliminated the effectiveness of the mace in favor of the battle-ax and metal-tipped spear. A helmet excavated from one of the richly adorned graves at the Royal Cemetery of Ur and dating from 2600 to 2400 B.C.E. was made of electrum, a gold and silver alloy, and hammered into shape from the inside.

The chariot appeared much earlier in Mesopotamia than elsewhere. Although it was in wide use as early as 3000 B.C.E., it was not the highly mobile, two-man, two-wheeled vehicle that appeared only after centuries of development. The war chariot of Sumer was a large, heavy, rather clumsy, four-wheeled vehicle that carried a driver, a warrior, and two shieldbearers commissioned to protect the warrior. The chariot warrior was armed with a spear, sometimes a battle-ax, but not a bow, which was used earlier and more regularly in other Near Eastern cultures, particularly in Egypt. Akkadian warriors under Sargon introduced Mesopotamia to the use of the composite bow, which provided this force with the necessary margin of superiority over the Sumerians. The bow fell into disuse until it began to be used again during the reunification of Mesopotamia under Hammurabi.

MILITARY ORGANIZATION

The Sumerian Stele of the Vultures, an artifact of singular importance dating from approximately 2500 B.C.E., supplies information about the organization and formation of combatants into fighting units in Mesopotamia. This limestone victory monument depicts King Eannatum of Lagash leading his troops into battle. The warrior-hero stands at the head of his advancing army, which is composed of a cadre of infantrymen packed shoulder to shoulder behind a barrier of interlocking, handheld rectangular shields, wearing matching helmets, and presenting a hedgehog formation of protruding spears. In other words, the infantry forms a genuine, full-fledged phalanx. This depiction is significant because it constitutes evidence that the phalanx was used two thousand years before it was implemented by the Greeks, and it emphasizes the importance of Sumerian military developments, which are often overlooked in the history of weapons and warfare. The Sumerian phalanx seems to have been a full-blown innovation rather than a product of an evolutionary technological process.

Additionally, the Stele of the Vultures depicts all of the phalangite infantrymen as outfitted and protected in the same fashion but distinct in dress from the single warrior-leader placed in front to direct the shock troops. Although the egalitarian outfitting of

troops is certainly predicated on the practical demands of the type of close-arm combat tactics employed in Mesopotamia, it also suggests to scholars that regalia determined one's standing and social status as well as the expectations and presumed responsibilities of office.

The campaign of Sargon the Great, empowered by the new technology used by his Akkadian bowmen against the Sumerian leader Lugalzaggesi of Uruk, is regarded as the factor responsible for the disappearance of the Sumerian phalanx. Sargon's empire consisted of a small warrior class living off the work of a few artisans and craftsmen and a large peasantry.

DOCTRINE, STRATEGY, AND TACTICS

The first organized battles in Mesopotamia occurred before 3500 B.C.E., when smaller groups armed only with crude stone weapons and without protective armor clashed with one another for control of food sources and land. Although cultures coalesced and armies increased in size, any cogent doctrine of warfare or sophisticated strategies seem to have been lacking. The key to effective combat was to find and kill the enemy's leader. If the king and his retainers were destroyed, so would be their army's chances for victory. With the development of city-states and walled towns in early Mesopotamia, siege warfare became increasingly important. The subjugation of all city-states and towns became the common goal of every competing army seeking to control the entire area. Warfare in early Mesopotamia was more frequent and less decisive strategically than in other parts of the ancient world precisely because of the constant intramural wars of the competing city-states. With the establishment of the first empires in Mesopotamia, warfare became directed outward, to-

North Wind Picture Archives

A mounted Babylonian warrior carrying a sword, spear, and bow and arrow.

ward the conquest of neighboring peoples and adjacent lands. For the most part Sumerian, Akkadian, and Babylonian styles of war remained confrontational, geared toward the frontal assault. This type of warfare, along with the types of weapons associated with such fighting, tended to emphasize the need for, and the prestige attached to, the attributes of bravery and physical prowess.

Because chariots in early Mesopotamia were not very mobile, they probably were not used in the same tactical way as were later two-man chariots. Later chariots could be deployed in quick shock attacks against an enemy's flank and in fighting against other chariots. However, the early four-man chariots had to be drawn by asses because they were so cumbersome, and, consequently, had to be maneuvered very close to enemy fortifications and forces in order to deliver any kind of effective firepower. Sources seem to agree that the early Mesopotamian chariots had little effective use as tools of destruction. They did, however, serve as instruments of intimidation.

ANCIENT SOURCES

The Sumerians kept records on clay tablets inscribed in cuneiform. One of the most famous stories from this culture, the Gilgamesh epic (c. 2000 B.C.E.; English translation, 1917) describes the life of Gilgamesh of Uruk, an actual person around whom legends formed, and who may be regarded as the first military hero in Near Eastern literature, serving as a model for warriors who followed. Gilgamesh was armed with a battle-ax bearing an actual name, "Might of Heroism," the first in a long line of titled weapons in the ancient world. The Gilgamesh epic also indicates that before the Mesopotamian warrior-leader decided to go into battle, he put the question before an assembly of the warrior class.

Various artifacts, including the Stele of the Vultures, uncovered by the work of archaeologists present visual images of ancient weapons and methods of war. Although physical evidence from the Akkadian period is slim, two cuneiform fragments depict the use of the composite bow, which scholars have hypothesized was made by carefully laminating bone, sinew, and keratin to a wooden core to create a weapon with tremendously magnified power.

BOOKS AND ARTICLES

Ferrill, Arthur. *The Origins of War: From the Stone Age to Alexander the Great.* New York: Thames and Hudson, 1986.

Humble, Richard. *Warfare in the Ancient World.* London: Weidenfield, 1980.

Laffont, Robert. *The Ancient Art of Warfare.* Greenwich, Conn.: New York Graphic Society, 1966.

O'Connell, Robert L. *Of Arms and Men: A History of War, Weapons, and Aggression.* New York: Oxford University Press, 1990.

Yadin, Yigael. *The Art of Warfare in Biblical Lands.* Vol. 1. New York: McGraw-Hill, 1963.

Andrew C. Skinner

THE HITTITES

DATES: C. 1620-1190 B.C.E.

MILITARY ACHIEVEMENT

The Hittites ruled a powerful empire in Asia Minor and northern Syria during the seventeenth to twelfth centuries B.C.E. One of their primary military achievements was in establishing a sphere of political influence in the Near East. Another was their creation of a professional army, in conjunction with refinements in siege warfare and the training of horses for use with the lightweight, single-axle chariot.

Weakened by royal family infighting, the Hittite Empire militarily secured by Mursilis I (r. c. 1620-c. 1590 B.C.E.) was in disarray two hundred years later when Suppiluliumas I (r. c. 1380-1346 B.C.E.) ascended to the throne. Hittite domination of central Anatolia, Syria, and territory stretching as far as the Amorite capital of Babylon was no longer assured.

Toward the mid-fourteenth century B.C.E., the Hittite capital of Hattusas (modern Bogazköy) was threatened, apparently with the assistance of the Hurrians of the Mitanni kingdom and of the Syrians at Aleppo. Around 1370 B.C.E., the Hittites under the leadership of Suppiluliumas I set out to reestablish their hold on Syria. The initial campaign against the Mitanni kingdom, a 300-mile march and attack on the Syrian kingdom's northwest corner, was unsuccessful. A second campaign (c. 1367 B.C.E.) took the Mitanni Nuhasse neighbor. A third (c. 1365 B.C.E.) resulted in Hittite control of Isuwa in northeast Anatolia. The fourth campaign advanced to threaten the southern Mitanni capital of Wassukkani. In 1366 B.C.E., Suppiluliumas captured Kadesh (Qadesh) in western Syria. Finally, in c. 1350 B.C.E., he succeeded in taking Carchemish, an important and strategic trade route on the west bank of the Euphrates River.

Suppiluliumas's military success reunited the Hittite Empire but introduced a third military power into the balance of the two dominant military forces in the Near East, Mesopotamia, and Egypt. Mur-silis II (r. c. 1345-c. 1320 B.C.E.) the heir to Suppiluliumas's expansionist policy, passed the Hittite Empire to his son, Muwatallis (r. c. 1320-c. 1294 B.C.E.). Over time, a growing internal unrest, stimulated partly by allied Mitanni and Assyrian forces, caused uprisings but received little response from the Hittite leader. Consequently, the Assyrians reconquered the region in a unified and formal manner. The Hittites, harassed by requests for defensive assistance from their allies but irritated by the sporadic raids made by their nominal vassal states, set out to reestablish Suppiluliumas's imperial holdings. The Hittites, rather than fight with their allies, the Assyrians, elected to engage the Egyptians in battle at Kadesh in Syria.

After about 1190 B.C.E., the Hittites faded as a major political and military power in the Near East. As the Assyrian Empire continued to expand systematically, the Hittite Empire eventually collapsed.

WEAPONS, UNIFORMS, AND ARMOR

The principal weapons used by the Hittites in battle were the bow and arrow, ax, and spear. The chariot was also used defensively. Suppiluliumas's strengths were his strategic tactics, his patience, and his ability to extract from defeat the seeds for future victory. His first defeat by the Mitanni illustrates his use of the chariot as a strategic weapon rather than a fighting wagon.

The Hittite spear, known from illustrations found at Egyptian ruins, consisted of a pointed metal blade attached to a wooden shaft with leather wrappings. Originally, the blade was made of copper, then bronze, and finally iron. The spear's structure consisted of a socket for the blunt blade end reinforced with leather strips attached to the wooden shaft. The spear shaft, for cutting and slashing, was fitted to maximize damage to the enemy in hand-to-hand combat. Although the spear has its advantages as a thrown weapon, there are no illustrations of Hittites actually using a spear offensively in this way. Instead, the spear seems to have been used primarily for defensive purposes, such as to guard the driver and bowman in the three-man chariot crew.

The design of both the ax and the battle-ax forms the shape of a human arm attached to a shaft. The flanged hand-end of the ax is flared in long bronze fingerlike forms. In hand-to-hand combat, the sharp-edged wrist section could not be grasped without cutting through the enemy's hand. The ax's extended, clawlike frontal section made it possible to slice through the neck of the enemy. In addition, the thumblike portion of the ax, just before the shaft, functioned as a hook for gouging. The dagger differs in design, with a shorter, double-edged blade for use in hand-to-hand combat.

Body armor worn by the Hittites consisted of 4.5-inch bronze plates bound together with linen or leather to form a small breast jacket. The jacket was made originally to protect the chariot driver and crew. A relief found in Luxor, Egypt, detailing the Battle of Kadesh (1274 B.C.E.) shows the Hittite infantry wearing ankle-length skirts made of leather without any metal plating. Because infantrymen required mobility, the metal plating may have been eliminated and the protective metal plates replaced with leather.

Hittite infantrymen were armed with javelins intended to be thrown either while on the run or from a stationary position. The lance was the traditional Hittite weapon for the chariot crew. Their use in battle is not recorded visually in the Luxor relief. Although Ramses II made claim that the Hittites were unable to use either their bows or their javelins because his chariots charged through their lines, thereby preventing a frontal assault, it is questionable whether such a tactic was actually used. The statement suggests that the throwers may have been not in the chariots but rather on foot, in retreat, or unable to immobilize the Egyptian chariots. Such a thesis implies that the throwers either were separated from their chariot crew or were in disarray.

Although the physical evidence indicates that bows and arrows tipped in bronze were used as a ma-

jor weapon in conjunction with the Hittite chariotry, there is little evidence that archers were used with chariots. Evidence for Hittite bowmen in action is scarce. Only Muwatallis, the king of the Hittites, is depicted in the Luxor reliefs in a chariot with an archer and bowcase. These reliefs show the Hittites with a defensive force and the Egyptian army with offensive weapons. Ironically, the intended purpose of this work was to show the heroic and invincible Egyptian pharaoh in the face of Hittite aggression. Contradictory information is contained in the Abydos inscriptions, where the Egyptian king records "killing horses, capturing chariots, bows, swords, all weapons of warfare."

The simple but sturdy Hittite chariot provided the army with an effective battlefield vehicle. The chariot design enabled the Hittites to retain flexibility and mobility in battle and to carry a three-man crew, consisting of driver, archer, and spearbearer.

The typical offensive use of the chariot by the Hittites was to taunt and encircle the enemy at a distance. After the chariot's forward advance toward the enemy, the infantry might advance using lances to inflict damage. The Hittite strategy suggests an emphasis on a defensive use of the chariot against an offensive line. Once the enemy line was broken by the chariotry, the Hittite infantry could strike effectively.

MILITARY ORGANIZATION

Upon his ascension to the Hittite throne in about 1380, Suppiluliumas I inherited an empire frayed by Hittite vassal-states. To restore the Hittite kingdom, he reinforced and restored the decaying fortifications of the Hittite capital, Hattusas, constructing a massive wall to encircle the city's vulnerable perimeter. Suppiluliumas also reorganized the professional Hittite army, which recruited and enlisted infantrymen. The infantry provided the Hittites with a regular standing army that could be increased as needed by vassal treaty. The infantry did not contain the protectorate citizens or native Hittite populations. Supposedly, the use of vassal-state infantry eliminated the need for mercenaries, although Egyptian sources suggest otherwise, listing a great number of mercenaries in the Hittite ranks.

Instructional specifics about the training of Hittite soldiers are scarce. It is thought that special locales or training camps existed and that training consisted of drill practice. A Hittite king might bring several army divisions with him on a campaign, depending on the conflict. Hittite strategy originally focused on fast-attack troops but quickly shifted to siege warfare, in which support troops and supply lines for men and horses were more crucial than battlefield encounters to the success of the siege.

For strategic purposes, the basic military unit was a platoon of fifty infantrymen under the command of the king. These infantry units were reinforced with elite troops or chariot warriors. Decision making

about battlefield tactics seems to have been left to the king alone. Acknowledged credit for battle success would lie respectively with the gods, the king, and then the king's generals. The different locations of unit types within the camp demonstrate a similar hierarchical arrangement.

Two principles defined the organization of the king's troops: chariotry and infantry. Within the reign of Suppiluliumas the leaders of each learned to work with the ten vassal-states. Although military professionals were incorporated into the Hittite army, they nonetheless remained identified with their individual vassal-states.

The Hittites had four types of troops: infantry, chariotry, outpost garrison, and elite guard. The sizes of the units are difficult to establish from existing de-

Library of Congress

A depiction of a relief on a wall at Giaur-Kala in modern Turkmenistan showing two Hittite soldiers.

scriptions, but evidence suggests that a division might have equaled about 5,000 men, a company about 250, a platoon approximately 50, and a squad as many as 10. In the Hittite military hierarchy, the king was the leader. Two generals represented the two protectorates, and they were followed in command by the generals of the vassal-states. Combat officers consisted of a platoon leader, garrison-troop leader, squad leaders, and the infantry and chariot soldiers.

The location of the Hittite capital shows the depth of Hittite defensive fears. The capital, Hattusas, was founded around 2000 B.C.E. within a natural defensive perimeter: a downward slope to the north, a dangerous gorge to the east, and a deep valley to the west.

The defensive fortifications of the upper city were located on the highest ground and designed of smooth rock to prevent an assault force from scaling the walls. Along the outer wall, there is another, inner wall. Parapets with round crenelations and high towers between them provided windows that allowed soldiers to survey the surroundings, guarding from attack. The massive walls were punctuated with several towers flanked by gateways. On the south, the outer wall was reached by a steep, sloping staircase defended from the ramparts. Between the outer and inner fortification walls, a ramp was built to inhibit free access. The main gateway was flanked with stone carved towers, double locking doors, and windows to decease potential assaults.

Access to the city could be gained through an underground postern, or back gate, about 230 feet long. It served a defensive military purpose by preventing massed groups from assaulting the city from beneath. The postern also had an offensive use, allowing Hittite soldiers to enter and leave the city undetected during a siege.

DOCTRINES, STRATEGY, AND TACTICS

Hittite strategy consisted of two parts: a military strategy for battle and a diplomatic strategy for treaties. The strategic weakness of the Hittite Empire is demonstrated by their treaties, of which the Hittites made two types: a treaty of parity with their two pro-

tectorate allies and a treaty of vassal-states. The Hittite treaty made the Hittites vulnerable to the petty raids and complaints of vassal-states. The other two major powers, Mesopotamia and Egypt, could leverage their treaties, but the Hittite treaty with vassal-states necessitated immediate response to calls for help by the vassal-states. If the Hittite Empire did not respond, it would be considered disinterested or too weak.

Egypt's sovereignty over the region during the second millennium B.C.E. reached from Canaan and the Levantine ports and the cities that bordered on the inland routes from Megiddo in modern Israel to the lands of the Hittite, Mitanni, and Babylonian kingdoms. Because control of the region was important to Egypt's continued trade with Near Eastern partners, Egypt kept pressure on the cities of Palestine simultaneously with the Hittites. Complaints contained in ancient letters indicate one catalyst for renewed hostilities: the emergence of the Amurru kingdom as a power. The nineteenth Hittite Dynasty witnessed renewed military activity throughout the region, threatening Hittite national unity and international expansionist policies. The result for both the Egyptians and the Hittites was the loyalty of Canaan and control of the Orontes Valley for trade with Syrian ports. The Egyptian campaigns of Sety I (c. 1306-1290) attempted to restore Egyptian hegemony in Canaan and the Amurru kingdom, which stood on the Hittite boundary. However, Sety succeeded only in Palestine. After the Egyptian king Ramses II (c. 1300-1213) ascended the throne, the provocation remained unresolved, and Ramses systematically began to retake control of Hittite territories along the Palestinian coastal plain to Byblos.

The Hittite strategy for the battle was designed to delude the Egyptians into thinking that the Hittite army was encamped beyond the city of Kadesh when they were hidden behind it, to the north. Ramses II, leading four divisions of his army: Amon, Re, Ptah, and Sutekh, made an unimaginable frontal attack for the city, leading the Amon division ahead of the other three divisions. The Hittite leader, Muwatallis, advanced around Kadesh on the west, while his chariots attacked the Re division from the south. Although the two armies were of virtually equal strength, Ramses was cut off from the rest of his army, with only one division.

In the Egyptian records, the Egyptians claim victory but it is possible that the Egyptians were prevented from recovering sufficient strength to oust the Hittites from Kadesh. The cunning strategy used by the Hittites demonstrates a keen understanding of the chariot's potential for subterfuge, coupled with speed and mobility.

ANCIENT SOURCES

Ancient Egyptian sources in relief and inscription at Luxor, Abu Simbel, and Abydos, and the Ramesseum, the funerary temple of Ramses II in western Thebes, all record strategic details of the Battle of Kadesh.

The reliefs reveal the strategy of Ramses: to penetrate as far as possible into enemy territory and to set up his offensive position before the city. The reliefs at Luxor illustrate Ramses' arrival and camp, and the Hittite ruse and subsequent surprise attack through the camp shield barriers. Ramses' counterattack, depicted on the walls of the Ramesseum, illustrates his second strategy: to make a full-force, frontal attack into the enemy lines. The Hittite charioteers were more intent on plundering the Egyptian camp than on fighting, and the Hittite forces fell into disarray. They were then chased by the Egyptians into retreat.

None of the Egyptian reliefs, however, shows the capture of Kadesh or Hittite surrender. Ramses claimed victory less for Egypt than for himself. There is some validity to his claim. After his army had fled, it was Ramses' leadership that sustained the Egyptian forces on the battlefield. Traditionally, historians interpret the outcome of the battle as a draw.

These ancient sources are significant in that they provide the names of ally groups, terminology for weapons, the organization and identification of types of soldier units and chariot warriors, and insight into strategies. The Hittites' use of subterfuge reveals an awareness of the tactical offensive role of the chariot in warfare.

BOOKS AND ARTICLES

Gurney, O. R. *The Hittites*. Rev. ed. London: Penguin, 1990.

Kitchen, K. A. *Pharoah Triumphant: The Life and Times of Ramesses II*. Warminster, England: Aris and Phillips, 1982.

Murname, W. *The Road to Kadesh: A Historical Interpretation of the Battle Reliefs of King Sety I at Karnak*. Chicago: University of Chicago Press, 1985.

Yadin, Y. *The Art of Warfare in Biblical Lands*. 2 vols. New York: McGraw-Hill, 1963.

Elizabeth L. Meyers

THE ASSYRIANS

DATES: C. 1950-612 B.C.E.

POLITICAL CONSIDERATIONS

Assyria was the ancient name of the area surrounding the upper Tigris River and its principal tributaries, the Greater Zab and the Lesser Zab, in northern Iraq. From an early period the Assyrians adopted many cultural features of the more civilized Sumerians of the lower Tigris and Euphrates River valleys, including cuneiform writing and a "hydraulic civilization," which required irrigation to take advantage of the available fertile alluvial plain. Although food could be produced locally, virtually all metals, luxury goods, and horses had to be imported or seized from surrounding mountains to the north and east, in modern Turkey and Iran, where the Assyrians frequently faced invasion from hostile tribes. The Assyrians' need to secure defensible borders beyond their homeland thus became intimately linked to the material prosperity of their empire.

MILITARY ACHIEVEMENT

Assyrian history can be divided into three periods. The empire first rose to power during the Old Empire period (1950-1500 B.C.E.). After the death of Shamshi-Adad I (r. c. 1813-1781 B.C.E.), Assyrian rule declined, leading to annexations by the Mitanni and to the revival of city-states, including Arrapha, Erbil, Ashur, and Ninevah. The Middle Empire period (c. 1500-900 B.C.E.) witnessed the rebirth of Assyrian domination. Ashur-uballit I (r. c. 1365-1330 B.C.E.) drove the Mitanni from Assyria and laid the foundations for further expansion. The Assyrians of the middle period reached their peak under Tiglath-pileser I (1115-1077 B.C.E.), who briefly expanded the empire as far as the Mediterranean Sea. After the death of Tiglath-pileser I, incursions of Aramaeans and dynastic struggles led to an alliance with Babylon and a retreat to the traditional Assyrian homeland.

Assyria's greatest era of military expansion came during the late imperial period (c. 900-600 B.C.E.). Ashur-dan II (934-912 B.C.E.) reestablished control of his kingdom, and his four successors all pushed forward Assyrian borders and expanded control of valuable trade routes. Under Ashurnasirpal II (r. 883-859 B.C.E.), the Assyrians crossed the Euphrates River, forcing most of the Aramaean, Phoenician, and neo-Hittite kings as far as the Mediterranean Sea, the Taurus and Zagros Mountains, and the Armenian Highlands to pay tribute. Reflecting the importance of these new borders, Ashurnasirpal II moved the Assyrian capital to Calah, modern Nimrud, nearer to the front. Shalmaneser III (r. 858-824 B.C.E.) waged almost continual war during his reign. Although he maintained Assyrian dominance in northern Syria, he was defeated at Karkar in central Syria (853 B.C.E.) by a coalition of Syro-Palestinian kings that included Ahab (r. c. 874-c. 853 B.C.E.) of Israel. Shalmaneser III failed on five occasions to subdue Damascus and southern Syria but did manage to subdue Tyre, Sidon, and Israel.

After eighty years of domestic turmoil, Tiglath-pileser III (r. 745-727 B.C.E.) reestablished control over the Assyrian homeland and initiated the campaigns that destroyed the independence of the kings of Syria and Israel. Between 743 and 732 he drove the Urartians back into the Taurus Mountains and captured Damascus. In 729 he conquered Babylon. Israel was finally subdued during the first year of the reign of Sargon II (r. 721-705 B.C.E.), and Jerusalem, the capital of the southern Israelite kingdom of Judah, was unsuccessfully besieged by Sargon's son Sennacherib (r. 704-681 B.C.E.). The last great Assyrian king, Ashurbanipal (r. 668-627 B.C.E.), completed the conquest of Egypt that had been undertaken by his father. Continually harassed by the Elamites in the east (modern Iran), in 639 he led a massive campaign of extermination. The Assyrian Empire had never been greater, stretching from Thebes in southern Egypt to Tarsus in Asia Minor, to Babylonia in the south, and to Elam in the east. In fewer than thirty years, however, overextension, harsh treatment of subject peoples, and a disastrous struggle with the Medes led to the conquest of Nineveh (612 B.C.E.) by a combined army of Medes and Babylonians and to the final destruction of the Assyrian Empire. The Hebrew prophet Nahum (fl. seventh century B.C.E.) echoed the common sentiment of all Near Eastern peoples when he said, "All who hear the news of you clap their hands at your downfall, for who has not felt your unrelenting cruelty?"

WEAPONS, UNIFORMS, AND ARMOR

Assyria's offensive power initially rested upon development and use of the war chariot. The vehicle evolved from the more mobile two-man chariot, used for reconnaissance, communication, and combat, to the heavy, four-horse, four-man chariot common during Ashurbanipal's reign. By the time the empire fell, cavalry units had taken over many of the duties of the chariots, which were then being used principally as firing platforms for archers and as shock vehicles in frontal attacks. Effective use of the chariot in combat was limited to flat or nearly flat terrain, making it less valuable as Assyria expanded into surrounding mountainous terrain.

The first record of Assyrian cavalry units is found in the ninth century B.C.E., when riders were deployed in pairs, with one man holding the reins of both mounts while the other fired a bow. As riders gained expertise, each horse and rider became an autonomous unit, with riders carrying long lances. By the seventh century B.C.E., the cavalry had largely displaced the chariot as the mobile force of the military, and horsemen were typically armed with both bows and lances. Riders covered their torsos with lamellar armor, consisting of bronze plates stitched to a leather underjacket, whereas fabric armor was used to protect their mounts.

The bow and arrow and the lance were the most common weapons among infantry units, but slings, knives, and swords were also utilized. In the late imperial period, archers were deployed in pairs, with one man serving as a shieldbearer. Shields made from plaited reeds were often taller than a man and curved at the top to deflect incoming arrows. Both simple and compound bows were used, with ranges of between 250 and 650 meters. The bow used by particular units was often linked to the ethnicity of the unit. Records indicate, for instance, that there were distinctive Akkadian, Assyrian, and Cimmerian bows. Tiglath-pileser III introduced both the lance-spear, for close-order thrusting, and lamellar armor, known among elite infantry units as the *zuku sa sheppe*. Ordinary units and native levies had only a helmet and shield for personal protection.

In an age in which the art of fortification was highly developed, the Assyrians were innovators in siegecraft and siege orga-

TURNING POINTS

1950-1500 B.C.E.	Assyrians first rise to power during the Old Empire period.
c. 1500-900 B.C.E.	During their Middle Empire period, the Assyrians drive the Mitanni from Assyria, laying foundations for further expansion.
c. 1000 B.C.E.	Iron begins to replace bronze in the making of weapons in Assyria.
900-600 B.C.E.	Assyria undergoes Late Empire period, its greatest era of military expansion.
745-727 B.C.E.	After years of domestic turmoil, Tiglath-pileser III reestablishes control over Assyrian homeland and institutes military reforms.
721 B.C.E.	Sargon II conquers Israel.
612 B.C.E.	Assyrian city of Nineveh is conquered by Medes and Babylonians, marking the final destruction of the Assyrian Empire.

An Assyrian battle scene at the palace of Ashurnasirpal.

nization. They built movable wooden towers covered by dampened leather hides, which enabled expert archers to clear the parapets above while troops below worked to undermine the walls. They sometimes used a swinging "ram" to batter the walls and sometimes a ram with a wide, iron blade that would be inserted between stones and rocked in order to pry the stones apart.

MILITARY ORGANIZATION

Assyrian military success owed much to superior preparation, which allowed large armies to be quickly assembled. Shalmaneser III, for instance, reportedly invaded Syria in 845 B.C.E. with 120,000 troops. Marshaling cities were kept in readiness to receive corn, oil, battle equipment, and troops in preparation for a new campaign, thus enabling forces to be quickly organized and provisioned. This led to the creation of Ashurnasirpal's Greater Assyria, a large area of northern Mesopotamia that could be controlled by relatively short campaigns and raids. In

keeping with the agricultural basis of society, campaigning was seasonal, with conscripts called to arms by July, shortly after harvest.

Despite successes, more extensive campaigns, attrition, and battle losses made campaigning under the old system difficult. Tiglath-pileser III initiated important military reforms that created the most efficient army of the ancient world until the rise of Rome, enabling emperors to vastly increase the size of the empire. Instead of calling up agricultural workers during the summer, he introduced a standing army and personal bodyguard that was augmented as necessary by contingents raised in the provinces and levies drawn from vassal states. The Assyrian army may have been the first in which ethnic units were integrated largely on a basis of equality, though they frequently performed functions for which they were already expertly prepared.

On campaign, the Assyrian king frequently led the army, but sometimes he delegated authority to senior field marshals, known as *turtans*. Below these wing commanders, rank designations indicated control of 1,000, 500, or 100 troops. Although much remains unknown about Assyrian military organization, it is clear that it enabled the Assyrians to create the first army capable of sustained, long-distance campaigning. An efficient system of supply depots, transport columns, and bridging trains enabled the Assyrian army to advance as rapidly as any army before the modern industrial age, fighting effectively at distances of up to 300 miles from their base of operations.

Assyria's unmatched striking capability was based upon its chariot force, which enabled it to wage lightning attacks across the plains of Mesopotamia and Syria, shocking enemy troops and paving the way for the lancers and archers of the infantry. From the ninth century onward, the cavalry became increasingly important, sometimes operating in units of 1,000 or more and eventually replacing the charioteers as the mobile arm of the military. This dependence upon cavalry forced the Assyrians to remain militarily aggressive in order to provide a continuous stream of remounts that could come only from capture, tribute payments, or taxation.

DOCTRINE, STRATEGY, AND TACTICS

Given the lack of geographical barriers, Assyria's grand strategy was to wage offensive wars that would push Assyrian boundaries far beyond the cities of the Tigris River Valley. As a part of this plan, terror was used as a deliberate tactic. The ultimate goal was to secure *adu*, or "pacts of loyalty," which required payment of tribute. If enemies refused to submit, it was not uncommon for all men, women, and children in a resisting city to be killed. Assyrians commonly laid waste to enemy lands, destroying granaries and irrigation systems and cutting down orchards. Sur-

rounding territories would then be annexed, with native populations deported to distant cities. The magnitude of deportations rose dramatically during the reign of Tiglath-pileser III. In 744 B.C.E., for instance, Tiglath-pileser III deported 65,000 people from Iran. Two years later, he resettled 30,000 Syrians in the Zagros Mountains of Persia. The use of deportation, torture, and other forms of terror was designed both to convince enemies to surrender and to deter future rebellious activity among conquered peoples. Tributary (vassal) states were allowed to maintain considerable autonomy, especially in the area of religion, whereas annexed territories, with imported foreign populations, were forced to worship Ashur and treated in every way as Assyrians.

Assyrian strategy involved building a series of fortresses in annexed territories, manned by prisoners of war, which would ensure control of trade routes. Control of roads enhanced trade and brought valuable commodities to a land that was not rich in natural resources, whereas fortresses were used as bases from which tribute raids could be launched into surrounding areas.

In terms of tactics, Assyria deployed infantry, cavalry, and charioteers in combined operations. Skirmishers, archers, and slingshot specialists harassed and demoralized opponents in the opening rounds of conflict. Infantry, armed with their lances, swords, and daggers, followed with a frontal assault against enemy lines. Cavalry and chariots would ideally provide the decisive thrust from the flanks or from the center of the Assyrian army toward a weak point in the enemy line. After the horses and chariots charged, a rout of the enemy could often be expected. However, if the forces were evenly matched, the cavalry and chariot charges might well be indecisive and yield a chaotic melee rather than a decisive victory.

ANCIENT SOURCES

There are extensive records on campaigns of the late imperial period. The most important Assyrian sources include the annals of the Assyrian kings, which provide campaigning records; and many inscribed carvings and palace reliefs uncovered principally in Nineveh, Lachish, and other cities of the Assyrian homeland. Outside Assyria, victorious kings erected stelae, or carved stone pillars, on which they recorded their victories and reminded subjugated peoples of their tributary status. One of the most accessible sources of ancient information regarding the

Assyrians is from the Old Testament of the Bible, principally in the books of 2 Kings, 2 Chronicles, Isaiah, and Hosea. Finally, there are scattered references to Assyrian warfare in Sumerian and Greek sources, including those of Josephus (c. 37-c. 100 C.E.) and Herodotus (c. 484-c. 424 B.C.E.).

BOOKS AND ARTICLES

Gallagher, William R. *Sennacherib's Campaign in Judah*. Leiden, Netherlands: Brill, 1999.

Gwaltney, William C., Jr. "Assyrians." In *Peoples of the Old Testament World*, edited by Alfred J. Hoerth, Gerald L. Mattingly, and Edwin M. Yamauchi. Grand Rapids, Mich.: Baker Books, 1994.

Healy, Mark. *The Ancient Assyrians*. Botley, England: Osprey Publishing, 1991.

Saggs, Harry W. F. *The Might That Was Assyria*. London: Sidgwick and Jackson, 1984.

Yamada, Shigeo. *The Construction of the Assyrian Empire: A Historical Study of the Inscriptions of Shalmaneser II Relating to the Campaigns in the West*. Leiden, Netherlands: Brill, 2000.

Mark Polelle and John Powell

THE CHALDEANS

DATES: 626-539 B.C.E.

MILITARY ACHIEVEMENT

The Chaldeans, or Neo-Babylonians, are credited with destroying the Assyrian Empire and establishing a new one in the Near East that was responsible for sacking Jerusalem, razing the Jewish temple located there, and destroying and deporting the kingdom of Judah in 586 B.C.E. The Chaldean culture was known not for military innovation but rather for honing previously used policies, weapons, and tactics in campaigns and battles that were fought over most of the ancient Near East.

During the period of Assyrian domination in the Near East (1300-700 B.C.E.), a new group of Semitic desert dwellers infiltrated southern Mesopotamia and established a culture that came to be known as Chaldean, named after the dominant tribe, the Kaldu. Discontent within the Assyrian Empire grew steadily during the reign of Ashurbanipal (r. 668-627 B.C.E.), the last great king of ancient Assyria. After his death, an imperial governor named Nabopolassar Nebuchadnezzar (r. 626-605 B.C.E.), a member of the Kaldu tribe, became leader of the insurrection. In 626 B.C.E., after a year of guerrilla war, Nabopolassar Nebuchadnezzar ascended the throne of the city-state of Babylon, inaugurated the Eleventh Babylonian dynasty, and established the Chaldean or Neo-Babylonian kingdom, to distinguish it from the Old Babylonian Empire of Hammurabi's (c. 1810-1750 B.C.E.) day.

For twelve years, from 626 to 614 B.C.E., war between the Chaldean, or Neo-Babylonian, kingdom and the remnants of the Assyrian Empire consisted of a series of battles over control of a network of fortified cities and towns in southern Mesopotamia, in modern-day Iraq. The Assyrians made an alliance with the Egyptians, who had become alarmed at the successes of the Chaldeans and of the Medes in what is now Iran. In 615 B.C.E. the Medes invaded Assyria and one year later captured the important city of Ashur. Significant emphasis was given by the Chaldeans to what might be termed coalition warfare in its early stages of development, and an alliance between the Chaldeans and the Medes was forged when Nabopolassar Nebuchadnezzar and the Median ruler Cyaxares (r. 625-585 B.C.E.) met under the walls of Ashur after the Median victory.

In 612 B.C.E. Nabopolassar Nebuchadnezzar led a final assault against Assyria's main city, Nineveh. Although it was strongly fortified, the city fell after a two-month siege, and, for all intents and purposes, the empire fell with it. In 610 B.C.E. the Medes and the Neo-Babylonians marched against Harran to the north and took it. The last of the Assyrian pretenders to the throne disappeared. The Medes did not lay claim to any part of the empire they helped to overthrow. Apparently content with their share of the booty, they withdrew to the east and turned their attention toward Armenia and Asia Minor. The Neo-Babylonians built their empire on the ruins of the Assyrian Empire, though they did not repair much of the damage they had inflicted.

TURNING POINTS

1300-700 B.C.E.	Semitic desert dwellers infiltrate southern Mesopotamia to establish Chaldean culture during period of Assyrian domination in Near East.
626 B.C.E.	Nabopolassar Nebuchadnezzar leads revolt against Assyrian rule and establishes Chaldean, or Neo-Babylonian, kingdom.
587-586 B.C.E.	Nebuchadnezzar II uses siege warfare to conquer Jerusalem.
539 B.C.E.	Chaldean Empire is conquered by Persian king Cyrus the Great.

After his final victory over the Assyrians, the aging Nabopolassar Nebuchadnezzar relied increasingly on his son, Nebuchadnezzar II (c. 630-562 B.C.E.) for the conduct of military operations. In 607 B.C.E. the crown prince attacked the Egyptian stronghold of Carchemish on the northern Euphrates River, routed the Egyptian army under Pharaoh Necho II (r. 610-595 B.C.E.), and gained military and economic control over areas to the west of Mesopotamia. However, just as all of Syria-Palestine now lay open to the Chaldeans, Nabopolassar Nebuchadnezzar died and Nebuchadnezzar II had to return to Babylon. He was crowned king in 605 B.C.E. For the next seven years he found himself quelling rebellion after rebellion in both Mesopotamia and Syria-Palestine. During the winter of 598 B.C.E. the king of Judah refused to pay tribute, forcing Nebuchadnezzar II to march on the kingdom's capital, Jerusalem, subjugating the city and installing a new king, Zedekiah.

Eleven years later, the kingdom of Judah was again at the center of rebellion against the Neo-Babylonian Empire. Nebuchadnezzar II personally directed operations against the rebellious Jews. In 586 B.C.E., after a siege of eighteen months, Jerusalem was captured, the city looted, the Jewish temple destroyed, and thousands of Jews rounded up and deported to Babylon. Thus, 135 years after thousands of citizens of the Northern Kingdom of Israel were deported by the Assyrians, thousands more Jews were once again carried away out of their lands in one of history's monumental turning points, the Babylonian Exile. One of the last actions of Nebuchadnezzar II in Syria was the siege of the coastal town of Tyre, which lasted thirteen years. A fragmentary text now housed in the British Museum alludes to a Neo-Babylonian campaign against Pharaoh Ahmose II (570-526 B.C.E.) in 568 B.C.E., but it cannot be determined if the Neo-Babylonians ever actually set foot in the Nile Valley.

The last years of Nebuchadnezzar II's reign are obscure and seem to have ended amid internal chaos. His son, Evil-Merodach (d. 560 B.C.E.), of Old Testament fame, ruled for only two years (561-560 B.C.E.). After another four years of political instability, the Babylonians installed Nabonidus (r. 556-539 B.C.E) on the throne. A government official of Aramaean origin, Nabonidus was the last king of an independent Babylon. In 539 B.C.E. the founder of the Achaemenid Dynasty and first king of the Persian Empire, Cyrus the Great (c. 601 to 590-c. 530 B.C.E.), conquered the Neo-Babylonian Empire.

North Wind Picture Archives

Chaldean king Nebuchadnezzar II directs operations against rebellious Jews in 586 B.C.E., capturing and looting the capital of Jerusalem, destroying the Jewish temple, and rounding up and deporting thousands of Jews to Babylon.

WEAPONS, UNIFORMS, AND ARMOR

The Chaldeans do not appear to have been innovators in weapons development; they used the weapons of their immediate predecessors in Mesopotamia, including spears, daggers, and battle-axes. They also employed the composite bow first developed by Akkadian king Sargon the Great (c. 2334-2279 B.C.E.) and reintroduced by Hammurabi of the Old Babylonian Empire.

Babylonian infantry units are described fighting with metal helmets and carrying lances and wooden clubs. Friezes and reliefs show that the mace, though one of the oldest weapons employed in the Near East, was still being used in the seventh century B.C.E. Weapons used by the Neo-Babylonians were the product of the Iron Age technological revolution. By 900 B.C.E. smiths throughout the Near East had learned how to combine carbon with red-hot iron to produce carburized, or steel-like, iron weapons. Biblical as well as Babylonian texts imply the unmatched virtues of such weapons, referring to both their hardness and their sharpness. Other important pieces of equipment used in Neo-Babylonian warfare included scaling ladders, used in siege operations against walled cities, and war chariots.

MILITARY ORGANIZATION

Neo-Babylonian armies pursued their grand strategy by organizing together troops with different kinds of weapons and different tactical objectives: infantry units armed with spears and clubs, cavalry warriors on horseback, charioteers, and siege units that also included scaling parties composed of archers. Their strategy was to overwhelm the enemy. Although the Greek historian Herodotus (c. 484-424 B.C.E.) later indicated that the greatest of the Median kings, Cyaxares, was the first ruler who divided his troops into companies and distinct bodies of spearmen, archers, and others, all evidence indicates that Nabopolassar Nebuchadnezzar would have known of this well-coordinated, systematic arrangement of troops long before he formed his alliance with the Median ruler.

The Chaldeans undoubtedly followed the example of their predecessors, the Assyrians, in collecting horses for their cavalry troops from the many villages specifically cultivated for that purpose in Mesopotamia. Characteristic chariots of the period were large-wheeled, maneuverable, high-platformed vehicles accommodating three or four persons: a driver, an archer, and one or two shieldbearers to protect them. Late seventh century B.C.E. reliefs show chariots being preceded by two archers mounted on horseback, with slingers ahead of them.

DOCTRINE, STRATEGY, AND TACTICS

Because the major cities and towns in the Near East were walled, strongly fortified complexes by the time the Neo-Babylonians appeared on the scene, siege warfare was the dominant tactical principle employed in the seventh and sixth centuries B.C.E. The first-attacked cities in a region were usually those that supported the most important city, the capital, because of their strategic military value, their economic importance, and their symbolic value. These cities were usually of religious importance, because they were the home of either a region's patron deity or priestly class, or both. The capital city of a kingdom or group of people was often reserved for the final siege, because it was the most strongly fortified of the cities, and also because it could be greatly weakened in both supply and morale by the loss of its network of supporting towns.

A specific purpose of the siege was the attempt to starve the holdouts into submission, as in the Siege of Jerusalem (586 B.C.E.). Information about an opponent's troop strength, tactical weaknesses, fortifications, and other areas of possible exploitation was obtained either by spies who infiltrated the enemy camp or by internal informers. Once a city was captured, further resistance was often preempted by razing its walls. The rebuilding of a city's walls was usually regarded as a symbol of renewed revolt. The Neo-Babylonians also applied the policy of torching conquered cities. Modern archaeological excavations in Jerusalem attest to a great conflagration that swept over the whole city but that was especially prominent in the residential district, data which harmonizes well with the report presented in the Bible's Book of 2 Kings (25:9).

Campaign plans of the Neo-Babylonian military machine were often based on tradition and long-established patterns of warfare. The Neo-Babylonian conquest of Syria-Palestine followed much the same strategy and order employed by the Assyrians more than a century earlier. Like the Assyrians before them, the Neo-Babylonians also used the policy of deportation of vanquished foes with great effectiveness, especially as a tool of psychological warfare to break the will and ability of opponents to recombine against their oppressors.

Alliance warfare was an important strategy to the Chaldeans, or Neo-Babylonians, in their conquest of Assyria and the establishment of their own empire. Royal marriages during war sometimes sealed coali-tion agreements, as when Nabopolassar Nebuchad-nezzar's son, Nebuchadnezzar II, was wed to Amytis, the daughter of the Median ruler, Cyaxares. From that point on, the Chaldeans and the Medes fought side by side and the fate of the Assyrians was doomed.

ANCIENT SOURCES

Perhaps the most valuable resource regarding Neo-Babylonian warfare is a series of ancient texts collectively translated and known in English as *The Babylonian Chronicle* (1887). Begun in 626 B.C.E., the same year Nabopolassar Nebuchadnezzar ascended the throne of Babylon, this record describes the many wars and campaigns of the Chaldeans and allows military histo-rians to follow, almost day by day, the history of the Neo-Babylonian Empire. It includes invalu-able accounts of the fall of Nineveh and other Assyrian cities.

The Hebrew Bible, or Old Testament, also provides important commentary on the strategy and tactics used by the Neo-Babylonians and reports on their destruction of various cities both in Syria-Palestine and Mesopotamia. For example, Nahum (3:1-7) preserves not only the sense of vengeance unleashed during the destruction of Nineveh, but also the tools of war in use:

> Cursed be the city of blood, full of lies, full of violence. . . . The sound of the whip is heard, the gal-lop of horses, the rolling of chariots. An infinity of dead, the dead are everywhere! My anger is on thee, Nineveh, saith Jehovah. . . . I will show thy nakedness to the nations and thy shame to the king-doms. And then it will be said: Nineveh is destroyed! Who will mourn her?

Other important sources on Chaldean or Neo-Babylonian warfare include the writings of classical authors as well as Flavius Josephus's (c. 37-c. 100 C.E.) *Ioudaikē Archaiologia* (c. 93 C.E.; in Latin, *Antiquitates Judaicae*; in English, *Antiquities of the Jews*, 1926-1965).

BOOKS AND ARTICLES

Ferrill, Arther. *The Origins of War: From the Stone Age to Alexander the Great*. New York: Thames and Hudson, 1988.
Roux, Georges. *Ancient Iraq*. 2d ed. New York: Penguin, 1986.
Wiseman, D. J. *Nebuchadrezzar and Babylon*. New York: Oxford University Press, 1987.
Yadin, Yigael. *The Art of Warfare in Biblical Lands*. Vol. 2. New York: McGraw-Hill, 1963.

Andrew C. Skinner

THE HEBREWS

DATES: 1400 B.C.E.-FIRST CENTURY C.E.

POLITICAL CONSIDERATIONS

The history of the Hebrew people contains a large number of military campaigns and battles. The biblical stories of the walls of Jericho falling down and of David standing against Goliath with a slingshot are familiar ones to many people. These are, however, only two of many well-known war stories from the Bible. Initially, warfare was one of the methods the Israelites employed to first settle a homeland. The location of that homeland, the strategic Syro-Palestinian corridor, guaranteed that they would be engaged in continual warfare, trying to secure the land and to protect themselves from invasions from Mesopotamia and Egypt.

MILITARY ACHIEVEMENT

The first military engagements of the Hebrew people of the late Bronze Age were wars of conquest. These included, in Transjordan, the defeat of Sihon, king of Heshbon, and Og, king of Bashan, and the campaign against Midian, both of which are described in the biblical Book of Numbers. Later, Joshua ben Nun accomplished the occupation of Canaan, the Hebrew "promised land" west of the Jordan, through three strategic military actions, all of which are described in the biblical Book of Joshua. First, the Hebrews crossed the Jordan River opposite Jericho into the heart of the land, capturing Jericho, Ai, and Bethel. Second, a coalition of kings from five Canaanite city-states in the south were defeated and routed in battle at Gibeon, and a number of cities of the southern Shephelah were taken or destroyed. Finally, a league of Canaanite kings under the leadership of Jabin, king of Hazor, were defeated in battle at the "waters of Merom," in northern Galilee, and their cities were taken by the Israelites (Joshua 11). These achieve-ments were accomplished with a unified militia of Is-raelite tribes.

Although the unified strategy of Joshua ben Nun succeeded in defeating the coalition of forces capable of threatening Israel's position in Canaan, the task of mopping up fell to individual tribes at the beginning of the Iron Age (1200-1000 B.C.E.). The lack of tribal unity within the Israelite confederacy during this period allowed a resurgence of Canaanite power and the emergence along the Mediterranean coast of the Philistines, one group from among the earlier invading Sea Peoples that had been repulsed from Egypt by Ramses III (r. 1184-1153 B.C.E.) around 1168 B.C.E. According to extrabiblical records, the Philistines held a well-deserved reputation for martial skill and organization. In addition, they controlled a monopoly on iron metallurgy. Due to these factors, the Israelite leaders, the judges Samuel and Saul, found themselves fighting defensive engagements. The lack of tribal unity also contributed to a period of civil war, described in the biblical Book of Judges.

After consolidating his reign in Judah and Israel, David (c. 1030-c. 962 B.C.E.) besieged and captured the Jebusite city of Jerusalem around 1000 B.C.E., making it the capital of his kingdom, as described in the biblical Book of 2 Samuel. After the Philistines heard that David had been made king of Israel, they moved to attack, but were defeated by David in the Valley of Rephaim and pursued to Gezer. David then campaigned to expand his kingdom, conquering the Moabites, Edomites, Ammonites, Aramaeans, and others. He instituted a standing army and placed garrisons throughout his growing empire. By such means he gained control of the trade along the Kings Highway east of the Jordan as well as the Via Maris, a lowland passage running through Israel to Damascus. Israel reached the zenith of its military and political power under David. Solomon (c. 991-930 B.C.E.), David's heir, maintained the same control and

TURNING POINTS

c. 14th cent. B.C.E.	The Hebrews conquer Transjordan and Canaan under the leadership of Joshua.
1000-990 B.C.E.	David consolidates the reign of Judah and Israel and defeats neighboring kingdoms of Moab, Edom, Ammon, and Aramaea, among others.
705-701 B.C.E.	Judean king Hezekiah leads rebellion against Assyrian domination.
587 B.C.E.	Jerusalem falls to the Neo-Babylonians.
167-161 B.C.E.	Judas Maccabeus leads campaigns against Greek rule.
39-37 B.C.E.	Herod is named king of Judea by the Roman Senate and leads campaigns to establish his kingdom.
66-70 C.E.	The Jews wage war against the Romans.
70	Jerusalem falls to the Romans.
73	The stronghold of Masada falls to the Romans after a three-year siege.

reigned from the great bend of the Euphrates to Elat on the Red Sea.

During the years of the divided monarchy, the southern kingdom of Judah and the northern kingdom of Israel were reduced to fighting each other in civil war or supporting each other in defensive battles against outside invasion. Two particular examples of the latter stand out. In 853 B.C.E. Ahab (c. 874-c. 853 B.C.E.), king of Israel, joined other small Canaanite and Syrian kingdoms in a coalition against Shalmaneser III (r. 858-824 B.C.E.), king of Assyria. Ahab was able to field 2,000 chariots and 18,000 infantrymen, some of them probably from Judah. The coalition met Shalmaneser III at Karkar in the Orontes Valley and stopped his advance. In 725 B.C.E. Shalmaneser V (r. 726-722 B.C.E.) laid siege to Samaria, the capital of Israel. Although the city held out for several years, it finally surrendered, and the kingdom of Israel disintegrated.

Judah remained a vassal-state of Assyria. However, at the end of the eighth century B.C.E. King Hezekiah of Judah (r. c. 715-c. 686 B.C.E.) revolted along with rulers of other smaller kingdoms. The Neo-Assyrian king Sennacherib's (r. 704-681 B.C.E.) response was brutal. Every town in Judah was captured, and in 701 B.C.E. Sennacherib trapped Hezekiah in Jerusalem. In response to the Assyrian threat, Hezekiah reorganized the army, refortified Jerusalem and redirected its water source, constructing the Siloam tunnel to bring water into the city. Senna-

cherib failed in his siege and returned to Assyria, where he was assassinated. The kingdom of Judah lasted until 587 B.C.E., when Jerusalem fell to the Neo-Babylonians.

For several centuries after the fall of Jerusalem the Hebrews were subject to foreign masters. Successively conquered by Babylon, Assyria, Persia, and Greece, they generally cooperated with rulers who tolerated their religious practices. Despite the pacifist strains of Isaiah and other prophets, the Jews could be quite bellicose in defending their religion. When Alexander the Great (356-323 B.C.E.) conquered Judea, he did not interfere with Jewish worship. However, one of his successors, Antiochus IV Epiphanes (c. 215-164 B.C.E.), decided to impose Greek culture on subject peoples and around 167 B.C.E. constructed a statue of Zeus in the Holy Temple of Jerusalem and forbade such practices as circumcision and observing the Sabbath. Rebellion again broke out in 167 B.C.E. under the Maccabees, a priestly family. The uprising began as a guerrilla war, but Judas Maccabeus (d. 160 B.C.E.) organized the army along the old traditional lines. Fighting with small outnumbered forces, Judas proved to be a brilliant tactician accomplishing many difficult military feats. Judas and his brothers liberated Jerusalem and established a new independent Jewish state, with the kings and high priests both coming from the Maccabee family. Once independent, the Maccabees continued to wage war in Samaria, Transjordan, and among the descendants of the Edomites, forcing them to convert to Judaism. They also suppressed Jews who adopted Greek values and practices. For all their militarism, the Maccabees refused to fight on the Sabbath.

The later Maccabees allied with Rome and allowed Judea to fall under Roman control. Initially, the Romans tolerated the religion of Jews who did not challenge Roman authority. Jews were allowed to live and prosper throughout the empire, especially in Alexandria and Rome. The Roman Senate designated Herod the Great (r. 37-4 B.C.E.) king of Judea, but he had to fight for every inch of his kingdom. In the winter of 39 B.C.E. Herod returned to Palestine with the help of the Roman army. By 37 B.C.E. Herod had taken Jerusalem. Five years later Herod defeated the Nabateans and annexed a portion of their territory. Finally, by 20 B.C.E. Herod's kingdom had almost reached the size of that of David and Solomon.

Commonly, the Romans permitted conquered peoples to continue worshiping their gods, providing they acknowledged the Roman gods, including Caesar. However, monotheistic Judaism did not allow this accommodation, and guerrilla movements to resist Rome emerged in Judea. The Romans executed Jewish prophets and messiahs who challenged them. Among them may have been Jesus of Nazareth. One party, the Zealots, committed to purging Judea of all pagan elements, allegedly kidnapped and killed Jews who cooperated with Rome. In 66 C.E. the Jews revolted against Rome. The rebels set up a government in Jerusalem and divided the country into seven military districts. The emperor Nero (37-68 C.E.) sent his best general, Vespasian (9-79 C.E.), to quell the uprising. Vespasian systematically defeated the rebels until the Jews held only Jerusalem and the territory surrounding the city. Vespasian returned to Rome to be crowned

emperor, leaving his son Titus (39-81 C.E.) in charge of the Siege of Jerusalem. By August 30, 70 C.E., Titus had taken the entire population of Jerusalem captive and leveled its buildings to the ground. A small group of rebels fled to the stronghold at Masada. They lasted until 73 C.E., when the Romans breached the walls. Approximately 960 defenders at Masada committed suicide during the night rather than surrender to the Romans.

WEAPONS, UNIFORMS, AND ARMOR

A wide range of offensive and defensive weapons are mentioned in biblical texts. None of these are in essence unique to the Israelite soldier. By the time of the Iron Age, the Hebrew soldier employed the same weaponry used in the surrounding ancient Near eastern area.

The most practical offensive weapon was the small sword or dagger. It was fewer than 50 centimeters in length and generally used in short-range, hand-to-hand combat. The sword was carried in a sheath attached to the belt. The Israelites also used

North Wind Picture Archives

Hebrew leader Joshua ben Nun begins the occupation of Canaan, the Hebrew "promised land" west of the Jordan, with the taking of Jericho.

javelins and lances. The most significant long-range offensive weapon, however, was the bow and arrow. Arrowheads were first made of bronze and later iron. They were designed to pierce armor. David used a sling against Goliath, and soldiers from the tribe of Benjamin developed a deadly accuracy with this weapon.

The most common defensive arm, the leather buckler or shield, could be made in several sizes. Body armor, coats of mail, and helmets were available although probably were not common until the time of David. The defenders of Lachish, besieged by the forces of Sennacherib in 701 B.C.E., are shown wearing bronze helmets in the famous Assyrian bas-relief in the palace of Sennacherib at Nineveh.

MILITARY ORGANIZATION

At the end of the Bronze Age, military service was a part of the life of every capable male. Although some exceptions were granted, as described in the biblical Book of Deuteronomy, the survival of the nation as a whole depended upon the tribal fighting units that could be called up for battle as needed. These forces were voluntary and functioned on an as-needed basis. Soldiers returned to their homes and fields after the war.

A major change took place during the monarchy. Saul (r. c. 1020-1000) was the first to begin to recruit a more permanent army. David developed his own personal bodyguard and a professional army including several mercenaries. The Hebrew army was divided into units of 1,000 commanded by a leader. These units could be further divided into smaller groups of 100 and 50. Solomon was the first to establish a strong chariot force. Chariots were effective on the open plain, but they proved useless in the mountain terrain of much of Palestine.

Archive Photos

David, the Hebrew king of Judah and Israel, who besieged and captured the Jebusite city of Jerusalem and made it the capital of his kingdom.

DOCTRINE, STRATEGY, AND TACTICS

The early Hebrew army did not seem to do well in pitched battles on open terrain. Usually outnumbered, they often employed guerrilla tactics. Some of these included feints, decoys, ambushes, and diversionary maneuvers. Night movements and night attacks were also used. The Hebrews also developed a battle cry that would frighten or dishearten the enemy.

David instituted a particular military and political doctrine that provided great wealth for himself and his son Solomon. Even later, when the kings of Israel and Judah also followed this doctrine, political power and prosperity followed. First, David sought peace between Israel and Judah. Second, he exercised a strong hand in matters east of the Jordan. His plan was to subjugate the Aramaeans, Ammonites, Moabites, and Edomites, and thus to control the trade along the Kings Highway in Transjordan. Finally, David opened trade relations with the maritime nation of Hiram of Tyre (r. 969-936 B.C.E.).

ANCIENT SOURCES

A fair knowledge of the military achievements of the nations of the ancient Near East is revealed by the numerous paintings, drawings, reliefs, and inscriptions left behind. Even peace treaties describe the titles and functions of individuals in the army. However, information about the military organization of Israel from 1400 B.C.E. to the first century C.E. is not so complete. The Hebrew Bible remains the primary resource for understanding the military achievements of the Hebrew people. However, the Bible is not a military history. Therefore, it must be supplemented with archaeological and epigraphic discoveries from elsewhere in Egypt, Mesopotamia, and Palestine.

BOOKS AND ARTICLES

Aharoni, Yohanan, and Michael Avi-Yonah. *The Macmillan Bible Atlas*. 3d ed. New York: Macmillan, 1993.

Bright, John. *A History of Israel*. 4th ed. Louisville, Ky.: Westminster John Knox Press, 2000.

De Vaux, Roland. *Ancient Israel: Its Life and Institutions*. Grand Rapids, Mich.: Wm. B. Eerdmans, 1997.

Gonen, R. *Weapons of the Ancient World*. London: Cassell, 1975.

Yadin, Yigael. *The Art of Warfare in Biblical Lands in the Light of Archaeological Study*. 2 vols. New York: McGraw-Hill, 1963.

Stephen J. Andrews

THE EGYPTIANS

DATES: C. 3000-30 B.C.E.

MILITARY ACHIEVEMENT

The chief innovations of Egyptian military thought were more in strategy and tactics than in weapons development. Although Egyptian military armaments remained relatively unchanged for millennia, the Egyptians' emphasis on indirect engagement and speed of movement—more than cultural conservatism—accounts for this lack of innovation.

Egyptian armies early enlisted large numbers of foreign troops, foremost among whom were Nubian auxiliaries, renowned for their archery skills. The geology of southern Egypt, and the southern armies' early use of Nubian troops, who were adept at desert warfare, led to wars of maneuver in the desert. Predynastic Period (c. 5300-3000 B.C.E.) and First Intermediate Period (c. 2160-2055 B.C.E.) forces used desert roads in order to outflank Nile Valley opponents. This emphasis on an indirect approach, and the Egyptians' apparent preference for projectile weapons and battles of speed, led to an increasing reliance on foreign troops during the first millennium B.C.E., as foreign troops became increasingly important. During the reign of Ptolemy IV Philopator (r. 221-205 B.C.E.), Egyptian soldiers were armed and trained in Hellenistic fashion.

WEAPONS, UNIFORMS, AND ARMOR

The bow was the most important weapon in the Egyptian arsenal. Early bows were the simple bow and a bow with animal horns as the tip elements. The composite bow appeared in Egypt during the Second Intermediate Period (c. 1650-1550 B.C.E.) and became increasingly popular during the New Kingdom (c. 1550-1069 B.C.E.), partly in response to the increased use of body armor by many of Egypt's enemies. The bows of Libyan auxiliaries were small composite bows; Nubian troops preferred the self bow. New Kingdom Egyptian chariots served as mobile archery platforms.

Pointed, and sometimes barbed, Egyptian arrows caused deep wounds. Broad, and sometimes flat-tipped, Egyptian arrows caused broad, stunning injuries. Arrow tips were made from flint, horn, wood, and bone; copper tips had appeared by the time of the Middle Kingdom (c. 2055-1650 B.C.E.), and bronze tips by the time of the New Kingdom. There is slight evidence for the use of poisoned arrows. Arrows were carried in quivers; primarily during the Middle Kingdom bows and arrows together were at times held within a sleevelike quiver, open at each end.

Slings are attested, and slingers appear in the crows' nests of Egyptian warships. Late Coptic sources portray Egyptian women as adept at the use of the sling. The Egyptians also employed throwsticks in combat.

Spears appeared early in the Egyptian arsenal, both long, thrusting spears and short, stabbing spears. By the time of the Nineteenth Dynasty (1295-1186 B.C.E.) two spears had appeared in the arsenal of Egyptian chariot soldiers, to be used if the chariot became disabled. Throwing spears are also attested. New Kingdom troops at times carried both spear and battle-ax, possibly throwing spears prior to closing with axes.

Battle-axes, with blades of stone, copper, or bronze as technology evolved, were the preferred close-combat weapons. Early metal battle-axes had rounded blades. From the time of the Second Intermediate Period the standard shape was a long, roughly rectangular blade, convex on the cutting edge, with slightly concave sides. New Kingdom Libyan auxiliaries carried battle-axes with archaic, rounded blades.

The mace administered the *coup de grâce* to the heads of the mortally wounded, the origin of the pharaonic image of the ruler smiting the enemies of Egypt. Apparently common in earlier Egyptian forces as actual weapons with pear- and disc-shaped heads, the mace is rarely depicted outside of smiting scenes and royal regalia. The mace becomes more visible in later New Kingdom scenes, in which it is larger, with a curved blade attached, beginning at the base of the mace head and coming to a point beyond the top of the mace head. The weight of the mace was apparently intended to help the blade pierce body armor.

A variety of staves and clubs were employed. A First Intermediate Period warrior refers to a staff of copper, perhaps a metal-sheathed staff, and fighting rods are relatively common in Ramessid Period (1295-1069 B.C.E.) battle scenes. These weapons, like the biblical "rod of iron," delivered crushing blows and became more prevalent during the later New Kingdom as a means of combating armored foes. Nubian foes and allies of the Egyptians often wielded wooden clubs with relatively narrow handles, swelling below the tip.

Soldiers carried daggers of various lengths, which could be used to remove a hand, or the phallus of an uncircumcised foe, from each slain enemy, a well-attested New Kingdom practice that allowed an accurate estimate of the strength of enemy forces. The slashing scimitar appeared in Egypt during the New Kingdom; mounted troops developed long, stabbing rapiers. Long swords and body armor appeared with Mediterranean mercenaries during the New Kingdom.

As in hunting, so in warfare dogs frequently accompanied Egyptian soldiers into battle. Old Kingdom (c. 2686-2125 B.C.E.) and Middle Kingdom desert rangers often appeared with their dogs, usually basenjis. During the New Kingdom greyhound- and saluki-like hounds became more common in battle scenes. Ramses II (c. 1300-1213 B.C.E.) was accompanied into battle by a pet "battle-lion."

Early shields depicted on the Hunters Palette, a stone carving from the Predynastic Period, were small and irregular, perhaps made from turtle shells, like some more recent shields of Red Sea nomads. Shields during the Early Dynastic Period (c. 3000-2686 B.C.E.) were often large; tall, full-coverage shields are known from the time of the Middle Kingdom. Shields became smaller during the New Kingdom, rounded at the top and square at the bottom. During the New Kingdom they were often covered in animal hide, often with a metal boss in the upper middle. During melees New Kingdom soldiers often slung their shields over their shoulders with a diagonal strap, protecting their backs and necks while freeing both hands. At the end of the New Kingdom period, Mediterranean mercenaries introduced round shields into the Egyptian arsenal.

ARMOR AND ATTIRE

Climate and Egyptian emphasis on speed of movement and flanking maneuvers through the deserts flanking the Nile Valley discouraged the development of body armor. A metal breast protector appears in a Middle Kingdom scene, but during the Old Kingdom and Middle Kingdom the only garments common on soldiers' torsos were crossed textile bands. Quilted and leather protection for the torso appeared during the New Kingdom, usually in the form of bands wrapped around the chest and over one shoulder. Textile or leather shirts with metal and leather scale armor also appeared during the New Kingdom, primarily providing protection for chariot warriors. During the New Kingdom Mediterranean pirates and mercenaries in Egyptian service began to wear significant metal body armor; however, it is unclear to what extent native troops adopted such armor.

Nubian auxiliaries wore leather sporrans, or pouches, during both the First Intermediate Period and Middle Kingdom. Large, heart-shaped, quilted sporrans appeared during the New Kingdom. These elements of clothing appear to have functioned as protection for the groin area. Soldiers often wore a leather overkilt, cut to have the appearance of a leather net with a seat patch.

Middle Kingdom soldiers, as revealed by mummified remains at Deir el-Bahri, a temple site on the west bank of the Nile near Thebes, wore their hair thick and greased, forming a natural protection against blows to the head and neck. Textile head coverings are well attested, and there is sporadic evidence for helmets during the New Kingdom.

CHARIOTRY

The chariot appeared in Egypt's arsenal at the beginning of the Eighteenth Dynasty (1550-1295 B.C.E.) and presumably had entered the land during the Second Intermediate Period, when the Hyksos, an Eastern Mediterranean maritime power, dominated northern Egypt. Egyptian chariots were light, usually with a rear-mounted wheel, and carried a driver and an archer. Horses wore protective armor, or bardings. Egypt's opponents followed this pattern until the Hittites, under pressure from heavily armored troops in their western marches, adopted a heavier chariot with three occupants, used for rapid transport of infantry rather than for archery. Egyptian chariotry did not adopt such a response to the rise of heavy infantry. Runners accompanied chariots; many were foreign mercenaries who protected the chariots and horses and attempted to capture those of the enemy.

North Wind Picture Archives

An Egyptian chariot team of driver and archer.

The earliest Egyptian chariots had wheels with four spokes. During the middle of the Eighteenth Dynasty, six spokes became standard. Egyptian chariots had a cab with a roughly D-shaped floor plan; a curved wooden banister at waist level in front stretched back and down to the rear floor. The light bodies could be partially closed with wood or leather sidings. Floors of rope or leather mesh absorbed the shock of rough terrain. Side-mounted cases held bows and arrows and, from the time of the Nineteenth Dynasty, spears.

The infrequently attested use of mounted troops was primarily as reconnaissance patrols and couriers. Many of these cavalry troopers were Nubians. Roads and remount stations were maintained for these patrols.

SIEGE EQUIPMENT

Wheeled siege ladders appeared during the late Old Kingdom and the First Intermediate Period. Sapping is attested, often performed by soldiers with hand weapons. In one Middle Kingdom scene, three men within a protective testudo siege engine work a long, crowbarlike pole against the walls of a fortress. The use of sloping glacis at the base of fortress walls by the time of the Middle Kingdom suggests the use of similar sapping, and would also have deterred the use of battering rams.

Supposed evidence for stone-throwing machines from the Twenty-fifth Dynasty (747-656 B.C.E.) is based on faulty translations. Siege ramps, apparently of earth and wood, with platforms for archers and slingers, are attested. When the Nubian ruler Piye (747-716 B.C.E.) attacked Memphis by land and river, his marines used their ships' spars to scale the river walls of the city, and the construction of a siege ramp held down many of the defenders of the land walls.

MILITARY ORGANIZATION

Early Egyptian forces were divided between infantry and archers; during the New Kingdom the chief divisions were between chariotry and foot soldiers. The smallest independently operating units appear to have been of ten men, with a squad leader; during the New Kingdom the smallest units appear to have been fifty men. The New Kingdom saw the emergence of a complex military hierarchy. Armies were equipped by various temples, institutions that fulfilled many important economic functions in Egypt. The four armies of Ramses II (r. 1279-1213 B.C.E.) at Kadesh were named for four deities. Mercenaries were important, and there were early units of Nubian troops, usually archers. Libyans and Mediterranean mercenaries and pirates were also important. Each independently operating unit had at least one scribe. During the Ptolemaic (332-30 B.C.E.) and Roman (30 B.C.E.-395 C.E.) Periods, Hellenistic and Roman military practices supplanted earlier Egyptian practices.

DOCTRINE, STRATEGY, AND TACTICS

FORTIFICATIONS

Fortified positions first appeared during the Predynastic Period. During the Middle Kingdom, a series of fortresses, watch posts, and patrol roads created an elaborate system of defense in depth at the Second Cataract of the Nile in Nubia, the southern boundary of direct Egyptian control and influence in the south. The complexity and extent of this system presaged later Roman achievements. Roman border defenses, and their Egyptian precursors, consisted of three types: defense by client states, with lightly defended legionary camps; perimeter defense; and defense in depth. Perimeter defense involved main fortresses behind outer defenses, with patrol roads and watchtowers stretching back to the fortresses. In defense in depth, larger and more heavily fortified fortresses were intended to stand alone in areas periodically overrun by foes.

Middle Kingdom Egyptian forts in Nubia developed in almost the opposite way. Initially they were well-fortified outposts in a perimeter defense, part of an elaborate system of patrol roads and watchposts, befitting their location in the low desert plain. Later Middle Kingdom forts on the southern end of the Second Cataract were, like later Roman fortresses, heavily fortified, with spur walls for enfilading fire, atop granite outcroppings, a response to the rise of the powerful Kerman state in Nubia. The Middle Kingdom fortresses in Nubia were supply depots and strongholds allowing the extension of Egyptian patrols into the far south.

By the time of Thutmose II (r. 1492-1479 B.C.E.) there were client states in Nubia, and the New Kingdom fortress of Buhen was less heavily defended, like the later Roman fortresses of the perimeter defense system. During the New Kingdom Egypt had a *foederati*-like arrangement with more developed Nubian client states. Nubia was important to Egypt as a source of military manpower, and the point of origin or transshipment of many goods, including gold and incense.

A network of patrol roads, camps, and watchposts stretched through the Western Desert during the Middle Kingdom, and the Theban Seventeenth Dynasty (c. 1580-1550 B.C.E.) maintained and elaborated upon certain elements of this system. Fortresses also guarded the eastern Nile Delta; a Middle Kingdom fortress in the Wadi an-Naṭrūn implies a similar line guarding the Western Delta. During the reign of Ramses II a line of fortresses guarded the approach to the Delta between the Mediterranean coast and the Qattara Depression.

Chariotry dominated late Bronze Age battlefields, on which the vehicles initially served as mobile archery platforms. A reliance on the expensive chariot arm was possible only for the wealthiest states of the ancient Near East, allowing those states to rely on small, elite forces, a desirable situation for complex societies in which labor was needed in many fields. Chariotry was ineffective against massed barbarian infantry and unsuited to mountainous or forested terrain. In battles in which chariotry was the principal arm, infantry provided support. At the Battle of Kadesh (1274 B.C.E.) under Ramses II, an infantry division assured the Egyptians' tactical success.

Unlike the Nubians, the Egyptians never permanently occupied Asia. In the northeast, Egypt supported the lesser of two conflicting powers, thereby seeking to create buffer states that, with Egyptian aid, might oppose a third power, but could not alone pose a threat to Egypt.

NAVAL ACTIVITY AND STRATEGIES

Amphibious infantry landings are known from the late Old Kingdom and the First Intermediate Period.

During the Seventeenth Dynasty, Kamose (r. 1555-1550 B.C.E.) employed warships in three lines ahead, the central line breaking the enemy line and flanking lines preventing enemy escape. Kamose could thereby break the line of the Hyksos battle squadron and capture its merchant fleet. Thutmose III (r. 1479-1425 B.C.E.) constructed ships in sections on the Mediterranean coast and transported them overland for an amphibious attack on the Euphrates.

When invasions of marauding Sea Peoples occurred during the reign of Ramses III (r. 1184-1153 B.C.E.), various ships, including smaller Nile warships, protected the Nile Delta. Archers and grappling hooks and lines for capsizing enemy warships were the main offensive weapons. Large ships filled with troops appear to have broken the formations of the attacking enemy. Smaller vessels, able to operate in the treacherous areas of sandbanks near the mouths of the Nile, completed the destruction of the enemy. Ramming apparently was not practiced until the Ptolemaic and Roman periods.

MAGIC

Considering the importance of religion in Egyptian culture, it is to be expected that religion should serve military purposes as well. The names of foreign and domestic foes were written on small, usually clay images of bound enemies, and buried in execration rituals. Warfare was equated with hunting, both activities asserting Egyptian authority and control over chaotic forces and contributing to the proper order of the cosmos.

ANCIENT SOURCES

The considerable accomplishments of the ancient Egyptians in the realm of tactics must be reconstructed from much disparate and indirect evidence, and the lack of any true military treatise from ancient Egypt means that much information has been lost. Numerous scenes and inscriptions recounting military activity survive, the earliest from the late Gerzean Period (c. 3500-3200 B.C.E.). Military scribes kept daybook accounts of expeditions, excerpts of which appeared occasionally in inscriptions, such as those of Thutmose III at Karnak. The ancient Egyptians stressed the timeless importance of events and of history as festival, an emphasis leading to a lack of what might be considered truly historical accounts of military activities.

BOOKS AND ARTICLES

Drews, Robert. *The End of the Bronze Age*. Princeton, N.J.: Princeton University Press, 1993.

Shaw, Ian. *Egyptian Warfare and Weapons*. Princes Risborough, England: Shire, 1991.

Spalinger, Anthony John. *Aspects of the Military Documents of the Ancient Egyptians*. New Haven, Conn.: Yale University Press, 1982.

Wachsmann, Shelley. *Seagoing Ships and Seamanship in the Bronze Age Levant*. College Station: Texas A&M University Press, 1998.

Yadin, Yigael. *The Art of Warfare in Biblical Lands in the Light of Archaeological Study*. New York: McGraw-Hill, 1963.

John Coleman Darnell

THE PERSIANS

DATES: TO 651 C.E.

The Persians were an Iranian-speaking, Indo-European people. As described in both the *Rig Veda* and the *Avesta*, the sacred texts of Hinduism and Zoroastrianism respectively, warriors played an important part in Persian society. The warrior class, from which chiefs and kings were chosen, was second in status only to that of the priests. However, these religious texts, written by priests, may overemphasize the importance of the priest class within Persian society. Horses were important to the Persians, who used them effectively against both the native inhabitants of the Iranian plateau and their Mesopotamian neighbors, especially the Assyrians, whose military technology was the most advanced in the world in the first millennium B.C.E. Ancient Persian history can be divided into three periods: the Achaemenid Persian period (550-330 B.C.E.), the Hellenic and Parthian period (330 B.C.E.-224 C.E.), and the Sassanid period (224-651 C.E.).

MILITARY ACHIEVEMENT

ACHAEMENID PERSIAN PERIOD

The Achaemenid Persians achieved supremacy by 550 B.C.E. after their leader, Cyrus the Great (r. 550-529 B.C.E.), had conquered the Iranian plateau, Mesopotamia, Levant, and Anatolia. The Achaemenid Persians defeated their cousins, the Medes, who had previously defeated the Assyrians. Cyrus's successors, Cambyses II (r. 529-522 B.C.E.) and Darius I (r. 522-486 B.C.E), conquered Egypt, Nubia, Libya, and Central Asia, forming the largest empire known to the world at that time. The Achaemenid Persian Empire was matched only by that of Alexander the Great (356-323 B.C.E.), who later conquered the Persian Empire. For two centuries the Persians maintained a vast empire with a large army requiring a large administrative apparatus. Only the Greeks were able to resist the Persians, and the struggle between the two civilizations became a focal point of Greek and Western historiography.

HELLENIC AND THE PARTHIAN PERIOD

After the Greek conquest of Persia in 330 B.C.E., Seleucus I (between 358 and 354-281 B.C.E.), one of Alexander's generals, took over the Asiatic portion of the Persian Empire and formed the Seleucid Dynasty. The Seleucid Empire centered on Syria and extended, at its peak, from the Mediterranean Sea to as far east as India's Indus Valley. By 238 B.C.E. an Iranian group known as the Parthians had established themselves in the eastern portion of the Persian Empire, in the area that encompasses the modern Iranian province of Khurāsān and part of southern Turkmenistan. Because the Parthians were a nomadic group, the cavalry remained the most important aspect of the Persian army during this period. The Parthians were able to defend themselves against the Roman forces, defeating the Romans in several key battles.

SASSANID PERIOD

The Sassanid Dynasty was established in 224 C.E. by Ardashīr I (r. c. 224-241 C.E.), who revived the Achaemenid religious tradition of Zoroastrianism and made it the official religion. From the outset of their reign, the Sassanids were able to defeat the Romans and all other competing forces in Southwest Asia. The Sassanids controlled Central Asia, the Iranian Plateau, and Mesopotamia, and made major incursions into Syria. Throughout the third century they repeatedly defeated Roman forces, killing one emperor, capturing another, and forcing a third to pay a ransom for the safety of his army. Seventh century Sassanid forces conquered Palestine, Egypt, and Anatolia, laying siege to the Byzantine capital, Constantinople. For four centuries, the Sassanids successfully defended their empire from invasions by the Turkic tribes and the Kushans from the east, the Romans, Byzantines, and Arabs from the west, and the nomadic tribes from the north.

WEAPONS, UNIFORMS, AND ARMOR

The sacred Zoroastrian text, the *Avesta*, mentions weapons and war sporadically. Certain Zoroastrian gods, such as Wahrām, had been worshipped by the military since well before the time of the Achaemenid Persians. Wahrām, whose name means "offensive victory," could take on many forms, mainly those of fierce beasts. The goddess Anahitā was another deity from whom the Persians sought aid in battle against their enemies. Prayers were usually accompanied with sacrifices and ritual acts.

Greek and Iranian sources indicate that the elite Persian forces wore long, draped robes with trousers, as well as coats of mail covering their chests. The Greek historian Xenophon (430-354 B.C.E.) states that Persian cavalry forces carried javelins and wore breastplates, armor, and helmets. Xenophon also mentions various standards, or banners carried in battle, specifically the royal standard, a spread-winged eagle on a shield.

The Persian infantry wore loose tunics with corslets of metal scales underneath for protection from spear thrusts. They wore felt hoods and helmets for head protection and carried short swords, lances with wooden shafts and metal points, quivers full of arrows with bronze or iron points, bows with ends shaped like animals' heads, and wicker shields of different shapes.

Greek sources tend to exaggerate the numbers of Persian forces, with estimates ranging from 900 thousand to 5 million. The main reason for such exaggeration was to boast the Greeks' ability to repel Achaemenid aggression during the Greco-Persian Wars (499-448 B.C.E.). The Persian navy, stationed at Cilicia on the Mediterranean coast, was composed mainly of foreigners, such as the Phoenicians, Greeks, and Egyptians. The mercenary status of the Persian navy was a reason for its defeat against the Greek navy; when the war became difficult or its outcome unsure, the Persian naval commanders either retreated or left altogether. The lack of a competent naval force would be a major reason that the Achaemenid Persians were ultimately unsuccessful against the Greek city-states.

MILITARY ORGANIZATION

The success of the Persian military was based on the capability of its military leaders and its army. Greek sources provide ample information on the composition of the Persian army, especially during the Greco-Persian Wars. The Persian nomadic forces that conquered the Medes were turned into organized standing forces composed of both Persians and Medians. These forces consisted of both cavalry, which included chariots, horses, and camels, and infantry, which included lance-bearers and bowmen. As more people, including Greeks, Lydians, and Mesopotamians, were incorporated into the Persian Empire, they were also brought into the army. Greek mercenaries were used from the time of Cambyses in the sixth century B.C.E.

The Persian army's sophisticated training regiment of elite forces was drawn from the ranks of the nobility. In a system resembling that of the Spartans, who trained soldiers from youth, the Persians selectively trained certain youths, who passed required tests, to be warriors. According to Greek sources, the youths who were accepted into warrior society were taught various athletic, farming, and craft skills. As they matured, they were trained in the military arts, such as archery, spear and javelin throwing, and marching. In addition to these elite warrior forces, there were special forces composed of hardened warriors who acted as a sort of secret service.

The Persian army was divided according to the decimal system, in units of tens, hundreds, and thousands. Greek sources mention an elite Persian force known as the Immortals, composed of ten thousand men and so called because previously selected men waited to fill the places of casualties in battle. The Immortals reportedly included spearmen of Persian nobility: one thousand in the cavalry and ten thousand in the infantry. Of these ten thousand infantrymen, one thousand had golden pomegranates instead

PERSIAN EMPIRE, C. 500 B.C.E.

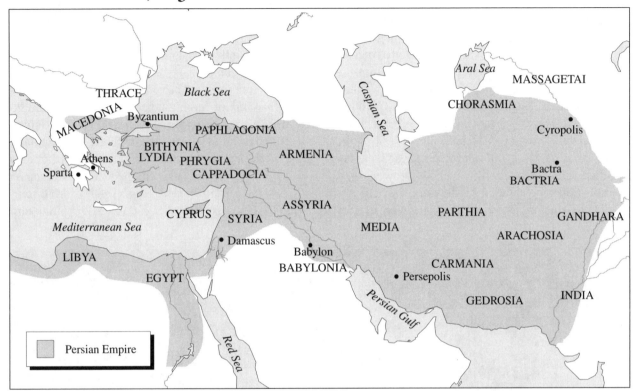

of spikes on the butt-ends of their spears. They marched in two sections, one ahead of and the other behind the remaining nine thousand Immortals, whose spears had silver pomegranates.

After 238 B.C.E. when the Parthians came to dominate the Persian Empire, the heavily armored cavalry, known as *cataphracts*, became the elite forces of the army. The extremely accurate mounted bowmen of the Parthian cavalry repeatedly defeated the Romans with their famed maneuvering techniques. The most famous of these techniques, riding a horse while shooting arrows backward, came to be known as the Parthian shot. Parthian horses were covered with mail to protect them from attacks by Roman infantrymen. Another unit of lighter, more mobile cavalry also carried bows and arrows. At the Battle of Carrhae in 53 B.C.E., Roman troops under the general Crassus were destroyed by the Parthian cavalry, which harassed the Roman infantry until it broke ranks, at which point the Parthian cavalry pursued

and cut the Roman foot soldiers to pieces. People from other regions were also used in the Parthian forces as either light cavalry or infantry. The infantry was the second group of the army and it was usually considered to be weak and untrained and less reliable in wars.

In the fourth century C.E. Roman soldier and historian Ammianus Marcellinus (c. 330-395) described the Persian cavalry as clad in body armor, mailed coats, breastplates, leg armor plates, and helmets with holes only for the eyes. The Persian cavalry horses were also covered with armor. The grotto of King Xusrō II (590-628 C.E.) at Tāq-i Bustān in northern Persia represents the culmination of the advancement in armor. The Persian weapons, based on the descriptions of Muslim historians, included swords, lances, shields, maces, battle-axes, clubs, bow cases containing two bows with their strings, thirty arrows, and two plaited cords. By the sixth century the chancery of warriors set a stable stipend for cavalry. It was from among these soldiers that the the Immortals, the elite corps of the Achaemenid Persians, were chosen. Their leader was probably the *puštigbān-sālār*, or "commander of the royal guard."

There was also a light cavalry composed of mercenaries or tribespeople in the empire, including the Dailamites, Gēlānīs, Georgians, Armenians, Turks, Arabs, Kushans, Khazars, and Hephtalites. The other form of cavalry used in wars were the elephant corps, or *pīl-bānān*. Ammianus Marcellinus described the elephants as having awful figures and savage, gaping mouths. They looked like walking towers and scarcely could be endured by the faint-hearted. According to Muslim historians, elephants were used as

early as the third century C.E. by the Sassanids, who used them to raze such cities as Hatra. Sassanian king Pērōz I (r. 457/459-484 C.E.) used fifty elephants in his campaign against the Ephthalites in the fifth century. Elephants were again used against the Arabs in the seventh century.

The infantry, or *paygān*, was headed by the *paygān-sālār*, or "commander of the infantry." Infantrymen were fitted with shields and lances. Behind them in formation were the archers, who actually started the war with volleys of shots into the enemy camp before the cavalry charged. The *Strategikon* (c. 580 C.E.; English translation, 1984) of Mauricius Flavius Tiberius (c. 539-602 C.E.), a Byzantine em-

Library of Congress

The Persian forces of Darius I the Great employ elephants in battle against the forces of Alexander the Great at Gaugamela (331 B.C.E.).

peror who reigned from 582 to 602 C.E., gives detailed information on the differences in strategies between the Persian and the Roman soldiers, as well as the intricacies and differences in their weapons and their uses. Naturally the cavalry and infantry forces required a huge logistical apparatus that was sustained by conscripts from the general population. These forces prepared food, repaired weapons, tended to the wounded, and established camps, among other tasks. The Sassanids also utilized Roman techniques in the use of siege weapons including ballistae, battering rams, moving towers, and catapults. The Sassanian navy had been instrumental from the beginning of the Sassanian period, when the founder of the Sassanid Persian dynasty, Ardashīr I (r. 224-241), conquered the Arab side of the Persian Gulf. The control of the Persian Gulf was necessary both militarily and economically, to make it safe from piracy and Roman encroachment. Based on the accounts of Muslim historians, it appears that the Persian ships held one hundred men but were not very important to the military.

Other Persian titles and classifications are from later sources that describe several other military positions, including commander of the forts, warden of marches, the hereditary title of the general of Tus, in northeastern Persia, and the army general. The warrior estate also had a designated Zoroastrian fire-temple known as Adur Gušnasp. This fire-temple was at Šēz, in northwestern Persia, where the king and the warriors went to worship. Rulers such as the Sassanid king Bahrām V, or Bahrām Gūr (fl. fifth century C.E.), sent the booty of jewelry to be hung in the Zoroastrian fire-temple after defeating the Turks in his campaign against them. Ardashīr I also made offerings—the heads of rebels—to the fire-temple of Anāhīd.

During the Sassanid period the warrior class formed the second tier of the social structure; the function of the warrior was to protect the empire and its subjects. There were several divisions within the military, and within the cavalry and infantry. As clergy attended seminaries, the soldiers attended academies where they were trained in the military sciences. The alliance between the priests and the warriors was of paramount importance; the idea of *ērān-sahr*, which had manifested itself under the Sassanids as that of a set territory ruled by the warrior aristocracy, had been developed and revived by Zoroastrian priests. Under the Zoroastrian religion, which was made the official state religion during the Sassanid period, church and state were considered inseparable from each other. In reality, however, each group attempted to impose its will on the other, and this long battle caused the final fragmentation and the weakening of the Persian Empire.

DOCTRINE, STRATEGY, AND TACTICS

Although Achaemenid Persian forces were superior on the ground, their weakness was on the seas, where they mainly employed mercenary forces. At the battles, it was the norm for the king to be present to watch over the battle lines and to engage in battle as well. Before each individual battle a council decided the plan and the strategy the forces would follow. In terms of the military attack, the foot soldiers and the foot archers were stationed in the front and in the middle, flanked by the cavalry and the armed forces. To begin the war, the archers began sending volleys of arrows toward the enemy, then the spearmen and the cavalry came into action. These tactics were successful against the people of the Near East, but they did not crush the Greeks, who, with their hoplite forces, were able to withstand the Persians. Man-to-man combat was also known, and it was a sign of heroic deed to defeat one's enemy in this manner. Cyrus the Younger (c. 424-401 B.C.E.), versed in the Greek tactics, was able to strengthen the Persian military capabilities by enlisting Greek hoplite forces into his army. This group was aided by a heavily armored but ineffective cavalry. Xenophon mentions the Persian cavalry kept their seat only through the pressure of their knees, indicating that they lacked stirrup and saddle.

During the Sassanian period, there existed manuals of warfare that have since been lost. Portions, however, remain extant in Middle Persian and Arabic texts. The Middle Persian text known as the *Dēnkart* (ninth century C.E.; acts of religion) contains a section devoted to the military. This manual informed soldiers about tactics and rations for food, methods for dealing with war prisoners, and the positions for specific forces. For example, the text mentions that the cavalry should be in front and that left-handed archers should be put on the left flank to defend the army. The center should be on an elevated place, where the army commander be supported by the infantry. The army should also be placed with the sun and the wind at their backs to blind and hamper the capability of the enemy.

ANCIENT SOURCES

Sources for the earliest history of the Persians come from the sacred book of the Zoroastrians, the *Avesta*, in which references to combat and weapons are made. The Old Persian sources of the Achaemenid period also give some terminology on weapons, but the Greek sources furnish much more. Herodotus (c. 484-424 B.C.E.), Xenophon, and Strabo (64 or 63-after 23 B.C.E.) are the chief Greek sources, providing many details of the Persian army and their tactics. For the Hellenic and the Parthian period classical authors such as Herodian (third century C.E.), Pliny (23-79 C.E.), and Plutarch (c. 46-after 120) are the major sources. For the Sassanian period, there are a variety of sources not limited to the classical authors. Among the Greek and Latin sources, Ammianus Marcellinus is quite informative on Persian siege tactics, armor, and military. Sassanian sources such as the *Dēnkart* are primary sources, whereas the Arabic and Persian sources after the seventh century C.E., the best of which is *Al-Tabari*, give much information.

BOOKS AND ARTICLES

Briant, P. "The Achaemenid Empire." In *War and Society in the Ancient and Medieval Worlds*, edited by K. Raaflabu and N. Rosenstein. Cambridge, Mass.: Harvard University Press, 1999.

Shahbazi, A. "Army in Pre-Islamic Iran." In *Encyclopaedia Iranica*, edited by Ehsan Yarshater. Vol. 2. London: Routledge & Kegan Paul, 1985.

Wiesehöfer, J. *Ancient Persia.* London: I. B. Taurus, 1996.

Touraj Daryaee

THE ANCIENT WORLD

WORLD

EUROPE AND THE MEDITERRANEAN

GREEK WARFARE TO ALEXANDER
DATES: C. 1600-336 B.C.E.

MILITARY ACHIEVEMENT

The period from 1600 to 336 B.C.E. saw the emergence in Greece of four distinct ways of war. The first of these, Mycenaean chariot warfare, did not survive past about 1100 B.C.E. It was succeeded by an infantry-based system of individual combat, often called "heroic" because of its prominence in Homer's *Iliad* and *Odyssey* (both c. 800 B.C.E.). This system in turn gave way to the close-order infantry warfare of classical Greece. A fourth way of war, the combined arms system developed by the Macedonians in the mid-fourth century B.C.E., ultimately overcame the classical Greeks and provided the basis for the conquests of Alexander the Great.

Mycenaean civilization, named after the citadel of Mycenae in southern Greece, emerged about 1600 B.C.E. and reached its height between 1400 and 1200 B.C.E. Mycenaean monarchs ruled from fortified royal palaces, which were economic as well as political and religious centers. Palaces flourished at Mycenae, Pylos, Tiryns, Thebes, and elsewhere on mainland Greece, as well as at Knossos on the island of Crete. These citadels shared a common culture but were not politically unified. Mycenaean society was hierarchical and bureaucratic; professional scribes used clay tablets and a script called Linear B to track everything that entered or left the palaces. Although little conclusive evidence survives, it appears that Mycenaean armies relied heavily on chariots, perhaps supported by infantry. As in the contemporary Egyptian and Hittite military systems, these chariots probably served as mobile fighting platforms for aristocratic archers and spearmen.

For uncertain reasons, Mycenaean civilization began to collapse around 1250 B.C.E. Indeed, there were upheavals throughout the Mediterranean at this time; the fictional story of the Trojan War reflects later poetic memories of these disturbances. In mainland Greece, the palaces were burned, the countryside was depopulated, and Linear B script disappeared. The chariot forces, dependent on logistical support from the palaces, also declined. Consequently, foot soldiers seem to have gained greater prominence in late Mycenaean warfare. By 1100 B.C.E., however, the great Mycenaean centers and the military system they supported had disappeared completely.

The centuries (1100-750 B.C.E.) following the destruction of Mycenaean civilization are often designated the Greek Dark Age. As petty chieftains replaced Mycenaean kings, warfare became sporadic and local, in the form of raids for booty and individual duels between aristocratic champions. The Homeric poems suggest that Dark Age or heroic warriors preferred spears to swords; spears could be thrown from a distance or used hand-to-hand. Archery, however, was disdained as barbaric and unfair. Chariots may have continued in limited use, perhaps as transports to and from battle. Eventually aristocrats also began to fight from horseback, as cavalry. Yet the most significant military development of the Dark Age was metallurgical: By 900 B.C.E., iron weapons were in widespread use.

By 800 B.C.E. Greece was recovering from the Dark Age. Renewed commerce with the wider Mediterranean world led around 750 B.C.E. to the introduction of the alphabet. During the eighth century B.C.E., increased population and prosperity throughout Greece fostered the rise of the polis, or city-state. A polis (plural, poleis) was a self-governing political unit with a defined territory. Eventually there were more than a thousand poleis in Greece, each one with its own laws, calendar, and military organization. Athens and Sparta, the best known of these states, were exceptionally large in territory and population. Most other poleis were relatively small, with perhaps a few hundred citizens each. Polis governments came in many forms, but all included an assembly of adult male citizens and a council of elders. Political rights and military service were closely linked, so the new emphasis on community over individualism soon transferred into warfare. By about 650 B.C.E. a communal way of war, the hoplite system, had supplanted the individual aristocratic fighting of the Dark Age.

The hoplite was a heavily armored spearman who fought alongside his fellow citizens in a close-order formation called a phalanx. Because hoplites were required to provide their own equipment, most hoplites were middle-class farmers who could afford metal arms and armor. Because citizen farmers could not spare time for extensive training, hoplites were militia, rather than professional, forces. Battles were limited, ritualized affairs, fought on the borderlands between poleis during lulls in the agricultural schedule. There was little in the way of tactics or strategy: Opposing phalanxes lined up against each other on flat open ground, listened to speeches and performed sacrifices, then marched forward against each other. Inevitably one side won the shoving match that followed. Although the losers broke and ran, the victors usually preferred to strip the enemy dead, erect a trophy, and head home. Pursuit after battle was rare. Hoplite warfare, then, did not often result in the complete subjugation of the losing opponent.

TURNING POINTS

1400-1200 B.C.E.	Mycenaean civilization flourishes, with a wealth of political, economic, and religious centers.
1200-1100 B.C.E.	Mycenaean order collapses during a period of upheaval.
1100-750 B.C.E.	In the period known as the Greek Dark Age, petty chieftains replace the Mycenaean kings.
c. 900 B.C.E.	Iron weapons become increasingly popular.
750-650 B.C.E.	Hoplite armor and tactics are developed.
499-448 B.C.E.	The Greco-Persian Wars are fought between Persia and the Greek city-states.
431-404 B.C.E.	The Peloponnesian Wars are fought between Athens and Sparta.
371 B.C.E.	Thebes defeats Sparta at Leuctra, ending Spartan supremacy in hoplite warfare.
338 B.C.E.	The Macedonian army of Philip II defeats Athens at Chaeronea.

The great achievement of the hoplite system was not so much military as political. Hoplite warfare demanded teamwork. There was no room for displays of individual heroism. The communal structure of the phalanx thus reinforced the community spirit of the polis. The hoplite system also helped confine the destructiveness of war to decisive single-day struggles that would not interfere with farming. It therefore gave middle-class agrarians a monopoly on organized violence. Aristocrats were relegated to the cavalry, which usually played only a minor battlefield role. Poor men who could not afford arms and armor were left out of battle altogether, unless they served as slingers or rock throwers.

Sparta was the exception to the hoplite rule. Threatened by military defeat and internal disorder during the mid-seventh century B.C.E., the Spartans responded by turning their state into an armed camp. Spartan boys began military training at age seven. For most of their adult lives, even when married, they lived in sex-segregated barracks rather than private homes. Girls also received military training. Adult male Spartan citizens, or Spartiates, practiced almost constantly for war, giving Sparta the only professional phalanx in all of Greece. Unlike the militiamen of other city-states, Spartan hoplites marched in step to the sound of flutes and could carry out complex tactical maneuvers. This drill and discipline made the Spartan army invincible on the battlefield. Yet in order to free its citizens for war, Sparta's economy had to rely on the labor of helots, serfs who worked the land for their Spartiate masters. Fear of helot revolts often kept the Spartan army at home, thus inhibiting Spartan control of the whole Greek world.

For more than two centuries, the hoplite reigned supreme on Greek battlefields. The Greco-Persian Wars (499-448 B.C.E.) reinforced Greek beliefs in their own military superiority. At the Battle of Marathon in 490 B.C.E., for example, some 10,000 Athenian and Plataean

ATHENIAN EMPIRE, 5TH CENTURY B.C.E.

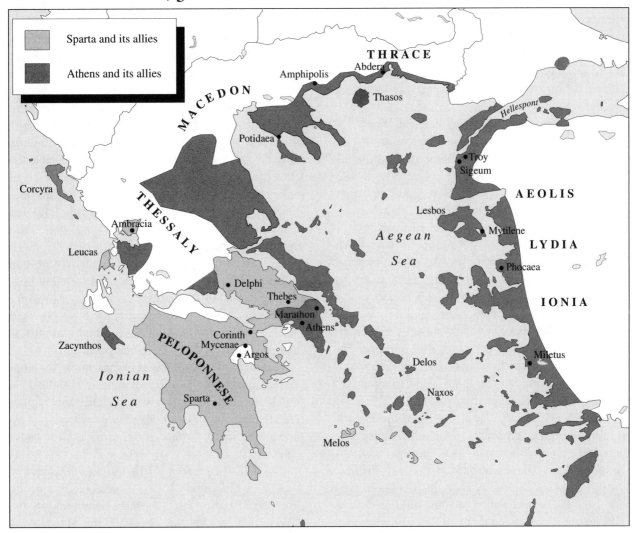

Sparta and its allies

Athens and its allies

hoplites routed about 25,000 lightly armed Persian invaders. Even the Greek defeat at Thermopylae (480 B.C.E.), where 300 Spartiates held off perhaps 70,000 Persians for several days, represented in some sense a victory for the hoplite system. To the Greeks, Thermopylae showed that only treachery and vastly superior numbers could overwhelm free citizens fighting in a hoplite phalanx.

In the last half of the fifth century B.C.E. the hoplite way of war confronted several challenges. In particular, during the Greco-Persian Wars several city-states had developed fleets of oared galleys called triremes.

Athens took the lead in naval warfare and by 450 B.C.E. had a skilled professional fleet numbering two hundred ships, the best and largest in the Greek world. Navies added strategic mobility to the military equation. No longer were battles confined to the borderlands between neighboring poleis. Fleets could now launch amphibious assaults hundreds of miles away from their home cities.

To take advantage of this mobility, a new type of soldier began to appear: the peltast. The original peltasts were Thracian mercenaries equipped with a small shield, or *peltê*, in Greek; later the term "peltast" denoted a wide variety of lightly armored foot soldiers equipped primarily with javelins. Peltasts fought in loose skirmishing formation. Although they could not confront a phalanx head-on, they were more mobile than heavily armored hoplites and so excelled at quick attacks in difficult terrain. Other light infantry, including slingers and archers, also became more common.

The long and agonizing Peloponnesian War (431-404 B.C.E.), fought between opposing coalitions led by Athens and Sparta, clearly demonstrated the effects of these military innovations. Near Pylos in 425 B.C.E., for instance, an amphibious assault by Athenian peltasts and other light infantry overwhelmed Spartiate hoplites stationed on the rocky island of Sphakteria. The next year, at Amphipolis in northern Greece, the Spartan general Brasidas used a surprise attack combining hoplites, peltasts, and cavalry to rout a superior Athenian force. In this period, battle lost its limited and ritual character, and fighting occurred instead in both summer and winter, in both rain and snow, at night, on mountains, and even inside cities. The growing importance of fleets and light troops, in sum, was bringing an end to the agrarian monopoly on organized violence.

The Peloponnesian War also spurred the growth of military professionalism. Commanders, once amateurs, became skilled tacticians through constant campaigning. Some states imitated Sparta by drilling units of picked troops—*epilektoi*, in Greek—to provide a trained corps for their phalanx militias. Along with growing professionalism, the economic devastation caused by the war prompted many men to seek employment outside Greece. By the end of the fifth century, tens of thousands had enlisted as mercenaries with the Persian army in Asia Minor. In fact, twelve thousand of these soldiers supported the Achaemenid prince Cyrus the Younger (c. 424-401 B.C.E.) during his abortive attempt to usurp the Persian throne (401 B.C.E.).

Although shaken, the hoplite system was not totally overthrown by the Peloponnesian War. Indeed, its best practitioners, the Spartans, took comfort in the fact that they had triumphed in the major phalanx clashes of the conflict. During the Corinthian War (395-386 B.C.E.), though, Spartan military confidence suffered when a Spartan unit was attacked and nearly destroyed near Corinth by Athenian troops under the general Iphicrates (c. 410-353 B.C.E.) Iphicrates is said to have trained his hoplites as peltasts, lightening their armor and lengthening their spears.

The real blow came in 371 B.C.E., when the Thebans defeated the Spartans in a pitched hoplite battle at Leuctra. The Theban commander, Epaminondas (c. 410-362 B.C.E.), took advantage of many of the military innovations of the preceding century. He deployed cavalry and light troops to screen his advance and protect his flanks and used his force of picked troops, the Sacred Band, to spearhead his hoplite assault. Epaminondas also drew up the left wing of his phalanx fifty men deep; the usual depth was eight men. The Thebans easily crushed the much thinner opposing Spartan wing. For the first time in centuries, a Spartan army had been defeated in hoplite battle; the era of Spartan invincibility was over.

Thus by the mid-fourth century B.C.E. the classical Greek way of war had undergone many modifications. Nonetheless, as long as the polis remained the characteristic Greek political organization, the hoplite phalanx of citizen militia persisted. Ultimately, a fourth military system evolved to challenge the phalanx. It arose not in the poleis, but in Macedon, a region of northern Greece long considered a backwater.

Philip II of Macedon (382-336 B.C.E.), father of Alexander the Great (356-323 B.C.E.), came to the throne in 359 B.C.E. He inherited a kingdom in crisis; Illyrian invaders had just smashed the Macedonian army, killing King Perdiccas III, Philip's brother. Macedon was large and populous but in danger of being dismembered by its neighbors. To save his monarchy, Philip reformed his army. He began by creating a new mass infantry force. These soldiers, peasants rather than middle-class agrarians, fought as a phalanx but wore significantly less armor than hoplites. They carried a long pike, the sarissa, rather than the hoplite spear. Philip also reorganized Macedon's aristocratic cavalry, equipping it with lances and training it for mounted charges. In battle, cavalry and infantry functioned as hammer and anvil. The sarissa phalanx, with its hedgehog of pikes, would pin the enemy in place until the cavalry could charge a flank or other vulnerable spot. Specialized troops, including archers, light cavalry, slingers, and spearmen, protected the army's flanks, screened infantry advances, and conducted reconnaissance before battles. Finally, Philip created a corps of engineers and a siege train, enabling the Macedonians to capture fortified cities.

The new Macedonian army, then, was a true combined arms force. Many of its elements had surfaced before in Greek warfare—Philip reputedly drew inspiration from both Iphicrates and Epaminondas—but they had never been fully developed. Only a large monarchy such as Macedon, not a traditional polis, could afford to maintain such an army. Philip himself added the final ingredient to the Macedonian way of war. A master diplomat, he combined intrigue and negotiation with swift military strikes. By 348 B.C.E., Macedon not only had recovered from crisis but also reigned supreme in northern Greece. Philip then moved gradually south, threatening the independence of the city-states. After much squabbling, Athens and its allies took the field against the Macedonians. The two sides met at Chaeronea in 338 B.C.E., the citizen phalanx against Philip's new model army. First the Macedonian infantry pinned their hoplite opponents. Then Philip's cavalry, led by his eighteen-year-old son Alexander, charged through a gap in the line and fell on the Greek rear. The Greeks broke and ran. Only the Theban Sacred Band stood its ground and fought to the death. The day of the independent polis and its citizen militia hoplites was over; the ascendancy of Macedon's military system was just beginning.

Philip never lived to enjoy the fruits of his victories. He was assassinated in 336 B.C.E., bringing his son Alexander III, known as Alexander the Great, to the Macedonian throne. Within two years, Alexander would embark on a journey of world conquest that eventually took him to the banks of the Indus River. Alexander's conquests, though, owed at least part of their success to the professional combined arms approach created by Philip II. The Macedonian way of

THE PELOPONNESIAN WARS

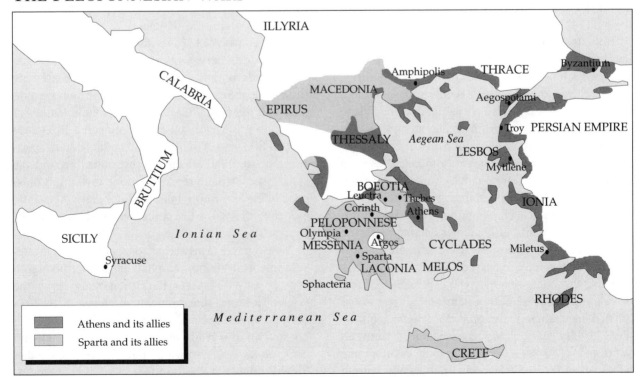

war would reign supreme in the eastern Mediterranean until the second century B.C.E., when the successors of Alexander confronted the legions of Republican Rome.

WEAPONS, UNIFORMS, AND ARMOR

The earliest Mycenaean weapons, dating from the sixteenth century B.C.E., include long rapiers, daggers, large spearheads, and arrows of bronze, flint, or obsidian. Bows were of the simple, noncomposite type. Slings were certainly deployed in this period and in all following ones. Little evidence for armor exists, although small metal discs found in early graves at Mycenae may be the remnants of otherwise perishable leather or fabric armor. The famous boar's tusk helmet, known from Homer's *Iliad* as well as from Mycenaean art, was also in use during this period. Artistic representations show two kinds of large shield: an oblong "tower" shield and the more common "figure eight," both of animal hide with metal reinforcement. Neither type had handles. Instead the shield was suspended by a shoulder strap, so a warrior could easily throw it over his back to protect a retreat.

Both weapons and armor improved during the height of Mycenaean power. Sword redesign eliminated weak tangs and provided better hand guards. A new large spearhead, some 50 centimeters long, appeared by the fifteenth century B.C.E.; its ribbed blade ran straight into its socket for greater strength. Composite bows, a borrowing from Minoan Crete, also came into use. Bronze body armor made its debut in the late fifteenth century B.C.E. An example from Dendra, constructed of overlapping metal plates with greaves and a high neck, seems designed for chariot-borne use. A boar's tusk helmet accompanies the Dendra armor; at Knossos and elsewhere conical bronze helmets have appeared. Shields became less popular; the "figure eight" type especially became more a ritual than a military item.

Striking changes in weapons and armor accompanied the last years of Mycenaean power. Between 1250 and 1150 B.C.E., long thrusting swords gave way to new types, shorter and stouter, with strong hilts and flat, straight-edged blades. The so-called *Griffzungenschwert*, most distinctive of these types, was mass-produced and widely distributed. Examples appear in central Europe, Cyprus, the Levant, and Egypt as well as in Greece. Spearheads became smaller and less ornate, and spears began to be equipped with end spikes. Late Mycenaean arrowheads were invariably bronze and joined with a tang instead of slotted into shafts, like earlier arrowheads. Art of the period shows soldiers wearing reinforced leather or fabric, rather than bronze armor. Contemporary helmets may also have been made of reinforced hide rather than metal. Small circular or elliptical shields with handgrips appear alongside this armor.

Dark Age weaponry made a major shift from bronze to iron. Lighter, tougher and sharper than bronze, iron came into widespread use during the eleventh century B.C.E. The late Mycenaean *Griffzungenschwert* sword, translated into iron, remained common in the early Dark Age, but in the ninth and eighth centuries, shorter, broader swords appeared. Spearheads, often with wide leaf blades, initially remained bronze but became iron by the tenth century B.C.E. Dark Age graves often included multiple spearheads but no swords, perhaps reflecting the long-range warfare in Homer. The paucity of early Dark Age arrowhead finds also reflects the Homeric disdain for archery. Only on Crete did long, tanged arrowheads remain relatively common. Extremely little evidence exists for early Dark Age metal armor, although there may have been perishable leather or fabric armor. Metal corselets reappeared in Greece around 800 B.C.E. Conical metal helmets, with transverse or fore-and-aft crests, resurfaced around the same time. Artistic representations reveal the presence of cavalry throughout the later Dark Age; little evidence exists for the continued battlefield use of chariots.

New types of arms and armor accompanied the development of the hoplite phalanx during the eighth century B.C.E. Hoplites took their name from the *hoplon*, a large, round shield of leather or bronze-covered wood, some 3 feet in diameter. The *hoplon* boasted an arm band, or *porpax*, as well as a hand grip, or *antilabê*, making it far easier to handle. Shields might have borne either a state emblem or individual insignia. Hoplite equipment also included a bronze helmet, greaves, and corselet. The most common helmet was the Corinthian, beaten from a single piece of metal and offering all-around protection at the expense of vision and hearing. The hoplite's main weapon, the spear, or *doru*, was roughly 6 feet long, with a bronze point and end spike. A variety of short swords served as secondary weapons. Among these was the single-edged *machaira*, a machete-like slashing blade. Over time the hoplite panoply got lighter. By the fifth century B.C.E., greaves were discarded, leather and fabric composite corselets often substituted for bronze, and metal helmets sometimes replaced with felt ones. Although Spartiates all wore red cloaks, no polis army had standardized equipment or a real uniform.

Peltasts wore little or no armor and carried light animal-hide shields. Often they attached a throwing-loop to their javelins for increased range. Greek archers generally used a short, weak bow to shoot bronze- or iron-tipped arrows. The recurved Scythian type arrow was known but not widely used. Slingers, their weapons made of gut or sinew, often outranged archers. They used stones or almond-shaped lead bullets as ammunition. Classical Greek cavalry was weak and suited mostly for pursuit. Horsemen carried javelins and wore light armor; they had no stirrups.

In the fourth century B.C.E., Macedonian phalangites usually wore only light fabric or leather armor. Their pike, or sarissa, required both hands, so they carried a small light shield on a neck strap. Like the hoplite spear, the sarissa had a bronze tip and end spike. Both cavalry and infantry versions of the sarissa existed; the infantry version was 12 to 15 feet long, and the cavalry type relatively shorter. As shock troops, Macedonian cavalry often wore metal armor. They were expert lancers even without the aid of stirrups.

MILITARY ORGANIZATION

Virtually nothing is known about Mycenaean military organization. Linear B tablets from Pylos suggest an army divided into ten units with attached officers. The tablets also mention an official called the *lawagetas* ("people-leader"), who might have been

the kingdom's wartime commander. Dark Age military structure remains similarly obscure. Chieftains together with clansmen and retainers probably fought as loose warrior bands.

In the hoplite era, each polis had its own military structure, usually reflecting its civic organization. At Athens, for example, the phalanx was divided into ten tribal regiments or *phylai* (singular *phylê*), also called *taxeis* (singular *taxis*). The *phylê* or *taxis* was not a tactical unit, and it varied in strength according to the number of men called up for any given campaign. Athens's cavalry was also divided into ten tribal regiments. The early Athenian army was commanded by its *polemarchos*, or war leader; later a board of ten elected generals (*strategoi*, singular *strategos*) took over.

The Spartan phalanx possessed a defined tactical organization, but its details remain disputed. According to Thucydides, it consisted of seven *lochoi* (singular *lochos*), each divided into four *pentekostyes* (singular *pentekostys*) of 128 men apiece. The *pentekostys* in turn comprised four *enomotiai* (singular *enomotia*) of 32 men apiece. Xenophon in contrast describes an army of six *morai* (singular *mora*), each containing four *lochoi* of 128 men. These *lochoi* mustered only two *pentekostyes* of two *enomotiai* apiece. Thucydides and Xenophon agree that each subunit had its own regular officers. The army as a whole was commanded by Sparta's two kings.

During the fifth and fourth centuries B.C.E., a number of states experimented with units of picked troops, or *epilektoi*. Their size varied; the most famous of these elite units, the Theban Sacred Band, comprising 150 pairs of homosexual lovers, was maintained at state expense. Greek mercenaries in Asia Minor, perhaps following Persian military principles, were regularly organized into *lochoi* of one hundred men each. These *lochoi* were independent tactical and administrative units, with regular officers, called *lochagoi* (singular *lochagos*).

The basic unit of the Macedonian phalanx was the *syntagma* of 256 men, comprising 16 files of 16 men apiece. Macedonian *syntagmata* were maneuverable tactical units, with regular officers. Cavalry was organized into squadrons of two hundred horsemen called *ilai* (singular *ilê*). Units of elite infantry and cavalry functioned as vanguards in battle. Macedonian kings bestowed the coveted status of "Companions" (*hetairoi*) on both horse and foot soldiers in order to reward and encourage valor.

DOCTRINE, STRATEGY, AND TACTICS

Nothing certain can be said of Mycenaean or Dark Age military doctrine. The essential doctrine of the hoplite system, however, is clear: to engage in decisive phalanx battle. This principle undergirded Greek warfare from the rise of the polis on through the fourth century B.C.E. Its rationale was as much political as military: Short, decisive clashes kept war limited and allowed farmers to devote maximum time to agriculture. As long as hoplite warfare depended on mutual agreement to fight, moreover, strategy was not an issue.

The Peloponnesian War did see the development of Greek strategy. Athens, a sea power, sought to avoid hoplite battle by relying on its navy. Sparta, supreme on land, undertook annual invasions of Athenian territory in a fruitless attempt to lure the Athenian phalanx out to battle. These disparate strategies ensured that although neither side lost, neither side won a clear victory. Attempts in the middle years of the war by both belligerents to break the deadlock failed. Although each side had minor successes in the other's territory, neither side could win the war unless it beat the other at its own game. Ultimately the Spartans did exactly this. They deployed their own fleet, defeated Athens at sea, and blocked the city's grain imports. The Athenians could have prevented this outcome, but they overconfidently squandered much of their naval strength in a failed attempt to capture the island of Sicily.

As with strategy, there was not much to traditional hoplite tactics. Commanders were aware that advancing phalanxes tended to drift to the right, each man trying to get behind the shield of the man next to him, and they sometimes took measures to forestall

this. The Spartans, with their intricate tactical organization, were able to maneuver effectively on the battlefield. This ability won them the day on several occasions. Otherwise, the main tactic of phalanx battle, even for the Spartans, was head-on collision. The development of light troops in the late fifth century B.C.E. gave impetus to flanking movements and surprise attacks. Using hit-and-run tactics, peltasts, slingers, and spearmen could discomfit the traditional phalanx. Greek armies, though, still relied on hoplites to strike the decisive blow. Two strategies for increasing the strength of this blow were a deeper phalanx—the tactic of Epaminondas at Leuktra—and the use of picked troops.

On the battlefield, the combined arms tactics of the Macedonians gave them a decisive edge over even the best Greek troops. Perhaps more important, though, was Macedon's consistent strategy. From his accession, Philip proceeded methodically first to stabilize his kingdom, then to subjugate its neighbors, and finally to consolidate power over all Greece. Unlike the Greeks, the Macedonians were not tied to the doctrine of decisive battle. Indeed, Philip achieved some of his major victories through diplomacy and political intrigue.

The Macedonians also made logistics a keystone of strategy. The hoplite system gave little consideration to the requirements of extended campaigning. Traditional phalanx clashes, after all, occurred close to home. Furthermore, classical hoplites went to battle followed by slave servants bearing rations and equipment. When hoplites deployed far afield, as in the Peloponnesian War, they could usually depend on a fleet to carry supplies. The Macedonians, on the other hand, learned to conduct extended land campaigns without naval supply. Philip eliminated slave porters and made his troops travel light. He successfully employed coercion to ensure that food supplies would be ready and waiting when his troops entered new territory. Just as he trained Alexander's army, Philip developed the logistical and strategic thought that made feasible his son's conquests.

ANCIENT SOURCES

For all periods of Greek warfare from 1600 to 336 B.C.E., archaeological excavation provides the basic evidence for Greek arms and armor. A. M. Snodgrass, in *Arms and Armor of the*

Greeks (1999), collects this evidence in a format accessible to nonspecialists. For the late Bronze Age, excavated Linear B tablets from Mycenae, Pylos, and elsewhere furnish information about the military organization and equipment of the Mycenaean kingdoms.

The *Iliad* and the *Odyssey* (both c. 800 B.C.E.), epic poems ascribed to Homer, are among the earliest literary sources for information about Greek warfare. Scholars continue to debate the veracity of Homeric descriptions of warfare; most would agree that the poems reflect the battle conditions of the Greek Dark Age rather than those of the Mycenaean period.

In his *Historiai Herodotou* (c. 424 B.C.E.; *The History*, 1709), Herodotus (c. 484-424) recounts the major land and naval battles of the Persian Wars. Likewise, Thucydides (c. 459-402 B.C.E.) narrates the course of the long and agonizing Peloponnesian Wars. Both Herodotus and Thucydides provide useful information on Greek strategies, tactics, and military organization during the fifth century B.C.E.

The works of the Athenian author Xenophon (431-354 B.C.E.) are essential for any understanding of Greek warfare. In addition to a memoir of his experiences as a mercenary commander during 401-399, *Kurou anabasis* (*Anabasis*, 1623; also known as *Expedition of Cyrus* and *March Up Country*), Xenophon composed a history of Greece, *Ellēnika*, also known as *Helenica* (*History of the Affairs of Greece*, 1685), and technical treatises on the cavalry, horsemanship, and hunting. His *Lakedaimoniōn politeia* (*Polity of the Lacedaemonians*, 1832; also known as *Constitution of Sparta*) describes Spartan army organization and training in the fourth century B.C.E.

Finally, the Roman magistrate and writer known as Arrian (c. 86-160 C.E.) produced several texts that furnish important evidence for the organization, equipment, and tactics of the Macedonian army. These texts include a history of the campaigns of Alexander as well as a tactical manual.

BOOKS AND ARTICLES

Anderson, J. K. *Military Theory and Practice in the Age of Xenophon.* Berkeley: University of California Press, 1970.

Ducrey, Pierre. *Warfare in Ancient Greece.* Translated by Janet Lloyd. New York: Schocken Books, 1986.

Ferrill, Arther. *The Origins of War: From the Stone Age to Alexander the Great.* London: Thames and Hudson, 1985.

Hanson, Victor Davis. *The Western Way of War: Infantry Battle in Classical Greece.* 2d ed. Berkeley: University of California Press, 2000.

Snodgrass, A. M. *Arms and Armor of the Greeks.* Rev. ed. Baltimore, Md.: Johns Hopkins University Press, 1999.

John W. I. Lee

GREEK WARFARE AFTER ALEXANDER

DATES: 336-30 B.C.E.

MILITARY ACHIEVEMENT

One of the most important developments in Greek warfare during the approximately 300-year period from 336 to 30 B.C.E. was its evolution as the exclusive province of regularly trained, professional armies. The most successful of these armies consisted of tactically integrated forces derived from a variety of sources. This change in the style of Greek warfare favored large political units with access to significant material resources. Only those cities able to submerge their political identities within a federal system of some sort were able to survive independently. No such attempt worked very well, or for very long, in the classical Greek city-states, such as Athens and Sparta, which were rendered impotent and irrelevant as political players.

The rise of Macedonian king and conqueror Alexander the Great (356-323 B.C.E.) and the reign of his successor kingdoms in the east were the culmination of significant long-term changes in the financing and organization of armies and in the waging of war in the Greek world. The Greek city-states, or poleis—chiefly Athens, Sparta, and Thebes—had been engaged during the fifth and fourth centuries B.C.E. in a series of bitter struggles for the establishment and preservation of political hegemony on the Greek mainland. The series of indecisive and mutually destructive conflicts was not so much the result of attempts to establish domination over each other as it was to dominate the countless smaller cities in the areas between and adjacent to them. For the individual city-states, armed conflict discouraged interlopers from interfering in their ancestral relationships with neighbors. These relationships among supposed protectorates provided regular causes of specific conflict among the major Greek city-states. As might be expected, no such hegemony was ever lasting or even stable.

Athens, for example, had been the most successful of these city-states for the longest period of time because it possessed the largest fleet of ships and was therefore both easily able and politically willing to isolate and punish recalcitrant members of its alliance. In fact, Athens initially gained this position of power as the leading naval power in an alliance against an outside force, the Persians. After the Persian threat had receded, Athens failed to give up its leadership position, preferring instead to maintain the leadership of the alliance for its own benefit. This one exception notwithstanding, no single city-state possessed sufficient military power to enforce political compliance for very long. The military forces of the Greek city-states were, in most cases, constituted primarily of citizen soldiers whose interest in wars tended to be relatively short-lived and philosophically defensive. The financing of wars was a duty that fell to those who could afford it. No conflict could therefore be sustained without some short-term prospect of financial return. Absent some extraordinary event, the natural limiting factor in warfare of the fifth and fourth centuries B.C.E. was the cost-benefit ratio, which prevented any real change in the status quo.

Persian subsidies had financed the creation of competing naval forces intended to undermine Athenian supremacy in the seas adjacent to their own borders. The apparent result was a round-robin of competing hegemonies. The substantive result was an overall increase in the human cost of war, even as the financial costs were underwritten by the Persians. Persian gold was available only to some, however, and it suited the Persians to keep the Greeks fighting each other. A growing supply of mercenaries willing to fight for hire met the military demand. The desperate competition for new sources of cash led one previously unimportant city to seize the treasury of Apollo's Oracle at Delphi and, with that gold, to finance a well-equipped mercenary army that threatened to unbalance the status quo in Greece. The inability of the traditional Greek power brokers to overcome their historically particularist concerns provided a political opportunity for Philip II of Macedonia (382-336 B.C.E.) to intervene decisively. Philip's outside intervention alarmed the Greeks sufficiently that they picked a fight with Philip in 338 B.C.E. This last gasp of classical Greece proved futile when Philip dealt the Greeks a shocking defeat at the Battle of Chaeronea in that year.

In the process of conquering Greece, Philip forever changed its political formula. He did so at the head of a new kind of army, a permanent professional army whose leadership was derived, not from one city, but from a more broadly conceived federal structure that included newly consolidated areas of Thrace and Greece outside Macedonia. He called his aristocratic corps of leaders his Companions, and they acted as senior officers in his government and as elite cavalry in warfare. As such, they were enormously powerful. An inner circle of Philip's Companions formed a council of state without whose support neither Philip nor his charismatic son, Alexander the Great, could have moved.

Perhaps more important to the success of Philip's army was the bullion dug from the ground in newly consolidated areas around Macedon. This financial advantage allowed Philip to invest in engines of war that his disunited neighbors could not afford. No longer was it possible to wage war effectively within the context of homogenous citizen militias. The political organs of the classical city-states were mirror images of their military structures. A fundamentally new approach to waging war required the creation of a new, more inclusive, political model: a fundamental anathema to the political citizen of the classical city-states of Greece. The cities of Greece, reflecting a fossilized model of military organization, were therefore destined to sink into political obscurity.

Philip's new styles of government and war cost a great deal of money to sustain. He began to look eastward, toward the Persian kingdom whose inherent military weaknesses were made obvious by its hiring of Greek mercenaries for its own army. Philip's last military act was to send the lead elements of an invasion force to Persia in 336 B.C.E. He fell to an assassin's blade a few months later. In 334 B.C.E. his son, Alexander the Great, moved across into Persian territory with about 50,000 men, at the core of which was the 15,000-man Macedonian phalanx. In three major battles over the course of four years, Alexander smashed the Persian army with a combination of his father's flexible military organization and his own prominent and effective personal leadership, as well as good luck. He took key cities that preferred to hold out against him by siege, usually with terrible consequences for the inhabitants. Other cities more wisely yielded. Alexander employed all the best and latest technologies of artillery and siege engines developed up to that point. The Persians, fighting a defensive war with outdated technology and tactics that depended on numbers, were no match for Alexander's flexible tactics and relentless advances. Whereas civilized Greeks went home in the winter, Alexander did not stop until his army mutinied in 325 B.C.E.

After Alexander died, probably from poison, in 323 B.C.E., the leaders among his Companions fell to bickering over his empire. The ensuing period from the death of Alexander in 323 B.C.E. to the death of the final Hellenistic ruler in 30 B.C.E. is commonly termed the Hellenistic period, the cultural hallmarks of which endured until the spread of Islam a thousand years later. The period is associated with the greatest mathematical and engineering advances made before the European Renaissance, although few of these theories were ever applied practically. The exceptions were those with obvious military applications. Alexan-

TURNING POINTS

399 B.C.E.	Dionysius I of Syracuse sponsors catapult research.
338 B.C.E.	Philip II of Macedon defeats united Greek army at Chaeronea.
333 B.C.E.	Alexander defeats main army of Darius III at Issus.
332 B.C.E.	Alexander the Great begins Siege of Tyre.
331 B.C.E.	Alexander defeats main army of Darius III at Gaugamela.
197 B.C.E.	Romans defeat main army of Philip V at Cynoscephalae.

der's successors were not content merely to rule their respective kingdoms, and they engaged in frequent attacks on each other's possessions. Their conflicts were financed by the enormous reserves of gold and silver the Persian kings had amassed in the preceding period. The Hellenistic period is thus especially noted for systematic research and trials in various sciences of war. In fact, all the most successful designs and techniques of warfare that developed before the early modern period were perfected during this 300-year period. For example, Egyptian rulers Ptolemy I (367-283 B.C.E.), Ptolemy II (r. c. 283-246 B.C.E.), and their descendants sponsored research in ballistics for their catapults. Many types of elaborate warships were designed and deployed by the various players whose possessions bordered the Mediterra-

nean Sea. Archimedes of Syracuse (287-212 B.C.E.), arguably the greatest mathematician in antiquity, is renowned for, among other things, the ingenious antisiege engines he developed as the Romans surrounded his home city in 212. Despite these advances, however, infantry armament remained relatively moribund and continued to depend on the essential principles laid down by Philip II and Alexander the Great in the fourth century B.C.E.

WEAPONS, UNIFORMS, AND ARMOR

The Macedonian pike was the signature weapon of the Macedonian infantry. A 20-foot pike also known as a sarissa, it evolved from the shorter spear carried

ALEXANDER'S CAMPAIGN AGAINST PERSIA, 334-331 B.C.E.

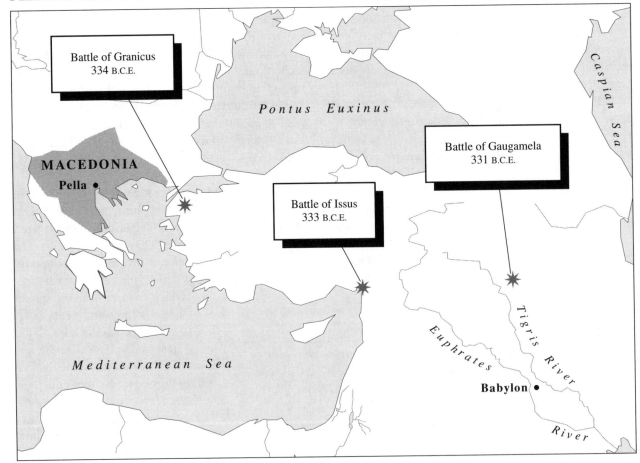

by traditional Greek hoplites, or infantry. The longer pike was useful in projecting contact between forces to a point farther forward of the advancing formation. Naturally this advantage was somewhat nullified if both formations were similarly equipped. The infantrymen advanced in a body called a phalanx. The formation was deeper than the traditional line of hoplites and depended essentially on pinning an enemy formation in advance of some other form of attack, usually by cavalry. Such a formation was practically invulnerable on even ground. The most surprising and distinctly Macedonian innovation might be that of training. There is little evidence to suggest that any of the Greeks before Philip II, with the exception of the Spartans, regularly trained in the art of moving as a formation.

The traditional Greek cavalry units were never decisive as offensive weapons, and few Greek cities placed any emphasis on their maintenance or deployment. Weapons carried by these earlier cavalries were usually restricted to various types of throwing javelins, giving the cavalry a limited role in any sustained action. An exception seems to be the Thessalian cavalry, famous among the Greeks throughout the classical period. No great success can be credited to the Thessalian cavalry by itself, however. It is perhaps no accident that the success of the Macedonian infantry came as a result of its integration with the Thessalian cavalry. The new Macedonian cavalry seemed to feature the use of lances rather than throwing javelins. Tactically, the cavalry was used to attack underdefended flanks of a formation already pressured by an advancing phalanx of pikemen or to exploit openings in enemy formations, created either during the infantry confrontation itself or after clumsy attempts by the opposing force to move laterally. Cavalry tactics were decisive in Alexander the Great's battles with the main Persian army. This sort of action reaffirms the essential maxim of Greek infantry warfare, that success—and survival—depends on the integrity of the formation.

Alexander routinely deployed auxiliary squadrons of lightly armed spearmen and archers in fast-moving columns alongside the cavalry. These units were particularly effective in his later campaigns in Central Asia, which took him on narrow tracks over mountains. Lightly armed troops had always been a part of Greek warfare, but their association with cavalry units was an innovation of Alexander.

The Indians were arguably the first to employ elephants in battle, primarily as moving platforms from which to launch projectiles, and Alexander first encountered elephants in his march to India. Although Alexander himself did not employ elephants actively, his successors routinely did so, with mixed results. In addition to the larger Indian elephants, the Hellenistic rulers used the smaller, now nearly extinct, African elephant, not as a platform, but as a weapon and a shock tactic against infantry formations. Pyrrhus of Epirus (r. 297-272 B.C.E.) brought these elephants to Italy and used them against the Romans, who had never seen them before. At Heraclea in 280 B.C.E., Pyrrhus's elephants drove off the Roman cavalry, whose horses also apparently had not seen elephants previously. In another confrontation at Ausculum in the following year, Pyrrhus deployed elephants successfully as a tactical substitute for Macedonian cavalry. However, after their rough introduction to elephants, the Romans had little trouble with them again. For their own part, the Romans rarely used elephants except for ceremony and ritual slaughter.

Although there are possible antecedents in the Near East, it is generally assumed that catapult technology was decisively advanced around 400 B.C.E., by the dictator Dionysius I of Syracuse (r. 405-367 B.C.E.) in his defense of Sicily against the Carthaginians. One early design was the *gastraphetes*, or belly bow, a powerful bow that required a mechanical device to cock. The operator would lean forward with his abdomen, pinning the weapon against the ground to force a slide backward. These designs were essentially oversized bows designed to launch oversized arrows. By the time of Philip II sixty years later, these catapult designs had been advanced along two lines: one for stones that launched overhead and one for projectiles fired along a track. The latter design was adapted both for regular bolts and for round projectiles made of lead. The most effective of these were powered by torsion created by wrapped bundles of human hair or animal sinew. Alexander brought these weapons on his advance into Persian territory, and they proved decisive in his early sieges along the

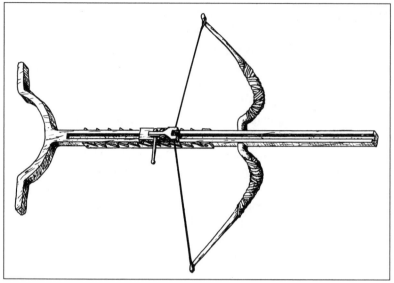

Kimberly L. Dawson Kurnizki

The gastraphetes, *or belly bow, developed by the Greeks around* 400 *B.C.E., was a significant advance in catapult technology. The operator would lean forward with his abdomen, pinning the weapon against the ground to force a slide backward.*

Mediterranean coastline. In the Roman period, artillery design rested upon that already developed by the Greeks and was lost as a science until the Middle Ages.

The advances made in artillery naturally revolutionized siege warfare. It became possible to sweep battlements clear while attempts were made to undermine city walls. Alexander built rolling towers on which teams armed with various forms of artillery could be deployed against defenders stationed on or near city walls. Similarly, towers and covering sheds could now more effectively shield engineers working against the wall itself. Although similar structures of various sorts had been used previously by many, including the Athenians, it was not until the development of effective artillery for covering fire that the advantage swung decisively to attackers in siege warfare.

The warships developed during the Hellenistic period were not revolutionary but were, rather, ambitious adaptations made on proven designs. The adaptations generally seemed to increase both the number of rowers and the overall size of the ships. Many of

these designs were impressive as engineering feats even if they were usually failures as advancements in warships. The most effective offensive ship remained the trireme, which had been developed in Corinth around the year 500 B.C.E. The trireme was 117 feet long and featured 170 rowers arranged in three tiers per side, a detachable ram of bronze on the front, and a platform from which a detachment of fifteen marines was prepared to attempt boarding of hostile vessels. Two sails could be erected to enhance speed downwind, although these were routinely put aside in battle conditions. A reconstructed trireme exists as a flagged vessel in the modern Greek navy, and teams of college students have tested its capabilities. There is only sketchy information on the exact configurations of the various Hellenistic models mentioned in ancient sources, but there is a consensus that however impressive was their appearance, their great size rendered them generally ineffective.

All of these ships were vulnerable to any serious wave action and as many warships were lost in rough waters as were lost in battle. The sheer expense of building and maintaining a serious naval capacity was a limiting factor preventing most cities from accumulating more than a few ships, suitable for controlling piracy. However, the mere existence of a decentralized naval capacity gave many smaller cities on the islands and coasts a bargaining potential that tended to prevent their absorption by their more ambitious neighbors. In essence, these cities loaned or provided ships in return for their protection or independence. It is on this basis that the Romans made their first treaty with the Greek Neapolitans of Italy in 326 B.C.E. One might also argue that a complex of such diplomatic arrangements was a key factor in Rome's first war with Carthage, known as the First Punic War (264-241 B.C.E.), wherein most of the conflict took place at sea. During the long, drawn-out war, both sides lost many hundreds of ships, many to weather. The Carthaginians capitulated essentially because their economy was ruined by competition in shipbuilding.

MILITARY ORGANIZATION

The most characteristic element of the Hellenistic armies was a core phalanx of ten to thirty thousand pikemen, usually but not necessarily Macedonian, armed and trained in the Macedonian style. This core phalanx was augmented by attached units of various sizes devoted to specialty weapons or beasts, such as bows, slings, cavalry, and elephants. The phalanx was a permanent professional force; the auxiliary units, entirely allied or mercenary, were called upon in campaigns as needed. The amassing of military forces large enough to be credible threats to similarly configured rivals was an expensive proposition that militated against integrated training. Likewise, the resulting short nature of Hellenistic campaigns prevented the sort of successful integrated tactics that are associated with Alexander's long and extremely profitable campaign to conquer and subdue Persia. One of the most debilitating qualities of such armies was the fickle loyalty of mercenaries.

The Hellenistic organization differs both from the classical and Roman military organizations in ways that correspond with the differing political models of each culture. In the case of the classical organization, armies were recruited from citizen ranks of individual communities, and their armament corresponded to their economic class. War was essentially the privilege of those who could afford to equip themselves. The Hellenistic model freed the army from the constraints of a city construct but chained it anew to the finances of a few powerful kings. The later Roman system overcame the limitations of Hellenistic armies by inventing more inclusive political models that fostered the creation of very large armies without having to rely on mercenaries. The Romans did use auxiliary specialty units provided by allies, but these units never represented a numerical majority of the Roman army, whereas they were always the preponderant proportion of Hellenistic armies.

DOCTRINE, STRATEGY, AND TACTICS

Two types of warfare evolved significantly in the Hellenistic period. There were the innovations made in set-piece battle warfare and those made in the techniques of siege warfare. The second of these was largely a function of technology and finance. From the time of Alexander forward, no city could reasonably risk outlasting a well-equipped besieging army. The innovations in set-piece battles were, however, a function of tactics and training. In general, the most successful examples of Hellenistic warfare featured the functional flexibility of well-trained and tactically integrated infantry and cavalry forces deployed against opponents without these advantages. This clear distinction is evident in Alexander's battles against the main Persian army at Issus and Gaugamela.

In 333 B.C.E. Alexander faced the main army of the Persians commanded by King Darius III himself. The battle took place at Issus, where Asia Minor joins the Levantine coast, and a river divided the two forces. Darius, commanding a numerical advantage in troops, took an early lead with a cavalry advance from his left against Alexander's Thessalian cavalry on Alexander's right. The disciplined Thessalians held while Alexander's cavalry crossed through the weak left of the Persian infantry and wheeled against the Persian center. The right side of the Macedonian phalanx crossed over, and the battle was essentially won in that moment, despite Persian success on their own right side of the battle. The Persians could not counter the combined attack.

Two years later, Alexander and Darius faced each other again, this time at Gaugamela, east of the northern Tigris River. Here, once again, Darius seized the initiative with an attempt to stretch his own lines in a flanking move to Alexander's right and with a simultaneous chariot charge through Alexander's center. The chariot attack was easily nullified by lightly armed troops stationed in Alexander's front ranks, thereby frustrating Darius's diversion from his own flanking attempt. Alexander immediately exploited obvious gaps appearing in the Persian center as the Persian infantry attempted to extend to their own left. Alexander charged through that gap, cutting the Persian army in half. The advantage was won because the Persians were unable to make a simple lateral movement in formation.

The Macedonian generals dividing Alexander's empire styled themselves kings and continued to rely on the physical elements of army deployments developed by Philip and Alexander. All continued to rely on Macedonian-style phalanxes as the literal centerpieces of their armies. They augmented these forces from a variety of sources and employed specialist mercenary attachments, as did Alexander.

In most armies of the Hellenistic period, elephants were added. However, Alexander's true military advantages had come from his tactical integration of forces with deliberate flexibility. Nevertheless, the Hellenistic monarchs, to their ultimate peril, increasingly ignored these principles. One can see this clearly in the Battle of Raphia in 217 B.C.E. between the Hellenistic kings Ptolemy IV (died 205 B.C.E.; r. 221-205 B.C.E.) and Antiochus III (242-187 B.C.E.). Here, the armies, each including a large number of elephants, were more or less evenly matched. Both kings placed their phalanxes in the center of the lines. From the centers outward, various allied, specialist, and mercenary contingents, then cavalry, then elephants were deployed. Antiochus's elephants, stationed on his own right, charged Ptolemy's elephants directly opposite, successfully driving them off and leaving Ptolemy's cavalry holding the left. Antiochus sent his cavalry against Ptolemy's cavalry, then his mercenaries and allies against Ptolemy's. Although Antiochus was initially successful, he never committed his phalanx. Instead, intent upon chasing Ptolemy's left side from the field, he failed to notice that Ptolemy's right had prevailed against his own left, leaving his own phalanx dangerously vulnerable. The ensuing destruction was inevitable; all Antiochus got for this expense was the elephants he captured from Ptolemy. Both sides brought elaborate professional armies to the field; neither side understood integrated tactics.

This fundamental failure of integration was the critical factor in the ultimate demise of the once-dominant Macedonian armies. The Romans later learned the same lessons as had the Macedonians, but the Romans continued to apply those lessons to changing circumstances. The first two major confrontations between the two powers were Cynoscephalae and Pydna. In the Battle of Cynoscephalae (197 B.C.E.) the Roman and the Macedonian armies were marching in the same direction on either side of a series of ridges; the two armies were in contact and skirmishing intermittently. The Macedonian king Philip V (238-179 B.C.E.) attempted to seize the initiative by mounting the heights between the armies. Here, the decisive moment came when the Roman right reacted quickly to the Macedonian move and destroyed the Macedonian left side before the formation was fully deployed. The Romans wheeled immediately behind the Macedonian right and destroyed it as well, despite its success against the Roman left.

At Pydna in 168 B.C.E., Philip V's son Perseus (c. 212-c. 165 B.C.E.) faced the Romans in a similar contest. Here the Macedonians managed to deploy first but were unable to advance in good order over the uneven ground. The smaller detached Roman units, in contrast, were able to advance easily and sliced through the ragged Macedonian formations. They easily smashed the Macedonian left side and destroyed the entire Macedonian army shortly thereafter. In both of these battles, the Romans demonstrated clearly their superior tactical flexibility in the face of changing battlefield exigencies and against obvious advantages in training. Subsequent contests between Romans and Greeks tended to reaffirm these principles. Greek hegemony in the east existed after Pydna only on Roman sufferance.

ANCIENT SOURCES

Information on Alexander the Great comes primarily from the ancient authors Arrian, Curtius Rufus, Diodorus Siculus, and Plutarch. Arrian, a Greek citizen of Rome, served in the Roman government (c. 120-130 B.C.E.) and wrote in his retirement. His highly detailed and most reliable accounts of Alexander's military campaigns are believed to have come from the campaign notebooks of Alexander's general and friend, Ptolemy I, who later became king of Egpyt. Curtius Rufus lived and wrote in the first century C.E.; Diodorus Siculus lived and wrote in the first century B.C.E. and compiled a world history from the earliest times to the reign of Roman emperor Julius Caesar. Only the latter part of his work survives, however, covering Greek history in the fourth and third century B.C.E.

Plutarch (c. 50-125 C.E.), a Greek, is considered the greatest biographer of antiquity. He lived during the early days of the Roman Empire, and his work *Bioi paralleloi* (c. 105-115; *Parallel Lives*, 1579) compares and contrasts various pairs of Greek and Roman leaders. In this work, Alexander the Great is paired with Julius Caesar. Plutarch also provides biographies of some of Alexander's successors, including the colorful Demetrius the City Besieger. Polybius (c. 200-c. 118 B.C.E.) covers some of the Hellenistic conflicts in the years up through the Romans' arrival, as does Diodorus Siculus. Surviving chapters from the Roman writer Livy (59 B.C.E.-17 C.E.) also cover some of this conflict. Several ancient treatises on catapult technology by the authors Ctesibus, Heron, and Philon have survived and are available in English translations.

BOOKS AND ARTICLES

Billows, Richard A. *Antigonos the One-Eyed and the Creation of the Hellenistic State*. Berkeley: University of California Press, 1990.

Bosworth, A. B. *Conquest and Empire: The Reign of Alexander the Great*. Cambridge, England: Cambridge University Press, 1988.

Buckler, John. *Phillip II and the Sacred War*. New York: E. J. Brill, 1989.

Green, Peter. *Alexander to Actium: The Historical Evolution of the Hellenistic Age*. Berkeley: University of California Press, 1990.

Gruen, Erich S. *The Hellenistic World and the Coming of Rome*. Berkeley: University of California Press, 1984.

Morrison, J. S. *Greek and Roman Oared Warships*. Oxford, England: Oxbow Books, 1996.

Randall S. Howarth

CARTHAGINIAN WARFARE

DATES: 814-202 B.C.E.

MILITARY ACHIEVEMENT

Carthage, a historic city on the north coast of Africa, traditionally was founded in 814 B.C.E. by Phoenicians. Historically, the military achievements of Carthage, a maritime trading power, have been measured by its naval and land conflicts with Rome, the emerging power on land. This deadly hegemonic contest, however, was not the only formal measure of Carthage's military achievements. Long before its fateful clashes with Rome in the Punic Wars (264-146 B.C.E.), Carthage had made its military presence forcefully known throughout the western Mediterranean, Southern European, North African, and West African regions from the eighth to the third centuries B.C.E. This strategic presence was based on a powerful professional navy with a significant troop-transport capacity that sustained land forces that protected Carthage's home and overseas territories, important trade routes, and wide-ranging commercial fleets. Carthage's strategic ability to move significant military forces throughout the western Mediterranean region would, for a period of time, deter Rome both politically and militarily from challenging Punic control of Sardinia and Sicily.

The land and naval expeditionary forces of Carthage ranged widely in the Atlantic and the Mediterranean, resulting in the occupation of Corsica, Spain, Sardinia, Sicily, and territories of North Africa. This first phase of Carthage's expansionism (264-237 B.C.E.) was characterized by a strict civilian control by the Council of Elders of senior army and navy commanders and their mercenary troops. During this period of civilian supremacy over political and military policy, Punic generals and admirals who were successful in battle were rewarded, and those who were not were either exiled or killed.

During the twenty-three years of the First Punic War, Rome had 400,000 casualties. At the same time,

Carthage suffered major defeats in the Battles of Mylae (260 B.C.E.), Ecnomus (256 B.C.E.), Adys (256 B.C.E.), and Panormus (250 B.C.E.). Carthage won a major battle at Tunis in 255 B.C.E., led by the Spartan general Xanthippus, who defeated the Roman consul Regulus and forced the latter's retreat from Africa. At the Battle of Drepana (249 B.C.E.), the Punic naval commanders Adherbal, Carthalo, and Himilico defeated a large Roman fleet under admiral Claudius toward the end of the First Punic War. Despite this victory, Carthage's surrender at the Aegates Islands (241 B.C.E.) ended the First Punic War. The defeat resulted in a severe loss of Carthaginian territory, including Sicily, Corsica, and Sardinia. Carthage also suffered large reparations, a vastly reduced battle fleet, and a weakened land army.

Rome, a weaker naval power, owed much of its success in the First Punic War to its acquisition of a new naval technology: the *corvus*, a nautical grappling hook. This device was simply a long, spiked gangplank mounted on the bow of a Roman warship and dropped onto the deck of a Carthaginian ship, securing the two ships together and allowing a Roman contingent to board and capture the opposing vessel. The *corvus* effectively ended Carthage's naval supremacy and had a long-term negative impact on Carthage's national security and overseas military operations.

The second phase of Carthaginian expansionism occurred from 237 to 202 B.C.E. The military achievements and the very survival of the Carthaginian Empire during this time rested on the strategic leadership and tactical genius of its talented military commanders, the Barcid family. The commanders—Hamilcar Barca (c. 270-228 B.C.E.), Hannibal (247-182 B.C.E.), Mago (died c. 203 B.C.E.), Hasdrubal (died 207 B.C.E.), Hanno (fl. third century B.C.E.), and Maharbal (fl. c. 216 B.C.E.)—would train the physically tough and hard-fighting indigenous and mercenary troops

TURNING POINTS

247 B.C.E.	Hamilcar Barca is appointed Carthaginian military commander; Carthage emerges as a major military threat.
237 B.C.E.	Hamilcar begins Spanish military campaign, in preparation for ultimate war with Rome.
221 B.C.E.	Hamilcar's son Hannibal takes command of military.
218 B.C.E.	Hannibal leads a force of elephants, cavalry, and foot soldiers across the Alps to trap and defeat the Romans at Trebia.
216 B.C.E.	Hannibal issues Rome its greatest defeat in battle at Cannae.
202 B.C.E.	Scipio Africanus defeats Carthage at the Battle of Zama.
146 B.C.E.	The Third Punic War ends; Carthage's threat to Rome's domination is defeated.

through the force of their personalities, charisma, and personal courage. This period also signaled the masterly control of the political and military policies of Carthage by these strong-willed and militarily gifted generals.

In 247 B.C.E. the Council of Elders' appointment of Hamilcar Barca as the military commander of Sicily began a dynamic new phase in the military history of Carthage. After the end of the disastrous First Punic War, the Barcid clan began to question the competency of the mercantilist faction of the Council of Elders to conduct political policy and wage war against Rome. This fierce internal struggle within the Council of Elders between the mercantilist faction and the Barcid clan and among other Punic interest groups would have long-term consequences.

The end of the First Punic War found Carthage without sufficient bullion to pay its mercenary army adequately, which revolted and attacked Carthage and its surrounding provinces. Hamilcar Barca was appointed by the Council of Elders to put down the revolt and moved quickly to defeat the rebellious mercenary forces. In the summer of 237 B.C.E., Hamilcar and his sons Hannibal, Mago, and Hasdrubal landed in Spain. After eight years of military campaigning, Hannibal subjugated important Spanish territories in preparation for the coming military conflict with Rome. He was the first in a dedicated group of highly trained and dedicated Punic military commanders who would practice strategic endurance, exercise tactical brilliance, and exert complete

control over Carthage's political policy in the grand military conflict with Rome. In the winter of 229-228 B.C.E. Hamilcar died and his son-in-law Hasdrubal (died 221 B.C.E.) took over in Spain. After Hasdrubal was assassinated in 221 B.C.E., Hannibal came to power in Spain and in Carthage and strengthened the Punic army of 50,000 foot soldiers, 6,000 cavalry, and 200 battle elephants. In 218 B.C.E. Rome declared war against Carthage in response to Hannibal's defeat of Rome's ally in Spain, the city-state Sarguntum.

In late 218 B.C.E., Hannibal descended victoriously into Italy's Po River Valley with 20,000 soldiers and 6,000 cavalry. He had designed a major trap for the two Roman generals Scipio Africanus (236-184 or 183 B.C.E.) and Tiberius Sempronius Longus, who were meeting at Scipio's camp near Trebia, and routed the Roman forces. In June, 217 B.C.E., Hannibal designed another large ambush at Lake Trasimeno and killed 20,000 soldiers in the army of Gaius Flaminius. In August, 216 B.C.E., the co-consuls Lucius Aemilius Paulus (died 216 B.C.E.) and Gaius Terentius Varro (fl. c. 216 B.C.E.) arrived at Cannae with more than 87,200 soldiers. Hannibal's army of 50,000 men was prepared for battle. With losses of 47,000 infantry and 2,700 cavalry, and with 19,000 prisoners, the Roman army was decimated in what became known as the first battle of annihilation in history.

However, the military achievements of Hannibal and Carthage came to a final end with his military defeat by Scipio Africanus at the Battle of Zama in 202 B.C.E.

WEAPONS, UNIFORMS, AND ARMOR

There is little historical evidence relating to the weapons, uniforms, and armor used by the Carthaginian army and navy. The polyglot army that Hannibal fielded in the Second Punic War was a unique mixture of Africans, Spaniards, Celts, Numidians,

CANNAE, 216 B.C.E.

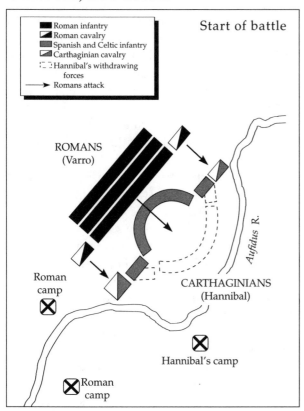

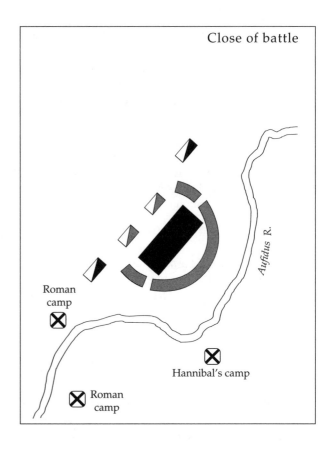

and Libya-Phoenicians, along with Greeks, Persians, and Egyptians. Hannibal's army was international in its racial and ethnic composition and was extremely loyal in its dedication to its supreme military leader. Hannibal used his heavy and light infantry divisions as maneuver units to unbalance enemy forces and his heavy and light cavalry divisions as his main strike force on the battlefield to annihilate the enemy forces.

The weapons, armor, and uniforms of Hannibal's infantry reflected the rich diversity of its fighting soldiers. The famous African heavy infantry were formidable, tenacious, and highly trained fighters from northern and western Africa. They wore a variety of colorful uniforms and clothing and were heavily armed with long and short battle swords, bows and arrows, and lances, as well as an assortment of other exotic weapons, which they used with deadly efficiency in battle. The African heavy infantry, which proved itself at the Battle of Cannae (216 B.C.E.),

wore chain mail and carried shields for protection.

Hannibal recruited the courageous and tough-fighting Spanish infantry, heavy and light, from the Iberian tribes of Spain. The Spanish light infantry were armed with javelins, darts, slings, and wooden shields, whereas the Spanish heavy infantry was dressed in chain mail and armed with javelins, as well as the noted heavy steel sword later adopted by the Roman heavy infantry. The Celtic light infantry were recruited from the Po River Valley in Italy and were armed with swords. They wore no armor and fought nude or half naked. Finally, the proud and sagacious Libya-Phoenicians were recruited from the Carthaginian elite classes, wore chain mail armor, and expertly used the battle weapons of the Greek hoplite. The Libya-Phoenicians formed the elite backbone of Hannibal's Carthaginian army in Italy, and they would prove their mettle repeatedly in countless battles and campaigns.

The heavy and light cavalry forces in Hannibal's army were also a polyglot mixture of nationalities, races, and languages. The cavalry corps were Hannibal's strategic strike force and implemented his orders on the battlefield with both precision and decisiveness. The elite heavy cavalry were composed of a small number of Carthaginians and Libya-Phoenicians, highly expert fighters on or off their battle horses and drilled in every conceivable cavalry maneuver. The Spanish heavy infantry comprised the bulk of Hannibal's heavy cavalry force, and they dressed in helmet and mail armor and were armed with short and long lances, short swords, buckler-shields, and greaves (armor for the leg below the knee).

The magnificent light cavalry force comprised the Numidians, a North African people famous throughout the Mediterranean region for their outstanding mobility and expert fighting abilities. In battle, the Numidians wore their famous leopard skins and used swords, short javelins, and lances to maneuver expertly around and through their enemies, seeking a fatal weakness before striking. Finally, Hannibal used African battle elephants both to anchor his lines and to launch, along with heavy and light cavalry, combined-arms shock assaults to disorient and defeat the enemy on his front and rear. It has been argued that Hannibal also used his elephants along his route of march to impress and frighten European tribes to join his army.

The battle-hardened Carthaginian army constantly changed its weapons systems, military uniforms, and body armor after each successful battle with the Romans. This exchange of military technology and weapons systems was an integral component of Hannibal's war in Italy and proved decisive in allowing his forces to fight against Rome.

MILITARY ORGANIZATION

The military organization of the Carthaginian army stands unique in the history of the ancient world. Car-

Hannibal's army crosses the Rhone River in 218 B.C.E. on its way to invade Italy. Hannibal made the most famous use of war elephants with his crossing of the Alps in this Italian campaign.

thaginian leaders had decided early on that a standing professional army recruited from the general population of eligible men would ensure neither national security nor the worldwide advancement of Carthage's foreign economic policy interests. After enduring a period during which Punic generals and admirals sought to control the state's political policy, Carthage's Council of Elders ruled that the recruitment of trained mercenaries from the western Mediterranean region and elsewhere would be sufficient to meet military requirements in case of war.

The traditional military organization of the Carthaginian army was the Greek hoplite phalanx. Carthage inherited this military tactical system from the Phoenician cities of Tyre and Sidon, and it was a prominent tactical system in most ancient militaries, including that of Rome. However, Hannibal fundamentally altered the hoplite system to gain flexibility and tactical maneuverability in battle. His changes were designed to ensure maximum coordination and communication between the main strike force, the cavalry, and the main maneuver force, the infantry.

The importance of decisive battlefield communications, rapid logistical support, accurate military intelligence, and sound battlefield leadership was constantly communicated to officers and soldiers. As the historical record indicates, Hannibal tried to maximize surprise and shock against the enemy, attacking the enemy in difficult geographical areas, making the enemy fight up hilly terrain, or driving the enemy cavalry from the field of battle in order to launch attacks against the remaining enemy on his front or rear. In this context, Hannibal developed and trained an effective corps of officers, known for their toughness, wisdom, bravado, and discipline.

DOCTRINE, STRATEGY, AND TACTICS

The strategic political doctrine of the Carthaginian Empire was based both on satisfying its national security interests and on maintaining its worldwide commercial relations and trade routes. After the negative outcome of the First Punic War, Carthage's strategic doctrine took into account the empire's depleted resource base, its weakened battle fleet and

naval troop transport capability, and its severe manpower limitations in any future conflict with Rome. Carthage had a military manpower base of 100,000 to 120,000 fighting men for its army and navy and a 30,000- to 35,000-man cavalry force, out of an estimated total population base of 700,000 citizens. In contrast, Rome and its allied states had a strategic military manpower base of 700,000 foot soldiers and 70,000 cavalry forces, and, for combat operations, Rome could deploy within a year more than 250,000 foot soldiers and a 23,000-man cavalry force. Based on these comparative manpower data, a war of attrition was out of the question for Carthage.

For this reason, the Barcid clan reasoned that any future war with Rome would have to be fought in Italy, in order to break the wills of the Roman Senate and the Roman people. This position, advocated by Hannibal, argued that Carthage could prevent Rome from launching major invasions of Carthage, Spain, or other important overseas territories only by launching aggressive combat operations in the heart of the Roman state. The Barcid clan also reasoned that Carthaginian military land forces executing a major land war against Rome and contiguous territories could not expect military reinforcements from the sea while facing overwhelming Roman land armies. In this specific context, the Carthaginian forces would need to inflict serious manpower losses on the Roman army while minimizing their own losses until military reinforcements could arrive from either Carthage or Spain.

At a deeper level, Rome's increasing land and naval power operations in the western Mediterranean region proved a challenge to Carthaginian military strategy. Carthage could no longer adequately control sea lanes for military and commercial purposes; transport troops to danger spots; supply, reinforce, or extradite troops from overseas bases; or protect Carthage and Africa from Roman raids and invasion. For the Punic military and naval planners, the lack of robust naval forces to deter the powerful Roman navy had a profound impact on subsequent strategic military planning and tactical operations.

The implementation of Carthage's strategic military doctrine in the light of Rome's military resources and manpower preponderance was not easy. Hannibal's rise to power injected a new strategic dynamic factor, namely Hannibal's military genius and leadership capabilities, into Roman and Carthaginian foreign security relations. On the ground, Hannibal's offensively oriented strategy was based on the following principles: to win battlefield victories and encourage the defection or the neutrality of Rome's allies and, if militarily decisive in battle, to force Rome to negotiate a compromise peace on Carthaginian terms.

On the battlefield, Hannibal's operational doctrine was to execute the war against Rome using Rome's own material resources, instead of those of Carthage. Hannibal's decision to engage Rome in its own territory and use its resources was consistent with Punic strategic military doctrine against fighting wars of attrition. The objective was to fight a war for victory in Italy and, at the very least, to achieve a

negotiated settlement, which would leave Carthage and its territories free of Rome. The implementation of this tactical doctrine required Hannibal to utilize a variety of military factors to engage, fight, and defeat the much larger and better equipped Roman army in Italy for more than fifteen years. Among the tactics he employed were successful battlefield maneuvers, strategic and tactical surprise, psychological warfare, mastery of the geographical terrain, and military intelligence.

However, Hannibal's war strategy was ultimately unsuccessful. Rome's military manpower and preponderance of material resources, combined with its improved military generalship, very powerful battle fleets, and large land forces, proved strategically overwhelming. The direct result was the inevitable dissolution of the Carthaginian Empire.

ANCIENT SOURCES

Ab urbe condita libri (c. 26 B.C.E.-15 C.E.; *The History of Rome*, 1600), by the ancient Roman historian Livy (59 B.C.E.-17 C.E.), is one of the primary reference sources that classical and modern scholars have used to "reconstruct" the great political, economic, and military struggle between the mature African power, Carthage, and the rising Italian power, Rome. Livy's critical analysis of the Punic Wars was based in the prevailing Roman worldview, and in his writings Livy painted both Hannibal and Carthage in less than friendly terms. He provides the student of Carthaginian warfare, however, with some insights into the character, intensity, and implications of Hannibal's military engagements with Rome from a Roman point of view.

Polybius (c. 200-c. 118 B.C.E.), a Greek historian taken as a prisoner to Rome in 168 B.C.E., wrote a series of histories of Rome and nearby countries from 220 to 146 B.C.E. (*The General History of Polybius: In Five Books*, 1773). His work contributed to the development of historiography as a significant area of inquiry away from previous leanings toward didacticism. Tiberius Catius Asconius Silius Italicus (25 or 26-101 C.E.), a Latin epic poet and politician, authored a seventeen-volume epic on the Second Punic War, entitled *Punica* (*Punica, with an English Translation*, 1934). Appianos, also known as Appian, a second century C.E. Greek historian, authored *Romaica* (*Appian's Roman History*, 1912-1913), a history of Rome and its conquests, including that of Carthage.

A more modern work that provides an interesting analysis of the origins of the First and Second Punic Wars using ancient sources exclusively is B. D. Hoyos's *Unplanned Wars: The Origins of the First and Second Punic Wars* (1997). Hoyos uses Roman historical writers such as Polybius, among others, to look deeply into the origins of the conflict between Carthage and Rome. The tightly argued historical analysis reexamines both ancient evidence and recent findings about the origins of the Punic Wars and the major personalities and events of the great struggle.

BOOKS AND ARTICLES

Bagnall, Nigel. *The Punic Wars*. London: Hutchinson, 1990.

Bradford, Ernle. *Hannibal*. New York: McGraw-Hill, 1981.

Cornell, Tim, Boris Rankov, and Philip Sabin, eds. *The Second Punic War: A Reappraisal*. London: Institute of Classical Studies, University of London, 1996.

De Beer, Sir Gavin. *Hannibal: Challenging Rome's Supremacy*. New York: Viking, 1970.

_____. *Hannibal: The Struggle for Power in the Mediterranean*. London: Thames and Hudson, 1969.

Hoyos, B. D. *Unplanned Wars: The Origins of the First and Second Punic Wars*. Berlin: Walter de Gruyter, 1998.

Lazenby, J. F. *Hannibal's War: A Military History of the Second Punic War*. Warminster, England: Aris and Phillips, 1978. Reprint. Norman: University of Oklahoma Press, 1998.

FILMS AND OTHER MEDIA

Carthage. Documentary. Films for the Humanities, 1990.

Michael J. Siler

ROMAN WARFARE DURING THE REPUBLIC

DATES: 753-27 B.C.E.

MILITARY ACHIEVEMENT

According to tradition, the city of Rome was founded on the banks of the Tiber River in 753 by Romulus, one of the twin sons of Mars, the Roman god of war. At the time of its founding, Rome's proud future still lay far in the distance. A dynasty of foreign kings from neighboring Etruria eventually settled at Rome and dominated the institutions of the city. Although this early history is uncertain, Rome's levy seems to have relied on the wealthy, because they could afford their own equipment for battle. Armed like Greek hoplites, Roman soldiers fought with thrusting spears, and, using a Greek formation—the phalanx—they stood shoulder to shoulder, with shields locked together.

After expelling the last of the Etruscan monarchs in 510, the Romans installed a Republican government, dominated by the Senate, and kept the Greek style of fighting. About a century later, however, some changes were introduced during a long war with Veii, an Etruscan stronghold north of Rome. In need of more soldiers, the Romans began recruiting more broadly. These new recruits, unable to afford full protective armor, adopted the *scutum*, a long Italic shield, in place of the hoplite's round buckler. Moreover, the Romans introduced pay for military service and, for the first time, provided at public expense a horse for every new member of the cavalry.

The Roman victory over Veii was followed by defeat on the Allia, a stream about 11 miles north of Rome. There in around 390 B.C.E.

Gallic warriors overwhelmed the Republic's forces, capturing and plundering the city before moving on. The conquering Gallic chieftain Brennus uttered the harsh words *Vae victis*, meaning "Woe to the vanquished!" This disaster revealed Rome's military weaknesses and stirred reform. No longer fighting as a single compact body, the Romans came to employ a looser formation, composed of small units, or maniples. After abandoning the thrusting spear, Rome's soldiers also came to adopt a throwing spear.

Eventually Rome's influence managed to spread beyond the neighboring communities of Latium and into southern Italy. Greek cities, established there centuries earlier, called on Pyrrhus of Epirus (r. 297-272 B.C.E.) to stop the advance. With his war elephants, Pyrrhus defeated Rome's forces at Heraclea (280 B.C.E.) and Ausculum (279 B.C.E.) but also suffered enormous casualties. He exclaimed that another victory such as his last would be the ruin of his army. After Beneventum in 275 B.C.E. he withdrew from Italy, never to return. By 264 Rome controlled

TURNING POINTS

753 B.C.E.	The city of Rome is said to be founded on the banks of the Tiber River by Romulus, one of the twin sons of Mars, the Roman god of war.
c. 390 B.C.E.	Gallic warriors overwhelm the Republic's forces, capturing and plundering the city of Rome.
202 B.C.E.	Rome defeats Carthage at the Battle of Zama.
168 B.C.E	The Roman Republic defeats Macedonia at Pydna, eventually organizing Macedonia as a Roman province.
146 B.C.E.	Rome defeats Carthage in the Third Punic War, destroying its greatest enemy and assuring its long-term dominion.
60 B.C.E.	The First Triumvirate is formed.
27 B.C.E.	Augustus establishes the Roman Empire.

BATTLES OF THE SECOND PUNIC WAR, 218-202 B.C.E.

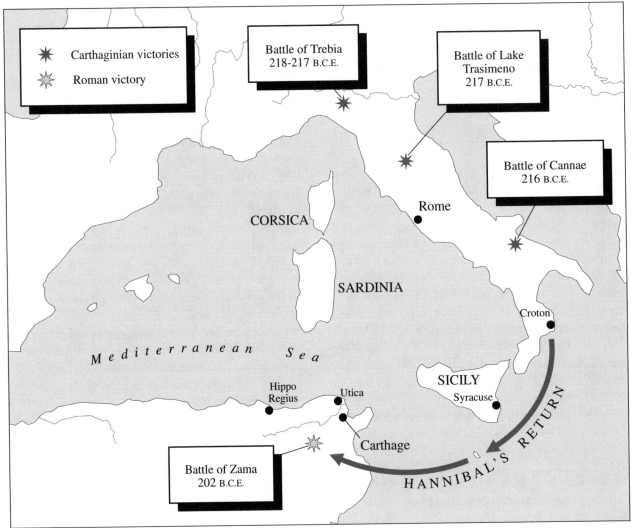

* Carthaginian victories

* Roman victory

Battle of Trebia
218-217 B.C.E.

Battle of Lake
Trasimeno
217 B.C.E.

Battle of Cannae
216 B.C.E.

CORSICA

Rome

SARDINIA

Croton

Mediterranean Sea

SICILY

Hippo
Regius   Utica   Syracuse

Carthage

Battle of Zama
202 B.C.E.

HANNIBAL'S RETURN

all of the Italian peninsula, except the Po valley in the north.

Rome then turned to Sicily, vying for control of the island with Carthage, a powerful city on the North African coast. During the First Punic War (264-241 B.C.E.), Rome mobilized large fleets for the first time. Although inexperienced at sea, Rome's invention of a grappling hook and boarding bridge allowed soldiers to cross over to enemy ships and fight on their decks like infantry. With a final naval victory in 241 B.C.E., Rome expelled the Carthaginians from Sicily.

A generation later, the Second Punic War (219-201 B.C.E.) revived old grudges. With an eternal hatred of Rome, the Carthaginian general Hannibal (247-182 B.C.E.) planned to win the war through a bold surprise invasion of the Italian peninsula. Hannibal made a winter crossing of the Alps to enter Italy and gain victories at Trebbia (218-217 B.C.E.), Trasimeno Lake (217 B.C.E.), and Cannae (216 B.C.E.). However, Rome sent forces against his base in Spain and eventually confined him to the "toe," or southernmost tip, of Italy. After sixteen years in enemy territory, Hannibal finally withdrew to Africa, where he was crushed at Zama (202 B.C.E.) by Scipio

Africanus (236-184 or 183 B.C.E.). Hannibal escaped the battlefield and urged his countrymen to surrender. Carthage lost some of its African territory to Rome's allies, and Spain was eventually organized as Roman territory.

Hannibal's alliance with Philip V (238-179 B.C.E.) of Macedonia led to two Macedonian Wars, in which Roman troops crossed the Adriatic Sea and at last secured victory at Cynoscephalae in 197 B.C.E. Although Macedonia survived and Greece was declared free, Rome's influence came to dominate the whole area. Once involved in the eastern Mediterranean, Rome's forces also accepted the challenge of Syria's Antiochus III (242-187 B.C.E.), also known as Antiochus the Great. After victory at Magnesia in 190 B.C.E., the Republic refused to annex any new territory, but it now arranged the affairs of Hellenistic Asia as it wished.

At Pydna (168 B.C.E) the Republic defeated Philip's son, Perseus (c. 212-c. 165 B.C.E.). Macedonia was eventually organized as a Roman province,

North Wind Picture Archives

Soldiers of the Roman Republic, bearing spears, swords, shields, and standards with the initials SPQR, for "Senatus Populusque Romanus," or, "the Senate and People of Rome."

and its governor was made responsible for Greece. Moreover, Egypt was treated like a dependency. When Antiochus IV (c. 215-164 B.C.E.) invaded the Nile Delta, a Roman ambassador is said to have drawn a circle around the Syrian king and commanded him to order a retreat before stepping out of it. The Third Punic War (149-146 B.C.E.) resulted in the complete destruction of Carthage in 146, and the city's remaining territory became the province of Africa. Thus with the defeat of Carthage and Hannibal's allies, the Republic had destroyed its greatest enemies. Although more wars lay in the future, Rome's long-term dominion was assured.

WEAPONS, UNIFORMS, AND ARMOR

The ancient sources present a reasonably clear picture of the Republic's military affairs as it emerged from the struggle with Hannibal. All Roman citizens between the ages of seventeen and thirty-six were liable for service. The maximum length of service was likely sixteen years for infantry and ten for cavalry, but in normal circumstances a soldier would probably serve for up to six years and then be released.

The number of the main infantry division, the legion, is given as 4,200 soldiers, but in emergencies it could be higher. The legion was drawn up in three lines of *hastati*, *principes*, and *triarii*, with the youngest and poorest forming the *velites*. As lightly armed skirmishers, the *velites* carried a sword, javelin, and small circular shield. The *hastati* and *principes*, in contrast, were heavily armed. Protected by the long Italic shield, they relied upon a short Spanish sword, or *gladius*, and two throwing spears, or *pila*. Like the *hastati* and *principes*, the *triarii* were also heavily armed, but they carried a thrusting spear, or *hasta*, instead of the *pilum*. All soldiers wore a bronze breastplate, a bronze helmet, and a pair of greaves, or shin guards. In order to be distinguished from a distance, the *velites* covered their helmets with wolfskin, and the *hastati* wore three tall feathers in their helmets. To preserve a degree of exclusiveness, wealthy recruits wore shirts of ring mail, whether serving among the *hastati*, *principes*, or *triarii*.

MILITARY ORGANIZATION

The supreme magistrates of the state, the two consuls, usually served also as generals of the army. Elected to serve for one year, each consul traditionally commanded two legions. His authority, called imperium, was absolute beyond the walls of the city. The fasces, a bundle of rods and axes bound together by red thongs, symbolized the consul's power of life and death. After victory, the consul was decked with laurel and borne before the general by twelve attendants, or lictors, proceeding in single file.

The general's senior officers included the military tribunes. With six in each legion, all tribunes were required to have significant military experience and to meet stringent property qualifications. Usually most, if not all, were elected. They had some important military responsibilities. As elective officers, they more often tended to the welfare of the soldiers. By the early second century, it was also customary for the general to be accompanied by legates. Appointed by the Senate on the general's advice, these were often ambitious young men from prominent families, who had little military experience.

The real strength of Rome's military were the centurions, career officers who, as one contemporary observed, held their ground when worsted and stood ready to die at their posts. There were sixty centurions in each legion, with two in each of thirty maniples. Selected by the tribunes, the centurions were organized into a hierarchy with a well-defined order of promotion. Every centurion's ambition was to serve as *primus pilus*, senior officer of the first maniple, because the holder of that title was recognized as the best soldier of the legion and given a seat on the general's war council.

In addition to infantry, the legion had three hundred cavalrymen. They wore linen corselets and relied on strong circular shields and long spears. They were divided into ten units, or *turmae*. Each of these had three decurions, and the most senior of the three always exercised command. Allied contingents, recruited from throughout Italy, also campaigned with Rome's citizen army. In fact, there was at least one legion of allies, if not more, for every legion of citizens. Known as *socii*, they were organized and equipped like Romans. They were also commanded by Roman citizens called *praefecti*. An elite corps, the *extraordinarii*, was selected from the best of the allies, horse and foot. The rest were divided into *alae*, right and left wings, reflecting their positions on the army's flanks. The great numbers of the *socii* especially contributed to the might and effectiveness of Rome's forces.

DOCTRINE, STRATEGY, AND TACTICS

After assembling with their arms, the soldiers would be ordered to pitch camp. It resembled a city, complete with a forum and tents arranged in neat rows. The *via principalis*, or "first street," ran past the tents of the senior officers, and the *via quintana*, or "fifth street," paralleled the main boulevard. During the time of the Republic, these camps were usually temporary. Because commanders always employed the same plan, every soldier knew the camp's layout and could find his way around, even in the dark. In addition to soldiers and officers, the camp also housed animals, equipment, baggage, and sometimes plunder taken from the defeated enemy. Moreover, there were hosts of camp followers. In 134 B.C.E., for example, numerous traders, soothsayers, and diviners, as well as two thousand prostitutes, were cast out of a camp near Numantia in Spain.

Yet the camp remained an integral part of Republican strategy. As an entrenched fortress, it provided a base for attack and a safe retreat in the event of defeat. The guarding of its gates therefore required discipline. Those who fell asleep during the night watch were usually stoned to death. This harsh discipline extended to the field of battle, where a maniple, giving ground without good reason, could be, literally, "decimated." A tenth part of its men, selected by lot, would be clubbed to death, while the rest would be ordered to sleep outside the camp's fortifications on an unprotected spot. In contrast, there was also a system of military decorations to reward exceptional bravery. The general praised heroic soldiers before the assembled army and gave them prizes. To the first man mounting the enemy's walls, for example, he conferred a crown of gold.

On breaking camp, procedure had to be followed. On the first signal, the soldiers took down their tents. On the second, they loaded the pack animals. On the third, their march began. When attack was not expected, all moved in one long train, the *extraordinarii* leading the way. In times of danger, a different marching order prevailed. The *hastati*, *principes*, and *triarii* formed three parallel columns. When the enemy appeared, the maniples turned to the left or to the right, clearing the baggage trains and confronting the enemy from whichever side necessary. Thus in a single movement, the army placed itself in good battle order.

When engaging the enemy, the legion approached in three lines. First, the *hastati*. Second, the *principes*. Third, the *triarii*. Each line consisted of ten maniples, drawn up with gaps between them, equal in width to the maniples. These gaps usually alternated in each row, like dark spaces on a checkerboard. Thus the gaps in the first line adjoined the maniples in the second line. Likewise, gaps in the second line adjoined maniples in the third.

Traditionally, the battle followed a more or less schematic plan. Forming a light screen, the *velites* opened with a hail of javelins and retired to the rear through the gaps. Then the *hastati*, closing the gaps in the first line, offered a united front against the enemy. After surging forward in unison and striking with their swords, the soldiers soon recoiled, rested, and tried again. If the assault continued to fail after many attempts, the *hastati* retired through the gaps in the line of the *principes*, who next advanced and attacked in the same manner. If the *principes* also failed, then they retired through the gaps in the line of the *triarii*, who proceeded to the final trial of strength, reinforced by survivors from the first and second lines. The Romans thus refused to expose all

their forces to a frontal assault, keeping part of them in reserve, while the rest engaged the enemy.

On the whole, Roman strategy aimed at the destruction of the enemy in pitched battle. This strategy sometimes employed flexible tactics. In 169 B.C.E., for example, the Romans borrowed a formation from the gladiatorial arena. In this formation, called the "tortoise," or *testudo*, several ranks locked their shields together and formed a sloping roof over their heads. They advanced to the lowest part of the enemy's wall, where some of the Romans then mounted the roof of shields. After moving up its slope, they occupied the high end, where they fought face to face with the wall's defenders. Finally overwhelming their opponents, the victorious Romans crossed over into the enemy city and captured it.

Under a strong general, the storming and plundering of a city proceeded by well-defined stages, announced by signals. First the troops slaughtered. Next they looted. Finally they disposed of their spoils, with the profits distributed equally among all the soldiers. More often, however, the general made little attempt to restrain them. They held the power of life and death, and they did whatever they wished to the inhabitants of a captured city. In these cases, of course, every soldier looted for himself, and everything he laid his hands on became his private property.

Saluted as *imperator* by his troops, the successful general looked forward to a triumph, the most distinguished reward conferred by the Senate for military achievement. This ceremony celebrated important victories and was granted only under certain conditions, such as extraordinarily numerous enemy casualties and significant expansion of Roman territory. The triumph was a magnificent procession in which the victorious general, with laurel wreath on his brow and ivory scepter in his hand, mounted a chariot drawn by white horses and paraded through the streets of Rome. Before him were the spoils of conquered cities and captive leaders imprisoned in chains. After him followed his troops in military array, enjoying unusual license and singing bawdy songs. The procession formed upon the Campus Martius, the field of the war god Mars, and entered the city through the Triumphal Gate. It then ascended the Capitol, where the general offered sacrifice and dined with Jupiter, the king of the gods and goddesses. The entire population participated with unbounded jubilation in this ceremony of great pomp and circumstance. After all, the general was, at least temporarily, a god-king. However, as a reminder, a slave would be stationed near the general throughout the parade, occasionally whispering in his ear, "Remember! Thou art a man."

REFORMS OF THE LATE REPUBLIC

Although late second century Roman legions again met defeat, eventually Gaius Marius claimed victory for the Republic, in Africa over King Jugurtha (c. 160-104 B.C.E.) of Numidia and in northern Italy over the Teutons (102 B.C.E.) and the Cimbri (101 B.C.E.). While holding an unprecedented series of consulships in 107 and from 104 to 100, Marius encouraged military reform, and he has been credited by some with the conversion of Rome's citizen militia into a standing professional force. Marius undoubtedly played an important role in the evolution of Rome's military.

As in past crises of state, Marius opened the ranks to the *capite censi*, citizens who failed to meet prescribed property qualifications for military service. He likely viewed this measure as a temporary emergency action, but later generations followed his example. Immersed in wars both foreign and domestic, Marius's successors abandoned all restrictions on liability for service and recruited more troops than ever before. Because most of these soldiers came from poor families, the State equipped them at public expense. So variations in arms and armor soon disappeared.

Marius also made fundamental changes in tactical organization, preferring the cohort to the maniple as the basic unit within the legion. Marius's new cohort consisted of three maniples, one drawn from each line: *hastati*, *principes*, and *triarii*. As a result, his cohort was a microcosm of the old legion. The First Cohort consisted of the three maniples situated on the extreme right of the old lines. The last cohort, the Tenth, moving from right to left, consisted of the three maniples on the extreme left.

Marius's new legion drew up for battle in three lines. There were four cohorts in the first line, three in the second line, and three in the third. The cohorts likely had a standard size, which under the Empire was 480 men. Thus the new legion seems to have had a strength of 4,800 men, organized into ten cohorts and thirty maniples. The *velites* were apparently abolished. Eventually the Roman army incorporated contingents raised outside Italy. These new contingents carried their national weapons and were called *auxilia*. Some came from independent allies, others came from forced levies, and still others were paid as mercenaries.

In the press of battle, standards, banners on long poles, served as a rallying point. Marius gave preeminence to the *aquila*, or eagle, as the legion's chief standard. The legion had previously used a variety of standards, including the eagle, wolf, minotaur, horse, and boar, among others. Yet by the Republic's close, the eagle shared importance only with the standards of the *hastati* and *principes*, which consisted of slender poles decorated with circular bosses. The *primus pilus*, the best soldier in the legion, acted as *aquilifer*, or eaglebearer. To lose or surrender the *aquila* was, of course, a great disgrace for the entire legion.

Along with these changes, Marius modified the *pilum*. The iron tip of Rome's heavy spear was joined to its wooden shaft by two iron rivets. Marius replaced one of these with a wooden pin, and on striking a target the shaft now snapped off. The spear could no longer be picked up and thrown back at its owner. Moreover, Marius wished to reduce the great numbers of pack animals, because they slowed the army's march, so he required his troops to carry equipment and rations on forked poles flung over their shoulders. As the general's beasts of burden, the legionaries came to be called "Marius's Mules."

WARS OF THE LATE REPUBLIC

In Marius's later years, violence spread across the Italian peninsula, with serious repercussions for the Republic. Weary of Rome's stern ascendancy, the Italian allies rose in revolt. Fearful but wise, Rome promised citizenship to all who laid down their arms. Although the Social War (91-88 B.C.E.), as it was called, soon ended, the riot of its daily warfare created an angry generation whose sons found lodging in Rome's legions, filling them with a spirit of apathy and callousness. These soldiers cared little for the Republic and were loyal only to the general who paid them.

Almost inevitably, civil war followed the Social War. As one of its leaders, Marius died in 86, before destroying all of his opponents. His archenemy, Lucius Cornelius Sulla (138-78 B.C.E.), survived to conduct a great bloodbath and hold untrammeled authority until his own death. Under these chaotic conditions, only small military gains were made abroad. Yet when Mithridates VI of Pontus seized Asia Minor and invaded Greece, he was defeated by Pompey the Great (106-48 B.C.E.), who annexed Syria and Palestine, thereby enlarging Rome's Asiatic dominion.

Only a few years later, bold adventures began to unfold in Gaul. Julius Caesar (100-44 B.C.E.) embarked on a war of conquest against warrior Celts and their powerful priests, the Druids. With his small force, Caesar opposed the large Celtic armies and eventually defeated the Gallic tribes, organizing their territories as a province. At the same time Caesar accelerated the gradual professionalization of the Roman army.

Caesar followed tradition by relying upon the cohort and the centurion, although his military tribunes were mostly young men with political charges. Yet Caesar's legates, ten in number, played an essential role in his command structure. Acting as subordinate commanders, some commanded legions and auxiliary forces, while others managed the camp and secured the surrounding region. Perhaps even more important, Caesar's battle order responded dramatically to topography. He exploited flank attacks, for example, and often held troops in reserve for the decisive onslaught. Caesar thus helped to liberate Roman warfare from the traditional scheme of advance and assault.

Like a great Hellenistic king, Caesar raised siege towers, built bridges to span fierce rivers, and dug elaborate entrenchments around enemy bases. His formidable artillery included giant catapults, which fired heavy stones, and smaller *scorpions*, which fired arrows with extraordinary accuracy. Apart from his tactical expertise Caesar's personal qualities also invited his success as a commander. More often than not, his decisiveness and instinct compensated for his reckless daring.

Despite the continued Roman military success, by 49 B.C.E. the Republic was again divided by civil war. Caesar crossed the Rubicon and swept through Italy into Greece, where he defeated Pompey. Embroiled in Rome's affairs, the pharaoh of Egypt soon fell to Caesar's arms as well. Then Pharnaces (r. 63-47 B.C.E.), son of Mithradates the Great, took his turn, losing at Zela (47 B.C.E.). To underscore the rapidity of this victory, Caesar employed three short words, *Veni, vidi, vici*, meaning, "I came, I saw, I conquered." Other civil war battles followed in Africa and Spain. Caesar prevailed in all and returned to Rome with unprecedented power, as dictator for life. However, by the Ides of March, 44 B.C.E., he lay dead, murdered by conspirators.

Through civil war Caesar's heir, Octavius (63-14 B.C.E.), claimed unrivaled supremacy. He then adopted a new name, Caesar Augustus, and, ruling as Rome's first emperor, he replaced the citizen militia of the Republic, which had become increasingly unmanageable and restless, with a smaller professional force. Legionaries eventually served for twenty-five years, enjoyed promotion through the ranks, and received generous cash payments on discharge. Except for a special corps, they were stationed in the frontier provinces, at a safe distance from the imperial capitol. Augustus's reign thus signaled a new epoch in Roman political and military history, as well as the end of the Republic in 27 B.C.E.

In conclusion, the military institutions of the Republic proved extremely durable and successful. With great adaptability, the Romans learned from their opponents, borrowing weaponry and improving tactical structure. Rome's forces were also guided in a few critical moments by generals of genius. Yet the most fundamental reason for the Republic's success lay in its manpower, fueled by the populations of Italy, which allowed the Romans to ignore defeats. Thus Rome's military evolved from obscurity into a remarkable institution, which eventually dominated the ancient Mediterranean and shaped one of history's longest-lived empires.

ANCIENT SOURCES

Most historians contemporary with the Republic discussed military affairs. Yet few of these scholars were actually eyewitnesses to councils of war and victories on the battlefield. However, there are two notable exceptions. First, the Greek author Polybius (c. 200-c. 118 B.C.E.) saw the Roman army in action against fellow Greeks, and later he seems to have accompanied a Roman general on military campaign. In his *Histories* (first appearing in English as *The General History of Polybius: In Five Books*, 1773), Polybius gives an important description of the Roman army as it emerged from the struggle against Hannibal. Second, Julius Caesar provides a valuable narrative of the Roman army at war. He recounts his own activities as general in Gaul, Germany, and Britain throughout a period of almost ten years. Caesar's *Comentarii de Bello Gallico* (51-52 B.C.E.; *Commentaries*, 1609) explores a wide range of the Republic's military institutions and activities as they existed in the first century B.C.E.

BOOKS AND ARTICLES

Bishop, M. C., and J. C. N. Coulston. *Roman Military Equipment: From the Punic Wars to the Fall of Rome*. London: Batsford, 1993.

Keppie, Lawrence. *The Making of the Roman Army from Republic to Empire*. Totowa, N.J.: Barnes & Noble Books, 1984.

Rich, John, and Graham Shipley, eds. *War and Society in the Roman World*. London: Routledge, 1993.

Salvatore, John Pamment. *Roman Republican Castrametation: A Reappraisal of Historical and Archaeological Sources*. Oxford, England: Tempus Reparatum, 1996.

Denvy A. Bowman

ROMAN WARFARE DURING THE EMPIRE

DATES: 27 B.C.E.-476 C.E.

MILITARY ACHIEVEMENT

The imperial Roman army was arguably one of the most impressive fighting forces the world has ever known. Its military campaigns greatly expanded the territory of the Roman Empire. In the first century C.E., Rome began the conquest of Britain, and in the second century, it conquered Dacia, modern Romania, as well as parts of modern Jordan and Iraq. The Roman army also defended the Empire against a wide range of enemies along its frontiers, including the Caledonians in northern Britain, various Germanic tribes, the Sarmatians, the Parthians, the Sassanid Persians, and desert peoples in North Africa. Roman soldiers were highly skilled in pitched battle, siegecraft, and military engineering. In the course of their campaigns Roman troops built military roads, bridges, and large permanent camps, many of which eventually became cities in Europe, the Middle East, and North Africa.

WEAPONS, UNIFORMS, AND ARMOR

At the beginning of Augustus's reign as emperor in 27 B.C.E., Roman legionary infantrymen wore a simple round helmet with a horsehair tail at the top as well as a chain mail shirt known as a *lorica hamata*. The latter consisted of interlocking metal rings and provided good protection, but was, however, very heavy and took a long time to manufacture. Later in Augustus's reign infantrymen began to use a new type of helmet, of Gallic origin, which was more closely fitted to the skull and included neck and cheek guards. In addition, possibly due to a major loss of military equipment in the German defeat of three legions in the Battle of Teutoburg Forest (9 C.E.), the Roman infantry began to use a new type of breastplate known as the *lorica segmentata*. This armor consisted of horizontal metal bands covering the chest and abdomen as well as vertical metal bands protecting the shoulders. This could be manufactured much more quickly than mail armor and was very flexible. However, the fittings that held the bands together were easily damaged; as a result, this type of armor was in constant need of repair. Early imperial infantrymen also wore greaves, or shin guards, on their legs as well as leather strips called *pteurages* that were attached to their body armor and provided protection for their thighs and upper arms.

The principal weapon of early imperial legionary infantrymen was a short sword called a *gladius*, which was modeled after that of the Spanish Celts and used for hand-to-hand combat. Infantrymen also carried a javelin, or *pilum*, which was hurled at the enemy from a distance, as well as a thrusting spear known as a *hasta*. The large semicylindrical shield, or *scutum*, was probably of Celtic origin and derived from flat oval shields. By the first century C.E. its upper and lower curved edges had been removed, giving it a more rectangular shape. Legionary infantrymen were also equipped with a dagger, which, like the *gladius*, was of Spanish origin.

Roman officers of the early Empire wore the same Gallic-type helmets worn by the infantry and a variety of body armor, including mail shirts, cuirasses that were modeled after the human torso, or scale shirts known as *loricae squamatae*. The latter consisted of overlapping metal scales arranged in horizontal rows and fastened to a foundation of linen or hide. This type of armor was easy to make and repair and, when polished, gave the wearer an impressive appearance. However, it was not very flexible, and its wearer was vulnerable to a sword or spear thrust from below.

Under the early Empire, troops of the *auxilia* used equipment that was generally inferior to that of the legionaries; however, they began to receive better-quality equipment during the reign of the emperor

TURNING POINTS

27 B.C.E.	Augustus establishes the Roman Empire.
9 C.E.	Roman legions are defeated by the Germans at the Battle of Teutoburg Forest.
70	The Romans besiege Jerusalem, taking the city's population captive and leveling its buildings.
122	Construction of Hadrian's Wall begins in Britain.
476	The weakened western Roman Empire finally falls.

Trajan (c. 53-c. 117 C.E.). The infantry wore a variety of helmets as well as leather tunics covered with metal plates or mail, and used narrow, flat, sometimes oval shields. Their principal weapons were the *hasta* and the *spatha*, a long sword that became the dominant form of sword throughout the Roman army by the early third century. Cavalrymen wore iron helmets that covered the entire head except for the eyes, nose, and mouth. They wore either mail or scale body armor and used the same weapons as did the infantry of the *auxilia* cohorts. Although they did not use stirrups, they were firmly anchored on horseback by the four projecting horns of their saddles.

During the crisis of the third century C.E. the Roman Empire experienced increased invasion and internal chaos but lacked a centralized military supply system. Armies were consequently forced to salvage equipment from battlefields or to obtain it on their own from other sources, which, in turn, led to an end to uniformity in the appearance of soldiers. During this period, the *lorica segmentata* was gradually abandoned, and soldiers increasingly made use of mail shirts as well as an improved form of scale armor. In this type of armor, which did not require a foundation, the scales were ringed together vertically as well as horizontally. The scales were therefore locked down, and the wearer was much less vulnerable to a thrust from below. Moreover, the older Gallic helmet was replaced by a new helmet of Sarmatian origin, the *spangenhelm*, which consisted of several metal plates held together in a conical shape by reinforcement bands. This helmet, which included cheek, neck, and nose guards, was used by both infantry and cavalry. In addition the *scutum* was re-

placed by a large-dished oval shield covered with hide or linen. Cavalry units used a similar type of shield that featured the insignia of the bearer's unit.

In the late third century C.E., the emperor Diocletian (c. 245-316 C.E.) established a series of state-run arms factories, or *fabricae*, in an attempt to remedy the supply problem. However, these factories failed to restore uniformity in military equipment due to the fact that a wide range of barbarian peoples were serving in the Roman army by this time and used their own native weapons. In the fourth century the factories did mass-produce a new type of helmet of Parthian-Sassanid origin, known as a ridge helmet, because it consisted of two metal halves held together by a central ridge. During this period, soldiers also received monetary allowances for the purchase of clothing, arms, and armor. By the late fourth century C.E., the army came to include increased numbers of barbarians who had little need for armor and therefore little desire to purchase it for regular use. Instead, soldiers relied primarily on large circular shields for protection. When an army was on the march, its armor was carried in wagons and was normally used only during an actual pitched battle.

The Roman army also used various types of artillery both in battle and when conducting a siege. These included a device known as a *tormenta*, which fired arrows, javelins, and rocks, as well as larger *ballistae* and catapults that hurled larger arrows or stones.

MILITARY ORGANIZATION

During most of its history, the basic unit of the Roman army was the legion, which consisted only of Roman citizens and during the time of the early Empire numbered about 5,000 men. Each legion was organized into ten infantry cohorts, one of which consisted of five centuries of 160 men each, while the remaining nine cohorts were each composed of six centuries of 80 men each. The centuries were grouped into maniples, each consisting of two centuries. During the first to third centuries C.E., each legion also included a cavalry detachment of 120 men. The command structure of the legion consisted of the fifty-nine centurions, who commanded the centuries; five tribunes, each of whom commanded two cohorts; a prefect of the camp; a tribune of senatorial rank; and the legions' commanders, the legates.

The legions were supported by units known as *auxilia*, which consisted of troops recruited from subject peoples. These included infantry cohorts of 480 men divided into six centuries, and cavalry detachments (*alae*) consisting of sixteen troops (*turmae*) of thirty-two riders each. In the late first century C.E. these were enlarged to cohorts of ten centuries and *alae* composed of twenty-four *turmae*; the new cohorts and *alae* each theoretically numbered 1,000 men but were actually somewhat smaller in number. There were also mixed units, known as *cohortes equitatae*, consisting of one infantry cohort and four troops of cavalry, and units known as *numeri*, which were not grouped as cohorts or *alae* but retained their own ethnic characteristics in terms of organization and weaponry. In addition to infantry and cavalry units, the *auxilia* included specialized troops such as archers and slingers.

The early imperial army also included certain elite

ROMAN EMPIRE, C. 117

units based in Rome. The most important of these was the Praetorian Guard, which was created by the emperor Augustus (63-14 B.C.E.) and originally consisted of nine cohorts. It supervised public life in the capital, escorted the emperor, and eventually came to play a major political role by occasionally helping to determine the succession to the imperial throne. The emperor was also protected by an elite personal cavalry unit known as the *equites singulares Augusti*. In the fourth century, the emperor Constantine the Great (c. 275 to 285-337 C.E.) disbanded both of these units because they had supported his rival Maxentius (died 312), and replaced them with a new bodyguard of German cavalry, the *scholae Palatinae*.

In the late second and third centuries C.E., the imperial army underwent some notable changes. The emperor Lucius Septimius Severus (146-211 C.E.) increased both the pay and the size of the army, adding new *auxilia* units as well as three new legions. One of these was stationed near Rome, serving as a reserve unit and ensuring that Severus remained in power. In 212 C.E. Severus's son, the emperor Caracalla (188-217 C.E.), extended Roman citizenship to most of the Empire's population; this action essentially ended the distinction between legions and *auxilia*. At the start of the third century crisis (235-284 C.E.), the Empire lacked reserve forces that could deal with invasions by German tribes. As a result, the emperors of this period formed reserve field armies that could readily respond to such invaders. The cavalry of the early imperial army were essentially light cavalry, but by the fourth century the army included two types of heavily armored cavalry, known as *catapractarii* and *clibanarii*, which were modeled after Sarmatian and Persian cavalry respectively.

In the fourth century, Constantine the Great established a single large mobile field army known as the *comitatus*. This was led by two newly created officers, the *magister peditum*, who commanded the infantry, and the *magister equitum*, the commander of the cavalry. Constantine thus established a clear division between the field army and the frontier troops, the *limitanei*, who during this period were organized into legions of 1,000 men. However, due to the inability of this single field army to respond to simultaneous attacks on various parts of the frontier,

Constantine's successors divided the *comitatus* into a number of regional field armies.

In the late fourth century, the Roman army faced mounting manpower shortages, which became particularly acute following a disastrous campaign against the Persians (363 C.E.) and a major defeat at Adrianople (378 C.E.). As a result, units of *limitanei* were transferred to the field armies. Moreover, the Romans permitted individual German tribes to settle within Roman territory as allies, or *foederati*, who were obliged to provide military service to the emperor. However, the field armies fell into decline, and individual military commanders and other wealthy individuals consequently organized private armies known as *bucellarii*, which continued to exist after the fall of the western Roman Empire in 476 C.E.

DOCTRINE, STRATEGY, AND TACTICS

During the early imperial period Roman leaders believed that it was Rome's destiny to rule the entire world, a view that is reflected in book 6 of Virgil's (70-19 B.C.E.) *Aeneid* (c. 29-19 B.C.E.; English translation, 1589). However, during this same period they came to recognize major factors that limited further territorial expansion. One of these was the sometimes formidable resistance by enemies such as the Caledonians, the Germanic tribes, and the Parthians and Sassanids. Moreover, some territories open to conquest, such as the Arabian deserts to the far southeast, were of little economic or strategic value. Finally, the empire simply did not possess the military manpower or resources to expand indefinitely. Augustus stationed most of the legions on the frontiers and recommended to his successors the basic strategy of defending Rome's existing frontiers rather than conquering additional territory.

Despite Augustus's recommendation, emperors of the first to third centuries C.E. did not completely abandon the policy of expansion. Notable examples of this policy can be seen in the conquests of Britain, Dacia, certain Middle Eastern territories, and in Septimius Severus's campaigns in Mesopotamia and northern Britain. In addition, Roman emperors and their generals sometimes carried out preemptive attacks or reprisals in order to eliminate potential threats to the Empire. However, for the most part Roman emperors developed and adhered to a strategy of defense of the Empire's frontiers. In doing so, they gradually established defensive zones, or limes, along the frontiers. The central feature of such zones was a military road running along the actual frontier. At various intervals along such roads the Romans built various defensive fortifications, including large legionary camps, smaller forts, watchtowers, and fortified ports along rivers. In the first and second centuries emperors sometimes implemented a policy of "forward defense," in which Roman forces took control of adjacent enemy territory and built roads, watchtowers, and forts in order to monitor enemy activity and discourage possible attack.

Sometimes the Romans built continuous defensive barriers in the limes in order to prevent barbarian entry into imperial territory as well as to define the Empire's actual boundaries. These include three barriers built in the second century: Hadrian's Wall and the Antonine Wall in northern Britain, as well as a 240-mile-long wooden palisade built to protect the strategic area between the upper Rhine and Danube Rivers. Such fortifications consisted of a ditch, an embankment, and a rampart, with smaller forts and military camps of varying size built at intervals along the wall. A military road was built along the entire wall for the purpose of communication and moving troops in the event of an enemy threat.

During the early imperial period, frontier provinces were guarded by armies composed either of legions and *auxilia* or simply of *auxilia* cavalry and infantry units. The northern frontiers consisted of three regions: northern Britain and the Rhine and Danube frontiers, each of which was threatened by warlike barbarian peoples. Rome's eastern provinces lacked natural geographical barriers and were therefore vulnerable to attack from the Parthians and, beginning in the third century, the Sassanid Persians. During the reign of Augustus, the Rhine and North African frontiers were considered the most dangerous in the Empire. However, as these frontiers were stabilized, their garrisons were reduced, and those on the Danube and eastern frontiers were gradually increased during the first to third centuries.

During the third century crisis, frontier defenses collapsed and emperors consequently developed a new strategy of imperial defense. During this period Germanic tribes and Sassanid armies frequently penetrated the limes and sometimes moved virtually at will within Roman territory. They sometimes posed a threat to cities located in interior areas away from the frontiers. The inhabitants of such cities consequently began to build defensive walls around them; in the late third century the emperor Aurelian (c. 215-275 C.E.) began construction of a wall around Rome itself. Moreover, third century emperors began to develop a strategy of "defense in depth," which featured less emphasis on frontier forces and greater use of mobile field armies that centered on heavy cavalry units. Such armies were stationed in cities away from the frontier and then sent to intercept and defeat invaders. Moreover, in an attempt to deal with a shortage of manpower, some barbarians (*laeti*) were allowed to settle in Roman territory and entrusted with defense of part of the frontier; they were also required to provide recruits for the army.

In the fourth century, Constantine the Great and his successors made increased use of mobile field armies. During this period, some emperors also attempted to strengthen the frontier defenses. Under Diocletian, frontier defenses were rebuilt, and new forts were built along the Danube and eastern frontiers and in North Africa. Valentinian I (321-375 C.E.) strengthened defenses on the Rhine and Danube and directed preemptive attacks against barbarians along both frontiers. However, by the late fourth century the Empire was confronted with mounting manpower shortages as well as growing barbarian pressure on the frontiers. The manpower shortage resulted in understrength garrisons on the Rhine frontier being grouped together at a few vital points. In the fifth century C.E. Germanic invaders simply bypassed such strongpoints, which led to a complete collapse of the Rhine frontiers and, ultimately, to the end of the western Roman Empire.

The principal tactical objectives of a Roman commander were to move his army safely and swiftly and ultimately to defeat the enemy in open battle. A Roman army was most vulnerable when on the march, and therefore it had to be arranged in an order of march that would enable it to deal effectively with an enemy attack. Moreover, army commanders had to provide maximum protection for the baggage train because if enemy forces captured it and began looting, soldiers might break ranks in order to retrieve their belongings and consequently place the entire army in peril. In order to ensure safe and rapid passage through enemy territory, Roman troops often built roads and bridges. Moreover, at the end of each day's march they built temporary marching camps for protection. These camps were surrounded by earthen ramparts and ditches and were disassembled the following morning before the army resumed its march.

When preparing for battle, Roman commanders sought to gather information about the enemy and to position the army in a manner best suited to the terrain on which it would fight. In battle, the Roman army was normally deployed in three parts, including a center or main body with flanking forces to its right and left that could be used to encircle the enemy. The legions were the most important component of the army. By the second century C.E. their basic battle formation was a solid phalanx consisting of several ranks of legionaries; however, the legion's subdivisions of cohorts, maniples, and centuries gave it great flexibility in battle.

A Roman army normally began a battle with an artillery salvo designed to demoralize and disrupt the enemy. Next archers and slingers fired on the enemy, and the infantry hurled javelins. This was followed by a great shout from the Roman lines that was intended to frighten the enemy. If the enemy then fled, the Roman cavalry was sent in pursuit; the advance cavalry units moved rapidly to make sure that the enemy retreat was not a tactical deception, while the remaining cavalry advanced carefully in battle formation. If the enemy attacked, the front ranks of the legions held firm while other ranks hurled javelins, and archers fired arrows upon the attackers; the cavalry was sent to meet any enemy flank attacks. However, if the Roman army made the initial move, it directed its attack against the weakest point in the enemy position. *Auxilia* units carried out the initial assault. They were followed by the legions, who advanced in a "tortoise," or *testudo*, formation, with

their shields locked together in the front, sides, and overhead in order to protect the legionaries from enemy javelins or arrows. After the enemy position was broken, hand-to-hand combat followed until the enemy either surrendered or fled. If the enemy did flee, Roman troops first searched the immediate surroundings to avoid falling into an ambush, and then the cavalry was sent in pursuit of the enemy.

When conducting sieges of enemy fortresses or cities, Roman armies first set out to confine the enemy within their defenses by means of a series of fortified positions. The defenders were surrounded by a ditch and earthen rampart as well as a system of forts. Once this was constructed, the Romans set out to penetrate the enemy's defenses and force them to surrender. In some cases, as in the Siege of Masada (73 C.E.), the Romans built a high approach platform or ramp, which they would use to move a large siege tower close to the enemy wall. Archers positioned at the top of the tower could then fire on the defenders below; sometimes siege towers also were equipped with battering rams that were used to break through the enemy wall. Another method was to approach the enemy position under cover of a movable protective structure and then attempt to undermine the wall. If these methods did not work, the Romans would launch a frontal assault on the weakest point in the enemy defenses. This was preceded by a major artillery bombardment. The legionaries would then approach under cover of a *testudo* and scale the walls. After the top of the walls was secured, enemy cities were then sacked.

During the late imperial period, Roman warfare changed considerably. By the fourth century, most military action consisted of small-scale skirmishes involving small detachments of troops. However, in large-scale battles Roman commanders still sought to defeat barbarians such as the Goths by means of a decisive infantry clash in which the Roman infantry was deployed in a phalanx formation. When the enemy approached, they came under fire from archers deployed behind the phalanx; this might slow or even halt the enemy advance. If it did not, both sides would shout a battle cry, or *barritus*, and the enemy would resume their advance. The Roman archery fire continued, while Roman infantrymen in the rear ranks hurled their javelins and moved forward to support the troops in the front ranks. After the enemy made contact with the Roman phalanx, the two sides pressed upon each other until one side lost heart and gave way. The cavalry then pursued the soldiers of the defeated army; it was in this last stage of battle that the largest number of casualties were inflicted.

Roman infantry employed the same tactics against enemy cavalry attacks. However, such attacks were relatively rare since it was difficult for cavalrymen to make their horses charge up against tightly packed infantry positions. If the infantry held firm, they could easily repel such attacks.

During the fifth century C.E., cavalry replaced infantry as the most important element in Roman armies. They generally used one of two different attack formations: a wedge, or rhomboid, formation, which was effective when carrying out elaborate maneuvers or seeking to pierce enemy formations, and a square, or oblong, formation, which was used when carrying out a full-scale charge. During the late imperial period, Roman cavalry used both skirmishing and shock tactics. In the former, the cavalry rode up to an enemy formation and fired their arrows; if the enemy held firm, they would fall back and attack again. If the enemy broke ranks, they then charged and engaged in close combat. *Foederati* and other German cavalry in the late Roman army used shock tactics in which they simply charged, sometimes with the support of mounted archers, and attempted to defeat the enemy in close combat.

ANCIENT SOURCES

The noted Roman historian Cornelius Tacitus (c. 56-120 C.E.) wrote a number of works that offer valuable insights into early imperial warfare. These include a biography of his father-in-law, a governor of Britain, that describes Rome's military campaigns in that province. Tacitus also wrote *Ab Excessu Divi Augusti*, also known as *Annales* (c. 116 C.E.; *Annals*, 1598), an account of events in the Empire in the period from 14 to 68 C.E., and the *Historiae* (c. 109; *Histories*, 1731) on the period from 68 to 96 C.E., of which only the portions on the period from 69 to 70 C.E. have survived. The Jewish historian Flavius Josephus (c. 37-c. 100 C.E.) wrote a history of the Jewish revolt of 66-70, which includes descriptions of the Roman army in action.

Arrian (c. 86-160 C.E.), a governor of Cappadocia under the emperor Hadrian, wrote a first-hand account of a campaign that he conducted against the Alani in 134. He also wrote the *Ars Tactica*, a manual on the training of cavalry. Pseudo-Hyginus, an obscure figure who probably lived during the second century C.E., wrote *De Munitionibus Castrorum* (second century C.E.; *Fortifications of the Camp*, 1993), a discussion of the planning and construction of Roman military camps. The fifth century Roman military theorist Flavius Vegetius Renatus wrote *De Re Militari* (383-450 C.E.; *The Fovre Bookes of Flauius Vegetius Renatus: Briefelye Contayninge a Plaine Forme and Perfect Knowledge of Martiall Policye, Feates of Chiualrie, and Vvhatsoeuver Pertayneth to Warre*, 1572; also translated as *Military Institutions of Vegetius*, 1767), a treatise in which he called for a restoration of traditional military drill and training, and in doing so discussed various aspects of the Roman army in earlier periods.

Ammianus Marcellinus (c. 330-395 C.E.), an officer who served in the Roman army in the 350's and 360's, wrote a history of the Roman Empire that continued Tacitus's account from 96 to 378 C.E. However, only the books on the period from 353 to 378 C.E. have survived; these are a major source for political and military events of this period. The *Notitia Dignitatum* (c. 395 C.E.) is an illustrated manuscript that lists the officers of the late fourth century army, as well as their units and where each was stationed.

BOOKS AND ARTICLES

Dixon, Karen R., and Pat Southern. *The Late Roman Army*. New Haven, Conn.: Yale University Press, 1996.

Goldsworthy, Adrian. *Roman Warfare*. London: Cassell, 2000.

Le Bohec, Yann. *The Imperial Roman Army*. Translated by Raphael Bate. London: Routledge, 1994.

Mattern, Susan P. *Rome and the Enemy: Imperial Strategy in the Principate*. Berkeley: University of California Press, 1999.

Simkins, Michael. *The Roman Army from Caesar to Trajan*. London: Osprey, 1993.

_____. *The Roman Army from Hadrian to Constantine*. London: Osprey, 1991.

Thomas I. Crimando

"Barbarian" Enemies of Rome

Dates: Eighth Century B.C.E.-Fifth Century C.E.

Military Achievement

Etruscans

The most powerful early influence on developing Rome, Etruscan civilization arose in the early eighth century B.C.E. Because the Etruscans were not a unified state but a collection of individual chieftains fighting for their own glory and wealth, their conquests were limited. Nevertheless, they expanded their power west across the Etrurian Sea to Corsica, south to Latium and Campania, and north as far as the Po Valley. Because these conquests did not rest on a firm political infrastructure, they were short-lived. Etruscan power declined rapidly after the founding of the Roman Republic in 509 B.C.E. In about 400 B.C.E., Celts from Gaul entered the Po Valley and expelled the Etruscans. Etruscan culture survived only in its influence on Rome. Its language has thus far eluded decipherment.

Celts

The Celts, who originated in Germany, had overrun most of Western Europe by the fifth century B.C.E. In the fourth century B.C.E. they moved into Italy, where they established Milan as their principal town. The last of the Celtic tribes to come into Italy was the Senones, the tribe that sacked Rome (389 B.C.E.). Later during the fourth century they moved eastward into the Balkans, finally settling in Asia Minor, in Galatia. The Romans treated the Celts as their foulest enemies, massacring them in northern Italy, Spain, and Gaul. In the aftermath of the Second Punic War (219-202 B.C.E.), when the Romans reconquered the Po Valley that had been lost to Hannibal (247-182 B.C.E.), they so exterminated the remaining Italian Celts that few were left by the middle of the second century.

In the seven-year Gallic Wars (58-52 B.C.E.) with Julius Caesar (100-44 B.C.E.), the Celts of Gaul made the most of their local marshes and forests, which were very difficult to attack, and astonished the Romans under Caesar by forcing them to fight to their fullest strength. The tribal nature of the Gauls was probably their undoing in their war with the Roman general, for it enabled Caesar to exploit the jealousies

A Celt depicted in battle with a Roman on the column of Roman emperor Antoninus.

213

and intense hatreds that invariably exist among closely related peoples. As a result, Caesar was able to enlist contingents of Gauls to fight alongside his troops. Caesar's greatest foe was Vercingetorix (died c. 45 B.C.E.), who became leader of a confederation of Gauls in 52 B.C.E. Vercingetorix's strategic genius employed a policy first of systematic destruction of Caesar's supply lines and then of forcing Caesar to attack on highly unfavorable ground. When Vercin-

getorix, however, was himself led to attack in the field, he was defeated. He retreated to a fortress, where Caesar successfully besieged him and forced his surrender. Vercingetorix spent six years in prison before he was exhibited in Rome in a triumph and subsequently strangled. His defeat meant the submission of Gaul to Rome.

Britons also enjoyed partial success against Rome. Caesar, writing about his second campaign

FINAL ROMAN CAMPAIGN AGAINST GALLIC TRIBES, 52 B.C.E.

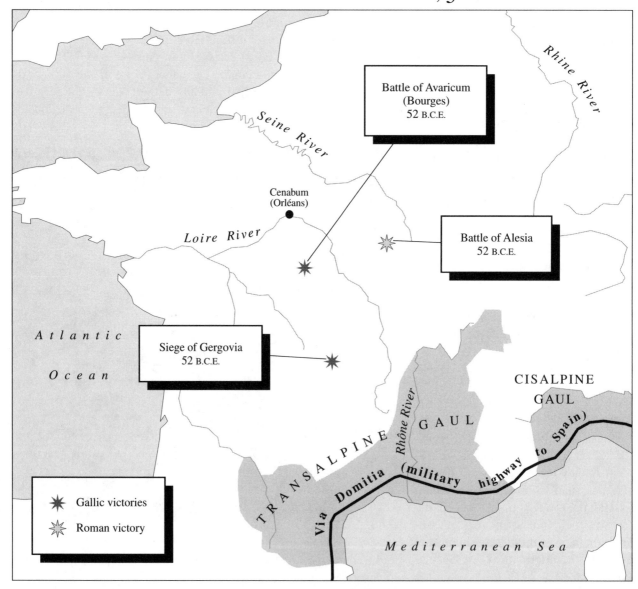

against Britain in 54 B.C.E., expressed some admiration for the British chariots, which were able to throw his army into confusion and, even when the chariots were repulsed, to withdraw safely into the woods. It was only when he had rethought his strategy and attacked immediately, before the Britons could draw up into a defensive file, that he was able to defeat them. The Roman historian Cornelius Tacitus (c. 56-120 C.E.) describes how, about a century after Caesar, during the reign of Nero (37-68 C.E.), Boudicca (died 62 C.E.), queen of the Iceni Celts, led an initially successful revolt from 60 to 61 C.E., in which she was able to destroy a Roman legion. Later, however, in a disastrous encounter with Gaius Suetonius Paulinus, she and her army were destroyed in a battle that cost the British 80,000 dead to 400 Roman dead.

NUMIDIANS

The Numidians of northern Africa had the best light cavalry in the ancient world. They served as mercenaries in Hannibal's (247-182 B.C.E.) war with Rome, where they participated in mopping up operations at the close of the Battle of Cannae (216 B.C.E.). Later, they fought in the Jugurthine War (112-106 B.C.E.) against Rome, successful until they were finally subdued by Gaius Marius (157-86 B.C.E.). Eventually, they served in the Roman military, earning a place on Trajan's Column, a monument to Roman military might. They developed a civilization under Roman rule as Numidia Constantina until they were destroyed by the Vandals in 428 C.E.

GERMANS

The German military leader Arminius (died 19 C.E.), also known as Hermann, changed the history of the world in ways still felt, when he defeated and thoroughly annihilated a Roman army of three legions in the Teutoburg Forest (9 C.E.). As a consequence, the Roman emperor Augustus (63 B.C.E.-14 C.E.), who had hoped to push into Central Europe to create a Roman Germany, abandoned this plan in favor of more conservatively defensible borders along the Rhine and Danube Rivers. If Arminius had not defeated Rome or had not defeated Rome so decisively, the Empire might have continued its expansion, and the linguistic borders of Europe would not

have been drawn where the Roman Princeps established the Roman boundary. It is at this boundary where the Romance languages yield to the Germanic. The Romans, deceived by Arminius into a long march during a wet season, were trapped and butchered in the forest's dark ravines.

VANDALS

A Teutonic nation, Vandals began to migrate from Pannonia and Dacia in the early fifth century C.E., invading Gaul and Spain and crossing into Africa where they continued to fight and began to develop into a maritime power. Under Gaiseric, who became king in 428 C.E., Vandals conquered the Roman province of Africa, and in 455 Gaiseric's army sacked Rome, taking the empress and her daughters as hostages. Gaiseric's death in 477 spelled the end of Vandal greatness, and when, in 533, the army of Justinian captured Carthage, the Vandals ceased to exist as a separate people.

GOTHS

Migrating from Sweden in the first century C.E., Goths were blond warriors whose contribution to warfare in the West consisted of increasing the functional importance of cavalry. Historians usually distinguish between the East Goths, or Ostrogoths, and the West Goths, or Visigoths, when writing about events after the end of the fourth century C.E. In 378 C.E., the East Goths, driven to desperation when Roman leaders offered the Gothic chiefs dogs in exchange for their men as slaves, rampaged through Thrace and instigated the Romans to fight at Adrianople. The Gothic leader Fritigern (died after 382 C.E.) employed the clever ruse of luring the Roman emperor Valens (c. 328-378) to battle by the offer of a humiliating peace and then caught the Romans with a mass of troops, destroying 40,000 of them, among whom was the emperor himself. The historical importance of this victory was immense: The Romans stopped taking the initiative against barbarian invaders. In a treaty after the war, the Romans allowed the Goths freedom from taxation and also granted them self-rule in Thrace in return for supplying troops to the imperial armies. This was the first time that imperial lands passed from Roman control.

Etruscan warriors in uniform, armed with short swords and carrying shields for protection.

HUNS

Excluded from China in the third century B.C.E. by the Great Wall, which had been built to keep them out, the Huns settled in North China until, in the third century C.E., they moved west, where they displaced the Goths, who moved further west in the great waves of migration that ultimately undermined the Roman Empire. In 432 C.E., the Huns themselves crossed the Danube into the Empire, where their leader Attila (c. 406-453 C.E.) forced the Roman emperor to pay tribute. When Rome refused to increase the tribute (450 C.E.), Attila invaded Italy, and though the Huns were defeated by Aetius (c. 390-454 C.E.) in 451 C.E., they ravaged Italy until, at Attila's death in 453 C.E., they departed for eastern Europe and obscurity.

WEAPONS, UNIFORMS, AND ARMOR

ETRUSCANS

The earliest historical enemy of Rome, the Etruscan military was much like that in Greece, where each city had its own force and where the continual warfare among the cities was more in the manner of cattle raids than of pitched battles. The Etruscan soldiers seem to have been organized into phalanxes, with units consisting of four officers and seventy-two hoplites ranked twelve wide and eight deep. Under Etruscan king Lucius Tarquinius Priscus (fl. fourth century B.C.E.), an Etrusco-Roman army probably engaged its enemies with a combination of Etruscans fighting in phalanxes in the center and Romans on each wing fighting in a freer style with spears, axes, and javelins. Soldiers in an Etruscan field army would have been armed like Greek hoplites, with several units of medium spearmen, equipped with spears, swords, helmets (usually with a crest, the meaning of which has not been determined), greaves, cuirasses, and Italic shields. Other units would have had lighter spears, and still others, slings.

CELTS

A typical Celt fought naked, armed with a long sword hung by a bronze or iron chain from his waist. Celtic swords were famous for their length, a length perhaps exaggerated in the historical accounts, though some swords have been uncovered as long as 80 centimeters. The Celts carried spears or javelins and long shields recorded as being as tall as a soldier. Archaeologists, however, have not uncovered any Celtic shields more than waist-high. Shields were often adorned with figures and embossed in bronze. Some shields were oak; some were covered with hides to protect the bare wood from splintering when struck. A few warriors wore mail shirts and bronze helmets. Archaeologists have uncovered elaborate helmets fitted with multiple crest-holders. These helmets, known as the Montefortino type, from the cemetery where they were first found, are supposed to have been worn only by the chiefs. This style of helmet, originating in Italy and spread throughout the Celtic world, has been found wherever the Celts migrated, even as far as Galatia.

British tribal warriors wore colored trousers made of wool and were crisscrossed with leather straps below the knee. Warriors' torsos were painted with blue stripes. Their wealthier compatriots, who manned the front line, wore multicolored cloaks, brightly colored shields, and pointed helmets. Because the Britons were, for the most part, taller and broader than the Romans, they must have presented a frightening spectacle.

Numidians

The Numidian cavalrymen portrayed on Trajan's Column are riding horses that have only a neck strap. Lacking bridles and bits, Numidians used only their legs to control their steeds. They wore no armor, only a short tunic, and carried a round shield and light javelins with iron heads. Excavations in Algeria have uncovered swords with blades 60 centimeters long.

Germans

Germans were, in general, armed with a short spear that was sometimes thrust like a lance and sometimes thrown, and a double-edged sword for slashing, like that used by the Celts. German cavalrymen carried long spears with a sharp but narrow iron point and a shield. They had little in the way of defensive armor, most wearing only animal skins and shields of osier, or willow rods. Their clothing consisted of a loose mantle. Very few Germans, even among chieftains, wore cuirasses or helmets.

Goths

Goths were skilled archers, but it was their expertise in the use of cavalry that changed the art of warfare. Cavalrymen, heavily armored, carried a heavy lance and rode a large horse. Gothic armor was made of heavy iron plates or of thick leather. Some infantrymen carried a long broadsword, called a *spatha*, and a lasso, in the use of which they also excelled.

Huns

Stocky ponies were part of the personal equipment of the Huns, who were said to eat, drink, sleep, and negotiate treaties while riding. Although they were particularly skilled archers, their equipment also included the lasso and the lance. They dressed in thickly padded quilted clothing and fur hats. They sported so many iron charms around their necks that from a distance they appeared to be wearing chain mail.

Military Organization

Etruscans

The Etrusco-Roman army in the sixth century B.C.E. was organized by wealth into six classes. The richest class was formed into eighty centuries heavily armed with ornate shields, cuirasses, greaves, javelins, and swords. The twenty centuries of the second class substituted an oblong shield made of boards covered with leather, known as a *scutum*, for the more expensive and ornate Argive shield of the wealthier class and omitted the cuirass. The twenty centuries of the third class omitted the greaves. It is uncertain whether the twenty centuries of the fourth class were armed only with the spear and javelin or also with the shield and sword. The fifth class was formed of thirty centuries of slingers. The rest of the citizens, the sixth class, were so poor that they were exempted from military service.

Celts

Like other primitive peoples, Celts had a warrior class drawn from the two wealthiest strata of their society. The army comprised heavy infantry, light infantry, cavalry, and charioteers. The wealthy class did the fighting, while the free poor seem to have served as chariot drivers.

NUMIDIANS

The Numidians, nomadic herdsmen in North Africa, in the area of present-day Algeria, virtually lived on horseback. Sometimes they practiced a simple agriculture. They lived in small clans with no political union, and their cavalry was leased to the various military powers.

GERMANS

The Germans were all soldiers and their villages were grouped together by clans to form units, traditionally referred to as Hundreds. The Hundreds were formed into battle groups of between 5,000 and 6,000 soldiers. The bravest warrior was called upon to lead the members of his tribe into a military engagement, but his leadership was by example rather than by command, and his authority ended with the battle.

North Wind Picture Archives

A German warrior shown with a Roman general.

GOTHS

A compilation of the laws of the West Goths gives a sense of the military hierarchy by which the leadership was organized. There were, in declining rank, leaders of Thousands, leaders of Hundreds, and leaders of Tens. Because Goths had virtually no nobility, except for the families of royalty, most officers, certainly at the level of leaders of Hundreds, were freemen. In the early period the leaders of Hundreds were probably elected; as time passed, leaders remained in the same families by the choice of the electorate. Eventually, after a few generations, a transition to hereditary command would have been barely noticed.

HUNS

Although the command hierarchy of the Huns is not known, the army was divided into long range archers, who would harass an enemy formation before the pitched battle, and light cavalrymen, who would dismount and fight with sword and lasso. Leaders were kept informed of the ongoing battle by messengers and would then direct the separate cavalry units by special whistling arrows shot into the air.

DOCTRINE, STRATEGY, AND TACTICS

ETRUSCANS

The Etrusco-Roman phalanx functioned like the Greek phalanx developed in the eighth century B.C.E. An orderly battle line several ranks deep was divided into files of men, one behind the other. Each file was a unit, and when a man fell, his place could be taken by a man in the rank behind. The phalanx fought with only a pace or two for each man. Thus the shield in close-order formation was wide enough to offer protection to the unguarded side of the man on the left.

CELTS

The Celts were accomplished fighters whose principal methods were ambush and surprise. According to ancient writers, Celts fought in confused and disorganized fashion, responding only to the urgency of immediate passions. Yet this criticism is undermined by the very accounts of Celtic battles and, indeed, by the terror exhibited by Romans at the marshaled ranks and noise of the Celts. Horns and trumpets and standards, regular items of Celtic spoils, suggest an organization and system to their warfare. Polybius (200-118 B.C.E.), the Greek historian who described Celtic battles, determined that it was not inferiority in organization that led to the Celts' defeat by the Romans, but rather inferiority in weapons. Caesar himself describes how Roman heavy javelins adhered to a formation of overlapping shields, a suggestion of a well-disciplined phalanx-like formation. Though the closely packed Celtic formation was apparently cohesive, it lacked mobility against Caesar's legions, and this immobility was its fatal disadvantage.

When fighting from a chariot, a warrior first threw his javelin, in the manner of a Homeric warrior, then dismounted to fight with his sword. The ancients report that a Celtic warrior whirled his sword over his head, shrieking terrible war cries, slashed the air from side to side, and then struck his enemy. Everything he did was aimed at inspiring fear in his enemy. If the warrior killed his enemy, he cut off the dead man's head and hung the skull around his victorious neck, a vision that must have inspired even more dread in subsequent enemies. He then stripped the body of its armor and sang a victory song over the spoils. Archaeological excavations have uncovered numerous heads, embalmed in cedar oil, and it is believed that these were used in religious rituals.

By the time of Caesar's campaign against the Celts of Gaul, the strongest part of the Celtic army was the cavalry, which charged in a mass attack. Caesar reports a few narrow escapes from defeat, suggesting that the Celts, despite their lack of formal military scientific doctrine, were formidable enemies in the field.

NUMIDIANS

The lightly armed Numidians were unable to break the Roman cavalry. At the Battle of Cannae, they were used to pursue the fleeing enemy, a maneuver in which they excelled. Their general tactic was to fly upon the enemy, throw their javelins, and ride off, never venturing too close.

GERMANS

Caesar considered the German cavalry better than the Gallic, so much so that he recruited horsemen from the German tribes to help him against Vercingetorix. The real German strength, however, lay in its infantry. Infantry soldiers would draw up in deep columns according to their tribes and then rush into battle with discordant war cries in no disciplined formation. Their aim was to overcome their Roman enemies in a single rush or die. In fact, death was the only result apart from victory, for this type of onrush did not allow for the orderly retreat that would favor survival.

GOTHS

Perhaps the Goths' strategic use of cavalry is best illustrated by their engagement in the Battle of Adrianople in 378 C.E. There the Romans attacked with cohorts of heavy infantry against a small number of Gothic infantry fighting behind a barricade of wagons. A large force of heavily armed cavalry charged the Roman army in the flank. The Roman cavalry was surprised and fled, allowing the Gothic cavalry to attack the legionary formation. The Romans were left in a confused mass as the Gothic infantry emerged from behind the wagons and commenced the butchery. Surrounded on all sides, the Romans lay helpless.

HUNS

Because their numbers were never great, Huns relied on guerrilla tactics and terror for their success. They fought under the stern discipline of their leaders and employed surprise, rapid mobility, and trickery to defeat their enemies. In order to diminish the effectiveness of a far larger opponent, they aimed at breaking up enemy formations. To do so they feigned retreat so that the enemy would break ranks and give chase; then, at a sudden command, they turned in order upon the enemy and killed the now-undisciplined soldiers. When forced to fight defensively, Huns retreated behind an encircling encampment of wagons.

ANCIENT SOURCES

The works of Livy (59 B.C.E.-17 C.E.) and Dionysius of Halicarnassus (fl. 20 B.C.E.), who both appear to have drawn on the account by Quintus Fabius Pictor (fl. c. 200 B.C.E.), are the main sources on the Etruscans.

The main sources for the Celts are Diodorus Siculus (fl. first century B.C.E.), who gives a full description of the Celtic warrior, and Polybius, who describes several battles with the Celts, including the Battle of Telamon (225 B.C.E.). Julius Caesar is the principal source for his wars with the Gauls and Britons. Tacitus supplies information about Claudius's annexation of Britain (43 C.E.) and of the subsequent rebellions.

The role of the Numidians in the Punic Wars is narrated by Livy; their role in the Jugurthine War, by Sallust (86-35 B.C.E.). Sources for the Germans include the Roman historians, who are not without bias. For the character of the Germans and a description of their weaponry there is Tacitus's *De origine et situ Germanorum* (c. 98 C.E.; also known as *Germania*; *The Description of Germanie*, 1598). For the Battle of Teutoburg Forest, there survive the contemporary account of Velleius Paterculus (c. 19 B.C.E.-30 C.E.) and the later accounts of Dio Cassius (c. 150-235 C.E.) and Publius Annius Florus (fl. second century C.E.).

The main sources on the Vandals are the *Historian naturalis* (77 C.E.; *The Historie of the World*, 1601; better known as *Natural History*) of Pliny (23-79 C.E.), and the *History of the Wars of Justinian* by Procopius (fl. 540).

Ammianus Marcellinus (c. 330-395 C.E.) left an exciting account of the Goths in his history of the Roman Empire, the extant part of which covers the years from 353 to 378. The main ancient sources for the Huns are the works of Ammianus Marcellinus, sixth century Gothic historian Jordanes, and the sixth century Byzantine historian Menander Protector.

BOOKS AND ARTICLES

Connolly, Peter. *Greece and Rome at War.* London: Greenhill Books, 1998.

Delbrück, Hans. *History of the Art of War Within the Framework of Political History.* Translated by Walter J. Renfroe, Jr. Westport, Conn.: Greenwood Press, 1975.

Featherstone, Donald. *Warriors and Weapons in Ancient and Medieval Times.* London: Constable, 1997.

Lloyd, Alan B., ed. *Battle in Antiquity.* London: Duckworth, 1996.

May, Elmer C., Gerald P. Stadler, and John F. Votaw. *Ancient and Medieval Warfare.* Wayne, N.J.: Avery, 1984.

FILMS AND OTHER MEDIA

Attila: The Scourge of God. Documentary. History Channel, 1994.

The Great Commanders: Julius Caesar. Documentary. History Channel, 1993.

Julius Caesar. Documentary. Kultur, 1996.

Julius Caesar and the Battle of Alesia. Documentary. Ambrose Video, 1993.

The Legions of Rome: The Gallic Wars. Documentary. Cromwell, 1992.

Roman War Machine. Documentary. History Channel, 1999.

James A. Arieti

THE ANCIENT WORLD

WORLD

EASTERN AND SOUTHERN ASIA

China

Dates: c. 1523 b.c.e.-588 c.e.

Military Achievement

Chinese tradition holds that throughout most of its history, China has relegated warfare and military matters to a secondary role within society. From the earliest dynastic records onward, the Chinese have deliberately differentiated *wen* (cultural or civil) and *wu* (martial) matters. The perfectly ordered society is one in which literate culture triumphs over mere force, and military matters are disdained. Civilized Chinese need not use brute force to maintain internal peace or repulse external aggression. Instead, cultural superiority and demonstrated moral virtue suffice in the pursuit of peace.

Despite these ideals, China's early history revolved around conquest and the centralization of the state. Every major dynasty was founded through warfare, and once unified, China guarded its frontiers with military force and sought to expand its territory at the expense of southern and western neighbors. Inevitably, each dynasty in turn fell as a result of warfare.

The Shang (Chang) are the first historically identifiable ancestors of the Chinese. Chengtang (Ch'eng T'ang) is credited with founding the dynasty, following his decisive victory over Emperor Jie (Chieh) of the Xia (Hsia) Dynasty in 1523 b.c.e. at the Battle of Ming Jiao (Ming Chiao). In a recurring pattern of Chinese historiography, the victorious commander's success is attributed to his moral superiority and his opponent's wretchedness.

Accordingly, the Shang fell as a result of Emperor Zhou Xin's (Chou Hsin) overall bad character and practice of mutilating pregnant women and murdering innocents with abandon. King Wu (the Martial King) led the Zhou into a decisive battle at Muye (Mu-yeh) in 1027 b.c.e. According to the *Shiji* (*Shih Chi*) annals, the Zhou were vastly outnumbered, confronting a Shang army of 700,000 with a lilliputian force of 300 chariots, 3,000 Tiger Guards, and 45,000 foot soldiers. Despite the Shang's overwhelming numbers, the Zhou routed them in a matter of hours. Following an initial charge of one hundred infantry, the chariots were deployed to the astonishment of the Shang troops, who reportedly had never encountered such a mass attack. After their king fled, the Shang forces "inverted their weapons" and gave up the fight. After the death of King Wu, his brother, the duke of Zhou, acted as regent for his young nephew. During his regency, the Zhou domain expanded eastward and purportedly brought fifty states under Zhou control.

The Zhou policy of decentralized rule in its peripheral territories eventually led to its decline in 722 b.c.e., when an alliance of disgruntled vassals and a nomadic tribe killed the Zhou king. Despite moving the capital farther east to avoid further incursions, the Zhou never fully recovered, inaugurating nearly five hundred years of unremitting violence and warfare.

The remaining half of the Zhou dynastic age is subdivided into two sections: the Chunqiu (Ch'un Ch'iu) or Spring and Autumn period (c. 770-476 b.c.e.) and the Warring States period (c. 475-221 b.c.e.). This was an age characterized by the growth of powerful independent states, shifting alliances, and open warfare. Beside a dozen major states, innumerable smaller states existed, some no more than a town surrounded by a thick earthen wall and a few square miles of marginal territory. As Zhou power declined, the major states asserted increasing independence, until, by the Warring States period, their rulers had assumed the title of king. New technologies, ranging from the long sword, crossbow, and iron implements, allowed the larger states to conquer and control surrounding territories.

Around 307 b.c.e. King Wu Ling of Zhao (Chao) took a cue from the nomadic tribes to the north and introduced the deployment of cavalry. Faster and far more mobile than the war chariot, cavalry revolution-

TURNING POINTS

1600-1066 B.C.E.	Shang Dynasty rules in China.
1200 B.C.E.	The chariot is introduced to China from the northwest and is later adapted for use in siege warfare.
1066-256 B.C.E.	Zhou (Chou) Dynasty rules in China.
5th cent. B.C.E.	The crossbow is developed in China, providing more power, speed, and accuracy than the composite bow.
307 B.C.E.	King Wu Ling of Zhao, inspired by steppe nomad tribes to the north, introduces the use of cavalry in China.
221-206 B.C.E.	Qin (Ch'in) Dynasty rules in China.
206 B.C.E.-220 C.E.	Han (Han) Dynasty rules in China.
220-280	Wei (Wei), Shu (Shu), and Wu (Wu) Dynasties rule in China during Three Kingdoms period.
265-316	Western Jin (Chin) Dynasty rules.
4th cent.	The use of stirrups is introduced in China, allowing cavalry armor to become heavier and more formidable.
317-420	Eastern Jin Dynasty rules.
386-588	Southern and Northern Dynasties rule concurrently in China.

ized Warring States conflicts and prompted a change in Chinese uniforms: In place of their traditional long robes, Chinese soldiers now adopted the short tunics and trousers of their northern neighbors. Infantry also took on greater importance, as wars spread into the mountainous terrain and marshy valleys of the Chang (Yangtze) region.

Final unification occurred in 221 B.C.E. when the Qin (Ch'in) systematically defeated its rivals and imposed centralized control over the region. The Qin victory has been traced to two important factors: the strict and ruthless policies of Legalism, which brought Qin subjects under the iron hand of the state, and a highly efficient military structure in which cavalry, iron weapons, and massed infantry overwhelmed their opponents. Following unification, the Qin ordered the confiscation of their opponents' weapons, which were subsequently melted down and molded into twelve statues at the new capital. Old states were abolished, the country was divided into

thirty-six commanderies headed by a civil governor and military commander, and prominent families moved to the capital. Once in power, the First Emperor Qin Shihuang-diiqin Shihuangdi (Ch'in Shih huang-ti; 259-210 B.C.E.) secured his northern borders and took control of the southern coast near Guangzhou (Canton).

Upon Shihuangdi's death in 210 B.C.E., the Qin Dynasty immediately fell into chaos, and by 206 B.C.E., the Han Dynasty had been established. Despite constant invasions from the north by the nomadic Xiongnu (Hsiung-nu), the Han managed to retain control of the country, and under the leadership of Wu Di (Wu Tii, 156-87 B.C.E.), the Martial Emperor, greatly expanded their territorial holdings. Between 136 and 56 B.C.E., twenty-five major expeditions were sent, fourteen to the northwest and west, three to the northeast, and eight to the south. In one case, a force of more than 300,000 launched an attack on the Xiongnu (133 B.C.E.). To safeguard his conquests, Wu Di established garrisons along the military routes and sent more than 2,000,000 Chinese to the northwest as colonists. One legendary encounter is reported to have occurred in 42 B.C.E. While on an expedition in the northern district of Sogdiana, a Chinese force purportedly engaged a group of Xiongnu accompanied by Roman legionaries. The Chinese victory is attributed to the use of the crossbow, the arrows of which apparently easily penetrated Roman armor and shields.

By 190 C.E., the Han had begun its decline, and in 194 General Cao Cao (Ts'ao Ts'ao; 155-220 C.E.) had emerged victorious in the ensuing civil war. Upon his death however, the southern states refused to recognize the central authority of the upstart Cao Cao family, and the Han Empire was quickly divided into three major regions, inaugurating yet another 400-year period of almost-constant warfare.

Following the breakup of the Han, three kingdoms emerged. The Wei (220-265) dominated the north and moved into Korea; Shu-Han (221-263) in the southwest subdued several indigenous tribes; and the southern Wu (222-280) expanded as far as Vietnam. In 265, following the conquest of the Shu-Han and the Wu, a Wei general announced the creation of a new dynasty, the Jin (Chin), which would survive until 420. Southern China would then experience a succession of four southern dynasties, lasting into the sixth century. Meanwhile, a series of northern tribes ruled Northern China until 386, when the northern Wei successfully defeated the last kingdom and secured rule until 533.

WEAPONS, UNIFORMS, AND ARMOR

Weaponry evolved considerably over the period from 1500 B.C.E. to 500 C.E. During the Shang Dynasty, metallurgy had advanced to the point that nobility was primarily armed with bronze weapons, whereas commoners fought with arms made of wood, stone, or animal bones. Among the common weapons found in grave sites are bronze-tipped spears, probably the earliest known weapons in Chinese history; daggers; the composite reflexive bow and arrow, with the bow both longer and more powerful than its Western counterpart; and the *ge-* (*ko-*) halberd, a battle-ax with a curved bronze blade horizontally mounted atop a long wooden shaft approximately 43 inches long. Used primarily to hook and then slash one's opponent, late variations added a spear to the tip, a hooked blade behind the first, and another to the butt.

The war chariot also played a central role in early Chinese warfare. First introduced to China from the northwest in 1200 B.C.E., the chariot evolved from a symbol of royal power and prestige to a vehicle adapted to the exigencies of siege warfare during the Warring States period. Typically, a chariot team consisted of three men: the driver in the center, a warrior armed with a *ge*-halberd on the right, and an archer to the left. Each would be accompanied by a platoon of foot soldiers armed with spears. Whereas Shang chariots were used primarily as elevated, mobile command posts for royalty, their Zhou counterparts

were employed extensively in battle. States were judged by the number of chariots they could field, and battle records routinely reported the numbers captured. The *Zuo Zhuan* (*Tso chuan*, c. 475-221 B.C.E.; *Tso chuan*, 1872) attributes 4,900 chariots to the large Jin state, whereas the much smaller Zhu (Chu) boasted 600 chariots.

As the Warring States period progressed, the chariot was adapted to the emergence of armored infantry and new siege warfare tactics. To ward off infantry, knife blades were added to wheel hubs. Furthermore, whereas previous armies had routinely avoided fortified cities rather than expending manpower on their capture, the newly significant role of cities as economic and political centers now warranted aggressive assaults. Accordingly, chariots were outfitted with large shields, towers, battering rams, movable ladders, and multiarrow crossbows. In defense, towns employed a bewildering array of iron and wooden caltrops, collapsible fences, and sharp iron stakes, "mined" moats, and a variety of long axes, halberds, fire-lances, and hammers. Vessels containing water, iron, sand, and human excrement were also available to hurl upon the heads of besiegers.

Swords do not appear until the middle of the Chunqiu, or Spring and Autumn, period, when they were probably adopted from steppe nomads. The earliest were fashioned from bronze, with iron swords becoming widespread during the Qin Dynasty. Although long, double-edged swords are mentioned as early as the seventh century B.C.E., most would appear to have been relatively short and used principally for thrusting rather than slashing. By the Warring States period, they had become standardized as the *jien* (*chien*), a double-edged sword with a blade measuring approximately 2 feet, eventually reaching a length of 3 feet during the Han Dynasty.

Clearly the most important innovation in early Chinese warfare was the crossbow. Developed in China some time in the fifth century B.C.E., the new weapon was more powerful and far more accurate than the composite bow. The standard crossbow consisted of a wooden stock, a bow of laminated bamboo, and an intricately designed bronze trigger mechanism. The mortised stock supported the bow and included both a channel for the arrow and a pistol grip. Trigger mechanisms were complicated devices containing three moving pieces on two shafts that could hold a very heavy-tension load while firing easily and delivering a bolt with greater impact than that of a high-velocity rifle. By removing two pins, the mechanism could be dismantled in case of capture, and the Chinese would guard the secret of its construction well into the Han Dynasty. The earliest bows could be hand-cocked, whereas the later, more powerful versions required either leg strength or a rope tied to the waist. By the time of the Qin Dynasty, crossbows had evolved into repeating models, those which could fire two bolts simultaneously, and larger, winch-powered versions mounted on carts and chariots.

The first Chinese armor appeared during the Shang Dynasty as simple, lacquered leather breastplates secured with leather thongs. Leather continued to be used as late as the sixth century C.E. By contrast, the first helmets were bronze and highly decorated. The construction of Zhou armor became more detailed, with body armor composed of small rectangular pieces strung into rows and fastened with leather thongs, a process known as lamellar construction. Individual pieces and the rows themselves were then lacquered and colored.

A great deal about Qin armor is known from the life-size terra-cotta figures unearthed near the first emperor's tomb. Several styles of armor are noted, including short mail jackets of lamellar construction designed to cover the entire upper body; lamellar chest protectors; lamellar armor for charioteers, which includes both neck guards and armor extending to the wrists with plates to protect the hands; and that of the cavalry, shorter than the others and missing shoulder guards. Under the armor, each warrior wears a long-sleeved robe reaching to the knees, along with a heavy cloth bundle at the neck. Short trousers are also discernible.

Not until the time of the Han Dynasty was iron used for certain types of armor. Most armor consisted of plates arranged in the lamellar construction, designed to protect the neck, front, back, and thighs. One such suit contained 500 plates and weighed nearly 22 pounds. By the late Han Dynasty, authors begin referring to brilliant dark armor, which may suggest a suit made of decarburized steel, although none have been recovered as yet.

Infantry typically appeared without armor and were generally equipped with little more than a shield and helmet. Most infantrymen wore a simple tunic, trousers, and leather shin guards. Helmets varied from the simple head-covering tied under the chin to heavier versions with straight earflaps. Iron helmets began to appear during the Warring States period but did not become prevalent until the Han Dynasty. Cavalry were furnished with a helmet, a mail jacket with a high collar and flared bottom, and a chaplike protector for the front of the leg.

Horse armor, or barding, appears in some of the earliest histories, but no evidence exists for its use until the end of the Han Dynasty. By that time, the cavalry had become an integral part of warfare, and as the cavalryman's armor improved, measures were also taken to insure the safety of the horse. Early barding was of a single piece, protecting the top and underside of the horse's neck down to the chest, with some also covering the underside of the belly. As it evolved, barding became five separate pieces: head mask, neck guard, chest and shoulder guards, side armor, and rump armor. Lamellar construction was again used, with materials varying based on period and geographic region. After stirrups were introduced in the fourth century, the armor for cavalrymen and horses became heavier and more formidable.

Shields varied according to usage, with those carried by charioteers slightly longer than the ge-halberd, and those for the infantrymen somewhat shorter. Built on wooden frames, shields were made of either leather or lacquered cloth stretched across the front. Occasionally the leather was fortified by bronze and in some cases painted with patterns and designs. Iron shields appeared alongside iron weapons and the crossbow, although in relatively small quantities until the Qin and Han Dynasties.

MILITARY ORGANIZATION

Shang Dynasty military organization is open to a great deal of speculation. Given the paucity of reliable literary sources, scholars are dependent on archaeological evidence and speculation concerning the actual role of chariots in early warfare. It is clear that Shang social structure centered on clan units designated as *zu* (*tsu*). Most scholars believe that the *zu* represent military units assigned to protect the walled towns in which they resided. The *zu* chief functioned as the local military leader; the same arrangement applied to the royal capital, with the king acting as military leader for the kingdom. Each *zu* may have numbered one hundred members of the nobility, all under the command of the chief or king. A standing army consisting of selected *zu* members maintained order during peacetime, and all members were subject to mobilization when necessary. In such cases, ten *zu* were combined to form an army of 10,000. Oracle records suggest that infantry and archers alike were organized into companies of one hundred warriors. Three such companies comprised a regiment, deployed as left, middle, and right companies.

Under the Zhou Dynasty, the chariot emerged as the most important factor in organizing the military. Later tradition holds that each three-man chariot team was accompanied by a platoon of twenty-five infantry, arranged into five squads. Five companies of four chariots were further organized into brigades, then into platoons of 25, divisions of 2,500, and armies of 12,500. Command originated with the emperor, who often led many campaigns himself. A variety of commanders served under him; unfortunately, little is known concerning their functions. Included are such ministers as the Director of Horses, the Runner of Horses, the Commandant, and the Commander. None, however, appear to have been entrusted with full command over imperial forces.

Apart from local variations, this organizational structure held throughout the Spring and Autumn and Warring States periods. However, whereas warfare in the former was conducted by the nobility following strict codes of honor and chivalrous behavior, the latter was marked by increasing violence and retributive combat. As war intensified, the need for manpower increased dramatically, with forced conscription becoming the norm. Although only a single male from each family was required to serve during the Spring and Autumn period, every male became subject to military levy during the Warring States period.

Qin armies were filled through the conscription of peasants into local militia units available for immediate call-ups. Every male between the ages of seventeen and sixty served as either a warrior or a laborer. The Han modified this policy, filling its ranks with conscripts, volunteers, and convicts. Every male between the ages of twenty-three and fifty-six was required to serve two years, one in training, the other in active service at a garrison. Following their stint, soldiers joined the local militia until age fifty-six.

Both the Qin and Han used increasingly sophisticated armies combining infantry, chariots, crossbowmen, and cavalry. The first Qin emperor implemented the use of mounted crossbowmen and their coordination with the composite bow. These combined armies allowed the Chinese to deploy small independent units, as well as traditionally organized larger armies, in the field.

Although the nobility continued to fill the highest command positions, junior officers began to emerge from the general rank and file, being chosen on the basis of ability. Advancement was based on merit, with an elaborate system of differentiated pay relative to one's seniority and rank. Officers were assigned as a particular need arose. Titles and roles related specifically to the campaign, with several generals assigned to each to avoid possible coups.

The Han military was organized into three principal units: a standing garrison at the capital, a task force on the march, and a permanent frontier defense. Once mobilized in an emergency, the military was organized into divisions led by the generals, regiments led by colonels, companies led by captains, and platoons led by commanders. Although local variations would appear in the chaos that followed upon the collapse of the Han, this basic organizational structure as established by the Qin and Han continued to prevail.

The size of Chinese armies has been notoriously difficult to calculate, particularly for the earliest Shang and Western Zhou periods. As noted above, the war between the Zhou and Shang was said to have been fought by a Shang army of 700,000 and a Zhou force of 300 chariots, 3,000 Tiger Guards and 45,000 foot soldiers. By the Spring and Autumn period, when warfare had become highly ritualized and was dominated by aristocratic charioteers, field armies typically numbered in the thousands but would appear to have rarely exceeded 10,000. As the scale of war increased in the Warring States period, the size of armies grew dramatically. In order to lay siege to fortified cities and to conduct wars that often took years to complete, hundreds of thousands of men were required. According to one contemporary account, the typical army consisted of "one thousand chariots, ten thousands of cavalry, and several hundred thousand armored warriors." The smallest of the warring states fielded armies of more than 300,000; the largest, such as Qin, commanded more than 1,000,000. Likewise, Han expeditions numbering from 50,000 to 300,000 were routinely sent out to quell rebellions and punish nomadic invaders.

A member of the Tiger Guard, with his sword and shield and distinctive uniform.

DOCTRINE, STRATEGY, AND TACTICS

Throughout the Shang and early Zhou periods, warfare was violent and fought in the Homeric style. Chariots served as transport or observational platforms, and warriors fought with spears, axes, and composite bows. If the military classic the *Taigong* (*T'ai Kung*, c. third century B.C.E.; *Tai Kung's Six Secret Teachings*, 1993) is to be trusted in its account of the Zhou triumph over the Shang, total warfare was to be fought by utilizing every conceivable method and resource necessary to achieve victory. The state's resources and all customary means of production were to be employed in the campaign's execution. Strategically, the capable general would analyze the entire situation before engaging the enemy, gauging such factors as terrain, methods of attack and counterattack, escape routes, and techniques for psychological warfare. The *Taigong* advocates employing subterfuge and deception as the most effective means of securing victory. Among other tactics, the successful campaign would utilize feints, false attacks, and limited encounters to confuse and disorient the enemy before the main attack. In prosecuting the war, the best strategies would promote confusion within the enemy's ranks through aggression, misinformation, and speed. The humane treatment of prisoners would encourage others to surrender.

A new era of warfare began in the Spring and Autumn period. This was the great age of chivalry, in which honor and virtue dictated both strategy and the conduct of warfare. Fighting was ideally a game played between members of the nobility, mounted in chariots and accompanied by platoons of foot soldiers. During the heyday of chariot warfare, gentlemen studied the arts of charioteering, archery, and virtuous conduct. Actual combat followed an excessively strict code of conduct calling for bravery, valor, and honor. War was to be pursued with moderation and respect for the opponent. For instance, the duke of Song (Sung) waited for his enemy to cross a river and arrange his battle forces before launching his attack. Following his humiliating defeat, the duke justified his action by referring to the sage, who "does not crush the feeble nor order the attack until his enemy has formed his ranks." In another instance, "Yen Hsi shot a man in the eyebrow and retired, saying 'I have no valor. I was aiming at his eye.'"

Such sentiments were forgotten during the Warring States period. However, even as the violence escalated, strategists continued to advocate deception and speed as the primary means of securing victory. Siege warfare introduced new strategies and tactics, as massive armies sought to wrest control of fortified cities from their occupants, who in turn deployed new technologies designed to repulse the aggressors. In this regard, the Mohists became the undisputed masters of defensive warfare in ancient China.

Sunzi's (Sun Tzu; fl. c. 500 B.C.E.) *Bingfa* (c. 510 B.C.E.; *The Art of War*, 1910) is certainly the most famous text from this period. A general in the service of Wu, Sunzi had the primary objective of obtaining victory without combat. He argued that a more comprehensive victory could be forged by using diplomatic means, breaking up alliances, and thwarting the enemy's own strategy. In general, one should gain victory at the least cost possible, for both oneself and the enemy. "Thus attaining one hundred victories in one hundred battles is not the height of excellence. Subjugating the enemy's army without fighting is the true height of excellence." Failing that, he emphasized the manipulation of the enemy through the use of terrain, psychology, and the employment of both unorthodox and orthodox methods. Sunzi believed that "warfare is the way [*dao/tao*] of deception," advancing where least expected and attacking where the enemy is least prepared. Although he advocated unorthodox methods such as flanking movements and circular thrusts, Sunzi also insisted that orthodox measures could be effective, if they were employed in an unorthodox manner.

While specific tactics and strategies evolved and adapted to new technologies and the changing face of war, the fundamental principles espoused by Sunzi and other classical theoreticians continued to hold sway. From the Warring States period to the chaos following the fall of the Han, Chinese warfare emphasized the doctrine of maneuverability. Beginning with the fundamental organization of armies into flexible, self-reliant units of five, military maneuvers sought to exploit enemy weaknesses through speed, deception, and misdirection. Every strategist sought to manipulate the enemy into disadvantageous positions by using surprise, by exploiting climatic and topographical factors, and by psychologically and physically destabilizing the enemy to gain temporary, context-specific advantages.

Thus, even as the Han adapted the cavalry, they devised new strategies to defeat it. In 99 B.C.E., Li Ling defeated a cavalry of 30,000 using only 5,000 infantrymen. Behind a line of infantry armed with shields and pikes, Li Ling positioned archers with powerful multiple-firing crossbows. The nomadic horsemen continually charged unsuccessfully. Zhuge Liang (Chu-ko Liang, 181-234), who served as adviser to the founder of the Shu-Han Dynasty (221-263), was a brilliant mathematician, mechanical engineer, and military strategist who both used and wrote a commentary on Sunzi's *The Art of War*. Said to have never fallen in battle, Zhuge became one of China's most celebrated heroes, was named a Confucian saint in 1724, and was immortalized in Luo Guanzhong's (Lo Kuan-chung; c. 1320-c. 1380) fourteenth century historical novel, *San kuo chi yen-i* (*Romance of the Three Kingdoms*, 1925). Subsequent generations of tacticians continued to revere and employ the stratagems formulated by Sunzi and his contemporaries.

ANCIENT SOURCES

The most important primary sources fall into two basic categories. The first are the numerous histories compiled throughout this period. These include the *Shujing* (*Shu ching*), or *Book of History* (1918), which purports to cover the years 2357-627 B.C.E.; the *Chunqiu* (*Ch'un ch'iu*), translated as *Ch'un ts'ew* in 1872 and also known as the *Spring and Autumn Annals*, chronicling the period from 722-481 B.C.E.; the *Zuo Zhuan* (*Tso chuan*), or *Tradition of Zuo*, a commentary that carries Zhou history down to 468 B.C.E.; and the first official Chinese history, the *Shiji* (*Shih-chi*, 104 B.C.E.; *Records of the Grand Historian of China*, 1961), compiled by Sima Qian (Ssu-ma Ch'ien, c. 145-90 B.C.E.).

The second principal resource consists of several military texts brought together during the Song (Sung) Dynasty (960-1126 C.E.) and placed in a collection known as the Seven Military Classics. Each provides varying degrees of detail concerning the art of warfare, military strategy and organization, along with references to the types of weapons used. As traditionally arranged, the Seven Military Classics consist of Sunzi's *Bingfa*; the *Wuzi* (*Wu-tzu*, c. 400 B.C.E.; *Wu-tzu*, 1993); *Sima Fa* (*Ssu-ma Fa*, c. fourth century B.C.E.; *The Methods of the Ssu-ma*, 1993); *Lei Weigong Wen Dui* (*Lei Wei-kung Wen Tui*, c. 600 C.E.; *Questions and Replies Between T'ang T'ai-tsung and Li Wei-kung*, 1993); the *Wei Liaozi* (*Wei Liao Tzu*, c. fourth century B.C.E.; *Wei Liao-tzu*, 1993); the *Huang Shigong San Lüe* (*Huang Shi-kung San Lüeh*, c. first century C.E.; *Three Strategies of Huang Shih-kung*, 1993); and the *Taigong*.

BOOKS AND ARTICLES

Kierman, Frank A., Jr., and John K. Fairbank, eds. *Chinese Ways in Warfare*. Cambridge, Mass.: Harvard University Press, 1974.

Needham, Joseph. *Military Technology: Missiles and Sieges*. Vol. 5 in *Science and Civilisation in China*. Cambridge, England: Cambridge University Press, 1994.

Sawyer, Ralph D., trans. and comm. *The Seven Military Classics of Ancient China*. Boulder, Colo.: Westview Press, 1993.

Twitchett, Denis, and John K. Fairbank, eds. *The Ch'in and Han Empires, 221 B.C.-A.D. 220*. Vol. 1 in *The Cambridge History of China*. Cambridge, England: Cambridge University Press, 1986.

Jeffrey Dippmann

Nomadic Warriors of the Steppe

Dates: To c. 500 c.e.

Military Achievement

The most significant of the steppe warrior societies included the Scythian, Xiongnu (Hsiung-nu), Yuezhi (Yüeh-chih), Saka, Sarmatian, Avar, Hun, and White Hun. Some, such as the Yuezhi, were Indo-European peoples, and others, such as the Huns, were Turko-Mongolian peoples. Population growth was marked by competition for pasture lands in the north and by irrigation networks to the south. Nomadic societies looked to towns for trade but at other times were tempted to raid their accumulated produce and crafts. Until the emergence of cannons and muskets, the settled communities were easy prey for the mounted nomad warriors.

Scyths spread their nomadic influences across the Eurasian continent from Mongolia in the east to the Russian grasslands in the west. Believed to be Iranians from Turkestan who had refused to succumb to the settled existence of the Persian state to the south, some of the Scyths moved into the plains north of the Black Sea, displacing the Cimmerians in the Russian steppes after 750 B.C.E. From that base they attacked the fleeing Cimmerians, who penetrated the Assyrian lands to the south. Under a leader named Madyas, the Scyths subjugated the Medes about 628 B.C.E. Although the Medes rebelled and turned the Scyths northward, the Scyths were the first of the mounted nomad warriors to threaten the classical cultures south of the Black Sea. With iron implements forged by craftsmen from the Urals, the Scyths created the first recognized northern Eurasian empire, with territory extending from the Danube to Mongolia. Although divisions within their ranks were common, their federations remained threats to all the nearby communities for centuries. Although the Scyths who remained in Turkestan when the others moved across the Volga were called Sakas by the Persians, they were of the same Iranian nomad stock.

Steppe nomads were not always on the offensive. In the sixth century B.C.E. Cyrus the Great (c. 601 to 590-c. 530 B.C.E.) of Persia invaded Scythian Parthia, in the area of present southern Turkmenistan, before leading an army through the deserts of Gedrosia, in present Baluchistan, to defeat the Amyrgian Sakas of the mountains. Later his armies overran the Uzbek steppes between the Amu Dar'ya and the Syr Dar'ya Rivers. Along the latter Cyrus constructed a town named Cyropolis, later known as Khudzhand and Leninabad. To protect his territories he constructed seven forts to guard against the aggressive Sakas. In September, 529 B.C.E., the Massagetae Scyths defeated Cyrus even though other Scythian mercenaries had been recruited against these Saka tribes east of Khiva. In 512 B.C.E. Darius the Great (550-486 B.C.E.) attacked and defeated the Tigrakhanda Sakas, also called the "Pointed Hat Sakas," of the Aral Sea region, capturing their chieftain. Other Sakas to the north and east were out of the range of Darius's conquests. Hence, Darius established twenty satrapys, or provinces, in his lands, including Bactria, Saka, and Khorezm-Sogdia.

Farther west, Scythian ruler Ateas (d. 339 B.C.E.) led his forces to challenge the Macedonian forces of Philip II (382-336 B.C.E.) in 340 B.C.E. but was killed the following year in battle against the Macedonians, after which the Scythians were absorbed by the Sarmatians, another Iranian nomad people of the Russian steppes. By 350 B.C.E. the Sarmatians were already governing the Pontic steppes, where they founded Kamenskoye, present Dniprodzerzhyns'k. Like the Scyths, these mounted nomads wore coats of mail and depended more on the lance than on the bow. By the late third century the Sarmatians had forced the Scyths south toward the Crimea and occupied the Russian steppes west of the Volga.

The Scyths of Central Asia, however, continued to menace the wealthy oases and towns to the south.

Macedonian leader Alexander the Great (356-323 B.C.E.), after conquering Persia, had failed to extend his rule over the nomads of that region. On the south bank of the Jaxartes River he founded a frontier outpost, Alexandria Eschate, but in 329 B.C.E. rebellious Sakas in Sogdiana threatened his new frontier town. Alexander then launched a campaign of terror enabling him to regain command of most of Sogdiana, including Maracanda, present Samarqand. The Scyths in Parthia seceded from Alexander's successors in the third century B.C.E., and during the Seleucid civil wars nomad strength was revived. More Scythian nomads from the northern steppes invaded Parthia to aid the local nomads led by Arsaces (fl. third century B.C.E.), who established an independent state with Nisa as its capital.

Farther east, a Turko-Mongolian people had begun attacking the Chinese empire as early as the ninth century B.C.E. Like the Scyths, these were nomadic, mounted warriors whose aggressiveness later caused the Chinese to construct the Great Wall. They were probably the ancestors of the Xiongnu, the earliest of the famous Huns. At any rate the Chinese were to adopt a more mobile style of warfare better suited to defense against these mounted neighbors. Only by the second half of the third century did these Xiongnu unite under a leader called the Shanyu (Shan-yü). Under Shanyu Duman (Shan-yü Tuman, died c. 210 B.C.E.), they moved into western Gansu (Kansu). Duman's son and successor, Mao Dun (Mao-tun), fought several wars with the Chinese and then turned

westward in 177 B.C.E. to complete the conquest of western Gansu from the Yuezhi, driving the remnants into the Gobi Desert. However, the Xiongnu had been compelled to sign a treaty with China's Han rulers in 198 B.C.E., the beginning of Chinese ascendancy over the nomads. Han emperor Wu Di (Wu Ti, 156-87 B.C.E.) attacked the Xiongnu of the Ordos west of China and ended the payment of tribute to the horde in 133 B.C.E. Within twelve years China overcame the Xiongnu in Gansu and initiated Chinese settlements there. Han troops then attacked the Xiongnu in Mongolia. By 48 B.C.E. the Xiongnu presence had disintegrated in Mongolia, and the southern branch recognized Chinese hegemony to inhabit the Ordos region as subjects.

Meanwhile, after 140 B.C.E. Saka nomads had overwhelmed the Bactrian kingdom of Heliocles I (r. 150-140), bringing an end to the Greco-Bactrian state. They themselves were being pushed south by the Yuezhi. Chinese sources place them in Xingjiang province, present eastern Turkestan, as early as the fifth century. The Yuezhih, also called Tochari, were an Indo-European people dwelling in Gansu (part of Xinjiang), just south of the Gobi Desert, by the early second century B.C.E. In approximately 177 B.C.E. they were driven from that region to the Ili Valley by chief Mao Dun of the Xiongnu and twelve years later were forced south by the Wu Sun (Wu-sun), ancestors of the Sarmatian Alans and vassals of the Xiongnu. Part of the Yuezhi formed a confederacy and moved south to the Tibetan mountains. Most, however, occupied territories between the Amu Dar'ya and Syr Dar'ya Rivers in Sogdia, driving Saka tribes south into Khorāsān and Bactria. The Yuezhi established their capital at Kienshih, previously known as Maracanda and Samarqand. In 138 B.C.E. the Chinese Han emperor Wu Di dispatched an ambassador to the Fergana Valley to secure the Yuezhi's assistance against the Xiongnu. However, the embassy came to nothing, because the Yuezhi were more interested in the southern lands. Hence the Yuezhi invaded Bactria between 141 and 128 B.C.E., after which

TURNING POINTS

1000 B.C.E.	Cimmerians first produce bronze battle-axes.
900 B.C.E.	Scyths and succeeding steppe warriors master the use of bows while on horseback.
6th cent. B.C.E.	The lance is first used by the Alans and Sarmatians, and the chariot is first used by various tribes in battle.
4th-3d cent. B.C.E.	The use of protective bone breastplates is regularly adopted.
2d cent. C.E.	The use of armor spreads from the Ukraine to Manchuria.
451	Attila the Hun invades Roman Gaul.

the region was renamed Tocharistan. One branch of the Yuezhi, the Kushans, moved into the Sistan and Kabul river valleys and crossed the Indus River in 50 C.E. to establish the Kushan Dynasty in northwestern India. Nevertheless, a Yuezhi state continued to exist into the next century in Bactria.

In 380 C.E. a chieftain named Toulun led his Mongolian people, called the Juan-juan, westward from China. These warriors defeated the Xiongnu to establish a large steppe empire. About a generation later Toulun adopted the title of "khan" or "khagan." The Juan-juan were eventually overwhelmed, however, by the Toga Turks, who controlled northern China in the fifth century. The remaining Juan-juans migrated to the Yenisei region in Siberia to launch the Avar Empire that spread westward through the steppes. That empire lasted until it was overthrown by the Altai Turks under a leader named Tuman or Duman, who took the title Khan of the Blue (or Celestial) Turks. Meanwhile, the western tribes of the Avars migrated to the Russian-Ukrainian steppes, eventually invading Eastern Europe to threaten the Byzantines for two hundred years.

The Huns emerged in fourth century B.C.E. Mongolia. Although little is known about them for several centuries, they most probably descended from the Turkic Xiongnu. After they had established control of Inner and Outer Mongolia, a rift occurred in their ranks by the year 44 C.E. Some of the Huns formed a new confederation and moved the nation into what is now Kazakhstan. By 48 C.E. the eastern branch further split into northern and southern factions, and the former were conquered by Mongol tribes called the Xianbi (Hsien-pi). Those in the south became confederates of the Chinese emperor and resided south of the Great Wall in Shansi. These southerners, under Liu Cong (Liu Ts'ung, died c. 334), eventually overthrew the Chinese emperors and became rulers of North China by 318. However, by 348 this Hun or Xiongnu Empire in China had collapsed.

The western Huns took their federation farther west, across the Volga, in 374, defeating first the Sarmatian Alans and then the Ostrogoths. All of the Goths were pressured to leave the steppes for Roman East Europe, and the Huns then followed them, terrifying the inhabitants with their mounted archers. The

Roman historian Ammianus Marcellinus (c. 330-395 C.E.) described them as "skilled in unimaginable ferocity." In 432 the Romans were compelled to pay tribute to the Huns. When the Romans later balked at further exactions, Attila (c. 406-453), the Hun chieftain, led the Huns farther into the Roman world, as the emperor ceded vast lands to them south of the Danube River. Early in 451 Attila moved his nation into Roman Gaul. After crossing the Rhine, he set Metz ablaze but failed to take the fortified town of Orléans. He was stopped to the west of Troyes by a Frankish-Roman confederacy under Aëtius (d. 454) in 451. A year later the Huns ravaged Milan and Pavia in Italy before retiring northward, following the promise of tribute by the bishop of Rome. After the death of Attila in Pannonia in 453, no new leader could manage to hold the nation together. The forced allies revolted and killed Attila's eldest son. Another son, Dengizich (died 469), at first directed the Huns back toward the steppes but then altered course to attack the Eastern Roman Empire. The Huns were defeated, Dengizich was killed, and his head was placed on exhibit in the circus of Constantinople in 468.

In Central Asia another horde, called the Ephthalite or White Huns, moved south from the Altai Mountains to the Aral Sea region of Turkestan in the mid-fifth century. This horde occupied Sogdiana, Transoxiana, and south to Bactria. Later in the fifth century they attacked Khorāsān, killing the Sassanian king Peroz. Subsequently the White Huns took Merv and Herat, eventually replacing the Yuezhi and Kushans in Bactria, Kandahar, and Kabul. They were stopped, however, when they attempted to conquer the Punjab. Sources describe these White Huns as barbarians eschewing all the elements of settled civilization. Like their counterparts in the West, they seem to have passed out of history in the same era.

WEAPONS, UNIFORMS, AND ARMOR

Paleolithic grave sites reveal the use of knives and spear points. Those of the Andronovo population of 1750 to 800 B.C.E. show flint arrowheads and bronze weapons. However, such evidence may indicate more of a hunting than a military culture. The Okunev peoples, who engaged in metalworking in the Altai Mountain region in the era from 1800 to 1500 B.C.E., may have been the first Siberians to develop metallurgy, especially bronze casting, for military enterprises, although armed horsemen arose much later. The Cimmerians had produced bronze battle-axes by 1000 B.C.E. Early in that first millennium sword-length daggers with hollow handles were typically found in grave sites. The first militant horsemen appeared in north Central Asia at about this time.

With the rise of organized warfare, the dominant weapon in the steppe was the bow and arrow. The Scyths and their successors in the steppes surpassed all other peoples in their ability to fire with accuracy from both sides (50-60 meters) while galloping on horseback at great speed. After dismounting they could fire also with amazing agility while running at full speed. Their arrows were usually of sharp bone points, shot from composite bows made from different materials, usually with a wooden core backed with sinews and bellied with horn. The length of the bow was 140 to 160 centimeters, and the string was permanently attached to one end. Such bows were found in graves from the fourth century B.C.E. Characteristic of the Scythian bow was its short length and double-curved nature. They were made by professional craftsmen, not by the steppe warriors themselves. Much later the Huns improved the composite bow, which was copied by the Romans.

Among other common steppe weapons was the lance, used since the sixth century B.C.E. The longest one was extended 10 feet and its weight was such that the user held it with two hands while on horseback. First used by the Alans and Sarmatians, it was still employed by the Huns one thousand years later. The lasso, used to entangle an opponent before hand-to-hand combat, was a device employed by the Alans, the Sarmatians, and later the Huns.

As for armor, the steppe warriors for centuries fought without breastplates, until they were first worn by nobles. Gradually, the practice of wearing protective cuirasses made from bone or horn began to be regularly adopted. By the fourth or third centuries

B.C.E. bone breastplates were found in use from evidence in burial mounds of the lower Ob River, although bone lamellae from as early as the eighteenth century B.C.E. have been discovered in the Cis-Baikal region. From 100 B.C.E. to 100 C.E. scale armor was introduced by steppe warriors in the Altai region and in Western Siberia.

The Xiongnu wore leather and bone armor and sometimes even bronze. Iron scales were used in Tuva as early as the second century B.C.E. Within a century, chain mail had appeared among the Sarmatians in the Kuban Basin. Use of armor spread from the Ukraine to Manchuria by the second century C.E. By the early fifth century the nobles among the Huns wore a metal thorax that covered the sides as well as the breast. By this time the same Huns wore helmets that protected even the nose, a device that may have been Sassanian in origin. In the East, tribes wore such helmets by the beginning of the modern era. To decrease their weight, shields were made of wicker and supported by leather; they were made smaller for use on horseback and larger for use on foot. As for dress, common to the both the Scyths and Huns were wide trousers, gripped tight at the ankles to facilitate horse riding. The sleeves of the loose robes were also wound close to the wrists. Ammianus wrote that the Huns wore "ratskin" and linen tunics until they "rotted away on their bodies."

MILITARY ORGANIZATION

Steppe warriors were ruled by khagans, or khans, who exercised total authority over their troops. Organization was primitive, but the warriors gave allegiance to the tribal nobles who administered the wishes of the khagan. Military federations were formed, reformed, disintegrated, and overwhelmed. Armies depended upon the charismatic appeal of the leader and, upon his death, civil wars usually erupted among the followers of each son until the strongest was able to meld together a new federation. Grave sites confirm the existence of class among the warriors, and the elites were the first to wear armored protection. Armies also included women warriors, who may have constituted between 15 and 18 percent of the fighting forces. Most steppe warriors of the early centuries had no known military organization, similar to that of the medieval Mongols, yet the Huns were organized into right and left provinces, each of which was under a king who governed his army commanders. They in turn supervised the chiefs of either one thousand, one hundred, and even ten soldiers. Most, however, were simply organized into hordes, living off the conquered lands by pillaging. As they moved over long distances, their allegiances were fragile, often breaking down over competing grazing rights or plunder.

DOCTRINE, STRATEGY, AND TACTICS

Nomad military success depended upon speed, surprise, and psychology. The rapid advance of the cavalry would be highlighted by volleys of arrows from the horsemen followed by hand-to-hand fighting by scattered bands who appeared to fight in disarray, but whose intent was to destroy any unity among the opposition. Often, when fighting other steppe tribes, the strategy of feigned flight was successfully employed. Sometimes steppe warriors fled quickly when encountering opposition and then suddenly reversed direction to attack again with amazing speed. There was no strategy employed to attack fortified positions, because, in

Mounted Hunnic warriors on a raid carry a collection of weapons, including spears, swords, maces, and bows and arrows.

most cases, warriors' accuracy with bows was sufficient to overcome the defenders. In many cases, combat was accompanied by "howling" typical of the Avars, Magyars, Huns, and others. Another psychological weapon was the well-advertised practice of scalping their defeated foes, whose heads were used for drinking vessels during victory feasts. From the Scyths in the West to the Xiongnu in the East, the

steppe warriors were known for their swift, unexpected raids for plunder. If pursued, they would lead their opponents into an open field, where they could not be pinned down and where their horses could work to the best advantage. The nomads would employ volleys of arrows to exhaust their foes before engaging them in hand-to-hand combat.

As early as the fourth millennium B.C.E. the skill

of horse riding may have existed in the region of modern Kazakhstan. The horse culture became so pervasive among the steppe peoples that the warriors, men and women, spent a great portion of their lives on horseback, eating, fighting, negotiating, and even sleeping. Such traits were common throughout the long history of nomadic peoples, whether Turk, Mongol, or Indo-European. Early steppe horsemen wore neither metal stirrups nor spurs, and they directed their horses with whips. Surely, however, the Avars used the stirrup with great success in their attacks on Eastern Europe. The early warriors used few saddles, though pillow saddles stuffed with deer hair were discovered in graves at Pazyryk. At the same site was evidence of earmarks to discern ownership of horses, and by the second century C.E., the Sarmatians were branding horses. From the era of the Scyths, steppe peoples castrated their male horses to better manage their herds.

Grave sites and burial mounds also reveal the use of chariots for carrying war booty from battle, as well as for fighting. Such practice was true of the Scyths (Saka), Sarmatians, Xiongnu, Alans, and Huns from the sixth century B.C.E. Two-wheeled chariots drawn by steppe horses provided formidable fighting forces. The custom of burying chariots in the graves of rulers was common in Mesopotamia, the steppe cultures of Eurasia, and China. By 900 B.C.E. steppe warriors had mastered the art of attacking with bows and arrows while on horseback. When on march the warriors consumed fermented horse milk, horse blood, and sometimes a mixture of the two, as well as horse meat and cheese. It is said they even tenderized the meat by pounding it under their saddles.

ANCIENT SOURCES

Ancient sources on the earliest history of steppe warfare depend more on the findings of modern archaeologists than upon the ancient writers. Nevertheless, valuable information still rests upon classic works such as Sunzi's (Sun Tzu) *Bingfa* (c. 510 B.C.E.; *The Art of War*, 1910), which deals in part with the Chinese wars with the Xiongnu nomads. The military exploits of the Scyths, Massagetae, Cimmerians, and even the Amazons are fully described by the Greek historian Herodotus (c. 484-424 B.C.E.), especially in chapter 4 of his *Historiai Herodotou* (c. 424 B.C.E.; *The History*, 1709).

The Roman historian Ammianus Marcellinus (c. 330-395 C.E.), who was born a Greek and later served as an officer in the Eastern Roman armies, wrote a history describing the plight of the Roman Empire in its struggles with the barbarians, including the Huns and Avars. He did not know the Huns directly but relied upon Gothic intermediaries, ending his account in the 390's. The sixth century Gothic historian Jordanes tells much about the Huns from his knowledge of the writings, which survive only in fragments, of the Roman philosopher Helvidius Priscus (d. c. 70-79 C.E.).

BOOKS AND ARTICLES

Davis-Kimball, Jeanine, Vladimir A. Bashilov, and Leonid T. Yablonsky, eds. *Nomads of the Eurasian Steppes in the Early Iron Age*. Berkeley, Calif.: Zinat Press, 1995.

Frye, Richard N. *The Heritage of Central Asia: From Antiquity to the Turkish Expansion*. Princeton, N.J.: Marcus Weiner Publishers, 1996.

Grousset, René. *The Empire of the Steppes: A History of Central Asia*. Translated by Naomi Walford. New Brunswick, N.J.: Rutgers University Press, 1970.

Mänchen-Helfen, Otto J. *The World of the Huns: Studies in their History and Culture*. Edited by Max Knight. Berkeley: University of California Press, 1973.

John D. Windhausen

INDIA AND SOUTH ASIA

DATES: C. 1400 B.C.E.-500 C.E.

MILITARY ACHIEVEMENT

Compared with those of other ancient civilizations, the interstate relations and warfare of India were the weakest aspects of Indian political affairs. Although the role of a *kṣatriya* warrior was extolled and ancient epics glorified war, India displayed little skill in military matters. Generally peaceful and docile, the people of ancient India offered little resistance to hordes of invaders from the north. Even medieval Hindu kingdoms could not create lasting empires, maintain strong alliances, or sustain large military forces. Ancient traditions, cumbersome pedantic theories, and outmoded military techniques hampered the progression of military science. None of these burdened the invaders of India. Although war was accepted as an essential state activity, condemnation of it was rarely voiced in Indian literature. The quintessential Jain-Buddhist doctrine of ahimsa, or nonviolence, was never interpreted as a condemnation of war until the Mahatma Gandhi (1869-1948) took up the banner in

the twentieth century. Even Aśoka the Great (c. 302-c. 232 B.C.E.), the only monarch to repudiate war, as well as most Buddhist kings accepted the use of warfare as necessary to achieve the cultural unit of Bhāratavarṣa, the ancient name of India—a dream constantly challenged by invaders of Indian soil.

The military history of South Asia coincides with the influx of Indo-European invaders, who, hardened by migrations from the steppes of Eastern Europe, entered the Indus Valley and made contacts with the indigenous, dark-skinned Dravidians. The innate aggressiveness, superior military technology, iron weaponry, and horse-drawn chariots of the steppe nomad warriors successfully overwhelmed the local population. However, little is actually known of the conflicts between the two cultures. Archaeological finds present scant evidence of military conflict. Integration of the Indus Valley seems to have been achieved by means other than military absorption. The synthesis of the two cultures resulted in a Hindu civilization after 1400 B.C.E. in which small states

TURNING POINTS

c. 1800-1000 B.C.E.	Aryan invaders conquer India, mixing with earlier cultures to produce a new Hindu civilization in the area of the Ganges River Valley.
c. 1000-600 B.C.E.	Aryan Hindu civilization comes to dominate most of northern and central India while smaller states wage war for control in the South.
327 B.C.E.	The Indian king Porus employs war elephants against the forces of Alexander the Great at the Battle of the Hydaspes, seriously disrupting the Macedonian phalanx.
c. 321 B.C.E.	Chandragupta Maurya expels Alexander's forces from India and establishes the Mauryan Dynasty.
4th cent. B.C.E.	The *Arthaśāstra*, an influential treatise on Indian politics, administration, and military science, is reputedly written by the prime minister Kauṭilya.
c. 274 B.C.E.	Aśoka the Great, grandson of Chandragupta Maurya and a military genius in his own right, solidifies the strength of the Mauryan Empire.
320 C.E.	Chandragupta I establishes the Gupta Dynasty, recalling the glory days of the Mauryan Empire and employing a feudal system of decentralized authority.

pursued incessant warfare for dominance. Against this background developed the *Vedas*, the most ancient and sacred writings of Hinduism, which give tantalizing clues to military events of the Vedic period.

The post-Vedic era, however, produced reliable histories describing military events and weaponry in South Asia. The format of war that continued well into the modern era had its birth around 400 B.C.E. Between 600 and 400 B.C.E. a patchwork of feudal tribal states consolidated into sixteen republics, *māhajanapadas*, four of which in the eastern Gangetic Valley—Kosala, Kasi, Magadha, and Vrjji—gained ascendancy. Magadha emerged victorious under Chandragupta Maurya (r. c. 321-297 B.C.E.), who founded the Mauryan Empire and expelled the forces of Alexander the Great (356-323 B.C.E.) from India. The Mauryan Empire achieved its grandeur under Chandragupta's son, Bindusāra (r. c. 297-272 B.C.E.), and grandson, Aśoka. Of these, Alexander, Chandragupta, and Aśoka represent the first great military geniuses of Indian history. Although the art of warfare that Chandragupta learned from the Macedonians helped him solidify India under the banner of the Mauryas, dramatic developments in warfare remained static for approximately 2,200 years. Aśoka even renounced war and its effects in favor of Buddhist pacifism, although later Buddhist monarchs such as Harṣa of Kanauj (c. 590-647 C.E.) and Dharmapāla of Bihār and Bengal (r. c. 770-810 C.E.) pursued their political aims as ruthlessly as their Hindu neighbors.

Between 200 and 180 B.C.E. Mauryan power steadily declined, setting the stage for invasions by the Scythians, Parthians, and Yuezhi, with ensuing warfare and chaos. Dynasties rose and fell, with the Scythians, or Sakas, establishing a foothold in North India between 80 and 40 B.C.E. that was held by the efforts of the Andhra king. At the dawn of the Christian era the Andhra Dynasty controlled central India, and the Sakas the Indus Valley. South India, although independent, was engulfed in constant warfare between the Chola, Pandya, and Cheras kingdoms.

The first two hundred years of the Christian era continued as a period of confusion throughout Hindu India with no significant developments in design or employment of weaponry. Between 1 and 50 C.E. an offshoot of the Saka, the Kushan, entered the Punjab and carved out a vast empire under Kaniṣka (fl. c. 78-103) between 78 and 103 C.E. It was a short-lived attempt at empire building. Upon Kaniṣka's death, Saka authority was usurped by satraps and feudal lords who maintained a state of confusion for ninety-seven years. During this period wars in South India were marked by copious bloodshed, violence, ferocity, and treachery, while in the north warfare was a sport of the monarchs, rarely a struggle for existence. Northern wars usually had limited objectives and were less savage than wars elsewhere in the world.

During the third and fourth centuries, kingdoms continued to rise and fall with no major power appearing on the scene. The Kushan Dynasty lingered into the mid-third century, and the An-

North Wind Picture Archives

The Indian prince Porus is defeated by Alexander the Great at the Battle of the Hydaspes (327 B.C.E.), during the ancient Vedic period of Indian history.

dhra Dynasty in the south collapsed and was replaced by the Pallava Dynasty of warrior kings, who dreamed of expansion. In 300 C.E. another Chandragupta, claiming descent from the founder of the Maurya Dynasty, consolidated the central Ganges, crowned himself Chandragupta I (r. 320-c. 330), or "King of Kings," and established the glorious Gupta Empire in 320 C.E. He conquered territory almost equal to that governed by Aśoka, but he employed a feudal decentralized authority. The golden age of the Gupta Empire was reached by the third emperor, Chandragupta II (r. c. 380-415) who added Vikramaditya to his name. With the approach of the Middle Ages, Ephthalite, or White Hun, invasions from the north challenged the now-weakened Guptas, who proved helpless against them. The Ephthalites established a kingdom in the Punjab and Rajputana between 500 and 530 C.E. but held sway for only twenty years. A patchwork of warring Hindu states ensued, with violent wars waged for territorial control.

The first five hundred years of the Christian era, then, were characterized by semisuccessful attempts at reestablishing Mauryan and Gupta glory, but ancient militarism did not result in a permanent empire. Only the Mauryans and Guptas exhibited the genius of empire building. The remainder of Indian history is a maelstrom of invasions and petty struggles toward creating a recognized cultural unit of *Bhāratavarṣa*.

WEAPONS, UNIFORMS, AND ARMOR

Although the military history of South Asia coincides with the influx of Aryan invaders, Stone Age weaponry in the form of celts, knives, and arrowheads have been discovered. Between 3500 and 3000 B.C.E. Mesopotamia and Egypt utilized weapons of copper which, a few hundred years later, were hardened with tin to usher in the Bronze Age throughout the Near East and Indus Valley cultures. The following Iron Age enhanced the manufacture of weapons. In major cultural centers a highly developed art of war with land and water transport, chariots, cavalry, and iron-steel weaponry ensued. Primitive military organization and combat techniques began to surface. By the sixth century B.C.E. continuous warfare records reveal the more sophisticated military trends.

The Aryans who entered India in the second millennium B.C.E. proved formidable adversaries, skilled in warfare and bronze metallurgy as seen in spear, dagger, arrowhead, mace, and sword specimens found in the mounds of Mohenjo-daro. The most significant improvement during the early historic period, then, was the use of metal for implements of war. Metallurgical skill permitted the working of malleable metal, a skill that produced highly sophisticated weaponry to ensure conquest of the Indus River Valley.

The primary weapon was the bow and arrow, which was used from the Stone Age until the end of the Middle Ages. Four to five feet in length, the bow was constructed of bamboo, horn, wood, or metal. Its strings were made of *saṇa* fiber, hemp, skin, or animal hide. An invaluable weapon, its effective range was 100 to 120 yards, fewer if heavy, antielephant arrows were used. It was carried into battle on the left shoulder or carried aloft in the left hand. So great was its importance in ancient times that a code of rules regarding archery was ennobled as a subsidiary *Veda*, the *Dhanur Veda*. The title of *Dhanurdhāra*, or "master of the bow," was the highest accolade paid to a warrior.

Arrows, fabricated from deer horn or iron, were barbed, crescent-shaped, needle-pointed, and dentiform, or serrated, and they were carried in a quiver made of hide, basket-work, or metal plates. The quiver was slung on the back and tied in front by a cross-belt. Fire-arrows and other incendiary missiles, often used against elephants, were disapproved by *smrti* writers. The *Arthaśāstra* (300 B.C.E.-300 C.E.; *Treatise on the Political Good*, 1961) of the Indian philosopher Kauṭilya (fl. 300 B.C.E.), a treatise on Indian polity from the Mauryan period, stressed the value of birds and monkeys to carry fire to enemy rooftops. Arrows tipped with metal and poison were used but were also condemned in religious texts.

Warriors also used a variety of hacking, stabbing, and felling weapons in the form of pikes, lances, spears, and battle-axes, as well as an assortment of swords, daggers, and javelins. The javelin, or *śela*, used by the infantry was highly praised, and a special long lance, the *tomara*, was used by warriors mounted on horses or elephants. Swords were double-edged, thick and heavy, and always borne in the hand. Sabers, on the other hand, were short-bladed, curved, single-edged, and worn on the left side. The *mushṭika*, a dagger of varied shape and form, was especially favored by the warriors. Siege machinery in the form of artillery, battering rams, and ballistae for hurling rocks, boiling oil, melted rosin of the *sal* tree (*kalpala*), and fire-tipped darts became common during the Mauryan period.

Beside traditional weapons, charioteers and infantry used a *nāgapāśa*, or lasso, to snare the enemy, as well as a boomerang that returned to the spot from which it was thrown.

Hindu warriors wore protective armor for head, torso, and legs, usually fabricated from leather reinforced with metal. Helmets, which had generally appeared by the Middle Ages, as well as breastplates and greaves, to protect the leg below the knee, were made entirely of bronze and iron. Prior to the Middle Ages warriors had depended on the thick folds of a turban to protect the head. To protect hands and arms from bowstring friction, leather guards were used. A wooden or wicker shield covered with buffalo or rhinoceros hide was carried in the left hand on the left arm. Archers without shields were protected by a front rank of oblong or circular shieldbearing javelin throwers. By the Middle Ages coats of mail were common protective gear for both man and beast.

Around the sixth century B.C.E. two decisive war machines appeared, namely the chariot, which developed after the Persian invasions, and the war elephant, which was considered as valuable as the chariot.

Elephants were outfitted with a housing, or howdah, covered with cloth or carpet and bells around the neck and rump. Lower-ranked warriors armed with bows and other missiles were seated in the howdah. According to the Greek historian Megasthenes (c. 350- c. 290 B.C.E.), sent as a representative to the royal court of India, three archers and a driver outfitted each elephant.

Primary reliance was placed upon the chariot or *śaṭangaratha*, a two-wheeled, open vehicle similar to those used in other ancient cultures. Drawn by horses, the chariot became a decisive fighting instrument in Indian warfare. Chariot wheels were occasionally outfitted with scythelike blades projecting from the axles, making the chariot a most dangerous weapon. Sanskrit literature describes chariots ornamented with precious materials and armed with an array of weapons. Large numbers were used in battle. Battalions of 405 infantry, 81 chariots, and 243 horses are commonly described in Sanskrit literature.

Cavalry armed with lances and short swords dominated the warfare of North India, whereas infantry was most important in South India, because southern geography and climate did not support the raising of sufficient horses for large cavalry units. Most of the superior horses of southern India were used for chariots. Although cavalry gave way to more disciplined and maneuverable infantry in Asia, India continued to rely heavily upon cavalry. India generally lagged behind other civilized cultures in military development. Its major contribution to military technology was the stirrup, which provided lancers stability in the saddle and was used by the Indian army as early as the first century B.C.E.

MILITARY ORGANIZATION

The Hindu army consisted of various categories of warriors but its backbone of seasoned hereditary troops were the *Kṣatriya* professionals. Its ranks were filled by southern mercenaries from Chera, Karnata, and other areas; troops that generally protected caravans or trading posts of *śreṇi*, or merchant guilds; troops supplied by subordinate allies; army deserters; and wild guerrilla tribesmen. All castes were incorporated into the army, but *Kṣatriya* represented the warrior par excellence. Brāhmans held high military ranks, whereas the lowest two castes, Vaiśya and Śūdra, fought as auxiliaries. Warriors were arranged according to the clans and districts to which they belonged. During the Vedic period, all free men were subject to military service, but this obligation vanished as caste rules solidified. After the Mauryan period general conscription was rare.

The army was divided into four sections, the whole forming a *caturangam*: elephants, chariots, cavalry, and infantry. Elephants, the first line of defense, were trained with extreme care and utilized as battering rams, to frighten horses, to trample troops underfoot, and to ford rivers. Although they were difficult to wound, they were protected by infantry. However, there was constant danger that elephants could easily be unnerved by fire and panic. Elephants were used well into the nineteenth century by later Muslim monarchs.

The cavalry, long considered indispensable, ultimately proved a weak element in Indian armies. The mounts were often wretched, failed to cover great distances, and proved vulnerable to mounted invaders from the northwest. It was not relied upon to any great extent. Chariots, on the other hand, were major fighting units in the Vedic period. They were used widely in Mauryan armies but by Gupta times, the light two-horsed car had evolved into a larger, more cumbersome transport vehicle.

The strength of the army rested in the infantry. In most Indian kingdoms an elite corps was pledged to protect the king to the death. Generally, however, they represented a miscellaneous horde of men that fell upon an enemy without any method or concerted plan. Each recruit usually provided his own mount and received a stipend for himself and for the upkeep of his horse. Undisciplined mercenaries often deserted. Some reference is made to armies having mutinied in face of the enemy until pay was received. Yet the infantry, numerically the army's largest contingent, represented its main strength and was relied upon heavily.

Thousands of noncombatants also accompanied the fighting force to battle. They were especially evident in disorderly camps pitched during campaigns. Soothsayers, astrologers, dancers, prostitutes, acrobats, quacks, merchants, cooks, fakirs, religious mendicants, entire families of the fighting men, and royal family, wives, and concubines often slowed the pace of the army. The *Arthaśāstra* speaks of physicians and veterinarians attached to the army to care for man and beast.

The size of the Hindu army usually was enormous. In ancient and medieval times, according to various sources, the army engaged 600,000 to 900,000 men. The king led his army personally into battle. Under him were a number of superintendents with a *senāpati*, or general, at the head of all military affairs. The Mauryan army, according to Megasthenes, was organized under a committee of thirty with subcommittees that controlled infantry, cavalry, chariot, elephant, navy, and commissariat elements. Captains from feudal nobility served under the general. Standards identified all regiments, divisions, and squadrons.

DOCTRINE, STRATEGY, AND TACTICS

Three reasons are given in the *Arthaśāstra* for pursuing war: *dharmavijaya*, or victory for justice or virtue; *lōbhavijaya*, or pursuit of booty and territory; and *āsuravijaya*, or incorporation of territory into that of the victor and political annihilation. The Mauryan kingdom waged wars for glory and homage rather than wealth and power. The Guptas, on the other hand, stressed political annihilation and incorporation of territory. However, *dharmavijaya*, or victory for justice, was the ideal that Hindu kings were expected to pursue. War, however, became a sport of kings, profitable and always serious. Defeat was usually expunged by suicide. Dravidian South India, never fully influenced by Aryan culture, waged wars of annexation. Captives and noncombatants were treated with ruthlessness, but the ideal of *dharmavijaya* was still present.

War was considered a religious rite, the highest sacrifice of a warrior. Battle was preceded by purification rituals, and astrologers determined the time and day for battle. The *Arthaśāstra* advised the employment of elephants and infantry in the center, light infantry, chariots, and cavalry on the wings, and archers behind spearmen. Emphasis was placed on single combat between selected warriors, but mass encounter of rank and file proved decisive. Morale was provided by leaders; if a leader was slain, the army generally fled. Elite *Kṣatriya* warriors were expected to fight to the death. Prisoners were treated honorably, usually released upon payment of ransom or after ransom was fulfilled by labor. Massacre was deprecated in Sanskrit literature.

The king and his nobles, the *rājanya*, fought from

chariots. Infantry marched along with charioteers to the accompaniment of martial music that inspired them toward victory. Laying siege was considered dangerous and was rarely pursued. Generally a town was attacked and starved into capitulation.

Armies met each other face to face, approaching in parallel lines, infantry in the center, chariots and cavalry on the flanks, with swarms of archers and slingers in the foreground raining harassing fire with shouts and clashing arms. The usual objective was to outflank an enemy, because the ten to thirty ranks of infantry were deemed vulnerable. Until 700 B.C.E. chariots provided the striking force, and the infantry provided a solid base around which more important groups could operate. Little organization was pres-

ent, because the primary objective was to reach a suitable battle site and overwhelm the enemy. When charioteers struck terror in the enemy, the battle resulted in a chase. Usually each side converged and fought for an hour or more until one side would sense defeat. After 1000 B.C.E. more order, discipline, and organization entered the military system.

India generally lagged behind other civilized cultures in military theory, strategy, and tactics up to the dawn of the common era. Although training and discipline were well known to the Hindus, they found it difficult to impose military fundamentals upon the troops. The *Arthaśāstra* of Kauṭilya became the primary guide for military organization, tactics, ethics, and doctrine well into the medieval period.

ANCIENT SOURCES

Early Indian literary sources such as the *Rig Veda*; the *Mahābhārata* (c. 400 B.C.E.-200 C.E.; *The Mahabharata*, 1834), including the *Bhagavad Gītā* (c. fifth century B.C.E.); and the *Manusmṛti* (compiled 200 B.C.E.; *The Laws of Manu*, 1886) describe the power of weaponry, the religious duty of war, the importance of strong leadership, and the ethical aspects of waging war. The comprehensive Mauryan *Arthaśāstra* of Kauṭilya, composed between 300 B.C.E. and 300 C.E., looked upon war as a "continuation of polity by other means," as a legitimate last resort for achieving the aims of government and not to be embarked upon lightly. Although earlier literature had stressed a warrior's *dharma*, or duty, the motive of the *Arthaśāstra* was the establishment of a great empire. Around 500 C.E. the *Śiva Dhanur Veda*, of unknown authorship, stressed the skills of archery and military science in general. Its importance is seen in the application of the term *Dhanur Veda* to all writings on the art of war.

BOOKS AND ARTICLES

Basham, E. L. *The Wonder That Was India: A Survey of the History and Culture of the Indian Subcontinent Before the Coming of the Muslims*. New York: Grove Press, 1954.

Bull, Stephen. *An Historical Guide to Arms and Armour*. London: Cassell, 1991.

Mitra, Rajendralala. *Indo-Aryans: Contributions Towards the Elucidation of Their Ancient and Mediaeval History*. 2 vols. Delhi, India: Indological Book House, 1969.

Spaulding, Oliver L. *Warfare: A Study of Military Methods from the Earliest Times*. 1925. Reprint. New York: Barnes & Noble Books, 1993.

George Hoynacki

THE MEDIEVAL WORLD

WORLD

THE ROMAN LEGACY

BYZANTIUM

DATES: 312-1453 C.E.

POLITICAL CONSIDERATIONS

In 312 C.E. Constantine the Great (c. 272 to 285-337) won a key battle at Milvian Bridge outside of Rome that ensured his domination over rivals in the Roman Empire. The victory relied on Roman divisions who counted numerous Christians among them, and Constantine announced that his victory had been blessed by heaven when he saw a cross in the sky with the words, "By this sign you shall conquer." Constantine built a new eastern capital, in addition to the one in Rome. This city, Constantinople (modern Istanbul), was built on the old Greek colony of Byzantium, and historians regard its establishment as a capital in 324

The Roman emperor Constantine, who in 312 C.E. established a new, eastern Roman capital at Constantinople, which became the seat of the Byzantine Empire. He is pictured here experiencing his legendary vision of Christ.

as the beginning of the Byzantine Empire. At this time Constantine also legalized Christianity and ordered its organization, although the pagan religion was not outlawed until 385.

The early Byzantine Empire still regarded itself as part of the Roman Empire, and its legions were formed in the Roman way. In its early centuries the Empire concerned itself with the increasing Germanic, Slavic, and Hunnic invasions into the Danubian region and the western portions of the Empire, where a co-emperor remained in Rome until 476. From the east the Byzantines also faced incursions of the Persian Empire. Unlike Rome, Constantinople was able to resist the German invasions mainly due to its fabulous defense system, created by its early emperors. In contrast to the modern city of Istanbul, which spans two continents, Europe and Asia, old Constantinople was confined to the southwestern tip of a peninsula on the European side of the Bosporus Strait linking the Black Sea and the Sea of Marmara. Constantinople was bounded by the Sea of Marmara, the Bosporus, and to the north, the Golden Horn, an inlet on the Bosporus. In the fourth and fifth centuries Byzantine emperors constructed a series of impenetrable walls, whose ruins can still be seen, across the land side from Marmara to the Golden Horn. An additional sea wall was built around the Sea of Marmara and the Bosporus to the Golden Horn, and a large boom blocked the entrance to the latter. The Byzantines, with a majority Greek population, would in fact, after the seventh century, be considered Greeks. They were the best sailors in the Mediterranean. Just as their wall held off land armies until the Fourth Crusade of 1204 and the Ottoman Invasion of 1453, their navies protected the city from sea attack.

In addition to foreign wars, the Byzantines fought civil wars against pagan generals opposed to the new Christian order and against heretical Christians associated with the old Hellenistic centers, such as Antioch and Alexandria. By the time of Justinian I (483-565), the religious wars had died down, but the emperor himself had almost lost his throne in the Nika Uprising of 532, which began after a fight between fans of competing chariot teams. The steadfastness of Justinian's wife, Theodora (c. 497-548), a commoner, saved the throne. Justinian continued with a glorious career, building the magnificent church of Santa Sophia, definitively codifying Roman law, and waging war against the Germans and Persians. In the last, however, he ultimately failed. Although his commander-in-chief Belisarius (c. 505-565), one of the four great generals of antiquity, regained much land in North Africa and Spain and won significant battles against the Persians, he did not restore the old Roman Empire, and those lands gained were lost just a few years after Justinian was succeeded by his nephew, Justin II (r. 565-578).

Justinian changed the nature of the Empire from that of a constitutional to that of an absolute monarchy. The emperor now bore the title "autocrat." In the early seventh century, under Heraclius (c. 575-641), the Byzantine Empire became Hellenized, with Greek replacing Latin as the official language. Although citizens of the Byzantine Empire still called themselves Romans, they were now really Greek. Heraclius also fought against the Persians in the field, winning victories that exhausted the empire's resources.

TURNING POINTS

324	Roman emperor Constantine builds a new eastern capital at Constantinople.
527-565	Emperor Justinian reigns, definitively codifying Roman law, waging war against the Germans and Persians, and changing the nature of the Empire from that of a constitutional to that of an absolute monarchy.
610-641	Heraclius reigns, Hellenizing the Byzantine Empire and introducing the theme system of Byzantine provinces ruled by military governors.
1096-1204	The First through Fourth Crusades are waged by Christians seeking to protect the Byzantine Empire and to recapture the Holy Land from Muslims.
1453	Constantinople is captured by the Ottoman Turks, ending the Byzantine Empire.

In the years from 632 to 670 the Muslim Arabs, storming out of the Arabian desert and filled with religious zeal inspired by the recently deceased prophet Muḥammad (c. 570-632), easily conquered the Near Eastern and North African lands even while they fought among themselves for leadership of the faithful. The resentment of the Christian dissidents who still lived in those regions and who were tolerated by the Muslims played an important part in these defeats.

From the north the Byzantine Empire contended with the Slavic invasions of the sixth and seventh century that culminated in the creation of the first Bulgarian empire on both sides of the Danube. The next four centuries witnessed periods of peace and alliance alternating with wars between the Greeks and Bulgarians. During this period the Byzantine emperors established the "theme system" of Byzantine provinces ruled by military governors. During times of war the peasants of the theme manned the Byzantine army and navy. The themes of the sea embraced the islands and hence were the major contributor to the navy.

Beginning in 711 the Byzantine Empire went through its most critical internal struggle until its downfall—a period of civil war over Iconoclasm. Iconoclasts were religious dissidents who wanted to remove religious pictures and icons from the Christian service, and one of their proponents, Leo III (c. 680-741), became emperor. Even though he won important victories against the Arabs and Bulgarians, his Iconoclast views were unpopular. At the end of the century Byzantine ruler Irene (c. 752-803) restored the veneration of icons and was later made a saint in the Christian church.

In 867 Basil I (c. 812-886) established the 189-year Macedonian Dynasty (867-1056), which brought the Byzantine Empire to new heights. In the tenth century the dynasty repulsed an attempt of the Bulgarian king Simeon I (died 927), claiming to be the Byzantine emperor, to seize the capital and the throne. In 1018 Basil II (c. 958-1025) defeated the Bulgarians and incorporated their empire into his own.

However, within forty years the Macedonian Dynasty had ended for lack of a male heir, and a series of intrigues and bloody rivalries among the noble fami-

lies ensued, which gave the term "Byzantine" its pejorative connotation. The conflicts of this period led to the losses of southern Italy to Norman adventurers at the Capture of Bari (1071) and of Asia Minor to the Seljuk Turks (Battle of Manzikert, 1071). Furthermore, in 1054 during the height of the struggles, the Christian church had split into Eastern and Western branches. In response Emperor Alexius I (c. 1048-1118) of the Comnenus Dynasty (1081-1118) asked Pope Urban II (c. 1042-1099) to send some Western knights to Constantinople as military assistance to heal the breach by helping the Greeks reconquer Asia Minor. The pope embraced the enterprise, with a grander vision of expanding the Christian community, calling for the First Crusade (1095-1099).

Alexius initially welcomed the knights but was unhappy to see the throngs of peasants who also took up the cross and came on crusade. Furthermore, when the Crusaders conquered the Arab land, they would not agree to hold it as Alexius's vassals but instead set up their own feudal hierarchy under Godfrey of Bouillon (c. 1060-1100), the Crusade leader who became the king of Jerusalem. When the Muslims reconquered the Crusader states, and Western Christians launched the Second (1145-1149) and Third Crusades (1187-1192) led by kings, the Greeks became less hospitable. After the failure of the Third Crusade, the spirit declined even in the west. In the meantime there had been a family rupture in the Byzantine Angelus Dynasty (1185-1204). Alexius III (r. 1195-1203) had overthrown and blinded his brother Isaac II (r. 1185-1195; 1203-1204) and had him imprisoned with his son, Alexius IV (r. 1203-1204). In 1202 a new group of Crusaders had gathered at Venice for another attempt to retake the Holy Land. However, the project did not have enough funds to begin. The Crusaders relied on the doge of Venice to give them the needed resources in exchange for the conquest of the merchant city-state of Zara, which had recently broken away from the Venetian empire. Because of the destruction of this Christian city, Pope Innocent III (1160 or 1161-1216) abandoned the enterprise. Isaac II's son Alexius IV escaped from Constantinople and promised to finance the Crusaders further if they could help him reestablish his father's claim to the Byzan-

BYZANTINE EMPIRE, C. 1250

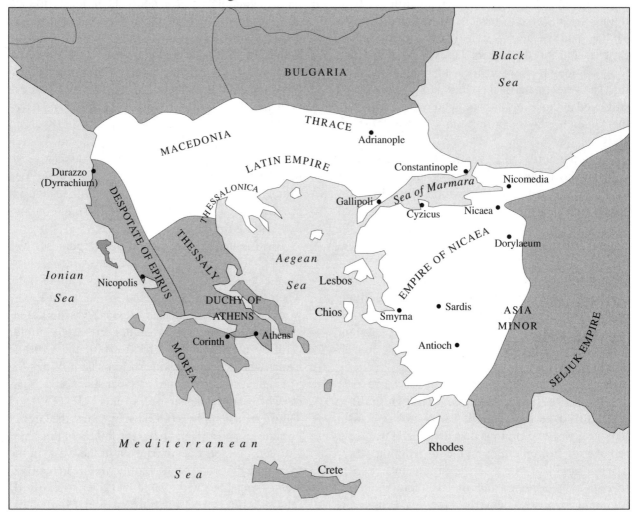

tine throne. The Crusaders agreed to the diversion, invaded Constantinople, expelled the blind emperor's brother, and put Isaac back on the throne with his son as co-ruler. Alexius IV, however, was unable to honor his commitment to supplying the Crusaders. Furthermore, a popular uprising in the city turned against Isaac and Alexius in favor of another member of the family. After realizing that Constantinople was an even better and easier prize than Jerusalem, the Crusaders and their Venetian allies seized the city and established themselves as rulers of the empire. Baldwin of Flanders (1172-1205), sponsored by the Venetian doge, became Baldwin I of Constantinople,

and he distributed the themes among his followers as vassal fiefs.

This Latin Empire (1204-1261) continued for only fifty-seven years, but the damage it did continued until the end of the Byzantine state in 1453. While Western rulers established a dozen new states in the themes of the empire, other rulers established independent realms as well. The great medieval Slavic empires—Serbia, Bulgaria, and Croatia—flourished in this age. There were several independent merchant cities, such as the Italian and Hungarian enclaves of Venice and Dubrovnik, as well as the Ottoman sultanate, which appeared in the thirteenth century and within two hundred years had steadily engulfed all of the Christian states, culminating in the conquest of Constantinople in 1453.

Military Achievement

The key to Byzantine endurance was its magnificent defense system, beginning with the walls of Constantinople and the boom at the entrance of the Golden Horn. Added to this was the best navy in the region, which was used primarily as a defensive force. The Greeks also effectively employed both peasant infantry and noble cavalry. However, throughout its history the empire alternated between periods of military victory and defeat. It reached its heights during the reigns of Justinian and Heraclius and later during the Macedonian Dynasty, but constant civil and religious wars, popular uprisings, and internal rivalries and intrigues revealed its weaknesses and flaws. The Greeks suffered at various times major defeats at the hands of the Slavs, Arabs, Turks, Normans, Crusaders, the pagan Patzinaks, and other adversaries.

Weapons, Uniforms, and Armor

The most spectacular and renowned weapon of the Byzantines was Greek fire, a paraffin mixture whose exact formula remains unknown. When set aflame it could not be doused by water. Greek fire was especially effective in naval warfare when the Greeks catapulted balls of the flaming wax onto enemy ships, spreading general panic. In the last years of the empire, it was shot through tubes using a form of gunpowder. Individual sailors and soldiers carried small amounts of Greek fire in a type of hand grenade that exploded on contact. Greek fire was also used in land warfare and dropped from the walls of besieged cities against soldiers trying to scale the defenses.

At the height of the Byzantine Empire, from the sixth to eleventh centuries, the cavalry was the mainstay of the Byzantine land forces. The heavy cavalry, known as *cataphracts*, dressed in mail covering their bodies in the Persian fashion and wore steel helmets. Their weapons included swords, daggers, bows that

were also borrowed from the Persians, and lances. They protected their horses with breast and frontal armor. Light cavalry and light infantry also used the bow, which was employed on long attacks. Some light infantry carried lances. Heavy infantry wore mail, as did their cavalry counterparts, and fought with swords, spears, battle-axes, and shields.

In the navy there were several classes of warships, known as *dromons*. Battleships of different sizes had sails and two banks of oars with an average crew of two to three hundred men. Seventy of the crew were marines who fought both on land and ship-to-ship. The remainder were rowers and sailors. Cruiser-type ships, *pamphyli*, were lighter, swifter, and more maneuverable, having only two banks of oars. They also fought in set battles. A special *pamphylus* stood as the admiral's flagship. Light ships with one bank of oars served for reconnaissance and carrying dispatches. Byzantine ships had ramming rods, which the lighter maneuverable vessels used very effectively.

Military Organization

The first Byzantine army was Constantine's Roman army, which followed the organization of the late third and early fourth century. These were divided into the border divisions, or *limitanei*, composed of the peasants of the region; the mobile units, or *comitatensis*, who fought in the field; and the guards, or *palatini*, the best troops. Under the emperor the highest ranks were prefects and two commanders-in-chief, or *magistri militum*, the senior for the cavalry and the junior for the infantry. However, when on independent campaign, either commander led mixed cavalry and infantry. At the end of the fourth century Emperor Theodosius the Great (346 or 347-395) settled the original commanders in Constantinople and added three more in the provinces. The commanders then operated independently, subject only to the emperor. Justinian added one more. The generals, or *dux*, of the provincial armies served under the commanders and had administrative and supervised judicial bureaus headed by chiefs, *princips*, from the imperial bureaucracy.

In principle the state subjected all Byzantine males subject to conscription. In practice landowners could pay to keep their peasants out of military service, and the draft affected mostly the urban population. The sons of soldiers were also regularly recruited. In fact most of the military was filled with volunteers, including foreigners and mercenaries called allies or *foederati*. Generals also maintained, at their own expense, troops called *bucellarii*, who took an oath to their leaders as well as to the emperor, thus presenting a danger to the throne. Nevertheless by Justinian's time the *bucellarii* had increased so much that they formed a major part of the army. The Roman army continued, with divisions composed of soldiers from regions such as Asia Minor, Thrace, and Armenia, and was held in special esteem. In the sixth century the cavalry replaced the infantry as the main force, and the financial difficulties caused by Justinian's ambitious wars and projects, together with a threat from the Russian steppe in the form of the pagan Avars, reduced the mercenary forces and increased conscription.

Heraclius introduced the theme system as a military measure to strengthen the provincial armies. Theme governors known as *strategoi*, literally generals, and division leaders, or *comes*, replaced the infantry and cavalry commanders-in-chief. Each theme provided an army *thema*, the equivalent of an army corps, divided into two or three division-strength *turmai*, about five thousand troops, commanded by *turmachs* serving both as army generals and civilian administrators in their provincial district. Smaller units included *moirai* (brigades), *tagmata* (regiments), *banda*, *pentarchies*, *pentakontarchies* (companies of forty men), and *dekarchies* (platoons of about ten men). *Banda* contained five *pentarchies* and *pentarchies* contained five *pentakontarchies*. *Banda* officers included *drungarii* and *kometes*. *Komes* commanded *pentarchies* and *pentakontarchos* the *pentakontarchies*. In addition special troop *kleisurai* (literally "mountain passes") commanded by *kleisuriarchs* guarded frontiers subject to invasion. If these districts became themes, the theme organization was applied. *Akritai*, the legendary frontier warriors of the Byzantine folk epics, at times fought beside the *kleisurai* and at other times independently. Higher officers were usually of noble rank. Each *bandon* had its own baggage train and accompanying noncombatants, such as slaves, servants, and physicians. The train brought engineering equipment, for building bridges and field camps, as well as siege equipment.

Apart from the theme armies there were special corps assigned to the capital. They included four cavalry *tagmata* named *scholarii*, *excubitores*, *hikanatai*, and *arithmos*, sometimes called *vigla*. *Domestici* commanded the first three, and a *drungarius* led the latter, the imperial guard. However, the real protectors of the emperors were the *hetairia*, or retinue, which had a large number of mercenaries and was led by the *hetairiarchos*. There was also an infantry *tagmata*, the *numeri* commanded by a *domesticus*, and additional infantry troops. The Constantinople soldiers fought with the emperor except for a battalion under the *domesticus* of the walls that always remained to protect the city.

From the sixth century the highest army commander was the *strategos* of the Theme of the East, and the next in rank was the *domesticus* of the *scholarii*. In the tenth century, after the emperors no longer regularly led the army in battle and the number of themes had increased, the *scholarii domesticus* became the commander-in-chief of the entire army. The army strength of the Byzantine Empire varied over time, but at its maximum it was about 150,000. Although military pay was small, soldiers' rights as peasants on theme land made up for the deficiency.

After the eleventh century the losses in Asia Minor and the Balkans brought about the decline and finally the end of the theme system. Citizens could purchase exemptions from the conscription, and the number of mercenaries increased to include Slavs, Arabs, Turks, Mongols, "Latins," Germans, and Caucasians. The elite Varangian corps of the Comnenus Dynasty was composed of Anglo-Saxons. The fortunes of the empire became more precarious. In a 1204 battle with Crusaders, the mercenary army, which had not been paid, refused to fight. By the last years of the Byzantine Empire, under the Paleologus Dynasty (1261-1453), the regular organization had dissolved and the army was a patchwork of troops, mainly mercenary soldiers.

Although the Byzantine army had evolved from that of the Romans, the Byzantine navy was created afresh. The Roman fleet was hardly more than a coast guard, and even up until the time of Justinian, the navy had played only a supplementary role. However, during the height of the empire the navy was a key part of the Byzantine military, especially in the empire's defense. The threat of the Arabs forced the Greeks to increase the size of the navy and to integrate it into the theme system. The fleet commander-in-chief was the strategos of the *carabisiani*, named after the *carabos*, a type of ship. Under him were one or two *drungarii*, with the responsibility of admirals although the equivalent rank in the army is similar to a modern colonel—a discrepancy stemming from the higher position of the army in the empire. Sailors came from the coastal regions and islands, the best being the Cibyhrrhaeots, from the Pamphylian city of Cibyra in southern Asia Minor. In the eighth century the Muslim caliphate moved inland to Persia and lessened the threat from the sea, after which the imperial navy declined. Because of a renewed Muslim threat in the Mediterranean in the following century, the Macedonian Dynasty paid more attention to the naval fleet. They added a third theme of the sea and established naval stations in the European themes. After the crisis of the eleventh century, the navy, as did the army, suffered a steady and eventually irreparable decline.

DOCTRINE, STRATEGY, AND TACTICS

Byzantine commanders paid detailed attention to military science. The Greeks, including emperors themselves, wrote manuals and commentary of military affairs, for example the *Strategikon*, (before 630; *Maurice's Strategikon*, 1984) attributed to Mauricius Flavius Tiberius (c. 539-602), a Byzantine emperor who reigned from 582 to 602, which gives detailed information on the differences in strategies between the Persian and the Roman soldiers, as well as the intricacies and differences in their weapons and their uses. The *Taktika* (compiled c. 905; tactics) of the emperor Leo VI (866-912) was another well-studied

text. The commanders studied the character of the enemy and the nature of the region for battle and applied their findings in the preparation and execution of both offense and defense. Surprisingly, the Greeks, who throughout history had been renowned for their seamanship, did not pay as much attention to naval science.

Special emphasis was laid on defense, and the Greeks used attack as their main strategy only in siege operations. Byzantine defense followed the frontier tactics of the late Roman Empire; the Greeks built fortified camps and small forts and posted troops at strategic passes and areas from which the enemy might invade. They fortified interior towns and cities and erected a chain of warning signals throughout the empire. If enemy forces succeeded in invading past the border defenses, the infantry would fall in behind them and block their retreat, while light infantry harassed their troops until the theme commander could assemble support from neighboring provinces in sufficient number to attack. In battle heavy cavalry, the main force of the army, attacked in mass formation. Light cavalry fought in quick sorties, made harassing raids, and carried out reconnaissance.

Byzantine military manuals carefully laid down the rule of field operations, but the commanders were also expected to show innovation and independence. The guiding principle in battle was to minimize casualties. Among the stratagems used to gain victory with the least loss were intelligence and espionage, negotiation, delaying tactics, ambushes, moving troops for their protection, feigning retreat. Training, discipline, and experience enabled the Greeks to use these doctrines effectively. The Greeks knew the value of esprit de corps, rewarding special service and recognizing valor. The emperor and commanders appointed orators to emphasize the glory of courage, arousing the spirit and enthusiasm of the troops for God, Christianity, the emperor, and the Empire. Religion played a major part in the life and spirit of the troops. Greek wars were holy wars. Solemn masses were celebrated on the battlefield. Every day began with morning prayers, and the Greek battle cries were, "God is with us" and "The cross is victorious."

MEDIEVAL SOURCES

There exists a large body of primary sources for the Byzantine Empire, many of which have been translated into English and published. Among the best known are the sixth century Byzantine historian Procopius's *Anekdota, e, Apokryphos Historia* (c. 550; *Secret History*, 1674), an account of the reign of Justinian I and Theodora; Michael Psellus's (1018-c. 1078) *Chronographia* (English translation, 1953) on the eleventh century; and princess Anna Comnena's (1083-c. 1148) *Alexiad* (English translation, 1928), an account of reign of her father, Alexius I, which includes Comnena's impressions of the Crusaders and the war with Patzinaks. Although these are general histories, they contain valuable information on the Byzantine military. Procopius, who was secretary to the general Belisarius, also wrote the official court histories of Justinian, which included accounts of his wars. Information about the military hierarchy of the early centuries is found in the *Notitia Dignitatum* of the fifth century and John of Lydia's (fl. sixth century) *De Magistratibus* (after 554; *On the Magistracies of the Roman Constitution*, 1971) of the sixth. Descriptions of the wars of Heraclius are found in the poetry of George Pisides (fl. seventh century).

There are a number of seventh and eighth century chronicles of the Byzantine Empire. Those of the monk Theophanes the Confessor (c. 752-c. 818) and the patriarch Nicephorus are valuable. The tenth century historian Joseph Genisius wrote about the end of the Iconoclast struggle and the first years of the Macedonian dynasty. Leo Diaconus (fl. tenth century) recounted in his history the military achievements of the emperors Nicephoras II Phocas (r. 963-969) and John I Tzimisces (r. 969-976). The chronicle of Byzantine historian John Scylitzes (fl. eleventh century) covers the years 811 to 1057. Some non-Byzantine sources important to this period include *Provest' Vremennykh Let* (twelfth century; *Russian Primary Chronicle*, 1930), partly attributed to Nestor (c. 1056-1113), and the Latin *Antapodosis* (tenth century; *Antapodosis*, 1930) of Liutprand of Cremona (c. 922-c. 972). The emperor Constantine VII (905-959) wrote on a number of subjects, including the themes. Two military manuals of this period are the *Taktika* of Leo VI and the *Sylloge Tacticorum* (compiled tenth century; *Sylloge Tacticorum*, 1938). For the eleventh century in addition to Psellus and Comnena there is also the *Strategicon* of Cacaumenus, a Byzantine general. John Cinnamus and Nicetas Choniates wrote on the twelfth century. For the crusades there are many Western works with tangential reference to Byzantine military affairs. Important historians of the last years of the Byzantine Empire include George Pachymeres (1242-c. 1310), Nicephorus II Phocas, and the emperor John VI Cantacuzenus (1292-1354), all of whom wrote before the fall of the empire in 1453. Those who wrote after the fall include Laonicus Chalcocondyles (c. 1423-c. 1490), Ducas (fl. mid-fifteenth century), Critobulos of Imbros (fl. fifteenth century), and George Sphrantes (fl. fifteenth century), whose description of the fall of Constantinople is a standard account.

BOOKS AND ARTICLES

Bartusis, Mark C. *The Late Byzantine Army: Arms and Society, 1204-1453*. Philadelphia: University of Pennsylvania Press, 1997.

Haldon, John F. *Warfare, State, and Society in the Byzantine World, 565-1204*. London: UCL Press, 1999.

Heath, Ian, Angus McBride, and Lee Johnson. *Byzantine Armies, 1118-1461*. London: Osprey, 1995.

Nicolle, David. *Romano-Byzantine Armies, Fourth-Ninth Centuries*. London: Osprey, 1992.

Treadgold, Warren T. *Byzantium and Its Army, 284-1081*. Stanford, Calif.: Stanford University Press, 1995.

FILMS AND OTHER MEDIA

Byzantium. Documentary. Discovery Channel, 1997.

Byzantium: The Lost Empire. Documentary. Artisan Home Entertainment, 1997.

Civilizations in Conflict: Byzantium, Islam, and the Crusades. Documentary. United Learning, 1998.

Fall of Byzantium: May 29, 1453. Docudrama. Zenger Video, 1989.

The Fall of Constantinople. Documentary. Time-Life, 1970.

Justinian: The Last of the Romans. Documentary. A&E Home Video, 1997.

The Siege of Constantinople. Documentary. Ambrose Video, 1995.

Frederick B. Chary

HOLY ROMAN EMPIRE

DATES: 482-918 C.E.

POLITICAL CONSIDERATIONS

During the last days of the Roman Empire, the Western European landscape was divided among various Germanic tribes, remaining bastions of Roman administrative rule, and surviving Roman military settlements, or *laeti*. The Franks alone were divided into at least four subgroups that competed for control with various Gallo-Roman magnates whose cities and surrounding territories comprised lands sufficient for them to be called *sub reguli*, or "sub-kings," in the sources. It is little wonder that any military commander with enough drive and power to stitch together an identifiable fabric from this crazy quilt of disarray would be hailed as more than just another king. Such a man was Clovis I (c. 466-511), a king of the Sicambrian Franks who created something approaching a unified Gaul at the point of his lance. Although this first Francia would be a heterogeneous kingdom, it would suffer from two major flaws that were principally Frankish in origin: the practice of partible inheritance among royal sons, which divided lands and encouraged disunion and often outright civil war, and the eventual usurpation of royal power by the chief executive officer of the king, the major domo, or "mayor of the palace." The former flaw acted as a check on Frankish expansion and the latter

eventually led to a change of dynasty from the ruling house of the Merovingians to that of the House of Charles, or Carolingians.

Although Clovis was named consul by the eastern emperor Anastasius (c. 430-518) after gaining control of most of Gaul, this title was imperiled upon his death in 511. Clovis's four sons each received an equal portion of his holdings and spent the next fifty years battling for his inheritance. No sooner had it all fallen into the hands of the surviving son, Chlotar I (c. 497-561), than he died, redividing the kingdom once again among his own four sons, who showed even less inclination toward cooperation than had the preceding generation. Gaul was torn by incessant civil war for yet another fifty years. With the execution of the matriarch queen Brunhilde in 613, Chlotar II (r. 613-629) introduced a brief period of effective Merovingian rule.

At this point, an office originally intended to relieve the kings of burdensome daily administrative duties began to encroach on royal prerogatives. The position of major domo had been created to oversee supplies and the smooth running of the royal estates. During the turbulent civil wars, the office came to be occupied by key magnates of the realm who could bring military power to the side of their king. By the mid-600's, the Merovingian kings had begun to place more military authority in the hands of the mayors.

By 687 the mayor Pépin of Herstal (r. 687-714) had defeated his rivals and solidified his rule over all Franks. Pépin's illegitimate son, Charles (688-741), later known as Charles Martel, or the Hammer, furthered the power of the position by seizing control in a palace coup in 714. The stage was now set for a contest between the king and the mayor for mastery of Francia. However, there was no contest. The later Merovingian kings, long characterized by French historians as *rois*

TURNING POINTS

482	Clovis I accedes to the Frankish throne.
507	Clovis defeats the Visigoths at Vouillé and unifies Gaul.
687	Pépin of Herstal solidifies Frankish rule.
714	Charles Martel seizes control over Frankish kingdom.
800	Charlemagne is crowned Holy Roman Emperor.
843	The Treaty of Verdun divides the Frankish Empire.
918	Feudalism disintegrates the Frankish Empire as Saxons and northern raiders infiltrate.

faineants, or "fainting kings," were unable, or unwilling, to contend seriously for power. By 752 Charles Martel's son, Pépin III (714-768), known as Pépin the Short, had sent the last Merovingian to a monastery and assumed the throne as the first Carolingian king with the blessing of the Pope.

This move inaugurated an efflorescence of Frankish power under Pépin and his legendary son, Charles (742-814), known as Charlemagne, or, literally, Charles the Great. During this period the Franks reassembled a large portion of the old Roman Empire—Gaul, Italy, and extreme northern Spain—and

CAROLINGIAN EMPIRE

conquered most of Germany as well. In 800 Pope
Leo III crowned Charlemagne as Holy Roman Emperor, reviving the concept of a Roman Empire and
solidifying the division between the Roman Empire
in the west and the Byzantine Empire in the east. By
the time of Charlemagne's grandsons, and the Treaty
of Verdun in 843, however, the issue of partible inheritance had once again divided the Frankish Empire
and diluted its power. This fact, coupled with the increasing pressure of Viking invasions, brought an end
to any dreams of unity as the newly emerging concept
of feudalism further subdivided the West.

MILITARY ACHIEVEMENT

The Frankish legacy is one of military conquest.
Clovis's accession to the Frankish throne in 482
came at a time in which there was no one overarching
military presence in northern Gaul. Therefore, with a
fairly small contingent of troops, Clovis was able, in
486, to conquer the Kingdom of Soissons, a sub-
Roman territorial remnant under the command of the
patrician Syagrius (c. 430-486), the last Roman governor in Gaul. By 491 Clovis had absorbed Paris and
campaigned victoriously against Thuringian settlements in eastern Gaul. The incursion of the Alemanni
into Frankish lands in 496 provided Clovis with opportunities for leadership over all the northern
Franks. He used this leverage to good effect with a
decisive victory that same year over the Alemanni at
Tolbiac, southwest of Cologne. Although Clovis's
subsequent conversion to Christianity somewhat
eroded his Frankish coalition, he was still able to intervene in Burgundy, come to terms with the Alan
laeti in Armorica, in present-day Brittany, and finally
secure his Rhineland borders. In 507 he moved on the
biggest prize: the Visigothic kingdom of southern
Gaul under Alaric II (r. 484-507). In the late spring
and early summer of 507, Clovis's forces crushed the
Visigoths at Vouillé, killing Alaric II and opening the
way for the conquest of the south. Clovis took most of
the key cities in the south and the Visigothic royal
treasury but could not take the province of Septi-
mania. He finished his career of expansion from 508
to 511 by incorporating holdout Frankish subgroups

in the north, notably at Cambrai and Cologne.

The sons of Clovis were mostly concerned with
one another's patrimony, but they did cooperate long
enough to effect the conquest of Burgundy in 534, at
the prompting of the queen mother, Clotilde, herself a
Burgundian princess. After the old queen died in 544,
the remaining brothers gave themselves over to inter-

*Charlemagne, crowned Holy Roman Emperor in
800, united the Frankish kingdoms and solidified the
division between the Roman Empire in the West and
the Byzantine Empire in the East.*

necine strife. Matters only worsened with the succession of the four sons of Chlotar in 561. Only an occasional raiding campaign into Lombard, Italy, broke the monotony of civil war.

After unity was restored under Chlotar II in 613, two major developments occupied the Frankish military: the extension of control into Austrasia, the territories east of the Rhine, and the growth of the positions of the major domos, or mayors of the palace. By the 660's, the mayors of Neustria (central France) and Austrasia were openly influencing the choice of Frankish kings. In 687 Pépin of Herstal, the Austrasian mayor, was able to defeat his Neustrian rival and proclaim one king with one mayor for all of Francia. As he passed this on to his son, Charles Martel, the Franks found themselves governed by the mayor much more than the king. This was the situation when the Saracens, under leader ʿAbd-ar-Raḥmān (died 732), encountered the Franks near Poitiers on October 25, 732. Charles Martel, the mayor, formed his men into a defensive infantry position, and the Muslim forces, mostly foot soldiers with some cavalry, broke on the Frankish shield wall.

In the ensuing years, as the Carolingians made their rule officially royal, Pépin the Short conquered central Italy for the Pope, the so-called Donation of Pépin of 756. Charlemagne subdued northern Italy in 774 and ultimately Saxony, at the end of a bitter decades-long campaign. Frankish military power had won a realm extending from the Spanish March to the Elbe River and from the plains of Hungary well into central Italy.

Throughout this period the Franks evolved from a fragmented Germanic tribe to become the single strongest military force in Europe. By incorporating into their fighting forces the strengths of the various peoples they conquered, the Franks became so powerful that the Pope, when threatened in the 750's with Lombard invasion and Byzantine control, intentionally sought an alliance with them. By the end of Charlemagne's reign in 814, the Franks were supreme on the continent. Only the old malaise of a divided empire and the new threat of recurrent Viking raids, which challenged even the most formidable military of the era, brought an end to Frankish power. After 918 the local military agreements collectively known as feudalism would fragment both the land and the military might of Francia, as it did most of Europe.

WEAPONS, UNIFORMS, AND ARMOR

The disparate nature of Frankish armies worked against any uniformity in their appearance. The concept of "personality of the law," wherein each man was judged by his ethnic background, had military applications as well. Whether Frank, Saxon, Sarmatian, Alan, Gallo-Roman, or from some group less well known, the individual soldier would be expected to wear into combat that which conformed to his own tastes, abilities, and national dress. Any uniformity in dress or equipment would have derived from a soldier's military function, such as cavalry, infantry, or siege operator. Even after Charlemagne's rule took on the characteristics of a centralized empire, the use of territorial levies precluded uniforms. Because there was no government issue of battle dress or equipment, there could be no uniformity assured.

Despite these variations, the typical infantryman in a Frankish army most likely carried a spear and a shield. The spear could be of two types; the *hasta*, or *lancea*, was a thrusting spear for close engagement, whereas the *angon* was a shorter, barbed throwing spear with an iron housing extending down from the head to encase almost the entire length of the weapon. The typical length of the lance was about 8 feet, although longer ones are known. The *angon*, generally no longer than 6 feet, also could be used for thrusting, but its long, narrow shaft made it more suited for throwing. The theory behind the *angon* was that once it impacted the enemy's shield, its weight could not be cast off due to its barbed head, thereby pulling down the shield. Battle descriptions also tell of Frankish warriors stepping on the trailing *angon* shafts in order to deprive their opponents of their shields. Should the *angon* penetrate the opponent's body, its barbed spearhead ensured maximum damage when removed. The *angon*'s long metal casing prevented the easy hacking away of the shaft and created quite a problem for the victim.

Frankish shields appear to have been round, or occasionally elliptical, and of 32 to 36 inches in diame-

DIVISION OF CHARLEMAGNE'S EMPIRE

West Frankish Kingdom
under Charles the Bald

Middle Frankish Kingdom
under Lothar I

East Frankish Kingdom
under Louis II, the German

ter. A metal stud in the center permitted the soldier to strike his opponent with a punching motion, giving the shield offensive as well as defensive possibilities. The shield was usually made of wood, rimmed with iron or, in lesser instances, wicker covered by hides.

Swords seem to have been fairly rare in the Frankish world, as they were throughout early medieval Europe. Those that did exist were of two types: the long sword and the *scramasax*. The long sword was a double-edged weapon of 30 to 36 inches in length. Because its center of gravity was somewhat closer to the tip of the blade, it was better suited for cutting rather than thrusting motions, which may explain why the long sword made the transition from foot to mounted combat. The short sword, or *scramasax*, a single-edged weapon, ranged in length from 8 inches to a more formidable 16 inches. Its obvious use was for close combat, and its lethal impact could be enhanced by the judicious use of poison in its blood-gutter groove.

A favorite weapon of the Frankish infantryman, particularly in the early years of the period, was the *francisca*. This small ax, with a 16-inch haft attached to its 7-inch single-edged head, weighed only about 2.5 pounds, making it suitable for both striking and throwing. When thrown, the *francisca* could have an effective range of up to 39 feet on three in-air rotations; sources mention the Franks engaging their opponents in this way. In hand-to-hand combat, the *francisca* also worked much like a heavy tomahawk or hatchet.

Although some sources claim that the Franks were without bows and arrows, evidence in Frankish graves indicates otherwise. Double-curved bows and arrowheads of more than 2.5 inches in length are suggested by the archaeology of the age. Frankish prelate and bishop Gregory of Tours (539-594), describing a particularly arrogant Frankish count, noted the count's habit of entering church with his quiver slung over his shoulder.

Body armor included the helmet, or *galea*, usually a variation on the simple iron cap, often without a nasal piece. The better-attired warriors would also have a *brunia*, or leather tunic covered in either ring-mail or mail of iron plates that overlapped like scales. Even as late as Charlemagne's day, the high cost of these pieces of equipment made them rare; the *brunia* itself could cost the equivalent of six cows in the early 800's. Consequently the vision of Frankish armies with little or no body armor has taken hold. The heterogeneous nature of the Frankish forces meant that some of their early armies contained elements of Roman *laeti,* who were frequently outfitted in mail. By the time of Charlemagne, the heavy cavalry, or *caballarii*, were protected by the *brunia*, whereas the *lantweri*, or general levy, would be less heavily armed.

MILITARY ORGANIZATION

Despite the general impression of early medieval warfare as undertaken by ignorant armies, the military organization of this period in Francia was quite complex. When Clovis began his career of conquest he assembled warbands of Frankish sub-kings, the armed retainers of Gallo-Roman magnates, descendants of Roman garrisons, armed colonists, or *laeti*, from late Imperial days, and barbarian allies. Each of these components could be expected to contribute their distinctive abilities. For example, the Alan *laeti* of Armorica were noted for their cavalry, the Gallo-Romans for their siegecraft, and the erstwhile Roman garrison personnel for their archery and missile weapons expertise. The end result would be an army capable of a combined-arms approach to war, as well as one that conceivably could be available nearly year-round. The army of the first great Merovingian king, Clovis I, bore a much greater resemblance to a late Roman force than to a barbarian, tribal army.

The major addition to this system, introduced in Francia during the time of Clovis's warring grandsons (c. 560-590), was the introduction of levies. Based on a double heritage of Frankish and Roman custom, each king could call out his populace in time of war. The Franks had held that all able-bodied men owed military service and had developed a procedure for bringing this into effect. It was called the *campus Martius*, which could mean either "field of Mars" or "Marchfield." It is assumed this was originally an early spring muster of all available fighting men, but the sources indicate that it eventually became a muster of combatants at any time of the year. Warriors were to bring their own equipment and supplies, because pillaging was restricted until the army reached enemy territory.

The Roman tradition was one of each landowning group supplying a man from their land to serve in the army. This was called *praebitio tironum*, and it meant that the Roman populace was accustomed to regularly furnishing troops to the government. Once again these soldiers were financed and thus equipped and provisioned by those satisfying the *praebitio*. The sixth century grandsons of Clovis simply accessed an old notion when they began calling up levies of troops for their incessant civil wars.

There were, however, distinctions among the levies, of which there appear to have been two types. Local levies, only affecting the *territorium* of certain cities, did not include the poor or those whose absence from farming or commerce would cause disruption to the flow of society. The city would make the determination as to who would be called up and who would be excused. General levies, on the other hand, were just that: a general call to arms of every able-bodied man. Even general levies were restricted to the areas under direct threat. The general levies, owing to the low level of military fitness among the troops, were not particularly helpful. As the Frankish presence expanded throughout Gaul and into Germany and Italy, so did the concept of local and general levies.

By late Carolingian times, the Franks had virtually re-created the old Roman *praebitio tironum*. Charlemagne's edict of 806 required men of a certain level of landholding to fight and those of lesser landholdings to pool their responsibility with others to share in the provision of a warrior. A man whose small landholding was not enough for him to serve personally, but who joined with others to furnish a warrior and supplies, was said to have done his military service. All this could be seen to offer great numerical potential for Frankish armies. Yet out of a possible thirty-five thousand horsemen and some hundred thousand foot soldiers available to Charlemagne, his usual victorious army numbered from fifteen to twenty thousand, at the most. Given the shrunken state of early medieval armies, however, this was more than enough to dominate.

DOCTRINE, STRATEGY, AND TACTICS

The issue of doctrine, strategy, and tactics to a large degree revolves around the question of how "Roman" or how "barbarian" armies in Frankish Gaul were. Once again the heterogeneous nature of Frankish forces provides a clue to the mixed viewpoints of Frankish commanders and their armies. Much of the military action in the period from 482 to 918 appears

reactive and circumstantial, and thus more "barbarian," as if devised to conform to events rather than some far-sighted, state-driven strategic plan. Clovis, for example, is said to have invaded the Visigothic south because he felt angry that the Arian Visigoths should occupy an Orthodox land.

Despite this alleged barbarianism, there are certain strategic considerations that can be seen in the Frankish campaigns. Clovis seems to have intentionally sought territorial expansion and executed a systematic campaign of besieging cities after his decisive victory in the open field at Vouille. His sons and grandsons, however, appear to have begun and finished campaigns with little more than a grand raiding objective in mind. It would not be until the era of Pépin the Short and Charlemagne that the Franks would reattain a strategic view of conquest and the reduction of rebellious peoples. With that as their objective, the Franks invested their energies in the capture of key cities, using a type of scorched-earth policy to deny the strongholds their subsistence.

The Franks seem to have been somewhat deficient in siege warfare, at least until they incorporated into their empire those who had inherited knowledge of Roman siegecraft. Generally the Franks took fortified strongholds by deceit, which required abilities of a different sort. Although there is scant mention in source literature of them doing so, Franks do appear to have been able to construct many types of siege engines. They were, however, capable of circumvallation—building walls to deny the besieged city any outside contact. Frankish supply trains consisted of large wagons and carts, called *basternae*. So thorough could be the Frankish investment that the Avars, having fortified their strongholds for a 791 Frankish cavalry attack, simply gave up when they saw Charlemagne's approaching army with all its supplies in tow.

Frankish battle tactics included the basic barbarian charge, called the "wedge," which, in formation, was sometimes likened to the blunt snout of a wild boar, an animal generally revered by the Germans for its ferocity. As the charge was made, the Franks would let their *franciscas* and *angons* fly and would generally count on breaking the enemy's resolve in one rush. With the incorporation of other peoples and tactics in their armies, the Franks also supplemented thier cavalry with Alans, a warlike people from the steppes northeast of the Black Sea. With their practiced wheeling maneuvers, the Alani rendered the Frankish army a more diversified and dangerous fighting force. When faced with a stronger foe, the Franks would form a shield wall with their infantry and allow the enemy to beat itself into submission on it.

Toward the end of the Frankish period, as cavalry grew in prominence, the Carolingian armies were still dominated primarily by infantry. Even the advent of the stirrup did not give the horseman the leverage he would have two centuries later when the cantle enabled him to deliver a lance blow without being driven over the rump of his mount. Lances were used, as were the long swords, by the Carolingian cavalry in a downward thrusting manner.

MEDIEVAL SOURCES

Although sources are not lacking for the period from 482 to 918, many are flawed as reliable sources of information. A common problem is brevity; for example, the Viking invasions are frequently dismissed with a terse "this year the heathen ravaged." There is also a fundamental problem of worldview. The sources of the early medieval period more frequently recount facts than convey causation. They describe what happened, but not why. Despite an abundance of detail about an event, the lack of analysis often hinders a holistic understanding of the event. Information about weapons, tactics, and military matters must be gleaned from chance comments offhandedly dropped into narratives. It is revealed, for example, that as Count Leudast strode into church, he wore a mail shirt, had a bow and arrow, a javelin, and a cuirass, but his sword is mentioned only when, much later in the story, he is called to defend himself. When descriptions are offered, they can be maddeningly vague.

Nevertheless, the sources available for interpretation do include some gems of western historiography. They begin with Gregory of Tours' (539-594) *Historia Francorum* (c. 594; *The History of the Franks*, 1927), which covers the history of the Franks to 591. A work that provides an overlapping but slightly different view is the *Liber Historiae Francorum* (1973), translated by Bernard S. Bachrach from an earlier Latin text, as well as *The Fourth Book of the Chronicle of Fredegar* (1960), translated by J. M. Wallace-Hadrill, both of which take the Frankish saga up to the time of the Carolingians. A Lombard viewpoint covering many of the same events is offered by Paul the Deacon's (c. 720-c. 799) *Historia Langobardorum* (c. 786; *History of the Lombards*). Eastern views on Frankish warfare are available in small doses in the works of the Byzantine historians Agathias (c. 536-c. 582), whose work is contained in Averil Cameron's *Agathias* (1970), and Procopius of Caesarea's (between 490 and 507 and after 562) *Polemon* (c. 551; *History of the Wars*, 1960).

A Byzantine view on the Carolingian military is found in the *Tactica* of the emperor Leo VI (866-912), once again not translated into English. The greatest of the Carolingian personalities, the Holy Roman Emperor Charlemagne, is described in Einhard's *Life of Charlemagne*, translated by Sidney Painter. Because Einhard served in Charlemagne's court, he presumably had firsthand knowledge of his subject's governance.

A vast and disparate field of supplemental study is that of the lives of the various saints from the period. Once again, it is the accidental rather than the intentional inclusion of material that repays the search.

BOOKS AND ARTICLES

Bachrach, Bernard S. *Armies and Politics in the Early Medieval West.* Brookfield, Vt.: Ashgate, 1993.

_____. *Merovingian Military Organization, 481-751.* Minneapolis: University of Minnesota Press, 1972.

Contamine, Philippe. *War in the Middle Ages.* Translated by Michael Jones. Oxford, England: Basil Blackwell, 1984.

Elton, Hugh. *Warfare in Roman Europe,* A.D. *350-425.* Oxford, England: Oxford University Press, 1996.

Burnam W. Reynolds

ARMIES OF CHRISTENDOM AND THE AGE OF CHIVALRY

DATES: C. 918-1500 C.E.

POLITICAL CONSIDERATIONS

Most historians agree that warfare in the Middle Ages cannot be studied in isolation. By its very definition, war—organized violence by groups against other groups—reflects the societies involved and, in turn, shapes them. This dynamic was especially true in the high medieval period, when military needs fueled administrative developments in finance, organization, recruitment, supply, and the tools of government itself. Before then, however, the very deterioration of such structures would limit the forms that warfare could take. Larger cultural issues would likewise play off of, and be played upon, by war. The Christian Church spent centuries trying to restrain or redirect the violence of its newest converts, the Germanic peoples. In time, however, the Church would find itself inextricably entangled in violent endeavors. On the secular side, the cult of chivalry developed first as the expression of a new, knightly identity; once in place, this new ethos sometimes had its own power to shape the contours of battle.

Although scholarly ideas about its dominance and character are undergoing continual revision, the network of feudal relations that lay across most of Europe in this period was the hallmark of medieval politics and war. In summary, these arrangements were coming into being even during the reign of Charlemagne (r. 768-814), but their evolution was speeded by the breakup of his empire and of effective central government, coupled with foreign invasions by Vikings and Magyars. By the end of the first millennium, the Western European population's overwhelming need for protection had caused feudalism to be cobbled together in varying ways across the former Carolingian lands. The typical model of feudalism appeared thus: Men in need (vassals) would ap-

proach someone (a lord) capable of protecting them because of his already collected followers. In officially entering this lord's entourage, the vassals would swear faithfulness or fealty to that lord. The price of protection for the vassal was his own service in the lord's retinue, or mesne, as it was later called. Other obligations later became standard, but military service was the original and fundamental one. These early vassals depended on the lord for upkeep, and in the absence of a money economy, the institution of the fief evolved. Usually in the form of land, the fief provided the economic component of feudal relationships; with it, the vassal had the wherewithal to report with all the panoply of war: horse, armor, weapons, and supplies for campaign.

Military historians have recognized for some time that feudalism did not accurately describe all the means whereby medieval armies came together. The idea of the "nation-at-arms" still compelled many to answer a summons. This was as true of the Anglo-Saxon *fyrd* before 1066 as it would be 150 years later when King John (1166-1216) of England summoned even the most recently liberated serfs to repel French invaders. On the continent, King Louis VI (1081-1137) in 1124 gathered more of his vassals together to face a German attack than he had ever commanded as a feudal lord. In addition, money was never truly absent; its role in recruiting and maintaining armies continued throughout the High Middle Ages. Thus, military historians see less incongruity than do legal historians in the use and prevalence of contracts to engage soldiers in the late medieval period.

It would be difficult to overstate the reciprocal influences on each other of the Church and medieval warfare. At first, though, the Church saw little success in its efforts to curtail the violence of its members. Before the year 1000, it had already proposed the idea of the Truce of God. The Truce endeavored to set certain days aside as inappropriate for any violence: Days of religious significance obviously dominated this agenda, thereby "officially" making large parts of the yearly calendar off-limits for warfare. The Peace of God quickly followed, which insisted that certain groups, primarily the unarmed populace such as clergy, women, children, and peasants, were also off-limits. Although both movements had limited success, constant appeals indicate how often they were violated by combatants. Such calls on the conscience of medieval warriors went unheard for the most part, but the many gifts to the church by soldiers testify to the soldiers' uneasiness about their profession.

When Pope Urban II (c. 1042-1099) preached in 1095 that Europe's knights could actually earn redemption instead of condemnation by going on armed pilgrimage to Jerusalem, he struck a more responsive chord than he had anticipated. The success of the First Crusade (1095-1099) guaranteed that generations of Europe's knights would "take up the cross" both as penance for their violent misdeeds and as a novel continuance of their profession. The Church would rail against Christians who killed Christians in wars, including even those simulations of war, tournaments, which were condemned in numerous councils. Against infidels and heretics, however, warfare was deemed more than licit; it was divinely approved. As the later Crusades not only failed to achieve similar success but also went terribly awry, as did the Fourth Crusade (1198-1204) at Constantinople, the Church found its military involvement more problematic. The Church got further involved in the development of the knightly caste, as it sanctioned some of the trappings of chivalry. The vigils that preceded formal dubbing ceremonies as well as the oaths taken by new knights seemed to confirm that the Church had indeed domesticated its most troublesome sons. Such an appearance was deceptive, though, because chivalry always remained more a secular creation than an ecclesiastical one.

In fact it ought to be remembered that chivalry was the province not only of a secular group but also of a knightly caste that was not alone on Christendom's battlefields. In the early 1100's writers such as Or-

dericus Vitalis (1075-c. 1142) remarked that the absence of fatalities among knights came from a mutual Christian desire to hold violence in check. This idea of brotherhood among foes continued throughout the Middle Ages. The national orders of chivalry of the fourteenth and fifteenth centuries regularly welcomed foreign members who displayed the requisite chivalric virtues. Although chivalry might restrain lethal tendencies among knights, however, it hardly mattered when aristocratic warriors met their social inferiors. With ransoms or honor rarely at stake, this combat was far more vicious and far more deadly.

MILITARY ACHIEVEMENT

The conviction that the Middle Ages was above all the Age of Cavalry is primarily a legacy of the great military historians of the nineteenth and early twentieth centuries. For them, this was the military contribution, and a questionable one at that, of the Middle Ages to history. The British historian Sir Charles Oman (1860-1946) wrote of the "complete superiority of heavy cavalry" and drew a compelling picture of the massed charge of horsemen with their couched lances. Although this image continues to be propagated in film and general histories, even very good ones, military historians have revised their view of the role of heavy cavalry to one of more limited importance. Some suggested that the end of cavalry's dominance originally seemed to lie in the successes of the Swiss pikemen of the 1300's. Others focused on the Hundred Years' War (1337-1453), in which the longbow supposedly played the more decisive role. This interpretation, however, has since evolved to place more emphasis on the combined use of forces by the English to cripple the French charge. Other historians credit the Flemish infantry, who withstood the French in the opening years of the 1300's. The motion picture *Braveheart* (1995), even though it transposed the actions of Bannockburn (1314) and Stirling Bridge (1297), validated, with some dramatic license, those who credit the Scots with teaching the English the value of foot soldiers. Historians of the Angevins and Anglo-Normans have demonstrated the pivotal role of infantry, or dismounted knights, at multiple battles. Although the mounted knight was a hallmark of the Middle Ages, he was not the period's definitive warrior.

As a result of this improved understanding of medieval combat, a better appreciation of the military achievement of the Middle Ages is possible. Rather than seeing an epoch of heedless courage and pell-mell charges that appear as an endless cycle of fruitless violence, late-twentieth century historians have come to appreciate the sophisticated answers of medieval commanders to problems that were peculiarly their own. At first, the emphasis on cavalry grew

MAJOR SITES IN THE HUNDRED YEARS' WAR, 1337-1453

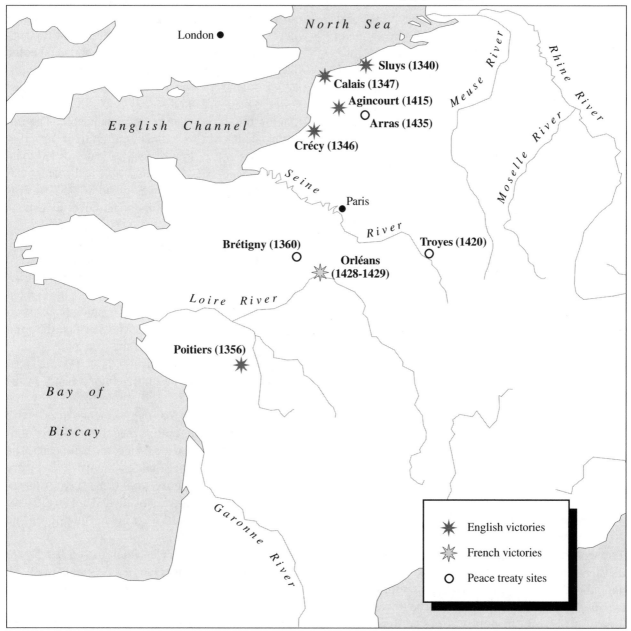

quickly because of the need to counter the mobility of Viking, Magyar, and Muslim raiders. Other military issues came into play, however, as the new feudal blocs began to compete with each other. This competition drove innovation: in tactics, weaponry, fortification, and behind the lines, in the very creation and provisioning of armies. The crucible of invasions and internal fighting honed the overall military practice of Christendom so that it was able for centuries after 1095 to field armies far away in the Middle East. The experiences of Crusader forces sharpened European armies, as veterans returned with an appreciation of the successes to be gained by discipline and practice. Although Europe would effectively give up crusading after 1291, other conflicts, especially the Hundred Years' War, would further the development of military establishments. Amending the thesis of historian Geoffrey Parker on a "military revolution" in the early modern period, medievalists have traced the outlines for earlier changes that might account for Europe's later military preeminence.

The Saxon Dynasty came to power in 918 in the Germanic territories of Charlemagne's former empire. Reviving not only Charlemagne's imperial title but even some of his political and military power, this dynasty managed to withstand the double threats to any medieval government: internal factiousness and external invaders. The victory of Otto the Great (912-973) at the Battle of the Lechfeld (955) confirmed their success. By the end of the medieval period—a date open to much dispute—an entirely different military and political situation prevailed. The nation-state was replacing the feudal system, permanent armies appeared by the 1470's, and Charles VIII's (r. 1483-1498) invasion of Italy in 1494 showed that old styles of warfare no longer applied against national armies wielding powerful gunpowder weapons.

WEAPONS, UNIFORMS, AND ARMOR

Two weapons especially dominated the personal medieval arsenal: the sword and the spear. The latter was undoubtedly the most popular weapon employed, but the former was the most prized. The expense and time involved in the manufacture of swords restricted their availability and thus contributed to their importance as status symbols. Not surprisingly, those who could afford a mount also owned swords, and the sword became associated with cavalry and medieval society's elite. The long sword tended to be between 75 and 100 centimeters in length with a blade of up to 6 centimeters in width, double-edged, and counterweighted by an enlarged pommel behind the hilt. A fuller, or groove, ran much of the length of the blade's center, removing some of the weapon's weight without sacrificing any strength; the result was a sword that averaged 1.5 kilograms in weight. Some time before the tenth century, blacksmiths began to taper the blade so that it began a gradual narrowing immediately from the cross-guard. This development helped shift the blade's center of gravity closer to the hand, making the sword even more manageable. The importance attached to swords ensured their preservation across generations of owners and thus led to an increasing number of them available in the later Middle Ages. At one muster in England in 1457, swords were second only to bows in the number of weapons brought.

The innovations in gunpowder and armor in the later medieval period caused rapid changes in sword design. As the transition from chain mail to plate armor became more widespread after 1350, the emphasis in sword design moved from slashing to perforating. Blades grew shorter and stiffer, because the point was now the offensive part of the weapon.

For both infantry and cavalry, however, the spear was the weapon that lay most often at hand. In the wake of some efforts at standardization by the Carolingians, spears for both branches averaged 2 meters in length, but both archaeology and contemporary art evidence a wide variety of spearheads. The basic similarity testifies that for infantry and cavalry alike it was a thrusting weapon. If the Bayeux tapestry's representation is true-to-life and not an effect of the weaving, spear shafts were rather flimsy even late in the eleventh century.

The medieval cavalry's switch to sturdier lances came with its implementation of "mounted shock combat." This form of attack is the archetypal view of medieval combat: The horse-borne warrior, lance couched under his armpit, charges his enemy. The combined weight of the knight and his horse are thus concentrated in the irresistible point of the lance. At least, contemporaries saw it this way. Byzantine princess and historian Anna Comnena (1083-c. 1148) suspected that the walls of Babylon would not withstand a charge by the Frankish Crusaders she witnessed passing through Constantinople in 1095. Popular poems such as the French epic *Le Chanson de Roland* (eleventh century; *The Song of Roland*, c. 1100) painted a far more graphic, if exaggerated, picture, making reference to a knight charging his foe, cutting through his bones, and tearing the whole spine from his back.

The necessary prerequisite to such mounted combat is the stirrup, which holds the rider on his horse, and this small piece of equipment has created quite an industry among scholars trying to date its first appearance in Europe. The old assumption that mounted shock dominated the entire medieval period was unseated in 1951 when D. J. A. Ross contended that references to such assaults came no earlier than the late eleventh century *chansons de geste* such as that of Roland. Lynn Townsend White, Jr., challenged this argument a decade later when he tried to date the stirrup (and shock combat) as early as the 700's. A bevy of historians, among them Bernard R. Bachrach and David Charles Nicolle, arose to counter White's assertion, and, on the whole, their arguments have focused on the early twelfth century as the moment when mounted shock combat became the primary cavalry tactic of Christendom. To date, their contentions have carried the field.

Infantry weapons, such as the spear, remained mostly unchanged until the late medieval period. However, there were experimental modifications. King Philip II (1165-1223) of France and his retinue at Bouvines (1214) faced mercenary foot soldiers who endeavored to pull the king and his knights from their horses with hooked spears that caught their chain mail links. Unhorsed, the knights were threatened by the soldiers' daggers, which could reach unarmored areas, such as the groin or armpit. In the 1300's and 1400's the Flemish and Swiss levies began utilizing pikes in regular formations that achieved repeated victories against cavalry. Other alterations of the spear resulted from combinations:

spear and ax became the halberd; the billhook had a curved blade on the side of a lance.

There was no shortage of other handheld weapons. The Vikings often used axes in battle, as did the Anglo-Saxons. The Bayeux tapestry may show one of the earliest representations of a mace, which had by the twelfth century become a popular weapon in tournament melees and on the battlefield. The dagger, like the sword, evolved in form to whatever shape was most effective at penetrating the weak points of armor.

Armies of the High Middle Ages understood the value of missile weapons and relied upon a variety of them. Slings were still used as late as the thirteenth century, especially in the form of staff slings, which propelled the missile more forcefully. For the early part of the period, short bows and composite, or Turkish, bows predominated. The latter were adopted by Christians from their Muslim foes, particularly in Spain, where the Christians even went so far as to emulate Muslims in the use of horse archers. In the Crusader kingdoms, warriors turned to native horse archers willing to fight for their new masters. The composite bow was less popular to the northwest, perhaps because the wetter climate affected the glue that held the bows together. Short bows were used by the Normans, including William the Conqueror (c. 1027-1087), who saw no dishonor in personally using the weapon. William took a great many archers with him to England, where they proved their worth by the attrition they caused in the formations of Harold II (c. 1022-1066).

The best-known bow of the Middle Ages is the Welsh longbow. Averaging 1.8 meter in length, with an exterior strip of sapwood and an interior strip of heartwood to increase its spring, the longbow was able to propel "cloth-yard shafts" from 365 to 400 meters. At 200 meters, the longbow's arrows could penetrate chain mail. After facing this formidable weapon in the thirteenth century, the English reacted by recruiting large numbers of Welshmen proficient with the bow to serve in their continental armies. The longbow had its heyday during the Hundred Years' War, playing a large role in British victories at the Battles of Crécy (1346), Poitiers (1356), and Agincourt (1415). However, the longbow was one weapon among several that the English used wisely in conjunction with others to assure victory. The longbow's use continued with English armies until the fifteenth century, when the government simply found itself unable to ensure that there were enough bows, arrows, and archers to fill the usual complements.

The counterpart of the longbow was the crossbow, which was known throughout the period but grew in usage as siege warfare became a larger component of campaigning. From that function, it developed also into a weapon of field armies. Its potential for lethality resulted in official bans of its use by the Church in the late eleventh century and 1139. The repeated bans also testify to the fact that medieval soldiers did not give up such a weapon easily. After 1200, the Church finally approved the crossbow's use against non-Christians. Nonetheless, Christians often used it against other Christians. English king Richard I (1157-1199) was so fond of using crossbows that he was erroneously credited with introducing the weapons to the French. Experimenters improved the bow across the Middle Ages, constantly increasing its power and range while attempting to decrease the time necessary for reloading. The original wooden bow and stock became a composite bow by the 1200's and would be made entirely of steel by the 1400's. Stirrups, ratchets, and levers were all added to ease the task of drawing the bow's string back to the trigger. Load times varied between 12 and 35 seconds, but the tremendous power was sufficient to puncture even the plate armor of the later Middle Ages. The advantages of the crossbow, power combined with a low level of training necessary for accuracy, would be the same ingredients that in the later fifteenth century would enable the gun to displace the crossbow on the battlefield.

Apart from personal weapons, successful armies also employed a siege train, a collection of raw materials, prefabricated weapons, and personnel who could build and operate such pregunpowder artillery. The importance of such weapons is reflected in the complaint that the so-called artists of war, knights, had been replaced by the new specialists: engineers, miners, crossbowmen, and artillerists.

The siege weapons handled by the new specialists worked by one of three means. The onager was a sur-

A fourteenth century English knight. In the late Middle Ages the cult of chivalry developed as the expression of a new, knightly identity, an ethos that sometimes shaped the contours of battle.

vivor from antiquity in which a single beam, inserted through a horizontal braid of animal tendons or hair, was pulled back into firing position. This torsion weapon was less powerful than its classical predecessors and was immensely heavy; one reconstruction weighed nearly 2 tons. The ballista of the Romans was probably a two-armed torsion weapon, but the term referred in the Middle Ages to a tension weapon that was essentially an oversized crossbow on a stable platform. Lever machines were the third variety of pregunpowder artillery. The use of lever artillery originated in China and spread via Byzantium and the Islamic lands. Lever artillery relied on either traction power or a counterweight. In the former case, a crowd of operators hauled downward on ropes attached to one end of the lever-arm, causing it to swing on a pivot and release its projectile in a high arc. This was the *petraria*, or stone-thrower. The trebuchet was the pregunpowder giant; it replaced the human hauler with a fixed counterweight that allowed truly impressive weights to be launched. Projectiles typically weighed between 50 and 75 kilograms, with a range of approximately 200 meters.

Given the impressive arsenal that both the well-to-do knights and common soldiers carried into battle, there is little wonder that medieval combatants also invested in sophisticated personal armor. The simplest, most efficient form of armor remained the shield, in use since ancient times. In the tenth century, the shield was still evolving, from a round shape to that of an elongated kite. The new shape better protected the legs of horsemen without adding too much weight. In addition, infantry could jam the shield's lower point into the ground for more stability when creating the formation called a "shield-wall." Although the shield would later be shortened, this triangular shape remained standard until the best plate armor made shields themselves redundant.

Armor itself underwent several changes throughout the medieval period. The primary body armor before 900 had been a leather jacket with metal scales attached. By the eleventh century this form of armor had grown more complex; the Bayeux tapestry shows coats of chain mail on most of the Normans. Made up of thousands of interlocked rings, this hauberk was probably worn over a padded undergarment both to prevent chafing and to soften opponents' blows should some of the links be broken and forced inward. This form of armor, with continued improvements, would dominate Europe and the Crusader kingdoms for several centuries. Extra pieces of mail would be added for the lower legs, the back of the neck, the lower face, feet, and hands. The helmet evolved from a conical shape with only a nasal guard to the "great helm," an enveloping, metal defense for the entire head. As missile weaponry evolved, plate armor became widely adopted. Steel, which had been tested especially against crossbows, began to be combined with chain mail and later replaced it. Eventually, knights would wear form-fitting plates that covered not only all major parts of the body but also protected complex joint areas such as the knees, elbows, and even fingers. Apart from such armor's protective benefits, its gleaming qualities also appealed to those who could afford it.

Because medieval warriors were usually responsible for outfitting themselves, there would be little use of standardized uniforms until the late Middle Ages, when powerful rulers and some cities would either provide or require them. Before that point, the emphasis fell more on individual insignia and costume. Although the Bayeux tapestry shows some painted shields, the earliest evidence for heraldic decoration comes from the reign of Stephen, king of England, also known as Stephen of Blois (r. 1135-1154). During his day, the Clare family began consistently to display its gold and red bands, and Geoffrey of Anjou (Geoffrey Plantagenet, 1113-1151) his two lions, which would in changed form become the English royal insignia. Although the participants in the Third Crusade (1187-1192) would adopt national identifiers such as differently colored crosses for the French, English, and Flemish, the real shift from personal to corporate designations came later. Wealthy cities such as Tournai were outfitting contingents in uniform livery in 1297 and again in 1340. Men from Wales and the adjoining marches wore green and white costumes and hats when serving on the Continent in the mid-1300's. As revenues increased, princes also began to outfit notable units within their forces; thus, French kings Charles VII (1403-1461) and Louis XI (1423-1483) contributed to the distinctiveness of their Scots Archers in the fifteenth century. The dukes of Burgundy would do likewise before their finances and power failed.

A turning point in medieval warfare came with the widespread adoption of gunpowder weapons. The first known recipe in Europe for gunpowder comes from 1267 in the works of Roger Bacon (c. 1220-c. 1292), more than two centuries after its first mention in Chinese texts. Within sixty years the first evidence for cannons appears in the illustrated margins of medieval texts, followed by their confirmed use at Puy-Guillaume (1338) and then against Lille (1341). Within twenty years, evidence of gunpowder artillery spread from Italy to Scandinavia and from Russia to England. The most dramatic example of the new technology was the bombard. With a weight of around 16,000 kilograms and firing balls of 380 kilograms, the largest of these giants could breach almost any wall with only several well-placed shots. On the battlefield, however, the effect of early cannons was more limited. They may have been used at Crécy in 1346 merely for the shock effect of the noise they made. The adoption by the early 1400's of smaller calibers made cannons more accurate, and a roll call of distinguished victims began.

Even though the overall battlefield effect of cannons remained negligible, the sudden vulnerability of elite warriors, the quick obsolescence of old defenses, and the new demands on military budgets spelled the end of chivalric warfare.

MILITARY ORGANIZATION

Medieval warfare, at its most proficient practice, was a sophisticated affair, marked by careful preparations, skillful analysis of risk and reward, and the use of multiple branches of service. This thesis, however, has been only recently accepted by a wide audience holding a more traditional image of feudal armies as violent mobs. The historian Oman claimed in 1885 that medieval troops were neither disciplined nor unified, and this idea has been long held. The conviction that chivalric ideals were "inimical" to battlefield discipline and organization appeared repeatedly in encyclopedia articles and surveys of military history

throughout the twentieth century. It was supposed that knights, ever desirous of increasing their personal glory, turned battles into giant melees of individual combats. However, closer attention to the original sources by recent scholars has shown otherwise.

Well before battle got under way, medieval knights reported to a muster less as individuals than as members of a group. At the very least, they came as part of a lord's retinue, following his banner and perhaps wearing colors or insignia indicating their corporate identity. By the 1300's, even individual knights typically reported with a coterie of aides. In fourteenth century France this group, often called a lance, consisted of two men; in the 1400's the standard composition was three. These units could then be organized as necessary into larger units called by multiple terms: banners, *conrois*, *échelles*, *batailles*, or battles. Such units were then spread in compact ranks across the perceived battlefield. The widespread use of these terms across Europe and in all vernaculars indicates such tactical units had a long history in medieval warfare.

Vernacular literature also reveals that these units stayed together compactly in battle rather than being dispersed enough to allow the individual combats supposedly characteristic of war in the Middle Ages. The *chansons de geste* (literally "songs of war") repeatedly describe the ranks of armies as being drawn up so tightly that objects thrown amid them would not have reached the ground. Latin prelate William of Tyre (c. 1130-1185) provides a particularly instructive example, describing a Crusade in 1180 to relieve the fortress of Darum. Partly out of fear and partly from lack of training, the crusading knights crowded so compactly together that their ability to launch an attack was hampered. Nonetheless, this dense group forced its way through the Muslim lines with steady pressure, rather than a dramatic charge. Their success was a testament more to their organization and discipline than to their reckless courage.

DOCTRINE, STRATEGY, AND TACTICS

A legacy of late nineteenth century medieval studies has been an appreciation of the quality of medieval military strategy and tactics. Until that time, medieval historians had been heirs to the military tradition of the decisive battle. Such historians often had been frustrated by the study of medieval military efforts, because they saw a quite random pattern of violence marking medieval campaigns. The historians could not find the decisive, battlefield resolution that they assumed was the natural goal of any expedition. The repetitive medieval cycle of raid and counterraid appeared only as senseless violence. The appearance was only made worse by the fact that medieval commanders had, in the fifth century Roman military theorist Flavius Vegetius Renatus's treatise *De Re Militari* (between 383 and 450 C.E.; *The Fovre Bookes of Flauius Vegetius Renatus: Briefelye Contayninge a Plaine Forme and Perfect Knowledge of Martiall Policye, Feates of Chiualrie, and Vvhatsoeuuer Pertayneth to Warre*, 1572; also translated as *Military Institutions of Vegetius*, 1767), a reputable guide to the tactics and strategy of late fourth century Rome. Numerous copies of this work in both Latin and native dialects survive as evidence of its popularity. There is also narrative evidence that commanders such as Geoffrey of Anjou consulted Vegetius's work for instruction on building incendiary devices. At the end of the Middle Ages, the dukes of Burgundy turned to Vegetius for counsel in building new siegeworks. Although the actual influence of Vegetius has been questioned, his work nonetheless served to introduce generations of medieval leaders to larger strategic issues.

One thing that medieval commanders understood quite well on their own was the utter uncertainty of battle. It was to be avoided not from fear, but from a sound recognition that far better means lay at hand to force an opponent to the bargaining table. The Latin kings of Jerusalem avoided battle as a policy, because the price of failure would be too high. In 1187 Guy de Lusignan (1129-1194) gambled at Hattin, and Saladin's (1138-1193) resulting victory left the rest of the kingdom incapable of defense. The destruction that attended so many raids was actually part of the medieval "science of war." Far more than daredevil heroes or wanton destroyers of countryside, good commanders such as William the Conqueror and Richard I conducted strategic raids that had the cumulative effect of enfeebling the opponent at the least

risk to one's own army. Richard's case is all the more dramatic; in nearly thirty years of campaigning, he fought only one pitched battle by his own choice.

There were, of course, times to seek battle, as evidenced by William the Conqueror at Hastings (1066), Frederick II (1194-1250) at Cortenuova (1237), and the French in the great battles of the Hundred Years' War. Each demonstrates a different aspect of strategy. The French doubtless felt they had met Vegetius's criteria for offering battle; they had superiority of numbers, and the foe was in pitiful condition. Their defeats at Crécy, Poitiers, and Agincourt served to reinforce the lesson of fickle fortune. Frederick II gambled in 1237 by dividing his forces, but he did so as a ruse; by convincing the Milanese that he was retiring for the winter, he engineered a devastating ambush. Under different conditions William worked to provoke Harold to battle in 1066, primarily because he could not hope to hold his invasion force together indefinitely. Many other battles, however, occurred in more accidental fashion; even though a clash was intended, Bouvines took place on a Sunday in 1214 because Otto IV's forces overtook those of Philip II more quickly than was expected.

Although anything might transpire when battle did occur, a few themes appear amid the varied actualities. Although many other elements of medieval warfare are often emphasized, knights and their potential charge remained the central concern in battles. The actual, successful delivery of such a charge as both initiation and conclusion of a battle seems to have been a rare occurrence. Of more concern were the reserve or flanking units of cavalry, which many commanders kept ready. This very disposition belies the contention of some scholars that once battle was joined, the possibility of giving orders disappeared in the chaos. The prebattle arrangement of forces varied over the years. From the eleventh through early thirteenth centuries, commanders formed several long shallow lines composed mostly of infantry but often augmented by dismounted knights. Its primary role was to withstand the opponent's charge. In protected positions, or even in front of this first line at the very start, archers would add their missile fire so as to disrupt the enemy assault. Variations on this line would appear. The Knights Templars had a "crown" formation they adopted for defense; the Flemings at Bouvines and the Scots a century later at Bannockburn withstood charges in circular formations. As the Flemings and later the Swiss fielded large numbers of infantry in the 1300's, they utilized massive arrangements of squares and wedges with no real center. Where the defending force was not wholly composed of infantry, the concern was to break the foe's charge or at least engage it until a counterattack came from reserve or flanking units. Once a formation broke, the pursuit naturally involved the mounted units; even here, the pursuers had to take care they were not being drawn out of their formation and into an ambush by a feigned retreat. In all cases, the charging knights constituted a minority on the battlefield but remained uppermost in the minds of leaders and combatants.

MEDIEVAL SOURCES

In the area of military affairs, and most especially combat, medieval sources present a number of intersecting problems. The authoritative writers of the age were churchmen, men unlikely to have witnessed combat, particularly if they were monks. Some, such as William of Tyre or Ordericus Vitalis, are noteworthy for having obviously sifted through their informants' accounts to give posterity as full and accurate a narrative as possible. However, the details of battle often did not concern such writers; they were more interested in the miraculous than the human aspects of battle. Thus they told more of the saints who appeared in the melee than of the actual tactics employed. Moreover, because the lesson to be drawn from a military event was far more important, ecclesiastical writers tended to treat numbers with some license. Medium-sized hosts numbered 300 so often as to defy belief, whereas truly large armies appear in multiples of 100,000, numbers quite beyond the administrative capabilities of any medieval government. Further complications arose when clerics adapted terms from antiquity to refer to peculiarly medieval items.

Such problems can be occasionally resolved, however, by relying also on secular, typically vernacular sources. The documents written for the military elite help us by using more precise language. Even the fanciful world of the *chansons de geste* can be instructive if carefully culled. Such songs had a practiced, knightly audience in mind who would have little appreciated an inaccurate picture of the realities of battle, apart from the superhuman accomplishments of the heroes. The *Histoire de Guillaume le Maréchal* (c. 1225; the story of Guillaume le Maréchal) often reads like the *chansons* but rather is a biography that has been found correct in many questionable details. Many of the poem's events were clearly witnessed in person. Firsthand accounts include those of Ambroise d'Évreux (fl. c. 1190), who was at Arsuf with Richard I; Jean (or John) de Joinville (c. 1224-1317), who was at Mansurah; and Jean le Bel (c. 1224-1317), who was in Scotland. These sources provide details on tactics, strategy, and weaponry, as well as a picture of the actual experience of the medieval warrior in combat. There were moments of both fear and courage.

Finally, there is the pictorial record. The Bayeux tapestry is a uniquely rich source. Numerous medieval manuscripts, even many that do not deal specifically with military topics, abound with decorated letter forms and illustrations of combat in the margins. Awareness of the dates of such manuscripts allows scholars to refine theories on the use of certain weapons and armor. Similarly, the carvings in churches and monasteries reveal much about medieval armaments. The seals of many feudal lords are also instructive, although only for the weapons of the elite. Where details of armaments can be discerned in these smaller figures, though, the dating is quite precise.

BOOKS AND ARTICLES

Contamine, Philippe. *War in the Middle Ages*. Translated by Michael Jones. Oxford, England: Basil Blackwell, 1984.

DeVries, Kelly. *Medieval Military Technology*. Lewiston, N.Y.: Broadview Press, 1992.

France, John. *Western Warfare in the Age of the Crusades, 1000-1300*. Ithaca, N.Y.: Cornell University Press, 1999.

Nicolle, David. *Arms and Armour of the Crusading Era, 1050-1350*. London: Greenhill Books, 1999.

Strickland, Matthew, ed. *Anglo-Norman Warfare*. Woodbridge, England: Boydell Press, 1992.

Verbruggen, J. F. *The Art of Warfare in Western Europe During the Middle Ages*. Woodbridge, England: Boydell Press, 1997.

Steven Isaac

THE MEDIEVAL WORLD

THE MIDDLE EAST AND AFRICA

ISLAMIC ARMIES

DATES: 622-1453 C.E.

POLITICAL CONSIDERATIONS

Arab successes in the expansion of Islam in the years between the Hegira, or the flight of the Islamic prophet Muḥammad (c. 570-632) from Mecca to Medina, in 622 and the Muslim Siege of Constantinople in 1453 were due to an innate style of warfare and value system developed by the Bedouin tribes during the pre-Islamic barbaric period of al-Jahliya. During this pre-Islamic period, tribes made raids, or *ghazwa*, to acquire camels, slaves, and booty to add to their store of goods. Every man bore arms and engaged in tactics that involved the element of surprise, hand-to-hand combat, confiscation of booty, and a speedy withdrawal. As external pressures from Byzantine and Sassanian sources began to appear, alliances were formed between tribes, or *qabila*, and clans, or *qaum*. Tribal solidarity demanded the virtue of *murūwa*, which included courage, honor, generosity, and chivalry. The *lex taliones*, or law of retaliation, governed pre-Islamic Arab society.

A strong Arab value, instilled by Muḥammad, was a fiery religious zeal that gained followers and consolidated Arabic tribes under the banner of Islam. Muḥammad raided Arabia far and wide, captured Mecca, and began the earliest expeditions against peripheral foes. His fiery zeal forged the religious instrument of *jihād fi sabil Allāh*, a "holy war" that legitimized conquest in the name of Allah and demanded faith and sacrifice in the spread of the Islamic order throughout the world. Death in this cause merited instant martyrdom and eternal reward in paradise.

After Muḥammad's death in 632, his successors, the Rāshidūn, the first four legitimate caliphs, developed a professional army that continued Muḥammad's zealous policies. The powerful Muslim army centered on volunteers and their families, resulting in a relocation of Arab populations and the creation of an Arab-Islamic region from the Middle East to the Atlantic Ocean.

The seventh and eighth centuries witnessed dynamic change in the Islamic world, marked by the rise and spread of Islam across one-half of the civilized world and by the opposition of cultures to its assault. Religious zeal resulted in unifying the Arabs to the extent that concern for death, hardship, and personal danger became secondary to the dissemination of Islam. This Islamic energy and missionary zeal coincided with Byzantine and Sassanian weaknesses brought about by prolonged external wars and internal religio-political strife. The Arabs expanded westward against Byzantine Anatolia, along the North African coast into Spain, eastward toward India, northwestward into Central Asia, and northward through the Caucasus. Some regions welcomed the Arabs as deliverers from tyranny; others fell into anarchy and merely succumbed to Arab rule. Byzantine and Frank resilience finally halted the Muslim onslaught in the early part of the eighth century.

Toward the end of the eighth century Muslims began to experience the effects of their far-flung expansion. They turned their energies toward internal dynastic disputes that threatened the caliphate and Muslim unity. Although the empire was generally stable on the perimeter, endemic warfare, strife, and coups continued for centuries. For two hundred years internal religio-political forces tore at the fabric of Islam and the caliphate, resulting in a rise of feudalism, numerous semi-independent principalities, and heretical religious communities. Islam eventually became fragmented, as local territories enhanced their military capabilities.

Amid the chaotic conditions erupting within the Muslim potentates as a result of their newly acquired military strength, the Middle East experienced three events that shaped the future of the land. In the first half of the eleventh century the region was overrun by

Seljuk Turks who threatened and captured the Holy Land and its sacred sites. In response Western military, religious, and cultural forces launched the Crusades (1095-1270) in the twelfth century. The primary purpose of the Crusades was the liberation of the sacred sites from Muslim control. Reaction to Western encroachment came in a temporary unification of Arab, Egyptian, and Turkish Muslims under the leadership of Nur al-Dīn (1118-1174) and his successor, Saladin (1138-1193), who waged a jihad against the Crusaders.

During the years between 1000 and 1200, the Muslim Empire was in turmoil from the Atlantic to South Asia. Northern Africa fragmented into various Islamized dynasties that struggled among themselves for control of local territories. The most enduring dynasty was the Fāṭimid caliphate of Egypt, which, together with Jerusalem, ultimately fell to the Turkish forces of Nur al-Dīn and Saladin in the mid-twelfth century. After most of Palestine yielded to the Turks, a compromise peace was negotiated with the Crusaders under Richard I (1157-1199) of England.

In South Asia, meanwhile, the Ghaznavids under Maḥmūd of Ghazna (971-1030), one of the most able conquerors in Asiatic history, invaded North India and weakened the power of the Hindu states. His successor, Muhammad of Ghor (c. 1206), completed the Muslim conquest of most of India, which was perpetuated by the Sultanate of Delhi.

The most formidable foe of the Muslims, the Byzantine Empire, was reduced in size and power by the encroachment of Ottoman Turks. Constantinople, the jewel in Byzantium's crown, which had withstood numerous assaults through the centuries, finally fell to the powerful military strength and superior assault weapons of Mehmed II (1432-1481) in 1453. The Islamic Empire ultimately reigned throughout northern Africa, the Middle East, and much of South Asia.

MILITARY ACHIEVEMENT

The first Arab military conquests were initiated by Muḥammad after 622. Prior to this date territorial acquisition had not been a part of the nomadic Bedouin life, and tribes had engaged in sporadic raids only to satisfy their immediate needs. Muḥammad

Library of Congress

The Islamic prophet Muḥammad, whose flight from Mecca to Medina in 622 marks the first year in the Muslim calendar.

successfully formed a small nucleus of an army, which eventually swelled into the thousands and changed the course of Arab history. The faith, determination, courage, and initiative of Muḥammad's followers resulted in a victory at the Battle of Badr (624). Three years of continuing skirmishes finally resulted in the fall of Mecca to Muḥammad's forces in 630. Integration of Bedouin desert tribes into the Islamic society followed until Muḥammad's death in 632.

With no guidelines for the government of the growing Muslim community after Muḥammad's death, his four successors, the Rāshidūn, formed a new government, the caliphate. Abū Bakr (r. 632-634) was appointed the first caliph. He was followed by ʿUmar I (r. 634-644), ʿUthman (r. 644-656), and ʿAlī ibn Abī Ṭālib (r. 656-661). With Islam as the new government's religious and political order, the caliphs looked to expand beyond Arabia while incorporating such regions as eastern Arabia, southern Yemen, and Ḥaḍramaut into Islamic society. Within thirty years Arab-Muslim conquests extended into all the Middle East, Mesopotamia, Persia, Byzantium, Palestine, Syria, Egypt, regions of North Africa, and Afghanistan. These territories supplied economic wealth for the Arabs and land for the migration of administrators, military units, and Arab settlers. They became permanently Islamized when Muʿāwiyah I (c. 602-680) emerged as caliph in 661 and founded the Umayyad Dynasty. One of the greatest Islamic leaders, Muʿāwiya was as successful on the battlefield as he was at arbitration. Initially the caliphate ingrained its subject peoples with Islamic values and ruled from Damascus with respect and justice. Opposition reared its head among Iraqi Arabs, who claimed Ḥusayn (624-680), Muḥammad's grandson, as the rightful leader of the Muslims. With his supporters, Ḥusayn was ambushed and massacred by Umayyad forces near Karbalā in 680, a battle that marked the beginning of Shia as a branch of Islam.

TURNING POINTS

622	In a journey known as the Hegira, the Islamic prophet Muḥammad (c. 570-632) flees from Mecca to Medina to avoid persecution.
632-661	Muḥammad is succeeded after his death in 632 by the four legitimate successors of the Rāshidūn caliphate.
680	The forces of Muḥammad's grandson Ḥusayn are ambushed and massacred at the Battle of Karbalā, marking the beginning of Shia as a branch of Islam.
Mid-8th cent.	Islam becomes the dominant religio-political power structure of the Middle East, from the Atlantic to the Indian frontier, including the Mediterranean coast and Spain.
1095	The Crusades are launched by Christian warriors seeking to reclaim the Holy Land for Christianity.
1187	Jerusalem is captured by Saladin from the Crusaders.
1260	Baybars I, the Mamlūk sultan of Egypt, defeats the Mongol hordes at Nabūlus.
1453	Muslim Turks besiege and capture Constantinople, extinguishing the Byzantine Empire.

The zenith of the Umayyad Dynasty was reached under al-Walīd (r. 705-715), under whose reign the Muslim Empire reached its greatest extent. Under effective rulers Muslim hold over the Islamic world was greatly extended. The primary goal of the Umayyads was the subjugation of the Byzantine Empire. In the process the Umayyads became highly skilled sea and land fighters. Islamic forces had swept into Europe by 718, but they were halted in 732 by Frankish king Charles Martel at the Battle of Tours. The Islamic navies' domination of much of the Mediterranean allowed continued control of the Mediterranean coastline and Spain. By the end of the Umayyad Dynasty in the mid-eighth century, Islam had become the dominant religio-political power structure from the Atlantic to the frontiers of India. A rebellious outbreak by the ʿAbbāsids of Khurāsān from 747 to 749 initiated the end of the Umayyad caliphate in Damascus. Abū al-ʿAbbās (r. 750-754) was proclaimed the first caliph of the ʿAbbāsid caliphate at Kūfa in 750. After a period of challenges that were suppressed, the ʿAbbāsid caliphate was firmly established at Baghdad in 758.

MUSLIM EMPIRE IN 760

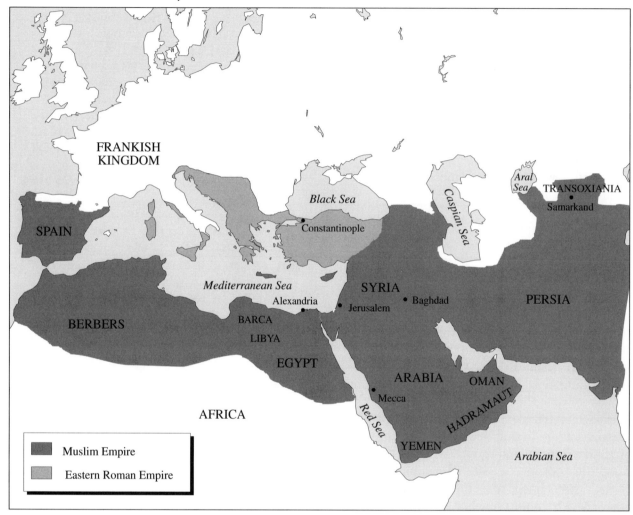

The zenith of the new caliphate was reached in the first half of the ninth century, during the reign of Hārūn ar-Rashīd (r. 786-809), continued under al-Maʾmūn (r. 813-833), and Abu Ishak al-Muʿtaṣim (r. 833-842), the last strong caliph. By the end of the century internal dynastic rivalries, conflicts between rival principalities, and innumerable foreign wars along the northern and eastern frontiers had weakened the caliphate.

Between 1000 and 1200 incessant warfare among numerous minor Muslim potentates in the Middle East initiated the appearance of three major forces on the scene. The eleventh century Seljuk Turk on-slaught and the twelfth century Crusades and Saladin's Arab, Egyptian, and Turkish military coun-terattack dominated events in the Middle Eastern ʿAbbāsid Islamic world. The authority and legitimacy of the ʿAbbāsid caliphate was seriously challenged by other Muslim groups from Central Asia, by the Persians, and by the Mongols, rendering the caliph a virtual prisoner in his own palace. In 1258 the Mongols burned Baghdad and executed the last ʿAbbāsid caliph.

The Mongol invasions caused constant strife and confusion in the Islamic world well after the fall of Baghdad. By the fifteenth century three great Islamic empires had arisen to dominate the areas from the Mediterranean and Europe to the subcontinent of India. The Mughal Dynasty ruled India; the Safavid Dynasty controlled Iran; and the great and powerful Ottoman Dynasty, which had originated in the thirteenth century and established small states in the fourteenth, captured Byzantine Constantinople in 1453. The Ottoman Empire ruled the lands of the eastern Mediterranean, Asia Minor, and southeastern Europe under the banner of Islam. It was totally Islamized, fundamentally Turkic, and ruled its domains from Constantinople.

WEAPONS, UNIFORMS, AND ARMOR

In the years between 600 and 800 Byzantine resistance to the sweep of Islam across the civilized world presented the Arabs with a new realization. Religious zeal alone could not justify the tremendous losses in manpower experienced by light cavalries armed only with lances and swords against powerful military forces. With the power and strength of superior and more modern armaments, the Muslims began to adopt many battlefield tactics learned from their foes.

Cavalry dominated Islamic battlefields, utilizing the bow and arrow as the primary weapons of distant engagement. Saddles and stirrups introduced by the ninth century gave riders a stable seat to support the use of swords, spears, and lances. Muslims, who had never achieved a great reputation in archery, used a simple bow fabricated from several sections of glued wood imported from Iran, Africa, or India. Infantry used a bow which was slung from the shoulder with a quiver of arrows. In confrontations with Byzantine archers, Arabs learned of the arrow-guide, which used flat, dartlike arrows in an ordinary bow and proved effective against harassing cavalry charges. Although the bow was adopted extensively by 800, the Muslims also used the crossbow, which, by the tenth century was included in a warrior's arsenal together with daggers, spears, and javelins.

In early military skirmishes the Arab infantry gained a reputation for skilled use of a short, straight sword frequently inlaid with precious metals and other materials. From the eleventh to the thirteenth

centuries craftsmen in Damascus and Toledo metallurgically perfected a curve-bladed scimitar, which further increased Muslim reputation on the battlefield. Although European swords used by the Crusaders were longer and heavier, steel scimitars were surprisingly supple and sturdy and could be sharpened to razor keenness.

Early Arab spears, the best of which originated in India and the Gulf Coast, were long with reed shafts. More typical was the *qanāh*, a heavy, large-bladed spear with a length that varied from 10 feet for infantry and 21 feet for cavalry. Although javelins were uncommon, a *zūpīn*, or heavy javelin, was carried as a symbol of command, as was a mace by Turks and Mamlūks. Large daggers, or *khanjars*, and single-handed axes (*ṭabar-i-zīn*) completed the hand weaponry.

During the first Muslim Siege of Constantinople (717-718) a major new weapon, known as Greek fire, was introduced by the Byzantines. Greek fire was a mixture of sulfur, naphtha, and quicklime, which was placed into a brass-bound wooden tube. The ignited flamethrower was then projected by water pressure to explode against Muslim naval ships. The use of Greek fire allowed the Byzantines to maintain their naval supremacy in the Mediterranean and resist Muslim attack. Muslim forces knew almost nothing about oil-based fire weapons, but in 712 they did use incendiary grenades against Indian war elephants. By 1453 projectile weapons in the form of gunpowder revealed their potential destructive power when the walls of Constantinople toppled to Turkish artillery.

Muslim infantry, cavalry, and cavalry horses were outfitted with armored body protection and shields. Shields of wood and hardened leather were used by various Islamic groups from India to the Atlantic. Larger leather shields were commonly employed by the Berbers of North Africa. Initially infantry and cavalry were lightly armored with helmets and mail shirts. After contact with Byzantine and Sassanian heavy cavalry, the Arabs adopted the heavier armor of their foes, and elite troops wore helmets that covered all but the wearer's eyes and provided protection against arrows. Mail and lamellar armor was adopted from Persia, and a highly effective lamellar cuirass was worn over a mail hauberk. Quilted armor without mail was worn by some warriors. In a few areas, such as Afghanistan, infantry wore armor made of cowhide stuffed with cotton and covered with decorative materials. It was borne on the shoulders as a protection for the body from head to foot. Limb defenses were rare and by the ninth century had completely disappeared as protection in the ʿAbbāsid army.

Although the use of horse armor, saddles, and stirrups was widespread after the tenth century in North Africa and Egypt, the use of these items by the early Arabs is unclear. The first equipment appears among Arab invaders of Nubia in the mid-seventh century. Arab and Berber nomads used padded leather saddles or simply rode bareback, controlling their steeds with leather or rope bitless bridles. For centuries Muslim Arabs considered the use of stirrups a Persian practice and a sign of weakness. It was not until the late seventh and early eighth centuries that they adopted metallic stirrups from the Turks. The hoofs of horses were outfitted with platelike horseshoes, an idea that originated in Arabia. Very few Umayyad cavalry used horse armor, lamellar cuirasses, or advanced forms of helmet and arm-defenses. The ʿAbbāsid cavalry elite, however, used quilted horse armor in the ninth century. By the tenth century Syrian horses were fully outfitted with mail or metallic lamellar armor.

MILITARY ORGANIZATION

Rigid military organization did not exist in pre-Islamic tribal Arabia. Raiding was the primary activity conducted by men recruited within a tribe for the purpose of gaining loot. The first organized Islamic field army developed between 622 and 750 and was made up of four elements: vanguard, center, wings, and rearguard. Each element was composed of troops from the same tribe or town. Cavalry troops generally were composed of nomadic Bedouin camel herders of the desert. Effectiveness was limited, because stirrups were not used in early campaigns and many warriors were undisciplined Muslims. Militias for garrison duty and field operations were also formed of town-dwelling Arabs. A major part of the army included highly efficient Yemeni infantry archers. Because manpower was limited, Islamic armies relied heavily on southern Syrians, Christians, pagan tribal members, and or non-Arab Muslim converts known as mawālī, black Africans, Christian Nubians, and even defeated Sassanians from Persia and Iraq.

The first Muslim armies were generally patterned on those of pre-Islamic South Arabia. All men had a military obligation to serve in the early army. The only distinctions in early Arabia existed between infantry and cavalry, most of which did duty in garrisons or in highly sensitive areas subject to external threats or internal rebellion. Cantonments, or temporary quarters, for warriors and their families were established in conquered areas. A high level of tribal military skill offset the lack of manpower and was responsible for Muslim battlefield success against forces of superior numbers.

The Umayyad Muslim army was a professional force of mostly Arab troops that settled in conquered territories. This regional organization, or jund, was attributed to ʿUmar, the second caliph, and was based on fortified provincial towns. A government ministry known as the dīwān met the military needs of all registered military personnel. The established junds were groupings of similar warriors such as elite urban-based ahl al-shām Syrian Arabs, Syrian desert tribals, Christian Nabataean Arabs of northern Syria, Persian, Turk, Afghan, Sijistan, Bukhari, Armenian, Coptic Egyptian, and African Berber mercenaries in eastern armies and even Ex-Visigothic forces in western armies, as well as local militias. Because the old tribal system had proved too small a fighting unit, tribes were united into large Umayyad divisions. Officers commanded regional units but Umayyad royal family members held senior positions.

During the eighth and ninth centuries the ʿAbbāsids reorganized the army, allowing all soldiers equal status regardless of ethnic origin. A large military base was provided in the Round City of Baghdad that served as a vast garrison at the center of the empire. Unique military skills of various regional groups were exploited in recruitment of army personnel. Arab khawariji were conscripted for their physical endurance and skill with the long spear. Turkish Mamlūk elite were sought for their maneuverability, self-sufficiency, and archery expertise. The caliph's palace, surrounded by cantonments of elite guard units, regiments, and paramilitary militias, was situated in the center of the military base. Security forces and police protected the perimeter. Well-supplied mobile provincial armies were used against invaders and rebels alike.

Infantry and light cavalry made up the earliest ʿAbbāsid army, which was divided into functional units. Garrison forces maintained internal security while expeditionary units defended the frontiers. Each comprised regulars, volunteers, professional heavy infantry, archers, and specialists in fire weapons. Generals led regiments of 1,000 men. A supreme commander commanded 10,000 men. Hereditary privilege and political reliability were criteria for selection of senior officers. The primary virtue in the army was loyalty to the ʿAbbāsid Dynasty and to officers and other soldiers. Military upkeep was provided by a tax structure, with the lion's share given to professional seasoned troops stationed in the provinces. Local forces and part-time militias protected peaceful regions.

Little is known about military organization of successor states after the fragmentation of the ʿAbbāsid caliphate. These states relied upon their own resources and rarely came to the aid of armies opposing Byzantine aggression. Loyalty in armies of successor states, especially those in North Africa, Fāṭimid Egypt, the Maghreb, and al-Andalus, was given not to the caliph but rather to local leaders.

DOCTRINE, STRATEGY, AND TACTICS

Prior to the appearance of Islam, warfare among the Arabs had consisted primarily of intertribal rivalries. The control of water and grazing sites, the promise of economic booty, and the domination of a tribal area to assure survival in a fixed ecological environment were all reasons for such rivalries. Hilly desert and wooded terrain provided sites for launching surprise ambushes and raids. There was no interest in serving in fixed positions or engaging in major confrontations with superior rivals. If confronted by a superior force, the Bedouins prudently retreated into the desert where their innate knowledge ensured their safety and survival. Most raids were executed rapidly

by light cavalry, who achieved their goals and then withdrew. Occasionally two or more allied tribes met at a prescribed site, seized an enemy town, or regained and defended their won terrain.

With Islam as a unifying force, the same strategy was followed in early campaigns against Byzantine and Sassanian forces. Extensive raids were executed, but major garrisons and fortified places were avoided. Overall strategy stressed caution, the involvement only of necessary troops, and the deployment of reinforcements only if needed. After the semiarid steppes along Byzantine and Sassanian frontiers were consolidated, small cavalry units were rapidly deployed to tip the balance in a campaign. As Ummayad armies gained knowledge and experience fighting Byzantine and Sassanian armies, they adopted new weaponry and military techniques which, together with great mobility, compensated for Arab numerical inferiority. Raiding forces would occasionally winter in Byzantine territory, seize a fortification, plant crops, and harvest in the spring.

During the seventh and eighth centuries campaigns were fought by infantry archers with small mailed cavalry units preceding them into battle. The bow was the preferred missile weapon, and the battle was one of fire and movement. Byzantines, on the other hand, demonstrated great infantry and cavalry coordination, which required intense training and control. Arab tactics centered on cavalry charges supported by horse archers and infantry fire. The intent was to break an enemy formation, cause panic, attack, and destroy each unit separately. After an initial charge, Arab warriors became engaged in hand-to-hand combat, as had the Bedouins in traditional intertribal skirmishes. This situation accounted for a major weakness and breakdown of unit cohesion in early Arab tactics. However, in spite of this weakness, Arab superior mobility, high moral and religious zeal, support from native populations, and skill in utilizing the desert to draw an enemy into favorable battle conditions accounted for Arab victories. Early Muslim forces tactically fought defensive battles within an offensive strategy, by which they placed themselves in naturally strong positions, engaged in repeated attacks, and then withdrew.

Early Muslim armies divided their forces into an

advance guard, a center, a right wing, a left wing, and a rearguard. The Umayyad caliphate continued this strategic practice but added an offensive cavalry that was divided into small units called *miqnab*. Infantry fought in close-ordered ranks. Later, smaller cavalry squadrons allowed for more maneuverability. The traditional infantry remained, but reconnaissance patrols and armored cavalry were added.

Although most great Arab-Islamic conquests had been made by 750, the ʿAbbāsid army retained great capability and highly sophisticated strategy. Small-scale raids continued to be used to acquire horses, prisoners for ransom, grain-storage sites, and booty with the aim of weakening the economic base of the enemy. The military continued to stress caution, the protection of communication lines, a strong intelligence system, and extreme planning for seizing enemy territory. As colonial armies began to appear in the ninth century, methods of warfare from non-Arab and non-Muslim sources were adopted. Non-Arabic peoples who served in colonial armies and converted to Islam produced some of the greatest Muslim leaders of Islamic history, most notably the Kurd al-Malik al-Nāṣir Ṣalāḥ al-Dīn aba ʾl-Mussafer Yūsuf ibn Ayyūb ibn Shadi, more commonly known as Saladin, who founded the Ayyubid Dynasty (1169-1250), fought the Crusaders, and took Jerusalem in 1187. Another great Islamic leader was Baybars I (r. 1260-1277), the Mamlūk sultan of Egypt who fought against the Crusade of Louis IX in 1250 and decisively defeated Hülegü and his Mongol warriors in 1260. The Arab art of war in the twelfth and thirteenth centuries reached a high point characterized by military discipline, religious unity and fervor, strategic mobility, effective mastery of siege machinery, an effective intelligence system, and a superb supply of manufactured war machinery. Tactically the Muslims, in their warfare with Crusading forces, concentrated upon separating cavalry units from solid infantry, destroying each in turn. However, the Arabs were eventually dismantled by Western armies, Mongol invasions, and the Turkish Seljuk and Ottoman Empires, the latter devouring the entire Arab world except for Morocco in the Western Maghreb.

MEDIEVAL SOURCES

Several medieval theoretical and practical military manuals have survived that provide a picture of warfare waged by Arab and Byzantine forces in the Middle East. A significant work was produced by the ninth century Arab writer Ibn Qutayba al-Dīnawarī (828-889), describing Arabic cavalry and guerrilla "shadow" warfare. It wielded significant influence on Arabic military campaigns after the ninth century. Two other works of importance present in detail warfare waged by the Byzantine Empire against Islam. The *Strategikon* (c. 580 C.E.; English translation, 1984) of Mauricius Flavius Tiberius (c. 539-602 C.E.), a Byzantine emperor who reigned from 582 to 602 C.E., is an encyclopedic theoretical manual on the science of war, covering leadership, tactical operations, administration, logistics, and various battlefield problems. It exercised a major influence on the Byzantine military system for centuries. The second work, the *Taktika* (compiled c. 905; tactics), was written by the Byzantine emperor Leo VI (886-912). Leo considered the Arabs prudent in their military operations and their adoption of Byzantine military practice, arms, and strategy but negligent in absorbing its organization and discipline.

BOOKS AND ARTICLES

Glubb, Sir John Bagot. *The Great Arab Conquests*. Englewood Cliffs, N.J.: Prentice Hall, 1964.
Hitti, Philip K. *History of the Arabs from the Earliest Times to the Present*. London: Macmillan, 1970.
Lewis, Bernard. *The Arabs in History*. New York: Oxford University Press, 1993.
Oman, Charles. *A History of the Art of War in the Middle Ages*. London: Greenhill Press, 1991.

George Hoynacki

CRUSADING ARMIES
DATES: 1095-1291 C.E.

POLITICAL CONSIDERATIONS

In the eleventh century C.E., the petty kingdoms of Western Europe were prospering as they had not done since the fall of the western Roman Empire six hundred years earlier. Political order had been established through vassal networks of nobles, who fought together as warriors called knights. Because the knights dominated society, their ethos of chivalry began to permeate most aspects of their contemporary culture, including religion. The knights took the idea of a pilgrimage, a pious journey granting forgiveness of sins, and combined it with the concept of war. Thus appeared the idea of the crusade, in which Christian warriors, properly sanctioned by a religious authority such as the pope, would defeat the supposed enemies of God as an act of virtue. Once this idea was established, the crusading movement provoked warfare on many fronts, from the Iberian Peninsula to the Baltic coast, and even against heretics in the south of France.

The most important crusades, however, took place in the Levant, the eastern coastline of the Mediterranean from Asia Minor to Egypt, namely modern Syria, Lebanon, and Israel. The Christians called this area the Holy Land because of the biblical history of the Hebrews and Jesus of Nazareth. Although the Holy Land had been under Muslim domination since the eighth century, many Christians continued to travel there on pilgrimages.

The impetus for the Levantine crusades had a curious origin. The Byzantine Empire had suffered a devastating defeat at the Battle of Manzikert (1071), in which it lost most of Asia Minor to the Seljuk Turks, an invading Asiatic people who were trying to dominate the Middle East. The emperor contacted the pope in Rome, seeking military support from Western mercenaries. Pope Urban II (c. 1042-1099), with a grander vision, proclaimed the first "official" crusade in 1095, announcing that God had called on Christian warriors to free Jerusalem. The surprising success of this First Crusade (1095-1099) began nearly two centuries of crusading warfare in Palestine.

MILITARY ACHIEVEMENT

The First Crusade brought a major army from the heartland of Europe to the Levant. The Crusaders succeeded in conquering most of the Mediterranean coastline from the local Muslim overlords, culminating in the capture of Jerusalem itself. They then came to dominate the local population, which consisted mostly of Muslims, but also of Jews and various Christians, usually through the demand of tribute and taxes. They also tried to expand their borders, in order render them less vulnerable to attack. The relatively small numbers of Christian Crusaders in the Holy Land required constant reinforcements, leading to subsequent crusades mounted on their behalf, which number between five and seven depending on how they are counted by historians, as well as small contingents of knights on personal missions.

Periodically, Christians and Muslims tried to live together in peace; however, zealots on both sides ensured that military conflict would remain inevitable. The Muslim goal, quite reasonably, came to be one of driving the Christians out of the Levant. By the mid-twelfth century, they also revived their own version of holy war, jihad, to inspire opposition to the Christians.

Nur al-Dīn's (1118-1174) conquest of the principality of Edessa in 1144 prompted the Second Crusade (1145-1149), led by the kings of France and Germany, whose failed attack on Damascus miserably ended that effort. Nur al-Din's successor, Saladin (1138-1193), a Kurd who united Egypt and Syria under his control, nearly destroyed all the Crusader

TURNING POINTS

1095-1099	During the First Crusade, initiated by Pope Urban II, European crusaders, fighting to protect the Holy Land for Christianity, capture Jerusalem.
1145-1149	The Second Crusade, unsuccessfully led by the kings of France and Germany, is prompted by Muslim conquest of the principality of Edessa in 1144.
1187-1192	The Third Crusade succeeds, especially through the efforts of English king Richard I, in restoring some Christian possessions.
1198-1204	The Fourth Crusade, initiated by Pope Innocent III, captures Constantinople and damages the Byzantine Empire.
1217-1221	The Fifth Crusade, organized to attack the Islamic power base in Egypt, succeeds in capturing the Egyptian port city of Damietta but ends in defeat when the crusading army attempts to capture Cairo.
1228-1229	In what is sometimes referred to as the Sixth Crusade, the excommunicated Holy Roman Emperor Frederick II sails to the Holy Land and negotiates a reoccupation of Jerusalem.
1248-1254	The Seventh (or Sixth) Crusade is led by Louis IX of France and follows a course similar to that of the Fifth Crusade.
1269-1270	Eighth (or Seventh) Crusade is organized by a now-elderly Louis IX, who dies upon landing in Tunisia, leading to the breakup of his army.
1270-1272	Edward I, the son of Henry III of England, decides to press on alone to Palestine after the French abandon the Eighth Crusade and achieves some modest success with a truce before the ultimate fall of Acre, the last bastion of the crusader states, in 1291.

states by the 1180's. The Third Crusade (1187-1192) succeeded, especially through the efforts of English king Richard I (1157-1199) in restoring some Christian possessions. After the Third Crusade, the Christians found it particularly difficult to mount offensives and depended upon their network of castles and fortified towns.

The goal of the Fourth Crusade (1198-1204), rather than assistance to the Levant, was the conquering of Constantinople, which severely damaged the Crusaders' nominal ally, the Byzantine Empire. The Fifth Crusade (1217-1221) tried to attack the Muslims at one source of their power, Egypt. This mission failed, as did another attempt from 1248 to 1254 led by King Louis IX (1214-1270) of France. Holy Roman Emperor Frederick II's (1194-1250) peacefully negotiated acquisition of Jerusalem in 1229 was an anomaly, widely criticized by bellicose Christians. A defeat of the Mongols in 1260 enabled the Mamlūk leader Baybars I (c. 1223-1277) to unite Egypt and Syria. Baybars conquered most Crusader possessions, and his third successor took the last Christian stronghold in the Levant in 1291.

WEAPONS, UNIFORMS, AND ARMOR

The knight was the main warrior of the Christian Crusaders. The knight's primary weapon was the couched lance, which he used in a horse charge to crash into an opposing force. For close combat the knight most often used the sword but also employed the ax and the mace. The knight's protective armor evolved over two hundred years of crusading. Knights initially wore heavy mail shirts and small, conical Norman-style helmets. By the end of the Crusades they wore lighter mail suits, made stronger with reinforcing pieces of plate armor on some joints and limbs, and pot helmets. A light surcoat gave knights protection from sun and wind. Their original large kite-shaped shields grew smaller as the armor became more protective.

Other forces were also essential to Christian armies, although their noble commanders often considered them unimportant. Knights were frequently supported, especially during sieges, by infantry armed with pole-arms or bows, particularly crossbows, as well as specialists such as miners and sappers. Land forces often required naval support. Warships provided by the Genoese, Venetians, or Pisans both captured and defended coastal towns and supplied and reinforced the Christians.

Christian Crusaders did not have an identifying uniform, any more than did contemporary Western medieval armies. In the course of the crusades, heraldic insignia developed to identify individual knights. All Crusaders could be identified by a cross, which they wore openly on their armor or clothing at all times. As time went on, the shape and color of crosses could identify a Crusader's national origin or religious order.

Muslim warriors were more diverse in their weapons, uniforms, and armor. The primary Turkish weapon was the light bow. Like other steppe peoples, the Turks employed attacks by archers mounted on swift horses, who repeatedly would strike with coordinated arrow barrages and retreat until their enemy broke ranks. If drawn into close combat, the riders wielded maces, war-hammers, and light swords such as the curved scimitar. They protected themselves with small, round shields and light body armor. The Arab armies fought with heavy cavalry and infantry in a fashion more similar to that of the Crusaders. Over time the Mamlūks began to dominate the Islamic world. Originally slave-soldiers of Turkish origin, they became highly professionalized armored horsemen wielding bow and lance. Thick robes and tunics both differentiated Muslim from Christian forces and served as protection from weather and weapons.

MILITARY ORGANIZATION

One of the greatest challenges facing the Christian forces was a lack of coherent organization. The vassal bonds that held knights together in European

EUROPE AND THE BYZANTINE EMPIRE DURING THE CRUSADES

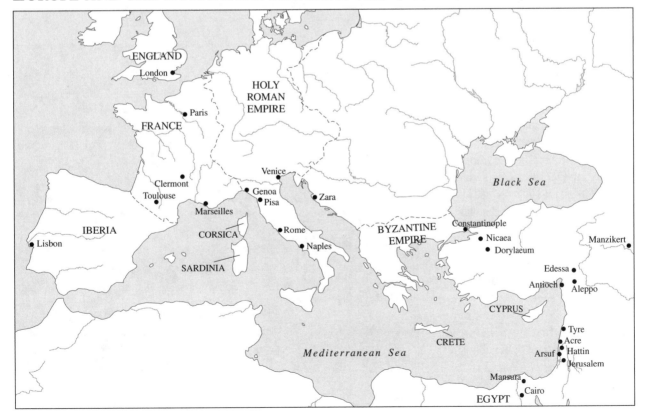

kingdoms weakened or disappeared entirely within the crusading armies. The First Crusade (1095-1099) nearly failed because of bickering and rivalries among the military commanders. National and ethnic differences also weakened the efforts of crusading armies, most famously during the Third Crusade, in which the kings of France and England quarreled both with each other and with the duke of Austria.

The monastic military orders added yet another layer of division within the Christian forces. Beginning in the 1120's, these orders were made up of monk-knights: men who took religious vows but also served as warriors. Soon groups such as the Knights Hospitallers and the Knights Templars had formed complex, wealthy institutions. Although they provided much needed financial resources and military reserves, their power also led them to assert leadership in the politics of the kingdom of Jerusalem and on campaigns.

Further, the Christians were usually short of manpower, never quite fully replenished by new waves of crusading pilgrims coming from Europe. Often those new Crusaders further complicated matters, since they frequently refused to accept the command of those already on the scene.

Muslim forces were similarly disunited. They were divided not only by religious schisms (between Shia and Sunni, for example) but also split in their main centers of power. For example, the city of Damascus was ruled by the Turks, and Cairo was ruled first by the Fāṭimid Arabs, later by the Ayyubid Kurds, and then finally by the Mamlūks. Quarrels between the Turks and Fāṭimid Egyptians initially enabled the Crusaders to succeed. However, when the two power centers stood united, first by Saladin in the 1160's and then by Baybars in the 1260's, they were able to inflict heavy defeats upon the Christians. Still, Muslim armies

were usually assembled on an as-needed basis, with most contingents returning to local areas after a campaign. Muslim commanders held the loyalty of their troops through an unreliable combination of pay, legal subjugation, nationalist sentiment, and religious fervor.

DOCTRINE, STRATEGY, AND TACTICS

The first problem for any crusading army was to reach the Holy Land intact. Armies who favored the land route faced challenges such as long marches, hostile populations, and vulnerability to surprise attack. Others favored the quicker sea route, with its own difficulties of high cost, piracy, and exposure to storm and shipwreck. Either way, Crusaders were constantly challenged to obtain enough supplies for the armies and camp followers. When food and water ran out, some even resorted to cannibalism. Crusaders were particularly vulnerable to diseases such as typhoid, cholera, and dysentery, but they had little sense of how to combat contagion.

Library of Congress

Crusaders under English king Richard I reach the holy city of Jerusalem.

Like that of Europe, most warfare of the Crusades centered on the raid: stealing from and destroying enemy resources. Slow-moving Crusader armies were most vulnerable while on the march. The Battle of Arsuf (1191) demonstrated Richard I's ability to control his troops and eke out a modest victory. When such pitched battles were fought, the invading Crusaders generally had to adapt to Muslim tactics. Against Turkish foes, the key to Christian victory often lay in enduring several waves of attacks by massed archers on horseback. Only when the Muslim horses had been exhausted could the heavier, slower knights succeed in striking the enemy or engaging in hand-to-hand combat. If, however, the Muslims were able to isolate units of knights, or avoid the shock of their cavalry charge, they would be victorious.

Most major battles were connected to sieges, such as that of Antioch (1097-1098) or Hattin (1187). Because armies in the field could not leave major forts in their rear, many campaigns sought to take strategically located cities and castles. Because a small number of defenders could usually hold a fortification against a much larger army, sieges were common. Assaults were risky and dangerous, so most armies preferred to wait and starve out the besieged. The besieged, in turn, hoped for the opposing army to give up or for a relief army to arrive and destroy the enemy.

The Christians put much effort and innovation into building castles and improving city defenses. The Christians used assault ladders and even a siege tower in the conquest of Jerusalem. The Muslims excelled in the use of Greek fire and stone-throwing artillery and in the undermining of fortifications. By the 1250's Muslim trebuchets could reputedly batter down castle walls within six weeks. Armies also took castles through betrayal, sneak attacks, and trickery.

Defeated enemies, both warriors and noncombatants, were often slaughtered, unless a prisoner was worthy of ransom, as was King Louis IX of France after Mansura (1249-1250). The butchering of the entire population of Jerusalem (1099) and Richard I's execution of 2,700 prisoners at Acre (1189-1191) were particularly notorious. To intimidate the enemy, armies also employed torture, mutilation, and desecration of the dead. Such atrocities committed by both sides have lent the Crusades a reputation for cruelty.

MEDIEVAL SOURCES

There exist many useful sources on the Crusades written from various points of view. For Western Christians, French priest and historian Foucher of Chartres (c. 1059-c. 1127) wrote a thorough account of the First Crusade. William of Tyre's (c. 1130-1185) *Historia Rerum in Partibus Transmarinis Gestarum* (1184; *A History of Deeds Done Beyond the Sea*, 1943) covers the crusades from 1095 to 1184. Geoffrey of Villehardouin (c. 1150-c. 1213) describes the conquest of Constantinople. John of Joinville, also known as Jean, sire de Joinville (c. 1224-1317), writes of Louis IX's crusades. The *Alexiad* (English translation, 1928), by the Byzantine princess Anna Comnena (1083-c. 1148), provides a Greek perspective. Of the Muslim sources, Ibn al-Qalānisī's (c. 1073-1160) continuation of the history of Damascus covers events to the mid-twelfth century. Usāmah ibn Munqidh's (1095-1188) memoirs offer an invaluable account of the middle of the twelfth century and the rise of Saladin. In 1251 Abū Shāma (1203-1268) finished a useful compilation of many earlier historians.

BOOKS AND ARTICLES

Bartlett, W. B. *God Wills It! An Illustrated History of the Crusades*. Stroud, England: Sutton, 1999.

Edbury, Peter. "Warfare in the Latin East." In *Medieval Warfare: A History*, edited by Maurice Keen. Oxford, England: Oxford University Press, 1999.

France, John. *Western Warfare in the Age of the Crusades, 1000-1300*. Ithaca, N.Y.: Cornell University Press, 1999.

Nicolle, David. *Arms and Armour of the Crusading Era, 1050-1350: Islam, Eastern Europe, and Asia*. London: Greenhill Books, 1999.

Riley-Smith, Jonathan, ed. *The Oxford Illustrated History of the Crusades*. Oxford, England: Oxford University Press, 1995.

Tate, Georges. *The Crusaders: Warriors of God*. New York: Harry N. Abrams, 1996.

FILMS AND OTHER MEDIA

Crusaders and Schism in the East: Christianity in the Eleventh and Twelfth Centuries. Vol. 6 in *Two Thousand Years: The History of Christianity*. Documentary. Films for the Humanities and Sciences, 1999.

The Crusades. Documentary. Arts and Entertainment Network, 1995.

Brian A. Pavlac

WEST AFRICAN EMPIRES

DATES: 400-1591 C.E.

POLITICAL CONSIDERATIONS

In the period from 400 to 1591, West Africa saw the rise and fall of the indigenous kingdoms and empires of Ghana, medieval Mali, and Songhai. Although many other petty states and kingdoms arose in West Africa during this time, only Ghana, Mali, and Songhai achieved the status of full-fledged and long-lived conquest states and expansionist empires, for which contact-era Islamic and European documentary histories are available.

Ghana's emergence as the first of the West African empires ultimately set the stage for subsequent developments identified with the establishment of the kingdoms of Mali and Songhai. In each instance the intensification of trade along the trans-Saharan trade network was a critical factor underlying the expansion, influence, and institutionalization of the military orders of the day. In fact, much of the wealth generated to support the maintenance of professional armies—documented by various Islamic writers to have ranged between 40,000 and 200,000 soldiers each—was derived directly from the military and police protections afforded foreign travelers and merchants on the trans-Saharan trade corridor. With the advent and spread of the Islamic faith out of North Africa in the eighth century, new forms of commercial, religious, social, cultural, and military interaction transformed the social and political landscape of West Africa. In some instances, as with the reign of Mansa Mūsā I of Mali (1312-1337 C.E.), Islamic influence transformed the organizational structure of the empire and the administration of justice and launched the religious wars of the Islamic jihad. Subsequent kings and kingdoms either waged war under the doctrines of the Islamic tradition or sought to eradicate the Muslim tradition altogether, setting the stage for much of the military history of the kingdoms of Mali and Songhai until the emergence of the

European slave trade and the introduction of firearms. These latter developments in turn fueled a long-standing pattern of internecine warfare that ultimately depopulated entire towns and regions subject to West Africa's colonial-era encounter with European merchants, militarists, and slave traders.

MILITARY ACHIEVEMENT

Military achievement during this period centered on the emergence and mobilization of professional armies and cavalry forces; the formalization of military protocols, organizational structures, propaganda, and tactics; and the adoption of new military technologies, fortifications, and weaponry. Whereas the primary achievements ascribed to the kingdom of Ghana center on the fact that it was the first of the western Sudanese empires to establish large professional armies for the maintenance of law and order over a vast territory, the medieval kingdom of Mali in turn contributed to the formal development and mobilization of cavalry forces in the thirteenth and fourteenth centuries in order to command the battlefields of the savanna and sahel regions of West Africa. Both within and beyond the context of indigenous warfare, the kingdoms of Songhai and Benin, among others, further advanced indigenous armaments, protective armor, fortifications, tactical mobilizations, and, ultimately, the adoption of firearms.

The combined impact of the Islamic faith and the deployment of cavalry forces on the military culture of the era were most forcefully felt during the reign of the Malian king Mansa Mūsā I. Mansa Mūsā undertook the military expansion of Mali and the concomitant control and taxation of the trans-Saharan trade in salt, gold, ivory, ebony, pepper, and kola nuts. His primary contribution was the military incorporation of the Middle Niger River region into the kingdom of

Mali through the use of cavalry forces and professional armies. In addition, his conquests ultimately led to the control and incorporation of the important mercantile centers and cities of Timbuktu and Gao, the trans-Saharan trading town of Walata, and the salt mines of Taghaza to the north. During Mansa Mūsā's reign the territory of Mali was doubled in size, and the capture and control of the primary salt- and gold-producing areas of the region secured the empire's wealth and stability. So famous were the cavalry exploits of Mansa Mūsā's day that one of the more notable art forms of this time consisted of relatively large terra-cotta figures of mounted cavalry troops replete with padded body armor, backpacks, elaborate helmets with chin straps, and a variety of weapons including swords and javelins. Ultimately, Mansa Mūsā's conquests and his organization of an imperial form of government transformed Mali from a regional to an international presence, with Malian ambassadors posted in Morocco and Egypt.

The kingdom of Songhai provides another prominent body of documented achievements in the use of light cavalry for the purposes of territorial gain and empire building. Malian and Songhai battle formations, or *mandekalu*, entailed the use of light cavalry forces bearing padded armor, spears or javelins, and imported swords. Such forces were highly effective in combat with enemy soldiers within the range of the savanna; however, these same cavalry forces were far less effective in the forested areas to the south of the Niger River or within tsetse-fly-ridden regions where horses were vulnerable. This was clearly the case for the Mandekalu horse warriors of the Mali Empire, whose realm was largely restricted to the West African sahel and savanna woodlands through much of the period extending from 1100 to 1500 C.E. Following on the heels of the cavalry were the infantrymen, who typically bore full armor, iron-tipped spears, and poisoned arrows.

Ultimately, the development of sophisticated military organizations, advanced strategies and tactics, effective diplomacy, and weaponry of the kingdoms of Mali, Songhai, and successor states of West Africa, was such that these kingdoms largely dictated the conditions of European and Arabic commerce in West Africa well into the eighteenth and nineteenth centuries.

Weapons, Uniforms, and Armor

The earliest indigenous forms of combat relied largely on the deployment of shock weapons, including short-handled wood, stone, and iron-tipped thrusting spears; javelins; iron swords; protective headgear; and bamboo shields. The use of these weapons provides a clear indication that hand-to-hand combat was a key strategy both in the sahel and savanna and in the jungle-shrouded landscapes that contained the West African kingdoms. As did the armies of other societies engaged in jungle or desert combat before the advent of firearms, those of the West African kingdoms employed thrusting spears and other shock weapons. To this ensemble of shock weapons were added projectiles, or "missile weapons," in the form of the hunting bow and iron-tipped arrow, which was a critical innovation for those infantry that accompanied the cavalry corps late in Ghana's military history. Much of this early weaponry constituted the warriors' toolkit for centuries to come. Primary innovations centered on the transition from stone-

Turning Points

700-1000	Ghana emerges as the dominant kingdom and military power of the Western Sudan.
1230	The kingdom of Mali is founded by a Mandinka prince after the defeat of the Susu kingdom.
1450	Songhai incorporates the former kingdom of Mali and comes to control one of the largest empires of that time.
1468	Songhai armies invade Timbuktu, execute Arab merchants and traitors, and sack and burn the city, thereby heralding a period of anti-Islamic sentiment in West Africa.
1591	Songhai is conquered by a Moroccan army consisting primarily of European mercenaries armed with muskets, the first to be used in West African warfare.

A mounted warrior of the Bornu, where cavalry was a dominant aspect of the savanna kingdom's military.

leg and ampleness in the seat." Combat insignia and ethnic accoutrements were also characteristically donned by warriors, and the role of insignia, such as feathers inserted into headgear, was intended to signify rank and status within the battle formations. Fifteenth century Bini swordsmen were depicted in brass castings wearing an elaborately standardized protective armor that included armored helmets, spiked collars and breastplates, massive curvilinear swords, and warhammers.

MILITARY ORGANIZATION

According to one Muslim history of West Africa, the Songhai military, known as the Tarikh al-Fattash, was organized under the aegis of three full-time commanders or generals. The *dyini-koy* or *balama* was the commander of the army, the *hi-koy* was the admiral of the war-canoe fleet, and the *tara-farma* was the full-time commander of the cavalry forces of the empire. Each of these commanders and his respective subordinates was identified by his uniform, clothing, and insignia.

West African kings typically rose to power through either inheritance or demonstrated success as a military leader, conqueror, or facilitator of a coup. All military organization and support in West African kingdoms was directly subject to the order and mandate of the ruling king in his capacity as commander in chief. The organizational culture of each kingdom's armies varied according to the nature of the military mobilization. Slaves or other captives often served a critical support function during major military operations. Although professional armies were often renowned for their cavalry corps, they often included tens, if not hundreds of thousands, of infantrymen, backed by slaves who facilitated the movement of cargo and supplies necessary to the deployment of troops in long-distance engagements. The combination of infantry, cavalry, and naval corps

tipped wooden arrows and spears, and bows and arrows, to iron-tipped projectiles in these same categories. The slingshot has also been documented among the weaponry utilized in combat within and between the West African kingdoms. The addition of North African, Spanish-Moorish, and German steel sabers and swords to the growing arsenals of West African weaponry indicates the growing international status and wealth of West African armies.

The kingdom of Mali eventually standardized its warriors' battle regalia and uniforms, as did the kingdoms of Ghana, Songhai, and Benin. In addition, Malian rulers introduced the so-called Honor of the Trousers. According to the twelfth century Arab author al-ʿUmarī (1301-1349), who chronicled the history of the Mali Empire, "Whenever a hero adds to the list of his exploits, the king gives him a pair of wide trousers, and the greater the number of a knight's exploits, the bigger the size of trousers. These trousers are characterized by narrowness in the proved a highly resilient and organizationally effective military method for maintaining the long-term stability of the West African kingdoms of Mali and Songhai.

DOCTRINE, STRATEGY, AND TACTICS

The doctrines, strategies, and tactics that characterized West African warfare varied considerably through time, reflecting cultural and technological influences that impacted the region through the course of nearly twelve hundred years of human interaction. The earliest recorded wars and military mobilizations of the Ghanaian peoples centered on the protection of the all-important salt trade. However, the nature of war and weaponry in West Africa evolved in response to the growing significance of iron for tools and weapons, the capture of war captives for the slave trade, and the mining of gold for commercial exchange with Arab and European merchants. Ultimately, the protection of the kingdom and its long-distance trade networks and merchants led to the formalization of professional armies and the formation of special military units within the kingdom. Despite this changing relationship between the king and his soldiers, Ghana is thought to have depended largely on civilian reserves for the mobilization of standing armies. The later kingdom of Mali expanded the role of the professional soldier and created large standing armies as well as highly disciplined cavalry forces. The kingdom of Songhai clearly epitomized the changing nature of military practice: Songhai's unceasing pattern of territorial and political expansionism served to justify the role and status of its formally institutionalized military.

Throughout the course of West African history, religious doctrine served to define and redefine the nature and transformation of military doctrine, political organization, and, ultimately, conquest interactions with neighboring states. Whereas Ghana was the dominant power of the western Sudan from 700 to 1000, the Islamic domination of North Africa and the growing role of Islam in West Africa provided a catalyst for the intensification of professional soldiering and the protection of trade with Arab merchants. Given the growing penetration of Islamic thought and culture in West Africa, the military took on a police function where trans-Saharan trade was concerned. During this period, although the protection of trade remained of paramount concern, the advent of the Islamic jihad, or holy war, signaled the beginning of wars devoted to spreading the Islamic faith and eliminating infidels, or nonbelievers. With the rise of Mali, the military took on an expansionist function, conquering the city of Gao and consolidating control over the salt and gold trade. The heavily Islamic character of Mansa Mūsā's reign reflected a long-standing pattern of Islamic influence and status. On one hand the adoption of the Islamic tradition in Western African kingdoms increased social and cultural cohesiveness over a vast geographic region and brought about a new era of prosperity. On the other hand, the scorched-earth policy of empire building and the role of the jihad ultimately fed the decline of the kingdom of Mali and, subsequently, that of Songhai.

MEDIEVAL SOURCES

Early Arab and Muslim accounts of the culture, society, technology, militarism, and urban settings of the West African kingdoms are among the most authoritative and complete. Such accounts include those of the eleventh century Arab geographer al-Bakri (died c. 1094), who describes ancient Ghana in *The Book of Routes and Kingdoms*; and Mahmud al-Kati, a Muslim scholar who authored the *Tarikh al-Fattash*, or *History of the Sudan*, which was largely incorporated into the accounts of Ibn Mukhtar in his publication of the *Tarikh al-Fattash*. Among the most important historians of later periods of the kingdoms of Mali and Songhai are Ibn Battuta, a fourteenth century Muslim traveler, and al-Ḥasan ibn Muḥammad al-Wazzān al-Zaiyātī (c. 1485-c. 1554), also known as Leo Africanus, who authored the fifteenth century chronicle of Songhai, *History and Description of Africa and the Notable Things Contained Therein* (1526).

BOOKS AND ARTICLES

Brooks, George E. *Landlords and Strangers: Ecology, Society, and Trade in Western Africa, 1000-1630*. Boulder, Colo.: Westview Press, 1993.

Connah, Graham. *African Civilizations: Precolonial Cities and States in Tropical Africa, an Archaeological Perspective*. New York: Cambridge University Press, 1987.

Davidson, Basil. *African Kingdoms*. New York: Time-Life Books, 1971.

_____. *West Africa Before the Colonial Era: A History to 1850*. London: Longman, 1998.

Law, Robin. "Warfare on the West African Slave Coast, 1650-1850." In *War in the Tribal Zone: Expanding States and Indigenous Warfare*, edited by R. Brian Ferguson and Neil L. Whitehead. Santa Fe, N.Mex.: School of American Research Press, 1992.

McKissack, Patricia, and Fredrick McKissack. *The Royal Kingdoms of Ghana, Mali, and Songhay: Life in Medieval Africa*. New York: Henry Holt, 1994.

Martin, Phyllis M., and Patrick O'Meara, eds. *Africa*. 3d ed. Bloomington: Indiana University Press, 1995.

Phillipson, David W. *African Archaeology*. Cambridge, England: Cambridge University Press, 1985.

Ruben G. Mendoza

ETHIOPIA
DATES: C. FOURTH CENTURY-1543 C.E.

POLITICAL CONSIDERATIONS

The military history of Ethiopia is closely tied to political and commercial relations of the highland regions to those in the surrounding lowlands. It is also tied to the caravan trade in Nubia and to sea-based trade along the Red Sea coast, and thus to the Arabian Peninsula. Related to these geopolitical factors are religious ones: first the fourth century spread of Christianity into areas dominated by animistic and pagan religious practice, and later the seventh century introduction of Islam in the lowlands. The areas to the east, north, and west of the Ethiopian highlands retained a lively Christian religious tradition and came to view themselves as isolated island bastions of Christianity surrounded by a sea of Islam.

The formation of states in the Ethiopian highlands, financed by thriving commerce, dates back to several centuries before the common era. These states were increasingly influenced by Arabian culture and later by commercial ties with the Ptolemaic dynasty subsequent to the Alexandrian imperial period in the late fourth century B.C.E. down to the emergence of the Roman Empire. The interplay of commercial wealth with the growth of numerous political states gave rise to a constant competition between the food-growing regions of the Ethiopian highlands and the commercial settlements along the Red Sea coast. Warfare increased in scale and importance during this period, as competition among local elites for the profits of trade drove them into violent confrontation. By the first century C.E., the powerful state of Aksum, centered in the Tigrayan highlands, emerged as the dominant player in the commercial contest, but Aksum acted more as a monitor over a feudal system of trade than as a monolithic state. Aksumite Ethiopians gradually expanded their dominance over the southwestern littoral of the Red Sea, attempting to dominate even the caravan trade to the north. They even established a considerable presence on the Arabian side of the Red Sea. Trade with the Roman Empire was considerable, and with the success of Christianity in that empire, it was only a matter of time before Aksumites also began to embrace the Christian faith in the third and fourth centuries. Tradition maintains that during the fourth century Christianity was more firmly established by the shipwrecked Syrian Frumentius (fl. c. fourth century). Frumentius later became bishop and successfully evangelized much of the Aksumite kingdom, which maintained a largely peaceful domination of Ethiopia and neighboring regions until its displacement from the Arabian coast by Persians in the mid-sixth century. The Aksumite kingdom was further weakened in the seventh and eighth centuries by the spread of Islam throughout Arabia, into north Africa, and along the lowland regions of the Eritrean and Somali coasts. The Aksumite Empire, deprived of its links to the Mediterranean and to lucrative trade, could no longer maintain large armies, nor rely on sea-based or caravan trade. In growing isolation from the rest of the world, the Aksumites moved south into the mountainous interior of the Abyssinian highlands, where they dominated Agau-speaking agriculturalists, assimilating much of the local population through intermarriage, cultural transplantation, and religious conversion. Still, Agau-speaking peoples fought back in peripheral areas that the centralized but by now weakened Aksumite state could not control during the tenth and eleventh centuries.

The cross-fertilization of Aksum with the Agau produced a new dynasty, the Zagwe, whose most celebrated figure was the emperor Lalibela (r. c. 1185-1225), who was Agau by bloodline but thoroughly assimilated into the Aksumite Christian culture. Lalibela was unable to hold the fractious and feudal empire together, however, and was eventually defeated by the Shewan rebel and Christian leader

Yekuno Amlak (fl. thirteenth century) after a series of battles that culminated in 1270 with Lalibela's death. Yekuno Amlak declared himself emperor and, to bolster his legitimacy, claimed to be a descendant from the line of King Solomon and Queen Sheba of the Old Testament. He quickly consolidated the existing empire and subdued neighboring Muslim areas. In the early thirteenth century, Emperor Amda Tseyon (r. 1314-c. 1344) expanded and solidified the Solomonid Dynasty over the divided feudal system. He established military garrisons throughout the highlands, areas difficult to govern even in the best of times, given their remoteness and inaccessibility. He also encouraged Christian evangelization. The order instituted by Amda Tseyon increased both the economic activity and wealth of the area, as he extracted tribute from his locally appointed administrators and feudal lords. Amda Tseyon attacked Ifat, a Muslim area that had earlier provided tribute. When troubles in the empire called his attention elsewhere, however, the Ifat Muslims responded by declaring a holy war in 1332. Amda

TURNING POINTS

3rd cent. C.E.	Aksumite Ethiopians emerge as dominant players in the control of Red Sea trade.
7th cent.	Aksumite kingdom is weakened by the spread of Islam throughout Arabia and North Africa.
1314	Emperor Amda Tseyon comes to power in Ethiopia, expanding and solidifying the Solomonid Dynasty.
1529	Muslim leader Aḥmad Grāñ defeats forces of Lebna Dengel at the Battle of Shimbra-Kure, opening southern Ethiopia to Islamic rule.
1541	Portuguese musketeers arrive to help defend Ethiopia, ending Islamic threat two years later, under the emperor Galawdewos.

Tseyon responded vigorously and with great military brilliance. Against the highly mobile Muslim units, he used his army effectively to isolate and attack the weakest Muslim units, fielding decoy columns to keep the Muslim-federated troops off-balance and always on the defensive. Eventually he thoroughly routed the Muslim forces and substantially expanded the extent of his empire. Subsequent Ethiopian kings built on his success by fostering Christianity as a unifying force in an otherwise feudal economic system. However, not all Muslims in the empire converted, and thus they remained a group susceptible to mobilization when outside Muslim forces intervened.

From the fifteenth to the sixteenth century, the greatest threat to Ethiopia proved to be the Islamic peoples of the northern and eastern lowlands and the Oromo peoples to the south. Under the reign of Lebna Dengel (fl. sixteenth century), Islamic rebellions were put down, but increasing pressures were placed upon the lowland grazing grounds of both Somali and Oromo peoples to the south and east. The Somalis and Oromos gradually migrated into Muslim upland areas under Lebna Dengel's control, precipitating con-

Two ancient Ethiopian warriors spar with each other.

stant turmoil in these areas. Muslims eventually responded with the jihad of Muslim leader Aḥmad ibn Ibrāhīm al-Ghāzī, known as Aḥmad Grāñ (1506-1543), "the left-handed," who trained a disciplined group of warriors in the art of highly mobile warfare, made more deadly by the introduction of firearms obtained from the Ottoman Turks. Aḥmad Grāñ's smaller fighting force defeated the larger but disunited armies of Lebna Dengel at the Battle of Shimbra-Kure (1529), opening much of the southern part of the Ethiopian Empire to Islamic rule.

Lebna Dengel died in 1540, still in control of the highland region of his country. His appeal to Portugal eventually paid off, when in 1541, about 400 Portuguese musketeers disembarked and made their way to Abyssinia's support. With this firepower, Ethiopian forces won their first victory over the forces of Aḥmad Grāñ, who, stung by defeat, turned to the Ottoman Turks for additional support, which was granted. With nearly a thousand Turkish mercenaries armed with muskets and cannons, Aḥmad Grāñ defeated the Ethiopian-Portuguese forces in 1542. Subsequently, however, under the emperor Galawdewos (r. 1540-1559) the Ethiopians shifted to hit-and-run warfare, and eventually Aḥmad Grāñ was killed in 1543, thus ending the Islamic threat to Ethiopia. The gradual rise of the largely animistic Oromo peoples along the periphery of the Ethiopian Empire in subsequent years further insulated Ethiopia from direct contact with Islamic forces.

MILITARY ACHIEVEMENT

Throughout the history of Ethiopia, military activity tended in its tactical and technological dimensions to lag behind that of other regions. Although Ethiopia was not known for its military innovation, military leaders of both the Ethiopian state and of rebel groups along its periphery were quick to adopt tactics and methods of warfare suited to their immediate needs. Their tactics were further reinforced by changing economic conditions over time. When the central state was stable and encouraging to economic growth and commerce, more revenues were available to maintain larger armies. Tactics for maintaining con-

trol of an expanding state included the garrisoning of soldiers in hinterland regions. The interconnection of military policy with that of religious evangelization was critical to the expansion of his empire during the reign of Amda Tseyon. Appeals by contending forces to external assistance and to the latest weaponry were hallmarks of warfare in the region during the sixteenth century, as each side sought to increase its firepower.

WEAPONS, UNIFORMS, AND ARMOR

The spear was the principal traditional weapon of the Ethiopian warrior. For defense, warriors carried shields. Uniforms consisted of full and colorful pants and long-sleeved shirts. Caps and capes of cloth or fur were worn for warmth in the cool of the highland regions. Rebel and Muslim armies in the lowlands also fought with spears and sabers, although their dress was much lighter, befitting the hotter and dryer conditions of the desert lowlands. Only in the early sixteenth century were firearms and cannon introduced into the warfare of the region, typically with the deployment of mercenary forces familiar with the new technologies. Rebel forces in the lowland regions used camels for transport and cavalry.

MILITARY ORGANIZATION

Military organization varied significantly throughout Ethiopian history. Feudal and clan warfare marked by temporary and shifting alliances of small militia-like forces were perhaps the most common and persistent manifestations of warfare during most of the period from the fourth to the sixteenth centuries. During periods of expansion of the central state such as those of the Aksum Dynasty from 300 to 500 and the Solomonid Dynasty of the fourteenth and fifteenth centuries, larger armies were maintained. During periods of central governmental weakness, the various isolated areas broke down along lines of feudal lordship, as did the armies. Under stronger emperors, greater unity of command and control over the military forces was in evidence.

DOCTRINE, STRATEGY, AND TACTICS

As in the area of military organization, so in the areas of military doctrine, strategy, and tactics, a great deal of variation is exhibited in Ethiopian military history, and this variation was itself the result of changing circumstances and necessity. For example, when Amda Tseyon was faced with full rebellion in the predominantly Muslim areas of his country in 1332, he deftly used his military forces in a highly mobile warfare that prevented the rebels from ever mounting a successful counterattack in force. By gradually defeating smaller units apart from any main body of forces, the emperor was able to win victory over otherwise fairly mobile rebel forces. By forswearing a conventional positional strategy and by using superior numbers, Amda Tseyon bested the rebels in their one potential advantage, mobility.

Similarly, Aḥmad Grāñ, by using hit-and-run tactics, largely crippled Lebna Dengel's forces during the jihad of 1527 to 1543. The Ethiopian forces, though far superior in number, fought a more conventional and positional war strategy that proved unable to match Aḥmad Grāñ's highly motivated and carefully trained forces, who were armed with some firearms and under a clear chain of command. Dengel's forces, though larger, were divided by feudal loyalties, proving no match for Aḥmad Grāñ's better-trained and better-led army. When Portuguese muskets arrived to tip the balance slightly against Aḥmad Grāñ, he sought further outside support and firepower, regaining the advantage. Under Emperor Galawdewos, Ethiopian forces shifted strategy and, like Amda Tseyon before them, employed hit-and-run tactics, thus turning Aḥmad Grāñ's own tactics against him. This plan eventually succeeded because Aḥmad Grāñ was fighting on unfamiliar ground, whereas the Ethiopians were defending their own mountainous territories. With this strategy, the Ethiopians caught Aḥmad Grāñ alone with only a small force and were thus able to trap and kill him. Clearly, Ethiopian military figures were capable of assessing the threats and forces they faced and of adapting their strategies and tactics to the demands of changing situations.

BOOKS AND ARTICLES

Abir, Mordechai. *Ethiopia: The Era of the Princes: The Challenge of Islam and the Reunification of the Christian Empire.* New York: Praeger, 1968.

Greenfield, Richard. *Ethiopia: A New Political History.* New York: Praeger, 1965.

Henze, Paul B. *Layers of Time: A History of Ethiopia.* New York: St. Martin's Press, 2000.

Levine, Donald. *Greater Ethiopia: The Evolution of a Multiethnic Society.* Chicago: University of Chicago Press, 2000.

Marcus, Harold G. *A History of Ethiopia.* Berkeley: University of California Press, 1994.

Robert F. Gorman

THE MEDIEVAL WORLD

EASTERN AND SOUTHERN ASIA

CHINA

DATES: 581-1644 C.E.

POLITICAL CONSIDERATIONS

After the collapse of the Han Dynasty in 220 C.E., China drifted into a period of political chaos during which it was controlled by a number of rival regional kingdoms. However, by the sixth century, Yang Jian (Yang Chien), also known as Wendi (Wen-ti; 541-604), a successful military commander, had won the support of the majority of the regional leaders in the north to reestablish a central authority that eventually brought most of traditional China under his control. By 589 the Sui (Sui) Dynasty (581-618) had set in motion a number of reforms that increased and stabilized the Chinese standard of living. Yang Jian instituted a new system of taxation that brought needed financial relief to most of the peasantry. He also constructed a series of regional granaries, which both lowered prices and ensured the equal distribution of food. This newfound prosperity was short-lived, however, because the emperor was assassinated by his eldest son, Yangdi (Yangti; 569-618). As emperor, Yangdi began a series of extensive civil engineering projects in an attempt to improve transportation and tie the vast empire together. He also started a series of military campaigns to gain control of the northern portion of the Korean Peninsula. Both actions greatly disrupted the economy and were especially hard on the peasant population. Violent political uprisings broke out in every corner of the empire, and Yangdi was finally assassinated by a group of his ministers in an attempt to quell the fighting and reestablish political order.

This internal dissent severely weakened the Sui Dynasty, and in 618 Li Yuan (Li yuan; 565-635), the duke of Tang, took advantage of the situation to establish the Tang (T'ang) Dynasty (618-907). Li Yuan's first action was to restore the traditional scholar gentry as the foundation of the government bureaucracy, returning the intellectual class to the study of Confucian philosophy and reinstating the national examination system as the entry into government positions. These actions produced a class of neo-Confucian scholars that would have a profound ethical impact upon China's civil and military services. Most important, this new intellectual class believed the major function of Confucian philosophy was to develop an individual moral code. This new philosophical system would impact Chinese society in important ways. The scholar gentry became very xenophobic and rejected all alternative worldviews as inferior. This narrow focus on a strict social structure stressed tradition and fought any political, economic, scientific, or technological innovation. The gentry's emphasis on individual moral growth clashed with the harsh realities of the martial arts and resulted in an antimilitary bias among the Chinese intellectual class.

Under both the Tang and Song (Sung) Dynasties (960-1279), China experienced widespread economic growth, which in turn gave birth to a Chinese golden age. This success was based upon the development of the agricultural potential of southern China, most significantly in the production of rice in the Yangtze (pinyin, Chang) River Valley. The future of China would now be determined by the link between the bureaucratic north and the agricultural south. To solidify this crucial relationship, the government constructed the Grand Canal, a magnificent civil engineering project that was, in its time, the largest human-made waterway in the world. The canal increased transportation throughout the country, both accelerating trade and creating a sense of unity. The maintenance and protection of the Grand Canal became a major focus of the Chinese military. In times of conflict, this waterway allowed the emperor to move troops swiftly to any trouble spot.

With China's great economic success came a softening of Chinese society, widespread political corruption, and a series of weak and incompetent emperors who eventually sapped the energy of the empire. In particular, the effectiveness of both the bureaucracy and the military was decreased, helping to create the conditions for the Mongol conquests at the beginning of the thirteenth century. These nomadic warriors first entered China at the invitation of the declining Song Dynasty. The emperor hoped that they would engage and destroy the Jürcheds and the Jin (Chin), two northern nomadic tribes that threatened to invade China. In 1234 the Jin were defeated by a Sino-Mongolian military alliance, but then, in direct violation of that agreement, the Song attempted to occupy the newly conquered land and extend their empire into the northern territories. This action shattered the alliance and set in motion the Mongol conquest of China and the establishment of the Yuan Dynasty (1279-1368).

The Mongols would have a significant impact upon Chinese history. They established their capital at Beijing and abolished the bureaucracy based upon Confucianism and the examination system. These actions were taken specifically to negate the influence of the scholar gentry. The Mongols eventually adopted many aspects of Chinese culture and aggressively promoted its literature and art. Despite this openness, the Mongols were never able to find a solution to the Sino-Mongolian ethnic rivalry. Most of the intellectuals from the gentry class considered the Mongols to be uncouth barbarians. This ethnocentricity was exacerbated by the gentry's resentment of the abolition of the state examination system, which blocked the gentry from gaining access to the highest levels of political power.

After the death of Kublai Khan (1215-1294), the Yuan Dynasty fell into a period of decline. There were essentially four reasons that this took place. First, the southern region was occupied by a large number of activists who had remained loyal to Song Dynasty. As the Yuan declined, many of these disenchanted groups were emboldened to take political action that eventually resulted in an empire-wide revolt. Second, Yuan military prestige also suffered a severe blow from two disastrous military expeditions against Japan in 1274 and 1280. Third, Yuan military failures were founded in the general weakness of the

post-Kublai Khan government that was beset by deep-seated corruption within the political bureaucracy. By the middle of the fourteenth century, the Mongol government was far too weak to maintain its control over all of China. Fourth, the increase in peasant uprisings and the rise of secret revolutionary societies resulted in a series of disastrous insurrections that finally forced the Mongols to withdraw to their ancestral homeland.

By 1368 the Ming Dynasty (1368-1644) had been firmly established, and, from the very beginning, the new leadership made a concerted effort to reinstate the important Chinese institutions that had been suppressed by the Mongols. Most important, the Ming emperor restored the power of the scholar gentry. Confucianism once again became the dominant philosophical system and served as the basis for the renewal of the civil service examination system. In the first decades of Ming rule, the emperor began to develop a truly global perspective. China became a major force in Eastern trade, and by the 1400's it controlled the extensive and profitable Indian Ocean trade. China experienced an unprecedented age of economic growth that impacted every sector of Ming society. China at this time truly ruled the oceans of the world. From 1405 to 1433 no other civilization could match China's marine technology. During this time the great Ming imperial fleet made seven extensive voyages to every major port from the South China Sea to the east coast of Africa. Products from throughout the Eastern Hemisphere flowed into the markets of the empire. Most important, the latest geographic, medical, and scientific knowledge became available to the Ming Dynasty. However, as China was poised to become the first world empire, the emperor decided to adopt an isolationist policy and completely dismantled his great world navy.

This profoundly important historical act was the result of an intellectual battle between the newly established Confucian scholar gentry and a group of Mongolian technocrats led by the famous admiral Zheng He (Cheng Ho; c. 1371-c. 1433). This controversy was fueled by a fifteenth century Chinese "postmodern" worldview based upon the scholar gentry's fear of the new scientific and technological class. The scholar gentry realized that this new group,

Bettmann Archive/Corbis

Marco Polo before the emperor Kublai Khan, Mongol founder of China's Yuan Dynasty.

with their knowledge and skill, could very well dominate the development of China's economic, defense, and social policies. These scholars were influenced by the strong Confucian ideal of isolationism and tradition, rejecting the idea of internationalism. Finally, the knowledge base upon which the scholar gentry entered government service was founded in their ancient classical texts. The new sciences of modern astronomy, navigation, and marine engineering were both foreign and threatening to this bureaucratic elite.

The gentry were victorious against the technologists because they successfully implemented a three-pronged attack. In their argument to the emperor they first appealed to the ethnocentric tendencies inherent to Chinese culture. The name "China" itself means "Middle Kingdom," and traditional Chinese thought regarded the country as occupying the prestigious position in the center of the world. This view lent credence to the argument that China had nothing to learn

from the world beyond its borders. Second, the gentry emphasized the superiority of classical knowledge, from which the traditional political philosophy of the Tian Ming (T'ien Ming), or "mandate of Heaven," the idea that an emperor was conferred directly from Heaven the right to rule, had evolved. Finally, because there still existed within Chinese society a profound hatred of the old Mongol regime, the Confucians were able to use the ethnicity of these technologists, most of whom were descendants of the Yuan Dynasty, against them to bring the emperor over to the gentry's side. Eventually, a decree came forth from the Ming Dynasty that China's navy would remain in port, and that future funding of this great fleet would be canceled. In just a few short years the most sophisticated navy in the world fell into decay and eventually disappeared.

At first glance, the Ming Dynasty would seem to have survived its neo-isolationist policy, but in fact the opposite was true. By the mid-sixteenth century it was evident that the empire had entered a state of decline. A series of incompetent emperors created an environment of corruption that led to a drastic reduction in the effectiveness of the government. This widespread inefficiency had the greatest impact in the area of public works. Corrupt officials allowed the agricultural infrastructure of dikes and irrigation canals to fall into a state of disrepair, creating conditions that resulted in famine and starvation. The government lost its mandate of Heaven, and the countryside was ravaged by peasant uprisings. The resulting political chaos led to the fall of the Ming Dynasty.

MILITARY ACHIEVEMENT

Military events also played an important role in Chinese affairs during the era between the rise of the Sui Dynasty and the fall of the Ming Dynasty. Yang Jian, the founder of the Sui Dynasty, used his prestige as a great military leader to bring all of China under his control. Despite his military success, however, he was unable to establish a lasting peace. His new government was beset by revolts, and he reacted to this chaos by implementing an authoritarian style of government. His greatest threat came from the disaffected population in the south, where he sent his two most trusted generals to crush any resistance to imperial authority. The emperor then instituted a policy of forced labor, which concentrated on the construction of the Grand Canal and the restoration of more than 1,000 miles of defensive walls on the empire's northern borders.

Yang Jian's two major military problems were the constant threat of invasion from the northern steppe and the fear of rebellion. In an attempt to control the military, he issued a series of decrees that placed all army units throughout the empire under the direct control of local civilian officials. These loyal bureaucrats were also directed to confiscate all privately owned weapons and store them for possible military use.

Yang Jian also began an expansionist policy, and his primary goal was to return Vietnam to Chinese control. In 602 he sent an expeditionary force to Vietnam, where his army was devastated by both stiff re-sistance on the part of the Vietnamese and a deadly virus that killed hundreds of soldiers.

The emperor's son Yangdi used this disaster to organize and execute an assassination plot, which brought him to the throne in 604. The young emperor also had plans for extending the borders of the empire, and in 607 he led an army that marched westward against the T'u-yü-hun, a band of nomadic warriors that had recently negotiated a military alliance with the Koguryo, the most powerful dynasty in the northern Korean Peninsula. Fear that such an agreement would prove a threat to China, Yangdi initiated a military campaign against this potential rival. The Koguryo took advantage of the mountainous landscape of northern Korea, fortifying their towns and implementing a defensive strategy against the invading Chinese. Stifled by this tactical policy, the emperor's army fought a long, difficult, and unsuccessful campaign, and Yangdi returned home to find his empire in open rebellion.

Li Yuan, the duke of Tang, took advantage of this military disaster to increase his power in the area. In 617 he successfully negotiated an alliance with the Turks, who agreed to supply men and horses to the duke's army. Secure in this new military arrangement, Li Yuan moved against the Sui. After a disastrous military campaign in which his forces were soundly defeated, Yangdi died. The duke of Tang, upon hearing of these events, declared himself the new emperor of China.

Li Yuan adopted a military policy that proved to be very successful. The Tang Dynasty used the mountains in the west as a natural fortification against invasion from the central Asian steppe. The new emperor was also very generous to the Sui army, and he implemented the enlightened policy of granting both the enlisted men and officers from defeated armies positions in his armed forces. This policy not only increased the effectiveness of his military but also ended any possibility of a future military uprising by the Sui forces.

Li Shimin (Li Shih-min; 600-649), the duke's son, was also a major factor in the military success of the Tang. He was a great tactician and was famous for his use of cavalry. Concerned about his father's advancing age and emboldened by an important victory against peasant rebels in the Yellow River Valley, Li Shimin forced his father's abdication and assumed the Tang throne. He governed China for twenty-three years and became one of the most successful military leaders in Chinese history. He launched an ambitious plan to enlarge the territory of the empire, beginning this quest with an important victory over the Turks in 629, during the Sino-Turkic War (629-630). The success of this campaign so enhanced his international reputation that both the Persian and Byzantine Empires sent representatives to his court. Li Shimin continued to expand his empire, and by the time of his death in 649, the borders of China stretched from Tibet in the south to Lake Balkhash in the west. Tang military power continued into the next century. From 663 to 668 the Chinese fought and defeated the Japanese in the War of Kokuryo, uniting all of Korea under one rule, subject to China.

After he had secured the eastern border, the Tang emperor returned his attention toward the west. From 736 to 755 a series of successful campaigns extended the borders of the empire to the Pamir range, bringing the Tang to the frontier of Islamic civilization and placing these two great eighth century powers on a collision course. This Sino-Islamic crisis reached a flash point at the Battle of Talas River (751), a bloody confrontation that lasted for five days. The armies of Islam ultimately defeated the Chinese forces, ending Tang westward expansion.

This defeat marked the beginning of the Tang Dynasty's decline. Decades of military campaigns had taken a toll on Chinese society, and the losses in both revenue and productivity were significant. These problems led to widespread civil unrest, which devastated Chinese society. For more than one hundred years, the emperors and their bureaucracies had failed to return the empire to a state of normalcy, and by 884 the Tang Dynasty was shattered.

With the final collapse of the Tang Empire in 907, China fell into a chaotic intermediate period referred to as the time of the Five Dynasties (907-960). None of the dynasties was able to unify China, and order was finally restored in 960, with the establishment of the Song. Most historians refer to the Song as the world's first modern state, and its emperors were traditionally antimilitary. The government, in constant fear of an armed takeover, made strong efforts to limit the army's power. The Song created a military model that placed their generals under the control of the civilian bureaucracy, resulting in the military's lowered prestige and appeal for the aristocratic class. In time, the military came to be dominated by the lower echelons of Song society, and by the middle of the eleventh century enlisted men were receiving one-tenth of their former wages. This lowered pay caused great economic hardship, and mutinies became commonplace.

The Song government was faced with significant financial difficulties. The population of China had reached 140 million, and vast amounts of money had been set aside for the construction of large-scale irrigation projects. The empire also had to import the vast majority of its cavalry horses, which also cost a considerable amount of money. China's underfinanced military was grossly ill-equipped to meet the security challenges of the nomadic horsemen of central Asia. The Song bureaucracy responded to this problem by adopting a military philosophy based upon the concept of strategic defense. Money was allocated for the construction of massive fortifications that would frustrate the light horse cavalry tactics of the nomadic armies. The military theory that all defensive structures are eventually neutralized by an opposition force came to pass in the last years of the Song Dynasty. When the Song-Mongol military alliance broke down, the aggressive Mongol warriors quickly defeated the demoralized forces of the emperor and established the Yuan Dynasty. Between 1200 and 1405 the Mongols conquered Tibet, Russia, Iraq, Asia Minor, and southern and eastern Europe.

By the middle of the fourteenth century, the Yuan Dynasty began to decline. Years of famine gave rise to peasant unrest, and a secret religious sect known as the White Lotus spread anti-Yuan propaganda concerning the reestablishment of the Song Dynasty. In turn, the White Lotus also supported a peasant rebel organization known as the Red Turban movement. Fighting broke out between the Yuan forces in the south and the rebel armies. The success of these armies was primarily due to the fact that the Yuan had failed to keep the system of defensive walls under repair. The Yuan's nomadic heritage and military success was based upon swift cavalry movements, and a defensive mindset was totally alien to them. Eventually, the Mongols were able to defeat the rebel armies, but they were never able to regain complete political control of southern China.

From 1351 to 1368 the Mongols were involved in a series of military campaigns against Chinese forces in the south, in which they suffered a series of disastrous setbacks. The Mongols decided to abandon much of their territory and returned to their ancient homelands in the north. This strategic withdrawal marked the beginning of the Ming Dynasty (1368-1644).

The new Ming emperor and his intellectual elite modeled themselves after the Song Dynasty. Like the Song the Ming adopted an isolationist policy that kept the government's focus on protecting the homeland.

WEAPONS, UNIFORMS, AND ARMOR

The development of Chinese weaponry between 589 and 1644 reflected the dominant military philosophy of the most prominent dynasties. The Sui, Tang, and Song military policies were oriented toward the defense of the "Middle Kingdom." This attitude was reinforced by Confucian philosophy, which questioned the ethical status of militarism. Finally, the emperors also feared the possibility of a *coup d'état*. These factors made the development of the infantry the major focus of these dynasties, and weapons development reflected this orientation. Every infantryman received training in the use of both the sword and the spear. The most important weapon in the early Chinese arsenal was the crossbow, which had a devastating impact on enemy ground forces. As tactics evolved, the crossbow became both more sophisticated and more specialized. The military developed different types of crossbows that were used against infantries and cavalries and finally a series of bows that propelled fire-arrows to aid in the penetration of defensive walls.

The most important weapon used in sieges was the catapult. This technology had existed since the time of the Han Dynasty, but it was perfected under the Song. Three basic types of stone-throwers were utilized by the Song, ranging from small, highly maneuverable machines to large siege weapons that were used to destroy permanent fortifications. The Arabs also introduced the Chinese to the use of naphtha, an oil-based chemical mixture that burned on contact with water. This weapon was oriented toward naval warfare and proved devastating when wind conditions allowed its use.

The defensive, infantry-oriented philosophy of the Song changed with the onset of the Yuan Dynasty. The nomadic heritage of the Mongols emphasized constant movement. The most important weapon in the Yuan arsenal was the horse, a small, sturdy, and highly maneuverable Asian breed. A Mongol cavalryman was taught to ride by his mother at the age of three, and by the time he was ready for military service, he could both eat and sleep in the saddle. These mounted warriors were armed with a compound bow that had a force of 166 pounds and a killing range of 300 yards. Each warrior carried two bows and two to three quivers of arrows, some with small heads for distance and larger ones for close-in fighting. Both the rider and horse were protected by armor that consisted of a series of leather or iron strips and was quite effective against swords and spears.

The Ming made improvements to traditional weapons, such as the crossbow and catapults, and initiated significant progress in the use of gunpowder and explosive devices. Small handheld grenadelike projectiles became commonplace in Ming infantry units, and the shrapnel produced in the explosion of these bombs was quite deadly. The Ming also developed accurate rockets that were used to bring down wooden fortifications. These projectiles were usually launched from wheelbarrows, and their maneuverability made them a valuable addition to the Ming arsenal. The most significant development in weaponry during the Ming Dynasty was the construction of the Great Wall. China, because of its emphasis on defense, had a long history of using defensive walls as part of their arsenal. This strategy extends back to the Qin (Ch'in) Dynasty (221-206 B.C.E.) in the third century before the common era. As the result of both internal problems and foreign invasion, most of these walls became inoperable. Soon after the Ming came to power they began to construct a series of defensive walls to protect China from invasion from the north. By the mid-sixteenth century China once again found itself threatened by a new Mongol army. To counteract this threat the Ming government began the construction of the Great Wall, actually a series of fortifications linked by a defensive wall. Ironically, China's main danger did not come from the central Asian steppe but from the sea. The European armies that entered China all possessed the technology to overcome this Great Wall.

MILITARY ORGANIZATION

The Sui based their military organization upon a military and social philosophy that emphasized the obligation of the social elite to provide service to the state. The military leadership of the Sui came from old, established, aristocratic families, and their traditional social values formed the foundation of the Sui military organization.

This orientation toward service continued during the Tang Dynasty but was tempered by the impact of Confucian philosophy. The Tang armed forces consisted of six hundred militia units that ranged in size from eight hundred to twelve hundred men. Control of the army was transferred from the old aristocratic families under the Sui to the scholar gentry that now ran the newly formed Ministry of the Army. The armed forces were divided into two basic groups, the infantry and cavalry with sections divided into smaller units consisting of two hundred, fifty, and ten men. The Tang also developed a permanent cadre of professional officers, and the enlisted ranks consisted of men who rotated to duty for a specific number of months. This system was established so that soldiers could support themselves through agriculture, thus reducing the government expense of supplying the army. In times of great military danger, the Tang would also employ mercenaries to increase the size of its armed forces.

By the early eighth century, the cost of sending a large expeditionary force to a particular trouble spot became too expensive. The ministry created nine frontier commands and adopted the philosophy of a defensive army. By 737 the militia was replaced by a totally professional armed force, and these units were placed in the region of a powerful provincial official who would make decisions about their deployment. Each group constructed a fortified base of operations that served as a regional sanctuary in times of trouble.

The military strength of China began to decline under the Song Dynasty. The emperors were so fearful of a military uprising that they dissolved the successful organizational model that had evolved during the Sui and Tang Dynasties. They took control of the military decision-making process away from the generals and placed it under the tight control of the civilian government. Most important, the Song emperors used the enlisted ranks of the army as a social welfare program, providing employment for the poorest sectors of society. This system lowered the status of the military, and by the middle of the eleventh century the average enlisted man was receiving about one-tenth of his formerly allotted wages. This great inequity decreased the operational effectiveness of the army and eventually caused numerous mutinies.

The military organization under the Yuan Dynasty reflected the aggressive, loyal heritage of nomadic warriors, and was based upon the decimal system, with the smallest and largest units consisting of ten and one thousand men, respectively. Within the Mongol organization, each individual soldier occupied a unique position in the unit and was responsible to perform a specific task. The Mongol army was always divided into three operational units that controlled the left, right, and center of any military operation. All individuals within the Yuan armed forces were expected to carry out the necessary functions of a successful soldier. Both generals and enlisted men stood guard duty, and every member of the unit strictly obeyed the orders of his superior. Promotion was based upon skill, and it was quite common for a commoner to rise to the level of a great general. The martial qualities of bravery, discipline, and strength made the Mongols a very successful military organization.

The Ming military organization mirrored that of the Song. Its focus was directed primarily toward the defense of China and the control of the military. The government implemented a system that divided the country into military districts under the control of the civilian leadership. The logistics, supply, and training for the military were controlled by a Board of War.

DOCTRINE, STRATEGY, AND TACTICS

Military strategy and doctrine in the period between 581 and 1644 were profoundly influenced by the writings of China's great ancient military philosophers. These theorists were in turn influenced by the important philosophical systems that dominated ancient Chinese intellectual life. The four most important early schools of thought were Confucianism, Mohism, Daoism, and Legalism. Both the ethical codes and social models espoused by these philosophies formed the intellectual framework in which China's military theories were constructed.

Confucius (551-479 B.C.E.), who wrote prior to the Warring States period (475-221 B.C.E.), believed that China's social and political chaos was due to the fact that the nation was divided into competing regional states. He stated that the only solution to this situation was the development of a strong centralized government. A philosophically strong ruler supported by a Confucian bureaucracy would bring the peace and prosperity the Chinese nation so desperately needed. This would be a government based upon the development of personal morality. Later military theorists used this Confucian system to develop their doctrines, believing that the most important factor in preparation for war is the stability of one's own nation. The emperor must be a virtuous ruler whose actions have created a harmonious state. Before an emperor goes to war, he must have both the loyalty of his people and the "Mandate of Heaven" behind him.

The fifth century B.C.E. philosopher Mozi (Motzu) challenged Confucianism with his Mohist philosophy of universal love, which rejected all offensive war as immoral. To attack one's neighbor would be in violation of this most basic principle, causing the ruler to lose the Mandate of Heaven. According to Mozi, the only justifiable war is a defensive one, conducted to protect the population.

These two opposing philosophical schools would have the deepest impact on the evolution of Chinese military doctrine. The Confucian emphasis on the development of a strong personal ethical code would always be in conflict with the aggressive nature of the martial arts. This would be the basis for placing the military under the control of the gentry-dominated bureaucracy. The Mohist stand against offensive war would lead to the development of a "Grand Defensive Strategy" that would greatly influence the development of training, tactics, and weaponry.

The philosophical foundation for tactical operations can be found in the writings of the Daoist military philosopher Sunzi (Sun Tzu; fl. c. fifth century B.C.E.). In keeping with the philosophical premise that the laws of nature were the ultimate reality, Sunzi developed a tactical doctrine that synthesized Confucian, Mohist, and Daoist beliefs. Sunzi, incorporating the Daoist concept of natural order, wrote that war is governed by five eternal elements. The correct application of all five by the military commander was necessary in order to carry out a successful campaign. Every military commander had to develop a plan of action that would take into consideration the moral law, weather, geography, the commander and his rules, and finally the military organization he was commanding. The success or failure of any military campaign depended upon all five of these factors operating in harmony with one another.

Finally the implementation of these theories under battlefield conditions was influenced by the philosophy of Legalism, which emphasized order and strength. Every successful leader, before he engaged the enemy, had to be assured that his orders would be executed without question and that his forces were always operating from a position of superior strength.

MEDIEVAL SOURCES

The vast majority of Chinese sources have yet to be translated into English, although some have been translated into French, German, and Russian. The most important medieval sources are three military manuals that were used by the Tang, Song, and Ming Dynasties. The earliest of these is Li Quan's (Li Ch'üan; fl. 759), *Shen chi chih ti T'ai-pai yin ching*, a manual that was utilized by the armies of the Tang Dynasty. The most respected source is the *Wujing* (*Wu-ching*), or "Five Classics," a collection of treatises written during the Song Dynasty giving detailed accounts of medieval Chinese military strategy.

Sunzi, the military theorist who wrote *Bingfa* (c. 510 B.C.E.; *The Art of War*, 1910), was active in military affairs during the Zhou (Chou) Dynasty and had a profound influence on later Asian military thought. He was largely unknown in the West until the eighteenth century and received widespread appreciation only in the twentieth.

The primary chronicle of the Yuan Dynasty is the *Yuan Shih* (1370), originally composed in ten volumes by Song Lian and Wang Wei, and revised and rewritten in 1934 by Ke Shaobin in 257 volumes as *Xin Yuanshi*. It contains not only the history of the conquests and the military in general but also includes biographies of most of the commanders throughout the Mongol Empire.

BOOKS AND ARTICLES

Peers, Chris, and Michael Perry. *Imperial Chinese Armies, 200 B.C.E. to 1260 C.E.* 2 vols. London: Osprey, 1995.

_____. *Late Imperial Chinese Armies, 1520 to 1840 C.E.* London: Osprey, 1997.

Roberts, J. A. G. *A History of China, Prehistory to c. 1800*. New York: St. Martin's Press, 1996.

Richard D. Fitzgerald

JAPAN

DATES: C. 600-1600 C.E.

POLITICAL CONSIDERATIONS

Two outstanding political institutions dominate most of Japanese history until 1867: the samurai warrior class and the shogun military dictators. It is not exactly clear when the first Japanese state appeared, but Chinese and Korean chronicles speak of a recognizable kingdom at least by the fourth century C.E. In the fifth and six centuries, powerful families and clans residing in the area of present-day Kyoto and Osaka became united into the Yamato Court, the first real political entity in Japanese history. These hereditary clans, known as *uji*, controlled the majority of the population: the peasants, or *be*, who were grouped in caste-like fashion by occupation, residence, and family.

The *uji-be* system was modified in 645, but a characteristic feature of Japanese government at this time was the use of outpost soldiers, or *sakimori*, who guarded the borders. *Sakimori* protected strategic locations, such as outlying islands in the south and mountain passes in the north. An incipient standing army, these frontier guards were also sent on expeditions of various kinds, such as fighting the indigenous Ainu people in the northern territories. Although troops were initially provided by only the most powerful clans, by the eighth century each provincial governor was expected to provide a certain number (sometimes up to one-third of the male population aged sixteen to fifty-nine) of peasant-soldiers for three-year commitments. This policy was intended to break up the monopoly on military power held by the influential families.

However, the government, unable to control the activities of the remnants of the local *uji* clans in certain distant provinces, sent officials to these areas to oversee its interests and supervise the local administrations. The government also began granting land and tax exceptions to loyal subjects and to the younger sons and relatives of the court who, under the system of primogeniture, would not inherit their family's wealth.

A two-year smallpox epidemic beginning in 735 decimated the country, killing at least a quarter of the population and causing a severe labor shortage. As a result the government was economically unable to provide for a standing army, and landowners and aristocrats—as well as the officials previously sent by the government—began recruiting kinsmen to form bands of warriors to guard their own estates. Eventually, these blood ties lessened, but the permanent use of groups of such soldiers, called "samurai," or "those who serve," became a common way for landowners to protect and expand their holdings. The relationship between these noble warlords, eventually termed "daimyo," or "great names," and their vassals became one of intense loyalty. The samurai themselves grew into a class of military elite, with leaders

TURNING POINTS

c. 750	Carbon-steel swords first appear in Japan.
1192	The samurai Minamoto Yoritomo establishes the first shogunate at Kamakura, bringing order to Japan after four centuries of feudal chaos and political vacuum.
1477-1601	Perpetual civil war is waged throughout the Sengoku, or "Warring States," period.
1543	Firearms are first used in Japan.
1575	Three thousand musketeers help General Oda Nobunaga win control of central Japan.
1600	After the Battle of Sekigahara, Japan is unified as Tokugawa Ieyasu establishes the Tokugawa shogunate, with its capital at Edo.

drawn from descendants from the imperial family.

Although it was nominally a monarchy, medieval Japan actually was not ruled by the reigning emperor. Since the mid-700's, true power had lain in the hands of the shogun, a military dictator who theoretically protected the emperor from revolutionaries or barbarous indigenous border tribes. Although emperors inherited their titles, shoguns were ambitious leaders who rose to power on the basis of individual military skill and political guile. These shogun warrior governments ruled Japan until the mid-nineteenth century.

Under the shogunate system, power was divided between court and regent, allowing social or political instability as each disputed matters of jurisdiction. Because the shogun ostensibly governed on behalf of the emperor, his control was never absolute. Often disgruntled daimyo warlords would have their own ambitions and might rebel. Some samurai were never even vassals of the shogunate to begin with and were reluctant to obey its commands. Occasionally emperors themselves would try assert direct authority and start revolutions of their own. Of course, too, there were many disputes over shogunal succession, both from within the ruling families and from outsiders.

North Wind Picture Archives

A group of samurai warriors, a class that served as Japan's military elite throughout the medieval period.

MILITARY ACHIEVEMENT

Much of Japanese history centers on the struggles of the various shogunates and the resulting countrywide conflicts. Civil war was rampant, brutal, and endemic.

The Sengoku, or Warring States, period was a particularly cruel time. Perpetual fighting went on for more than a century, from 1477 to 1601. By the 1580's two generals, Oda Nobunaga (1534-1582) and Toyotomi Hideyoshi (1537-1598), had succeeded in unifying Japan after fighting numerous battles against various clans and eliminating the last Ashikaga shogun, Yoshiaki (1537-1597). After the assassination of Nobunaga by one of his own generals and the death of Hideyoshi, the country again fell into civil war. Tokugawa Ieyasu (1543-1616), Hideyoshi's successor, defeated a coalition of generals and warlords at the Battle of Sekigahara in 1600.

The Battle of Sekigahara is considered the most important Japanese battle in premodern times, ending the almost constant warfare that had preceded it and finally uniting the country. Ieyasu moved the Japanese capital to present-day Tokyo and established a reign of peace that lasted some 250 years. During this time of peace, the samurai evolved from warriors to government bureaucrats, administrators, scholars, and intellectuals. Though still an armed elite, the samurai warrior caste had, after a thousand years of struggle, finally been tamed in probably the greatest military achievement in Japanese history.

North Wind Picture Archives

A collection of Japanese swords, which, from the tenth to the nineteenth centuries were considered the best in the world.

WEAPONS, UNIFORMS, AND ARMOR

SWORDS

The most famous Japanese weapon of this time is undoubtedly the Japanese sword, which had been made in the islands since the eighth century. More than two hundred schools of swordmaking could be found, each with its own distinctive style and characteristics. By the tenth century Japanese swords were considered the best in the world, a distinction that lasted until an 1868 imperial edict limiting their production.

Swords came in a number of sizes, weights, and lengths. During the Muromachi period of government (1338-1573), it became common for samurai to carry matching pairs of swords: a long *katana* sword with a blade about 2 feet in length and a short *wakizashi* sword with a blade about 16 to 20 inches in length. Only samurai were allowed to wear swords, tucked into sashes around the waist, in non-combat situations.

SPEARS

Although regular foot soldiers would often carry swords, usually of inferior quality, their primary weapon was the long spear. Spears of every possible length and weight could be found, but one popular type of spear was the *naginata*: a curved steel blade placed on a polished wood staff of about 5 or 6 feet in length. The *naginata* was particularly effective against mounted attacks. The straight *yari* was the most common type of spear, with a double-edged hardened steel blade placed at the tip.

BOWS AND ARROWS

Japan has always been famous for the art of archery, and for centuries the bow and arrow was the primary military weapon. Mounted archery was a favorite sport of the early imperial court, and troops of mounted archers played an important role in repelling the thirteenth century Mongol invasion led by Kublai Khan (1215-1294). Arrows were made of fine points of steel, and the layered bows were especially powerful. By the fifteenth and sixteenth centuries, units of foot soldiers would advance while firing their arrows in alternating rows. Although it was not especially accurate, this steady stream of arrows flying at the enemy often forced defenders to break ranks.

ARMOR

Although armor was used in Japan as early as 400, it was not until the ninth century that the distinctively Japanese style of armor known as *yoroi* first appeared. This style remained basically unchanged until the modernization of Japan in the mid-nineteenth century. Medieval Japanese armor was some of the most intricate and beautiful in the world. Squares of metal were laced together with leather straps, allowing for a great range of motion. This supple armor gave mounted archers and swordsmen the flexibility needed to ride and fight and also afforded foot soldiers solid protection against piercing lunges or deflected blows. Japanese iron helmets were works of art unto themselves, displaying everything from antler horns to flags to demon faces.

UNIFORMS

Uniforms were not standardized in Japan until the late sixteenth century. Each warlord or clan had its own distinctive crest or coat of arms. Individual samurai, too, were quite idiosyncratic in their choice of dress. By the mid-sixteenth century, battles had become colorful. Samurai wore small flags, or *sashimono*, on the backs of their armor to indicate their affiliations, and the foot soldiers and conscripts of a particular daimyo began to wear similar kinds of dress.

MILITARY ORGANIZATION

Even as late as the Battle of Sekigahara in 1600 the Japanese system of military organization differed from the regimental models found in Europe. The main operational unit was the individual daimyo's army. Forces were placed in the field according to family or warlord, and orders were given to each unit's individual leader, often without close coordination with the other field units. This lack of organized communication often caused severe logistical problems.

Unit specialization in the Japanese army was not particularly pronounced. Japanese armies generally consisted of foot soldiers and archers. Japanese horses tended to be small, making Japanese mounted attacks less effective than those of the European knights. Samurai often rode to battle but dismounted to fight; organized cavalry units, then, were not especially popular. Artillery units were also unusual. After Japanese daimyo learned that stone castles were necessary to withstand cannon attacks, all wood castles quickly disappeared. Japanese gunsmiths never really designed siege guns to destroy castle walls. Thus, individual artillery units were also rare.

DOCTRINE, STRATEGY, AND TACTICS

The famous battles of the Gempei Wars (1180-1185) and the Japanese Civil Wars (1331-1392) established the strategies and tactics of Japanese warfare that would last for more than two hundred years. Typical military formations employed samurai armed with swords or bows and arrows, peasant foot soldiers armed with pikes, and the occasional mounted samurai cavalry charge. It has been said by some military historians that these battles, for the most part, were little more than mass confusion. Although elaborate and colorful formations were often staged before the battle, no strict patterns were followed in fighting. Struggles often degenerated into numerous one-on-one fights pitting individual soldiers against one another, each man simply trying to stay alive and attempting to decapitate the nearest foe.

This form of battle owed much to the samurai ethos of personal bravery and honor. For example, Daidoji Yuzan (1639-1730), in his book *Budo shoshinshu*, translated as *The Code of the Samurai*, recommended that a true warrior "never neglects the offensive spirit" and that he should follow the proverb "When you leave your gate, act as though the enemy was in sight." According to the way of the samurai, the public demonstration of one's personal individual honor on the battlefield was more important than large-scale military or geographic objectives. In fact, some samurai even discouraged the study of military strategy altogether. In another famous treatise on the samurai way of life, the *Hagakure*, which translates literally as "in the shadows of leaves," and is often known as *The Way of the Samurai*, Yamamoto Tsunetomo (1659-1719) argues that "Learning such things as military tactics is useless. If one does not strike out by simply closing his eyes and rushing into the enemy, even if it is only one step, he will be of no use." Indeed, it could be argued from the perspective of a millennium's distance that these individual private battles were as much the real reason for fighting as anything else.

Japanese warfare before 1570, then, was a highly unstructured affair; troops underwent little training and few drills. Samurai leaders, too, paid little attention to a campaign's supposed military goals. In the mid-sixteenth century, however, all this changed. A century of protracted civil war had altered the political climate and power dynamics in Japan. The central government and the shogunate were now vastly weakened, and the daimyo sought to enlarge their individual domains by force of arms. War came to be defined as warlord against warlord, clan against clan. To maintain this constant state of siege and countersiege, larger armies were needed. As there were not enough samurai (never more than 5 or 10 percent of the population), more and more peasant troops had to be used. These *ashigaru*, or foot soldiers, made up increasing portions of each of the daimyo's forces.

By the 1580's Nobunaga had realized the need for major changes, and his initial successes were due at least in part to his new ways of military thinking. Previously, a general in command of a smaller army had been able personally to inspire his troops with his own charisma, persuasion, and bravery. Now, with 20,000- to 50,000-man armies often commonplace, a leader's method of training, tactics, and command control were as important as his swordsmanship. Nobunaga, for example, realized the importance of uniforms and unit insignias for his troops, both to

make identification during battle easier and to instill a sense of unit cohesion and identity.

Another major sixteenth century development was the introduction of firearms in 1543. The first guns brought to the country were Portuguese harquebuses, matchlocks, and muskets. Japanese daimyo immediately ordered their swordsmiths to start making copies. Within a few decades Japanese gunsmiths, working with high-quality Japanese copper, were some of the best in the world. Firearms became relatively inexpensive to produce and reliable to use. As early as 1549 Nobunaga bought five hundred matchlocks from a local daimyo and established the first musket brigade in a Japanese army. By the 1570's more than a third of all daimyos' armies had muskets, which became the most important weapon in the Japanese arsenal.

These new weapons forced major changes in tactics, as Nobunaga was quick to realize. Nobunaga pioneered the use of harquebus volley fire as a major offensive tool, and others followed suit. In response to the adoption of firearms, the infantry was reformed into structured formations and echelons, including second-line units held back as reserves, a notion not used effectively by the Europeans until the early seventeenth century. In skirmishes spearmen were placed to the rear and flanks of the infantry to protect against infiltrators, and musketeers guarded the infantry and spearmen from cavalry charges.

After a series of power struggles throughout the late sixteenth century, Ieyasu defeated a coalition of generals and warlords at the Battle of Sekigahara in 1600 and established peace in the land. At this point he issued an unprecedented series of decrees that would eventually remove firearms from the country. Gun manufacturing first was restricted to one location and eventually was abolished altogether. The decision to eliminate firearms had several possible motivations. First, there was a generally negative feeling at this time toward all things Western, including guns. Second, according to samurai ethics, it was considered cowardly to kill someone from a great distance without meeting him face-to-face on the battlefield. Third, swords and the art of their use held special symbolic and aesthetic meaning in the minds of the samurai, who apparently felt almost naked without them. Finally and most simply, the country did not seem to need firearms. After stabilization by the Tokugawa family, Japan effectively cut itself off from the rest of the world for the next two and one-half centuries. Ironically, it was American gunboats in the 1850's that reopened the door.

MEDIEVAL SOURCES

There are many surviving documents, books, images, and artifacts from medieval Japanese times that tell a great deal about the lives of the samurai, daimyo, shoguns, and emperors. For example, illustrated training manuals of the era include guides to musket marksmanship, fencing, hand-to-hand combat, and even ninja assassination techniques. Also, the extensive writings of individual warriors tell much about their personal lives and philosophies. For instance, the loneliness of the *sakimori* frontier guards is reflected in the *Man'yō-shū*, an anthology of *sakimori* poems collected around 800 C.E. and translated into English as *Collection of Ten Thousand Leaves* in 1967 by H. H. Fonda. The famous *Gorin no sho* (c. 1643; *The Book of Five Rings*, 1974), written by master swordsman and artist Miyamoto Mushashi (1584-1645), is still read for its timeless insights on the philosophy of martial arts. The intrigues of the court and the shoguns are documented in the genre of war tales writings, the most famous of which is the *Heike monogatari* (c. 1240; *The Tale of Heike*, 1988). This collection of traditional tales of the five-year Gempei Wars (1180-1185) is probably the best existing expression of the samurai code of Bushido, the virtue of martial loyalty.

BOOKS AND ARTICLES

Ratti, Oscar, and Adele Westbrook. *Secrets of the Samurai: The Martial Arts of Feudal Japan.* Edison, N.J.: Castle Books, 1999.

Sugawara, Mokoto. *The Ancient Samurai.* Tokyo: The East Publications, 1986.

_____. *Battles of the Samurai.* London: Arms and Armour Press, 1992.

Turnbull, Stephen. *Samurai Warlords: The Book of the Daimyo.* London: Blandford Press, 1992.

Varley, H. Paul, with Ivan Morris and Nobuko Morris. *Samurai.* New York: Dell, 1970.

FILMS AND OTHER MEDIA

Samurai Japan. Documentary. Cromwell Productions, 1997.

James Stanlaw

INDIA AND SOUTH ASIA

DATES: C. 500-1526 C.E.

POLITICAL CONSIDERATIONS

India's long history, with the exception of Aśoka's (c. 302-c. 232 B.C.E.) Mauryan rule between 269 and 232 B.C.E., has been one of constant internal strife and defensive warfare. Early Hindu literature considered war and duplicity as serious activities, extolling them as honorable duties of king and subject alike. A warrior caste, the *kṣatriya*, was dedicated to warfare, and the concepts of glory and honor were punctuated in works such as the *Mahābhārata* (c. 400 B.C.E.-200 C.E.; *The Mahabharata*, 1834); the *Manusmṛti* (compiled 200 B.C.E.-200 C.E.; *The Laws of Manu*, 1886); and the *Arthaśāstra* (300 B.C.E.-300 C.E.; *Treatise on the Political Good*, 1961). Prior to the Mauryan Empire and Aśoka's rule, war had been brutal and merciless. After the second century B.C.E., however, war was fought in a more humane manner.

Around 500 C.E., with the appearance in India of numerous invaders from Central Asia, where armies and fighting techniques were superior, Hindu warfare underwent a profound modification. War elephants, concentrated use of cavalry, and emphasis upon horses were integrated with Indian techniques to give the highly mobile invaders a distinct advantage over rigid Indian methods. Horses, which had not flourished in India, were hearty, strong, and durable in battle. The invaders' concentration upon cavalry with superior horses increased their mobility. With their entrance into the Punjab and their operation around trade routes, the invaders opened a new era in Indian warfare. Hindu principalities, for the most part, continued to engage in petty intertribal disputes.

The one thousand years between 500 and 1526 C.E. witnessed four critical periods characterized by internecine warfare and destruction. The sixth century introduced numerous invading hordes that opened India to centuries of defensive warfare. Mus-

lim influence in the tenth century, in the form of the Ghaznavid Turks from Afghanistan, began an early influx of Islamic and Muslim influence that continued almost uninterrupted into the early sixteenth century. The most traumatic period was the fourteenth century with the Mongol invasions of Tamerlane (1336-1405) in 1398, which left North India devastated. Two hundred years later, a turning point in Hindu history occurred with the invasions of Turkic armies out of Kabul, Afghanistan, under Bābur (1482-1530) and the founding of the first Mughal Empire of India.

MILITARY ACHIEVEMENT

Petty squabbles and interprincipality rivalries for territorial control characterized the approximately one-thousand-year period from 500 to 1526 C.E. Attempts were made at creating unified empires, but these were short-lived. During the first half of the seventh century two figures emerged who vied for supremacy. North India was conquered by Harṣa (c. 590-c. 647) who, in attempting a southward expansion, was repulsed by Pulakeśin II (r. 609-642), the greatest of the Chalukyan monarchs. After the death of Harṣa, constant endemic warfare erupted between numerous rival dynasties and local kingdoms amid frequent foreign invasions by steppe nomad warriors and by Arabs whose militant religious zeal left an indelible mark on Indian history.

During the ninth century North India witnessed a fierce three-way struggle between three dynasties—the Prātihara of Rajputana, the Pāla of Bengal, and the Rāṣṭrakūṭa of the Deccan—that left general chaos and disunity in its wake well into the tenth century. On the periphery of India a new power flexed its muscle in the form of the Central Asian Turks. Their Muslim emirate of Ghaznī in Kabul, Afghanistan, exploited the anarchy of the subcontinent by raiding northern Punjab. In the early years of the eleventh century, Maḥmūd of Ghaznī (971-1030), one of the most able military leaders of Asiatic history, exerted such pressure with his raids that Hindu princes swore allegiance to him. He weakened the power of Hindu states in North India and removed the Prātihara Dynasty of Kanauj, the greatest obstacle to the spread of Islam. These raids ceased in 1030, and the Turks turned to gaining control of Persia and Central Asia. Maḥmūd's successful attacks were a precursor of events to come later in the twelfth century. The Hindu rulers continued their wrangling using the same unwieldy military tactics, having learned nothing from their defeat at the hands of the Turks.

Muslim invasions continued during the twelfth century, led by Maḥmūd's successor, Muhammad of Ghor (died 1206), who completed the conquest of North India. Meanwhile, interdynastic war between the Chola, Chalukya, and Hoysala Dynasties raged for hegemony of South India, and Tamil invasions of Ceylon added to the area's struggles. With Muslim conquests and the spread of Islam, North India fell under the domination of a foreign power, a foreign religion, and a foreign language. The Muslim Sultanate of Delhi and its offshoot, the Slave Dynasty, dominated the Indian scene throughout the thirteenth century. Quttbuddin Aibak (died 1210), Shams al-Dīn Iltutmish (r. 1211-1236), and Ghiyās al-Dīn Balban (r. 1266-1287) extended the Sultanate, ruled with great ability, and attended to the safety of the empire, which was constantly threatened by various Mongol hordes on its borders. Periods of stability existed but were punctuated by anarchic dynastic changes, Hindu rebellions, and endemic civil war between Turkish nobility and the Mongol raiders of India.

In 1296 the ruthless monarch ʾAlāʾ al-Dīn Muḥammad Khaljī (r. 1296-1316) conquered the Deccan to unite most of India under one rule. By the end of the century, however, the empire collapsed in 1398 under the relentless onslaught of Mongol forces led by Tamerlane. For two hundred years North India

lived in utter chaos under the Mongol onslaught, while South India collapsed under the conflicts waged between various Hindu and Hindu-Dravidian dynasties as well as the assault of ʾAlāʾ al-Dīn Muḥammad Khaljī.

The rise of the new Hindu kingdom of Vijayanagar continued warfare with the Muslim Sultanate of Bahmani during a large part of the fourteenth century. The Muslims were victorious, but Vijayanagar remained independent. The Sinhalese of south Ceylon, meanwhile, waged war with the Hindu Kalingas of the north, against whom they were generally successful.

After Tamerlane's disastrous invasion, the central Gangetic Valley and south-central and southwestern India fell under the control of turbulent Muslim rulers. The Hindus took advantage of the situation and emerged as leading powers in eastern and western India, most notably in Orissa and Mewar. Intermittent warfare continued between the two powers until two great events of the sixteenth century ended the chaos of the fourteenth and fifteenth centuries and changed the course of Indian history. In 1498 Portuguese traders arrived on the Malabar Coast and exposed India for the first time to European ideas and influence. Simultaneously the Central Asian Turk Bābur succeeded in occupying Kabul in 1504. He took advantage of the chaotic political environment to invade India, defeat the Delhi Sultan Ibrāhīm Lodī (died 1526) and establish the first Mughal Empire of India in 1526. Such an empire had not been seen since the days of the Guptas.

The medieval period in South Asia was dominated by three outside forces that revealed the inherent

TURNING POINTS

500	Central Asian invaders appear in India, bringing superior fighting techniques and concentrated use of cavalry.
10th cent.	Ghaznavid Turks invade India from Afghanistan, introducing an Islamic influence that will continue almost uninterrupted until the early sixteenth century.
1398	Mongol invasions by Tamerlane devastate North India.
1526	The Asian Turk Bābur defeats Delhi Sultan Ibrāhīm Lodī at the Battle of Pānipāt and establishes the Mughal Empire.

weakness of the Hindus against less numerous but better trained and equipped mounted invaders. Turkic Muslims, Central Asian Mongols, and European Portuguese traders exerted an influence that forever altered the course of history in India, a history dominated by superior military skill and prowess.

WEAPONS, UNIFORMS, AND ARMOR

Before the time of written records, wars were waged between tribal units using clubs, spears, and knives to vindicate offenses. Rarely were wars waged to acquire territory or gain some economic advantage. During the ancient period in India battles were close-formation skirmishes fought by the *kṣatriya* warrior caste utilizing thrusting and throwing instruments. During the medieval age, from 500 to 1500 C.E., battles were dominated by heavy cavalry. The primary weapon of choice was the bow and arrow. The growing reliance upon cavalry and archers was due to technological advancements in archery and the introduction of the saddle and stirrup between 300 and 800 C.E., which provided stability for the rider and support for his sword, spear, and lance.

Weapons during the medieval age were generally the same as those used in ancient warfare. These included quivers (*bhastrā*) slung from a shoulder, broad-bladed swords (*khadga*), heavy broadswords (*niṣtrimśa*), spears (*śakti*), javelins (*śūla*), reverse-curved swords, ancient slings (*gophaṇa*), curved throwing sticks (*vālāri kāmbi*), and sharpened throwing discs (*jah*) thrown horizontally or dropped vertically upon attackers.

Head and body protection included shields of leather, the preferred material, scale or lamellar helmets, and a "coat of a thousand nails" scale-lined and fabric-covered or padded about the torso. Heavier lamellar armor of thin plates, common in premedieval times, was rarely worn, especially in the humid, tropical south. For climatic reasons soft cotton quilted armor was preferred, and its use eventually spread to the Middle East and even to Europe. Asbestos cloth appeared in an assortment of fireproof clothing by the twelfth century. Some protective armor for arms and legs was also used.

Horse harnesses were primitive at best. A leather toe-stirrup had been known in India since the first century B.C.E. and continued to be used well into the eighth century C.E. Horse armor seems rarely to have been used in Indian warfare.

Years of civil strife left Indian armies poorly equipped. The infantry, made up of peasants, farmers, Jats, Gujratis, and various robbers, used bamboo staffs and, at best, rusty swords. The bow and arrow, much relied upon as a primary weapon, could not pierce the armor worn by Central Asian Turkic forces. The Hindu rajas relied heavily on herds of war elephants to demoralize enemy ranks and disperse cavalry. Turkic forces, however, used steel-clad warriors mounted on superb, agile horses. These were kept in reserve in the center of battle, behind the front line of attack, and were used to decide the final outcome.

Hindus generally expended their energy pursuing Turkic horsemen who harassed them with firepower, counterattacked, and forced them into hopeless flight and slaughter. The Turkic nomadic invaders used a composite two-piece bow considered the most fearful weapon on the battlefield. Hindus possessed nothing that matched the success of the composite bow. They used mounted bowmen as light troops to harass the enemy, whereas Turks used heavy armor-clad cavalry equipped with long spears in mass charges.

Military superiority gave the Turks the advantage over the Hindus. Turkish horses were superior in speed, endurance, intelligence, and dependability in hostile desert terrain. Turks used swift camels to carry provisions while living off the land, whereas Hindus used slow and burdensome pack-oxen. Thousands of years on the steppes and deserts of Asia had trained the Turks in stamina and strength.

The Muslim forces utilized various weapons developed by superior metallurgy around the tenth century C.E. Of these the curve-bladed steel scimitar proved supple, tough, sturdy, and capable of being honed to razor sharpness. Arab and Mongol forces possessed artillery against grenades, fireworks, and rockets of the Delhi Sultans. The arrival of Bābur's hardy, disciplined, and seasoned troops signaled the end of the disorderly and poorly equipped forces of the Sultans of Delhi. The introduction of muskets and artillery turned the tide against Hindu forces at the

Battle of Pānīpat in 1526. Hindu rule in North India collapsed with the establishment of the first Mughal Empire of India, which lasted well into the nineteenth century. Gunpowder changed the course of warfare forever.

MILITARY ORGANIZATION

The organization of standing armies in India since the third century B.C.E was based on an ideal extolled in classic religious texts. An army (senā) was commanded by a supreme commander (senāpati) over a four-tiered structure of infantry, cavalry, chariots, and elephants. Harṣha's army consisted of 50,000 infantry, 20,000 cavalry, and 5,000 elephants. Support services and noncombatants complemented this huge, unwieldy army. Chariots, mentioned in the seventh century C.E., represented a continuation of the ancient form of warfare. The senāpati used a four-horse chariot surrounded by a bodyguard and officers (nāyaka). The ancient military organizational system continued well into the fourteenth century, when cavalry gained greater importance in confronting Muslim invasions. However, traditional Hindu ideals of military organization remained.

In South India there was a clear militarization of the state into military camps. The huge and effective fourteenth century Vijayanagar army was organized by a governmental department called the Kandāchāra and led by a dandanāyaka, or commander-in-chief. However, there was a notable absence of discipline among the military personnel.

Muslim invaders maintained a well-organized and effective army unlike anything they confronted in India. Muslim forces relied heavily upon superior leadership, seasoned troops of high quality, highly developed military science, and great metallurgical skill. Morale was of the highest nature, supported by a firm brotherhood and religious zeal that rationalized war and conquest in the name of religion. Primary goals were booty and destruction of heathen places of worship.

The backbones of the Delhi Sultan's army were cavalry and war elephants, the latter adopted from the Hindus. The effect of one elephant in battle was equal to that of 500 horsemen. Infantrymen were recruited slaves and individuals needing employment.

Bābur, descended from the Mongol leader Genghis Khan (between 1155 and 1162-1227), organized his Turkic army on that of Tamerlane (1336-1405). A first-rate military genius, Tamerlane had organized his fighting forces on a rational basis rather than one of ancient traditional practice, assuring him of unfailing success. He surrounded himself with loyal lieutenants whom he could safely trust with far-flung branch operations beyond his personal direction.

Muslim and Mongol organizational skills, complete mobility, and superior horses and weaponry overwhelmed Hindu forces governed by tradition and lack of discipline. Although Hindu rajas commanded close to one million men, lack of discipline made them vulnerable to highly structured outside forces.

DOCTRINE, STRATEGY, AND TACTICS

The Arthaśāstra remained the guide for military doctrine, strategy, and tactics well into the medieval period. After the Gupta monarch Skanda Gupta (r. c. 455-467) successfully repulsed the Ephthalite, or White Hun, invasion in 445 C.E., greater emphasis was placed on shock tactics and mobility of cavalry and archers. However, after Ephthalite leaders caused the collapse of the Gupta state early in the sixth century, Hindu armies again reverted to traditional use of inferior cavalry, war elephants, and less mobility in battle. Warriors continued to use quivers attached to the rear of a saddle. Chariot warfare declined, and shock-value use of war elephants increased. In the south, the Deccan army of the Vijayanagar kingdom used camel troops as mounted infantry. Certain troops long abandoned in most of Asia, such as slingers, were still maintained and used by Hindu rajas. Archers also remained a critical component of the army, guided by the Dhanur Veda, "science of archery," military manual.

Military tactics were heavily governed by the Artharva Veda (1500-1200 B.C.E.), one of the sacred writings of Hinduism. Archers shot from a kneeling position supported by spear, javelin, and shield-wielding infantry. Such immobility opened the army to ravaging attacks by extremely mobile Muslim and Mongol troops skilled in fighting on horseback. Elephants generally carried a driver, or *mahout*, and three to four warriors. In response the use of large caltrops, iron-pointed triangular devices set in the ground to impede elephant and cavalry advances, was developed. Such Indian tactics were old-fashioned by the tenth century, but they continued into the thirteenth. Hindu pride prevented leaders from learning from their foreign adversaries. Hindus valued strength in numbers over speed and mobility, a doctrine that rapidly caused their defeat.

Pre-Islamic India was, however, well fortified, with walls built of stone, brick, or wood, and protected by slopes and bastions. Towers projected a short distance from the wall. Towns and villages of the seventh century had inner gates, wide walls of brick or tiles, and bamboo or wood towers. Six hundred years later the military architecture of Muslim and Hindu added the *chatri*, a ceremonial kiosk above the main gate to allow a monarch an observation post. Countersiege was highly developed, utilizing scaling ladders secured to mud-brick walls and iron plates to breach them. Elephants with iron plates on their foreheads were used as battering rams. A *pāshtīb*, or raised platform of sandbags, filled ditches between walls, and a *gargaj*, or movable wooden

tower, reigned down firepower upon the enemy. Attacks were impeded by use of fire, smoke, and heated iron grills.

Turk, Muslim, and Mongol strategy revolved around hit-and-run tactics, the defeat and humbling of a raja into vassalship, the utilization of his kingdom as a base for further advances into India, and the eventual annexation of the territory. The strategy of nibbling away at border provinces allowed a deeper penetration of the subcontinent. Success was directly dependent upon a well-established line of communications with Central Asia, which provided fresh reinforcements and supplies to accomplish deeper penetration. Together with social solidarity, a brotherhood of equality, lust for loot, and a fiery Islamic zeal against the infidel, the invaders quickly overcame Hindu resistance. Rapid movement necessitated a strong cavalry, which paralyzed Hindu armies with sharp decisive blows that frustrated their battle plans and evacuation.

Unlike Muslim solidarity, interclan and intercaste Hindu feuding and stress upon tradition in military affairs led directly to their final demise at the hands of Bābur's forces at the Battle of Pānipāt. Here Muslim firearms dominated the field of battle. The result was the complete collapse of Hindu resistance in 1526 C.E. and the formation of the first Mughal Empire in India.

MEDIEVAL SOURCES

The *Manusmṛti* (compiled 200 B.C.E.-200 C.E.; *The Laws of Manu*, 1886), which stressed glory and power, and the *Arthaśāstra* (300 B.C.E.-300 C.E.; *Treatise on the Political Good*, 1961), the primary treatise on Indian polity, laid the standards for war and peace well into the medieval period. The latter established principles of warfare, military organization, strategy, tactics, the role of king, military leaders, and warriors, as well as weaponry of war. In a theory of concentric circles, the core state was seen as surrounded by enemy states, and the aim of policy was to achieve a series of mutual alliances. Its emphasis was upon the reality of war rather than glory. The critical arm of the army, the archers, was governed and guided by the *Dhanur Veda*, written in approximately 500 C.E., an important manual on the science of archery.

Muslim military science and government of the thirteenth century was guided by the *Ādāb-ul-Mulūk wa-kifāyat al-mamlūk* (c. thirteenth century; translated in part in *Fresh Light on the Ghaznavids*, 1938), written by Fakhir-i Mudabbir (fl. twelfth-thirteenth centuries) for Sultan Shams al-Dīn Iltutmish. It covered governmental policies and served as a war manual, laying out guidelines for camping sites, battle formations, subterfuge, spying and scouting, night warfare, equipment and arms, and the care of man and horse alike.

BOOKS AND ARTICLES

Majumdar, Ramesh Chandra, H. C. Raychaudhuri, and Kalikindar Dutta. *An Advanced History of India*. London: Macmillan, 1950.

Oman, Charles. *A History of the Art of War in the Middle Ages*. London: Greenhill Press, 1991.

Sarkar, Jadunath. *Military History of India*. Calcutta, India: M. C. Sarkar and Sons, 1960.

Wise, Terence. *Medieval Warfare*. London: Osprey, 1976.

George Hoynacki

SOUTHEAST ASIA
DATES: C. 500-1500 C.E.

POLITICAL CONSIDERATIONS

Although the early history of the Southeast Asian region is vague, and the origins of its peoples are unclear, it is certain that the neighboring civilizations of China and India had major influences upon Southeast Asian history. As a result of the infiltration of Indian culture in the fifth century, the Indian warrior class and methods of waging war were adopted by the new Southeast Asian empires. The migration of the Guptas led to the founding of the Funan Empire. The Pallava wave was the impetus for the vital empires of Cambodia and Srivijaya. The Pala Dynasty of Bengal profoundly influenced the Javan culture. The desire for aggressive imperial expansion was also subsequently embraced in Southeast Asia, and constant raids and sieges among Southeast Asian empires mark the early history of the region.

MILITARY ACHIEVEMENT

The earliest information that exists on the ways of war comes from the small Indianized states on the Malay Peninsula, many of which were within the Funan Empire to the north, in the area of present-day Cambodia. From the seventh to the tenth centuries, soldiers used bows, arrows, swords, lances, and armor of leather. As a result of the Indian influence, many fought mounted on elephants; one division of the army consisted of one hundred elephants, and a hundred men surrounded each elephant. On the elephant's back was a sort of cage, called a howdah, in which rode four men armed with bows, arrows, and lances. The elephant's tusks might also be sharpened or lengthened with sword blades, and it might pick up enemy soldiers with its trunk or trample them underfoot. The standard battlefield role of war elephants was in the assault, to break up the enemy ranks, but elephants were also used in sieges, to push over gates and palisades or to serve as living bridges.

The growth and expansion of the Srivijayan and Javanese Empires is a strong example of the common aggressive desire to expand, and the constant conflict between the two empires eventually led to the absorption of Srivijaya within the dominion of the Majapahit kingdom, which controlled most of Sumatra, the coastal regions of Borneo and Celebes, and the Lesser Sunda Islands. The earliest reference to war in Srivijaya dates from 686 C.E., in which it is stated that the king went in search of magical power with 20,000 troops.

WEAPONS, UNIFORMS, AND ARMOR

The weapons used by the Srivijayans were mainly Indian in style: bows, arrows, curved flat swords, broad short daggers, and long shields. The unusual arrows had crescent-shaped heads, which could cut a head from a body or divide a bow in two.

Battle scenes are depicted in many bas-reliefs of the late eighth century C.E. Although these images tell nothing of tactics, they are significant in revealing that only infantry took part in the melees. This was almost certainly an aspect of Javanese warfare; horses and elephants were mainly reserved for chiefs and high officers. Of note is the virtual absence of spears, because only the strongest Indianization could have replaced this favorite local weapon with the bow. The spear, however, shared the primary place with the flat and curved sword. Another local weapon was the blow-pipe, which probably fired some form of poisonous dart. There were daggers, but no trace at this time of the kris, a typical Malay dagger invented around the fourteenth century. The most commonly used bow was the Indian longbow, used with the arrows tied up in quivers. Shields were mostly oval or square. Some soldiers were also depicted wearing a cuirass, protective armor covering the torso.

After the formation of the Majapahit Dynasty, however, weapons and warfare underwent significant changes. The military dress completely evolved from the Indian to the East Javanese fashion. Weapons, notably axes, clubs, swords, and daggers, seem to have been Indian, though the curved swords are of a later type than those on the Central Javanese reliefs. The reappearance of the spear in these reliefs, while the use of the bow is confined to human heroes, suggests an increasing pressure to resume use of local types of weapons. Both swords and daggers have definitively Indian-type hilts, and the kris seems still to be absent from use. The kris may not have become popular until the fifteenth century when Majapahit krisses appear to be represented on a relief of a Javanese forge.

A Javanese inscription of 1323 speaks of "magically forged weapons," indicative of the belief that magic and proper worship and sacrifice to the gods would bring victory on the battlefield. Much importance was placed on the art of procuring talismans, incantations, or drugs, the knowledge of which was the education of every hero. Another piece of evidence concerning the character of Majapahit warfare is the reproduction through drawings of a battle array, a crayfish-type military formation in which the forces were distributed in order in preparation for an attack. The Javanese often gave up any idea of preserving their own lives in battle and would rush the enemy, committing indiscriminate slaughter and refusing to surrender alive.

From the fifth to the eighth centuries, the Khmers and the Chams of central Southeast Asia were also subject to tremendous Indian influence. For these empires, Chinese sources are particularly profitable, as the cultures often encountered one another in wars of expansion. For example, when the Chinese invaded Champa by sea, the Chinese strategy was revealed for how they overcame the difficulty of Cham elephant attacks. After the Chinese had landed, they directed all their arrow fire against the Cham elephants and subsequently obtained victory.

The Chams, however, had many enemies. Foremost among them were the Khmers, as the Chams continually invaded Funan. The military character of the Khmers in the seventh century, before the Pre-Angkorian kingdom had been disrupted, is described in a Chinese history as being defensive and quarrelsome. Thousands of guards wearing cuirasses and armed with lances protected the palace, and citizens habitually prepared for confrontation.

MILITARY ORGANIZATION

It is known that during the thirteenth century, the commanders of the Javanese army received an annual salary of twenty taels of gold, and the soldiers, 30,000 in number, also received fixed annual pay in varying amounts in gold. The reliefs of the temples of this time reveal little. An inscription of 1294, alongside reports in Chinese annals, tell much about the results of the fighting that took place in repelling the Mongol invaders and in establishing the Majapahit Dynasty, but almost nothing about the nature of the warfare.

During its Ankgor period (802-1431), the Khmer Empire, by force of arms, extended its commonwealth to encompass vast areas of Southeast Asia. The first attempts, in about 813, by a Cham general named Senāpati Par to test the united Khmer state were never more than raids, for Jayavarman II (c. 770-850) kept the empire firmly in his grasp. The strategies of the Chams, however, had been sharpened by their constant quarrelling with the Chinese on their northern frontier. As the Khmers and Chams battled, the Khmers too learned of new strategies and weapons, and a fairly homogeneous art of war was established. For example, the ballista, first used by the Chams, also became incorporated into the Khmer equipment.

The Hindu concept of war as a religious sacrifice was fully recognized by the Khmers. So, much like the Javanese, the Khmers associated the ancestor mountain god, Hinduized as Shiva, with military ventures and prayed for his aid on the battlefield. At about the same time in Champa, 1064, Rudravarman III, also made ornate gifts to the goddess of the kingdom to show his devotion.

The commander-in-chief of both the Khmers and Chams was usually a prince, often the king's brother. Of other officers there is little detailed knowledge, but it seems that they would begin in the Royal Guard and then ascend to captain roughly a thousand men for war. The officers were distinguished by the red parasols that they carried into battle. Moreover, as in Java, in the Khmer and Champa Empires, the use of horses and elephants was confined to officers. Unlike the Indian custom, there was only one rider per elephant with a shield on his left arm. The number of horses was limited, as they were difficult to procure from China; therefore, there probably did not exist a cavalry division in either army. An accurate number of soldiers for either side is also difficult to ascertain. It seems that there were roughly 50,000 soldiers assembled on one side in the fourth century, a number that increased with time. By the eighth century, the royal guards alone numbered 5,000. On both sides, the infantry formed the greatest part of the militaries' strength.

According to Chinese texts, Cham weapons consisted of shields, spears, halberds, bows, and crossbows. The arrows of bamboo, however, were not feathered, but the points were poisoned. Cham sculptures also show swords and daggers. The lance, or spear, was the most common of the Khmer weapons, and cases of them were attached to the sides of the elephant platforms. By the twelfth century, the lance had largely replaced the sword to become the most distinctive of Khmer arms. The club, which was the weapon of the Khmer gate guardian, was relatively rare in the hands of warriors. Bows and arrows were also used for distance fighting. For protection the Chams had cuirasses made of plaited cane in addition to their shields. The Khmers used this armor as well but in a more limited capacity; it seems it was used more for parades and than for actual fighting. The Khmers also fought bareheaded, though the Chams are shown in sculptured relief wearing a reversed flower headdress.

DOCTRINE, STRATEGY, AND TACTICS

The Khmer and Cham Empires also had considerable knowledge of fortification. The Cham capital was a mountain of bricks dominated by pavilions and towers reaching 70 or 80 feet. The Khmer capital of Angkor Thom was also built up of massive stone walls, which, in the twelfth century, replaced earlier defenses of moat and mound. Despite its seemingly impenetrable fortifications, in 1177 Angkor fell to an unexpected Cham naval attack. It was not only Champa that possessed a navy, however; the Khmers also practiced naval warfare. The Chams often employed fleets of more than one hundred vessels, which were almost exclusively barges propelled by rowers. The fleets on both sides operated in conjunction with armies that relied on boarding, not ramming. Both sides were armed with long spears and shields, and in one relief of the period, a Khmer barge is filled with archers. This suggests that the bow was used in naval warfare before the close combat began. Naval warfare was limited at this time, however, as navies could not venture far from a shore held by friendly forces, because of the need to frequently replenish fresh water supplies.

The ideal type of army exchange was to bring about a pitched frontal battle. In a battle such as this, once some important leaders had been slain or had run away, the defeated side usually fled to the sheltering jungle. Chinese accounts claim that the Cham soldiers fought in parties of five, and the members mutually helped one another. If one fled, the other four were liable to be punished with death. Once the battle was over and a victor clear, it was the custom for the conqueror to set up pillars to commemorate victory.

Concerning the early Mon warfare and that of the Burmans of the Pagan kingdom, there is no direct knowledge. These civilizations left no bas-reliefs illustrating their ways of war, and the spiritual practice of Buddhism did not condone the glorification of warfare in inscriptions. It can only be assumed that, because they were an Indianized people, the early Mons and Burmese adhered to Indian models of warfare. The capital of the Thai state was established at Ayutthaya in 1350 and, following this, the history of modern Siam is commonly traced. Although Siam ascended consistently in power and frequently kept its warlike neighbors of Japan, China, and India at bay, its history is plagued by centuries of quarrels between tribes, as the prominent provinces of Cheingmai, Ayudhya, and Sukhothai battled tirelessly for the semblance of a united kingdom under their respective rule. The second Siamese kingdom captured Angkor in 1352, after the Khmer kingdom had become weak and exhausted. In 1393 the Siamese took Angkor again, and in 1431 they captured it for the final time. Thus, although the Siamese had embraced Buddhism, they began to learn the ways of war from the dying Khmer Empire. A record of Siamese and Burmese weapons exists dating from after 1500 and includes bows, crossbows, lances, spears with curved heads, javelins, and swords.

MEDIEVAL SOURCES

Few written sources exist regarding warfare in Southeast Asia during this period, and most of these are questionable. The earliest knowledge, though limited, comes from various Chinese sources beginning in the fourth century. This is often found in the form of accounts drawn from Chinese pilgrimages to India, especially the seventh century account of Hsuan-tsang and I ching, and often relate to economic vitality. Much knowledge comes from temple inscriptions, as at Angkor, and monuments devoted to various kings, particularly in the Khmer Empire and Pagan. Statues and bas-reliefs throughout the region indicate the nature of weapons and battle dress. There are a number of annals that provide basic royal genealogies, especially from Cambodia, though these are often confused or incomplete. The dependencies of the Majapahit kingdom, for instance, are enumerated in Mpu Prapañcha's *Nagarakrtagama* (1365). Marco Polo recounts his twelfth century experiences in Southeast Asia in his *I Viaggi* (1298; *Travels of Marco Polo*, also known as *Description of the World*, 1818). Some information can also be gleaned from sixteenth century Portuguese accounts of their early voyages in East Indian waters.

BOOKS AND ARTICLES

Coedes, George. *The Indianized States of Southeast Asia*. Edited by Walter F. Vella. Honolulu: University of Hawaii Press, 1968.

Hall, D. G. E. *A History of Southeast Asia*. 4th ed. New York: St. Martin's Press, 1981.

Quaritch Wales, H. G. *Ancient Southeast Asian Warfare*. London: Bernard Quatrich, 1952.

Tarling, Nicholas. *The Cambridge History of Southeast Asia*. 2 vols. Cambridge, England: Cambridge University Press, 1992.

Aaron Plamondon

THE MEDIEVAL WORLD

MARAUDERS' WAYS OF WAR

THE MONGOLS

DATES: C. 600-1450 C.E.

POLITICAL CONSIDERATIONS

Numerous steppe nomad empires existed in Eurasia throughout the medieval period. Prior to 1200 the Mongols had been merely one of many tribes in the steppes of Mongolia. Mongolia had long been a training ground for the horse archers that formed the cores of steppe nomad armies. Between 600 and 1206 C.E. several empires rose in Mongolia. The first was the early Turkic T'u-chüeh Empire of the early 600's. The Uighurs, who formed an empire from 744 to 840, were driven south by the Kirghiz of the Yenisei River, who held Mongolia until 920, when the Khitans established an empire over part of Mongolia and northern China that lasted until 1125.

Most of the information concerning these empires indicates that their armies consisted primarily not of infantry but of horse archers who relied on mobility and barrages of arrows to defeat their enemies, rather than on the shock tactics of European cavalry. Indeed, the most difficult battles for the nomads usually were those fought against other armies of horse archers, and not those fought against their sedentary opponents in China, Central Asia, Europe, or Iran. Despite the long existence of these armies, it was not until the establishment of the Khitan Empire, also known as the Liao Dynasty (907-1125) of China, in southern Mongolia and Northern China, that a true standardized military organization took cohesive form. After the fall of the Liao, the nomads of Mongolia still maintained their military predominance, yet not until the ascendance of Genghis Khan (who lived from between 1155 and 1162 to 1227) did they become the premier military power of the medieval period.

Genghis Khan drew upon the military formations of the Khitans and the Jürcheds (1115-1234), a Manchurian people who defeated the Khitans, as well as nomadic traditions and technology from the lands he conquered, to create an army that surpassed contemporary foes not only in fighting ability but also in strategy, tactics, and organization. The innovations he introduced continued throughout the Mongol Empire and were adopted by later leaders such as the Turkish conqueror Tamerlane (1336-1405), whose talents for military and administrative leadership allowed him to become the first Central Asian leader to overthrow the Mongols. Although modifications of Mongol formations and equipment continued throughout the period following the Mongol Empire, it was not until the late fifteenth century that sedentary armies could match the achievements of the steppe nomads.

MILITARY ACHIEVEMENT

The Mongols' military achievements were impressive: The Mongols built, through mobility, superior discipline, and advanced strategies, the largest contiguous land empire of its time. Although the empire remained unified for roughly only seventy years after the death of Genghis Khan, its heritage was maintained by his successors, who included his grandson, Kublai Khan (1215-1294), and later successors such as Tamerlane.

Perhaps the most difficult achievement for Genghis Khan was the unification of the tribes of Mongolia. Once these tribes were united, Genghis Khan forged them into an army of unprecedented size and force. Although tribal confederations had appeared throughout history, none of them possessed the martial potency, discipline, and organization of the Mongols. Furthermore, the Mongols quickly learned to adapt those military methods of their opponents that they deemed effective, particularly siege warfare and the mobilization of resources.

The Mongol Empire at its height stretched from the Pacific Ocean to the Carpathian Mountains. Its armies ranged even farther, invading Vietnam and reaching the Adriatic Sea in Europe. In the early 1220's Jebe (fl. 1200-1230) and Sabutai (c. 1172-1245), two of Genghis Khan's top commanders, led roughly twenty thousand men into modern Iran, across the Caucasus Mountains into the Russian steppe, and back to Kazakhstan without the benefit of modern communication systems or even maps. This feat is even more impressive considering that the troops fought numerous battles along the way without reinforcements. The organization of the Mongol military allowed the empire to wage offensive wars on several fronts, from China to the Middle East. Although the empire gradually expanded over decades across Asia, individual invasions were rapid and fierce.

Successors such as Tamerlane carried on the Mongol tradition. His campaigns consisted of continuous marching, from India into Siberia and the Middle East. Tamerlane was victorious over many of the top commanders of the late medieval era, including the Ottoman sultan Bayezid (c. 1360-1403), who struck fear into Europe, as well as Toqtamish (fl. c. 1380-1390), who had reunified the Golden Horde, a tribe of Mongols that sacked and burned Moscow in 1382.

TURNING POINTS

553	Eastern T'u-chüeh Empire founded in Mongolia
740-840	Uighurs destroy T'u-chüeh Empire and dominate Mongolia.
840-920	Kirghiz invade Mongolia and drive out Uighurs, continuing to dominate the region.
920	Khitans drive out Kirghiz and establish empire in Mongolia and China.
1125	Jürcheds conquer northern China and drive out Khitans, and Mongolia descends into tribal warfare.
1206	Genghis Khan is named ruler of the Mongols.
1213	Mongols invade China.
1236-1242	Mongols make conquests in Russia, Eastern Europe, Iran, and Transcaucasia.
1258	Mongols capture Baghdad and end the ʿAbbasid Caliphate.
1260	Mongols invade Syria and capture Damascus but are defeated by Mamlūks at Ain Jalut.
1261	Civil war between Il-Khanate of Persia and the Golden Horde of Russia begins.
1272	Kublai Khan establishes the Yuan Dynasty.
1335	Il-Khanate of Persia ends.
1368	Yuan Dynasty ends in China, and Mongols are driven back to Mongolia, where a period of civil war ensues.
1369	Tamerlane becomes ruler of Central Asia.

WEAPONS, UNIFORMS, AND ARMOR

The average Mongol soldier's primary weapon was a composite bow. This multilayered bow was small enough to be used on horseback but possessed a range equal to, if not better than, that of the English longbow. Each Mongol warrior carried two or three such bows, often in a quiver attached to the saddle of his horse. For ammunition, each soldier carried approximately sixty arrows in multiple quivers, also often attached to the saddle. The arrows were divided into three categories. The first included arrows that could pierce the heavy armor of European knights when fired from the 80- to 160-pound draw of the Mongol bow. The second class of arrows were lighter arrows that had a greater range but little penetrating power. The third group of arrows were signal, or whistling, arrows, which were used to communicate within armies as well as to frighten enemies. The Mongols possessed a variety of other arrowheads for specialized purposes.

The Mongols also carried other weapons, such as sabers and axes, and often short lances, more often used for flying banners than in battle. However, these lances also possessed a hook forged into the blade, which enabled the Mongols to ensnare and then to pull more heavily armored foes off their mounts.

The single most important weapon or piece of equipment used by the Mongols and other steppe nomads was the horse. The Mongol horse was small, roughly the size of a pony, yet durable, with incredible stamina. Each warrior possessed a string of horses, ranging from three to six, although some records report higher figures. The large number of horses allowed the warrior to remain mounted for the entire campaign; if one horse was killed, he had a replacement. More important, this arrangement allowed the Mongols to maintain their superior mobility: As one horse tired, a warrior could switch to another.

For the most part, Mongol warriors were unencumbered by heavy armor. They wore little armor, apart from hardened leather, or leather reinforced with lamellar plates, considerably lighter than even the finest chain mail. Chain mail was worn occasionally, but because the art of Mongol warfare depended on mobility, the extra weight of the mail was considered a hindrance. Heavy cavalry units armored their horses with lamellar cuirasses, which covered the horses' upper bodies. In the Il-Khanate of Persia, a Mongol dynasty that ruled in Iran (1256-1353), the Mongols switched from a light cavalry to a heavier force that naturally required more armor.

Although the Mongols did not have a specific uniform, they did cut their hair in a certain manner to identify themselves. Even those conscripted from the conquered would receive the Mongol coif, which consisted of a tonsure similar to that of a monk, with only a tuft of hair remaining in front and two braids trailing from the back.

MILITARY ORGANIZATION

The Mongols drew upon the Khitan military system to base the organization of their armies on the decimal system. The largest unit was the *tumen*, a division of ten thousand men. Contained within each *tumen* were ten *minggans*, or one-thousand-man units. These in turn were divided into ten *jaghuns*, or one-hundred-man units. The *jaghun* was the basic tactical unit. The smallest unit consisted of ten men and was known as the *arban*.

During larger campaigns, the Mongols often instituted a *tamna* force, in which a certain number of men from every unit, approximately two out of ten, were mustered to form an army. Once the campaign ended, these troops were allowed to return to their units. The conquered were also included in conscription, but they were usually required to serve in foreign lands, in order to prevent rebellion. The most common method of preventing mutiny at a critical

THE MONGOL EMPIRE IN 1260

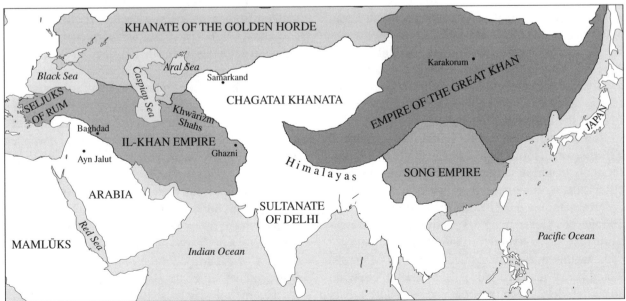

moment was simply to divide the new recruits into existing units. This arrangement prevented the new recruits from forming a cohesive and potentially disrupting force, and it helped to maintain the unit integrity of existing formations. Tamerlane, like Genghis Khan, divided members of recalcitrant tribes among various units in order to prevent mutiny.

DOCTRINE, STRATEGY, AND TACTICS

When the Mongols engaged an opponent's field army, they used a wide array of tactics to achieve victory. One such tactic, usually the opening one, was a barrage of arrows from a distance. Although this opening volley often inflicted little harm, it allowed the Mongols to see how the enemy would react. To remain in a position under constant fire probably became frustrating, especially for elite units. For massed infantry, often haphazardly armored, it became precarious.

From the Jürcheds, the Mongols adopted a troop composition of roughly 60 percent light cavalry and 40 percent medium-to-heavy cavalry. Army formations essentially consisted of five lines. The first three lines were light cavalry, and the last two were heavy cavalry. During battle the light cavalry released numerous barrages of arrows upon their opponents before retiring to regroup behind the heavy cavalry. After the opponent had become sufficiently disorganized, or after the Mongol commander decided to deliver the final blow, the heavy cavalry would trot forward in silence, accompanied only by the pounding of drums. Just before contact, the riders would release a terrific, collective scream, intended to frighten their opponents.

The key element in battle remained the Mongol barrage, or "storm," of arrows, after which the Mongols would base their ensuing actions on their observations of their enemy. They would opt either for an enveloping maneuver or for a continued arrow barrage, at a closer, more destructive range. Another tactic was the *mangutai*, or the so-called suicide attack. In this maneuver a select group of Mongols would harass the enemy lines, showering them with arrows at close range until the enemy finally broke ranks and charged. The Mongols would then flee, still firing their arrows by turning backward in their saddles, a technique known as the Parthian shot, perfected and made famous by Parthian warriors of ancient Persia. After the pursuing forces became strung out and disorganized, the majority of Mongol forces would then charge. Often these forces had been waiting in ambush along the flanks, or were in fact the *mangutai* troops, who had mounted fresh horses. The pursuing forces would be unable to withstand the cohesive force of the Mongol charge. This maneuver—the feigned rout—was an old steppe trick, one that the Mongols raised to perfection. In the encircling maneuver the Mongols often left a gap between their lines. Eventually, the encircled foe would detect the gap and attempt to escape through it, inevitably leading to a rout, during which the Mongols would pursue and cut down the fleeing soldiers.

The Mongols conducted the majority of their battles at a distance. They possessed a great advantage in the power of their bows and believed in the principle of massed firepower, coordinating their fire arcs through the use of banners, torches, and whistling arrows. Much like that of modern directed artillery fire, the effect of massed Mongol firepower could be devastating.

Mongol use of massed firepower also applied to sieges. At Aleppo in 1400, the Mongols arranged twenty catapults against one gate. The Mongol use of massed firepower—decades before the English use of massed longbow archers—reduced enemy armies, and with catapults and ballistae, demolished city defenses.

Other Mongol tactics included psychological maneuvers. The Mongols often lighted more campfires than normal to make their camps appear to be larger than they were. At times they also mounted dummies on their spare horses, so that their armies would appear from a distance to be larger than they were. Tamerlane contributed the trick of tying branches to the tails of his horses, so that enormous clouds of dust could be seen from a distance, deceiving his enemies. Merchants who served as spies spread rumors far in advance of the army. Furthermore, Mongols treated with leniency cities that surrendered, whereas they crushed mercilessly those that opposed or rebelled.

Mongol warriors harass their enemies in battle.

In terms of strategy, the Mongols had a set method of invasion that varied only slightly from campaign to campaign. The Mongol army invaded in several, usually three, columns: a center force and two flanking corps. The flanking units, in some instances, went into neighboring territories before a rendezvous with the center army, as in the Mongol invasion of Hungary in 1241. Armies sent into Poland distracted the Poles, the Teutonic Knights, and the Bohemians from joining the Hungarians. A screen of scouts and outriders constantly relayed information back to the column. Their preplanned schedule and use of scouts allowed the Mongols to march divided, but to fight united. Furthermore, because their forces marched in considerably smaller concentrations, the Mongols were not impeded by columns stretching for miles. They used their mobility to spread terror on many fronts at the same time; their opponents were rarely prepared to concentrate their forces against them.

The Mongols' use of many-pronged invasions also fit in with their preferred method of engaging the enemy. The Mongols preferred to deal with all field armies before moving deep into enemy territory. Because the enemy usually sought to meet the Mongols before they destroyed an entire province, reaching this goal was rarely difficult. Furthermore, the Mongols' use of columns and a screen of scouts enabled the gathering of intelligence that usually allowed the Mongols to unite their forces before the enemy was cognizant of all the different invading forces, thus better concealing their troop strengths. This arrangement also meant that an embattled force could receive reinforcements or, in the advent of defeat, could be avenged.

By concentrating on the dispersion and movement of field armies, the Mongols delayed assault on enemy strongholds. Of course, the Mongols took smaller or more easily surprised fortresses as they encountered them. The destruction of the field armies also allowed the Mongols to pasture their horses and other livestock without the threat of raids. Among the best examples occurred during Genghis Khan's Khwārizm campaign (c. 1220). The Mongols took the surrounding smaller cities and fortresses before capturing the principal city of Samarqand, in modern Uzbekistan. This strategy had two effects. First, it cut off the principal city from communications with other cities that might provide aid. Second, refugees from these smaller cities fled to Samarqand, the last stronghold. The sight of this streaming horde of refugees, as well as their reports, reduced the morale of the inhabitants and garrison of the principal city and also strained its resources. Food and water reserves were taxed by the sudden influx of refugees. Soon, what once had seemed a formidable undertaking became an easy task.

After conquering the surrounding territory, the Mongols were free to lay siege to the principal city without interference of a field army. Smaller forts and cities could not harry the Mongols, who either foraged or pursued other missions during the siege. Most important, the many Mongol columns and raiding forces had prevented the main city from effectively assisting its smaller neighbors without leaving itself open to attack. Finally, the capture of the outer strongholds and towns provided the Mongols more siege experience as well as raw materials in the form of labor either to man the siege engines or to act as human shields for the Mongols.

The Mongols also strove to destroy any hopes their opponents had to rally by harrying enemy leaders until they dropped. Genghis Khan first did this during his unification of Mongolia. In his first few encounters, the enemy leaders had escaped, which continually haunted him. After this lesson, the Mongols habitually hunted down opposing leaders. In Khwārizm Sultan ʿAlā al-Din Muḥammad (r. 1200-1220) died alone on an island in the Caspian Sea after being hounded by Jebe and Sabutai. Mongol units relentlessly pursued Jalāl ad-Dīn Mingburnu (r. 1220-1231), Muḥammad's son. Béla IV (1206-1270), king of Hungary, barely escaped the Mongols, led by Batu Khan (died 1255), in 1241, as his boat pushed off of the Dalmatian coast into the Adriatic Sea.

Constantly on the move to avoid the Mongol forces, an enemy leader was unable to serve as a rallying point for his armies, who were also required to keep moving in order to find him. In many reports, the enemy leaders were only a few steps ahead of the Mongols. This strategy also allowed the Mongols opportunities to acquire new intelligence on other lands, because fleeing leaders ran in the opposite direction of the Mongols. The pursuing Mongol forces could then wreak havoc in new territories. Local powers would keep their forces at home, instead of sending them to help their overlords. In many instances the Mongols would defeat local armies they encountered along the way while avoiding the strongholds, another example of the Mongol method of destroying field armies before laying siege. The most important aspect of these pursuit columns was their capacity for destruction and intimidation, which created a buffer between the currently occupied territories and those that recently had been subdued. Thus, the main army could finish its mission of subjugation while the surrounding environs were devastated and rendered harmless.

MEDIEVAL SOURCES

Medieval sources of information about the Mongol military are fairly rich, due to the fact that the Mongols covered a large territory. Most accounts were written by the conquered, or by individuals hostile to the Mongols. The one surviving Mongol source, *The Secret History of the Mongols* (c. 1240), is extremely important for the study of the Mongol military. It is the primary source for the unification of Mongolia under Genghis Khan, revealing his initial defeats and the lessons he learned from them. It also describes the organization and tactics of the Mongol army. Finally, this work also provides the best description of the *keshik*, or the bodyguard of Khan. The *keshik* also served as a training school for officers.

The *Jāmi 'at-tawārīkh* by Persian physician, historian, and politician Rashīd ad-Dīn (1247-1318), and the *Tārikh-i jehān-gushā* (1252-1256; *A History of the World Conqueror*, 1958) by ʿAṭā Malek Joveynī, also known as ʿAṭā Malek Juwaynī, are among the most important Muslim sources. Both authors were members of the civil government under the Mongols, and their works reveal much about Mongol conquests, organization, and strategies. Rashīd ad-Dīn's work also is the source of Maḥmūd Ghāzān's (1271-1304) reforms for the Il-Khanate's military. In addition, numerous Arab authors and later ones from the Mamluk period (1250-1517) discuss the Mongol invasions, as well as more minute details of strategy and tactics. Arab author Ibn al-Athīr (1160-1233), a historian and scholar of Mosul and Baghdad, wrote *al-Kāmil fi at-tārīkh*, whose title means "the complete history."

Among European sources, the travel accounts of French Franciscan friar and traveler Willem van Ruysbroeck (c. 1215-c. 1295) and missionary Giovanni da Pian del Carpini (c. 1180-1252) stand out. Both individuals traveled to the court of the Khans, a few years apart. Their accounts contain much anecdotal and incidental information and vary greatly in tone. Shortly after the Mongol invasion of Hungary Pope Innocent IV in 1246 sent del Carpini to the Mongols in an effort to determine the Mongols' intentions for the rest of Europe. Thus, del Carpini's account is that of a diplomat and a spy who is very concerned with the future of Christendom. Del Carpini notes the weapons and composition of the Mongols' armor and provides a lengthy treatise on how the Europeans should combat the Mongols. Had Europe heeded del Carpini's words, its military systems would have more closely resembled those of the Mongols. Del Carpini clearly recognized the inadequacies of the unruly masses of European knights and men-at-arms against the disciplined Mongol forces.

The vast majority of the Chinese sources have yet to be translated into English, although some have been translated into French, German, and Russian. The primary chronicle is the *Yuan Shih* (1370), originally composed in ten volumes by Song Lian and Wang Wei, and revised and rewritten in 1934 by Ke Shaobin in 257 volumes as *Xin Yuanshi*. It contains not only the history of the conquests and the military in general, but also biographies of most of the commanders throughout the Mongol Empire.

BOOKS AND ARTICLES

Biran, Michal. *Qaidu and the Rise of the Independent Mongol State in Central Asia*. Surrey, England: Curzon, 1997.

Hull, Mary. *The Mongol Empire*. San Diego, Calif.: Lucent Books, 1998.

Manz, Beatrice Forbes. *The Rise and Rule of Tamerlane*. Cambridge, England: Cambridge University Press, 1989.

Martin, H. D. *The Rise of Chingis Khan and His Conquest of North China*. Baltimore, Md.: Johns Hopkins Press, 1950.

Morgan, David. *The Mongols*. Oxford, England: Basil Blackwell, 1986.

Saunders, J. J. *The History of the Mongol Conquests*. London: Routledge & Kegan Paul, 1971. Reprint. Philadelphia: University of Pennsylvania Press, 2001.

FILMS AND OTHER MEDIA

The Storm from the East. Documentary. Films for the Humanities and Sciences, 1994.

Timothy May

THE VIKINGS

DATES: C. 700-1035 C.E.

POLITICAL CONSIDERATIONS

The Vikings were seaborne Scandinavian raiders and settlers who spread throughout Western Europe during the eighth through the eleventh centuries. Their assaults on the coastal areas of Western Europe, stretching as far south as the Mediterranean, and the Scandinavian expansion to the east into Russia had profound effects on European ways of war in the early Middle Ages. These effects, in turn, derived from the nature of the Viking attacks, which had their origins in Scandinavian politics, technologies, and culture.

Although individuals had occasionally been able to unite all of either Denmark, Norway, or Sweden under their rule, such unification had never lasted prior to the beginning of the eleventh century. Whenever central authority weakened, conflict among local notables and their followings had broken out, and the losers of these battles were forced to seek their fortunes elsewhere. The dominating political and social tie of the period was the *lid*, based on the loyalty earned by an outstanding warrior from those who followed him in battle. It has been postulated that a large population expansion in Scandinavia, an area with limited agricultural potential, also played a part in the Viking descent on Europe. The Viking warrior-leaders and their loyal followers, finding insufficient room within Scandinavia, turned their military aspirations toward Europe.

The political and military weaknesses of European rulers after Charlemagne, the king of the Franks who had died in 814, made their territories prime targets for the Vikings. Charlemagne's successors in France, the Low Countries, and Germany all relied, as did the rulers of Britain and Ireland, on local militias of unarmed peasants for a major part of their defense forces. These makeshift armies proved unequal to the military challenges posed by the Vikings.

The history of Viking raids can be divided into three major phases. The earliest phase of Viking expansion began in the late eighth century and lasted at least until the middle of the ninth. During this period the Vikings descended abruptly upon any part of Europe served by a major navigable river and terrorized the local populace, stealing any portable loot—especially the ornaments of the local monasteries—and immediately withdrawing and sailing for home. During the second phase of Viking expansion, from the mid-ninth century through most of the tenth, the Vikings established fortified bases in the Low Countries, France, England, and Ireland, from which they raided into the adjoining countryside. Finally, the last phase of Viking expansion took

TURNING POINTS

793	Vikings sack Lindisfarne Abbey in northern England.
843	Vikings sack Dorestadt and Utrecht.
845	Charles the Bald, king of the Franks, pays Vikings money to retreat.
886	Last Viking siege of Paris.
891	The Vikings suffer a rare defeat at Louvain.
911	Rollo receives county of Normandy from the French king.
930	Vikings settle Iceland.
954	English expel the last Viking king from York.
1013	Danish king Sveyn I Forkbeard defeats English king Ethelred I, forcing him into exile.
1017-1035	Sveyn's son Canute rules both England and Denmark.
1066	Norwegian king Harold Hardradi is defeated at Stamford Bridge in England; William of Normandy defeats English at Hastings.

VIKING RAIDS, 790-850

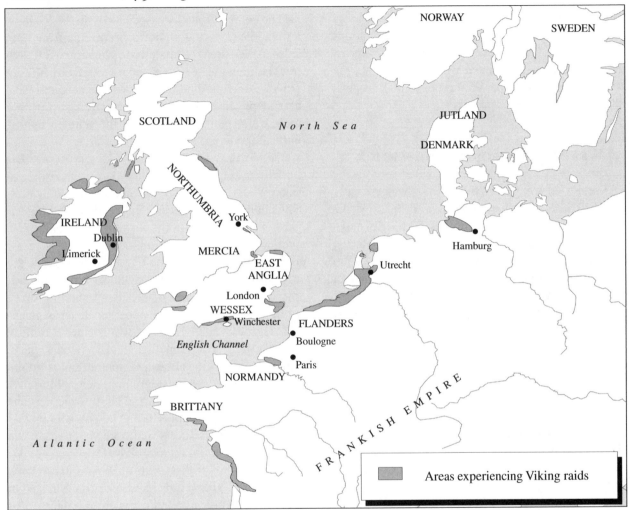

place during the eleventh century, when the Vikings, under the leadership of their own kings, took over either part or all of other lands. The effective defeat of the Norwegian king Harold III (1015-1066), at Stamford Bridge in 1066 in England, and the Norman conquest of England by William the Conqueror (c. 1027-1087), a descendant of Vikings who had previously settled in France, brought the Viking expansion essentially to an end. The Viking expansion to the east was ended in the tenth century, when they were defeated by the Byzantine emperor, under whom numerous individual Vikings later served as members of the emperor's famed Varangian Guard.

MILITARY ACHIEVEMENT

The Vikings' principal military achievement was that they forced their opponents to adopt a military system called feudalism, which proved the only effective defense against the Vikings. The system of feudalism was based on the tenure of land and derived from the need for a permanent force of knights to assist local kings with their wars and to protect the lands from raiders. Each territory relied on fortified positions and mounted, professional soldiers who defended these positions and barred the path of the Vikings. The armored knights on horseback proved to be the only means of overcoming the circle of Viking warriors wielding their shields and heavy battle-axes. Rivers navigated by the Vikings in their unique long-boats were fitted with bridges and other fortifications that barred the Vikings' passage. The dominance of the mounted, armed warrior evoked by the Viking raids long outlasted the Viking phase of European history.

WEAPONS, UNIFORMS, AND ARMOR

The preferred weapon of the Vikings was the two-handed battle-ax, which enabled warriors to strike down an enemy with one blow. Viking warriors also carried swords, many with inscriptions on the blades. Swords were popular at least in part because of the abundance of iron that was available in Scandinavia and the exceptional skill of Scandinavian iron workers. Nevertheless, the battle-ax was the weapon most feared by the victims of Viking raids.

The Vikings also carried javelins and often began battles by throwing their javelins at the enemy. Although the Vikings used bows and arrows, they did not rely on these weapons to the extent that English armies later did. The bow and arrow did, however, play a part in Viking tactics, making it possible to disable some enemy fighters before closing in for the hand-to-hand combat that was characteristic of the Vikings.

The shields used by the Vikings have been a source of historical controversy. Depictions of Scandinavian warriors, such as those on the Bayeux tapestry (c. 1080), show the Vikings carrying the characteristic kite-shaped shield of medieval fighters. There is some evidence that early Viking raiders carried round shields and later copied the kite-shaped shield from their Frankish opponents.

Although most depictions of the Vikings show them in chain mail, the earliest Viking raiders probably did not wear armor. They most likely dressed in heavy, woolen garments produced from the wool of the sheep raised on Scandinavian farms. They picked up, or probably captured, chain mail from their opponents. By the tenth century, however, all Vikings wore chain mail, except for those who journeyed east

to Russia and may have worn armor composed of small plates laced together.

The helmet typically associated with the Vikings, a round headpiece with horns protruding from both sides, is a figment of modern imagination. Although few helmets have been recovered from Viking graves, some pointed helmets with nosepieces have been depicted in art. Early Viking raiders probably wore round helmets, adopting the pointed helmet only after adopting chain mail.

One of the most important Viking weapons was the Viking ship. The technology, confirmed by excavated vessels, appears to have developed in Scandinavia in the years immediately preceding Viking expansion. The vessels were clinker-built, that is, with overlapping boards forming the sides, yet were astonishingly watertight. The Vikings had mastered the art of using pitch and other sealants in their shipbuilding. The vessels were of relatively shallow draft, which enabled them to forge up rivers to an astonishing degree, yet were designed to move rapidly through the water, propelled chiefly by oars. Sails, added as the Vikings began to venture out from the coasts into open waters, were essential in Viking voyages to Iceland, Greenland, and North America. The English, Irish, and Franks had no vessels comparable to the Viking warships, which were vital to the basic Viking raid strategy. Interestingly, the success of Alfred the Great (849-899), king of Wessex in England, in halting the Viking attacks on his country rested in part on his decision to build a navy that intercepted the Viking ships before they could land. Faced with this kind of opposition, the Vikings temporarily turned their attention to other parts of the European continent.

MILITARY ORGANIZATION

The basic military organization of the Vikings was the *lid*, a band of warriors under the leadership of one man with an exceptional military record. The primarily Danish Vikings who settled in France as Normans were led by a young Norwegian named Hrólfr Kraki (fl. sixth century), who accepted the invitation of the Frankish king to become the ruler of what is now known as Normandy, on the lower reaches of the Seine River around the town of Rouen. His mission was to defend the river against attack by other Viking bands. This individual took the Frankish name of Rollo and was the ancestor of William the Conqueror, who captured the throne of England in 1066, utilizing the armored cavalry that proved the only means of counteracting the Vikings.

As Viking strategy evolved from brief raids to occupations, the Viking leaders were increasingly drawn from the nobility, mostly younger sons who had no prospect of achieving prominence in their home countries. Some of these leaders became kings in the lands they occupied, although they rarely lasted long in that capacity.

By the eleventh century, however, Viking armies were led by Scandinavian kings, seeking to expand their empires beyond their homelands. Briefly, they succeeded. In 1014 Danish king Sweyn I Forkbeard (r. c. 987-1014) and his son Canute the Great (c. 995-

1035) defeated the English army led by King Ethelred II, who was forced into exile. Sweyn was accepted as king of England but died immediately thereafter. In 1017 Canute became the king of England, remaining its ruler until his death in 1035.

DOCTRINE, STRATEGY, AND TACTICS

The Viking military doctrine was based on the swift attack on undefended lands, after which the raiders would return home to enjoy their booty. Vikings focused first on monasteries, and indeed, the "Viking Age" is often dated from the sacking and looting in 793 of the monastery of Lindisfarne, also known as Holy Island, in northern England. The Vikings soon expanded their reach to the Scottish Isles, Ireland, the Low Countries, and the coast of modern France, going wherever there was loot to be pillaged. Western Europe, suffering no major invasions since the sixth

North Wind Picture Archives

A Viking raid carried out in Norse longboats.

century, with the exception of Muslims defeated in southern France in 732, had become peaceful and relatively wealthy. This wealth, which tended to be held in the possession of religious foundations, especially monasteries, attracted the attention of the Vikings.

The technological superiority of Viking vessels and the many navigable rivers on the Western European coastline, particularly those flowing into the North Sea and the English Channel, allowed the Vikings to approach their targets easily and swiftly. For the most part, monasteries were undefended. Wherever the Vikings met with opposition, it was generally in the form of loosely organized levies of local farmers who were no match for the discipline of fighting bands of Vikings. In the rare cases where the Vikings met with organized opposition from trained soldiers, they tended to withdraw rather than risk a battle.

The Vikings fought on foot. They never adopted the horse for use in battle but soon discovered that, should they meet with a force they could not easily overcome, there was value in having horses on which to escape. Early on, when the Vikings landed in a coastal area or river valley, they rounded up the horses of the local farmers and used them for a quick getaway when necessary.

Beginning in the mid-ninth century, many Viking bands began to spend the winter months at or near the point where the rivers they used to access the interior entered the sea instead of returning to their homelands with their loot in the fall. Their preferred locations for such camps, which they quickly fortified with wooden palisades, were on islands. Their first such camp, at Île de Noirmoutier in the Loire River, was established in 843. In the succeeding years they established camps in the Seine River, on the Isle of Man, and on the Isle of Thanet in Britain. These were always safe from attack until a camp at modern-day Louvain, built on a peninsula in a tributary of the Rhine River and protected on its landward side by a marsh, was overrun by the ruler of Germany in 891.

The Vikings' strategy involved getting their local opponents to attack them first. Because the only way to prevent the Vikings from wreaking havoc was to defeat them in battle and force them to reenter their ships and flee the area, the Franks, the English, and the Irish were essentially forced to fight the Vikings on their own terms. The Vikings' opponents were thus forced to develop a strategy that could beat the Vikings in the pitched battles that were the only way of sending the Vikings back to their ships. This strategy evolved during the course of the ninth century and was based on the development of well-fortified bases manned by professional soldiers mounted on horses. The Vikings practically never attacked well-fortified places and would eventually withdraw. In many cases, the local forces riding on horseback from within the fortifications could force the Vikings to leave the area.

Viking tactics were invariably based on finding a favorable site, often on a hill or a river, that would compel opponents to attack them frontally. The Vikings would form a tightly packed circle with interlocking shields facing the enemy. Occasionally, their opponents mounted on horseback would be able to break the shield wall, but they would then be forced to accept battle on the Vikings' terms, in hand-to-hand combat. In these situations, the Vikings' discipline and their skill with the two-handed ax generally prevailed. Successful attacks on Viking shield walls on horseback seldom led to victory on the ground, as the attackers were then forced to dismount and fight individually with the Vikings. When the Vikings anticipated an attack by mounted warriors, they often dug pits in front of their positions to prevent the horses from getting through. Sometimes such pits would be strengthened by palisades, or fences made from stakes, which further prevented the horses from reaching the Vikings.

Because the victims of the Vikings possessed considerable treasure that was generally the object of Viking raids, much of it in the form of silver coin, the victims of the Vikings soon found that their best defense was to buy off the Vikings. Enormous quantities of silver were transferred from England and the rulers of Western Europe to the Vikings during this period. Silver coins, particularly English coins, have been excavated in large quantities in Scandinavia. In the East, numerous coins originating either in the Byzantine Empire or in the Islamic kingdoms of the Middle East have been found in excavated Viking graves.

Medieval Sources

Two principal medieval sources provide information on the Vikings' military achievements. One is the wealth of accounts written by the victims of the Vikings. Because the Vikings' preferred objectives were generally monasteries, and because literacy during this period was largely confined to the Church, the written accounts are virtually all by monks whose monasteries were pillaged by the Vikings. It is from their writings that the prayer "From the fury of the Northmen dear Lord, deliver us!" originated. The Vikings themselves had a rudimentary written alphabet, the runic, which survives in the form of short legends inscribed on stones.

For information about this period from the Viking point of view, modern historians have been obliged to turn to Scandinavian literature, largely that of the twelfth and thirteenth centuries. Much of this literature originated in Iceland, which was settled by the Norse between 870 and 930. Although many of these accounts provide some vivid details, they have been questioned for their accuracy because of the long time lag of three to four centuries between the dates described and the time of composition. In the oral tradition of storytelling, it is possible that inaccuracies may have crept into the accounts in their repeated telling and retelling.

Two important medieval sources that are believed to be a bit less biased than the typical monastic accounts are *The Anglo-Saxon Chronicle* (c. 900) and the *Gesta Hammaburgensis ecclesiae pontificum* (c. 1072-1076; *The History of the Archbishops of Hamburg-Bremen*, 1959) by the German ecclesiastical historian Adam of Bremen (died 1081-1085). *The Anglo-Saxon Chronicle* arose from instructions issued by King Alfred of Wessex to the various monasteries in his kingdom, requesting monks to keep accounts of developments in their areas. The results of these monastic accounts were welded together into what are generally referred to as *The Anglo-Saxon Chronicle*, covering the period from the late ninth century to the mid-eleventh century. Adam of Bremen's *The History of the Archbishops of Hamburg-Bremen* covers a great deal of Viking history, in part because the archbishops of Hamburg-Bremen were responsible for many of the Christian missionaries sent into Scandinavia from 800 onward.

A good deal of information is contained in Icelandic sagas, but most of it survives in the form of twelfth to thirteenth century literary compositions, and it is often difficult to separate the literary element from the historical. Moreover, many of these stories are based on oral traditions in Iceland, which was widely separated from the bulk of the Viking raiding activity, because it was relatively uninhabited when the Vikings arrived there in the late ninth century and stayed to settle.

Books and Articles

Jones, Gwyn. *A History of the Vikings*. New York: Oxford University Press, 1984.

Oman, Charles. *A History of the Art of War in the Middle Ages*. 2d ed. New York: Burt Franklin, 1924.

Page, R. I. *Chronicles of the Vikings*. Toronto: University of Toronto Press, 1995.

Roesdahl, Else. *The Vikings*. 2d ed. London: Penguin Books, 1998.

Sawyer, P. H. *The Oxford Illustrated History of the Vikings*. New York: Oxford University Press, 1997.

Films and Other Media

Nova: The Vikings. Documentary. WGBH, 1974.

Nancy M. Gordon

THE MEDIEVAL WORLD

THE AMERICAS

THE MAYA AND AZTECS

DATES: C. 1500 B.C.E.-1521 C.E.

POLITICAL CONSIDERATIONS

Warfare in Mesoamerica can be reconstructed only from the cultural remains that have been left behind in the portable art, sculpture, architecture, and documents of the ancient Maya and Aztecs. Although this incomplete record allows only a partial glimpse of the politics, military achievements, weapons, and strategies of these early people, archaeologists and historians have been able to reconstruct much of their ancient military and warfare history. The cultures and chronologies of the ancient Maya and Aztecs differed greatly, but many parallels can be drawn between their politics and warfare strategies.

THE MAYA

The ancient Maya were once thought to have been gentle stargazers; however, discoveries such as that in 1946 of the murals at Bonampak in Chiapas, southern Mexico, depict violent and bloody scenes of warfare and sacrifice. Because the Maya are a much older culture, there is less abundant information about their methods of warfare than those of the Aztecs. The ancient history of the Maya region is typically divided into three periods: the Formative (c. 1500 B.C.E.-300 C.E.), the Classic (250-900), and the Postclassic (900-1500). Whereas much of the contemporary knowledge of Aztec society stems from contact-period documents, the Maya population had already gone into severe decline by the time that the Spanish conquistadores arrived in the Americas in the fifteenth and sixteenth centuries. Nonetheless, it is known that the Maya engaged in extensive civil war, often capturing the kings and other elite officials of competing city-states. It has been said that militarism and conquest were instrumental in creating and perpetuating a ruling elite and political centers. The success of an individual ruler was measured by his successful taking of captives, as depicted in much of the art and sculpture

of the ancient Maya. Hieroglyphic texts often refer to the conquests of kings, and naked and defeated captives are frequently depicted below the feet of triumphant captors. Early conflicts were generally not waged over long distances; instead, small-scale warfare was limited to local polities. As conflict grew over limited resources, warfare remained localized but became endemic. Captives became a necessary element in the inauguration of a new king, at the dedication of a new building, or for other sacred events; this need continued to motivate the Maya to invade neighboring polities. The intent of Mayan warfare was not to expand territory but to increase the prestige and power of the successful raiders.

THE AZTECS

The Aztecs, wandering barbarians, arrived late in Mesoamerica, settling at the site of Tenochtitlán in 1345 C.E. Over the next century, they assembled inexhaustible armies that marched hundreds of miles from the Valley of Mexico to confront and defeat rival cultures. Although they were a dominant power for only slightly more than one hundred years (1400-1521 C.E.), they were able to create an empire, maintain extensive economic trade routes, and appropriate the military organization, arts, and cultures of their subjects, incorporating them into their own civilization.

Religious fervor drove the Aztecs into constant war to capture political prisoners for sacrifice to their gods. Gory images of war captives with their hearts gouged out have been inextricably tied to the Aztecs.

MILITARY ACHIEVEMENT

THE MAYA

The greatest military achievement for the ancient Maya was the successful capture and sacrifice of a king from a neighboring and competing polity. Although this was a relatively rare event, it was depicted with both hieroglyphic text and images on the monuments of the victorious king. This visual and textual propaganda legitimized the power of the ruling king and often had profound effects on the cities of both the victor and loser. For example, in the first millennium C.E., when the king of the less powerful center of Quiriguá captured the ruler of the dominant center of Copán, Quiriguá was able to catapult itself into a more powerful position, while Copán went into a minor decline in authority and influence. The defeat of a ruler was an exacting blow to any city, and it placed

An Aztec warrior, carrying a wooden sword with stone blades and a decorated shield and dressed in cotton armor and an animal-head helmet.

the losing city in a state of flux. According to tradition, a new ruler could not be put in place until the preceding ruler had died, and in some cases, captured rulers were kept alive in order to weaken the power of the competing polity.

THE AZTECS

Military achievement for the ancient Aztecs was measured by the expansion of territory through intimidation of enemies in battle or simply the threat of battle. After the Aztecs had successfully moved into a new area, they became reliant on local leaders to successfully maintain their domains. Rather than install their own leaders in newly conquered areas, at the expense of their own human resources, the Aztecs would allow local leaders to remain in their positions under Aztec power. The Aztecs allowed the vanquished to maintain their traditional systems of trade and markets, while at the same time extracting some of the local resources as tribute. This system of loose military alliances allowed the Aztecs to spread their forces across a much broader region. The Spanish noted at the time of contact that the Aztecs were a fierce people, with a skilled military that lacked a fear of battle. Although there are few monuments dedicated to the successful military achievements of individuals, extensive records of tribute were documented, indicating the territory that was maintained and the resources that were extracted. Successful soldiers were highly valued and were rewarded for their valor with the special recognition of promotions and distinctive uniforms.

WEAPONS AND ARMOR

WEAPONS

Due to the fragmentary archaeological record, it is unlikely that a conclusive inventory of the weapons, uniforms, and armor of the ancient Maya and Aztec will ever be cataloged. However, depictions in art and documents from the pre- and post-contact periods do give insight into the more common and important weapons of warfare employed by these cultures.

Projectile weapons, used at a distance to strike at an enemy, include the bow and arrow, the sling, the dart, and the all-important atlatl. The atlatl, or spear-thrower, allowed the user to launch darts at greater distances than hand-thrown darts could be thrown. Depictions of the atlatl indicate that it had been used since the Classic period (250–900 C.E.). Atlatls were often ornately decorated with low-relief carving and even gold. The few existing examples are about 2 feet long, with a hook at one end where the barbed darts were attached. In some cases, loops were affixed to the other end of the weapon and used as finger grips. Many of the more extravagant atlatls were probably used only in ceremonies but were nonetheless extremely effective weapons in war. Spanish accounts attest to this potency, asserting that the darts could penetrate any armor and deliver a fatal wound. Experimental archaeology has confirmed that an experienced atlatl thrower could hurl a dart up to a distance of 243 feet and that altatls allowed up to 60 percent more accuracy than did an unaided spear.

The bow and arrow was another commonly used weapon in Mesoamerica. Bows measured up to 5 feet in length, and bowstrings were often made of animal sinew or deerskin. Arrows used in war had heads made of obsidian or fishbone and included barbed, blunt, and pointed styles. There is no indication that either the Maya or the Aztecs put poison on their arrow tips, but apparently both used fire-arrows to shoot at buildings. Experiments indicate that traditional arrows could be shot to ranges between 300 and 600 feet and that skilled archers could easily penetrate quilted cotton armor.

Slings made of maguey fibers, from agave plants, were used to catapult rounded, hand-shaped stones at adversaries. Stones were often collected in advance and apparently could be thrown more than 1,300 feet. Slings were often used with bows and arrows and could be extremely effective for penetrating the heavy Spanish armor.

Weapons used in close combat included the thrusting spear, which was actually most productive for slashing and parrying. Depictions from contact-period drawings indicate that the weapon was approximately 6 to 7 feet in length, with a roughly triangular head that was laced with closely set stone blades forming an unbroken cutting edge. The Aztecs also had one-handed and two-handed wooden

swords, with obsidian or flint blades adhered into grooves along the edge of the weapon. According to the Spanish, these blades were more effective than Spanish swords. Other weapons included wooden clubs, sometimes with a circular ball on the end that was most forceful on downward blows. Axes, blow-guns, and knives were also known in Mesoamerica but were more likely used in hunting than in warfare.

DEFENSIVE ARMOR

Shields, helmets, and armor were used in Mesoamerica as defensive weapons. Shields were usually made of hide, wood, palm leaves, or woven cane with cotton backing. They were decorated with feathers, paint, gold, silver, and copper foils and were round, square, or rectangular in shape. A shield's decorations were often reflective of the status and caliber of its user. The shield's primary use was as protection from projectiles; it probably was not very effective against clubs and swords.

Armor was made of a quilted cotton consisting of unspun cotton placed between two layers of cloth and stitched to a leather border. The thickness of the armor protected wearers from darts and arrows and was better suited than metal to the heat and humidity of Mesoamerica. Soldiers wore various styles of jackets and pullovers, which protected their upper bodies and thighs. Lower legs were protected with cotton leggings, although few weapons targeted this area of the body. War suits of feathers and fabric, or feathered tunics, were worn by higher-ranking warriors over their cotton armor. Some helmets were made of wood and bone and decorated with feathers, whereas others were made out of the heads of wild animals, such as wolves, jaguars, and pumas, placed over a wooden frame. The soldier's face could be seen in the gaping mouth of the animal's open jaw.

MILITARY ORGANIZATION

THE MAYA

The Maya's military organization appears to have been much less formalized than that of the Aztecs. However, those involved in conquest appear to have been afforded high status in society. Warriors, with their ability to seize captives, played a critical role in bringing power to a king and his city. Considered members of the elite class, they wore elaborate regalia and participated in rich ceremonies when they brought captives back to their king. Warriors also participated as ballplayers in the ball game that reenacted the ritual capture and eventual sacrifice of important rulers and elites from other sites. Although ballplayers and warriors were frequently depicted on portable art, they are almost never identified as individuals in texts. Kings, however, were recognized and regularly depicted as warriors, and the military prowess of their warriors was broadcast as their own success. Battles were generally short, limited in geographic scope, and usually timed around significant historical events. This system of warfare, unlike that of the Aztecs, afforded the Maya the luxury of not needing to maintain a huge standing army.

THE AZTECS

Aztec society was highly stratified, and military ranking was intimately tied to this overall social organization. The ruling nobles were placed in positions of higher rank, based on their birthright and social status, whereas the commoners often earned their military status through their skills in warfare. Most commoners paid their dues to society through the production of goods for tribute and labor, and many of them served in the Aztec military. All those who assisted the military were given extensive training in the use of weapons and the taking of captives, although those of higher status were provided with more thorough instruction. Soldiers who successfully took multiple captives were rewarded with promotions and uniforms signifying their accomplishments. Appropriate jewelry, hairstyles, body paint, and other insignia were also indicative of a soldier's status, and higher-ranking individuals were given privileges such as the rights to consume human flesh in public, to have mistresses, and to feast in the royal palaces.

DOCTRINE, STRATEGY, AND TACTICS

All Mesoamerican cultures were limited by the lack of efficient transportation beyond human foot traffic.

Although Mesoamerican cultures did have knowledge of the wheel, the harsh environment limited their ability to use it effectively. Draft animals were not introduced to the area until after the contact period. Transportation difficulties limited the cultures' abilities to control regions and their resources from long distances. The Maya and the Aztecs each developed different systems to maintain their political control over competing cities.

THE MAYA

The most effective method through which the Maya gained control over a competing city was either that of a royal marriage or that of a conquest, which was often the preferred choice. Ancient monuments at several Mayan cities depict both such events. Many sites, including the major city of Tikal, exhibited earthen walls along their boundaries as a form of protection from these battling neighbors, although they often proved ineffective. Numerous depictions in both text and art indicate that kings would send elite soldiers to raid smaller, less powerful polities and to capture and bring back important personages as prisoners. Low-ranking captives were often put into slavery or other service, while higher-ranking officials were displayed to the public and eventually sacrificed. These raids were important to validate the power of new polities and were frequently reenacted in the ritual ball game, an event held in elaborately built ball courts. The triumphant city would host the ball game as a ritual competition, after which the losers would be sacrificed. The Maya, believing in the cyclical nature of time, often planned their raids and reenactments to coincide with meaningful anniversaries of past events.

THE AZTECS

The Aztecs instituted a system in which local rulers of conquered areas were allowed to remain as heads of these areas, which were then required to produce and transport goods as a form of tribute to their conquerors. The Aztecs decided that, rather than leave behind their own garrisons to maintain controlled areas and extract large amounts of resources, they would instead lower the costs of administration and leave the control of conquered areas in the hands of local officials. Although this policy meant that Aztecs could not extract the maximum amount of goods from these conquered areas, it freed up soldiers and officials to continue their expansion into more distant areas. Campaigns were often scheduled around practical factors, including agricultural and seasonal cycles, such as the rainy season. This schedule often limited the ability of the Aztecs to run year-round crusades, and they had to depend on the local politicians to maintain their power.

The rulers of the Aztec Empire kept the local rulers of their loose alliance in line by continually intimidating them and engaging in warfare. Those who did not comply were harshly punished, and members of neighboring cities were often used to aid in these raids. Aztecs often pitted traditional adversaries against one another, and the threat of impending attack often allowed them to coerce loyalties without ever having to do battle. The Aztecs often used spies to gain military intelligence. Individuals were sent into rivals' territories dressed in their clothing and speaking their language. Spies were useful for obtaining strategic information about their foe's fortifications and preparations but were often caught or turned against their own. Although the overall military strategy of the Aztecs was fraught with problems, their system allowed them to maintain the largest political domain in all of Mesoamerica.

CONTEMPORARY SOURCES

Maya

Although the Maya codices do not deal with the topic of Mayan warfare and the contact-period documents deal with a culture in severe decline, some recent volumes have begun using the Maya's own texts and documents to look at aspects of elite society, including war and conquest. In Linda Schele and Peter Mathews's *The Code of Kings: The Language of Seven Sacred Maya Temples and Tombs* (1998), the authors decipher the ancient hieroglyphs on the monuments and buildings of seven Classic-period sites to reveal what the ancient Maya had to say about themselves. In it, there are numerous discussions of warfare between major cities, including war tactics, sacrifice, the ballgame, and war imagery. Matthew Restall's *Maya Conquistador* (1998) retells the Spanish encounter with the Maya from the Maya point of view. Using documents written by the Maya at the contact period, Restall allows the Maya to retell what the conquest was like. This book allows the reader to see that these brutal interactions with the Spanish fit into the Maya's cyclical worldview, and that they continued to deal with outsiders the way they had for hundreds of years. Both of the volumes offer an innovative and inside view of the native perspective of warfare and conquest. For a more traditional look at the contact period, a classic document is the 1941 translation by Alfred M. Tozzer of the original *Relación de las cosas de Yucatán* (1566; English translation, 1941); also known as *Yucatan Before and After the Conquest* (1937) by Bishop Diego de Landa, available in the papers of the Peabody Museum of American Archaeology and Ethnology at Harvard University. This significant document provides great insight into the contact period from the perspective of a Spanish bishop attempting to save the souls of the Mayan natives. In it, he describes the expeditions of the conquistadores in Yucatán, as well as Mayan culture and warfare, with information obtained from native informants and his own observations.

Aztecs

When the Spanish encountered the Aztecs in 1519, they discovered an empire that covered much of Mexico. Numerous contact-period documents describe the process of the Spanish conquest: the individual battles and the eventual taking over of Aztec society and its empire's tribute. Various chronicles, including *Historia de las Indias de Nueva-España y Islas de Tierra*

Firme: Mexico (1579-1581; *The Aztecs: The History of the Indies of New Spain*, 1964), by Diego Durán; *Obras Historicas* (1891-1892), by Fernando de Alva Ixtlilxóchitl; *Crónica Mexicana* (1598), by Fernando Alvarado Tezozómoc; and *Relaciónes Originales de Chalco Amequemecán* (c. 1620), by Domingo Chimanlpahín, describe Aztec military campaigns, dynastic relationships, and political and military strategies of assassination, bribery, and manipulation. These documents also reveal that Aztecs were more concerned in warfare with acquiring goods and services from a region than with occupying the territory themselves. *Historía Verdadera de la Conquista de la Nueva España* (1568; *The Discovery and Conquest of Mexico, 1517-1521*, 1844), considered the classic volume on the Spanish conquest, was written by Bernal Díaz del Castillo (1496-1584), a conquistador under Hernán Cortés who witnessed and documented wartime events, including more than one hundred battles, and the imprisonment of the Aztec king Moctezuma II (c. 1480-1520).

BOOKS AND ARTICLES

Culbert, T. Patrick, ed. *Classic Maya Political History: Hieroglyphic and Archaeological Evidence*. Cambridge, England: Cambridge University Press, 1991.
Hassig, Ross. *Aztec Warfare: Imperial Expansion and Political Control*. Norman: University of Oklahoma Press, 1995.
Sharer, Robert. *The Ancient Maya*. 6th ed. Stanford, Calif.: Stanford University Press, 1994.
Townsend, Richard. *The Aztecs*. London: Thames and Hudson, 2000.

FILMS AND OTHER MEDIA

In Search of History: The Aztec Empire. Documentary. History Channel, 1997.
Lost Kingdoms of the Maya. Documentary. National Geographic, 1993.

Jennifer P. Mathews

THE INCAS

DATES: C. 1200-1500 C.E.

POLITICAL CONSIDERATIONS

The Incas were one of many South American tribes engaged in a power struggle in the Andean highlands from the thirteenth century through the middle of the fifteenth century. Prior to this time, this region had been occupied by many different tribes. Between 500 and 1000 C.E. the Tiahuanco and Huari cultures, for example, developed large urban settlements and organized state systems. During the years from 1000 to 1456, however, the region encompassing modern Colombia, Ecuador, Peru, and Chile experienced a process of fragmentation that resulted in the development of small, regional states. Although warfare between different tribes was common, no one group was clearly dominant. The Incas were just one of the many tribes involved in warfare in the southern highlands near modern Bolivia. They were not especially strong at this time and had to form alliances to survive. The Chanca and Quechua tribes in the Apurímac Basin and the Lupaca and Colla tribes in the Titicaca Basin presented the biggest threats to the Incas, who, until the fifteenth century, dominated only a small area near Cuzco.

MILITARY ACHIEVEMENT

Under the leadership of the Incan warrior Pachacuti (c. 1391-1471), the Incas defeated the Chanca tribes in a battle at Cuzco in 1438. According to legend, the boulders on the battlefield became warriors who fought for the Incas. After this victory, Pachacuti became emperor, and the Incas began to expand their territory by conquering other tribes. Under Pachacuti the Incas emerged as the strongest military power in the southern highlands, and their territory stretched as far south as the Maule River in modern south-central Chile. Unlike other peoples, however, the In-

cas did not loot and abandon vanquished tribes, but rather they incorporated these former foes into their own military. The Incas conquered the western Titicaca Basin and nearly all of the Urubamba, Apurímac, and Mantaro Basins during the twenty-five years following their defeat of the Chancas. The military and logistical support provided by the vanquished tribes enabled the Incas to control the territory of the southern highlands and to begin expanding their territory through conquests along the northern coast. The defeated Chancan tribes, now fighting for the Incas, began conquering the northern tribes, which formed a part of the Chimú Empire.

The Incas attacked and defeated the Chimú tribes after Topa Inca Yupanqui (r. 1471-1493), Pachacuti's son, led attacks as far north as Ecuador before returning south along the coast. He extended the Incan Empire and maintained his father's policy of incorporating the vanquished tribes into the military. His son, Huayna Capac (r. 1493-1525), succeeded him as emperor and solidified the empire by conquering smaller areas throughout Ecuador, expanding Incan territory as far north as Colombia and establishing boundary markers to the Angasmayo River. Huayna Capac made Quito the northern capital of the empire, which spanned 2,500 miles. The Incas called their empire Tabuantinsuyu, meaning "the land of the four quarters." Geographic division of Incan territory was divided into four regions and subdivided into more than eight provinces.

WEAPONS, UNIFORMS, AND ARMOR

The Incas had an advanced Bronze Age technology in the fifteenth century that served as the foundation of the military force. The sling was the deadliest projectile weapon. Other effective weapons included bows and arrows, lances, darts, a short variation of a sword, battle-axes, spears, and arrows tipped with copper or bone. The weapons used by the Incan lords were decorated with gold or silver. For protection military leaders wore casques, or helmets, made from wood or the skins of wild animals and decorated with precious stones and the feathers of tropical birds. Soldiers wore the costume of the province from which they came; their armor consisted of a wooden helmet covered with bronze; a long, quilted tunic; and a quilted shield. The soldiers, who jogged at a pace of about 3 miles per hour and traveled nearly 20 miles per day, carried only their own supplies, while an army of soldiers was responsible for carrying baggage on their backs. Garrisons were housed in fortresses, whereas detachments occupied storehouses, which consisted of magazines filled with weapons, grain, and ammunition. Sacsahuamán, the site where the Incas defeated the Chancas, was the only fortress garrisoned by the Inca people. Sacsahuamán was only one of many Incan fortresses; others included Paramonga, a fortress constructed like a mountain of adobe bricks that had once been a part of the Chimú kingdom. These storehouses provided the army with food and clothing, thus avoiding the necessity to pillage villages as the army traveled across the country.

MILITARY ORGANIZATION

The Incan military was highly organized and consisted of nearly 200,000 soldiers. The military served as a public service organization that brought food and materials from one region of the country to another and trained specialists who contributed to the growth of the empire. In order to prepare future soldiers, military training took place on a bimonthly basis and began with boys as young as ten years old, who took part in physical activities such as wrestling, weight lifting, and sling shooting. This training enabled the Incan commanders to determine which soldiers could be used as specialists, such as builders, stonemasons, bridge experts, and assault leaders. Village elders reported on the progress of the boys, whom the military drafted as either warriors, carriers, or craftsmen. Short-term service drafting ensured an ample supply of young men in each district. The peri-

ods of service depended upon climatic conditions, and not all men returned to civilian life. The commanders ordered the most outstanding soldiers, those who were the bravest, the most disciplined, and the most adept at fighting, to remain permanently in the military.

The organization of the army was similar to that of the decimal system utilized by the Romans. Although the commanders were usually members of the Incan royal family, many ascended from the ranks because of their extraordinary ability and devotion to the emperor. One of the demands placed upon the commanders, who had to deal with the logistical problems of the roads and supplies, was to calculate the most efficient way to move their military across the country. Because the strategy was to fight only if absolutely necessary, the commanders had to ensure a deployment of soldiers superior to that of the enemy and would not waste manpower by sending too many. On important occasions, the emperor personally assumed command of a campaign. Topa Inca Yupanqui, for example, took personal command of an effort to expand the empire by overseeing the extension of the main highways, a task too difficult for an army commander to handle alone. Soldiers were required to participate in battles as far away from their homes as possible in order to avoid fraternization and to allow them experience the vastness of the country and the grandeur of the empire. Because the purpose of the military was both to defend and to extend Tahuantinsuyu and to serve the Sun God, individual glory in battle was not valued by the Incas.

DOCTRINE, STRATEGY, AND TACTICS

The primary aim of the Incan military was to spread the worship of the Sun and to seek harmony through the integration of so-called barbarians—who lacked military discipline, worshiped false gods, and practiced human sacrifices and cannibalism—into the Incan culture. The Incas believed, therefore, that their conquests were justifiable and were motivated by a desire to improve the quality of life of their vanquished tribes. The Incas traveled with the purpose of disrupting the lives of Peru's inhabitants as little as

An Inca-style battle scene in which warriors wear helmets and quilted tunics and wield swords, axes, and spears in hand-to-hand combat.

possible. Specialized engineering corps designed and constructed the travel routes, which extended through the mountains and along the coastal desert. The same corps of engineers also constructed giant suspension bridges where necessary. Different armies followed each route, and they eventually met before advancing. Because the idea behind the creation of Tahuantinsuyu was to spread universal peace, the Incas often showed mercy to the vanquished tribes and pursued peaceful resolutions whenever possible. The principal strategy utilized by the Incas to defeat their enemies was to destroy harvests and inflict famine. War, however, was often the only option. The slingers, due to their accuracy, began the attack on a fortress. Their sling bolts easily pierced the Peruvian helmets worn by their enemies. Feints were often used to draw defenders away from the center of an attack. Soldiers assembled human pyramids to attack the higher walls of enemy fortresses; the pyramid shape enabled the soldiers to attack quickly with their maces. The skin of the captured leaders was often made into drums used at festivals celebrating Incan victories. After killing the leaders, the Incas ripped out their intestines, dried the bodies as carefully as possible, fitted the abdominal skin over a bentwood frame, and finally placed the skin on a carrying frame. Although these drums were not very musical, they served as amusement for the Incas and as a warning of the fate of those who dared to resist the Incan emperor. Most leaders, however, surrendered and were incorporated into the Incan system of government. The Incas roped their prisoners together and sacrificed a few to the Sun God. Most of the prisoners, however, were detained long enough to ensure that they would cooperate with the Incas and contribute to the empire. The only prisoners who endured slave labor were the ones assigned to maintain the Incas' standards for roads and villages.

The evolution of the Inca Empire was an ongoing process, as each succeeding Incan emperor tried to continue the military plans of his predecessor. After each conquest, the Incas allowed time for the settlement of the new territory before pursuing the next one. This interval also gave the vanquished time to assimilate the Incan culture and to prepare to fight in the name of their new god. The receptions given to Incan sovereigns in the capital after a conquest rivaled Roman triumph celebrations in pomp and ceremony. Dressed in the colorful costumes of their provinces of origin, the people greeted their victorious ruler, who was borne aloft in a golden chair raised on the shoulders of his nobles, as he passed beneath arches erected along the route to the Temple of the Sun. Alone in the temple, because attendants were not permitted to enter, the sovereign, barefoot and stripped of his regal costume, gave thanks for his victory. A large celebration followed in which music, dancing, and bonfires commemorated the addition of a new territory. The Inca Empire, in reality, was a confederation of tribes with the Incas in control of a common government, a common religion, and a common language. A council of rulers ruled each of the tribes, which pledged its allegiance to the emperor, who, as a descendant of the Sun God, was considered divine. The conquered tribes maintained their individual cultural identities, but they paid Incan labor taxes; payment ensured that every individual received fulfillment of all of his or her basic needs. Although the inhabitants of each conquered town spoke their native languages, the Incas also imposed the Quechua language on them in order to enable communication among the different peoples.

MEDIEVAL SOURCES

El Inca Garcilaso de la Vega (1539-1616), the son of an Incan princess and a Spanish explorer, provides a detailed account of the Incan civilization both before and after the arrival of the Spaniards in his *Los Comentarios Reales de Los Incas* (1609-1617; *The Royal Commentaries of the Incas*, 1688), which remains one of the most complete and accurate available sources of information about the Incas. In the first part of this book, completed in 1609, Garcilaso de la Vega chronicles the development of the Inca Empire and discusses the political and social status of the Incas, as well as their legends, traditions, customs, and methods of warfare. The second part, written in 1617, describes the wars of the Spanish conquest, in which Garcilaso de la Vegas's father was a primary figure. "El Inca" bases the second part of his history on the stories told to him by soldiers and conquerors who fought alongside his father.

BOOKS AND ARTICLES

Avalle-Arce, Juan Bautista. *El Inca Garcilaso en sus "Comentarios."* Madrid: Editorial Gredos, 1970.
Burland, C. A. *Peru Under the Incas*. London: Evans Brothers, 1967.
Lanning, Edward P. *Peru Before the Incas*. Englewood Cliffs, N.J.: Prentice-Hall, 1967.
Stern, Steven J. *Peru's Indian Peoples and the Challenge of Spanish Conquest*. 2d ed. Madison: University of Wisconsin Press, 1993.

FILMS AND OTHER MEDIA

The Incas. Documentary. PBS Video, 1980.
The Incas Remembered. Monterey Home Video, 1986.

Michael J. McGrath

North American Indigenous Nations

Dates: c. 12,000 b.c.e.-1600 c.e.

Political Considerations

Among the southeastern and southern North American chiefdoms of the Mississippian period (900-1540 c.e.), there were cities designated as "peace towns" and "war towns," which were occupied alternately during times of peace and war. There were also chieftains who bore the same designations and alternately led their people during these times. The "Red Chief" led in times of war, and the "White Chief" led in times of peace. During the early eighteenth century, the Chickasaw of northern Mississippi, who were in periodic conflict with the Choctaw and their English allies, would turn leadership over to their Red Chief and remove their people to the red towns when hostilities loomed. It is assumed that this elaborate tradition of response to war and peace was in place long before the European contact.

Apparently, there was no effort on the part of Native American groups in the South and Southeast to develop what could be called empires. The chiefdoms controlled large areas that included many towns, but distance was an important factor in the amount of control a small group of native nobles and priests could have over a large territory. The Natchez of western Mississippi, near the city now bearing that name, along the Mississippi River, were probably the best and most advanced example of centralized control over people. The Great Sun was the absolute ruler, presiding over a tightly controlled class system that included four distinct classes: the Great Sun and his immediate family, the Nobility, the Honored Ones, and the Stinkards, or agricultural peasants. It is unlikely, however, that the total Natchez population ever exceeded 5,000 or 6,000, and the territory controlled by the central government was, by modern standards, extremely small. Some distance had to be maintained between chiefdoms to prevent encroachment upon one another's territories. These buffer zones also served as hunting territory.

Other politically advanced chiefdoms were groups later known to the Europeans as the Chickasaw, Choctaw, Seminole, Timucua, Quapaw, Catawba, Tunica, Caddo, Shawnee, Chitimacha, Calusa, Tuscarora, Pamlico, and Powhatan. This Mississippian, or "temple mound," group of cultures extended from Virginia to Oklahoma and from the Ohio River to the Gulf and Atlantic coasts. The Mississippian peoples also extended some distance up the Mississippi River into Wisconsin. At the peak of their development in the late fifteenth century, they probably included no more than one-half million people. They, like most of the Native American groups, periodically fought small battles with each other, but the fighting was mainly precipitated by encroachments into hunting territories or misunderstandings stemming from language differences. For instance, the Chickasaw often drove the Kickapoo out of their hunting grounds in present Tennessee and Kentucky, east of the Tennessee River. The Cherokee and the various Muskogean peoples—the Chickasaw, Choctaw, those who later made up the Creek Confederation, and the Seminole—were generally hostile to each other because the Cherokee, who had arrived in the Southeast in the twelfth or thirteenth century, spoke an Iroquoian language. The Muskogeans all spoke closely related dialects of the Muskogean language.

One of the most politically advanced groups in the East and Northeast was the Iroquois Confederacy, a United Nations-type alliance that had been organized by the sixteenth century. An increase in separate tribal identities had begun in the fourteenth century, perhaps as a male response to the increasing impor-

NATIVE PEOPLES OF EASTERN NORTH AMERICA, C. 1600

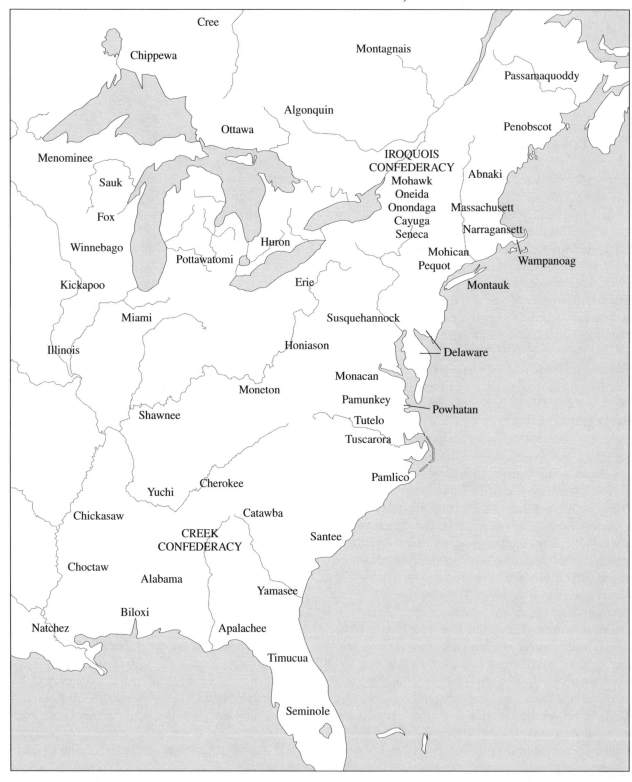

Cree

Chippewa

Montagnais

Passamaquoddy

Algonquin

Penobscot

Ottawa

Menominee

IROQUOIS
CONFEDERACY

Abnaki

Sauk

Mohawk
Oneida
Onondaga
Cayuga
Seneca

Massachusett

Fox

Narragansett

Winnebago

Huron

Mohican
Pequot

Wampanoag

Pottawatomi

Kickapoo

Erie

Montauk

Miami

Susquehannock

Illinois

Honiason

Delaware

Monacan

Moneton

Pamunkey

Powhatan

Shawnee

Tutelo

Tuscarora

Pamlico

Cherokee

Yuchi

Catawba

Chickasaw

Santee

CREEK
CONFEDERACY

Choctaw

Alabama

Yamasee

Biloxi

Natchez

Apalachee

Timucua

Seminole

tance of women in food production, with the spread of maize agriculture in the Northeast during this time. Male prestige, which had previously resulted from the successful hunting and auspicious bravery during the hunt, declined, and men roamed farther from home for longer periods of time, encroaching on the territories of others with whom they engaged in violence, all in search of prestige. Another view involves the trade in prestige items such as copper, obsidian, sea shells, and exotic furs. As male prestige suffered among the Iroquois, raiding to obtain these items by force brought about increased warfare between related groups that had once traded peacefully. By the time of European contact, the Iroquois Confederacy was responsible for a somewhat peaceful coexistence between formerly hostile tribes in the East Lakes region, New England, and southern Canada. These tribes often joined forces to fight their hostile western and southern neighbors.

Another significantly developed political entity were the Anasazi, who were a fundamentally agricultural people occupying a large area of Colorado, Arizona, New Mexico, and Utah. They built great pueblos in such places as Chaco Canyon and Mesa Verde in the Four Corners region. Some believe that the farflung Anasazi confederation was destroyed in the thirteenth century by raids conducted by Utes, Apaches, Navajos, and Comanches who had been driven out of adjacent habitats by a great and prolonged drought that impacted almost all of western North America during what was called the Little Ice Age. During this time, crops failed and the courses of rivers changed. The successors to the Anasazi, known as the Pueblo peoples, an amalgam of the raiding groups, occupied, and continue to occupy, villages consisting of great adobe apartment complexes. These peoples were not, however, part of any large confederation, but rather were more like bands who often fought with one another for a variety of reasons, many trivial.

Along the coast of British Columbia, reaching into southern Alaska and Washington state, lived tribes such as the Tlingit, who were highly developed both socially and politically. These tribes maintained some degree of peace by engaging in the periodic practice of the potlatch, the ceremonial act of giving a great deal of a group's material possessions to another group, which was expected to reciprocate appropriately within a reasonable time. Northwestern tribes did, however, engage in frequent combat with their neighbors over hunting and gathering territory and perhaps in response to raids for obtaining women.

The archaeological record reveals that during the early fourteenth century there were hostilities between Native Americans who lived along the river valleys of the Dakotas and those who occupied the river valleys of Kansas and Nebraska. The southern group, probably responding to drought conditions, moved northward, forcibly encroaching upon the Dakota group. At the Crow Creek site on the Missouri River in South Dakota, more than five hundred scalped and mutilated bodies were unearthed from a shallow mass grave at one end of a defensive trench. Evidence indicates that this massacre occurred around 1325. Many other such occurrences have been documented by archaeologists.

It is certain that warfare did exist between Native American groups during the prehistoric period, though it was almost always on the small scale of war parties, perhaps the size of squads or platoons. Battles were seldom fought for the purpose of territorial conquest, but rather in response to encroachments into hunting territory, over misunderstandings due to

TURNING POINTS

c. 400	The bow and arrow is introduced in eastern North America.
c. 700	Triangular projectile points are developed.
c. 1200	Destruction of southwestern Anasazi culture, possibly by raiding Ute, Apache, Navajo, and Comanche tribes.
c. 1300	An increase in separate tribal identities develops in response to increasing importance of agriculture and clearer definition of gender roles.
c. 1500-1600	The Iroquois Confederacy, an alliance of separate tribes formed to fight hostile western and southern neighbors, is established in the Northeast.

language differences, for theft of prestige items, or in raids to obtain slaves or wives.

MILITARY ACHIEVEMENT

Because no written historical record exists for North America north of the Valley of Mexico before 1500 C.E., warfare between groups of Native Americans cannot be documented with precision. Archaeological record evidence, nevertheless, points to violent conflicts. Many towns were fortified with palisades, bastions, and defensive trenches that would have been unnecessary had there not been real or potential enemy incursions.

WEAPONS, UNIFORMS, AND ARMOR

The weapons of prehistoric Native American warfare would have been essentially, if not exactly, the same weapons as those used in hunting. These would have included the throwing and thrusting spear, dart, bow and arrow, hand ax, war club, hand pick or tomahawk, knife, accoutrements such as the atlatl (spearthrower), detachable projectile points, body armor, shields, quivers, and knife sheaths.

The spear was probably one of the earliest Native American weapons, arriving with the earliest immigrants across the Bering Strait land bridge fourteen thousand or more years ago. The evolution of its use in North America is believed to have roughly paralleled that in Eurasia. The spear was originally used as a thrusting instrument in the early Paleolithic period (c. 12,000 B.C.E.). It then progressed to the throwing spear by the late Paleolithic period (c. 8000 B.C.E.). The earliest evidence of the atlatl comes from the Fort Rock Cave in Oregon and dates to approximately 6500 B.C.E. At the Five Mile Rapids site east of The Dalles, Oregon, on the Columbia River, two atlatl spurs, which engage the tip of the spear at the throwing end, were discovered and found to be contemporaneous with the Fort Rock Cave atlatl. There are two basic types of atlatl: the compound, with the spur as a separate piece attached to the body of the atlatl, and the simple, which combines the two into one piece. The simple atlatl appears to have appeared somewhat later than the compound. By the late Woodland period (c. 400 C.E.), the simple atlatl and spear, or the shorter dart, were in use, along with the bow and arrow. They appear to have been used as a weapon until about the end of the Woodland period (c. 700 C.E.) in both the South and Southeast. The spear continued to be used after this time in the Great Plains and in the West.

The spear point was made of a variety of lithic materials. In the West, flint and basalt were used. Slate, being easily chipped, was common in the Northeast, whereas chert and flint were utilized in the South and Southeast, as well as the Great Plains. Horn was also known to be used. These points were hafted into a groove at the end of the shaft and secured with sinew and glue.

The spear was constructed from hard, straight woods such as hickory and oak in the East; yew and sometimes cedar in the West; and spruce, especially Sitka spruce, in the Northwest. Atlatls were often constructed of horn, such as that of the bighorn sheep, as well as wood. They had stone weights attached to their handles that enabled effective balance of the weapon in the hand of the thrower. The atlatl-thrown spear was a very effective weapon, but it was neither as effective nor as easily portable as the bow and arrow. During the temple mound period in the South and Southeast, the spear became a ritual item.

The bow and arrow appears to have been the principal weapon used during the period one thousand to twelve hundred years before European contact with native North Americans. Only the projectile points, or arrowheads, of spears have survived through time to the present day; the organic parts have been lost to decay. There are exceptions, however, in cases where weapons were deposited in dry caves. The date for the introduction of the bow and arrow and its diffusion throughout North America is a matter of dispute. Most archaeologists date its inception in the fourth or fifth century C.E. A few would put the introduction of this technology in about 500 B.C.E., and still fewer as far back as 4000 B.C.E. The earliest sites have been reported, and highly disputed, to be in the southern half of the Canadian Shield region, which includes Labrador and the southern taiga of eastern Canada. Some

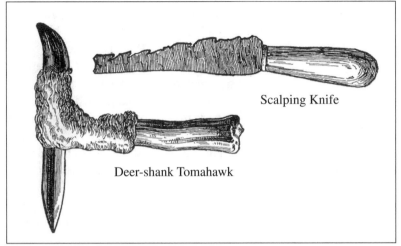

Scalping Knife

Deer-shank Tomahawk

North Wind Picture Archives

Two types of Mohawk weapons.

have suggested that bow and arrow weapons were diffused throughout this region through contact with Paleoeskimo (Inuit) peoples as early as 1500 B.C.E. At some pre-Dorset sites (1050 to 550 B.C.E.) in the eastern Arctic zone of North America, the region that includes Baffin Island, small, chipped, stone projectile points have been found and interpreted to be arrowheads.

In the lower and middle Columbia River region of Washington and Oregon, small projectile points inferred to be arrowheads date as early as 550 B.C.E. Sites in the Willamette Valley of Oregon and Saint Lawrence Island, Alaska, place the bow and arrow in use as early as 50 B.C.E. If these inferences are true, the bow and arrow may have diffused from Asia to the Paleoeskimo (Inuit) cultures of the North American Arctic. It is known that there were strong lines of communication between prehistoric Inuit peoples. At the time of European contact, their languages, from those of eastern Siberia to those of eastern Greenland, were fairly uniform. The bow and arrow could have diffused southward along both the Pacific and Atlantic coasts.

From these northwestern and northeastern locations, weapons technology moved into the Great Basin and the West Lakes regions by about 100 C.E. From these locations, diffusion into the East Coast and Southeast regions, the Colorado Plateau, and

California occurred by about 400 C.E. It was probably another few hundred years (525-950 C.E.) before the bow and arrow reached the bulk of the Great Plains region.

Before the introduction of the horse by Europeans in the early sixteenth century, bows were commonly from 1.5 to 2 meters in length and were fired from a vertical position. A bowman on horseback used a shorter bow and fired from a horizontal position. In the western and northern Great Plains, bows were often wrapped with sinew, which has elastic qualities. Because sinew-wrapped bows were prone to lose their tensile strength with exposure to high humidity, the craftsman would wrap the bow with rattlesnake skin, which is nonporous. Horn bows were also sometimes wrapped in a similar manner. Some bows resembled a curved lath, or rod, that was tapered in thickness from about 2.5 centimeters at the grip to about 1.5 centimeters at the tip. Other, compound, bows were elliptical in shape, bending outward from the grip; when strung, they bent gracefully in compound curves.

Bowstrings were fashioned from the tough shoulder sinew of the large male bison or elk. The sinew was separated into strands, soaked in water and a glue probably made from reduced vegetable and hoof materials, and finally twisted into a heavy cord. One end of the cord was always attached to one end of the bow, whereas the other end was attached to a notch on the other end only when the warrior was ready to string the bow for use. This allowed the bow to maintain its elasticity and tensile strength. The bowman often carried a spare string.

Arrows were made from essentially the same wood material as were bows. The length of arrows varied throughout North America. The Omaha, for instance, traditionally made arrows the length of the distance from the pit of the left elbow to the tip of the middle finger and back over the hand to the wrist bone, an average of 63 to 64 centimeters. Arrows were fletched with feathers—usually three—and some of the feather fletching extended a full one-third of the shaft length. The feathers had to be large enough to split, so the feathers of turkeys, prairie chickens, owls, chicken hawks, eagles, and vultures were preferred. The feathers, after splitting, were often tied to the shaft at both ends with sinew, allowing the middle section to be free from the shaft. The shafts were grooved from the fletching to the tip, and the design of the grooving varied from tribe to tribe. The purpose of this grooving has been lost through time, but some Native Americans of seventeenth and eighteenth centuries claimed that the grooves made the arrow fly a straighter course; some claimed they were bleeding channels, others claimed they kept the arrow from warping, and still others claimed they were occult symbols that ensured accuracy.

The notch on the arrow that fit on the bowstring was at the feather end of the arrow. This end was made a bit bulbous to facilitate a better grip with the thumb and index finger. The string was pulled with the other three fingers.

The arrowheads of war arrows were perpendicular to the bowstring, so that the arrows would easily pass between the ribs of the enemy. Hunting arrowheads were parallel to the string, so that they would pass through the ribs of game. Some reports claim that there was essentially no difference between hunting and war arrows, except that the arrowhead on the war arrow was longer for more effective penetration. Arrows were often distinctly decorated among the tribes and among individuals. This decoration facilitated retrieval by the owner and also emphasized tribal distinctiveness.

Arrowheads took many forms even in the early periods of bow and arrow usage. By the late Woodland period, points were side notched and corner notched on the hafting, or attaching, end and were of varying lengths to suit various purposes, such as hunting and warfare. The war arrowhead was the longest and most slender. Toward the end of the Woodland period and the beginning of the Mississippian, or temple mound, period, the triangular-shaped point became increasingly prominent.

These points were crafted by chipping and flaking any of several substances. Chert, flint, and obsidian were the most common materials; all are varieties of quartz. Chert, a poor-quality flint, was used when better qualities of raw materials were not available. Most arrowheads were made of good-quality flint. Flint, composed of extremely fine-grained sediment, has a concoidal fracture that easily lends itself to accurate chipping or pressure-flaking. Obsidian, or natural glass, is a volcanic rock and was available only in parts of the Rocky Mountains and the Cascade-Sierra Nevada ranges of the far West. Obsidian produced a super-sharp edge and could be easily sharpened when it became dull.

The arrowhead was hafted to the tip of the arrow shaft with sinew and glue. A notch was cut in the tip of the shaft, and the head was wedged into the notch. In the case of the war arrow, the head was sometimes detachable. It was loosely hafted to the shaft, and no sinew or glue was used. The head was simply wedged into the notch. If the arrow's victim attempted to pull the arrow out, the arrowhead would remain and increase the severity of the wound.

The bow and arrow was a very effective weapon of war. An arrow could be projected up to 500 meters and, in the hands of a skilled marksman, was extremely accurate at distances of 100 meters or more. The penetrating power of an arrow shot from a bow with a 40-pound pull had more penetrating potential than did a bullet shot from a Colt .45, and it was more accurate at long distances.

Bows were usually carried in highly decorated bow cases, and arrows were carried in equally elaborately decorated quivers that were slung over the shoulder and hung almost horizontally near the waist. Quivers were generally made of soft animal skins, such as that of the river otter.

In the Great Plains and in eastern North America, prehistoric bows often had a long flint blade or knife hafted to one end. These were used as bayonets in hand-to-hand combat. The Omaha called these weapons *mindehi*, which means "bowtooth."

The war club was a common weapon throughout North America. In very early times it was probably similar to the simple hand ax, made of ground sandstone with a groove near the top to permit it to be hafted onto a short wooden handle and lashed together with rawhide. During the temple mound period in the East and South, the war club was made of either stone or bone. The stone head, sometimes rounded, sometimes pointed, was hafted to a wooden handle with rawhide. Willow was a choice wood because it could be split on the hafting end and was pliable enough to wrap around the hafting groove. The whole assembly was wrapped with wet rawhide that shrunk tight while drying. A bone war club was a one-piece item made from one of the long bones of a large animal, the socket forming the rounded head of the club.

The Nootka of the Pacific Northwest often made their war clubs from whale bones. These war clubs were straight or slightly curved with a hole drilled in the handle end to facilitate a wrist thong. They were ornate objects, and intricate carvings of various designs are known. During the years of first European contact, war clubs of the Northwest were valuable trade items and carried great prestige.

Knives were bifacial instruments made of flaked or chipped flint or obsidian in most of North America. Ground or chipped slate knives have been found among the archaeological remains in the sub-Arctic Northeast. Some flint knives were as many as 75 centimeters in length and could be classified as short swords. Most, however, were considerably shorter and were hafted onto wooden handles in the manner of projectile points. The knife was often kept in a sheath made of leather, ornately decorated with shell and beads, and worn tucked in the waist belt. The knife, like the war club, was very effective in close combat.

A type of armor was sometimes worn by warriors in battle. Some of it was constructed of bent wooden laths that were drilled and sewn together with rawhide. Armor was also made of the thick leather of buffalo or elk, folded several times and worn as a vest that covered the entire torso. This same material was used by warriors in the Northwest to make thigh and shin guards. It was very difficult to penetrate, even with arrows and thrusting spears. Shields were also carried into battle. They were generally made of wood, covered with leather, and painted with various designs that were believed to have magical powers to protect the warrior.

It is not known whether the Native American warrior wore distinctive dress or a type of uniform that set him apart from the nonwarrior, because such items have not survived to the present day. At the time of European contact there was no indication that a particular type of uniform set any tribal warrior apart from others. It might be inferred, though, that someone wearing only a loincloth but carrying all of his weapons, body armor, and a shield could be identified as prepared to fight. European observers in all parts of North America often reported that, except for chiefs and shamans, all the men seemed to be dressed similarly.

MILITARY ORGANIZATION

It does not appear that any Native American group in prehistoric times had a standing army or even a warrior class. Warriors were able-bodied young men who, when called upon to engage in violence, left their normal duties as farmers, hunters, and craftsmen and assumed the role of warrior.

Most violent encounters between groups seem to have been conducted by small bands of warriors numbering no more than twenty or thirty. Oral tradition indicates that battles started with an ambush and concluded with hand-to-hand combat. It is true that some groups displaced others from their traditional territories. The traditions of the Shawnee tell of their former home somewhere in central Tennessee, and it is believed that they were displaced to the north of the Ohio River by pressures from some of the Southern tribes during the fifteenth or sixteenth century. Choctaw and Chickasaw migration legends claim that these peoples originally came from somewhere to the west of the Mississippi River. These removals, though, could have resulted just as easily from environmental conditions as from warfare. It would not have taken a vast army to cause the removal of small groups from their traditional homes. Persistent attacks by small raiding parties, which could not be successfully rebuffed or answered by counterraids, would have been enough pressure to force migrations. There is no record until after European contact of large military assemblages descending upon an enemy.

DOCTRINE, STRATEGY, AND TACTICS

Little or nothing is known of prehistoric military doctrine or strategies, and what is known of tactics is simple. The shock of ambush with bows and arrows followed by close fighting with clubs and knives seems to have been the favorite tactic used in hostile encounters. The strategies and tactics used by Native Americans after European contact, involving large numbers of warriors, probably were not traditional and could easily have been due to European influence.

MEDIEVAL SOURCES

Native Americans north of Mexico, prior to European contact, had no written languages; therefore, no information except the archaeological record remains. Apart from some Viking and Welsh legends, which may or may not have any historical foundation, little can be found. Castañeda de Nágera (fl. sixteenth century), chronicler for Francisco Vásquez de Coronado (1510-1554), recorded what he witnessed in the Southwest from February, 1540, until the fall of 1542. Alvar Nuñez Cabeza de Vaca (c. 1490-c. 1560) traded along the Gulf Coast in 1535 and left a journal describing his trade in bows and arrows. El Inca Garcilaso de la Vega's (1539-1616) chronicles of the 1539 to 1543 expedition of Hernando de Soto (c. 1496-1540) through the South offer a glimpse of Native American warfare at the close of the prehistoric period.

BOOKS AND ARTICLES

Ballentine, Betty, and Ian Ballentine, eds. *The Naïve Americans: An Illustrated History*. Atlanta: Turner, 1993.

Cressman, L. S. *Prehistory of the Far West: Homes of Vanished Peoples*. Salt Lake City: University of Utah Press, 1977.

Fagan, Brian M. *Ancient North America: The Archaeology of a Continent*. New York: Thames and Hudson, 1991.

Lewis, Thomas M. N., and Madeline Kneberg. *Tribes That Slumber: Indians of the Tennessee Region*. Knoxville: University of Tennessee Press, 1958.

Stewart, Hilary. *Indian Artifacts of the Northwest Coast*. Seattle: University of Washington Press, 1973.

Charles Mayer Dupier, Jr.

FROM MEDIEVAL TO MODERN

HANDARMS TO FIREARMS

DATES: Since c. 1130

NATURE AND USE

Firearms are a Chinese invention for which the earliest evidence dates to 1130. By that time the Chinese were using gunpowder in primitive flamethrowers made of bamboo, wood, or metal tubes. Within another century they had developed gunpowder projectile weapons that fired lances, arrows, and probably balls. Beyond these early weapons, however, development of firearms did not proceed much further in China. Although most historians agree that thirteenth century Mongols brought gunpowder to Europe, where its first definitive mention is dated to 1267, there is no consensus on whether the Mongols also brought Chinese gunpowder weaponry to the West.

An English illustration from 1326 shows the earliest known gunpowder weapon in Europe during a siege. The first certain use of gunpowder weaponry in Europe occurred in 1331 during a siege of Friuli in northeastern Italy. A French source for the Battle of Crécy (1346) states that the English fired three cannons at crossbowmen in the French army as they advanced toward the English lines, but many historians do not accept the report's accuracy. At the English siege of Calais following their victory at Crécy, there is good documentation for the use of small cannons called *ribaulds*, but these cannons had only a small role in the siege. Over the next twenty years cannons increased greatly in size. During his 1377 siege of Odruik in the Netherlands, Philip II, duke of Burgundy (1342-1404), used cannons called bombards, which were capable of firing 200-pound stone balls. This occasion was the first known instance of cannon fire breaching walls. Philip was the strongest early advocate of gunpowder weapons, encouraging experimentation with different sizes, gunpowder mixtures, and metals. Soon bombards weighing twenty tons and firing 1,000-pound balls were bringing sieges to quick conclusions across Europe.

DEVELOPMENT

FIFTEENTH CENTURY

By 1410 gunpowder weaponry had captured the attention of an unlikely commentator on military affairs, Christine de Pizan (c. 1365-c. 1430), a native of Italy who lived most of her life at the French court. Her *Le Livre des fais d'armes et de chevalerie* (1410; *The Book of Fayttes of Arms and of Chivalry*, 1489) discusses at length the use of the cannon as a siege weapon, recommending that the defenders of a fortification use twelve cannons using stone balls and ten pieces of mechanical artillery. Christine estimated the need for 1,500 pounds of gunpowder along with 200 stone balls and argued that attackers would need a much larger arsenal: forty-two cannon shooting 200-pound balls, along with many mechanical artillery pieces and smaller firearms. Attackers would also need 30,000 pounds of powder, 1,100 stone balls, and 500 pounds of lead for the smaller pieces, because working stone into balls small enough for these weapons was difficult and time-consuming. Christine also advocated mounting cannon on ships for war at sea.

The fact that Christine's work makes little mention of gunpowder weapons in battle suggests that, at least in France, they were not yet being widely used. In Flanders, *ribaulds* were placed on carts and used as field artillery. The first battle in which they had an impact was Beverhoudsveld (1382) in the Netherlands. The militiamen of the city of Ghent had some two hundred carts with several *ribaulds* apiece in the battle against the count of Flanders. Concentrated *ribauld* fire against the count's men as they charged caused them to panic and flee. These carts were difficult to move, and later the same year Ghent was defeated when its forces charged the enemy only to find that the *ribauld* carts could not keep up, depriving them of supporting fire at the crucial moment.

The solution was the development of handguns small enough to allow their bearers to move with the rest of the army. The first evidence for such weapons is found in an illustration from around 1400, which shows a soldier holding in one hand the breech end of a long narrow tube that rests on a tripod at the muzzle while he applies a burning stick to the touchhole. This device appears to be so clumsy that it was most likely used not in the field, but rather as a siege weapon. Walls provided a base on which to steady the weapons, and hooks attaching them to the walls absorbed much of the force of the recoil. Recoil was a serious problem in early handguns, which required two hands to use: one to hold either the burning stick or the match that appeared around 1420, and the other to hold the piece. Consequently early handguns were butted up against the middle of the user's chest, often resulting in a broken breastbone. The first hook guns probably were used in the Hussite Wars (1419-1434), an anti-Catholic revolt against King Sigismund of Bohemia (1368-1437). To counter the knightly forces of Sigismund, Hussite leader Jan Žižka (c. 1360-1424) devised the *Wagenburg*, a defensive line of wagons on which were placed men with firearms. Between the wagons, cannons were stationed. Men on horseback presented a large target for the gunpowder weapons in use, inaccurate as they were. These weapons had the additional advantage of frightening the horses with their smoke and noise. Even after Žižka's death, the *Wagenburg* continued to help the Hussites to victory over German knights. German efforts to replicate the *Wagenburg* failed, but Hussite hook guns appeared in Germany, where the German word for them is regarded as the source for the word "harquebus," used as the name for the first effective firearm.

The harquebus was a product of several German innovations that been made by 1460. Corned, or granulated, powder provided greater explosive power than had earlier powder and produced higher muzzle velocities. Gunsmiths found the right com-

TURNING POINTS

1130	Chinese use gunpowder in flamethrowers.
1331	First known use of gunpowder weaponry in the West occurs at the Siege of Friuli in Italy.
1377	Cannon are first used successfully to breach a wall at the Siege of Odruik, the Netherlands.
1420	Hussite leader Jan Žižka makes innovative use of firearms, with the *Wagenburg*, a defensive line of wagons and cannons.
1525	Spanish Square formation of pikemen and harquebusiers is perfected at the Battle of Pavia.
1631	Gustavus II Adolphus's military reforms prove their value at the Battle of Breitenfeld.

promise between ballistic performance and weight by using barrels of about 40 inches in length. Another major innovation was the match: a piece of string soaked in saltpeter that burned slowly but with a tip hot enough to touch off gunpowder. The match replaced the burning stick, which was both clumsy and unreliable. The match, however, created the same problem for its users as had the burning stick: It had to be held in a hand and touched down into the chamber to fire the powder, leaving only one hand to hold the piece. The solution was the matchlock, which brought together springs, a trigger, and a clamp for holding a smoldering match. When the trigger was pulled, the burning tip was thrust into the powder and touched it off. The shoulder stock, borrowed from the crossbow, reduced the impact of the recoil. The users of the matchlock device found that although overly coarse powder failed to be ignited by the match, overly fine powder created too forceful a recoil. The solution was the placement of a small pan behind the chamber of the barrel, into which fine powder was placed. Coarse powder was then put in the chamber. The match touched off the fine powder in the pan, blowing flame through a hole into the chamber, igniting the coarser powder there, and firing off the ball.

The harquebus's impact on the battlefield was slow to appear. Compared to longbows, the early harquebus performed poorly in its reliability, rate of fire, and accuracy. It found its first niche as a siege weapon, replacing the crossbow. Firearms were useful weapons for the militiamen who guarded the city walls across Europe. They did not require much training to be used effectively on walls, and the artisans and merchants who made up the urban militias could afford them. The earliest mentions of the harquebus appear in the weapons inventories of cities.

For a brief time, the use of the harquebus as a defensive weapon on walls reduced the advantage that heavy cannons had provided besiegers, but gunpowder artillery continued to improve more rapidly than did firearms. A problem with early cannons was the poor quality of cast iron used to make them, which resulted in pieces frequently bursting and killing gunners and bystanders. A solution was the use of bronze. Europeans were familiar with casting bronze bells, and that technology was easily transferred to the making of weapons. The use of bronze allowed founders to manufacture long-barreled pieces with small muzzles, which were capable of using iron or lead balls. Under Charles VII (1403-1461), the French led the way in developing high-quality cannons. The final years of the Hundred Years' War (1337-1453) saw dramatic improvements in the royal artillery train. Charles's masters of artillery organized a system of manufacturing cannon, procuring gunpowder and shot, and hiring gunners that played a significant role in reducing English-held locations in Normandy and Gascony. In the war's last major battles, Formigny (1450) and Castillon (1453), the French placed their guns all along the line of battle, routing the English. The king also promoted experimentation to improve the gun carriage, leading to the creation of the carriage with high wheels and long tail that defined gun carriages until the nineteenth century. Using an artillery train of around eighty bronze cannon on mobile carriages, Charles VIII (1470-1498) had great success in reducing Italian fortifications during the initial phase of the Italian Wars of

North Wind Picture Archives

A hand-cannon of the fifteenth century, fired from the shoulder or from a rest such as a wall with a lit match.

North Wind Picture Archives

The harquebus, popular by the sixteenth century, had a matchlock firing device that allowed for more reliable firing.

1494-1559. In the Battle of Fornovo (1495) the French artillery also played a role as a field weapon.

SIXTEENTH CENTURY

During the wars in Italy after 1494, field armies began to include harquebusiers. At the Battle of Cerignola (1503) in the French-Spanish War over Naples, the Spanish commander Gonzalo Fernández de Córdoba (1453-1515) devised a way to make effective use of harquebusiers by digging trenches in front of their lines. This action transformed the battlefield into a fort and imitated a siege, a situation in which the harquebus had long proven itself. Harquebus fire raked the French forces as they approached the Spanish trenches. Over the next twenty years the Spanish infantry was victorious as long as it had the time to dig entrenchments and the French and their Swiss mercenaries relied on frontal assault. At the Battle of Pavia (1525) the combination of harquebusiers and pikemen in the army of Holy Roman Emperor Charles V (1500-1558) formed without entrenchments and defeated the French. This infantry formation, in which pikemen and harquebusiers provided mutual support, was known as the Spanish Square.

During the Dutch Wars of Independence (1566-1648), Maurice of Nassau (1567-1625) made his infantry more effective by extensive drilling, which had special success in improving his handgunners' firepower. He broke down the process of loading and firing a matchlock firearm into forty-two steps; each step had a word of command shouted by the sergeant. Drill books showing the steps and providing the words of command spread across Europe. Gustavus II Adolphus (1594-1632) of Sweden built upon the Dutch system, emphasizing drills and increasing the rate of fire from firearms by providing a cartridge with a ball and a measured amount of powder. Intent on increasing firepower for his forces, he also introduced a light piece firing a 3-pound ball that could be moved with the infantry on the battlefield, thereby providing support fire for the infantry in a way that heavier cannon could not do. For Gustavus II Adolphus, the purpose of firepower was to create opportunities for shock forces to carry the attack into the ranks of the enemy. Pikemen continued to be a significant part of the European infantry until the development of the bayonet by 1700 combined shock and firepower in each soldier.

BOOKS AND ARTICLES

DeVries, Kelly. *Medieval Military Technology.* Peterborough, Ont.: Broadview Press, 1992.

Hall, Bert. *Weapons and Warfare in Renaissance Europe.* Baltimore: Johns Hopkins University Press, 1997.

Lugs, Jaroslav. *Firearms Past and Present: A Complete Review of Firearms Systems and Their Histories.* 2 vols. London: Grenville, 1973.

Parker, Geoffrey. *The Military Revolution.* Cambridge, England: Cambridge University Press, 1988.

Frederic J. Baumgartner

KNIGHTS TO CAVALRY

DATES: C. 1000-1600 C.E.

KNIGHTS

Although the roles of knights and cavalrymen are often confused, the two are actually different. Knights were mounted warriors who fought as an aggregate of individuals; cavalry were tactical bodies of horsemen who fought as a cohesive unit. Knights, who dominated the battlefields of central and Western Europe from the eleventh to the fourteenth centuries, were identified by their horses, armor, and weapons. Although it was not a violation of the knightly code for knights to fight on foot, knights generally fought on horseback, wearing armor, and engaged in hand-to-hand combat using couched lances, broadswords, and other shock weapons, such as maces. Knights' proper opponents were other knights, not the ill-disciplined and badly armed infantrymen who accompanied medieval armies.

The usual knightly tactic was the frontal charge, with the horsemen forming up in a line and riding toward the enemy's line, reaching a full gallop some 30 to 40 yards before colliding with the enemy. Unless one foe was badly inferior in number or morale, allowing the line to be broken, hand-to-hand combat ensued in the melee after the two lines collided, where individual combatants were nearly identical in equipment, strength, and training. The knights spent little time drilling together. Imbued with the old Germanic tradition that the best warrior led the others into battle, the knights competed to be the first into battle, making it difficult for commanders to coordinate simple tactical moves such as flanking maneuvers before the knights rode off to charge the enemy.

For all of their deficiencies, knights proved their mettle against Byzantine and Muslim forces, and for nearly 250 years after the Battle of Hastings (1066) they were all but invulnerable to the weapons used by European infantrymen. At the Battles of Courtrai (1302) in the Franco-Dutch War and the Morgarten (1315) in the First Austro-Swiss War, however, Flemish and Swiss pikemen demonstrated that the proper choice of terrain allowed resolute foot soldiers to defeat French and Austrian knights respectively. By then the use of powerful crossbows and longbows also put knights at greater risk of death on the battlefield at the hands of commoner bowmen. The combination of archer and dismounted knight used by the English throughout the Hundred Years' War (1337-1453) proved deadly effective against French knights. Men-at-arms responded to their new vulnerability by using plate armor for themselves and their horses, which were more likely than their riders to be killed in battle. Plate armor presented several problems. It was too expensive for the less wealthy nobles, so that the near equality in knightly equipment that had marked the previous era disappeared. Its weight required larger and more costly warhorses, which were slower and less maneuverable, allowing the men-at-arms to do little more than a straight-ahead charge. Despite defeat by the Swiss infantrymen in numerous battles throughout the fifteenth century, culminating at Nancy (1477) in the death of Charles the Bold (1433-1477), the duke of Normandy, armored horsemen remained a potent element, especially in the French army.

IMPACT OF GUNPOWDER WEAPONS

The development of gunpowder weapons after 1325 did little to change warfare for 150 years. Their first niche was in siege warfare. During the Hussite Wars (1419-1434) in Bohemia, Hussite leader Jan Žižka (c. 1360-1424) successfully brought the siege to the battlefield using the *Wagenburg*, which copied a fort by placing firearms and small cannon on wagons drawn up in a defensive line. Žižka's *Wagenburg* stymied the German knights who were his enemy in the

Medieval knights face a massed infantry pike formation, against which, in their heavy armor and their large un-wieldy horses, they became less and less effective.

war, but the tactic did not spread beyond Bohemia. The new weaponry, including both firearms and artillery, was too inaccurate, slow to reload, and clumsy to use on the battlefield to be effective against men-at-arms, although its ability to pierce plate armor increased knightly casualty rates.

During the Italian Wars of 1494-1559, which began in 1494 when French king Charles VIII (r. 1483-1498) led an army of 8,500 horsemen across the Alps, the men-at-arms continued to have a significant place in battle. At Seminara (1495) the French men-at-arms crushed the Spanish and Italian horsemen and then routed the enemy infantry by attacking its flank and rear. Faced with the need to reform his army after its crushing defeat, Ferdinand II of Aragon (1452-1516) decided to concentrate on the infantry, introducing the combination of firearms and pike that became known as the Spanish Square. This´ formation demonstrated its potential against the French men-at-arms at Cerignola (1503), when well-entrenched infantrymen using harquebuses and pikes held off their charge and killed the French com-

mander with a harquebus ball as he rode toward their line. The men-at-arms had their victorious moments, most notably at Marignano (1515), where they had a major role in the French victory over the Swiss. The last battle in which French men-at-arms using their traditional fighting style had a significant role in gaining victory was Cerisolles (1544) in northern Italy. Their foe, a Spanish and German force serving Holy Roman Emperor Charles V (1500-1558), placed too much faith in the ability of harquebusiers to withstand a cavalry charge without support from pikemen. The harquebusiers could not sustain fire strong enough to halt the men-at-arms as they charged through the balls into their ranks.

France was the last place in Europe where knights continued to be used as a major part of the army. This tradition reflected the attitude of the French nobles, who regarded fighting on horseback as their God-given right. The Spanish had never developed much of a force of armored horsemen because their principal foe through the Middle Ages had been the light cavalry of the Moors and because Spanish agriculture was incapable of breeding many of the heavy horses the knights required. The English had been using armored men as heavy infantry since conquering Wales in the thirteenth century. English ability to deploy armored men on horseback was severely limited by the lack of heavy horses. The Italians had used men-at-arms as their principal fighting force until 1494, but one consequence of the Italian Wars of 1494-1559 was a rapid decline in that system. A city such as Venice would keep some armored horsemen under arms until late in the sixteenth century, but this practice was more for the appeasement of its noble class than for any practical value the knights had on the battlefield.

THE PISTOL

The final challenge to the traditional man-at-arms appeared in Germany. German knights had continued to appear in war until 1540. Then, within a decade, the pistoler replaced the knight. The wheellock mechanism for the pistol was developed about 1505 in either Germany or Italy, but it evolved into the pistol first in Germany. By 1518, Holy Roman Emperor Maximilian I (1459-1519) had banned weapons small enough to be concealed in one's sleeve. The production of the wheel lock was a time-consuming task that required much smaller tolerances than the matchlock used in the harquebus did. Because the wheel lock had to be sturdy enough for use in a weapon, it was very expensive. Cost probably was the principal reason the pistol did not become a weapon for foot soldiers, although some wheel-lock muskets were made.

The nobles, who still insisted on their right to fight on horseback, found that the pistol could be effective from horseback, especially if they carried three or four of them, which could be loaded in advance, placed in slings or in their boots, and fired in rapid succession. The wheellock pistol was badly inaccurate at any distance beyond a few paces and only more so when fired from a moving horse. However, a horseman firing three or four pistols rapidly could have some hope of hitting a foe. The pistol was a one-handed weapon, which allowed the rider a free hand to control his horse. Although there had been mounted harquebusiers in most European armies since 1500, the sparking match of the harquebusiers' two-handed weapons frightened their horses, and the harquebusiers usually dismounted to fire. Pistols offered many benefits: Pistolers could shed much of their armor, making their mobility the key to what success they had; their horses could be smaller and cheaper; and it required less training to use a pistol than a lance.

Mounted pistolers first appeared in the war between Charles V and the Lutheran princes in Germany (1546-1555). When they served in Charles's army that fought the French for control of Lorraine (1553-1554), the French called them *reîtres*. The French men-at-arms were astonished when a force of *reîtres* little larger than their own band defeated them at Saint-Vincent in Lorraine (1553). The forces of Spanish king Philip II (r. 1556-1598) had great numbers of *reîtres* at the Battle of Saint Quentin (1557). Their speed played a major role in the deadly pursuit of the routed French forces. French king Henry II (r. 1547-1559) then recruited eight thousand *reîtres* for the French army. In the French Wars of Religion that followed Henry's accidental death while joust-

TURNING POINTS

1302	Flemish pikemen defeat French knights with advantageous choice of terrain at Courtrai.
1420	Hussite leader Jan Žižka stymies German knights during the Hussite Wars with his *Wagenburg*, a defensive line of wagons and cannons.
1503	Spanish infantry using Spanish Square formation of pikemen and harquebusiers defeat French knights at Cerignola.
1544	At Cerisolles, French knights fighting in the traditional style play a major role in gaining victory over the Swiss, the last battle in which they are to do so.
1562	The caracole maneuver is first executed by Huguenot pistolers against Catholic forces at the Battle of Dreux.
1631	Disciplined cavalrymen combine firepower and shock tactics at Breitenfeld.

ing (a further blow to the traditional style), the Protestant army had the larger number of *reîtres*, because most were Lutherans.

THE CARACOLE

In the Battle of Dreux (1562), between the Protestant Huguenots and the Catholics, the Protestant pistolers for the first time executed the tactic known as the caracole. The *reîtres* rode toward their enemy's line in successive ranks, fired their pistols a few yards from the foe as they wheeled their horses about, and returned to the rear of their formation to reload and wait their turn to repeat the maneuver. The caracole had success against an infantry force armed only with shock weapons, but it was ineffective against a well-equipped force of harquebusiers, who had greater range. The caracole was more successful against the men-at-arms because *reîtres* could rely on greater speed to keep clear of their shock weapons. In 1568 Marshal Gaspard de Tavannes (1509-1573), the royalist Catholic commander, ordered that each company of horsemen would ride together in the formation it would take on the battlefield, so that men would become accustomed to holding their positions, a clear statement of the change from the knight to the cavalryman. The pistolers formed up in depth, while the knights charged in a line one or two ranks deep. To be effective in their deep formation, *reîtres* required more organization, drill, and training than did knights. Cohesion in their units was more crucial to what success they had on the battlefield. François de La Noue (1531-1591), a Protestant captain, noted with distaste in his *Discours politiques et militaires* (1587; *The Politicke and Militarie Discourses*, 1588) that pistolers could defeat noble men-at-arms if they kept tight order and discipline.

By the time Henry IV (r. 1589-1610) became the French king, the pistol had largely replaced the lance in France. Henry regarded shock tactics as necessary, and he had his horsemen charge into the ranks of the enemy with swords after they had fired their pistols. The greater discipline in Henry's cavalry units made them effective in hand-to-hand combat. During the Dutch Wars of Independence (1566-1648), Maurice of Nassau (1567-1625) ordered his horsemen to abandon the lance entirely. When Gustavus II Adolphus of Sweden (1594-1632) went to war with Poland (1617-1629), he found that his pistolers lacked the discipline and training to counter the powerful Polish lancers, who still fought largely in the traditional style. The scarcity of firearms in eastern Europe meant that horsemen there had not increased the weight of their armor and thus were still mobile and effective. Although he allowed his horsemen to fire a pistol as they closed on the enemy, Gustavus reemphasized shock tactics using the sword. However, he also demanded that his horsemen drill extensively so that they would fight as a cohesive unit. In battles of the Thirty Years' War such as Breitenfeld I (1631), he demonstrated the success of his ideas and completed the transition from knight to cavalry.

BOOKS AND ARTICLES

Baumgartner, Frederic. "The Final Demise of the Medieval Knight in France." In *Regnum, Religio, et Ratio*, edited by Jerome Friedman. St. Louis, Mo.: Sixteenth Century Publishers, 1988.

Delbrück, Hans. *The History of the Art of War.* Translated by Walter Renfroe. 4 vols. Westport, Conn.: Greenwood Press, 1985.

Eltis, David. *The Military Revolution in the Sixteenth Century.* London: I. B. Tauris, 1995.

Hall, Bert. *Weapons and Warfare in Renaissance Europe.* Baltimore: Johns Hopkins University Press, 1997.

Frederic J. Baumgartner

GALLEYS TO GALLEONS
DATES: TO C. 1600 C.E.

THE MEDIEVAL GALLEY

The history of medieval naval warfare is the history of the galley. Since ancient times, battles at sea had taken place largely on the decks of ships and were fought much like land battles, with hand-to-hand combat. Medieval naval battles usually followed a similar pattern. First, smaller, more maneuverable ships would pin down the enemy fleet. Then the larger, more heavily armed galleys would attack, initially firing missiles and then ramming or grappling the enemy vessel in order to board it. Blasts of lime were often fired to blind the enemy and were then followed by volleys of stones. One of the most dreaded tactics was to fling onto the enemy ship what was known as Greek fire, a substance that, once ignited, was inextinguishable in water. Crossbows, lances, bows and arrows, and, by the late Middle Ages, guns and cannons served as well at sea as on land. However, the ship itself was the most powerful weapon, often determining the outcome of a naval battle. The warship at sea was likened to the warhorse on land and, like the warhorse, the warship was bred for fighting.

Equipped with sails for distance and oars for maneuverability, the medieval galley was ideally suited for the purpose of war. Medieval variations on the classical galley were many. The *dromon*, developed by the Byzantines, was a large galley that utilized one or two tiers of oars, a square sail set on a single mast, and a stern-hung rudder. In times of war, the *dromon* could carry troops, weapons, supplies, and cavalry horses, as well as engage in sea battles when necessary. The beam of the *dromon* permitted mounted cannons in the bow of the ship, which could be fired directly ahead of the vessel. A variation on the *dromon* was the Italian galley, which had one level of oars with two or three oarsmen to each rowing bench, a total of approximately 120 oarsmen. The Italian

galley was manned by about fifty soldiers and typically had a large catapult mounted on a platform on the front deck.

The galleass was another variation on the galley. Developed by the Venetians, the galleas had a gun deck, oars, and two to three masts. The triangular lateen sails, adopted from those of the Arab dhows, permitted the galleas to sail nearly straight into the wind, impossible with square sails. Sailors armed with crossbows and lances could fight on the ships' decks.

The last major naval battle in which galleys were employed was the Battle of Lepanto II, fought off the coast of southwestern Greece on October 7, 1571, between the Ottoman Turks, under the command of Ali Pasha (died 1616), and the Christian forces, under the command of Don Juan de Austria (1547-1578), half brother of King Philip II of Spain (1527-1598). The Turks' 273 ships (210 were galleys) and the Christians' 276 ships (208 were galleys) faced off in long lines across from one another, with the Christian forces hemming in the Muslim forces. Don Juan skillfully placed his most heavily armed galleys in the center of the line and his smaller, more maneuverable galleys on the outside, where they could dominate the flanks. The massive and heavily armed Christian galleys eventually triumphed over the lighter and less armed Arab ships, giving naval supremacy to the Christian forces in the Eastern Mediterranean. The Battle of Lepanto was the last major naval battle in which galleys were employed, and it was the first major naval battle in which guns and gunpowder played the decisive role. From this point on, guns and cannons would be increasingly important in naval warfare.

Although the galley was the vessel of choice in the Mediterranean Sea for more than four millennia, it was a typically unstable ship, particularly in rough waters. Maneuverability during battle was provided by oars, rather than by the sails, which had to be lowered during battles to prevent the enemy from tearing or setting fire to them. Despite their shortcomings, however, various forms of galleys continued to be employed in the Mediterranean until 1717 and in the Baltic Sea until 1809. In an effort to produce a more seaworthy craft, medieval shipbuilders turned to other designs for seagoing vessels.

THE COG

Developed in Northern Europe as a trading vessel, the cog was one step closer to the first true full-rigged ships, which relied on sails, rather than oars, for both distance and maneuverability. The cog was clinker-built, of overlapping planks. It had a broad beam, a rounded bow and stern, fore- and aft castles, and a single square sail hoisted on a yard. The castles were constructed primarily as high platforms for lookouts and archers and were useful in sea battles. Lower, oar-driven ships found it nearly impossible to conquer a taller ship due to its sheer height and to the superior positioning of its archers and fighting men. The cog was maneuvered by a rudder, attached like a hinge at the center stern and manipulated by a tiller. This steering system was a great technological advance, and it remains the basic means of control on ships.

The principal purpose of the cog was for commerce, but when enemies or pirates threatened, the cog became a warship. In 1234 and again in 1239, the Baltic German city of Lübeck, a central member of the Hanseatic League, sent a fleet of cogs against the king of Denmark when he threatened to take over the city. After pirates invaded the Mediterranean in 1304, the Genoese and Venetians began to use cogs in their navies. A psalter dating to 1330 depicts two cogs in a battle, with the soldiers engaged in hand-to-hand combat across the decks of the ships.

In naval battles the primary goal was not the sinking of the enemy's ship; in fact, it would have been considered foolish to sink a vessel that had been so expensive to construct. In 1340, during the Hundred Years' War, King Edward III of England (1312-1377) sailed in a cog to lead an English fleet of 250 vessels into battle against the French fleet anchored at Sluys, off the coast of Flanders. Although outnumbered, Edward was able to defeat the French fleet and capture 190 French ships. His chronicler estimated that Edward saved 200,000 florins in shipbuilders' wages.

By the fourteenth century cogs sailed the throughout the Mediterranean and the northern European seas. The cog was not without its shortcomings, among which were its inability to keep cargo dry and its insufficient leeway to allow navigation in shallow waters. As trade, exploration, and military challenges increased, so too did the need for more capable and seaworthy vessels.

TURNING POINTS

674-678	Greek fire, a flammable liquid, is used by the Byzantines against Arab ships during the Siege of Constantinople.
mid-13th cent.	The cog, with high sides that offer protection against other vessels, is developed in Northern Europe.
mid-14th cent.	The carrack, an efficient sailing ship with multiple masts, becomes popular in Atlantic and Mediterranean waters.
1501	The development of gunports allows a ship's heaviest guns to be mounted on its lowest decks, stabilizing its center of gravity.
1571	The Battle of Lepanto II, fought between the Ottoman Turks and the Christian forces of Don Juan de Austria, is the last major naval battle to be waged with galleys.
1588	The English employ galleons to individually attack the larger ships of the formidable Spanish Armada, defeating the Spanish and revolutionizing naval tactics.

THE CARRACK

From the fourteenth to the seventeenth century, a larger vessel called the carrack was the predominant trading vessel in Europe. The carrack combined the square sails of the northern ships with the lateen

The galleons of the Spanish Armada engage in battle with the British fleet in the English Channel (1588). Designed in the sixteenth century, the galleon marked the turn from medieval to modern naval warfare.

sails of the Mediterranean ships, along with three masts, a stern rudder, and very high fore- and aft castles, producing a vessel noted for its large cargo capacity and its ability to traverse great distances. Improvements in maps and charts greatly improved navigation, especially in the Mediterranean. Written sailing instructions called portolan charts described coastlines, ports, and dangerous sailing areas, and also provided information regarding the availability of supplies for seafarers. These charts aided sailors by mapping coastlines, marking locations of cities, and stating sailing distances.

Although primarily used in trade, the carrack was also employed in war. The English carrack HMS *Mary Rose* was built in 1510 as a ship of war. Like other warships of its day, the *Mary Rose* had gunports

with large guns mounted in its hull. Although the date of the first ship gunport is debated, it was most likely first developed by a Brest shipbuilder named Descharges in about 1501. The *Mary Rose* may have been the first of King Henry VIII's (1491-1547) ships to be equipped with gunports, perhaps installed when the *Mary Rose* was renovated in 1536. The guns on board the *Mary Rose* were cast of iron and bronze, with the heaviest guns mounted on the lowest deck in order to stabilize the ship's center of gravity. The *Mary Rose* carried a variety of guns, from smooth-bore barrel guns to oddly bored scatter guns. The low placement of the gunports, however, combined with the sheer weight of its eighty guns, led to the sinking of the *Mary Rose* when it was sent against the French on July 19, 1545, in a battle off Spithead, taking its crew and its captain, Roger Grenville, as well as the vice admiral, Sir George Carew, down with her.

THE GALLEON

The development of the galleon marked the turn from medieval to modern naval warfare. Designed in the sixteenth century by the admiral in charge of the Elizabethan navy, Sir John Hawkins (1532-1595), the galleon surpassed all previous ships. It was an adaptation of the carrack, eliminating the high forecastle to produce a ship with a lower profile and therefore with far better performance, particularly when sailing into the wind. This improved carrack design reached Spain about seventeen years after its introduction in England, and the result was the development of the Spanish war galleon. Within forty years, the galleon replaced the carrack as both the primary trading vessel and warship. For three centuries, the galleon ruled the world's seas.

Galleons differed from carracks in more than the absence of the high forecastle. On the aft was typically a quarterdeck instead of a deck-mounted aft castle. Gunports lined one or both of the main decks, and special, smaller decks served as fighting platforms. A galleon's hull was longer, narrower, and sleeker than that of a carrack. The result was a ship designed for speed, maneuverability, seaworthiness, and, especially, warfare.

By the late sixteenth century, commercial and religious rivalry between Catholic Spain and Protestant England brought the two countries to the brink of war. Spain, confident of its maritime supremacy, made the first move. In May, 1588, the Spanish Armada, assembled by King Philip II of Spain and under the command of the duke of Medina-Sidonia, Alonso Pérez de Guzmán (c. 1550-1619), sailed out of Lisbon harbor en route to the Low Countries to pick up the prince of Parma and his forces. Their goal was to invade England. The Spanish fleet consisted of 130 ships of varying sizes and types, the majority of which were galleons. Meanwhile, the English prepared for the Spanish invasion by dividing the English navy between Plymouth, with 94 ships under Charles Howard of Effingham (1536-1624), and Dover, with 35 ships under Lord Henry Seymour.

After heading into the English Channel, the Spanish positioned their ships in a crescent formation, which the smaller English ships could not break. The English turned this to their advantage by attacking the larger Spanish ships individually at close firing range. When the Spanish fleet anchored at Calais on July 27 to wait for the prince of Parma and his forces, the English sent in small fireships to attack the anchored Spanish vessels. The Spanish were forced to cut their lines and sail out into the bay, where they were met by the combined forces of Howard and Seymour. The Spanish Armada retreated to Spain with only 67 of its original 130 ships.

The difference between the Spanish loss and the English victory lay in the strategy of each. The Spanish relied on the traditional warfare technique, used since ancient times, of coming alongside and boarding enemy ships to engage in hand-to-hand combat. The English, however, did not attempt to board the enemy ships, but rather attacked them downwind at close range, disabling as many as possible. This was an important turning point in naval history. The naval tactics that were first employed by the English against the Spanish Armada continued in use in naval warfare from that point forward.

BOOKS AND ARTICLES

Keen, M., ed. *Medieval Warfare: A History.* Oxford, England: Oxford University Press, 1999.

Kirsch, P. *The Galleon.* London: Conway Maritime Press, 1991.

Lewis, A. R., and T. J. Runyan. *European Naval and Maritime History, 300-1500.* Bloomington: University of Indiana Press, 1990.

Unger, R. W., ed. *Cogs, Caravels, and Galleons.* London: Conway Maritime Press, 1994.

Sonia Sorrell